# WRITING FICTION
## A Guide to Narrative Craft

### Seventh Edition

## JANET BURROWAY
*Florida State University*

*with*

## ELIZABETH STUCKEY-FRENCH
*Florida State University*

PEARSON
Longman

New York    San Francisco    Boston
London    Toronto    Sydney    Tokyo    Singapore    Madrid
Mexico City    Munich    Paris    Cape Town    Hong Kong    Montreal

*In loving memory of David Daiches, mentor and friend*

Managing Editor: Erika Berg
Development Manager: Mary Ellen Curley
Development Editor: Adam Beroud
Executive Marketing Manager: Ann Stypuloski
Production Manager: Donna DeBenedictis
Project Coordination, Text Design, and Electronic Page Makeup:
    Elm Street Publishing Services, Inc.
Senior Cover Design Manager: Nancy Danahy
Cover Designer: Nancy Sacks
Cover Image: *New Ideas,* © Frances Hamilton, 1996.
Senior Manufacturing Buyer: Dennis J. Para
Printer and Binder: R.R. Donnelley & Sons Company/Crawfordsville
Cover Printer: Phoenix Color Corporation

For permission to use copyrighted material, grateful acknowledgment is made to the copyright
holders on pp. 424–425, which are hereby made part of this copyright page.

Library of Congress Cataloging-in-Publication Data

Burroway, Janet.
    Writing fiction : a guide to narrative craft/Janet Burroway with Elizabeth
Stuckey-French. -- 7th ed.
        p. cm.
    Includes bibliographical references and index.
    ISBN 0-321-27736-8
    1. Fiction--Technique.    2. Fiction--Authorship.    3. Narration (Rhetoric)
    4. Creative Writing.    I. Stucky-French, Elizabeth. II Title.
    PN3355.B79 2007
    808.3--dc22

                                                                        2006001281

Please visit us at www.ablongman.com

ISBN 0-321-27736-8

7 8 9 10—DOC—09 08

# CONTENTS

# PREFACE

## To Instructors: About This Book

The seventh edition of *Writing Fiction*, like its previous manifestations, attempts to guide the student writer from first impulse to final revision, employing concepts of fiction's elements familiar from literature study, but shifting the perspective toward that of the practicing writer. I have wanted to address the student, however inexperienced, as a fellow artist, whose concerns are both frightening and, often, also, a question of understanding and developing technique.

As experienced instructors are aware, the idea of a text for writing fiction is itself problematic. Unlike such subjects as math and history, where a certain mass of information needs to be organized and conveyed, the writing of fiction is more often a process of trial and error—the learning is perpetual and, paradoxically, the writer needs to know everything at once. If a text is too prescriptive, it's not true to the immense variety of possibilities; if it's too anecdotal, it may be cheering but is unlikely to be of use.

I'm also aware that *Writing Fiction* is used by many instructors in both beginning and advanced writing courses and for students at very different levels of understanding. I've tried therefore to make it practical, comprehensive, and flexible, and to keep the focus on the student writer and the process of the writing. My means of doing this is to cover discrete elements in separate chapters, yet to build in each chapter on what has been covered earlier. Focus on the writing process and suggestions for getting started have seemed to me a logical place to begin the book, but I have tried to keep subsequent chapters sufficiently self-contained that teachers may assign them in any order they prefer. In the seventh edition, in response to suggestions from writing teachers, the chapter order has been changed: two chapters have been combined and another chapter has been split into two separate chapters.

More than any previous edition, the seventh edition attempts to respond to teachers who use it in the classroom, those who write or e-mail me spontaneously throughout the life of the edition, colleagues in universities and the Associated Writing Programs, and those asked by the publisher to engage in a formal process of review. There is really no appropriate term for these people. A "reviewer" usually makes a take-it-or-leave-it judgment, whereas the reviewers of a text are collaborators in an ongoing attempt to keep the book vital among the changing needs of students, teachers, and the academic zeitgeist. Naturally these teacher/writers tend to nudge the new edition in the direction of their own pedagogical needs and methods, and inevitably some advice conflicts with other. Nevertheless, reviewers are surprisingly often in agreement and often thorough, thoughtful, practical, and inspired.

For the seventh edition of *Writing Fiction* I asked my friend, colleague, and fellow fiction writer Elizabeth Stuckey-French to plan and author the revisions, based on many dozens of suggestions from these teachers, students, and reviewers. The changes will be found in the readings, the exercises and the text itself, including many updated references and fresh examples. Elizabeth (indefatigably and ably aided by her husband, also a colleague at Florida State, and also a writer, Ned Stuckey-French), has been responsible for the sometimes daunting task of receiving, researching, collating, and incorporating suggestions for both the substance of the book and its apparatus. In particular she has found a way to respond to the often repeated requests for an expansion on the subject of setting (both time and place in fiction), and for a more direct and practical version of my somewhat academic discussion of point of view. She has also rearranged and clarified the chapters on character to make them more useful to the practicing writer. Elizabeth and Ned have made the arduous process a pleasure, for which I'm grateful.

### FEATURES OF THE SEVENTH EDITION

The seventh edition includes a significant expansion of the writing exercises at the end of each chapter, including both Individual and Collaborative assignments.

Except for the chapters on process, comparison, and revision, there are now three short stories at the end of most chapters. These stories have been chosen primarily from contemporary American fiction with attention to increased variety in form, mood, and content and emphasis on multicultural representation of authors and experiences. Excerpts from other short stories are used in the text to offer quick illustrations of concepts.

The former chapter on place and time has been divided into two chapters in order to provide a more comprehensive discussion of both topics. The two chapters on point of view have been condensed into one chapter to provide a more straightforward, practical discussion useful to beginning writing students.

The chapter on revision now includes the final draft of fiction writer Ron Carlson's story "Keith," as well as an essay he wrote about revising the story.

Boxed quotations from established authors—on topics such as writing from experience, story structure, openings and endings, and revision—offer students a quick and encouraging reminder of key chapter concepts.

Above all, for the new edition both Elizabeth Stuckey-French and I have kept the exigencies of the creative writing classroom in mind, intending to be catalytic rather than prescriptive, hoping to encourage both students and teachers to feel comfortable with themselves and the writing process.

### ACKNOWLEDGMENTS

Many people have helped with the seventh edition of *Writing Fiction*. Thanks go to my students and colleagues in the Writing Program at Florida State University. Elizabeth Stuckey-French wishes to especially thank Ned Stuckey-French and Caimeen Garrett, both of whose help with this edition has been invaluable.

I am also grateful to the following writers/teachers who have reviewed this edition: Lawrence Coates, Bowling Green State University; John Holman, Georgia State University; Susan Jackson Rodgers, Kansas State University; Arnie Johnson, Western Michigan University; Barry Lawler, Oregon State University; Jeanne M. Leiby, University of Central Florida; Colleen J. McElroy, University of Washington; Alyce Miller, Indiana University; Keith Lee Morris, Clemson University; Kimme

Nuckles, Baker College of Auburn Hills; R. Clay Reynolds, University of Texas at Dallas; Barry Rodman, University of North Texas; Sheryl St. Germain, Iowa State University; Stephen H. Watkins, University of Mary Washington; Charles Waugh, Utah State University; and Betty Wiesepape, University of Texas at Dallas.

We would like to acknowledge the writers Simone Poirier-Bures, Judith Slater, Anne Giles Rimbey, Gerald Shapiro, B. W. Jorgensen, Gordon Johnson, Tobey Kaplan, and Rachel Hall, whose exercises, which have appeared in the Associated Writing Programs' publication entitled *Pedagogy Papers*, have been adapted within this text. We would also like to acknowledge the writers Robert Olen Butler, Doug Bauer, Lee Smith, Jill McCorkle, Ron Hansen, Tom Batt, Wally Lamb, and Alan Gurganus, whose insightful words from interviews published in the Associated Writing Programs' publication *The Writer's Chronicle* have been quoted in this text. Among the many others who have shared exercises over the years, special thanks go to Nancy Huddleston Packer, John L'Heureux, Alice La Plante, Erin McGraw, Brad Owens, Rick Hillis, Bo Caldwell, Michelle Carter, and Leslee Becker. Some of the exercises were adapted from those appearing in *What If: Writing Exercises for Fiction Writers*, edited by Anne Berneys and Pamela Painter; *Writing Fiction Step by Step* by Josip Novakovich; and *Creating Fiction*, edited by Julie Checkoway.

—J. B.

## A Note from the Publisher

The following supplements can be value-packed at no additional cost or at a significant discount with *Writing Fiction*, Seventh Edition. Please contact your Longman representative to arrange a value-pack.

- **A Workshop Guide for Creative Writing** (0-321-09539-1) is a laminated reference tool, including guidelines for criticism, workshop etiquette, and more. Available at no additional cost when packaged with *Writing Fiction*, Seventh Edition.
- **The Longman Journal for Creative Writing** (0-321-09540-5) helps students explore and discover their own writing habits and styles. Available at no additional cost when value-packed with *Writing Fiction*, Seventh Edition.
- **Penguin Discount Program.** A variety of Penguin paperbacks are offered at a significant discount when packaged with *Writing Fiction*, Seventh Edition. To review the complete list of titles available, please visit: http://www.ablongman.com/penguin.
- **Merriam Websters Reader's Handbook: Your Complete Guide to Literary Terms** (0-321-10541-9) includes nearly 2,000 descriptions for every major genre, style, and era of writing. Available at no additional cost when value-packed with *Writing Fiction*, Seventh Edition.

## To Students: About the Writing Workshop

*Writing Fiction* is primarily intended for use in the college-level writing workshop—a phenomenon now so firmly established that nearly every higher institution in America offers some form of workshop-based creative writing course or program, and sufficiently evolved that it has given rise to a new verb—"to workshop."

To workshop is much more than to discuss. It implies a commitment on the part of everyone concerned to give close attention to work that is embryonic. The atmosphere of such a group is intense and personal in a way that other college classes are not, since a major text of the course is also the raw effort of its participants. At the same time, unlike the classic model of the artist's atelier or the music conservatory, the instruction is assumed to come largely from the group rather than from a single master of technical expertise. Thus the workshop represents a democratization of both the material for college study and its teaching.

Although workshops inevitably vary, a basic pattern has evolved in which twelve to twenty students are led by an instructor who is also a published writer. The students take turns writing, copying, and distributing stories, which the others take away, read, and critique. What is sought in such a group is mutual goodwill—the desire to make the story under scrutiny the best that it can be—together with an agreed-to toughness on the part of writer and readers.

This sounds simple enough, but as with all democratization, the perceived danger is that the process will flatten out the story's edge and originality, and that the result will be a homogenized "revision by committee." The danger is partly real and deserves attention. Partly, however, such fear masks protectiveness toward the image—solitary, remote, romantic—of the writer's life.

But those who have taken part in the process tend to champion it. John Gardner asserted that not only could writing be taught but that "writing ability is mainly a product of good teaching supported by a deep-down love of writing." John Irving says of his instructors, "They clearly saved me valuable time . . . [and] time is precious for a young writer." Isabel Allende says, "The process is lonely, but the response connects you with the world." Novelist and teacher Robert Morgan explains that "writing can't be taught as a body of knowledge to be passed from instructor to students, as with history or physics, say, because the young writer only really learns from practice." But, comparing writers to athletes, Morgan suggests that "We teach ourselves to write by doing it again and again, learning from our successes and mistakes . . . The writing teacher mostly builds up the confidence of the students that they can teach themselves, and tell when they are doing it right."

There are, I think, three questions about the workshop endeavor that have to be asked: Is it good for the most startlingly talented, those who will go on to "become" published professional writers? Is it good for the majority who will not publish but will instead become (as some of my most gifted students have) restaurateurs, photographers, technical writers, high school teachers? And is it good for literature and literacy generally to have students of all fields struggle toward this play and this craft? My answer must in all cases be a vigorous yes. The workshop aids both the vocation and the avocation. Writing is a solitary struggle, and from the beginning, writers have sought relief in the company and understanding of other writers. At its best the workshop provides an intellectual, emotional, and social (and some argue a spiritual) discipline. For the potential professionals there is the important focus on craft; course credit is a form of early pay-for-writing; deadlines help you find the time and discipline to do what you really want to; and above all, the workshop offers attention in an area where attention is hard to command. For those who will not be professionals, a course in writing fiction can be a valuable part of a liberal arts education, making for better readers, better letters home, better company reports, and better private memoirs. For everyone, the workshop can help develop critical thinking, a respect for craft, and important social skills.

There are also some pitfalls in the process: that students will develop unrealistic expectations of their chances in a chancy profession; that they will dull or provincialize their talents by trying to please the teacher or the group; that they will be buoyed into self-satisfaction by too-lavish praise or that they will be crushed by too-harsh criticism. On the other hand, workshop peers recognize and revere originality, vividness, and truth at least as often as professional critics. Hard work counts for more than anyone but writers realizes, and facility with the language can be learned out of obsessive attention to it. The driven desire is no guarantee of talent, but it is an annealing force. And amazing transformations can and do occur in the creative writing class. Sometimes young writers who exhibit only a propensity for cliché and the most hackneyed initial efforts make sudden, breathtaking progress. Sometimes the leap of imaginative capacity is inexplicable, like a sport of nature.

The appropriate atmosphere in which to foster this metamorphosis is a balance constructed of right-brain creative play and left-brain crafted language, and of obligations among readers, writers, and teachers. Of these obligations, a few seem to me worth noting.

### HOW WORKSHOPS WORK

The most basic expectation is that the manuscript itself should be professionally presented—that is, double-spaced on one side of white $8^1/_2$-by-11-inch paper, with generous margins, in clear copies, proofread for grammar, spelling, and punctuation. In most workshops the content is left entirely to the writer, with no censorship of subject. The reader's obligation is to read the story twice, once for its sense and story, a second time with pen in hand to make marginal comments, observations, suggestions. A summarizing end note is usual and helpful. This should be done with the understanding—on the parts of both writer and reader—that the work at hand is by definition a work in progress. If it were finished, then there would be no reason to bring it into workshop. Workshop readers should school themselves to identify the successes that are in every story: the potential strength, the interesting subject matter, the pleasing shape, or the vivid detail.

It's my experience that the workshop itself proceeds most usefully to the writer if each discussion begins with a critically neutral description and interpretation of the story. This is important because workshopping can descend into a litany of *I like, I don't like*, and it's the responsibility of the first speaker to provide a coherent reading as a basis for discussion. It's often a good idea to begin with a detailed summary of the narrative action—useful because if class members understand the events of the story differently, or are unclear about what happens, this is important information for the author, a signal that she has not revealed what, or all, she meant. The interpretation might then address such questions as: *What kind of story is this? What defining choices do the characters face? What is its conflict-crisis-resolution structure? What is it about? What does it say about what it is about? How sympathetic should the reader feel with the main character? How does its imagery relate to its theme?*

Only after some such questions are addressed should the critique begin to deal with whether the story is successful in its effects. The first speaker should try to close with two or three questions that, in his/her opinion, the story raises, and invite the class to consider these. Most of the questions will be technical: *Is the point of view consistent, are the characters fully drawn, is the imagery vivid and specific?* But now and again it is well to pause and return to more substantive matters: *What's the spirit of this story, what is it trying to say, what does it make me feel?*

## THE WRITER'S ROLE

For the writer, the obligations are more emotionally strenuous, but the rewards are great. The hardest part of being a writer in a workshop is to learn this: be still, be greedy for suggestions, take everything in, and don't defend.

This is difficult because the story under discussion is still new and may feel highly personal. The author has a strong impulse to explain and plead. If the criticism is "This isn't clear," it's hard not to feel "You didn't read it right"—even if you understand that it is not up to the workshop to "get it" but up to the author to be clear. If the reader's complaint is "This isn't credible," it's very hard not to respond "But it really happened!"—even though you know perfectly well that credibility is a different sort of fish than fact, and that autobiography is irrelevant. There is also a self-preservative impulse to keep from changing the core of what you've done: "Don't they realize how much time and effort I've already put in?"

But only the author's attempt at complete receptivity will make the workshop work. The chances are that your first draft really does not say the most meaningful thing inherent in the story, and that most meaningful thing may announce itself sideways, in a detail, within parentheses, an afterthought, a slip. Somebody else may see the design before you do. Sometimes the best advice comes from the most surprising source. The thing you resist the hardest may be exactly what you need.

After the workshop, the writer's obligation alters slightly. It's important to take the written critiques and take them seriously, let them sink in with as good a will as you brought to the workshop. But part of the obligation is also not to let them sink in too far. Reject without regret whatever seems on reflection wrongheaded, dull, destructive, or irrelevant to your vision. It's just as important to be able to discriminate between helpful and unhelpful criticism as it is to be able to write. More often than not, the most useful criticism will simply confirm what you already suspected yourself. So listen to everything and receive all criticism as if it were golden. Then listen to yourself and toss the dross.

(For further discussion of giving and receiving workshop feedback, please see Chapter 11, "Play It Again, Sam: Revision.")

—J. B.

# 1

## WHATEVER WORKS
### *The Writing Process*

+ *Get Started*

+ *Keep Going*

+ *A Word about Theme*

You want to write. Why is it so hard?

There are a few lucky souls for whom the whole process of writing is easy, for whom the smell of fresh paper is better than air, whose minds chuckle over their own agility, who forget to eat, and who consider the world at large an intrusion on their good time at the keyboard. But you and I are not among them. We are in love with words except when we have to face them. We are caught in a guilty paradox in which we grumble over our lack of time, and when we have the time, we sharpen pencils, check e-mail, or clip the hedges.

Of course, there's also joy. We write for the satisfaction of having wrestled a sentence to the page, for the rush of discovering an image, for the excitement of seeing a character come alive. Even the most successful writers will sincerely say that these pleasures—not money, fame, or glamour—are the real rewards of writing. Fiction writer Alice Munro concedes:

> It may not look like pleasure, because the difficulties can make me morose and distracted, but that's what it is—the pleasure of telling the story I mean to tell as wholly as I can tell it, of finding out in fact what the story is, by working around the different ways of telling it.

Nevertheless, writers may forget what such pleasure feels like when confronting a blank page, like the heroine of Anita Brookner's novel *Look at Me:*

Sometimes it feels like a physical effort simply to sit down at the desk and pull out the notebook. . . . Sometimes the effort of putting pen to paper is so great that I literally feel a pain in my head . . .

It helps to know that most writers share the paradox of at least wanting to do what we most want to do. It also helps to know some of the reasons for our reluctance. Fear of what could emerge on the page, and what it may reveal about our inner lives, can keep us from getting started. Dorothy Allison, author of *Bastard Out of Carolina*, describes the necessity of breaking through this form of self-censorship:

I believe the secret of writing is that fiction never exceeds the reach of the writer's courage. The best fiction comes from the place where the terror hides, the edge of our worst stuff. I believe, absolutely, that if you do not break out in that sweat of fear when you write, then you have not gone far enough. And I know you can fake that courage when you don't think of yourself as courageous—because I have done it. And that is not a bad thing, to fake it until you can make it. I know that until I started pushing on my own fears, telling the stories that were hardest for me, writing about exactly the things I was most afraid of and unsure about, I wasn't writing worth a damn.

There's another impediment to beginning, expressed by a writer character in Lawrence Durrell's *Alexandria Quartet*. Durrell's Pursewarden broods over the illusory significance of what he is about to write, unwilling to begin in case he spoils it. Many of us do this: The idea, whatever it is, seems so luminous, whole, and fragile, that to begin to write about that idea is to commit it to rubble. "The paradox of writing," says screenwriter Stephen Fischer, "is that you're trying to use words to express what words can't express." Knowing in advance that words will never exactly capture what we mean or intend, we must gingerly and gradually work ourselves into a state of accepting what words can do instead. No matter how many times we find out that what words can do is quite all right, we still shy again from the next beginning. Against this wasteful impulse I have a motto over my desk that reads: "Don't Dread; Do." It's a fine motto, and I contemplated it for several weeks before I began writing this chapter.

The mundane daily habits of writers are apparently fascinating. No author offers to answer questions at the end of a public reading without being asked: *Do you write in the morning or at night? Do you write every day? Do you compose longhand or on a computer?* Sometimes such questions show a reverent interest in the workings of genius. More often, I think, they are a plea for practical help: *Is there something I can do to make this job less horrific? Is there a trick that will unlock my words?*

## Get Started

The variety of authors' habits suggests that there is no magic to be found in any particular one. Donald Hall will tell you that he spends a dozen hours a day at his desk, moving back and forth between as many projects. Philip Larkin said that he wrote a poem only every eighteen months or so and never tried to write one that was not a gift.

Gail Godwin goes to her workroom every day "because what if the angel came and I wasn't there?" Julia Alvarez begins the day by reading first poetry, then prose, by her favorite writers "to remind me of the quality of writing I am aiming for." Like Hemingway, the late Andre Dubus advised students to stop writing midsentence in order to begin the next day by completing the thought, thereby reentering the creative flow more easily. Dickens could not deal with people when he was working: "The mere consciousness of an engagement will worry a whole day." Thomas Wolfe wrote standing up. Some writers can plop at the kitchen table without clearing the breakfast dishes; others need total seclusion, a beach, a cat, a string quartet.

There is something to be learned from all this, though. It is not an "open sesame" but a piece of advice older than fairy tales: Know thyself. The bottom line is that if you do not at some point write your story down, it will not get written. Having decided that you will write it, the question is not "How do you get it done?" but "How do *you* get it done?" Any discipline or indulgence that actually helps nudge you into position facing the page is acceptable and productive. If jogging after breakfast energizes your mind, then jog before you sit. If you have to pull an all-nighter on a coffee binge, do that. Some schedule, regularity, pattern in your writing day (or night) will always help, but only you can figure out what that pattern is for you.

## JOURNAL KEEPING

There are, though, a number of tricks you can teach yourself in order to free the writing self, and the essence of these is to give yourself permission to fail. The best place for such permission is a private place, and for that reason a writer's journal is an essential, likely to be the source of originality, ideas, experimentation, and growth.

Keep a journal. A journal is an intimate, a friend that will accept you as you are. Pick a notebook you like the look of, one you feel comfortable with, as you would pick a friend. I find a bound blank book too elegant to live up to, preferring instead a loose-leaf because I write my journal mainly at the computer and can stick anything in at the flip of a three-hole punch. But you can glue scribbled napkins into a spiral, too.

Keep the journal regularly, at least at first. It doesn't matter what you write and it doesn't matter very much how much, but it does matter that you make a steady habit of the writing. A major advantage of keeping a journal regularly is that it will put you in the habit of observing in words. If you know at dawn that you are committed to writing so many words before dusk, you will half-consciously tell the story of your day to yourself as you live it, finding a phrase to catch whatever catches your eye. When that habit is established, you'll begin to find that whatever invites your attention or sympathy, your anger or curiosity, may be the beginning of invention. *Whoever* catches your attention may be the beginning of a character.

Don't worry about being thorough. Your journal might consist of brief notes and bits of description only you can make sense of. F. Scott Fitzgerald (*The Great Gatsby*) used his journals to keep, among other things, snatches of overheard conversation and potential titles for short stories and novels. Many fiction writers use journals to jot down specific details about people, places, and things they observe and find intriguing. (See exercise #4 at the end of this chapter.) Later, when you're writing fiction and attempting to bring to life a teenager or a city street or a tractor, it's useful to have a bank of striking details in your journal to draw on. Often one or two details about something will be enough to trigger a fuller memory about a place or a person or a situation. Joan Didion, in her essay "On Keeping a Notebook," was puzzled when she first reread a recipe for sauerkraut she'd recorded in her journal. But then she remembered.

"It all comes back. Even that recipe for sauerkraut: even that brings it back. I was on Fire Island when I first made that sauerkraut, and it was raining, and we drank a lot of bourbon and ate the sauerkraut and went to bed at ten, and I listened to the rain and the Atlantic and felt safe. I made the sauerkraut again last night and it did not make me feel any safer, but that is, as they say, another story."

But before the journal-keeping habit is developed, you may find that even a blank journal page has the awesome aspect of a void, and you may need some tricks of permission to let yourself start writing there. The playwright Maria Irene Fornes says that there are two of you: one who wants to write and one who doesn't. The one who wants to write had better keep tricking the one who doesn't. Or another way to think of this conflict is between right brain and left brain—the playful, detail-loving creator, and the linear critic. The critic is an absolutely essential part of the writing process. The trick is to shut him or her up until there is something to criticize.

> The great Japanese film director Akira Kurosawa said that to be an artist means never to avert your eyes. And that's the hardest thing, because we want to flinch. The artist must go into the white hot center of himself, and our impulse when we get there is to look away and avert our eyes.
>
> Robert Olen Butler

## FREEWRITING

*Freewriting* is a technique that allows you to take very literally the notion of getting something down on paper. It can be done whenever you want to write, or just to free up the writing self. The idea is to put

> anything on paper and I mena anything, it doesn't matter as long as it's coming out of your head nad hte ends of your fingers, down ont the page I wonder if;m improving, if this process gets me going better now than it did all those— hoewever many years ago? I know my typing is geting worse, deteriorating even as we speak (are we speaking? to whom? IN what forM? I love it when i hit the caps button by mistake, it makes me wonder whether there isn;t something in the back or bottom of the brain that sez PAY ATTENTION now, which makes me think of a number of things, freud and his slip o tonuge, self-deception, the myriad way it operates in everybody's life, no not everybody's but in my own exp.

llike Aunt Ch. mourniong for the dead cats whenevershe hasn't got her way and can't disconnect one kind of sadness from another, I wonder if we ever disconnect kinds of sadness, if the first homesickness doesn;t operatfor everybody the same way it does for me, grandma's house the site of it, the grass out the window and the dog rolling a tin pie plate under the willow tree, great heavy hunger in the belly, the empty weight of loss, loss, loss

That's freewriting. Its point is to keep going, and that is the only point. When the critic intrudes and tells you that what you're doing is awful, tell the critic to take a dive, or acknowledge her/him (*typing is getting worse*) and keep writing. If you work on a computer, try dimming the screen so you can't see what you're doing. At times, you might find it liberating to freewrite to music, random or selected. If you freewrite often, pretty soon you'll be bored with writing about how you don't feel like writing (though that is as good a subject as any; the subject is of no importance and neither is the quality of the writing) and you will find your mind and your phrases running on things that interest you. Fine. It doesn't matter. Freewriting is the literary equivalent of scales at the piano or a short gym workout. All that matters is that you do it. The verbal muscles will develop of their own accord.

Though freewriting is mere technique, it can affect the freedom of the content. Many writers feel themselves to be *an instrument through which*, rather than a *creator of*, and whether you think of this possibility as humble or holy, it is worth finding out what you say when you aren't monitoring yourself. Fiction is written not so much to inform as to find out, and if you force yourself into a mode of informing when you haven't yet found out, you're likely to end up pontificating or lying some other way.

In *Becoming a Writer*, a book that only half-facetiously claims to do what teachers of writing claim cannot be done—to teach genius—Dorothea Brande suggests that the way to begin is not with an idea or a form at all, but with an unlocking of your thoughts on paper. She advises that you rise each day and go directly to your desk (if you have to have coffee, put it in a thermos the night before) and begin writing whatever comes to mind, before you are quite awake, before you have read anything or talked to anyone, before reason has begun to take over from the dream-functioning of your brain. Write for twenty or thirty minutes and then put away what you have written without reading it over. After a week or two of this, pick an additional time during the day when you can salvage a half hour or so to write, and when that time arrives, write, even if you "must climb out over the heads of your friends" to do it. It doesn't matter what you write. What does matter is that you develop the habit of beginning to write the moment you sit down to do so.

IF YOU HAVEN'T SURPRISED YOURSELF, YOU HAVEN'T written.

Eudora Welty

## EXERCISES

The American Dairy Association used to use the tagline "You never outgrow your need for milk." If you're a writer, the same might be said of exercises. Exercises, or prompts as they are sometimes called, can be helpful for all writers. They help you get started, and they can give you focus—whether you are writing in your journal, doing those early morning pages Brande suggests, sneaking in a bit of freewriting during the day, or trying to get to that next scene in a story.

Exercises are a way to tap your unconscious. The process of writing does not proceed clearly and obviously from point A to point B, but if you've been thinking about your story—sleeping on it, puzzling over it, mulling about it, working on a draft—you may well have a solution waiting for you in your unconscious. Stories do not begin with ideas or themes or outlines, so much as with images and obsessions, and they continue to be built by exploring those images and obsessions. Seemingly unrelated prompts can help you break loose that next page. Need to find out what should happen next with Sebastian and Nelly? Here's an exercise: write two pages about the two of them trying to decide what television show to watch. Pretty soon Sebastian and Nelly are fighting about the remote control, but more than that they're fighting about how Sebastian is remote and always wants control. Nelly is telling him that their relationship has got to change and he's acting like he doesn't have a clue. And you are off and running.

Robert Olen Butler has published two collections of stories that grew out of exercises. *Tabloid Dreams* was prompted by actual headlines Butler found in those outrageous supermarket tabloids. It includes such stories as "Jealous Husband Returns in Form of Parrot" and "*Titanic* Victim Speaks Through Waterbed." In *Had a Good Time* Butler wrote stories prompted by his collection of early twentieth-century postcards, on the backs of which were scribbled enigmatic and provocative messages— stories he felt were asking to be written.

Exercises can be shared. Early in their careers, two young writers, JoAnn Beard and Mary Allen, were splitting a job editing a physics journal at the University of Iowa. One worked one day, one the next. They shared a desk, but were never there at the same time. They decided to start leaving each other a daily writing exercise in the top drawer. "For tomorrow, write a scene that takes place in a car." Or, "Write a scene in which one character is lying." The exercises kept them going, broke the isolation of writing, tapped them into the material they would have written about anyway, and before too terribly long they each had a first book—Allen's *Rooms of Heaven* and Beard's *The Boys of My Youth*.

Gymnasts practice. Pianists practice. Artists sketch. Why shouldn't writers practice? Exercises are a way to exercise your skills, develop them, hone them, make them stronger. The novelist Stanley Elkin talked about sharing an office at the University of Illinois with his friend and fellow writer William H. Gass and being surprised to see Gass practicing sentences on the other side of the room.

Each chapter of *Writing Fiction* will end with some exercises designed to help you get started and move further into the issues discussed along the way. But don't stop there. Go to a bookstore or library and look through some of the books listed in Appendix B (Suggestions for Further Reading) to see which of their exercises intrigue you. (*What If? Writing Exercises for Fiction Writers* by Anne Bernays and Pamela Painter has deservedly become a classic.) Collect exercises as you might collect possible names for characters or words you like the sound of. Develop your own exercises. Ask writing friends what has worked for them. Note the ones that work for you and vary them and return to them again and again. Exercise. Exercise daily.

## THE COMPUTER

I think it's important for a writer to try a pencil from time to time so as not to lose the knack of writing by hand, of jotting at the park or the beach without any source of energy but your own hand and mind.

But for most writers, a computer is a great aid to spontaneity. Freewriting flows more freely on a computer. The knowledge that you can so easily delete makes it easier to quiet the internal critic and put down whatever comes. The "wraparound" feature of the computer means that you need never be aware that what you write is chopped into lines of type on the page. Turn down the screen or ignore it, stare out the window into middle space. You can follow the thread of your thought without a pause.

However, when you're rereading what you've written, you might want to step away from the screen. Scrolling through your work on a computer screen is not the same as reading it on a printed page—it's too easy to overlook problems. Most writers print out hard copies of their drafts and go over them with pen in hand, taking notes and making changes. This allows them to read more carefully, to easily jump back and skip ahead, to get a better sense of the story's pacing, to notice clunky sentences and weak word choices. Many writers will read also their drafts aloud, either to themselves or to a helpful critic, a process that will make the story's weaknesses even clearer. These revision strategies—and more—will be further discussed in chapter 11.

Computers are a wonderful tool, but they can't do everything.

## THE CRITIC: A CAUTION

The cautionary note that needs to be sounded regarding all the techniques and technology that free you to write is that the critic is absolutely essential afterward. Because revision—the heart of the writing process—will continue until you finally finish or abandon a piece of work, exercises for revision follow most chapters of this book. The revising process is continuous and begins as soon as you choose to let your critic in. Freedrafting allows you to create before you criticize, to do the essential play before the essential work. Don't forget the essential work. The computer lets you write a lot because you can so easily cut. Don't forget to do so.

I WANT HARD STORIES, I DEMAND THEM from myself. Hard stories are worth the difficulty. It seems to me the only way I have forgiven anything, understood anything, is through that process of opening up to my own terror and pain and reexamining it, re-creating it in the story, and making it something different, making it meaningful—even if the meaning is only in the act of the telling.

Dorothy Allison

## CHOOSING A SUBJECT

Some writers are lucky enough never to be faced with the problem of choosing a subject. The world presents itself to them in terms of conflict, crisis, and resolution. Ideas for stories pop into their heads day after day; their only difficulty is choosing among them. In fact, the habit of mind that produces stories is a habit and can be cultivated, so that the more and the longer you write, the less likely you are to run out of ideas.

But sooner or later you may find yourself faced with the desire (or the deadline necessity) to write a story when your mind is a blank. The sour and untrue impulse crosses your thoughts: Nothing has ever happened to me. The task you face then is to recognize among all the paraphernalia of your mind a situation, idea, perception, or character that you can turn into a story.

Some teachers and critics advise beginning writers to write only from their personal experience, but I feel that this is a misleading and demeaning rule. If your imagination never gets beyond your age group or off campus, never tackles issues larger than dormitory life, then you are severely underestimating the range of your imagination. It is certainly true that you must draw on your own experience (including your experience of the shape of sentences). But the trick is to identify what is interesting, unique, and original in that experience (including your experience of the shape of sentences) that will therefore surprise and attract the reader.

The kind of "writing what you know" that is *least* likely to produce good fiction is trying to tell just exactly what happened to you at such and such a time. Probably all good fiction is "autobiographical" in some way, but the awful or hilarious or tragic thing you went through may offer as many problems as possibilities when you start to turn it into fiction. The first of these is that to the extent you want to capture "what really happened," you remove your focus from what will work as narrative. Young writers, offended by being told that a piece is unconvincing, often defend themselves by declaring that *it really happened.* But credibility in words has almost nothing to do with fact. Aristotle went so far as to say that a "probable impossibility" made a better story than an "improbable possibility," meaning that a skillful author can sell us glass mountains, UFOs, and hobbits, whereas a less skilled writer may not be able to convince us that Mary Lou has a crush on Sam.

A SHORT STORY IS A WRITER'S WAY OF thinking through experience. . . . Journalism aims at accuracy, but fiction's aim is truth. The writer distorts reality in the interest of a larger truth.

John L'Heureux

The first step toward using autobiography in fiction is to accept this: Words are not experience. Even the most factual account of a personal experience involves choices and interpretations—your sister's recollection of the same event might be entirely different. If you are writing a memoir or personal essay, then it is important to maintain a basis in fact because, as Annie Dillard says, "that is the convention and the covenant between the nonfiction writer and his reader." But between fiction writer and reader it is the revelation of meaning through the creation of character, the vividness of scene, the effect of action that take priority over ordinary veracity. The test of this other truth is at once spiritual and visceral; its validity has nothing to do with whether such things did, or could, occur. Lorrie Moore says:

> ... the proper relationship of a writer to his or her own life is similar to a cook with a cupboard. What the cook makes from the cupboard is not the same thing as what's in the cupboard ...

Dorothy Allison strives to tell "the emotional truth of people's lives, not necessarily the historical truth"; similarly, Craig Nova stresses that

> The truth for a novelist isn't the same as the facts. . . . When a writer is successful in using a story taken from experience, it is not told exactly the way it happened, but in the way that reveals, through all one's beliefs, hopes, and fear, how the event should have happened.

Good. Now: what was it about this experience that made it matter to you? Try writing a *very* brief summary of what happened—no more than a hundred words. What kind of story might this be? Can the raw material of incident, accident, and choice be reshaped, plumped up, pared to the bone, refleshed, differently spiced? You experienced whatever it was chronologically—but is that the best way to tell it so as to bring its meaning out? Perhaps you experienced it over a period of months or years; what are the *fewest* scenes in the *least* amount of time that could contain the action? If "you" are at the center of the action, then "you" must be thoroughly characterized, and that may be difficult. Can you augment some revealing aspect of yourself, change yourself so you are forced to see anew, even make someone else altogether the central character? Use some of the suggestions in this chapter. Try freewriting moments from your memory in no particular order. Or freewrite the last scene first. Describe a place and exaggerate the description: if it's cold, make it murderously cold; if messy, then a disastrous mess. Describe the central character and be at least partly unflattering. All of these are devices to put some distance between you and raw experience so you can begin to shape the different thing that fiction is.

Writer Eudora Welty has suggested writing what you *don't* know about what you know—that is, exploring aspects of experience that remain puzzling or painful. In *Making Shapely Fiction*, Jerome Stern urges a broad interpretation of "writing what you know," recognizing that "the idea of *you* is complex in itself . . . your self is made of many selves . . . not only persons you once were, but also persons you have tried to be, persons you have avoided being, and persons you fear you might be." John Gardner, in *The Art of Fiction*, argues that "nothing can be more limiting to the imagination" than the advice that you write about what you know. He suggests instead that you "write the kind of story you know and like best."

This is a useful idea, because the kind of story you know and like best has also taught you something about the way such stories are told, how they are shaped, what kind of surprise, conflict, and change they involve. Many beginning writers who are not yet avid readers have learned from television more than they realize about structure, the way characters behave and talk, how a joke is arranged, how a lie is revealed, and so forth. The trouble is that if you learn fiction from television, or if the kind of story you know and like best is genre fiction—science fiction, fantasy, romance, mystery—you may have learned about technique without having learned anything about the unique contribution you can make to such a story. The result is that you end up writing imitation soap opera or space odyssey, second-rate somebody else instead of first-rate you.

The essential thing is that you write about something you really care about, and the first step is to find out what that is. Playwright Claudia Johnson advises her students to identify their real concerns by making a "menu" of them. Pick the big emotions and make lists in your journal: *What makes you angry? What are you afraid of? What do you want? What hurts?* Or consider the crucial turning points of your life: *What really changed you? Who really changed you?* Those will be the areas to look to for stories, whether or not those stories are autobiographical. Novelist Ron Carlson says, "I always write from my own experiences, whether I've had them or not."

Another journal idea is to jot down the facts of the first seven years of your life under several categories: *Events, People, Your Self, Inner Life, Characteristic Things.* What from those first seven years still occupies your mind? Underline or highlight the items on your page(s) that you aren't done with yet. Those items are clues to your concerns and a possible source of storytelling.

A related device for your journal might be borrowed from the *Pillow Book* of Sei Shonagun. A courtesan in tenth-century Japan, she kept a diary of the goings-on at court and concealed it in her wooden pillow—hence *pillow book.* Sei Shonagun made lists under various categories of specific, often quirky *Things.* This device is capable of endless variety and can reveal yourself to you as you find out what sort of things you want to list: *Things I wish had never been said. Red things. Things more embarrassing than nudity. Things to put off as long as possible. Things to die for. Acid things. Things that last only a day.*

Such devices may be necessary because identifying what we care about is not always easy. We are surrounded by a constant barrage of information, drama, ideas, and judgments offered to us live, printed, and electronically. It is so much easier to know what we ought to think and feel than what we actually do. Worthy authorities constantly exhort us to care about worthy causes, only a few of which really touch us, whereas what we care about at any given moment may seem trivial, self-conscious, or self-serving.

This, I think, is in large part the value of Brande's first exercise, which forces you to write in the intuitively honest period of first light, when the half-sleeping brain is still dealing with its real concerns. Often what seems unworthy is precisely the thing that contains a universal, and by catching it honestly, then stepping back from it, you may achieve the authorial distance that is an essential part of significance. (All you really care about this morning is how you'll look at the dance tonight? This is a trivial obsession that can hit anyone, at any age, anywhere. Write about it as honestly as you can. Now who else might have felt this way? Someone you hate? Someone remote in time from you? Look out: You're on your way to a story.)

Brande advises that once you have developed the habit of regular freewriting, you should read your pages over and pick a passage that seems to suggest a simple story. Muse on the idea for a few days, find its shape, and then fill that shape with people, settings, details from your own experience, observation, and imagination. Turn the story over in your mind. Sleep on it—more than once. Finally, pick a time when you are going to write the story, and when that time comes, go to the desk and write a complete first draft as rapidly as possible. Then put it away, at least overnight. When you take it out again, you will have something to work with, and the business of shaping the story may begin.

> Forget *INSPIRATION*. Habit is more dependable. Habit will sustain you whether you're inspired or not. Habit will help you finish and polish your stories. Inspiration won't. Habit is persistence in practice.
>
> Octavia Butler

Eventually you will learn what sort of experience sparks ideas for your sort of story—and you may be astonished at how such experiences accumulate, as if your life were arranging itself to produce material for you. In the meantime, here are a half dozen suggestions for the kind of idea that may be fruitful.

**The Dilemma, or Catch-22.** You find yourself facing—or know someone who is facing—a situation that offers no solution. Any action taken would be painful and costly. You have no chance of solving this dilemma in real life, but you're a writer, and it costs nothing to explore it with imaginary people in an imaginary setting, even if the outcome is a tragic one. Some writers use newspaper stories to generate this sort of idea. The situation is there in the bland black and white of this morning's news. But who are these people, and how did they come to be in such a mess? Make it up, think it through.

**The Incongruity.** Something comes to your attention that is interesting precisely because you can't figure it out. It doesn't seem to make sense. Someone is breeding pigs in the backyard of a mansion. Who is it? Why is she doing it? Your inventing mind can find the motives and the meanings. An example from my own experience: Once when my phone was out of order, I went out very late at night to make a call from a public phone at a supermarket plaza. At something like two in the morning all the stores were closed but the plaza was not empty. There were three women there, one of them with a baby in a stroller. What were they doing there? It was several years before I figured out a possible answer, and that answer was a short story.

**The Connection.**    You notice a striking similarity in two events, people, places, or periods that are fundamentally unlike. The more you explore the similarity, the more striking it becomes. My novel *The Buzzards* came from such a connection: The daughter of a famous politician was murdered, and I found myself in the position of comforting the dead girl's fiancé. At the same time I was writing lectures on the Agamemnon of Aeschylus. Two politicians, two murdered daughters—one in ancient Greece and one in contemporary America. The connection would not let go of me until I had thought it through and set it down.

**The Memory.**    Certain people, places, and events stand out in your memory with an intensity beyond logic. There's no earthly reason you should remember the smell of Aunt K's rouge. It makes no sense that you still flush with shame at the thought of that ball you "borrowed" when you were in fourth grade. But for some reason these things are still vivid in your mind. That vividness can be explored, embellished, given form. Stephen Minot in *Three Genres* wisely advises, though, that if you are going to write from a memory, *it should be a memory more than a year old.* Otherwise you are likely to be unable to distinguish between what happened and what must happen in the story or between what is in your mind and what you have conveyed on the page.

**The Transplant.**    You find yourself having to deal with a feeling that is either startlingly new to you or else obsessively old. You feel incapable of dealing with it. As a way of distancing yourself from that feeling and gaining some mastery over it, you write about the feeling as precisely as you can, but giving it to an imaginary someone in an imaginary situation. What situation other than your own would produce such a feeling? Who would be caught in that situation? Think it through.

**The Revenge.**    An injustice has been done, and you are powerless to do anything about it. But you're not really, because you're a writer. Reproduce the situation with another set of characters, in other circumstances or another setting. Cast the outcome to suit yourself. Punish whomever you choose. Even if the story ends in a similar injustice, you have righted the wrong by enlisting your reader's sympathy on the side of right. (Dante was particularly good at this: He put his enemies in the inferno and his friends in paradise.) Remember too that as human beings we are intensely, sometimes obsessively, interested in our boredom, and you can take revenge against the things that bore you by making them absurd or funny on paper.

## *Keep Going*

A story idea may come from any source at any time. You may not know you have an idea until you spot it in the random jottings of your journal. Once you've identified the idea, the process of thinking it through begins and doesn't end until you finish (or abandon) the story. Most writing is done between the mind and the hand, not between the hand and the page. It may take a fairly competent typist about three hours to type a twelve-page story. It may take days or months to write it. It follows that, even when you are writing well, most of the time spent writing is not spent putting words on the page. If the story idea grabs hard hold of you, the process of thinking through may be involuntary, a gift. If not, you need to find the inner stillness that will allow you to develop your characters, get to know them, follow their actions in your mind—and it may take an effort of the will to find such stillness.

The metamorphosis of an idea into a story has many aspects, some deliberate and some mysterious. "Inspiration" is a real thing, a gift from the subconscious to the conscious mind. Still, perhaps influenced by the philosophy (although it was not always the practice) of the Beat authors, some new writers may feel that "forcing" words is aesthetically false—and yet few readers can tell which story "flowed" from the writer's pen and which was set down one hard-won word at a time. Toni Morrison has said that she will frequently rewrite a passage eight times, simply to create the impression of an unbroken, inspired flow; Cynthia Ozick often begins with "simple forcing" until the breakthrough comes, and so bears with the "fear and terror until I've pushed through to joy."

Over and over again, successful writers attest that unless they prepare the conscious mind with the habit of work, the gift does not come. Writing is mind-farming. You have to plow, plant, weed, and hope for growing weather. Why a seed turns into a plant is something you are never going to understand, and the only relevant response to it is gratitude. You may be proud, however, of having plowed.

Many writers besides Dorothea Brande have observed that it is ideal, having turned your story over in your mind, to write the first draft at one sitting, pushing on through the action to the conclusion, no matter how dissatisfied you are with this paragraph, that character, this phrasing, or that incident. There are two advantages to doing this. The first is that you are more likely to produce a coherent draft when you come to the desk in a single frame of mind with a single vision of the whole, than when you write piecemeal, having altered ideas and moods. The second is that fast writing tends to make for fast pace in the story. It is always easier, later, to add and develop than it is to sharpen the pace. If you are the sort of writer who stays on page one for days, shoving commas around and combing the thesaurus for a word with slightly better connotations, then you should probably force yourself to try this method (more than once). A note of caution, though: If you write a draft at one sitting, it will not be the draft you want to show anyone, so schedule the sitting well in advance of whatever deadline you may have.

It may happen—always keeping in mind that a single-sitting draft is the ideal—that as you write, the story will take off of its own accord in some direction totally other than you intended. You thought you knew where you were going and now you don't, and you know that unless you stop for a while and think it through again, you'll go wrong. You may find that although you are doing precisely what you had in mind, it doesn't work—Brian Moore calls this "the place where the story gets sick," and often found he had to retrace his steps from an unlikely plot turn or unnatural character action. At such times, the story needs more imaginative mulching before it will bear fruit. Or you may find, simply, that your stamina gives out, and that though you have done your exercises, been steadfast, loyal, and practiced every writerly virtue known, you're stuck. You have writer's block.

Writer's block is not so popular as it was a few years ago. I suspect people got tired of hearing or even talking about it—sometimes writers can be sensitive even to their own clichés. But it may also be that writers began to understand and accept their difficulties. Sometimes the process seems to require working yourself into a muddle and past the muddle to despair; until you have done this, it may be impossible suddenly to see what the shape of a thing ought to be. When you're writing, this feels terrible. You sit spinning your wheels, digging deeper and deeper into the mental muck. You decide you are going to trash the whole thing and walk away from it—only you can't, and you keep going back to it like a tongue to an aching tooth. Or you decide you are going to sit there until you bludgeon it into shape—and as long as you sit there it remains recalcitrant. W. H. Auden observed that the hardest part of writing is not knowing whether you are procrastinating or must wait for the words to come.

"What's called writer's block," claims novelist Tom Wolfe, "is almost always ordinary fear." Indeed, whenever I ask a group of writers what they find most difficult, a significant number answer that they feel they aren't good enough, that the empty page intimidates them, that they are in some way afraid. Many complain of their own laziness, but laziness, like money, doesn't really exist except to represent something else—in this case fear, severe self-judgment, or what Natalie Goldberg calls "the cycle of guilt, avoidance, and pressure."

I know a newspaper editor who says that writer's block always represents a lack of information. I thought this inapplicable to fiction until I noticed that I was mainly frustrated when I didn't know enough about my characters, the scene, or the action—when I had not gone to the imaginative depth where information lies.

Encouragement comes from the poet William Stafford, who advised his students always to write to their lowest standard. Somebody always corrected him: "You mean your highest standard." No, he meant your lowest standard. Jean Cocteau's editor gave him the same advice. "The thought of having to produce a masterpiece is giving you writer's cramp. You're paralysed at the sight of a blank sheet of paper. So begin any old way. Write: 'One winter evening . . .'" In *On Writer's Block: A New Approach to Creativity*, Victoria Nelson points out that "there is an almost mathematical ratio between soaring, grandiose ambition . . . and severe creative block." More writers prostitute themselves "up" than "down"; more are false in the determination to write great literature than to throw off a romance.

A rough draft is rough; that's its nature. Let it be rough. Think of it as making clay. The molding and the gloss come later.

And remember: Writing is easy. Not writing is hard.

## A Word about Theme

The process of discovering, choosing, and revealing the theme of your story begins as early as a first freewrite and continues, probably, beyond publication. The theme is what your story is about and what you think about it, its core and the spin you put on it. John Gardner points out that theme "is not imposed on the story but evoked from within it—initially an intuitive but finally an intellectual act on the part of the writer."

What your story has to say will gradually reveal itself to you and to your reader through every choice you as a writer make—the actions, characters, setting, dialogue, objects, pace, metaphors and symbols, viewpoint, atmosphere, style, even syntax and punctuation, and even in some cases typography.

Because of this comprehensive nature of theme, I have placed the discussion of it in chapter 10, after the individual story elements have been addressed. But this is not entirely satisfactory, since each of those elements contributes to the theme as it unfolds. You may want to skip ahead and take a look at that chapter, or you may want to anticipate the issue by asking at every stage of your manuscript: What really interests me about this? How does this (image, character, dialogue, place . . .) reveal what I care about? What connections do I see between one image and another? How can I strengthen those connections? Am I saying what I really mean, telling my truth about it?

All the later chapters in this book include short stories or excerpts that operate as examples of the elements of fiction under consideration. What follows here, however, is an excerpt from a book about the writing process that takes a reassuring, "just do it" approach to getting started; the second selection, "Why I Write," offers examples of one writer's invention process.

## Shitty First Drafts

### ANNE LAMOTT

### FROM *BIRD BY BIRD*

Now, practically even better news than that of short assignments is the idea of shitty first drafts. All good writers write them. This is how they end up with good second drafts and terrific third drafts. People tend to look at successful writers, writers who are getting their books published and maybe even doing well financially, and think that they sit down at their desks every morning feeling like a million dollars, feeling great about who they are and how much talent they have and what a great story they have to tell; that they take in a few deep breaths, push back their sleeves, roll their necks a few times to get all the cricks out, and dive in, typing fully formed passages as fast as a court reporter. But this is just the fantasy of the uninitiated. I know some very great writers, writers you love who write beautifully and have made a great deal of money, and not *one* of them sits down routinely feeling wildly enthusiastic and confident. Not one of them writes elegant first drafts. All right, one of them does, but we do not like her very much. We do not think that she has a rich inner life or that God likes her or can even stand her. (Although when I mentioned this to my priest friend Tom, he said you can safely assume you've created God in your own image when it turns out that God hates all the same people you do.)

Very few writers really know what they are doing until they've done it. Nor do they go about their business feeling dewy and thrilled. They do not type a few stiff warm-up sentences and then find themselves bounding along like huskies across the snow. One writer I know tells me that he sits down every morning and says to himself nicely, "It's not like you don't have a choice, because you do—you can either type or kill yourself." We all often feel like we are pulling teeth, even those writers whose prose ends up being the most natural and fluid. The right words and sentences just do not come pouring out like ticker tape most of the time. Now, Muriel Spark is said to have felt that she was taking dictation from God every morning—sitting there, one supposes, plugged into a Dictaphone, typing away, humming. But this is a very hostile and aggressive position. One might hope for bad things to rain down on a person like this.

For me and most of the other writers I know, writing is not rapturous. In fact, the only way I can get anything written at all is to write really, really shitty first drafts.

The first draft is the child's draft, where you let it all pour out and then let it romp all over the place, knowing that no one is going to see it and that you can shape it later. You just let this childlike part of you channel whatever voices and visions come through and onto the page. If one of the characters wants to say, "Well, so what, Mr. Poopy Pants?" you let her. No one is going to see it. If the kid wants to get into really sentimental, weepy, emotional territory, you let him. Just get it all down on paper, because there may be something great in those six crazy pages that you would never have gotten to by more rational, grown-up means. There may be something in the very last line of the very last paragraph on page six that you just love, that is so beautiful or wild that you now know what you're supposed to be writing about, more or less, or in what direction you might go—but there was no way to get to this without first getting through the first five and a half pages.

I used to write food reviews for *California* magazine before it folded. (My writing food reviews had nothing to do with the magazine folding, although every single review did cause a couple of canceled subscriptions. Some readers took umbrage at my comparing mounds of vegetable puree with various ex-presidents' brains.) These reviews always took two days to write. First I'd go to a restaurant several times with a few opinionated, articulate friends in tow. I'd sit there writing down everything anyone said that was at all interesting or funny. Then on the following Monday I'd sit down at my desk with my notes, and try to write the review. Even after I'd been doing this for years, panic would set in. I'd try to write a lead, but instead I'd write a couple of dreadful sentences, xx them out, try again, xx everything out, and then feel despair and worry settle on my chest like an x-ray apron. It's over I'd think, calmly. I'm not going to be able to get the magic to work this time. I'm ruined. I'm through. I'm toast. Maybe, I'd think, I can get my old job back as a clerk-typist. But probably not. I'd get up and study my teeth in the mirror for a while. Then I'd stop, remember to breathe, make a few phone calls, hit the kitchen and chow down. Eventually I'd go back and sit down at my desk, and sigh for the next ten minutes. Finally I would pick up my one-inch picture frame, stare into it as if for the answer, and every time the answer would come: all I had to do was to write a really shitty first draft of, say, the opening paragraph. And no one was going to see it.

So I'd start writing without reining myself in. It was almost just typing, just making my fingers move. And the writing would be *terrible*. I'd write a lead paragraph that was a whole page, even though the entire review could only be three pages long, and then I'd start writing up descriptions of the food, one dish at a time, bird by bird, and the critics would be sitting on my shoulders, commenting like cartoon characters. They'd be pretending to snore, or rolling their eyes at my overwrought descriptions, no matter how hard I tried to tone those descriptions down, no matter how conscious I was of what a friend said to me gently in my early days of restaurant reviewing. "Annie," she said, "it is just a piece of *chicken*. It is just a bit of *cake*."

But because by then I had been writing for so long, I would eventually let myself trust the process—sort of, more or less. I'd write a first draft that was maybe twice as long as it should be, with a self-indulgent and boring beginning, stupefying descriptions of the meal, lots of quotes from my black-humored friends that made them sound more like the Manson girls than food lovers, and no ending to speak of. The whole thing would be so long and incoherent and hideous that for the rest of the day I'd obsess about getting creamed by a car before I could write a decent second draft. I'd worry that people would read what I'd written and believe that the accident had really been a suicide, that I had panicked because my talent was waning and my mind was shot.

The next day, though, I'd sit down, go through it all with a colored pen, take out everything I possibly could, find a new lead somewhere on the second page, figure out a kicky place to end it, and then write a second draft. It always turned out fine, sometimes even funny and weird and helpful. I'd go over it one more time and mail it in.

Then, a month later, when it was time for another review, the whole process would start again, complete with the fears that people would find my first draft before I could rewrite it.

Almost all good writing begins with terrible first efforts. You need to start somewhere. Start by getting something—anything—down on paper. A friend of mine says that the first draft is the down draft—you just get it down. The second draft is the up draft—you fix it up. You try to say what you have to say more accurately. And the third draft is the dental draft, where you check every tooth, to see if it's loose or cramped or decayed, or even, God help us, healthy.

What I've learned to do when I sit down to work on a shitty first draft is to quiet the voices in my head. First there's the vinegar-lipped Reader Lady, who says primly, "Well, *that's* not very interesting, is it?" And there's the emaciated German male who writes these Orwellian memos detailing your thought crimes. And there are your parents, agonizing over your lack of loyalty and discretion; and there's William Burroughs, dozing off or shooting up because he finds you as bold and articulate as a houseplant; and so on. And there are also the dogs: let's not forget the dogs, the dogs in their pen who will surely hurtle and snarl their way out if you ever *stop* writing, because writing is, for some of us, the latch that keeps the door of the pen closed, keeps those crazy ravenous dogs contained.

Quieting these voices is at least half the battle I fight daily. But this is better than it used to be. It used to be 87 percent. Left to its own devices, my mind spends much of its time having conversations with people who aren't there. I walk along defending myself to people, or exchanging repartee with them, or rationalizing my behavior, or seducing them with gossip, or pretending I'm on their TV talk show or whatever. I speed or run an aging yellow light or don't come to a full stop, and one nanosecond later am explaining to imaginary cops exactly why I had to do what I did, or insisting that I did not in fact do it.

I happened to mention this to a hypnotist I saw many years ago, and he looked at me very nicely. At first I thought he was feeling around on the floor for the silent alarm button, but then he gave me the following exercise, which I still use to this day.

Close your eyes and get quiet for a minute, until the chatter starts up. Then isolate one of the voices and imagine the person speaking as a mouse. Pick it up by the tail and drop it into a mason jar. Then isolate another voice, pick it up by the tail, drop it in the jar. And so on. Drop in any high-maintenance parental units, drop in any contractors, lawyers, colleagues, children, anyone who is whining in your head. Then put the lid on, and watch all these mouse people clawing at the glass, jabbering away, trying to make you feel like shit because you won't do what they want— won't give them more money, won't be more successful, won't see them more often. Then imagine that there is a volume-control button on the bottle. Turn it all the way up for a minute, and listen to the stream of angry, neglected, guilt-mongering voices. Then turn it all the way down and watch the frantic mice lunge at the glass, trying to get to you. Leave it down, and get back to your shitty first draft.

A writer friend of mine suggests opening the jar and shooting them all in the head. But I think he's a little angry, and I'm sure nothing like this would ever occur to you.

# Why I Write

### JOAN DIDION

Of course I stole the title for this talk from George Orwell. One reason I stole it was that I like the sound of the words: *Why I Write*. There you have three short unambiguous words that share a sound, and the sound they share is this:

*I*

*I*

*I*

In many ways writing is the act of saying *I*, of imposing oneself upon other people, of saying *listen to me, see it my way, change your mind*. It's an aggressive, even a hostile act. You can disguise its aggressiveness all you want with veils of subordinate clauses and qualifiers and tentative subjunctives, with ellipses and evasions—with the whole manner of intimating rather than claiming, of alluding rather than stating—but there's no getting around the fact that setting words on paper is the tactic of a secret bully, an invasion, an imposition of the writer's sensibility on the reader's most private space.

I stole the title not only because the words sounded right but because they seemed to sum up, in a no-nonsense way, all I have to tell you. Like many writers I have only this one "subject," this one "area": the act of writing. I can bring you no reports from any other front. I may have other interests: I am "interested," for example, in marine biology, but I don't flatter myself that you would come out to hear me talk about it. I am not a scholar. I am not in the least an intellectual, which is not to say that when I hear the word "intellectual" I reach for my gun, but only to say that I do not think in abstracts. During the years when I was an undergraduate at Berkeley I tried, with a kind of hopeless late-adolescent energy, to buy some temporary visa into the world of ideas, to forge for myself a mind that could deal with the abstract.

In short I tried to think. I failed. My attention veered inexorably back to the specific, to the tangible, to what was generally considered, by everyone I knew then and for that matter have known since, the peripheral. I would try to contemplate the Hegelian dialectic and would find myself concentrating instead on a flowering pear tree outside my window and the particular way that petals fell on my floor. I would try to read linguistic theory and would find myself wondering instead if the lights were on in the bevatron up the hill. When I say that I was wondering if the lights were on in the bevatron you might immediately suspect, if you deal in ideas at all, that I was registering the bevatron as a political symbol, thinking in shorthand about the military-industrial complex and its role in the university community, but you would be wrong. I was only wondering if the lights were on in the bevatron, and how they looked. A physical fact.

I had trouble graduating from Berkeley, not because of this inability to deal with ideas—I was majoring in English, and I could locate the house-and-garden imagery in *The Portrait of a Lady* as well as the next person, "imagery" being by definition the kind of specific that got my attention—but simply because I had neglected to take a course in Milton. For reasons which now sound baroque I needed a degree by the end of that summer, and the English department finally agreed, if I would come down from Sacramento every Friday and talk about the cosmology of *Paradise Lost,* to certify me proficient in Milton. I did this. Some Fridays I took the Greyhound bus, other Fridays I caught the Southern Pacific's City of San Francisco on the last leg of its transcontinental trip. I can no longer tell you whether Milton put the sun or the earth at the center of his universe in *Paradise Lost,* the central question of at least one century and a topic about which I wrote 10,000 words that summer, but I can still recall the exact rancidity of the butter in the City of San Francisco's dining car, and the way the tinted windows on the Greyhound bus cast the oil refineries around Carquinez Straits into a grayed and obscurely sinister light. In short my attention was always on the periphery, on what I would see and taste and touch, on the butter, and the Greyhound bus. During those years I was traveling on what I knew to be a very shaky passport, forged papers: I knew that I was no legitimate resident in any world of ideas. I knew I couldn't think. All I knew then was what I couldn't do. All I knew then was what I wasn't, and it took me some years to discover what I was.

Which was a writer.

By which I mean not a "good" writer or a "bad" writer but simply a writer, a person whose most absorbed and passionate hours are spent arranging words on pieces of paper. Had my credentials been in order I would never have become a writer. Had I been blessed with even limited access to my own mind there would have been no reason to write. I write entirely to find out what I'm thinking, what I'm looking at, what I see and what it means. What I want and what I fear. Why did the oil refineries around Carquinez Straits seem sinister to me in the summer of 1956? Why have the night lights in the bevatron burned in my mind for twenty years? *What is going on in these pictures in my mind?*

When I talk about pictures in my mind I am talking, quite specifically, about images that shimmer around the edges. There used to be an illustration in every elementary psychology book showing a cat drawn by a patient in varying stages of schizophrenia. This cat had a shimmer around it. You could see the molecular structure breaking down at the very edges of the cat: the cat became the background and the background the cat, everything interacting, exchanging ions. People on hallucinogens describe the same perception of objects. I'm not a schizophrenic, nor do I take hallucino- gens, but certain images do shimmer for me. Look hard enough, and you can't miss the shimmer. It's there. You can't think too much about these pictures that shimmer. You just lie low and let them develop. You stay quiet. You don't talk to many people and you keep your nervous system from shorting out and you try to locate the cat in the shimmer, the grammar in the picture.

Just as I meant "shimmer" literally I mean "grammar" literally. Grammar is a piano I play by ear, since I seem to have been out of school the year the rules were mentioned. All I know about grammar is its infinite power. To shift the structure of a sentence alters the meaning of that sentence, as definitely and inflexibly as the position of a camera alters the meaning of the object photographed. Many people know about camera angles now, but not so many know about sentences. The arrangement of the words matters, and the arrangement you want can be found in the picture in your mind. The picture dictates the arrangement. The picture dictates whether this will be a sentence with or without clauses, a sentence that ends hard or a dying-fall sentence, long or short, active or passive. The picture tells you how to arrange the words and the arrangement of the words tells you, or tells me, what's going on in the picture. *Nota bene:*

It tells you.
You don't tell it.

Let me show you what I mean by pictures in the mind. I began *Play It as It Lays* just as I have begun each of my novels, with no notion of "character" or "plot" or even "incident." I had only two pictures in my mind, more about which later, and a technical intention, which was to write a novel so elliptical and fast that it would be over before you noticed it, a novel so fast that it would scarcely exist on the page at all. About the pictures: the first was of white space. Empty space. This was clearly the picture that dictated the narrative intention of the book—a book in which anything that happened would happen off the page, a "white" book to which the reader would have to bring his or her own bad dreams—and yet this picture told me no "story," suggested no situation. The second picture did. This second picture was of something actually witnessed. A young woman with long hair and a short white halter dress walks through the casino at the Riviera in Las Vegas at one in the morning. She crosses the casino alone and picks up a house telephone. I watch her because I have heard her paged, and recognize her name: she is a minor actress I see around Los Angeles from time to time, in places like Jax and once in a gynecologist's office in the Beverly Hills Clinic, but have never met. I know nothing about her. Who is paging her? Why is she here to be paged? How exactly did she come to this? It was precisely this moment in Las Vegas that made *Play It as It Lays* begin to tell itself to me, but the moment appears in the novel only obliquely, in a chapter which begins:

Maria made a list of things she would never do. She would never: walk through the Sands or Caesar's alone after midnight. She would never: ball at a party, do S-M unless she wanted to, borrow furs from Abe Lipsey, deal. She would never: carry a Yorkshire in Beverly Hills.

That is the beginning of the chapter and that is also the end of the chapter, which may suggest what I meant by "white space."

I recall having a number of pictures in my mind when I began the novel I just finished, *A Book of Common Prayer*. As a matter of fact one of these pictures was of that bevatron I mentioned, although I would be hard put to tell you a story in which nuclear energy figured. Another was a newspaper photograph of a hijacked 707 burning on the desert in the Middle East. Another was the night view from a room in which I once spent a week with paratyphoid, a hotel room on the Colombian coast. My husband and I seemed to be on the Colombian coast representing the United States of America at a film festival (I recall invoking the name "Jack Valenti" a lot, as if its reiteration could make me well), and it was a bad place to have fever, not only because my indisposition offended our hosts but because every night in this hotel the generator failed. The lights went out. The elevator stopped. My husband would go to the event of the evening and make excuses for me and I would stay alone in this hotel room, in the dark. I remember standing at the window trying to call Bogotá (the telephone seemed to work on the same principle as the generator) and watching the night wind come up and wondering what I was doing eleven degrees off the equator with a fever of 103. The view from that window definitely figures in *A Book of Common Prayer*, as does the burning 707, and yet none of these pictures told me the story I needed.

The picture that did, the picture that shimmered and made these other images coalesce, was the Panama airport at 6 A.M. I was in this airport only once, on a plane to Bogotá that stopped for an hour to refuel, but the way it looked that morning remained superimposed on everything I saw until the day I finished *A Book of Common Prayer*. I lived in that airport for several years. I can still feel the hot air when I step off the plane, can see the heat already rising off the tarmac at 6 A.M. I can feel my skirt damp and wrinkled on my legs. I can feel the asphalt stick to my sandals. I remember the big tail of a Pan American plane floating motionless down at the end of the tarmac. I remember the sound of a slot machine in the waiting room. I could tell you that I remember a particular woman in the airport, an American woman, a *norteamericana*, a thin *norteamericana* about 40 who wore a big square emerald in lieu of a wedding ring, but there was no such woman there.

I put this woman in the airport later. I made this woman up, just as I later made up a country to put the airport in, and a family to run the country. This woman in the airport is neither catching a plane nor meeting one. She is ordering tea in the airport coffee shop. In fact she is not simply "ordering" tea but insisting that the water be boiled, in front of her, for twenty minutes. Why is this woman in this airport? Why is she going nowhere, where has she been? Where did she get that big emerald? What derangement, or disassociation, makes her believe that her will to see the water boiled can possibly prevail?

She had been going to one airport or another for four months, one could see it, looking at the visas on her passport. All those airports where Charlotte Douglas's passport had been stamped would have looked alike. Sometimes the sign on the tower would say "Bienvenidos" and sometimes the sign on the tower would say "Bienvenue," some places were wet and hot and others dry and hot, but at each of these airports the pastel concrete walls would rust and stain and the swamp off the runway would be littered with the fuselages of cannibalized Fairchild F-227's and the water would need boiling.

    I knew why Charlotte went to the airport even if Victor did not.

    I knew about airports.

These lines appear about halfway through *A Book of Common Prayer,* but I wrote them during the second week I worked on the book, long before I had any idea where Charlotte Douglas had been or why she went to airports. Until I wrote these lines I had no character called "Victor" in mind: the necessity for mentioning a name, and the name "Victor," occurred to me as I wrote the sentence. *I knew why Charlotte went to the airport* sounded incomplete. *I knew why Charlotte went to the airport even if Victor did not* carried a little more narrative drive. Most important of all, until I wrote these lines I did not know who "I" was, who was telling the story. I had intended until that moment that the "I" be no more than the voice of the author, a 19th-century omniscient narrator. But there it was:

    I knew why Charlotte went to the airport even if Victor did not.

    I knew about airports.

This "I" was the voice of no author in my house. This "I" was someone who not only knew why Charlotte went to the airport but also knew someone called "Victor." Who was Victor? Who was this narrator? Why was this narrator telling me this story? Let me tell you one thing about why writers write: had I known the answer to any of these questions I would never have needed to write a novel.

## Writing Exercises

### INDIVIDUAL

Keep a journal for two weeks. Decide on a comfortable amount to write daily, and then determine not to let a day slide. To get started, refer to the journal suggestions in this chapter—freewriting, pages 4–5; the Dorothea Brande exercise, page 5; a menu of concerns, page 10; a review of your first seven years, page 10; and a set of *Pillow Book* lists, page 10. At the end of the two weeks, assess your efforts and decide what habit of journal keeping you can develop and stick to. A page a day? A paragraph a day? Three pages a week? Then do it. Probably at least once a day you have a thought worth putting into words, and sometimes it's better to write one sentence a day than to let the habit slide. Like exercise and piano practice, a journal is most useful when it's kept up regularly and frequently. If you pick an hour during which you write each day, no matter how much or how little, you may find yourself looking forward to, and saving things up for, that time.

In addition to keeping a journal, you might try some of these story triggers:

1. In "Why I Write" Joan Didion says that she writes in order to explore the "images [in her mind] that shimmer around the edges." She says she is trying to answer the question "What is going on in these pictures in my mind?" What are some of the pictures in your mind? Pick a puzzling image from your memory that you often recall. Don't worry so much about figuring out why it has stuck with you. Just describe the moment in as much detail as you can.

2. Sketch a floor plan of the first house or apartment, or a map of the first neighborhood, you remember. Place an X on the spots in the plan where significant events happened to you—the tree house from which you used to look into the neighbors' window, the kitchen in which you found out that your parents were going to divorce, and so forth. Write a tour of the house as if you were a guide, pointing out its features and its history. If a story starts to emerge from one of the settings, go with it.

3. Identify the kernel of a short story from your experience of one of the following.
   - an early memory
   - an unfounded fear
   - a scar
   - a bad haircut
   - yesterday
   - a sudden change in a relationship
   - the loss of a small object
   - conflict over a lesson you were taught or never taught
   - an experience you still do not fully understand

   Freedraft a passage about it, then write the first page of the story.

4. Take your notebook and go to a place where you can observe people—a library, restaurant, bus station, wherever. Choose a few people and describe them in detail in your notebook. What are they wearing? What are they doing and why do you think they're doing it? If they are talking, can you overhear (or guess) what they're saying? What are they thinking?

   Next, choose one character and invent a life for him or her. Write at least two pages. Where does s/he live? Work? What relationships does s/he have? Worries? Fears? Desires? Pleasures? Does this character have a secret? Do you find yourself beginning a story?

5. Have you ever worked as a carpenter, cabdriver, janitor, dentist, bar pianist, waiter, actor, film critic, drummer, teacher, coach, stockbroker, therapist, librarian, or mailman? Or maybe you have the inside dope on a job that a close friend or family member has had. Make a list of jobs you've had or of which you have

secondhand knowledge of—no matter how odd or how mundane. Now list some incidents that happened at one or another of those jobs, then pick one incident and begin describing it. Don't limit yourself to what actually happened.

### COLLABORATIVE

6. Have everyone in the class work together to come up with a set of random elements that might prompt a story. (You may want to brainstorm together, vote on favorites, or even have small groups responsible for individual elements. Work together as a class to establish these common elements.) Here is an example of the kind of thing you might come up with:

Two characters: a dogcatcher and an ICU nurse

A place: First Baptist Church

Two objects: a bowling ball and a ballpoint pen

An adjective: scrumptious

An abstraction: fidelity

   Now each member of the class should begin a story using all the random elements decided upon by the class. Write for fifteen minutes. Be as silly or as serious as you wish.

7. Divide into small groups. Have each group member write two or three opening sentences. Pass the sentences around, and then each member should copy down someone else's sentence to use. (It doesn't matter if several people pick the same sentence.)

   Once you have a first sentence, take two or three words from that first sentence and use them again in the second sentence. In the third sentence, borrow two or three words from the second sentence. Continue on in this fashion until you gain momentum and can feel a story emerging.

   Variation: Use a "given" first sentence from another source. See how the same first sentence leads different writers in different directions.

8. Bring in a photograph, art print, postcard, or advertisement that suggests an intriguing situation. Put all the pictures on a table and have each class member choose one. Write for ten minutes through a pictured character's viewpoint, allowing yourself to discover the thread of a story. In small groups, show the picture, read your writing back to your small group, and together brainstorm possible directions for the story. Variations:

   a. With three others, individually write the exercise about the same picture. Then read your pieces aloud to observe the common and original elements that emerged.

   b. If you wish to write a fantastic or surreal story, try using as your source the paintings of George Tooker, René Magritte, or Salvador Dalí or the photographs of Jerry Uelsmann.

# 2

## SEEING IS BELIEVING
### *Showing and Telling*

- *Significant Detail*

- *The Active Voice*

- *Prose Rhythm*

- *Mechanics*

Literature offers us feelings for which we do not have to pay. It allows us to love, condemn, condone, hope, dread, and hate without any of the risks those feelings ordinarily involve, for even good feelings—intimacy, power, speed, drunkenness, passion—have consequences, and powerful feelings may risk powerful consequences. Fiction also must contain ideas, which give significance to characters and events. If the ideas are shallow or untrue, the fiction will be correspondingly shallow or untrue. But the ideas must be experienced through or with the characters; they must be felt or the fiction will fail also.

Much nonfiction writing, from editorials to advertising, also tries to persuade us to feel one way rather than another, but nonfiction works largely by means of logic and reasoning. Fiction tries to reproduce the emotional impact of experience. And this is a more difficult task, because unlike the images of film and drama, which directly strike the eye and ear, words are transmitted first to the mind, where they must be translated into images.

In order to move your reader, the standard advice runs, "Show, don't tell." This dictum can be confusing, considering that words are all a writer has to work with. What it means is that your job as a fiction writer is to focus attention not on the words, which are inert, nor on the thoughts these words produce, but through these to felt experience, where the vitality of understanding lies. There are techniques for accomplishing this—for making narrative vivid, moving, and resonant—which can be partly learned and always strengthened.

## Significant Detail

In *The Elements of Style*, William Strunk, Jr., writes:

> If those who have studied the art of writing are in accord on any one point, it is on this: the surest way to arouse and hold the attention of the reader is by being specific, definite and concrete. The greatest writers . . . are effective largely because they deal in particulars and report the details that matter.

Specific, definite, concrete, particular details—these are the life of fiction. Details (as every good liar knows) are the stuff of persuasiveness. Mary is sure that Ed forgot to go pay the gas bill last Tuesday, but Ed says, "I know I went, because this old guy in a knit vest was in front of me in the line, and went on and on about his twin granddaughters"—and it is hard to refute a knit vest and twins even if the furnace doesn't work. John Gardner in *The Art of Fiction* speaks of details as "proofs," rather like those in a geometric theorem or a statistical argument. The novelist, he says, "gives us such details about the streets, stores, weather, politics, and concerns of Cleveland (or wherever the setting is) and such details about the looks, gestures, and experiences of his characters that we cannot help believing that the story he tells us is true."

A detail is "definite" and "concrete" when it appeals to the senses. It should be seen, heard, smelled, tasted, or touched. The most superficial survey of any bookshelf of published fiction will turn up dozens of examples of this principle. Here is a fairly obvious one.

> It was a narrow room, with a rather high ceiling, and crowded from floor to ceiling with goodies. There were rows and rows of hams and sausages of all shapes and colors—white, yellow, red and black; fat and lean and round and long—rows of canned preserves, cocoa and tea, bright translucent glass bottles of honey, marmalade and jam.
>
> I stood enchanted, straining my ears and breathing in the delightful atmosphere and the mixed fragrance of chocolate and smoked fish and earthy truffles. I spoke into the silence, saying: "Good day" in quite a loud voice; I can still remember how my strained, unnatural tones died away in the stillness. No one answered. And my mouth literally began to water like a spring. One quick, noiseless step and I was beside one of the laden tables. I made one rapturous grab into the nearest glass urn, filled as it chanced with chocolate creams, slipped a fistful into my coat pocket, then reached the door, and in the next second was safely round the corner.

> Thomas Mann, *Confessions of Felix Krull, Confidence Man*

The shape of this passage is a tour through the five senses. Mann lets us see: *narrow room, high ceiling, hams, sausages, preserves, cocoa, tea, glass bottles, honey, marmalade, jam.*

He lets us smell: *fragrance of chocolate, smoked fish, earthy truffles*. He lets us hear: *"Good day," unnatural tones, stillness*. He lets us taste: *mouth, water like a spring*. He lets us touch: *grab, chocolate creams, slipped, fistful into my coat pocket*. The writing is alive because we do in fact live through our sense perceptions, and Mann takes us past words and through thought to let us perceive the scene in this way.

In this process, a number of ideas not stated reverberate off the sense images, so that we are also aware of a number of generalizations the author might have made but does not need to make; we will make them ourselves. Mann could have had his character "tell" us: *I was quite poor, and I was not used to seeing such a profusion of food, so that although I was very afraid there might be someone in the room and that I might be caught stealing, I couldn't resist taking the risk.*

Such a version would be very flat, and none of that telling is necessary as all these points are "shown." The character's relative poverty is inherent in the tumble of images of sight and smell; if he were used to such displays, his eyes and nose would not dart about as they do. His fear is inherent in the "strained, unnatural tones" and their dying away in the stillness. His desire is in his watering mouth, his fear in the furtive speed of "quick" and "grab" and "slipped."

The points to be made here are two, and they are both important. The first is that the writer must deal in sense detail. The second is that these must be details "that matter." As a writer of fiction you are at constant pains not simply to say what you mean, but to mean more than you say. Much of what you mean will be an abstraction or a judgment—*love requires trust, children can be cruel*. But if you write in abstractions or judgments, you are writing an essay, whereas if you let us use our senses and form our own interpretations, we will be involved as participants in a real way. Much of the pleasure of reading comes from the egotistical sense that we are clever enough to understand. When the author explains to us or interprets for us, we suspect that he or she doesn't think us bright enough to do it for ourselves.

A detail is *concrete* if it appeals to one of the five senses; it is *significant* if it also conveys an idea or a judgment or both. *The windowsill was green* is concrete, because we can see it. *The windowsill was shedding flakes of fungus-green paint* is concrete and also significant because it conveys the idea that the paint is old and suggests the judgment that the color is ugly. The second version can also be seen more vividly. (For further discussion of selecting detail, see chapter 10, "How Fictional Elements Contribute to Theme," page 370.)

Here is a passage from a young writer that fails through lack of appeal to the senses.

> Debbie was a very stubborn and completely independent person and was always doing things her way despite her parents' efforts to get her to conform. Her father was an executive in a dress manufacturing company and was able to afford his family all the luxuries and comforts of life. But Debbie was completely indifferent to her family's affluence.

This passage contains a number of judgments we might or might not share with the author, and she has not convinced us that we do. What constitutes stubbornness?

Independence? Indifference? Affluence? Further, since the judgments are supported by generalizations, we have no sense of the individuality of the characters, which alone would bring them to life on the page. What things was she always doing? What efforts did her parents make to get her to conform? What level of executive? What dress manufacturing company? What luxuries and comforts?

Debbie would wear a tank top to a tea party if she pleased, with fluorescent earrings and ankle-strap sandals.

"Oh, sweetheart," Mrs. Chiddister would stand in the doorway wringing her hands. "It's not *nice*."

"Not who?" Debbie would say, and add a fringed belt.

Mr. Chiddister was Artistic Director of the Boston branch of Cardin and had a high respect for what he called "elegant textures," which ranged from handwoven tweed to gold filigree, and which he willingly offered his daughter. Debbie preferred her laminated wrist bangles.

We have not passed a final judgment on the merits of these characters, but we know a good deal more about them, and we have drawn certain interim conclusions that are our own and not forced on us by the author. Debbie is independent of her parents' values, rather careless of their feelings, energetic, and possibly a tart. Mrs. Chiddister is quite ineffectual. Mr. Chiddister is a snob, though perhaps Debbie's taste is so bad we'll end up on his side.

But maybe that isn't at all what the author had in mind. The point is that we weren't allowed to know what the author did have in mind. Perhaps it was more like this version:

One day Debbie brought home a copy of *Ulysses*. Mrs. Strum called it "filth" and threw it across the sunporch. Debbie knelt on the parquet and retrieved her bookmark, which she replaced. "No, it's not," she said.

"You're not so old I can't take a strap to you!" Mr. Strum reminded her.

Mr. Strum was controlling stockholder of Readywear Conglomerates and was proud of treating his family, not only on his salary, but also on his expense account. The summer before, he had justified their company on a trip to Belgium, where they toured the American Cemetery and the torture chambers of Ghent Castle. Entirely ungrateful, Debbie had spent the rest of the trip curled up in the hotel with a shabby copy of some poet.

Now we have a much clearer understanding of *stubbornness, independence, indifference*, and *affluence*, both their natures and the value we are to place on them. This time our judgment is heavily weighed in Debbie's favor—partly because people who read books have a sentimental sympathy with people who read books—but also because we hear hysteria in "filth" and "take a strap to you," whereas Debbie's resistance is quiet and strong. Mr. Strum's attitude toward his expense account suggests that he's corrupt, and his choice of "luxuries" is morbid. The passage does contain two overt judgments, the first being that Debbie was "entirely ungrateful." Notice that by the time we get to this, we're aware that the judgment is Mr. Strum's and that Debbie has little enough to be grateful for. We understand not only what the author says but also that she means the opposite of what she says, and we feel doubly clever to get it; that is the pleasure of irony. Likewise, the judgment that the poet's book is "shabby" shows Mr. Strum's crass materialism toward what we know to be the finer things. At the very end of the passage, we are denied a detail that we might very well be given: *What* poet did Debbie curl up with? Again, by this time we understand that we are being given Mr. Strum's view of the situation and that it's Mr. Strum (not Debbie, not the author, and certainly not us) who wouldn't notice the difference between John Keats and Stanley Kunitz.

One may object that both rewrites of the passage are longer than the original. Doesn't "adding" so much detail make for long writing? The answer is yes and no. No, because in the rewrites we know so much more about the values, activities, lifestyles, attitudes, and personalities of the characters that it would take many times the length of the original to "tell" it all in generalizations. Yes, in the sense that detail requires words, and if you are to realize your characters through detail, then you must be careful to select the details that convey the characteristics essential to our understanding. You can't convey a whole person, or a whole action, or everything there is to be conveyed about a single moment of a single day. You must select the significant.

In fact, the greater significance of realistic details may emerge only as you continue to develop and revise your story, for, as Flannery O'Connor says, "the longer you look at one object, the more of the world you see in it." Certain details "tend to accumulate meaning from the action of the story itself" becoming "symbolic in the way they work," O'Connor notes. "While having their essential place in the literal level of the story, [details] operate in depth as well as on the surface, increasing the story in every direction."

No amount of concrete detail will move us, therefore, unless it also implicitly suggests meaning and value. Following is a passage that fails, not because it lacks detail, but because those details lack significance.

> Terry Landon, a handsome young man of twenty-two, was six foot four and broad-shouldered. He had medium-length thick blond hair and a natural tan, which set off the blue of his intense and friendly long-lashed eyes.

Here we have a good deal of generic sensory information, but we still know very little about Terry. There are so many broad-shouldered twenty-two-year-olds in the world, so many blonds, and so on. This sort of cataloging of characteristics suggests an all-points bulletin: *Male Caucasian, medium height, dark hair, last seen wearing gray raincoat.* Such a description may help the police locate a suspect in a crowd, but the assumption is that the identity of the person is not known. As an author you want us to know the character individually and immediately.

The fact is that all our ideas and judgments are formed through our sense perceptions, and daily, moment by moment, we receive information that is not merely sensuous in this way. Four people at a cocktail party may *do* nothing but stand and nibble canapés and may *talk* nothing but politics and the latest films. But you feel perfectly certain that X is furious at Y, who is flirting with Z, who is wounding Q, who is trying to comfort X. You have only your senses to observe with. How do you reach these conclusions? By what gestures, glances, tones, touches, choices of words?

It may be that this constant emphasis on judgment makes the author, and the reader, seem opinionated or self-righteous. "I want to present my characters objectively/ neutrally. I'm not making any value judgments. I want the reader to make up his or her own mind." Yet human beings are constantly judging: *How was the film? He seemed friendly. What a boring class! Do you like it here? She's very thin. That's fascinating. I'm so clumsy. You're gorgeous tonight. Life is crazy, isn't it?*

The fact is that when we are not passing such judgments, it's because we aren't much interested; we are indifferent. Although you may not want to sanctify or damn your characters, you do want us to care about them, and if you refuse to direct our judgment, you may be inviting our indifference. Usually, when you "don't want us to judge," you mean that you want our feelings to be mixed, paradoxical, complex. *She's horribly irritating, but it's not her fault. He's sexy, but there's something cold about it underneath.* If this is what you mean, then you must direct our judgment in both or several directions, not in no direction.

Even a character who doesn't exist except as a type or function will come to life if presented through significant detail, as in this portrait of an aunt in Dorothy Allison's story "Don't Tell Me You Don't Know." Like many of the female relatives the adult narrator mentions, the aunt embodies a powerful, nurturing force that nonetheless failed to protect the narrator from childhood abuse.

> My family runs to heavy women, gravy-fed working women, the kind usually seen in pictures taken at mining disasters. Big women, all of my aunts move under their own power and stalk around telling everybody else what to do. But Aunt Alma was the prototype, the one I had loved most, starting back when she had given us free meals in the roadhouse she'd run for awhile . . . Once there, we'd be fed on chicken gravy and biscuits, and Mama would be fed from the well of her sister's love and outrage.

For a character who is a "prototype," we have a remarkably clear image of this woman. Notice how Allison moves us from generalization toward sharpness of image, gradually bringing the character into focus. First she has only a size and gender, then a certain abstract "power" and an appeal to our visual memory of the grieving, tough women seen in documentary photographs; then a distinct role as the one who "had given us free meals" when the family hit hard times. Once in focus as manager of a particular roadhouse "on the Eustis Highway," Alma's qualities again become generalized to the adult women of the family.

> The power in them, the strength and the heat! . . . How could my daddy, my uncles, ever stand up to them, dare to raise hand or voice to them? They were a power on the earth.

Finally, the focus narrows to the individual again, whose body has been formed by the starchy foods that poverty made a necessity and that at least kept hunger temporarily at bay: "My aunt always made biscuits. What else stretched so well? Now those starch meals shadowed her loose shoulders and dimpled her fat white elbows."

The point is not that an author must never express an idea, general quality, or judgment. But, in order to carry the felt weight of fiction, these abstractions must be realized through the senses— "I smelled chicken gravy and hot grease, the close thick scent of love and understanding." Through details these abstract qualities live.

> GOOD WRITERS MAY "TELL" ABOUT ALMOST ANYTHING IN fiction except the characters' feelings. One may tell the reader that the character went to a private school . . . or one may tell the reader that the character hates spaghetti; but with rare exceptions the characters' feelings must be demonstrated: fear, love, excitement, doubt, embarrassment, despair become real only when they take the form of events—action (or gesture), dialogue, or physical reaction to setting. Detail is the lifeblood of fiction.
>
> John Gardner

## WRITING ABOUT EMOTION

Fiction offers feelings for which the reader doesn't pay—and yet to evoke those feelings, it is often necessary to portray sensory details that the reader may have experienced. Simply labeling a character's emotion as love or hatred will have little effect, for such abstraction operates solely on a vague, intellectual level; rather, emotion is the body's physical reaction to information the senses receive. The great Russian director Stanislavski, originator of realistic "Method" acting, urged his students to abandon the clichéd emotive postures of the nineteenth-century stage in favor of emotions evoked by the actor's recollection of sensory details connected with a personal past trauma. By recalling such details as the tingling of fingertips, the smell of singed hair, and the tensing of calf muscles, an emotion such as anger might naturally be induced within the actor's body.

Similarly, in written fiction, if the writer depicts the precise physical sensations experienced by the character, a particular emotion may be triggered by the reader's own sense memory. For example, in the story "Where Are You Going, Where Have You Been?" at the end of this chapter, the reader may reflexively identify with the protagonist's terror through a personal memory of fear in which vision became blurred and a pumping heart felt too big for its chest, or perhaps from a nightmare in which fingers were too weak to dial a telephone. To simply state that the main character is afraid would keep her at a dispassionate distance, but to dramatize her fear through physical detail allows a reader to share the experience.

THE PAST IS BEAUTIFUL BECAUSE ONE never realizes an emotion at the time. It expands later, and thus we don't have complete emotions about the present, only about the past . . . That is why we dwell on the past, I think.

Virginia Woolf

In his story "The Easy Way," author Tom Perrotta describes the moment in which a lottery winner learns of a jealous friend's death: "I stood perfectly still and let the news expand inside of me, like a bubble in my chest that wouldn't rise or pop. I waited for anger or grief to fill the space it opened, but all I felt just then was an unsteadiness in my legs, a faulty connection with the ground." By tracing the physical reaction and staying true to the shock of the moment, Perrotta conveys the initial impact of this loss.

"Get control of emotion by avoiding the *mention* of the emotion," urges John L'Heureux. "To avoid melodrama, aim for a restrained tone rather than an exaggerated one. A scene with hysteria needs more, not less control in the writing: keep the language deflated and rooted in action and sensory detail."

There are further reasons to avoid labeling emotion: emotion is seldom pure. Conflicting feelings often run together; we rarely stop to analyze our passions as we're caught up in them; and the reader may cease to participate when a label is simply given.

### FILTERING

John Gardner, in *The Art of Fiction*, points out that in addition to the faults of insufficient detail and excessive use of abstraction, there's a third failure:

> . . . the needless filtering of the image through some observing consciousness. The amateur writes: "Turning, she noticed two snakes fighting in among the rocks." Compare: "She turned. In among the rocks, two snakes were fighting . . ." Generally speaking—though no laws are absolute in fiction—vividness urges that almost every occurrence of such phrases as "she noticed" and "she saw" be suppressed in favor of direct presentation of the thing seen.

The filter is a common fault and often difficult to recognize—although once the principle is grasped, cutting away filters is an easy means to more vivid writing. As a fiction writer you will often be working through "some observing consciousness." Yet when you step back and ask readers to observe the observer—to look *at* rather than *through* the character—you start to tell-not-show and rip us briefly out of the scene. Here, for example, is a student passage quite competent except for the filtering:

Mrs. Blair made her way to the chair by the window and sank gratefully into it. *She looked out the window and there*, across the street, *she saw* the ivory BMW parked in front of the fire plug once more. *It seemed to her, though*, that something was wrong with it. *She noticed* that it was listing slightly toward the back and side, and *then saw* that the back rim was resting almost on the asphalt.

Remove the filters from this paragraph and we are allowed to stay in Mrs. Blair's consciousness, watching with her eyes, sharing understanding as it unfolds for her:

Mrs. Blair made her way to the chair by the window and sank gratefully into it. Across the street the ivory BMW was parked in front of the fire plug again. Something was wrong with it, though. It was listing toward the back and side, the back rim resting almost on the asphalt.

A similar filtering occurs when the writer chooses to begin a flashback and mistakenly supposes that the reader is not clever enough to follow this technique without a guiding transition:

Mrs. Blair *thought back to* the time that she and Henry had owned an ivory car, though it had been a Chevy. *She remembered clearly* that it had a hood shaped like a sugar scoop, and chrome bumpers that stuck out a foot front and back. And there was that funny time, *she recalled*, when Henry had to change the flat tire on Alligator Alley, and she'd thought the alligators would come up out of the swamp.

Just as the present scene will be more present to the reader without a filter, so we will be taken more thoroughly back to the time of the memory without a filter:

She and Henry had owned an ivory car once, though it had been a Chevy, with a hood shaped like a sugar scoop and chrome bumpers that stuck out a foot front and back. And there was that funny time Henry had to change the flat tire on Alligator Alley, and she'd thought the alligators would come up out of the swamp.

Observe that the pace of the reading is improved by the removal of the filters—at least partly, literally, because one or two lines of type have been removed.

## The Active Voice

If your prose is to be vigorous as well as vivid, if your characters are to be people who do rather than people to whom things are done, if your descriptions are to "come to life," you must make use of the active voice.

The active voice occurs when the subject of a sentence performs the action described by the verb of that sentence: *She spilled the milk.* When the passive voice is used, the object of the active verb becomes the subject of the passive verb: *The milk was spilled by her.* The passive voice is more indirect than the active; the subject is acted upon rather than acting, and the effect is to weaken the prose and to distance the reader from the action.

The passive voice does have an important place in fiction, precisely because it expresses a sense that the character is being acted upon. If a prison guard is kicking the hero, then *I was slammed into the wall; I was struck blindingly from behind and forced to the floor* appropriately carries the sense of his helplessness.

In general, however, you should seek to use the active voice in all prose and to use the passive only when the actor is unknown or insignificant or when you want to achieve special stylistic effects like the one above.

But there is one other common grammatical construction that is *in effect* passive and can distance the reader from a sense of immediate experience. The verbs that we learn in school to call *linking verbs* are effectively passive because verbs with auxiliaries suggest an indefinite time and are never as sharply focused as active verbs. (Further editing his example cited above, Gardner contrasts the phrase "two snakes were fighting" with the improved "two snakes fought," which pinpoints a specific moment; he further suggests substitution of active verbs, as in "two snakes whipped and lashed, striking at each other.")

Linking verbs also invite complements that tend to be generalized or judgmental: *Her hair* looked *beautiful. He* was *very happy. The room* seemed *expensively furnished. They* became *morose.* Let her hair bounce, tumble, cascade, or swing; we'll see better. Let him laugh, leap, cry, or hug a tree; we'll experience his joy.

The following is a passage with very little action, nevertheless made vital by the use of active verbs:

> At Mixt she neither drinks nor eats. Each of the sisters furtively stares at her as she tranquilly sits in post-Communion meditation with her hands immersed in her habit. *Lectio* has been halted for the morning, so there is only the Great Silence and the tinks of cutlery, but handsigns are being traded as the sisters lard their hunks of bread or fold and ring their dinner napkins. When the prioress stands, all rise up with her for the blessing, and then Sister Aimee gives Mariette the handsigns. *You, infirmary.*
>
> Ron Hansen, *Mariette in Ecstasy*

Here, though the convent meal is silent and action is minimal, a number of the verbs suggest suppressed power: *stares, sits, lard, fold, ring, stands, rise, gives.*

Compare the first passage about Debbie on page 27 with the second of the rewrites on page 28. In the generalized original we have *was stubborn, was doing things, was executive, was able, was indifferent.* Apart from the compound verb *was doing,* all these are linking verbs. In the rewrite the characters *brought, called, threw, knelt, retrieved, replaced, said, reminded, justified, toured, spent,* and *curled up.* What energetic people! The rewrite contains two linking verbs: Mr. Strum *was stockholder* and *was proud;* these properly represent static states, a position and an attitude.

One beneficial side effect of active verbs is that they tend to call forth significant details. If you say "she was shocked," you are telling us; but if you are to show us that

## On Active Verbs

A general verb creates a general impression, but a precise, active verb conveys the exact picture in the reader's mind. For example:

| General | Specific |
|---------|----------|
| walk | Does the waiter *scurry* or *amble?* |
| yell | Does the coach *demand* or *bellow?* |
| swim | Does the child *splash* or *glide?* |
| climb | Does the hiker *stumble up the hill* or *stride?* |

she was shocked through an action, you are likely to have to search for an image as well. "She clenched the arm of the chair so hard that her knuckles whitened." *Clenched* and *whitened* actively suggest shock, and at the same time we see her knuckles on the arm of the chair.

*To be* is the most common of the linking verbs and also the most overused, but all the linking verbs invite generalization and distance. *To feel, to seem, to look, to appear, to experience, to express, to show, to demonstrate, to convey, to display*—all these suggest in fiction that the character is being acted upon or observed by someone rather than doing something. She felt *happy/sad/amused/mortified* does not convince us. We want to see her and infer her emotion for ourselves. *He very clearly conveyed his displeasure.* It isn't clear to us. How did he convey it? To whom?

Linking verbs, like the passive voice, can appropriately convey a sense of passivity or helplessness when that is the desired effect. Notice that in the passage by Mann quoted earlier in this chapter, where Felix Krull is momentarily stunned by the sight of the food before him, linking verbs are used: *It was a narrow room, there were rows and rows,* while all the colors and shapes buffet his senses. Only as he gradually recovers can he *stand, breathe, speak,* and eventually *grab.*

I don't mean to suggest that as an author you should analyze your grammar as you go along. Most word choice is instinctive, and instinct is often the best guide. However, I do mean to suggest that you should be aware of the vigor and variety of available verbs, and that if a passage lacks energy, it may be because your instinct has let you down. How often *are* subjects portrayed in some condition or are they acted *upon,* when they could more forcefully *do?*

A note of caution about active verbs: Make sparing use of what John Ruskin called the "pathetic fallacy"—the attributing of human emotions to natural and man-made objects. Even a description of a static scene can be invigorated if the houses *stand,* the streets *wander,* and the trees *bend.* But if the houses *frown,* the streets *stagger drunkenly,* and the trees *weep,* we will feel more strain than energy in the writing.

## *Prose Rhythm*

Novelists and short-story writers are not under the same obligation as poets to rein-force sense with sound. In prose, on the whole, the rhythm is all right if it isn't clearly wrong. But it can be wrong if, for example, the cadence contradicts the meaning; on the other hand, rhythm can greatly enhance the meaning if it is sensitively used.

> The river moved slowly. It seemed sluggish. The surface lay flat. Birds circled lazily overhead. Jon's boat slipped forward.

In this extreme example, the short, clipped sentences and their parallel structures—subject, verb, modifier—work against the sense of slow, flowing movement. The rhythm could be effective if the character whose eyes we're using is not appreciating or sharing the calm; otherwise it needs recasting.

> The surface lay flat on the sluggish, slow-moving river, and the birds circled lazily overhead as Jon's boat slipped forward.

There is nothing very striking about the rhythm of this version, but at least it moves forward without obstructing the flow of the river.

> The first impression I had as I stopped in the doorway of the immense City Room was of extreme rush and bustle, with the reporters moving rapidly back and forth in the long aisles in order to shove their copy at each other or making frantic gestures as they shouted into their many telephones.

This long and leisurely sentence cannot possibly provide a sense of rush and bus-tle. The phrases need to move as fast as the reporters; the verbiage must be pared down because it slows them down.

> I stopped in the doorway. The City Room was immense, reporters rushing down the aisles, shoving copy at each other, bustling back again, flinging gestures, shouting into telephones.

> The poet Rolfe Humphries remarked that "*very* is the least very word in the lan-guage." It is frequently true that adverbs expressing emphasis or suddenness—*extremely, rapidly, suddenly, phenomenally, quickly, immediately, instantly, definitely, terribly, awfully*—slow the sentence down so as to dilute the force of the intended meaning. "'It's a very nice day,'" said Humphries, "is not as nice a day as 'It's a day!'" Likewise, "They stopped very abruptly" is not as abrupt as "They stopped."

The rhythm of an action can be imitated by the rhythm of a sentence in a rich variety of ways. In the previous example, simplifying the clauses helped create a sense of rush. James Joyce, in the short story "The Dead," structures a long sentence with a number of prepositional phrases so that it carries us headlong.

Lily, the caretaker's daughter, was literally run off her feet. Hardly had she brought one gentleman into the little pantry behind the office on the ground floor and helped him off with his overcoat than the wheezy hall-door bell clanged and she had to scamper along the bare hallway to let in another guest.

Lily's haste is largely created by beginning the sentence, "Hardly had she brought," so that we anticipate the clause that will finish the meaning, "than the bell clanged." Our anticipation forces us to scamper like Lily through the intervening actions.

Just as action and character can find an echo in prose rhythm, so it is possible to help us experience a character's emotions and attitudes through control of the starts and stops of prose tempo. In the following passage from *Persuasion*, Jane Austen combines generalization, passive verbs, and a staccato speech pattern to produce a kind of breathless blindness in the heroine.

> . . . a thousand feelings rushed on Anne, of which this was the most consoling, that it would soon be over. And it was soon over. In two minutes after Charles's preparation, the others appeared; they were in the drawing room. Her eye half met Captain Wentworth's, a bow, a courtesy passed; she heard his voice; he talked to Mary, said all that was right, said something to the Miss Musgroves, enough to mark an easy footing; the room seemed full, full of persons and voices, but a few minutes ended it.

Often an abrupt change in the prose rhythm will signal a discovery or change in mood; such a shift can also reinforce a contrast in characters, actions, and attitudes. In this passage from Frederick Busch's short story "Company," a woman whose movements are relatively confined watches her husband move, stop, and move again.

> Every day did not start with Vince awake that early, dressing in the dark, moving with whispery sounds down the stairs and through the kitchen, out into the autumn morning while groundfog lay on the milkweed burst open and on the stumps of harvested corn. But enough of them did.
>
> I went to the bedroom window to watch him hunt in a business suit.
>
> He moved with his feet in the slowly stirring fog, moving slowly himself with the rifle held across his body and his shoulders stiff. Then he stopped in a frozen watch for woodchucks. His stillness made the fog look faster as it blew across our field behind the barn. Vince stood. He waited for something to shoot. I went back to bed and lay between our covers again. I heard the bolt click. I heard the unemphatic shot, and then the second one, and after a while his feet on the porch, and soon the rush of water, the rattle of the pots on top of the stove, and later his feet again, and the car starting up as he left for work an hour before he had to.

The long opening sentence is arranged in a series of short phrases to move Vince forward. By contrast, "But enough of them did" comes abruptly, its abruptness as well as the sense of the words suggesting the woman's alienation. When Vince starts off again more slowly, the repetition of "moved, slowly stirring, moving slowly," slows down the sentence to match his strides. "Vince stood" again stills him, but the author also needs to convey that Vince stands for a long time, waiting, so we have the repetitions "he stopped, his stillness, Vince stood, he waited." As his activity speeds up again, the tempo of the prose speeds up with another series of short phrases, of which only the last is drawn out with a dependent clause, "as he left for work an hour before he had to," so that we feel the retreat of the car in the distance. Notice that Busch chooses the phrase "the rush of water," not the flow or splash of water, and how the word "rush" also points to Vince's actions. Here, meaning reinforces a tempo that, in turn, reinforces meaning. (An added bonus is that variety in sentence lengths and rhythms helps to hold readers' attention.)

"The Things They Carried" by Tim O'Brien, at the end of this chapter, demonstrates a range of rhythms with a rich variation of effects. Here is one:

> The things they carried were largely determined by necessity. Among the necessities or near-necessities were P-38 can openers, pocket knives, heat tabs, wristwatches, dog tags, mosquito repellent, chewing gum, candy, cigarettes, salt tablets, packets of Kool-Aid, lighters, matches, sewing kits, Military Payment Certificates, C rations, and two or three canteens of water. Together, these items weighed between 15 and 20 pounds . . .

In this passage the piling of items one on the other has the effect of loading the men down and at the same time increasingly suggests the rhythm of their marching as they "hump" their stuff. Similar lists through the story create a rhythmic thread, while variations and stoppages underlie shifts of emotion and sudden crises.

THE DIFFERENCE BETWEEN THE RIGHT WORD and the almost right word . . . is the difference between lightning and the lightning bug.

Mark Twain

## Mechanics

Significant detail, the active voice, and prose rhythm are techniques for achieving the sensuous in fiction, means of helping the reader "sink into the dream" of the story, in John Gardner's phrase. Yet no technique is of much use if the reader's eye is wrenched back to the surface by misspellings or grammatical errors, for once the reader has been startled out of the story's "vivid and continuous dream," that reader may not return.

Spelling, grammar, paragraphing, and punctuation are a kind of magic; their purpose is to be invisible. If the sleight of hand works, we will not notice a comma or a quotation mark but will translate each instantly into a pause or an awareness of voice; we will not focus on the individual letters of a word but extract its sense whole. When the mechanics are incorrectly used, the trick is revealed and the magic fails; the reader's focus is shifted from the story to its surface. The reader is irritated at the author, and of all the emotions the reader is willing to experience, irritation at the author is not one.

There is no intrinsic virtue in standardized mechanics, and you can depart from them whenever you produce a result that adequately compensates for a distracting effect. But only then. Poor mechanics signal amateurism to an editor and suggest that the story itself may be flawed. Unlike the techniques of narrative, the rules of spelling, grammar, and punctuation can be coldly learned anywhere in the English-speaking world—and they should be learned by anyone who aspires to write.

## *Big Me*

### DAN CHAON

It all started when I was twelve years old. Before that, everything was a peaceful blur of childhood, growing up in the small town of Beck, Nebraska. A "town," we called it. Really, the population was just under two hundred, and it was one of those dots along Highway 30 that people didn't usually even slow down for, though strangers sometimes stopped at the little gas station near the grain elevator or ate at the café. My mother and father owned a bar called The Crossroads, at the edge of town. We lived in a little house behind it, and behind our house was the junkyard, and beyond that were wheat fields, which ran all the way to a line of bluffs and barren hills, full of yucca and rattlesnakes.

Back then I spent a lot of time in my mind, building a city up toward those hills. This imaginary place was also called Beck, but it was a metropolis of a million people. The wise though cowardly mayor lived in a mansion in the hills above the interstate, as did the bullish, Teddy Roosevelt-like police commissioner, Winthrop Golding. There were other members of the rich and powerful who lived in enormous old Victorian houses along the bluffs, and many of them harbored dreadful secrets or were involved in one way or another with the powerful Beck underworld. One wealthy, respectable citizen, Mr. Karaffa, turned out to be a lycanthrope who preyed on the lovely, virginal junior high-school girls, mutilating them beyond recognition, until I shot him with a silver bullet. I was the city Detective, though I was often underappreciated and, because of my radical notions, in danger of being fired by the cowardly mayor. The police commissioner always defended me, even when he was exasperated by my unorthodox methods. He respected my integrity.

I don't know how many of my childhood years took place in this imaginary city. By the age of eight I had become the Detective, and shortly thereafter I began drawing maps of the metropolis. By the time we left Beck, I had a folder six inches thick, full of street guides and architecture and subway schedules. In the real town, I was known as the strange kid who wandered around talking to himself. Old people would find me in their backyard gardens and come out and yell at me. Children would see me playing on their swing sets, and when they came out to challenge me, I would run away. I trapped people's cats and bound their arms and legs, harshly forcing confessions from them. Since no one locked their doors, I went into people's houses and stole things, which I pretended were clues to the mystery I was trying to solve.

Everyone real also played a secret role in my city. My parents, for example, were the landlord and his wife, who lived downstairs from my modest one-room apartment. They were well-meaning but unimaginative people, and I was polite to them. There were a number of comic episodes in which the nosy landlady had to be tricked and defeated. My brother Mark was the district attorney, my nemesis. My younger sister Kathy was my secretary, Miss Kathy, whom I sometimes loved. I would have married her if I weren't such a lone wolf.

My family thought of me as a certain person, a role I knew well enough to perform from time to time. Now that they are far away, it sometimes hurts to think that we knew so little of one another. Sometimes I think if no one knows you, then you are no one.

In the spring of my twelfth year, a man moved into a house at the end of my block. The house had belonged to an old woman who had died and left her home fully furnished but tenantless for years, until her heir had finally gotten around to having the estate liquidated, the old furniture sold, the place cleared out and put up for sale. This was the house I had taken cats to, the hideout where I had extracted their yowling confessions. Then finally the house was emptied, and the man took up residence.

I first saw the man in what must have been late May. The lilac bush in his front yard was in full bloom, thick with spade-shaped leaves and clusters of perfumed flowers. The man was mowing the lawn as I passed, and I stopped to stare.

It immediately struck me that there was something familiar about him—the wavy dark hair and gloomy eyes, the round face and dimpled chin. At first I thought he looked like someone I'd seen on TV. And then I realized: he looked like me! Or rather, he looked like an older version of me—me grown up. As he got closer with his push lawnmower, I was aware that our eyes were the same odd, pale shade of gray, that we had the same map of freckles across the bridge of our noses, the same stubby fingers. He lifted his hand solemnly as he reached the edge of his lawn, and I lifted my opposite hand, so that for a moment we were mirror images of one another. I felt terribly worked up and hurried home.

That night, considering the encounter, I wondered whether the man actually *was* me. I thought about all that I'd heard about time travel, and considered the possibility that my older self had come back for some unknown purpose—perhaps to save me from some mistake I was about to make or to warn me. Maybe he was fleeing some future disaster and hoped to change the course of things.

I suppose this tells you a lot about what I was like as a boy, but these were among the first ideas I considered. I believed wholeheartedly in the notion that time travel would soon be a reality, just as I believed in UFOs and ESP and Bigfoot. I used to worry, in all seriousness, whether humanity would last as long as the dinosaurs had lasted. What if we were just a brief, passing phase on the planet? I felt strongly that we needed to explore other solar systems and establish colonies. The survival of the human species was very important to me.

Perhaps it was because of this that I began to keep a journal. I had recently read *The Diary of Anne Frank* and had been deeply moved by the idea that a piece of you, words on a page, could live on after you were dead. I imagined that, after a nuclear holocaust, an extraterrestrial boy might find my journal, floating among some bits of meteorite and pieces of buildings and furniture that had once been Earth. The extraterrestrial boy would translate my diary, and it would become a bestseller on his planet. Eventually, the aliens would be so stirred by my story that they would call off the intergalactic war they were waging and make a truce.

In these journals I would frequently write messages to myself, a person whom I addressed as "Big Me," or "The Future Me." Rereading these entries as the addressee, I try not to be insulted, since my former self admonishes me frequently. "I hope you are not a failure," he says. "I hope you are happy," he says. It gives me pause.

I'm trying to remember what was going on in the world when I was twelve. My brother Mark says it was the worst year of his life. He remembers it as a year of terrible fights between my parents. "They were drunk every night, up till three and four in the morning, screaming at each other. Do you remember the night Mom drove the car into the tree?"

I don't. In my mind, they seemed happy together, in the bantering, ironic manner of sitcom couples, and their arguments seemed full of comedy, as if a laugh track might ring out after their best put-down lines. I don't recall them drunk so much as expansive, and the bar seemed a cheerful, popular place, always full, though they would go bankrupt not long after I turned thirteen.

Mark says that was the year he tried to commit suicide, and I don't recall that either, though I do remember that he was in the hospital for a few days. Mostly, I think of him reclining on the couch, looking regal and dissipated, reading books like *I'm Okay, You're Okay,* and filling out questionnaires that told him whether or not he was normal.

The truth is, I mostly recall the Detective. He had taken an interest in the mysterious stranger who had moved in down the block. The Stranger, it turned out, would be teaching seventh grade science; he would be replacing the renowned girl's basketball coach and science teacher, Mr. Karaffa, who'd had a heart attack and died right after a big game. The Stranger was named Louis Mickleson, and he'd moved to Beck from a big city: Chicago or maybe Omaha. "He seems like a lonely type of guy," my mother commented once.

"A weirdo, you mean?" said my father.

I knew how to get into Mickleson's house. It had been my hideout, and there were a number of secret entrances: loose windows, the cellar door, the back door lock that could be dislodged with the thin, laminated edge of my library card.

He was not a very orderly person, Mr. Mickleson, or perhaps he was simply uncertain. The house was full of boxes, packed and unpacked, and the furniture was placed randomly about the house, as if he'd simply left things where the moving men had set them down. In various corners of the house were projects he'd begun and then abandoned—tilting towers of stacked books next to an empty bookcase, silverware organized in rows along the kitchen counter, a pile of winter coats left on the floor near a closet. The boxes seemed to be carefully classified. Near his bed, for example, were socks, underwear, white T-shirts—each in a separate box, neatly folded near a drawerless dresser. The drawers themselves lay on the floor and contained reams of magazines: *Popular Science* in one, *Azimov's Science Fiction* in another, and *Playboy* in yet another, though the dirty pictures had all been fastidiously scissored out.

You can imagine what a cave of wonders this was for me, piled high with riches and clues; each box almost trembled with mystery. There was a collection of costume jewelry, old coins, and keys. Here were his old lesson plans and grade books, the names of former students penciled in alongside their attendance records and grades and small comments ("messy," "lazy," "shows potential!") racked up in columns. Here were photos and letters: a gold mine!

One Afternoon I was kneeling before his box of letters when I heard the front door open. Naturally, I was very still. I heard the front door close, and then Mr. Mickleson muttering to himself. I tensed as he said, "Okay, well, never mind," and read aloud from a bit of junk mail he'd gotten, using a nasal, theatrical voice: "'A special gift for you enclosed!' How lovely!" I crouched there over his cardboard box, looking at a boyhood photo of him and what must have been his sister, circa 1952, sitting in the lap of an artificially bearded Santa. I heard him chuckling as he opened the freezer and took something out. Then he turned on the TV in the living room, and other voices leapt out at me.

It never felt like danger. I was convinced of my own powers of stealth and invisibility. He would not see me because that was not part of the story I was telling myself: I was the Detective! I sensed a cool, hollow spot in my stomach, and I could glide easily behind him as he sat in his La-Z-Boy recliner, staring at the blue glow of the television, watching the news. He didn't shudder as the dark shape of me passed behind him. He couldn't see me unless I chose to be seen.

I had my first blackout that day I left Mickleson's house, not long after I'd sneaked behind him and crept out the back door. I don't know wheather *blackout* is the best term, with its redolence of alcoholic excess and catatonic states, but I'm not sure what else to call it. I stepped into the backyard and remember walking cautiously along a line of weedy flowerbeds toward the gate that led to the alley. I had taken the Santa photo, and I stared at it. Yes, it could have been a photograph of me when I was five, and I shuddered at the eerie similarity. An obese calico cat hurried down the alley in front of me, disappearing into a hedge that bordered someone else's backyard.

A few seconds later, I found myself at the kitchen table, eating dinner with my family. I was in the process of bringing an ear of buttered corn to my mouth, and it felt something like waking up, only faster, as if I'd been transported in a blink from one place to another. My family had not seemed to notice that I was gone. They were all eating silently, grimly, as if everything were normal. My father was cutting his meat, his jaw firmly locked, and my mother's eyes were on her plate, as if she were watching a small round television. No one seemed surprised by my sudden appearance.

It was kind of alarming. At first, it just seemed odd—like, "Oh, how did I get here?" But then, the more I thought about it, the more my skin crawled. I looked up at the clock on the kitchen wall, grinning black cat with a clock face for a belly and a pendulum tail and eyes that shifted from left to right with each tick. I had somehow lost a considerable amount of time—at least half an hour, maybe forty-five minutes. The last thing I clearly recalled was staring at that photo—Mr. Mickleson, or myself, sitting on Santa's knee. And then, somehow, I had left my body. Where had I gone? I sat there, thinking, but there wasn't even a blur of memory. There was only a blank spot.

Once, I tried to explain it to my wife.

"A *blank* spot?" she said, and her voice grew stiff and concerned, as if I'd found a lump beneath my skin. "Do you mean a blackout? You have blackouts?"

"No, no," I said and tried to smile reassuringly. "Not exactly."

"What do you mean?" she said. "Listen, Andy," she said. "If I told you that I had periods when I. . . lost time. . . wouldn't you be concerned? Wouldn't you want me to see a doctor?"

"You're blowing this all out of proportion," I said. "It's nothing like that." And I wanted to tell her about the things that the Detective had read about in the weeks and months following the first incident—about trances and transcendental states, about astral projection and out-of-body travel. But I didn't.

"There's nothing wrong with me," I said and stretched my arms luxuriously. "I feel great," I said. "It's more like daydreaming. Only—a little different."

But she still looked concerned. "You don't have to hide anything from me," she said. "I just care about you, that's all."

"I know," I said, and I smiled as her eyes scoped my face. "It's nothing," I said, "just one of those little quirks!" And that is what I truly believe. Though my loved ones sometimes tease me about my distractedness, my forgetfulness, they do so affectionately. There haven't been any major incidents, and the only times that really worry me are when I am alone, when I am driving down one street and wake up on another. And even then, I am sure that nothing terrible has happened. I sometimes rub my hands against the steering wheel. I am always intact. It's just one of those things! There are no screams or sirens in the distance.

But back then, that first time, I was frightened. I remember asking my mother how a person would know if he had a brain tumor.

"You don't have a brain tumor," she said irritably. "It's time for bed."

A little later, perhaps feeling guilty, she came up to my room with aspirin and water.

"Do you have a headache, honey?" she said.

I shook my head as she turned off my bedside lamp. "Too much reading of comic books," she said and smiled at me exaggeratedly, as she sometimes did, pretending I was still a baby. "It would make anybody's head feel funny, Little Man!" She touched my forehead with the cold, dry pads of her fingertips, looking down into my eyes, heavily. She looked sad and for a moment lost her balance as she reached down to run a palm across my cheek. "Nothing is wrong," she whispered. "It will all seem better in the morning."

That night, I sat up writing in my diary, writing to Big Me. "I hope you are alive," I wrote. "I hope that I don't die before you are able to read this."

That particular diary entry always makes me feel philosophical. I'm not entirely sure of the person he is writing to, the future person he was imagining. I don't know whether that person is alive or not. There are so many people we could become, and we leave such a trail of bodies through our teens and twenties that it's hard to tell which one is us. How many versions do we abandon over the years? How many end up nearly forgotten, mumbling and gasping for air in some tenement room of our consciousness, like elderly relatives suffering some fatal lung disease?

Like the Detective. As I wander through my big suburban house at night, I can hear his wheezing breath in the background, still muttering about secrets that can't be named. Still hanging in there.

My wife is curled up on the sofa, sipping hot chocolate, reading, and when she looks up she smiles shyly. "What are you staring at?" she says. She is used to this sort of thing by now—finds it endearing, I think. She is a pleasant, practical woman, and I doubt that she would find much of interest in the many former selves that tap against my head, like moths.

She opens her robe. "See anything you like?" she says, and I smile back at her.

"Just peeking," I say brightly. My younger self wouldn't recognize me, I'm sure of that.

Which makes me wonder: what did I see in Mickleson, beyond the striking resemblance? I can't quite remember my train of thought, though it's clear from the diary that I latched wholeheartedly onto the idea. Some of it is obviously playacting, making drama for myself, but some of it isn't. Something about Mickleson struck a chord.

Maybe it was simply this—July 13: "If Mickleson is your future, then you took a wrong turn somewhere. Something is sinister about him! He could be a criminal on the lam! He is crazy. You have to change your life now! Don't ever think bad thoughts about Mom, Dad, or even Mark. Do a good deed every day."

I had been going to his house fairly frequently by that time. I had a notebook, into which I had pasted the Santa photo, and a sample of his handwriting, and a bit of hair from a comb. I tried to write down everything that seemed potentially significant: clues, evidence, but evidence of what, I don't know. There was the crowd of beer cans on his kitchen counter, sometimes arranged in geometric patterns. There were the boxes, unpacked then packed again. There were letters: "I am tired, unbelievably tired, of going around in circles with you," a woman who signed herself "Sandi" had written. "As far as I can see, there is no point in going on. Why can't you just make a decision and stick to it?" I had copied this down in my detective's notebook.

In his living room, there was a little plaque hanging on the wall. It was a rectangular piece of dark wood; a piece of parchment paper, burned around the edges, had been lacquered to it. On the parchment paper, in careful calligraphy, was written:

I wear
the chain
I forged
in life.

This seemed like a possible secret message. I thought maybe he'd escaped from jail.

From a distance, behind a hedge, I watched Mickleson's house. He wouldn't usually appear before ten in the morning. He would pop out of his front door in his bathrobe, glancing quickly around as if he sensed someone watching, and then he would snatch up the newspaper on his doorstep. At times, he seemed aware of my eyes.

I knew I had to be cautious. Mickleson must not guess that he was being investigated, and I tried to take precautions. I stopped wearing my favorite detective hat, to avoid calling attention to myself. When I went through his garbage, I did it in the early morning, while I was fairly certain he was still asleep. Even so, one July morning I was forced to crawl under a thick hedge when Mickleson's back door unexpectedly opened at eight in the morning, and he shuffled out the alley to dump a bag into his trash can. Luckily I was wearing brown and green, so I blended in with the shrubbery. I lay there, prone against the dirt, staring at his bare feet and hairy ankles. He was wearing nothing but boxer shorts, so I could see that his clothes had been concealing a large quantity of dark, vaguely sickening body hair; there was even some on his back! I had recently read a Classics Illustrated comic book version of *Dr. Jekyll and Mr. Hyde,* and I recalled the description of Hyde as "something troglodytic," which was a word I had looked up in the dictionary and now applied as Mickleson dumped his bag into the trash can. I had just begun to grow a few hairs on my own body and was chilled to think I might end up like this. I heard the clank of beer cans, then he walked away. I lay still, feeling uneasy.

At home, after dinner, I would sit in my bedroom, reading through my notes, puzzling. I would flip through my lists, trying to find clues I could link together. I'd sift through the cigar box full of things I'd taken from his home: photographs, keys, a Swiss army knife, a check stub with his signature, which I'd compared against my own. But nothing seemed to fit. All I knew was that he was mysterious. He had some secret.

Late one night that summer, I thought I heard my parents taking about me. I was reading, and their conversation had been mere background, rising and falling, until I heard my name. "Andrew . . . how he's turning out . . . not fair to anybody!" Then, loudly: "What will happen to him?"

I sat up straight, my heart beating heavily, because it seemed that something must have happened, that they must have discovered something. I felt certain I was about to be exposed: my spying, my breaking and entering, my stealing. I was quiet, frightened, and then after a while, I got up and crept downstairs. My mother and father were at the kitchen table, speaking softly, staring at the full ashtray that sat between them.

My mother looked up when I came in and clenched her teeth. "Oh, for God's sake," she said. "Andy, it's two-thirty in the morning! What are you doing up?"

I stood there in the doorway, uncertainly. I wished that I were a little kid again, that I could tell her I was scared. But I just hovered there. "I couldn't sleep," I said.

My mother frowned. "Well, try harder, God damn it," she said.

I stood there a moment longer. "Mom?" I said.

"Go to bed!" She glared.

"I thought I heard you guys saying something about that man that just moved in down the block. He didn't say anything about me, did he?"

"Listen to me, Andrew," she said. Her look darkened. "I don't want you up there listening to our conversations. This is grown-up talk, and I don't want you up there snooping."

"He's going to be the new science teacher," I said.

"I know," she said, but my father raised his eyebrows.

"Who's this?" my father said, raising his glass to his lips. "That weirdo is supposed to be a teacher? That's a laugh."

"Oh, don't start!" my mother said. "At least he's a customer! You better God damn not pick a fight with him. You've driven enough people away as it is, the way you are. It's no wonder we don't have any friends!" Then she turned on me. "I thought I told you to go to bed. Don't just stand there gaping when I tell you to do something! My God, I can't get a minute's peace!"

Back in my bedroom, I tried to forget what my parents had said—it didn't matter, I thought, as long as they didn't know anything about me. I was safe! And I sat there, relieved, slowly forgetting the fact that I was really just a strange twelve-year-old boy, a kid with no real playmates, an outsider even in his own family. I didn't like being that person, and I sat by the window, awake, listening to my parents' slow, arguing voices downstairs, smelling the smoke that hung in a thick, rippling cloud over their heads. Outside, the lights of Beck melted into the dark field; the hills were heavy, huddled shapes against the sky. I closed my eyes, wishing hard, trying to will my imaginary city into life, envisioning roads and streetlights suddenly sprouting up through the prairie grass. And tall buildings. And freeways. And people.

It has been almost twenty years since I last saw Beck. We left the town the summer before eighth grade, after my parents had gone bankrupt, and in the succeeding years we moved through a blur of ugly states—Wyoming, Montana; Panic, Despair—while my parents' marriage dissolved.

Now we are all scattered. My sister, Kathy, suffered brain damage in a car accident when she was nineteen, out driving with her friends. She now lives in a group home in Denver, where she and the others spend their days making Native American jewelry, which is sold at truck stops. My brother, Mark, is a physical therapist who lives on a houseboat in Marina Del Ray, California. He spends his free time reading books about childhood trauma, and every time I talk to him, he has a series of complaints about our old misery: at the very least, surely I remember the night that my father was going to kill us all with his gun, how he and Kathy and I ran into the junkyard and hid in an old refrigerator box? I think he's exaggerating, but Mark is always threatening to have me hypnotized, so I'll remember.

We have all lost touch with my mother. The last anyone heard, she was living in Puerto Vallarta, married to a man who apparently has something to do with real estate development. The last time I talked to her, she didn't sound like herself: a foreign-accented lilt had crept into her voice. She laughed harshly, then began to cough, when I mentioned old times.

For a time before he died, I was closest to my father. He was working as a bartender in a small town in Idaho, and he used to call me when I was in law school. Like me, he remembered Beck fondly: the happiest time of his life, he said. "If only we could have held on a little bit longer," he told me, "it would have been a different story. A different story entirely."

Then he'd sigh. "Well, anyway," he'd say. "How are things going with Katrina?"

"Fine," I'd say. "Just the usual. She's been a little distant lately. She's very busy with her classes. I think med school takes a lot out of her."

I remember shifting silently, because the truth was, I didn't really have a girlfriend named Katrina. I didn't have a girlfriend, period. I made Katrina up one evening, on the spur of the moment, to keep my dad from worrying so much. It helped him to think that I had a woman looking after me, that I was heading into a normal life: marriage, children, a house, etcetera. Now that I have such things, I feel a bit guilty. He died not knowing the truth. He died waiting to meet her, enmeshed in my made-up drama—in the last six months of his life, Katrina and I came close to breaking up, got back together, discussed marriage, worried that we were not spending enough time together. The conversations that my father and I had about Katrina were some of the best we ever had.

I don't remember much about my father from that summer when I was twelve. We certainly weren't having conversations that I can recall, and I don't ever remember that he pursued me with a gun. He was just there; I would walk past him in the morning as he sat, sipping coffee, preparing to go to work. I'd go into the bar, and he would pour me a glass of Coke with bitters, "to put hair on my chest." I'd sit there on the barstool, stroking Suds, the bar's tomcat, in my lap, murmuring quietly to him as I imagined my detective story. My father had a bit part in my imagination, barely a speaking role.

But it was at the bar that I saw Mr. Mickleson again. I had been at his house that morning, working through a box of letters, and then I'd been out at the junkyard behind our house. In those unenlightened times, it was called The Dump. People drove out and pitched their garbage over the edge of a ravine, which had become encrusted with a layer of beer cans, broken toys, bedsprings, car parts, broken glass. It was a magical place, and I'd spent a few hours in the driver's seat of a rusted-out Studebaker, fiddling with the various dashboard knobs, pretending to drive it, to stalk suspects, to become involved in a thrilling high-speed chase. At last I had come to the bar to unwind, to drink my Coke and bitters and recreate the day in my imagination. Occasionally my father would speak to me, and I would be forced to disengage myself from the Detective, who was brooding over a glass of bourbon. He had become hardened and cynical, but he would not give up his fight for justice.

I was repeating these stirring lines in my mind when Mr. Mickleson came into the bar. I felt a little thrum when he entered. My grip tightened on Suds the cat, who struggled and sprang from my lap.

Having spent time in The Crossroads, I recognized drunkenness. I was immediately aware of Mickleson's flopping gait, the way he settled heavily against the lip of the bar. "Okay, okay," he muttered to himself, then chuckled. "No, just forget it, never mind," he said cheerfully. Then he sighed and tapped his hand against the bar. "Shot o' rum," he said. "Captain Morgan, if you have it. No ice." I watched as my father served him, then flicked my glance away when Mickleson looked warily in my direction. He leveled his gaze at me, his eyes heavy with some meaning I couldn't decipher. It was part friendly, that look, but part threatening, too, in a particularly intimate way—as if he recognized me.

"Oh, hello," Mr. Mickleson said. "If it isn't the staring boy! Hello, Staring Boy!" He grinned at me, and my father gave him a stern look. "I believe I know you," Mr. Mickleson said jauntily. "I've seen you around, haven't I?"

I just sat there, blushing. It occurred to me that perhaps, despite my precautions, Mr. Mickleson had seen me after all. "Staring Boy," he said, and I tried to think of when he might have caught me staring. How many times? I saw myself from a distance, watching his house but now also being watched, and the idea set up a panic in me that was difficult to quell. I was grateful that my father came over and called me *son*. "Son," he said, "why don't you go on outside and find something to do? You may as well enjoy some of that summer sunshine before school starts."

"All right," I said. I saw that Mickleson was still grinning at me expectantly, his eyes blank and unblinking, and I realized that he was doing an imitation of my expression—Staring Boy, meet Staring Man. I tried to step casually off the barstool, but instead I stumbled and nearly fell. "Oopsie-daisy!" Mr. Mickleson said, and my father gave him a hard look, a careful glare that checked Mr. Mickleson's grin. He shrugged.

"Ah, children, children," he said confidingly to my father, as I hurried quickly to the door. I heard my father start to speak sharply as I left, but I didn't have the nerve to stick around to hear what was said.

Instead, I crept along the outside of the bar; I staked out Mickleson's old Volkswagen and found it locked. There were no windows into the bar, so I pressed myself against the wall, trying to listen. I tried to think what I would write in my notebook: that look he'd given me, his grinning mimicry of my state. "I believe I know you," he'd said. What, exactly, did he know?

And then I had a terrible thought. Where was the notebook? I imagined, for a moment, that I had left it there, on the bar, next to my drink. I had the dreadful image of Mr. Mickleson's eyes falling on it, the theme book cover, which was decorated with stylized question marks, and on which I'd written: Andy O'Day Mystery Series #67: The Detective Meets the Dreadful Double! I saw him smiling at it, opening it, his eyes narrowing as he saw his photo pasted there on the first page.

But it wasn't in the bar. I was sure it wasn't, because I remembered not having it when I went in. I didn't have it with me, I knew, and I began to backtrack, step by step, from the Studebaker to lunchtime to my bedroom, and then I saw it, with the kind of perfect clarity my memory has always been capable of, despite everything.

I saw myself in Mickleson's living room, on my knees in front of a box of his letters. I had copied something in the notebook and put it down on the floor. It was right there, next to the box. I could see it as if through a window, and I stood there observing the image in my mind's eye, as my mother came around the corner, into the parking lot.

"Andy!" she said. "I've been calling for you! Where the hell have you been?"

She was in one of her moods. "I am so sick of this!" she said and gave me a hard shake as she grabbed my arm. "You God-damned lazy kids just think you can do as you please, all the God-damn day long! The house is a pig sty, and not a one of you will bend a finger to pick up your filthy clothes or even wash a dish." She gritted her teeth, her voice trembling, and slammed into the house, where Mark was scrubbing the floor and Kathy was standing at the sink, washing dishes. Mark glared up at me, his eyes red with crying and self-pity and hatred. I knew he was going to hit me as soon as she left. "Clean, you brats!" my mother cried. "I'm going to work, and when I get home I want this house to shine!" She was in the frilly blouse and makeup she wore when she tended bar, beautiful and flushed, her eyes hard. "I'm not going to live like this anymore. I'm not going to live this kind of life!"

"She was a toxic parent," Mark says now, in one of our rare phone conversations. "A real psycho. It haunts me, you know, the shit that we went through. It was like living in a house of terror, you know? Like, you know, a dictatorship or something. You never knew what was next, and that was the scariest part. There was a point, I think, where I really just couldn't take it anymore. I really wanted to die." I listen as he draws on his cigarette and then exhales, containing the fussy spitefulness that's creeping into his voice. "Not that you'd remember. It always fell on me, whatever it was. They thought you were so cute and spacey; you were always checked out in La-La Land while I got the brunt of everything."

I listen but don't listen. I'm on the deck behind my house, with my cell phone, reclining, watching my daughters jump through the sprinkler. Everything is green and full of sunlight, and I might as well be watching an actor portraying me in the happy ending of a movie of my life. I've never told him about my blackouts, and I don't now, though they have been bothering me again lately. I can imagine what he would come up with: fugue states, repressed memories, multiple personalities. Ridiculous stuff.

"It all seems very far away to me," I tell Mark, which is not true exactly, but it's part of the role I've been playing for many years now. "I don't really think much about it."

This much is true: I barely remember what happened that night. I wasn't even there, among the mundane details of children squabbling and cleaning and my mother's ordinary unhappiness. I was the Detective!—driving my sleek Studebaker through the streets of Beck, nervous though not panicked, edgy and white-knuckled but still planning with steely determination: The notebook! The notebook must be re-trieved! Nothing else was really happening, and when I left the house, I was in a state of focused intensity.

It must have been about eleven o'clock. Mark had been especially evil and watchful, and it wasn't until he'd settled down in front of the television with a big bowl of ice cream that I could pretend, at last, to go to bed.

Outside, out the door, down the alley: it seems to me that I should have been frightened, but mostly I recall the heave of adrenaline and determination, the neces-sity of the notebook, the absolute need for it. It was my story.

The lights were on at Mickleson's house, a bad sign, but I moved forward anyway, into the dense and dripping shadows of his yard, the crickets singing thickly, my hand already extended to touch the knob of his back door.

It wasn't locked. It didn't even have to be jimmied; it gave under the pressure of my hand, a little electrical jolt across my skin, the door opening smooth and un-creaking, and I passed like a shadow into the narrow back foyer that led to the kitchen. There was a silence in the house, and for a moment I felt certain that Mickleson was asleep. Still, I moved cautiously. The kitchen was brightly fluores-cent and full of dirty dishes and beer cans. I slid my feet along the tile, inching along the wall. Silence, and then Mickleson's voice drifted up suddenly, a low mumble and then a firmer one, as if he were contradicting himself. My heart shrank. *Now what?* I thought as I came to the edge of the living room.

Mickleson was sitting in his chair, slumping, his foot jiggling with irritation. I heard the sail-like snap of a turning page, and I didn't even have to look to know that the notebook was in his hands. He murmured again as I stood there. I felt light-headed. *The notebook!* I thought and leaned against the wall. I felt my head bump against something, and Mr. Mickleson's plaque tilted, then fell. I fumbled for a mo-ment before I caught it.

But the sound made him turn. There I was, dumbly holding the slice of wood, and his eyes rested on me. His expression seemed to flicker with surprise, then terror, then annoyance, before settling on a kind of blank amusement. He cleared his throat.

"I believe I see a little person in my house," he said, and I might have fainted. I could feel the Detective leaving me, shriveling up and slumping to the floor, a suit of old clothes; the city of Beck disintegrated in the distance, streets drying up like old creek beds, skyscrapers sinking like ocean liners into the wheat fields. I was very still, his gaze pinning me. "A ghostly little person," he said, with satisfaction. He stood up for a moment, wavering, and then stumbled back against the chair for support, a look of affronted dignity freezing on his face. I didn't move.

"Well, well," he said. "Do I dare assume that I am in the presence of the author of this"—he waved my notebook vaguely—"this document?" He paused, thumbing through it with an exaggerated, mime-like gesture. "Hmm," he murmured, almost crooning. "So—imaginative! And—there's a certain—charm—about it—I think." And then he leaned toward me. "And so at last we meet, Detective O'Day!" he said, in a deep voice. "You may call me Professor Moriarty!" He made a strange shape with his mouth and laughed softly—it wasn't sinister exactly, but musing, as if he'd just told himself a good joke, and I was somehow in on it.

"Why so quiet?" he exclaimed and waggled the notebook at me. "Haven't you come to find your future, young Detective?" I watched as he pressed his fingers to his temples, like a stage medium. "Hmm," he said and began to wave his arms and fingers in a seaweed-like floating motion, as if casting a magic spell or performing a hula dance. "Looking for his future," he said. "What lies in wait for Andy O'Day? I ask myself that question frequently. Will he grow up to be . . ."—and here he read aloud from my journal—" . . . 'troglodytic' and 'sinister'? Will he ever escape the sad and lonely life of a Detective, or will he wander till the end of his days through the grim and withering streets of Beck?"

He paused then and looked up from my journal. I thought for a moment that if I leapt out, I could snatch it from him, even though the things I had written now seemed dirty and pathetic. I thought to say, "Give me back my notebook!" But I didn't really want it anymore. I just stood there, watching him finger the pages, and he leaned toward me, wavering, his eyes not exactly focused on me, but on some part of my forehead or shoulder or hair. He smiled, made another small effort to stand, then changed his mind. "What will happen to Andy O'Day?" he said again, thoughtfully. "It's such a compelling question, a very lovely question, and I can tell you the answer. Because, you see, I've come through my time machine to warn you! I have a special message for you from the future. Do you want to know what it is?"

"No," I said at last, my voice thick and uncertain.

"Oh, Andy," he said, as if very disappointed. "Andy, Andy. Look! Here I am!" He held his arms out wide, as if I'd run toward them. "Your Dreadful Double!" I watched as he straightened himself, correcting the slow tilt of his body. "I know you," Mr. Mickleson said. His head dropped, but he kept one eye on me. "You must be coming to me—for something?"

I shook my head. I didn't know. I couldn't even begin to imagine, and yet I felt—not for the last time—that I was standing in a desolate and empty prairie, the fields unraveling away from me in all directions, and the long winds running through my hair.

"Don't you want to know a secret?" he said. "Come over here, I'll whisper in your ear."

And it seemed to me, then, that he did know a secret. It seemed to me that he would tell me something terrible, something I didn't want to hear. I watched as he closed my notebook and placed it neatly on the coffee table, next to the *TV Guide*. He balanced himself on two feet, lifting up and lurching toward me. "Hold still," he murmured. "I'll whisper."

I turned and ran.

[∗∗∗]

I once tried to explain this incident to my wife, but it didn't make much sense to her. She nodded, as if it were merely strange, merely puzzling. "Hmmm," she said, and I thought that perhaps it *was* odd to remember this time so vividly, when I remembered so little else. It *was* a little ridiculous that I should find Mr. Mickleson on my mind so frequently.

"He was just a drunk," my wife said. "A little crazy, maybe, but . . ." And she looked into my face, her lips pursing. "He didn't . . . *do* anything to you, did he?" she said, awkwardly, and I shook my head.

"No—no," I said. And I explained to her that I never saw Mr. Mickleson again. I avoided the house after that night, of course, and when school started he wasn't teaching Science 7. We were told, casually, that he had had an "emergency," that he had been called away, and when, after a few weeks, he still didn't return, he was replaced without comment by an elderly lady substitute, who read to us from the textbook—*The World of Living Things*—in a lilting storybook voice, and who whispered, "My God," as she watched us, later, dissecting earthworms, pinning them to corkboard and exposing their many hearts. We never found out where Mr. Mickleson had gone.

"He was probably in rehab," my wife said sensibly. "Or institutionalized. Your father was right. He was just a weirdo. It doesn't seem that mysterious to me."

Yes. I nodded a little, ready to drop the subject. I couldn't very well explain the empty longing I had felt, the eager dread that would wash over me, going into the classroom and thinking that he might be sitting there behind the desk, waiting. It didn't make sense, I thought, and I couldn't explain it, any more than I could explain why he remained in my mind as I crisscrossed the country with my family, any more than I could explain why he seemed to be there when I thought of them, even now: Mark, fat and paranoid, on his houseboat; my mother in Mexico, nodding over a cocktail; Kathy, staring at a spider in the corner of her room in the group home, her eyes dull; my father, frightened, calling me on the phone as his liver failed him, his body decomposing in a tiny grave in Idaho that I'd never visited. How could I explain that Mickleson seemed to preside over these thoughts, hovering at the edge of them like a stage director at the back of my mind, smiling as if he'd done me a favor?

I didn't know why he came into my mind as I thought of them, just as I didn't know why he seemed to appear whenever I told lies. It was just that I could sense him. *Yes,* he whispered as I told my college friends that my father was an archaeologist living in Peru, that my mother was a former actress; *yes,* he murmured when I lied to my father about Katrina; *yes,* as I make excuses to my wife, when I say I am having dinner with a client when in fact I am tracing another path entirely—following a young family as they stroll through the park, or a whistling old man who might be my father, if he's gotten away, or a small, brisk-paced woman who looks like Katrina might, if Katrina weren't made up. How can I explain that I walk behind this Katrina woman for many blocks, living a different life, whistling my old man tune?

I can't. I can't explain it, no more than I can admit that I still have Mickleson's plaque, just as he probably still has my notebook; no more than I can explain why I take the plaque out of the bottom drawer of my desk and unwrap the tissue paper

I've folded it in, reading the inscription over, like a secret message: "I wear the chains I forged in life." I know it's just a cheap Dickens allusion, but it still seems important. I can hear him say, "Hold still. I'll whisper."

"Hmmm," my wife would say, puzzled and perhaps a bit disturbed. She's a practical woman, and so I say nothing. It's probably best that she doesn't think any more about it, and I keep to myself the private warmth I feel when I sense a blackout coming, the darkness clasping its hands over my eyes. It's better this way—we're all happy. I'm glad that my wife will be there when I awake, and my normal life, and my beautiful daughters, looking at me, wide-eye, staring.

"Hello?" my wife will say, and I'll smile as she nudges me. "Are you there?" she'll say. "Are you all right?" she'll whisper.

# The Things They Carried

### TIM O'BRIEN

First Lieutenant Jimmy Cross carried letters from a girl named Martha, a junior at Mount Sebastian College in New Jersey. They were not love letters, but Lieutenant Cross was hoping, so he kept them folded in plastic at the bottom of his rucksack. In the late afternoon, after a day's march, he would dig his foxhole, wash his hands under a canteen, unwrap the letters, hold them with the tips of his fingers, and spend the last hour of light pretending. He would imagine romantic camping trips into the White Mountains in New Hampshire. He would sometimes taste the envelope flaps, knowing her tongue had been there. More than anything, he wanted Martha to love him as he loved her, but the letters were mostly chatty, elusive on the matter of love. She was a virgin, he was almost sure. She was an English major at Mount Sebastian, and she wrote beautifully about her professors and roommates and midterm exams, about her respect for Chaucer and her great affection for Virginia Woolf. She often quoted lines of poetry; she never mentioned the war, except to say, Jimmy, take care of yourself. The letters weighed 10 ounces. They were signed Love, Martha, but Lieutenant Cross understood that Love was only a way of signing and did not mean what he sometimes pretended it meant. At dusk, he would carefully return the letters to his rucksack. Slowly, a bit distracted, he would get up and move among his men, checking the perimeter, then at full dark he would return to his hole and watch the night and wonder if Martha was a virgin.

The things they carried were largely determined by necessity. Among the necessities or near-necessities were P-38 can openers, pocket knives, heat tabs, wristwatches, dog tags, mosquito repellent, chewing gum, candy, cigarettes, salt tablets, packets of Kool-Aid, lighters, matches, sewing kits, Military Payment Certificates, C rations, and two or three canteens of water. Together, these items weighed between 15 and 20 pounds, depending upon a man's habits or rate of metabolism. Henry Dobbins, who was a big man, carried extra rations; he was especially fond of canned peaches in heavy syrup over pound cake. Dave Jensen, who practiced field hygiene, carried a toothbrush, dental floss, and several hotel-sized bars of soap he'd stolen on R&R in Sydney, Australia. Ted Lavender, who was scared, carried tranquilizers until he was shot in the head outside the village of Than Khe in mid-April. By necessity, and because it was SOP, they all carried steel helmets that weighed 5 pounds including the liner and camouflage cover. They carried the standard fatigue jackets and trousers. Very few carried underwear. On their feet they carried jungle boots—2.1 pounds—and Dave Jensen carried three pairs of socks and a can of Dr. Scholl's foot powder as a precaution against trench foot. Until he was shot, Ted Lavender carried six or seven ounces of premium dope, which for him was a necessity. Mitchell Sanders, the RTO, carried condoms. Norman Bowker carried a diary. Rat Kiley carried comic books. Kiowa, a devout Baptist, carried an illustrated New Testament that had been presented to him by his father, who taught Sunday school in Oklahoma City, Oklahoma. As a hedge against bad times, however, Kiowa also carried his grandmother's distrust of the white man, his grandfather's old hunting hatchet. Necessity dictated. Because the land was mined and booby-trapped, it was SOP for each man to carry a steel-centered, nylon-covered flak jacket, which weighed 6.7 pounds, but which on hot days seemed much heavier. Because you could die so quickly, each man carried at least one large compress bandage, usually in the helmet band for easy access. Because the nights were cold, and because the monsoons were wet, each carried a green plastic poncho that could be used as a raincoat or groundsheet or makeshift tent. With its quilted liner, the poncho weighed almost two pounds, but it was worth every ounce. In April, for instance, when Ted Lavender was shot, they used his poncho to wrap him up, then to carry him across the paddy, then to lift him into the chopper that took him away.

They were called legs or grunts.

To carry something was to hump it, as when Lieutenant Jimmy Cross humped his love for Martha up the hills and through the swamps. In its intransitive form, to hump meant to walk, or to march, but it implied burdens far beyond the intransitive.

Almost everyone humped photographs. In his wallet, Lieutenant Cross carried two photographs of Martha. The first was a Kodacolor snapshot signed Love, though he knew better. She stood against a brick wall. Her eyes were gray and neutral, her lips slightly open as she stared straight-on at the camera. At night, sometimes, Lieutenant Cross wondered who had taken the picture, because he knew she had boyfriends, because he loved her so much, and because he could see the shadow of the picture-taker spreading out against the brick wall. The second photograph had been clipped from the 1968 Mount Sebastian yearbook. It was an action shot—women's volleyball—and Martha was bent horizontal to the floor, reaching, the palms of her hands in sharp focus, the tongue taut, the expression frank and competitive. There was no visible sweat. She wore white gym shorts. Her legs, he thought, were almost certainly the legs of a virgin, dry and without hair, the left knee cocked and carrying her entire weight, which was just over one hundred pounds. Lieutenant Cross remembered touching that left knee. A dark theater, he remembered, and the movie was *Bonnie and Clyde*, and Martha wore a tweed skirt, and during the final scene, when he touched her knee, she turned and looked at him in a sad, sober way that made him pull his hand back, but he would always remember the feel of the tweed skirt and the knee beneath it and the sound of the gunfire that killed Bonnie and Clyde, how embarrassing it was, how slow and oppressive. He remembered kissing her good night at the dorm door. Right then, he thought, he should've done something brave. He should've carried her up the stairs to her room and tied her to the bed and touched that left knee all night long. He should've risked it. Whenever he looked at the photographs, he thought of new things he should've done.

What they carried was partly a function of rank, partly of field specialty.

As a first lieutenant and platoon leader, Jimmy Cross carried a compass, maps, code books, binoculars, and a .45-caliber pistol that weighed 2.9 pounds fully loaded. He carried a strobe light and the responsibility for the lives of his men.

As an RTO, Mitchell Sanders carried the PRC-25 radio, a killer, 26 pounds with its battery.

As a medic, Rat Kiley carried a canvas satchel filled with morphine and plasma and malaria tablets and surgical tape and comic books and all the things a medic must carry, including M&M's for especially bad wounds, for a total weight of nearly 20 pounds.

As a big man, therefore a machine gunner, Henry Dobbins carried the M-60, which weighed 23 pounds unloaded, but which was almost always loaded. In addition, Dobbins carried between 10 and 15 pounds of ammunition draped in belts across his chest and shoulders.

As PFCs or Spec 4s, most of them were common grunts and carried the standard M-16 gas-operated assault rifle. The weapon weighed 7.5 pounds unloaded, 8.2 pounds with its full 20-round magazine. Depending on numerous factors, such as topography and psychology, the riflemen carried anywhere from 12 to 20 magazines, usually in cloth bandoliers, adding on another 8.4 pounds at minimum, 14 pounds at maximum. When it was available, they also carried M-16 maintenance gear—rods and steel brushes and swabs and tubes of LSA oil—all of which weighed about a pound. Among the grunts, some carried the M-79 grenade launcher, 5.9 pounds unloaded, a reasonably light weapon except for the ammunition, which was heavy. A single round weighed 10 ounces. The typical load was 25 rounds. But Ted Lavender, who was scared, carried 34 rounds when he was shot and killed outside Than Khe, and he went down under an exceptional burden, more than 20 pounds of ammunition, plus the flak jacket and helmet and rations and water and toilet paper and tranquilizers and all the rest, plus the unweighed fear. He was dead weight. There was no twitching or flopping. Kiowa, who saw it happen, said it was like watching a rock fall, or a big sandbag or something—just boom, then down—not like the movies where the dead guy rolls around and does fancy spins and goes ass over teakettle— not like that, Kiowa said, the poor bastard just flat-fuck fell. Boom. Down. Nothing else. It was a bright morning in mid-April. Lieutenant Cross felt the pain. He blamed himself. They stripped off Lavender's canteens and ammo, all the heavy things, and Rat Kiley said the obvious, the guy's dead, and Mitchell Sanders used his radio to report one U.S. KIA and to request a chopper. Then they wrapped Lavender in his poncho. They carried him out to a dry paddy, established security, and sat smoking the dead man's dope until the chopper came. Lieutenant Cross kept to himself. He pictured Martha's smooth young face, thinking he loved her more than anything, more than his men, and now Ted Lavender was dead because he loved her so much and could not stop thinking about her. When the dustoff arrived, they carried Lavender aboard. Afterward they burned Than Khe. They marched until dusk, then dug their holes, and that night Kiowa kept explaining how you had to be there, how fast it was, how the poor guy just dropped like so much concrete. Boom-down, he said. Like cement.

In addition to the three standard weapons—the M-60, M-16, and M-79—they carried whatever presented itself, or whatever seemed appropriate as a means of killing or staying alive. They carried catch-as-catch-can. At various times, in various situations, they carried M-14s and CAR-15s and Swedish Ks and grease guns and captured AK-47s and Chi-Coms and RPGs and Simonov carbines and black market Uzis and .38-caliber Smith & Wesson handguns and 66 mm LAWs and shotguns and silencers and blackjacks and bayonets and C-4 plastic explosives. Lee Strunk carried a slingshot; a weapon of last resort, he called it. Mitchell Sanders carried brass knuckles. Kiowa carried his grandfather's feathered hatchet. Every third or fourth man carried a Claymore antipersonnel mine—3.5 pounds with its firing device. They all carried fragmentation grenades—14 ounces each. They all carried at least one M-18 colored smoke grenade—24 ounces. Some carried CS or tear gas grenades. Some carried white phosphorus grenades. They carried all they could bear, and then some, including a silent awe for the terrible power of the things they carried.

In the first week of April, before Lavender died, Lieutenant Jimmy Cross received a good-luck charm from Martha. It was a simple pebble, an ounce at most. Smooth to the touch, it was a milky white color with flecks of orange and violet, oval-shaped, like a miniature egg. In the accompanying letter, Martha wrote that she had found the pebble on the Jersey shoreline, precisely where the land touched water at high tide, where things came together but also separated. It was this separate-but-together quality, she wrote, that had inspired her to pick up the pebble and to carry it in her breast pocket for several days, where it seemed weightless, and then to send it through the mail, by air, as a token of her truest feelings for him. Lieutenant Cross found this romantic. But he wondered what her truest feelings were, exactly, and what she meant by separate-but-together. He wondered how the tides and waves had come into play on that afternoon along the Jersey shoreline when Martha saw the pebble and bent down to rescue it from geology. He imagined bare feet. Martha was a poet, with the poet's sensibilities, and her feet would be brown and bare, the toenails unpainted, the eyes chilly and somber like the ocean in March, and though it was painful, he wondered who had been with her that afternoon. He imagined a pair of shadows moving along the strip of sand where things came together but also separated. It was phantom jealousy, he knew, but he couldn't help himself. He loved her so much. On the march, through the hot days of early April, he carried the pebble in his mouth, turning it with his tongue, tasting sea salt and moisture. His mind wandered. He had difficulty keeping his attention on the war. On occasion he would yell at his men to spread out the column, to keep their eyes open, but then he would slip away into daydreams, just pretending, walking barefoot along the Jersey shore, with Martha, carrying nothing. He would feel himself rising. Sun and waves and gentle winds, all love and lightness.

What they carried varied by mission.

When a mission took them to the mountains, they carried mosquito netting, machetes, canvas tarps, and extra bug juice.

If a mission seemed especially hazardous, or if it involved a place they knew to be bad, they carried everything they could. In certain heavily mined AOs, where the land was dense with Toe Poppers and Bouncing Betties, they took turns humping a 28-pound mine detector. With its headphones and big sensing plate, the equipment was a stress on the lower back and shoulders, awkward to handle, often useless because of the shrapnel in the earth, but they carried it anyway, partly for safety, partly for the illusion of safety.

On ambush, or other night missions, they carried peculiar little odds and ends. Kiowa always took along his New Testament and a pair of moccasins for silence. Dave Jensen carried night-sight vitamins high in carotene. Lee Strunk carried his slingshot; ammo, he claimed, would never be a problem. Rat Kiley carried brandy and M&M's candy. Until he was shot, Ted Lavender carried the starlight scope, which weighed 6.3 pounds with its aluminum carrying case. Henry Dobbins carried his girlfriend's pantyhose wrapped around his neck as a comforter. They all carried ghosts. When dark came, they would move out single file across the meadows and paddies to their ambush coordinates, where they would quietly set up the Claymores and lie down and spend the night waiting.

Other missions were more complicated and required special equipment. In mid-April, it was their mission to search out and destroy the elaborate tunnel complexes in the Than Khe area south of Chu Lai. To blow the tunnels, they carried one-pound blocks of pentrite high explosives, four blocks to a man, 68 pounds in all. They carried wiring, detonators, and battery-powered clackers. Dave Jensen carried earplugs. Most often, before blowing the tunnels, they were ordered by higher command to search them, which was considered bad news, but by and large they just shrugged and carried out orders. Because he was a big man, Henry Dobbins was excused from tunnel duty. The others would draw numbers. Before Lavender died there were 17 men in the platoon, and whoever drew the number 17 would strip off his gear and crawl in headfirst with a flashlight and Lieutenant Cross's .45-caliber pistol. The rest of them would fan out as security. They would sit down or kneel, not facing the hole, listening to the ground beneath them, imagining cobwebs and ghosts, whatever was down there—the tunnel walls squeezing in—how the flashlight seemed impossibly heavy in the hand and how it was tunnel vision in the very strictest sense, compression in all ways, even time, and how you had to wiggle in—ass and elbows—a swallowed-up feeling—and how you found yourself worrying about odd things: Will your flashlight go dead? Do rats carry rabies? If you screamed, how far would the sound carry?

Would your buddies hear it? Would they have the courage to drag you out? In some respects, though not many, the waiting was worse than the tunnel itself. Imagination was a killer.

On April 16, when Lee Strunk drew the number 17, he laughed and muttered something and went down quickly. The morning was hot and very still. Not good, Kiowa said. He looked at the tunnel opening, then out across a dry paddy toward the village of Than Khe. Nothing moved. No clouds or birds or people. As they waited, the men smoked and drank Kool-Aid, not talking much, feeling sympathy for Lee Strunk but also feeling the luck of the draw. You win some, you lose some, said Mitchell Sanders, and sometimes you settle for a rain check. It was a tired line and no one laughed.

Henry Dobbins ate a tropical chocolate bar. Ted Lavender popped a tranquilizer and went off to pee.

After five minutes, Lieutenant Jimmy Cross moved to the tunnel, leaned down, and examined the darkness. Trouble, he thought—a cave-in maybe. And then suddenly, without willing it, he was thinking about Martha. The stresses and fractures, the quick collapse, the two of them buried alive under all that weight. Dense, crushing love. Kneeling, watching the hole, he tried to concentrate on Lee Strunk and the war, all the dangers, but his love was too much for him, he felt paralyzed, he wanted to sleep inside her lungs and breathe her blood and be smothered. He wanted her to be a virgin and not a virgin, all at once. He wanted to know her. Intimate secrets: Why poetry? Why so sad? Why that grayness in her eyes? Why so alone? Not lonely, just alone—riding her bike across campus or sitting off by herself in the cafeteria— even dancing, she danced alone—and it was the aloneness that filled him with love. He remembered telling her that one evening. How she nodded and looked away. And how, later, when he kissed her, she received the kiss without returning it, her eyes wide open, not afraid, not a virgin's eyes, just flat and uninvolved.

Lieutenant Cross gazed at the tunnel. But he was not there. He was buried with Martha under the white sand at the Jersey shore. They were pressed together, and the pebble in his mouth was her tongue. He was smiling. Vaguely, he was aware of how quiet the day was, the sullen paddies, yet he could not bring himself to worry about matters of security. He was beyond that. He was just a kid at war, in love. He was twenty-four years old. He couldn't help it.

A few moments later Lee Strunk crawled out of the tunnel. He came up grinning, filthy but alive. Lieutenant Cross nodded and closed his eyes while the others clapped Strunk on the back and made jokes about rising from the dead.

Worms, Rat Kiley said. Right out of the grave. Fuckin' zombie.

The men laughed. They all felt great relief.

Spook city, said Mitchell Sanders.

Lee Strunk made a funny ghost sound, a kind of moaning, yet very happy, and right then, when Strunk made that high happy moaning sound, when he went *Ahhooooo*, right then Ted Lavender was shot in the head on his way back from peeing. He lay with his mouth open. The teeth were broken. There was a swollen black bruise under his left eye. The cheekbone was gone. Oh shit, Rat Kiley said, the guy's dead. The guy's dead, he kept saying, which seemed profound—the guy's dead. I mean really.

The things they carried were determined to some extent by superstition. Lieutenant Cross carried his good-luck pebble. Dave Jensen carried a rabbit's foot. Norman Bowker, otherwise a very gentle person, carried a thumb that had been presented to him as a gift by Mitchell Sanders. The thumb was dark brown, rubbery to the touch, and weighed four ounces at most. It had been cut from a VC corpse, a boy of fifteen or sixteen. They'd found him at the bottom of an irrigation ditch, badly burned, flies in his mouth and eyes. The boy wore black shorts and sandals. At the time of his death he had been carrying a pouch of rice, a rifle, and three magazines of ammunition.

You want my opinion, Mitchell Sanders said, there's a definite moral here.

He put his hand on the dead boy's wrist. He was quiet for a time, as if counting a pulse, then he patted the stomach, almost affectionately, and used Kiowa's hunting hatchet to remove the thumb.

Henry Dobbins asked what the moral was.

Moral?

You know. *Moral.*

Sanders wrapped the thumb in toilet paper and handed it across to Norman Bowker. There was no blood. Smiling, he kicked the boy's head, watched the flies scatter, and said, It's like what that old TV show—Paladin. Have gun, will travel.

Henry Dobbins thought about it.

Yeah, well, he finally said. I don't see no moral.

There it is, man.

FUCK OFF.

They carried USO stationery and pencils and pens. They carried Sterno, safety pins, trip flares, signal flares, spools of wire, razor blades, chewing tobacco, liberated joss sticks and statuettes of the smiling Buddha, candles, grease pencils, *The Stars and Stripes*, fingernail clippers, Psy Ops leaflets, bush hats, bolos, and much more. Twice a week, when the resupply choppers came in, they carried hot chow in green mermite cans and large canvas bags filled with iced beer and soda pop. They carried plastic water containers, each with a two-gallon capacity. Mitchell Sanders carried a set of starched tiger fatigues for special occasions. Henry Dobbins carried Black Flag insecticide. Dave Jensen carried empty sandbags that could be filled at night for added protection. Lee Strunk carried tanning lotion. Some things they carried in common. Taking turns, they carried the big PRC-77 scrambler radio, which weighed 30 pounds with its battery. They shared the weight of memory. They took up what others could no longer bear. Often, they carried each other, the wounded or weak. They carried infections. They carried chess sets, basketballs, Vietnamese-English dictionaries, insignia of rank, Bronze Stars and Purple Hearts, plastic cards imprinted with the Code of Conduct. They carried diseases, among them malaria and dysentery. They carried lice and ringworm and leeches and paddy algae and various rots and molds. They carried the land itself—Vietnam, the place, the soil—a powdery orange-red dust that covered their boots and fatigues and faces. They carried the sky. The whole atmosphere, they carried it, the humidity, the monsoons, the stink of fungus and decay, all of it, they carried gravity. They moved like mules. By daylight they took sniper fire, at night they were mortared, but it was not battle, it was just the endless march, village to village, without purpose, nothing won or lost. They marched for the sake of the march. They plodded along slowly, dumbly, leaning forward against the heat, unthinking, all blood and bone, simple grunts, soldiering with their legs, toiling up the hills and down into the paddies and across the rivers and up again and down, just humping, one step and then the next and then another, but no volition, no will, because it was automatic, it was anatomy, and the war was entirely a matter of posture and carriage, the hump was everything, a kind of inertia, a kind of emptiness, a dullness of desire and intellect and conscience and hope and human sensibility. Their principles were in their feet. Their calculations were biological. They had no sense of strategy or mission. They searched the villages without knowing what to look for, not caring, kicking over jars of rice, frisking children and old men, blowing tunnels, sometimes setting fires and sometimes not, then forming up and moving on to the next village, then other villages, where it would always be the same. They carried their own lives. The pressures were enormous. In the heat of early afternoon, they would remove their helmets and flak jackets, walking bare, which was dangerous but which helped ease the strain. They would often discard things along the route of march. Purely for comfort, they would throw away rations, blow their Claymores and grenades, no matter, because by nightfall the resupply choppers would arrive with more of the same, then a day or two later still more, fresh watermelons and crates of ammunition and sunglasses and woolen sweaters—the resources were stunning—sparklers for the Fourth of July, colored eggs for Easter. It was the great American war chest—the fruits of science, the smokestacks, the canneries, the arsenals at Hartford, the Minnesota forests, the machine shops, the vast fields of corn and wheat—they carried like freight trains; they carried it on their backs and shoulders—and for all the ambiguities of Vietnam, all the mysteries and unknowns, there was at least the single abiding certainty that they would never be at a loss for things to carry.

After the chopper took Lavender away, Lieutenant Jimmy Cross led his men into the village of Than Khe. They burned everything. They shot chickens and dogs, they trashed the village well, they called in artillery and watched the wreckage, then they marched for several hours through the hot afternoon, and then at dusk, while Kiowa explained how Lavender died, Lieutenant Cross found himself trembling.

He tried not to cry. With his entrenching tool, which weighed five pounds, he began digging a hole in the earth.

He felt shame. He hated himself. He had loved Martha more than his men, and as a consequence Lavender was now dead, and this was something he would have to carry like a stone in his stomach for the rest of the war.

All he could do was dig. He used his entrenching tool like an ax, slashing, feeling both love and hate, and then later, when it was full dark, he sat at the bottom of his foxhole and wept. It went on for a long while. In part, he was grieving for Ted Lavender, but mostly it was for Martha, and for himself, because she belonged to another world, which was not quite real, and because she was a junior at Mount Sebastian College in New Jersey, a poet and a virgin and uninvolved, and because he realized she did not love him and never would.

Like cement, Kiowa whispered in the dark. I swear to God—boom, down. Not a word.

I've heard this, said Norman Bowker.

A pisser, you know? Still zipping himself up. Zapped while zipping.

All right, fine. That's enough.

Yeah, but you had to see it, the guy just—

I heard, man. Cement. So why not shut the fuck up?

Kiowa shook his head sadly and glanced over at the hole where Lieutenant Jimmy Cross sat watching the night. The air was thick and wet. A warm dense fog had settled over the paddies and there was the stillness that precedes rain.

After a time Kiowa sighed.

One thing for sure, he said. The lieutenant's in some deep hurt. I mean that crying jag—the way he was carrying on—it wasn't fake or anything, it was real heavy-duty hurt. The man cares.

Sure, Norman Bowker said.

Say what you want, the man does care.

We all got problems.

Not Lavender.

No, I guess not, Bowker said. Do me a favor, though.

Shut up?

That's a smart Indian. Shut up.

Shrugging, Kiowa pulled off his boots. He wanted to say more, just to lighten up his sleep, but instead he opened his New Testament and arranged it beneath his head as a pillow. The fog made things seem hollow and unattached. He tried not to think about Ted Lavender, but then he was thinking how fast it was, no drama, down and dead, and how it was hard to feel anything except surprise. It seemed unchristian. He wished he could find some great sadness, or even anger, but the emotion wasn't there and he couldn't make it happen. Mostly he felt pleased to be alive. He liked the smell of the New Testament under his cheek, the leather and ink and paper and glue, whatever the chemicals were. He liked hearing the sounds of night. Even his fatigue, it felt fine, the stiff muscles and the prickly awareness of his own body, a floating feeling. He enjoyed not being dead. Lying there, Kiowa admired Lieutenant Jimmy Cross's capacity for grief. He wanted to share the man's pain, he wanted to care as Jimmy Cross cared. And yet when he closed his eyes, all he could think was Boom-down, and all he could feel was the pleasure of having his boots off and the fog curling in around him and the damp soil and the Bible smells and the plush comfort of night.

After a moment Norman Bowker sat up in the dark.

What the hell, he said. You want to talk, *talk*. Tell it to me.

Forget it.

No, man, go on. One thing I hate, it's a silent Indian.

For the most part they carried themselves with poise, a kind of dignity. Now and then, however, there were times of panic, when they squealed or wanted to squeal but couldn't, when they twitched and made moaning sounds and covered their heads and said Dear Jesus and flopped around on the earth and fired their weapons blindly and cringed and sobbed and begged for the noise to stop and went wild and made stupid promises to themselves and to God and to their mothers and fathers, hoping not to die. In different ways, it happened to all of them. Afterward, when the firing ended, they would blink and peek up. They would touch their bodies, feeling shame, then quickly hiding it. They would force themselves to stand. As if in slow motion, frame by frame, the world would take on the old logic—absolute silence, then the wind, then sunlight, then voices. It was the burden of being alive. Awkwardly, the men would reassemble themselves, first in private, then in groups, becoming soldiers again. They would repair the leaks in their eyes. They would check for casualties, call in dustoffs, light cigarettes, try to smile, clear their throats and spit and begin cleaning their weapons. After a time someone would shake his head and say, No lie, I almost shit my pants, and someone else would laugh, which meant it was bad, yes, but the guy had obviously not shit his pants, it wasn't that bad, and in any case nobody would ever do such a thing and then go ahead and talk about it. They would squint into the dense, oppressive sunlight. For a few moments, perhaps, they would fall silent, lighting a joint and tracking its passage from man to man, inhaling, holding in the humiliation. Scary stuff, one of them might say. But then someone else would grin or flick his eyebrows and say, Roger-dodger, almost cut me a new asshole, *almost.*

There were numerous such poses. Some carried themselves with a sort of wistful resignation, others with pride or stiff soldierly discipline or good humor or macho zeal. They were afraid of dying but they were even more afraid to show it.

They found jokes to tell.

They used a hard vocabulary to contain the terrible softness. *Greased* they'd say. *Offed, lit up, zapped while zipping.* It wasn't cruelty, just stage presence. They were actors. When someone died, it wasn't quite dying, because in a curious way it seemed scripted, and because they had their lines mostly memorized, irony mixed with tragedy, and because they called it by other names, as if to encyst and destroy the reality of death itself. They kicked corpses. They cut off thumbs. They talked grunt lingo. They told stories about Ted Lavender's supply of tranquilizers, how the poor guy didn't feel a thing, how incredibly tranquil he was.

There's a moral here, said Mitchell Sanders.

They were waiting for Lavender's chopper, smoking the dead man's dope.

The moral's pretty obvious, Sanders said, and winked. Stay away from drugs. No joke, they'll ruin your day every time.

Cute, said Henry Dobbins.

Mind blower, get it? Talk about wiggy. Nothing left, just blood and brains.

They made themselves laugh.

There it is, they'd say. Over and over—there it is, my friend, there it is—as if the repetition itself were an act of poise, a balance between crazy and almost crazy, knowing without going, there it is, which meant be cool, let it ride, because Oh yeah, man, you can't change what can't be changed, there it is, there it absolutely and positively and fucking well is.

They were tough.

They carried all the emotional baggage of men who might die. Grief, terror, love, longing—these were intangibles, but the intangibles had their own mass and specific gravity, they had tangible weight. They carried shameful memories. They carried the common secret of cowardice barely restrained, the instinct to run or freeze or hide, and in many respects this was the heaviest burden of all, for it could never be put down, it required perfect balance and perfect posture. They carried their reputations. They carried the soldier's greatest fear, which was the fear of blushing. Men killed, and died, because they were embarrassed not to. It was what had brought them to the war in the first place, nothing positive, no dreams of glory or honor, just to avoid the blush of dishonor. They died so as not to die of embarrassment. They crawled into tunnels and walked point and advanced under fire. Each morning, despite the unknowns, they made their legs move. They endured. They kept humping, they did not submit to the obvious alternative, which was simply to close the eyes and fall. So easy, really. Go limp and tumble to the ground and let the muscles unwind and not speak and not budge until your buddies picked you up and lifted you into the chopper that would roar and dip its nose and carry you off to the world. A mere matter of falling, yet no one ever fell. It was not courage, exactly; the object was not valor. Rather, they were too frightened to be cowards.

By and large they carried these things inside, maintaining the masks of composure. They sneered at sick call. They spoke bitterly about guys who had found release by shooting off their own toes or fingers. Pussies, they'd say. Candy-asses. It was fierce, mocking talk, with only a trace of envy or awe, but even so the image played itself out behind their eyes.

They imagined the muzzle against flesh. So easy: squeeze the trigger and blow away a toe. They imagined it. They imagined the quick, sweet pain, then the evacuation to Japan, then a hospital with warm beds and cute geisha nurses.

And they dreamed of freedom birds.

At night, on guard, staring into the dark, they were carried away by jumbo jets. They felt the rush of takeoff. *Gone!* they yelled. And then velocity—wings and engines—a smiling stewardess—but it was more than a plane, it was a real bird, a big sleek silver bird with feathers and talons and high screeching. They were flying. The weights fell off; there was nothing to bear. They laughed and held on tight, feeling the cold slap of wind and altitude, soaring, thinking *It's over, I'm gone!*—they were naked, they were light and free—it was all lightness, bright and fast and buoyant, light as light, a helium buzz in the brain, a giddy bubbling in the lungs as they were taken up over the clouds and the war, beyond duty, beyond gravity and mortification and global entanglements—*Sin loi!* they yelled. *I'm sorry, motherfuckers, but I'm out of it, I'm goofed, I'm on a space cruise, I'm gone!*—and it was a restful, unencumbered sensation, just riding the light waves, sailing that big silver freedom bird over the mountains and oceans, over America, over the farms and great sleeping cities and cemeteries and highways and the golden arches of McDonald's, it was flight, a kind of fleeing, a kind of falling, falling higher and higher, spinning off the edge of the earth and beyond the sun and through the vast, silent vacuum where there were no burdens and where everything weighed exactly nothing— Gone! they screamed. I'm sorry but I'm gone!—and so at night, not quite dreaming, they gave themselves over to lightness, they were carried, they were purely borne.

On the morning after Ted Lavender died, First Lieutenant Jimmy Cross crouched at the bottom of his foxhole and burned Martha's letters. Then he burned the two photographs. There was a steady rain falling, which made it difficult, but he used heat tabs and Sterno to build a small fire, screening it with his body, holding the photographs over the tight blue flame with the tips of his fingers.

He realized it was only a gesture. Stupid, he thought. Sentimental, too, but mostly just stupid.

Lavender was dead. You couldn't burn the blame.

Besides, the letters were in his head. And even now, without photographs, Lieutenant Cross could see Martha playing volleyball in her white gym shorts and yellow T-shirt. He could see her moving in the rain.

When the fire died out, Lieutenant Cross pulled his poncho over his shoulders and ate breakfast from a can.

There was no great mystery, he decided.

In those burned letters Martha had never mentioned the war, except to say, Jimmy, take care of yourself. She wasn't involved. She signed the letters "Love," but it wasn't love, and all the fine lines and technicalities did not matter. Virginity was no longer an issue. He hated her. Yes, he did. He hated her. Love, too, but it was a hard, hating kind of love.

The morning came up wet and blurry. Everything seemed part of everything else, the fog and Martha and the deepening rain.

He was a soldier, after all.

Half smiling, Lieutenant Jimmy Cross took out his maps. He shook his head hard, as if to clear it, then bent forward and began planning the day's march. In ten minutes, or maybe twenty, he would rouse the men and they would pack up and head west, where the maps showed the country to be green and inviting. They would do what they had always done. The rain might add some weight, but otherwise it would be one more day layered upon all the other days.

He was realistic about it. There was that new hardness in his stomach. He loved her but he hated her.

No more fantasies, he told himself.

Henceforth, when he thought about Martha, it would be only to think that she belonged elsewhere. He would shut down the daydreams. This was not Mount Sebastian, it was another world, where there were no pretty poems or mid-term exams, a place where men died because of carelessness and gross stupidity. Kiowa was right. Boom-down, and you were dead, never partly dead.

Briefly, in the rain, Lieutenant Cross saw Martha's gray eyes gazing back at him.

He understood.

It was very sad, he thought. The things men carried inside. The things men did or felt they had to do.

He almost nodded at her, but didn't.

Instead he went back to his maps. He was now determined to perform his duties firmly and without negligence. It wouldn't help Lavender, he knew that, but from this point on he would comport himself as an officer. He would dispose of his good-luck pebble. Swallow it, maybe, or use Lee Strunk's slingshot, or just drop it along the trail.

On the march he would impose strict field discipline. He would be careful to send out flank security, to prevent straggling or bunching up, to keep his troops moving at the proper pace and at the proper interval. He would insist on clean weapons. He would confiscate the remainder of Lavender's dope. Later in the day, perhaps, he would call the men together and speak to them plainly. He would accept the blame for what had happened to Ted Lavender. He would be a man about it. He would look them in the eyes, keeping his chin level, and he would issue the new SOPs in a calm, impersonal tone of voice, a lieutenant's voice, leaving no room for argument or discussion. Commencing immediately, he'd tell them, they would no longer abandon equipment along the route of march. They would police up their acts. They would get their shit together, and keep it together, and maintain it neatly and in good working order.

He would not tolerate laxity. He would show strength, distancing himself.

Among the men there would be grumbling, of course, and maybe worse, because their days would seem longer and their loads heavier, but Lieutenant Jimmy Cross reminded himself that his obligation was not to be loved but to lead. He would dispense with love; it was not now a factor. And if anyone quarreled or complained, he would simply tighten his lips and arrange his shoulders in the correct command posture. He might give a curt little nod. Or he might not. He might just shrug and say, Carry on, then they would saddle up and form into a column and move out toward the villages west of Than Khe.

## *Where Are You Going, Where Have You Been?*

### JOYCE CAROL OATES

#### *FOR BOB DYLAN*

Her name was Connie. She was fifteen and she had a quick nervous giggling habit of craning her neck to glance into mirrors, or checking other people's faces to make sure her own was all right. Her mother, who noticed everything and knew everything and who hadn't much reason any longer to look at her own face, always scolded Connie about it. "Stop gawking at yourself, who are you? You think you're so pretty?" she would say. Connie would raise her eyebrows at these familiar complaints and look right through her mother, into a shadowy vision of herself as she was right at that moment: she knew she was pretty and that was everything. Her mother had been pretty once too, if you could believe those old snapshots in the album, but now her looks were gone and that was why she was always after Connie.

"Why don't you keep your room clean like your sister? How've you got your hair fixed—what the hell stinks? Hair spray? You don't see your sister using that junk."

Her sister June was twenty-four and still lived at home. She was a secretary in the high school Connie attended, and if that wasn't bad enough—with her in the same building—she was so plain and chunky and steady that Connie had to hear her praised all the time by her mother and her mother's sisters. June did this, June did that, she saved money and helped clean the house and cooked and Connie couldn't do a thing, her mind was all filled with trashy daydreams. Their father was away at work most of the time and when he came home he wanted supper and he read the newspaper at supper and after supper he went to bed. He didn't bother talking much to them, but around his bent head Connie's mother kept picking at her until Connie wished her mother was dead and she herself was dead and it was all over. "She makes me want to throw up sometimes," she complained to her friends. She had a high, breathless, amused voice which made everything she said a little forced, whether it was sincere or not.

There was one good thing: June went places with girl friends of hers, girls who were just as plain and steady as she, and so when Connie wanted to do that her mother had no objections. The father of Connie's best girl friend drove the girls the three miles to town and left them off at a shopping plaza, so that they could walk through the stores or go to a movie, and when he came to pick them up again at eleven he never bothered to ask what they had done.

They must have been familiar sights, walking around that shopping plaza in their shorts and flat ballerina slippers that always scuffed the sidewalk, with charm bracelets jingling on their thin wrists; they would lean together to whisper and laugh secretly if someone passed by who amused or interested them. Connie had long dark blond hair that drew anyone's eye to it, and she wore part of it pulled up on her head and puffed out and the rest of it she let fall down her back. She wore a pullover jersey blouse that looked one way when she was at home and another way when she was away from home. Everything about her had two sides to it, one for home and one for anywhere that was not home: her walk that could be childlike and bobbing, or languid enough to make anyone think she was hearing music in her head, her mouth which was pale and smirking most of the time, but bright and pink on these evenings out, her laugh which was cynical and drawling at home—"Ha, ha, very funny"—but high-pitched and nervous anywhere else, like the jingling of the charms on her bracelet.

Sometimes they did go shopping or to a movie, but sometimes they went across the highway, ducking fast across the busy road, to a drive-in restaurant where older kids hung out. The restaurant was shaped like a big bottle, though squatter than a real bottle, and on its cap was a revolving figure of a grinning boy who held a hamburger aloft. One night in midsummer they ran across, breathless with daring, and right away someone leaned out a car window and invited them over, but it was just a boy from high school they didn't like. It made them feel good to be able to ignore him. They went up through the maze of parked and cruising cars to the bright-lit, fly-infested restaurant, their faces pleased and expectant as if they were entering a sacred building that loomed out of the night to give them what haven and what blessing they yearned for. They sat at the counter and crossed their legs at the ankles, their thin shoulders rigid with excitement and listened to the music that made everything so good: the music was always in the background like music at a church service, it was something to depend upon.

A boy named Eddie came in to talk with them. He sat backwards on his stool, turning himself jerkily around in semi-circles and then stopping and turning again, and after a while he asked Connie if she would like something to eat. She said she did and so she tapped her friend's arm on her way out—her friend pulled her face up into a brave droll look—and Connie said she would meet her at eleven, across the way. "I just hate to leave her like that," Connie said earnestly, but the boy said that she wouldn't be alone for long. So they went out to his car and on the way Connie couldn't help but let her eyes wander over the windshields and faces all around her, her face gleaming with the joy that had nothing to do with Eddie or even this place; it might have been the music. She drew her shoulders up and sucked in her breath with the pure pleasure of being alive, and just at that moment she happened to glance at a face just a few feet from hers. It was a boy with shaggy black hair, in a convertible jalopy painted gold. He stared at her and then his lips widened into a grin. Connie slit her eyes at him and turned away, but she couldn't help glancing back and there he was still watching her. He wagged a finger and laughed and said, "Gonna get you, baby," and Connie turned away again without Eddie noticing anything.

She spent three hours with him, at the restaurant where they ate hamburgers and drank Cokes in wax cups that were always sweating, and then down an alley a mile or so away, and when he left her off at five to eleven only the movie house was still open at the plaza. Her girl friend was there, talking with a boy. When Connie came up the two girls smiled at each other and Connie said, "How was the movie?" and the girl said, "*You* should know." They rode off with the girl's father, sleepy and pleased, and Connie couldn't help but look at the darkened shopping plaza with its big empty parking lot and its signs that were faded and ghostly now, and over at the drive-in restaurant where cars were still circling tirelessly. She couldn't hear the music at this distance.

Next morning June asked her how the movie was and Connie said, "So-so."

She and that girl and occasionally another girl went out several times a week that way, and the rest of the time Connie spent around the house—it was summer vacation—getting in her mother's way and thinking, dreaming, about the boys she met. But all the boys fell back and dissolved into a single face that was not even a face, but an idea, a feeling, mixed up with the urgent insistent pounding of the music and the humid night air of July. Connie's mother kept dragging her back to the daylight by finding things for her to do or saying suddenly, "What's this about the Pettinger girl?"

And Connie would say nervously, "Oh, her. That dope." She always drew thick clear lines between herself and such girls, and her mother was simple and kindly enough to believe her. Her mother was so simple, Connie thought, that it was maybe cruel to fool her so much. Her mother went scuffling around the house in old bedroom slippers and complained over the telephone to one sister about the other, then the other called up and the two of them complained about the third one. If June's name was mentioned her mother's tone was approving, and if Connie's name was mentioned it was disapproving. This did not really mean she disliked Connie and actually Connie thought that her mother preferred her to June because she was prettier, but the two of them kept up a pretense of exasperation, a sense that they were tugging and struggling over something of little value to either of them. Sometimes, over coffee, they were almost friends, but something would come up—some vexation that was like a fly buzzing suddenly around their heads—and their faces went hard with contempt.

One Sunday Connie got up at eleven—none of them bothered with church—and washed her hair so that it could dry all day long, in the sun. Her parents and sister were going to a barbecue at an aunt's house and Connie said no, she wasn't interested, rolling her eyes, to let mother know just what she thought of it. "Stay home alone then," her mother said sharply. Connie sat out back in a lawn chair and watched them drive away, her father quiet and bald, hunched around so that he could back the car out, her mother with a look that was still angry and not at all softened through the windshield, and in the back seat poor old June all dressed up as if she didn't know what a barbecue was, with all the running yelling kids and the flies. Connie sat with her eyes closed in the sun, dreaming and dazed with the warmth about her as if this were a kind of love, the caresses of love, and her mind slipped over onto thoughts of the boy she had been with the night before and how nice he had been, how sweet it always was, not the way someone like June would suppose but sweet, gentle, the way it was in movies and promised in songs; and when she opened her eyes she hardly knew where she was, the back yard ran off into weeds and a fenceline of trees and behind it the sky was perfectly blue and still. The asbestos "ranch house" that was now three years old startled her—it looked small. She shook her head as if to get awake.

It was too hot. She went inside the house and turned on the radio to drown out the quiet. She sat on the edge of her bed, barefoot, and listened for an hour and a half to a program called XYZ Sunday Jamboree, record after record of hard, fast, shrieking songs she sang along with, interspersed by exclamations from "Bobby King": "An' look here you girls at Napoleon's—Son and Charley want you to pay real close attention to this song coming up!"

And Connie paid close attention herself, bathed in a glow of slow-pulsed joy that seemed to rise mysteriously out of the music itself and lay languidly about the airless little room, breathed in and breathed out with each gentle rise and fall of her chest.

After a while she heard a car coming up the drive. She sat up at once, startled, because it couldn't be her father so soon. The gravel kept crunching all the way in from the road—the driveway was long—and Connie ran to the window. It was a car she didn't know. It was an open jalopy, painted a bright gold that caught the sun opaquely. Her heart began to pound and her fingers snatched at her hair, checking it, and she whispered "Christ. Christ," wondering how bad she looked. The car came to a stop at the side door and the horn sounded four short taps as if this were a signal Connie knew.

She went into the kitchen and approached the door slowly, then hung out the screen door, her bare toes curling down off the step. There were two boys in the car and now she recognized the driver: he had shaggy, shabby black hair that looked crazy as a wig and he was grinning at her.

"I ain't late, am I?" he said.

"Who the hell do you think you are?" Connie said.

"Toldja I'd be out, didn't I?"

"I don't even know who you are."

She spoke sullenly, careful to show no interest or pleasure, and he spoke in a fast bright monotone. Connie looked past him to the other boy, taking her time. He had fair brown hair, with a lock that fell onto his forehead. His sideburns gave him a fierce, embarrassed look, but so far he hadn't even bothered to glance at her. Both boys wore sunglasses. The driver's glasses were metallic and mirrored everything in miniature.

"You wanta come for a ride?" he said.

Connie smirked and let her hair fall loose over one shoulder.

"Don'tcha like my car? New paint job," he said. "Hey."

"What?"

"You're cute."

She pretended to fidget, chasing flies away from the door.

"Don't cha believe me, or what?" he said.

"Look, I don't even know who you are," Connie said in disgust.

"Hey, Ellie's got a radio, see. Mine's broke down." He lifted his friend's arm and showed her the little transistor the boy was holding, and now Connie began to hear the music. It was the same program that was playing inside the house.

"Bobby King?" she said.

"I listen to him all the time. I think he's *great*."

"He's kind of great," Connie said reluctantly.

"Listen, that guy's *great*. He knows where the action is."

Connie blushed a little, because the glasses made it impossible for her to see just what this boy was looking at. She couldn't decide if she liked him or if he was just a jerk, and so she dawdled in the doorway and wouldn't come down or go back inside. She said, "What's all that stuff painted on your car?"

"Can'tcha read it?" He opened the door very carefully, as if he was afraid it might fall off. He slid out just as carefully, planting his feet firmly on the ground, the tiny metallic world in his glasses slowing down like gelatine hardening and in the midst of it Connie's bright green blouse. "This here is my name, to begin with," he said. ARNOLD FRIEND was written in tar-like black letters on the side, with a drawing of a round grinning face that reminded Connie of a pumpkin, except it wore sunglasses. "I wanta introduce myself, I'm Arnold Friend and that's my real name and I'm gonna be your friend, honey, and inside the car's Ellie Oscar, he's kinda shy." Ellie brought his transistor up to his shoulder and balanced it there. "Now these numbers are a secret code, honey," Arnold Friend explained. He read off the numbers 33, 19, 17 and raised his eyebrows at her to see what she thought of that, but she didn't think much of it. The left rear fender had been smashed and around it was written, on the gleaming gold background: DONE BY CRAZY WOMAN DRIVER. Connie had to laugh at that. Arnold Friend was pleased at her laughter and looked up at her. "Around the other side's a lot more—you wanta come and see them?"

"No."

"Why not?"

"Why should I?"

"Don'tcha wanta see what's on the car? Don'tcha wanta go for a ride?"

"I don't know."

"Why not?"

"I got things to do."

"Like what?"

"Things."

He laughed as if she had said something funny. He slapped his thighs. He was standing in a strange way, leaning back against the car as if he were balancing himself. He wasn't tall, only an inch or so taller than she would be if she came down to him. Connie liked the way he was dressed, which was the way all of them dressed: tight faded jeans stuffed into black, scuffed boots, a belt that pulled his waist in and showed how lean he was, and a white pull-over shirt that was a little soiled and showed the hard small muscles of his arms and shoulders. He looked as if he probably did hard work, lifting and carrying things. Even his neck looked muscular. And his face was a familiar face, somehow: the jaw and chin and cheeks slightly darkened, because he hadn't shaved for a day or two, and the nose long and hawk-like, sniffing as if she were a treat he was going to gobble up and it was all a joke.

"Connie, you ain't telling the truth. This is your day set aside for a ride with me and you know it," he said, still laughing. The way he straightened and recovered from his fit of laughing showed that it had been all fake.

"How do you know what my name is?" she said suspiciously.

"It's Connie."

"Maybe and maybe not."

"I know my Connie," he said, wagging his finger. Now she remembered him even better, back at the restaurant, and her cheeks warmed at the thought of how she sucked in her breath just at the moment she passed him—how she must have looked to him. And he had remembered her. "Ellie and I come out here especially for you," he said. "Ellie can sit in back. How about it?"

"Where?"

"Where what?"

"Where're we going?"

He looked at her. He took off the sunglasses and she saw how pale the skin around his eyes was, like holes that were not in shadow but instead in light. His eyes were like chips of broken glass that catch the light in an amiable way. He smiled. It was as if the idea of going for a ride somewhere, to some place, was a new idea to him.

"Just for a ride, Connie sweetheart."

"I never said my name was Connie," she said.

"But I know what it is. I know your name and all about you, lots of things," Arnold Friend said. He had not moved yet but stood still leaning back against the side of his jalopy. "I took a special interest in you, such a pretty girl, and found out all about you like I know your parents and sister are gone somewheres and I know where and how long they're going to be gone, and I know who you were with last night, and your best friend's name is Betty. Right?"

He spoke in a simple lilting voice, exactly as if he were reciting the words to a song. His smile assured her that everything was fine. In the car Ellie turned up the volume on his radio and did not bother to look around at them.

"Ellie can sit in the back seat," Arnold Friend said. He indicated his friend with a casual jerk of his chin, as if Ellie did not count and she should not bother with him.

"How'd you find out all that stuff?" Connie said.

"Listen: Betty Schultz and Tony Fitch and Jimmy Pettinger and Nancy Pettinger," he said, in a chant. "Raymond Stanley and Bob Hutter—"

"Do you know all those kids?"

"I know everybody."

"Look, you're kidding. You're not from around here."

"Sure."

"But—how come we never saw you before?"

"Sure you saw me before," he said. He looked down at his boots, as if he were a little offended. "You just don't remember."

"I guess I'd remember you," Connie said.

"Yeah?" He looked up at this, beaming. He was pleased. He began to mark time with the music from Ellie's radio, tapping his fists lightly together. Connie looked away from his smile to the car, which was painted so bright it almost hurt her eyes to look at it. She looked at that name, ARNOLD FRIEND. And up at the front fender was an expression that was familiar—MAN THE FLYING SAUCERS. It was an expression kids had used the year before, but didn't use this year. She looked at it for a while as if the words meant something to her that she did not yet know.

"What're you thinking about? Huh?" Arnold Friend demanded. "Not worried about your hair blowing around in the car, are you?"

"No."

"Think I maybe can't drive good?"

"How do I know?"

"You're a hard girl to handle. How come?" he said. "Don't you know I'm your friend? Didn't you see me put my sign in the air when you walked by?"

"WHAT SIGN?"

"My sign." And he drew an X in the air, leaning out toward her. They were maybe ten feet apart. After his hand fell back to his side the X was still in the air, almost visible. Connie let the screen door close and stood perfectly still inside it, listening to the music from her radio and the boy's blend together. She stared at Arnold Friend. He stood there so stiffly relaxed, pretending to be relaxed, with one hand idly on the door handle as if he were keeping himself up that way and had no intention of ever moving again. She recognized most things about him, the tight jeans that showed his thighs and buttocks and the greasy leather boots and the tight shirt, and even that slippery friendly smile of his, that sleepy dreamy smile that all the boys used to get across ideas they didn't want to put into words. She recognized all this and also the singsong way he talked, slightly mocking, kidding, but serious and a little melancholy, and she recognized the way he tapped one fist against the other in homage to the perpetual music behind him. But all these things did not come together.

She said suddenly, "Hey, how old are you?"

His smile faded. She could see then that he wasn't a kid, he was much older—thirty, maybe more. At this knowledge her heart began to pound faster.

"That's a crazy thing to ask. Can'tcha see I'm your own age?"

"Like hell you are."

"Or maybe a coupla years older, I'm eighteen."

"Eighteen?" she said doubtfully.

He grinned to reassure her and lines appeared at the corners of his mouth. His teeth were big and white. He grinned so broadly his eyes became slits and she saw how thick the lashes were, thick and black as if painted with a black tar-like material. Then he seemed to become embarrassed, abruptly, and looked over his shoulder at Ellie. "*Him*, he's crazy," he said. "Ain't he a riot, he's a nut, a real character." Ellie was still listening to the music. His sunglasses told nothing about what he was thinking. He wore a bright orange shirt unbuttoned halfway to show his chest, which was a pale, bluish chest and not muscular like Arnold Friend's. His shirt collar was turned up all around and the very tips of the collar pointed out past his chin as if they were protecting him. He was pressing the transistor radio up against his ear and sat there in a kind of daze, right in the sun.

"He's kinda strange," Connie said.

"Hey, she says you're kinda strange! Kinda strange!" Arnold Friend cried. He pounded on the car to get Ellie's attention. Ellie turned for the first time and Connie saw with shock that he wasn't a kid either—he had a fair, hairless face, cheeks reddened slightly as if the veins grew too close to the surface of his skin, the face of a forty-year-old baby. Connie felt a wave of dizziness rise in her at this sight and she stared at him as if waiting for something to change the shock of the moment, make it all right again. Ellie's lips kept shaping words, mumbling along with the words blasting his ear.

"Maybe you two better go away," Connie said faintly.

"What? How come?" Arnold Friend cried. "We come out here to take you for a ride. It's Sunday." He had the voice of the man on the radio now. It was the same voice, Connie thought. "Don'tcha know it's Sunday all day and honey, no matter who you were with last night today you're with Arnold Friend and don't you forget it!—Maybe you better step out here," he said, and this last was in a different voice. It was a little flatter, as if the heat was finally getting to him.

"No. I got things to do."

"Hey."

"You two better leave."

"We ain't leaving until you come with us."

"Like hell I am—"

"Connie, don't fool around with me. I mean—I mean, don't fool *around*," he said, shaking his head. He laughed incredulously. He placed his sunglasses on top of his head, carefully, as if he were indeed wearing a wig, and brought the stems down behind his ears. Connie stared at him, another wave of dizziness and fear rising in her so that for a moment he wasn't even in focus but was just a blur, standing there against his gold car, and she had the idea that he had driven up the driveway all right but had come from nowhere before that and belonged nowhere and that everything about him and even the music that was so familiar to her was only half real.

"If my father comes and sees you—"

"He ain't coming. He's at a barbecue."

"How do you know that?"

"Aunt Tillie's. Right now they're—uh—they're drinking. Sitting around," he said vaguely, squinting as if he were staring all the way to town and over to Aunt Tillie's back yard. Then the vision seemed to clear and he nodded energetically. "Yeah. Sitting around. There's your sister in a blue dress, huh? And high heels, the poor sad bitch—nothing like you, sweetheart! And your mother's helping some fat woman with the corn, they're cleaning the corn—husking the corn—"

"What fat woman?" Connie cried.

"How do I know what fat woman. I don't know every goddam fat woman in the world!" Arnold Friend laughed.

"Oh, that's Mrs. Hornby. . . . Who invited her?" Connie said. She felt a little light-headed. Her breath was coming quickly.

"She's too fat. I don't like them fat. I like them the way you are, honey," he said, smiling sleepily at her. They stared at each other for a while, through the screen door. He said softly, "Now what you're going to do is this: you're going to come out that door. You're going to sit up front with me and Ellie's going to sit in the back, the hell with Ellie, right? This isn't Ellie's date. You're my date. I'm your lover, honey."

"What? You're crazy—"

"Yes, I'm your lover. You don't know what that is but you will," he said. "I know that too. I know all about you. But look: it's real nice and you couldn't ask for nobody better than me, or more polite. I always keep my word. I'll tell you how it is, I'm always nice at first, the first time. I'll hold you so tight you won't think you have to try to get away or pretend anything because you'll know you can't. And I'll come inside you where it's all secret and you'll give in to me and you'll love me—"

"Shut up! You're crazy!" Connie said. She backed away from the door. She put her hands against her ears as if she'd heard something terrible, something not meant for her. "People don't talk like that, you're crazy," she muttered. Her heart was almost too big now for her chest and its pumping made sweat break out all over her. She looked out to see Arnold Friend pause and then take a step toward the porch lurching. He almost fell. But, like a clever drunken man, he managed to catch his balance. He wobbled in his high boots and grabbed hold of one of the porch posts.

"Honey?" he said. "You still listening?"

"Get the hell out of here!"

"Be nice, honey. Listen."

"I'm going to call the police—"

He wobbled again and out of the side of his mouth came a fast spat curse, an aside not meant for her to hear. But even this "Christ!" sounded forced. Then he began to smile again. She watched this smile come, awkward as if he were smiling from inside a mask. His whole face was a mask, she thought wildly, tanned down onto his throat but then running out as if he had plastered makeup on his face but had forgotten about his throat.

"Honey—? Listen, here's how it is. I always tell the truth and I promise you this: I ain't coming in that house after you."

"You better not! I'm going to call the police if you—if you don't—"

"Honey," he said, talking right through her voice, "honey, I'm not coming in there but you are coming out here. You know why?"

She was panting. The kitchen looked like a place she had never seen before, some room she had run inside but which wasn't good enough, wasn't going to help her. The kitchen window had never had a curtain, after three years, and there were dishes in the sink for her to do—probably—and if you ran your hand across the table you'd probably feel something sticky there.

"You listening, honey? Hey?"

"—going to call the police—"

"Soon as you touch the phone I don't need to keep my promise and can come inside. You won't want that."

She rushed forward and tried to lock the door. Her fingers were shaking. "But why lock it," Arnold Friend said gently, talking right into her face. "It's just a screen door. It's just nothing." One of his boots was at a strange angle, as if his foot wasn't in it. It pointed out to the left, bent at the ankle. "I mean, anybody can break through a screen door and glass and wood and iron or anything else if he needs to, anybody at all and specially Arnold Friend. If the place got lit up with a fire, honey, you'd come running out into my arms, right into my arms and safe at home—like you knew I was your lover and'd stopped fooling around. I don't mind a nice shy girl but I don't like no fooling around." Part of those words were spoken with a slight rhythmic lilt, and Connie somehow recognized them—the echo of a song from last year, about a girl rushing into her boy friend's arms and coming home again—

Connie stood barefoot on the linoleum floor, staring at him. "What do you want?" she whispered.

"I want you," he said.

"What?"

"Seen you that night and thought, that's the one, yes sir. I never needed to look any more."

"But my father's coming back. He's coming to get me. I had to wash my hair first—" She spoke in a dry, rapid voice, hardly raising it for him to hear.

"No, your daddy is not coming and yes, you had to wash your hair and you washed it for me. It's nice and shining and all for me, I thank you, sweetheart," he said, with a mock bow, but again he almost lost his balance. He had to bend and adjust his boots. Evidently his feet did not go all the way down; the boots must have been stuffed with something so that he would seem taller. Connie stared out at him and behind him Ellie in the car, who seemed to be looking off toward Connie's right, into nothing. This Ellie said, pulling the words out of the air one after another as if he were just discovering them, "You want me to pull out the phone?"

"Shut your mouth and keep it shut," Arnold Friend said, his face red from bending over or maybe from embarrassment because Connie had seen his boots. "This ain't none of your business."

"What—what are you doing? What do you want?" Connie said. "If I call the police they'll get you, they'll arrest you—"

"Promise was not to come in unless you touch that phone, and I'll keep that promise," he said. He resumed his erect position and tried to force his shoulders back. He sounded like a hero in a movie, declaring something important. He spoke too loudly and it was as if he were speaking to someone behind Connie. "I ain't made plans for coming in that house where I don't belong but just for you to come out to me, the way you should. Don't you know who I am?"

"You're crazy," she whispered. She backed away from the door but did not want to go into another part of the house, as if this would give him permission to come through the door. "What do you. . . . You're crazy, you. . . ."

"Huh? What're you saying, honey?"

Her eyes darted everywhere in the kitchen. She could not remember what it was, this room.

"This is how it is, honey: you come out and we'll drive away, have a nice ride. But if you don't come out we're gonna wait till your people come home and then they're all going to get it."

"You want that telephone pulled out?" Ellie said. He held the radio away from his ear and grimaced, as if without the radio the air was too much for him.

"I toldja shut up, Ellie." Arnold Friend said, "You're deaf, get a hearing aid, right? Fix yourself up. This little girl's no trouble and's gonna be nice to me, so Ellie keep to yourself, this ain't your date—right? Don't hem in on me. Don't hog. Don't crush. Don't bird dog. Don't trail me," he said in a rapid meaningless voice, as if he were running through all the expressions he'd learned but was no longer sure which one of them was in style, then rushing on to new ones, making them up with his eyes closed, "Don't crawl under my fence, don't squeeze in my chipmunk hole, don't sniff my glue, suck my popsicle, keep your own greasy fingers on yourself!" He shaded his eyes and peered in at Connie, who was backed against the kitchen table. "Don't mind him, honey, he's just a creep. He's a dope. Right? I'm the boy for you and like I said you come out here nice like a lady and give me your hand, and nobody else gets hurt, I mean, your nice old bald-headed daddy and your mummy and your sister in her high heels. Because listen: why bring them in this?"

"Leave me alone," Connie whispered.

"Hey, you know that old woman down the road, the one with the chickens and stuff—you know her?"

"She's dead!"

"Dead? What? You know her?" Arnold Friend said.

"She's dead—"

"Don't you like her?"

"She's dead—she's—she isn't here any more—"

"But don't you like her, I mean, you got something against her? Some grudge or something?" Then his voice dipped as if he were conscious of rudeness. He touched the sunglasses on top of his head as if to make sure they were still there. "Now you be a good girl."

"What are you going to do?"

"Just two things, or maybe three," Arnold Friend said. "But I promise it won't last long and you'll like me that way you get to like people you're close to. You will. It's all over for you here, so come on out. You don't want your people in any trouble, do you?"

She turned and bumped against a chair or something, hurting her leg, but she ran into the back room and picked up the telephone. Something roared in her ear, a tiny roaring, and she was so sick with fear that she could do nothing but listen to it—the telephone was clammy and very heavy and her fingers groped down to the dial but were too weak to touch it. She began to scream into the phone, into the roaring. She cried out, she cried for her mother, she felt her breath start jerking back and forth in her lungs as if it were something Arnold Friend were stabbing her with again and again with no tenderness. A noisy sorrowful wailing rose all about her and she was locked inside it the way she was locked inside this house.

After a while she could hear again. She was sitting on the floor, with her wet back against the wall.

Arnold Friend was saying from the door, "That's a good girl. Put the phone back."

She kicked the phone away from her.

"No, honey. Pick it up. Put it back right."

She picked it up and put it back. The dial tone stopped.

"That's a good girl. Now you come outside."

She was hollow with what had been fear, but what was now just an emptiness. All that screaming had blasted it out of her. She sat, one leg cramped under her, and deep inside her brain was something like a pinpoint of light that kept going and would not let her relax. She thought, I'm not going to see my mother again. She thought, I'm not going to sleep in my bed again. Her bright green blouse was all wet.

Arnold Friend said, in a gentle-loud voice that was like a stage voice, "The place where you came from ain't there any more, and where you had in mind to go is cancelled out. This place you are now—inside your daddy's house—is nothing but a cardboard box I can knock down any time. You know that and always did know it. You hear me?"

She thought, I have got to think. I have to know what to do.

"We'll go out to a nice field, out in the country here where it smells so nice and it's sunny," Arnold Friend said. "I'll have my arms tight around you so you won't need to try to get away and I'll show you what love is like, what it does. The hell with this house! It looks solid all right," he said. He ran a fingernail down the screen and the noise did not make Connie shiver, as it would have the day before. "Now put your hand on your heart, honey. Feel that? That feels solid too but we know better, be nice to me, be sweet like you can because what else is there for a girl like you but to be sweet and pretty and give in?—and get away before her people come back?"

She felt her pounding heart. Her hands seemed to enclose it. She thought for the first time in her life that it was nothing that was hers, that belonged to her, but just a pounding, living thing inside this body that wasn't hers either.

"You don't want them to get hurt," Arnold Friend went on. "Now get up, honey. Get up all by yourself."

She stood.

"Now turn this way. That's right. Come over here to me—Ellie, put that away, didn't I tell you? You dope. You miserable creepy dope," Arnold Friend said. His words were not angry but only part of an incantation. The incantation was kindly. "Now come out through the kitchen to me honey and let's see a smile, try it, you're a brave sweet little girl and now they're eating corn and hotdogs cooked to bursting over an outdoor fire, and they don't know one thing about you and never did and honey you're better than them because not one of them would have done this for you."

Connie felt the linoleum under her feet; it was cool. She brushed her hair back out of her eyes. Arnold Friend let go of the post tentatively and opened his arms for her, his elbows pointing up toward each other and his wrists limp, to show that this was an embarrassed embrace and a little mocking, he didn't want to make her self-conscious.

She put out her hand against the screen. She watched herself push the door slowly open as if she were safe back somewhere in the other doorway, watching this body and this head of long hair moving out into the sunlight where Arnold Friend waited.

"My sweet little blue-eyed girl," he said, in a half-sung sigh that had nothing to do with her brown eyes but was taken up just the same by the vast sunlit reaches of the land behind him and on all sides of him—so much land that Connie had never seen before and did not recognize except to know that she was going to it.

## Writing Exercises

### INDIVIDUAL

1. *Story Trigger.* One way to test your skill in the use of concrete, significant detail is to create a reality that is convincing—and yet literally impossible. To begin, draft a three-to-five-page story in which a single impossible event happens in the everyday world. (For example, a dog tells fortunes, a secret message appears on a pizza, the radio announcer speaks in an ex-husband's voice—supermarket tabloids can be a good source of ideas.) First, focus on using detail to create the reality of both the normal world and the impossible event—the more believable the reality is, the more seamlessly readers will accept the magic.

2. In the movie *Wait Until Dark*, Audrey Hepburn plays a blind woman being pursued by a killer through a darkened house. Audiences usually jump out of their seats during the film's climactic final scene because they identify so thoroughly with her character. Write a scene where your character is deprived of one of his five senses. Then, set the character in a situation where missing that particular sense would have an especially significant impact. The situation might put him at an advantage or disadvantage, but in any case, he will have to compensate, wringing every bit of useful information he can out of his other senses. Make the situation dramatic, one in which he is driven by a pressing need or desire. Here are some examples:
   - a child standing blindfolded in front of a piñata really wants to be the one to break it and get first crack at the candy inside,
   - a man (who is spying) can see, but not hear, his wife as she talks to her ex-husband,
   - someone on a very strict diet is at a party and stuck in a boring conversation near the buffet table.

3. *Touch*. We sometimes neglect to use tactile descriptions in our writing, but we do touch—all the time. Shopping for clothes, shaking hands, playing with pets, shuffling cards, scrubbing pots, shooting baskets. Think of what it means to touch an odd, rare, or even holy object. Consider temperature (*tepid, frigid*), moisture content (*arid, greasy, sticky, crisp*), texture (*crinkled, gritty, silky*), and weight (*ponderous, buoyant*). All of these sensations provide us with great descriptive words. Use some of them and find others.

   Describe the way an action or event *feels*—putting on a piece of clothing, engaging in exercise, eating a tough or squishy item of food, dancing, moving across a crowded room, carrying groceries in from the car, kissing, waking up, washing the car, whatever. What impression does your description give? Does it prompt a scene? Can you make some characters talk while they're doing one of these activities?

4. *Taste*. There are four main types of taste and each has its own words—sweet (*saccharine, sugary*), sour (*acidic, tart*), bitter (*acrid, biting*), and salty (*briny, brackish*). There are also lots of objects that have familiar, but distinctive tastes and so are useful in description (*fish, lemons, onions, candy, chocolate, pickles, beer, coffee, and so on*).

   Take some characters out for dinner—Chinese or Greek, burgers or gourmet, it doesn't matter. Describe a particular course or even a whole meal. What impression does your description give? What do the characters have to say about their meal? How do they communicate with each other through their appreciation of the food?

5. Imagine a crowded, overwhelming scene (a rock concert, a political rally, the mall, an accident, a big city emergency room, a theme park, a college town after their team won the championship, a Wall Street trading floor, etc.). Use sensory details to convey this particular experience. Don't *tell* how your character feels about this scene; instead, use significant details to suggest his emotional state. For example, your character is *exhilarated* by the music, ready to pass out from the heat, and afraid of being trampled by the frenzied fans. When writing your scene, consider reasons your character has an atypical response: for example, a paramedic who is either energized or bored by an accident scene.

6. Write about something familiar from the point of view of a stranger—a foreigner, a time-traveler from the past, a prisoner released after twenty years in jail, an orphan. Pick a situation that might seem commonplace to your readers and imagine how she would perceive it through all her available senses. Send the urbanite to a small town in the Midwest, introduce the time-traveler to his own future, have the ex-prisoner spend the evening in a karaoke bar, let the orphan be adopted by a previously childless couple. The goal is to make the everyday seem strange and new again. Avoid using familiar words (your character won't know them). You might even try not to *name* the situation but let your reader figure out where the character is through your use of sensory details.

7. Do your own version of "The Things They Carried." Imagine that some characters you have invented are going somewhere they've never been. Describe what each one is carrying in his pocket, purse, briefcase, or backpack. Let the objects be as odd and distinctive as you like. *What's he doing with that kumquat? Why does she have a screwdriver?* Use the items to explode stereotypes and individualize your characters. *Why is that atheist packing a Bible? Should it be a Snickers bar or Cadbury chocolates? A fountain pen or golf pencil? A Zippo lighter or matches?* Write for ten minutes.

## COLLABORATIVE

8. Make exercise #7 into a collaborative activity by having the class break up into small groups. Then, each member of the group reads his or her exercise aloud to the others. Finally, the groups decide which character has the most potential to be the main character in a story.

9. Bring an object to class that is for some reason important to you. It need not be valuable and its importance shouldn't be obvious (don't bring in your Oscar statuette, for instance). Perhaps when you were a kid, you helped your grandmother sort eggs on her farm and you still have the egg scale the two of you used. Maybe you brought a rock back from the Grand Canyon or still have the first model airplane you ever built.

   Step 1. Pass the objects around and study them in silence.

   Step 2. Now, choose an object other than your own to write about as if it were your own, explaining how you got it and why it's important to you. Write as fast as you can for ten minutes, not stopping to censor or edit yourself.

   Step 3. Read the fictitious accounts aloud and compare them with what the real owner has to say.

10. As a class, pick four emotions and make two lists for each (eight lists in all)—one that describes the body language of a person experiencing that emotion (external), and the other describing that person's physical sensations (internal). Review the lists: which symptoms seem overly familiar (his hair stood on end; her heart was racing) and which seem fresh and original?

    *Follow-up:* Circle a passage of high emotion in your own story and exchange manuscripts with a partner. Do you see a place where emotion could be physically shown rather than labeled? Do you see a clichéd or melodramatic description that could be replaced with a more precise and original physical detail?

# 3

# BUILDING CHARACTER
## *Characterization, Part I*

* *The Direct Methods of Character Presentation*

* *Appearance*

* *Action*

* *Dialogue*

* *Thought*

Human character is in the foreground of all fiction, however the humanity might be disguised. Attributing human characteristics to the natural world may be frowned on in science, but it is a literary necessity. Bugs Bunny isn't a rabbit; he's a plucky youth in ears. Peter Rabbit is a mischievous boy. Brer Rabbit is a sassy rebel. The romantic heroes of *Watership Down* are out of the Arthurian tradition, not out of the hutch.

Henri Bergson, in his essay "On Laughter," observes:

> . . . the comic does not exist outside the pale of what is strictly human. A land-scape may be beautiful, charming or sublime, or insignificant and ugly; it will never be laughable.

Bergson is right, but it is just as true that only the human is tragic. We may describe a landscape as "tragic" because nature has been devastated by industry, but the tragedy lies in the cupidity of those who wrought the havoc, in the dreariness, poverty, or disease of those who must live there. A conservationist or ecologist (or a novelist) may care passionately about nature and dislike people because they pollute oceans and cut down trees. Then we say he or she "identifies" with nature (a wholly human capacity) or "respects the natural unity" (of which humanity is a part) or wants to keep the earth habitable (for whom?) or "values nature for its own sake" (using standards of value that nature does not share). By all available evidence, the universe is indifferent to the destruction of trees, property, peoples, and planets. Only people care.

If this is so, then your fiction can be only as successful as the characters who move it and move within it. Whether they are drawn from life or are pure fantasy—and all fictional characters lie somewhere between the two—we must find them interesting, we must find them believable, and we must care about what happens to them.

> YOU ARE GOING TO LOVE SOME OF YOUR CHARACTERS, because they are you or some facet of you, and you are going to hate some of your characters for the same reason. But no matter what, you are probably going to have to let bad things happen to some of the characters you love or you won't have much of a story. Bad things happen to good characters, because our actions have consequences, and we do not all behave perfectly all the time.
>
> Anne Lamott

## The Direct Methods of Character Presentation

There are six basic methods of character presentation. The four direct methods—*appearance, action, dialogue,* and *thought*—will be discussed in this chapter. The indirect methods—*authorial interpretation* and *interpretation by another character*—will be discussed in chapter 4. Employing a variety of these methods can help you draw a full character.

It is through the four methods of direct characterization—*appearance, action, dialogue,* and *thought*—that a character is captured in print and transformed from a concept in the writer's mind to a living presence in the reader's. While each method will be examined separately, it is their combination that convinces, for while appearance and action convey a strong impression, characters reveal themselves most profoundly in the ways they speak and think. Like every other kind of "showing," the techniques explored in this chapter appeal to the senses, allowing readers to draw their own conclusions and to either accept or resist the narrator's judgment.

## Appearance

Of the four methods of direct presentation, appearance is especially important because our eyes are our most highly developed means of perception, and we therefore receive more nonsensuous information by sight than by any other sense. Beauty is only skin deep, but people are embodied, and whatever beauty—or ugliness—there is in them must somehow surface in order for us to perceive it. Such surfacing involves speech and action as well as appearance, but it is appearance that prompts our first reaction to people, and everything they wear and own presents some aspect of their inner selves.

Concerned to see beyond mere appearances, writers are sometimes inclined to neglect this power of the visible. In fact, much of the tension and conflict in character does proceed from the truth that appearance is not reality. But in order to know this, we must see the appearance first. Features, shape, style, clothing, and objects can make statements of internal values that are political, religious, social, intellectual, and essential. The man in the Ultrasuede jacket is making a different statement from the one in the holey sweatshirt. The woman with the cigarette holder is telling us something different from the one with the palmed joint. Even a person who has forsaken our materialistic society altogether, sworn off supermarkets, and gone to the country to grow organic potatoes has a special relationship with his or her hoe. However indifferent we may be to our looks, that indifference is the result of experiences with our bodies. A twenty-two-year-old Apollo who has been handsome since he was six is a very different person from the man who spent his childhood cocooned in fat and burst the chrysalis at age sixteen.

Following are four very brief portraits of women. Each is mainly characterized by such trivialities as fabric, hairdo, and cosmetics. It would nevertheless be impossible to mistake the essential nature of any one of them for that of any of the others.

Mrs. Withers, the dietician, marched in through the back door, drew up, and scanned the room. She wore her usual Betty Grable hairdo and open-toed pumps, and her shoulders had an aura of shoulder pads even in a sleeveless dress.

Margaret Atwood, *The Edible Woman*

My grandmother had on not just one skirt, but four, one over the other. It should not be supposed that she wore one skirt and three petticoats; no, she wore four skirts; one supported the next, and she wore the lot of them in accordance with a definite system, that is, the order of the skirts was changed from day to day . . . The one that was closest to her yesterday clearly disclosed its pattern today, or rather its lack of pattern: all my grandmother Anna Bronski's skirts favored the same potato color. It must have been becoming to her.

Günter Grass, *The Tin Drum*

How beautiful Helen is, how elegant, how timeless: how she charms Esther Songford and how she flirts with Edwin, laying a scarlet fingernail on his dusty lapel, mesmerizing.

She comes in a chauffeured car. She is all cream and roses. Her stockings are purest silk; her underskirt, just briefly showing, is lined with lace.

Fay Weldon, *Female Friends*

As soon as I entered the room, a pungent odor of phosphorus told me she'd taken rat poison. She lay groaning between the quilts. The tatami by the bed was splashed with blood, her waved hair was matted like rope waste, and a bandage tied round her throat showed up unnaturally white . . . The painted mouth in her waxen face created a ghastly effect, as though her lips were a gash open to the ears.

Masuji Ibuse, "Tajinko Village"

Vividness and richness of character are created in these four passages, which use nothing more than appearance to characterize.

Note that sense impressions other than sight are still a part of the way a character "appears." A limp handshake or a soft cheek; an odor of Chanel, oregano, or decay—these sense impressions can characterize much the way looks do if the narrative allows the reader to touch, smell, or taste a character.

The sound and associations of a character's name, too, can give a clue to personality: The affluent Mr. Chiddister in chapter 2 is automatically a more elegant sort than the affluent Mr. Strum; Huck Finn must have a different life from that of the Marquis of Lumbria. Although names with a blatant meaning—Joseph Surface, Billy Pilgrim, Martha Quest—tend to stylize a character and should be used sparingly, if at all, ordinary names can hint at traits you mean to heighten, and it is worth combing any list of names, including the telephone book, to find suggestive sounds. My own telephone book yields, at a glance this morning, Linda Holladay, Marvin Entzminger, and Melba Peebles, any one of which might set me to speculating on a character.

Sound also characterizes as a part of "appearance" insofar as sound represents timbre, tenor, or quality of noise and speech, the characterizing reediness or gruffness of a voice, the lift of laughter or stiffness of delivery.

The way a character physically moves is yet another form of "appearance." The almost feral nature of the sick child in "The Use of Force" (see chapter seven) is reinforced when "suddenly with one catlike movement both her hands clawed instinctively for my eyes and she almost reached them too." In "Gryphon" (see below in this chapter) Mr. Hibler's rigidity and inane way of stifling imagination is shown even in the way he reacts to a terrible cold: "Twice he bent over, and his loose tie, like a plumb line, hung straight down from his neck as he exploded himself into a Kleenex."

It is important to understand the difference between *movement* and *action*, however, for these terms are not synonymous. Physical movement—the way he crosses his legs, the way she charges down the hall—characterizes without necessarily moving the plot forward. Often movement is part of the setup of the scene, a way of establishing the situation before change-producing action begins.

## Action

The significant characters of a fiction must be both capable of causing an action and capable of being changed by it.

WHAT'S VITAL FOR THE FICTION WRITER to remember is that the wicked, the violent, and the stupid do also love, in their way. Just as humble and loving and thoughtful people also hate. Hate humbly, hate lovingly, hate thoughtfully, and so on.

Doug Bauer

If we accept that a story records a process of change, how is this change brought about? Basically, human beings face chance and choice, or discovery and decision—the first involuntary and the second voluntary. Translated into action, this means that a character driven by desire takes an action with an expected result, but something intervenes. Some force outside the character presents itself, in the form of information or accident or the behavior of others or the elements. The unknown becomes known, and then the discoverer must either take action or deliberately not take action, involving readers in the tension of the narrative query: and then what happens?

Here is a passage from Toni Morrison's "Recitatif" that demonstrates first movement, then discovery, then decision:

It was August and a bus crowd was just unloading. They would stand around a long while: going to the john, and looking at gifts and junk-for-sale machines, reluctant to sit down so soon. Even to eat. I was trying to fill the coffeepots and get them all situated on the electric burners when I saw her. She was sitting in a booth smoking a cigarette with two guys smothered in head and facial hair. Her own hair was so big and wild I could hardly see her face. But the eyes. I would know them anywhere. She had on a powder-blue halter and shorts outfit and earrings the size of bracelets. Talk about lipstick and eyebrow pencil. She made the big girls look like nuns. I couldn't get off the counter until seven o'clock, but I kept watching the booth in case they got up to leave before that. My replacement was on time for a change, so I counted and stacked my receipts as fast as I could and signed off. I walked over to the booth . . .

Here, unloading, milling around, and filling coffeepots is *movement* that represents scene-setting and characterization. The significant *action* begins with the discovery, "I saw her." Notice that "she" is characterized directly by appearance whereas the narrator is mainly characterized by her movements (expressed in active verbs)—watching, counting, stacking, signing off—until the moment when she acts on her decision. At the points of both the discovery and the decision we anticipate the possibility of change: what happens next?

In the next passage from John Cheever's "The Cure", the initial movement is seemingly innocuous before abruptly shifting toward suspense:

I turned on a light in the living room and looked at Rachel's books. I chose one by an author named Lin Yutang and sat down on a sofa under a lamp. Our living room is comfortable. The book seemed interesting. I was in a neighborhood where most of the front doors were unlocked, and on a street that is very quiet on a summer night. All the animals are domesticated, and the only night birds that I've ever heard are some owls way down by the railroad track. So it was very quiet. I heard the Barstows' dog bark, briefly, as if he had been waked by a nightmare, and then the barking stopped. Everything was quiet again. Then I heard, very close to me, a footstep and a cough.

    I felt my flesh get hard—you know that feeling—but I didn't look up from my book, although I felt that I was being watched.

This scene is set with movement and one choice—that book—that offers no particular opportunity for change and no particular dramatic force. With the moment "Then I heard," however, a discovery or realization of a different sort occurs, and there is suddenly the possibility of real change and so, suddenly, real dramatic tension. Notice that in the second paragraph the narrator discovers a familiar and entirely involuntary reaction—"I felt my flesh get hard"—followed by the decision *not* to take what would be the instinctive action. In fiction as in life, restraint, the decision to do nothing, is fraught with possible tension.

    In most cases, writers do not want their technique to be too conspicuous so they usually conceal the decision and discovery structure. In the next example, from Raymond Carver's "Neighbors," the pattern of change—Bill Miller's gradual intrusion into his neighbor's house—is based on a series of decisions that Carver does not explicitly state. The passage ends with a turning point, a moment of discovery.

When he returned to the kitchen the cat was scratching in her box. She looked at him steadily for a minute before she turned back to the litter. He opened all the cupboards and examined the canned goods, the cereals, the packaged foods, the cocktail and wine glasses, the china, the pots and pans. He opened the refrigerator. He sniffed some celery, took two bites of cheddar cheese, and chewed on an apple as he walked into the bedroom. The bed seemed enormous, with a fluffy white bedspread draped to the floor. He pulled out a nightstand drawer, found a half-empty package of cigarettes and stuffed them into his pocket. Then he stepped to the closet and was opening it when the knock sounded at the front door.

There is hardly grand larceny being committed here, but the actions build toward tension through two distinct techniques. The first is that they do actually "build": At first Bill only "examines." The celery he only sniffs, whereas he takes two bites of the cheese, then a whole apple, then half a pack of cigarettes. He moves from the kitchen to the bedroom, which is a clearer invasion of privacy, and from cupboard to refrigerator to nightstand to closet, each a more intimate intrusion than the last.

    The second technique is that the narrative subtly hints at Bill's own sense of stealth. It would be easy to imagine a vandal who performed the same actions with complete indifference. But Bill thinks the cat looks "steadily" at him, which is hardly of any importance except that he feels it to be. His awareness of the enormous white bed hints at sexual guilt. When the knock at the front door sounds, we start, as he must, in a clear sense of getting caught.

Thus it turns out that the internal or mental moment of change is where the action lies. Much movement in a story is mere event, and this is why descriptions of actions, like stage directions in a dull play, sometimes add little or nothing. When the wife picks up a cup of coffee, that is mere event. If she finds that the lipstick on the cup is not her shade, that is a dramatic event, a discovery; it makes a difference. She makes a decision to fling it at the woman with the Cherry Ice mouth. Flinging it is an action, but the dramatic change occurs with the second character's realization (discovery) that she has been hit—and so on.

Every story is a pattern of change (events connected, as the author E.M. Forster observed, primarily by cause and effect) in which small and large changes are made through decision and discovery.

## Dialogue

Speech characterizes in a way that is different from appearance, because speech represents an effort, mainly voluntary, to externalize the internal and to manifest not merely taste or preference but also deliberated thought. Like fiction itself, human dialogue attempts to marry logic to emotion.

### SUMMARY, INDIRECT, AND DIRECT DIALOGUE

Speech can be conveyed in fiction with varying degrees of directness. It can be *summarized* as part of the narrative so that a good deal of conversation is condensed:

> At home in the first few months, he and Maizie had talked brightly about changes that would make the company more profitable and more attractive to a prospective buyer: new cuts, new packaging, new advertising, new incentives to make supermarkets carry the brand.
>
> Joan Wickersham, "Commuter Marriage"

It can be reported in the third person as *indirect speech* so that it carries, without actual quotation, the feel of the exchange:

> Had he brought the coffee? She had been waiting all day long for coffee. They had forgot it when they ordered at the store the first day.
> Gosh, no, he hadn't. Lord, now he'd have to go back. Yes, he would if it killed him. He thought, though, he had everything else. She reminded him it was only because he didn't drink coffee himself. If he did he would remember it quick enough.
>
> Katherine Anne Porter, "Rope"

But usually when the exchange contains the possibility of discovery or decision, and therefore of dramatic action, it will be presented in *direct quotation:*

"But I thought you hardly knew her, Mr. Morning."

He picked up a pencil and began to doodle on a notebook page. "Did I tell you that?"

"Yes, you did."

"It's true. I didn't know her well."

"What is it you're after, then? Who was this person you're investigating?"

"I would like to know that too."

Siri Hustvedt, "Mr. Morning"

These three methods of presenting speech can be used in combination to take advantage of the virtues of each:

They differed on the issue of the holiday, and couldn't seem to find a common ground. (*Summary*.) She had an idea: why not some Caribbean island over Christmas? Well, but his mother expected them for turkey. (*Indirect*.)

"Oh, lord, yes, I wouldn't want to go without a yuletide gizzard." (*Direct*.)

Summary and indirect speech are often useful to get us quickly to the core of the scene, or when, for example, one character has to inform another of events that we already know, or when the emotional point of a conversation is that it has become tedious.

Carefully, playing down the danger, Len filled her in on the events of the long night.

Samantha claimed to be devastated. It was all very well if the Seversons wanted to let their cats run loose, but she certainly wasn't responsible for Lisbeth's parakeets, now was she?

But nothing is more frustrating to a reader than to be told that significant events are taking place in talk and to be denied the drama of the dialogue.

They whispered to each other all night long, and as he told her all about his past, she began to realize that she was falling in love with him.

Such a summary—it's *telling*—is a stingy way of treating the reader, who wants the chance to fall in love, too.

### ECONOMY IN DIALOGUE

Because direct dialogue has a dual nature—emotion within a logical structure—its purpose in fiction is never merely to convey information. Dialogue may do that (although information often is more naturally conveyed in narration), but it needs simultaneously to characterize, provide exposition, set the scene, advance the action, foreshadow, and/or remind. William Sloane, in *The Craft of Writing*, says:

There is a tentative rule that pertains to all fiction dialogue. It must do more than one thing at a time or it is too inert for the purposes of fiction. This may sound harsh, but I consider it an essential discipline.

In considering Sloane's "tentative rule," I place the emphasis on *rule*. With dialogue as with significant detail, when you write you are constantly at pains to mean more than you say. If a significant detail must both call up a sense image and *mean*, then the character's words, which presumably mean something, should simultaneously suggest image, personality, or emotion.

Dialogue, therefore, is not simply transcribed speech, but distilled speech—the "filler" and inert small talk of real conversation is edited away, even as the weight of implication is increased. "You don't simply copy what you heard on the street," says fiction writer Alice LaPlante. "You want to make it *sound* natural, but that doesn't mean it *is* natural. It takes careful editing to create natural-sounding dialogue. Generally, that means keeping things brief, and paying attention to the rhythm of the sentences. Sentences are short. They're not particularly grammatically correct, but rather quirky and characteristic of the speaker."

## CHARACTERIZING DIALOGUE

Even rote exchanges, however, can call up images. A character who says, "It is indeed a pleasure to meet you" carries his back at a different angle, dresses differently, from a character who says, "Hey, man, what's up?"

The three very brief speeches that follow portray three fictional men, sharply differentiated from each other not only by the content of what they say, but also by their diction (choice and use of words) and their syntax (the ordering of words in a sentence). Like appearance, these choices convey attributes of class, period, ethnicity, and so forth, as well as political or moral attitudes. How much do you know about each? How does each look?

"I had a female cousin one time—a Rockefeller, as it happened—" said the Senator, "and she confessed to me that she spent the fifteenth, sixteenth and seventeenth years of her life saying nothing but, No, thank you. Which is all very well for a girl of that age and station. But it would have been a damned unattractive trait in a male Rockefeller."

Kurt Vonnegut, *God Bless You, Mr. Rosewater*

"You think you the only one ever felt this way?" he asked. "You think I never felt this way? You think she never felt this way? Every last one of them back there one time in they life wanted to give up. She want to give up now. You know that? You got any idea how sick she is? Soon after he go, she's going too. I won't give her another year. I want her to believe he'll be up there waiting for her. And you can help me do it. And you the only one."

Ernest Gaines, *A Lesson Before Dying*

The Knight looked surprised at the question. "What does it matter where my body happens to be?" he said. "My mind goes on working all the same. In fact, the more head downward I am, the more I keep inventing new things.

"Now, the cleverest thing of the sort that I ever did," he went on after a pause, "was inventing a new pudding during the meat course."

Lewis Carroll, *Through the Looking Glass*

There are forms of insanity that condemn people to hear voices against their will, but as writers we invite ourselves to hear voices without relinquishing our hold on reality or our right to control. The trick to writing good dialogue is hearing voice. The question is, what would he or she say? The answer is entirely in language. The choice of language reveals content, character, and conflict, as well as type.

It's logical that if you must develop voices in order to develop dialogue, you'd do well to start with monologue and develop voices one by one. Use your journal to experiment with speech patterns that will characterize. Some people speak in telegraphically short sentences missing various parts of speech. Some speak in convoluted eloquence or in rhythms tedious with qualifying phrases. Some rush headlong without a pause for breath until they're breathless; others are measured or terse or begrudge even forming a sentence. Trust your "inner ear" and use your journal to practice catching voices. Freewriting is invaluable to dialogue writing because it is the manner of composition closest to speech. There is no time to mull or edit. Any qualifications, corrections, and disavowals must be made part of the process and the text.

To increase your ability to "hear" dialogue, try carrying a small pocket notebook with you and noting vivid lines or exchanges of eavesdropped dialogue verbatim. At home, look back through your notebook for speech that interests you and freedraft a monologue passage of that speech in your writing journal. Don't look for words that seem right; just listen to the voice and let it flow. You'll begin to develop your own range of voices whether you catch a particular voice or not, and may even develop your ear by the very process of "hearing" it go wrong at times.

## OTHER USES OF DIALOGUE

You can also limber up in your journal by setting yourself deliberate exercises in making dialogue—or monologue—do more than one thing at a time. In addition to revealing character, dialogue can *set the scene*.

"We didn't know no one was here. We thought hit a summer camp all closed up. Curtains all closed up. Nothing here. No cars or gear nor nothing. Looks closed to me, don't hit to you, J.J.?"

Joy Williams, "Woods"

Dialogue can *set the mood*.

"I have a lousy trip to Philadelphia, lousy flight back, I watch my own plane blow a tire on closed-circuit TV, I go to my office, I find Suzy in tears because Warren's camped in her one-room apartment. I come home and I find my wife hasn't gotten dressed in two days."

Joan Didion, *Book of Common Prayer*

Dialogue can *reveal the theme* because, as William Sloane says, the characters talk about what the story is about.

"You feel trapped, don't you?"
Jane looks at her.
"Don't you?"
"No."
"O.K.—You just have a headache."
"I do." . . .
Milly waits a moment and then clears her throat and says, "You know, for a while there after Wally and I were married, I thought maybe I'd made a mistake. I remember realizing that I didn't like the way he laughed. I mean, let's face it, Wally laughs like a hyena . . ."

Richard Bausch, "The Fireman's Wife"

In all of the preceding passages, the dialogue fulfills Sloane's rule because in addition to conveying its content, the dialogue either moves the story forward or enriches our understanding.

Dialogue is also one of the simplest ways to *reveal the past* (a fundamental playwriting device is to have a character who knows tell a character who doesn't know); and it is one of the most effective, because we get both the drama of the memory and the drama of the telling. Here is a passage from Toni Morrison's *The Bluest Eye* in which the past is evoked, the speaker characterized, the scene and mood set, and the theme revealed, all at the same time and in less than a dozen lines.

"The onliest time I be happy seem like was when I was in the picture show. Every time I got, I went. I'd go early, before the show started. They'd cut off the lights, and everything be black. Then the screen would light up, and I'd move right on in them pictures. White men taking such good care of they women, and they all dressed up in big clean houses with the bathtubs right in the same room with the toilet. Them pictures gave me a lot of pleasure, but it made coming home hard, and looking at Cholly hard. I don't know."

## DIALOGUE AS ACTION

If the telling of a memory *changes the relationship* between the teller and the listener, then you have a scene of high drama, and the dialogue can *advance the action*.

This is an important device, because dialogue is most valuable to fiction when it is itself a means of telling the story.

In the following passage, for example, the mother of a seriously ill toddler looks anxiously to a radiologist for information:

> "The surgeon will speak to you," says the Radiologist.
> "Are you finding something?"
> "The surgeon will speak to you," the Radiologist says again. "There seems to be something there, but the surgeon will talk to you about it."
> "My uncle once had something on his kidney," says the Mother. "So they removed the kidney and it turned out the something was benign."
> The Radiologist smiles a broad, ominous smile. "That's always the way it is," he says. "You don't know exactly what it is until it's in the bucket."
> "In the bucket," the Mother repeats.
> "That's doctor talk," the Radiologist says.
> "It's very appealing," says the Mother. "It's a very appealing way to talk."

> Lorrie Moore, "People Like That Are the Only People Here"

Here the radiologist's speech alters the mother's feeling toward him from hopeful to hostile in one short exchange. The level of fear for the child rises, and the dialogue itself has effected change.

A crucial (and sometimes difficult) distinction to make is between speech that is mere discussion or debate and speech that is drama or action. If in doubt, ask yourself: Can this conversation between characters really change anything? *Dialogue is action when it contains the possibility of change.* When two characters have made up their minds and know each other's positions on some political or philosophical matter, for instance, they may argue with splendid eloquence but there will be no discovery and nothing to decide, and therefore no option for change. No matter how significant their topic, we are likely to find them wooden and uninteresting. The story's question *what happened next?* will suggest only *more talk:*

> "This has been the traditional fishing spot of the river people for a thousand years, and we have a moral responsibility to aid them in preserving their way of life. If you put in these rigs, it may undermine the ecosystem and destroy the aquifer of the entire county!"
> "Join the real world, Sybil. Free enterprise is based on this kind of technological progress, and without it we would endanger the economic base."

Ho-hum. In order to engage us emotionally in a disagreement, the characters must have an emotional stake in the outcome; we need to feel that, even if it's unlikely they would change their minds, they might change their lives.

> "If you sink that drill tomorrow morning, I'll be gone by noon."
> "Sybil, I have no choice."

Further, if you find your characters getting stuck in a repetitive conflict ("yes-you-are, no-I'm-not"), you can jump-start the action if you remember that people generally change their tactics—become charming, threatening, seductive, guilt-inducing, and so on—when they are not succeeding in getting what they badly want. And if *each* character in the scene wants something from the other, although it probably won't be the same thing, the momentum will build. It's much harder (although not impossible) to maintain dramatic energy when one of the characters simply wants to get off stage.

## TEXT AND SUBTEXT

Often the most forceful dialogue can be achieved by *not* having the characters say what they mean. People in extreme emotional states—whether of fear, pain, anger, or love—are at their least articulate. There is more narrative tension in a love scene where the lovers make anxious small talk, terrified of revealing their feelings, than in one where they hop into bed. A character who is able to say "I hate you!" hates less than one who bottles the fury and pretends to submit, unwilling to expose the truth.

Dialogue can fall flat if characters define their feelings too precisely and honestly, because often the purpose of human exchange is to conceal as well as to reveal—to impress, hurt, protect, seduce, or reject. Anton Chekhov believed that a line of dialogue should always leave the sense that more could have been said. Playwright David Mamet suggests that people may or may not say what they mean, but always say something designed to get what they want.

In this example from Alice Munro's "Before the Change," the daughter of a doctor who performed illegal abortions up until his recent death takes a phone call:

> A woman on the phone wants to speak to the doctor.
> "I'm sorry. He's dead."
> "Dr. Strachan. Have I got the right doctor?"
> "Yes but I'm sorry, he's dead."
> "Is there anyone—does he by any chance have a partner I could talk to? Is there anybody else there?"
> "No. No partner."
> "Could you give me any other number I could call? Isn't there some other doctor that can—"
> "No. I haven't any number. There isn't anybody that I know of."
> "You must know what this is about. It's very crucial. There are very special circumstances—"
> "I'm sorry."

It's clear here that neither woman is willing to mention abortion, and that the daughter will also not (and probably could not) speak about her complicated feelings toward her father and his profession. The exchange is rich with irony in that both women and also the reader know the "special circumstance" they are guardedly referring to; only the daughter and the reader are privy to the events surrounding the doctor's death and to the daughter's feelings.

Notice that this is not a very articulate exchange, but it does represent dramatic action, because for both women the stakes are high; they are both emotionally involved, but in ways that put them at cross-purposes.

The idea of "reading between the lines" of dialogue is familiar to most people, for in life we tend to react more to what is implied in dialogue than to what is actually said. The linkage of text and subtext—that is, the surface, plot-related dialogue and its emotional undercurrent—was famously described by Ernest Hemingway with the analogy of an iceberg: "There is seven-eighths of it under water for every part that shows. Anything you know you can eliminate and it only strengthens your iceberg. It is the part that doesn't show."

When an unspoken subject remains unspoken, tension continues to build in a story. Often the crisis of a story occurs when the unspoken tension comes to the surface and an explosion results. "If you're trying to build pressure, don't take the lid off the pot," Jerome Stern suggests in his book *Making Shapely Fiction*. "Once people are really candid, once the unstated becomes stated, the tension is released and the effect is cathartic. . . . you want to give yourself the space for a major scene. Here you do want to describe setting and action vividly, and render what they say fully. You've taken the lid off the pot and we want to feel the dialogue boil over."

IF YOU TAKE TWO STICKS AND HOLD THEM PARALLEL, you can capture that image in a photograph because it doesn't change. But if you rub those two sticks together, harder and harder, faster and faster, they will burst into flame—that's the kind of change you can capture in a story or on film. Friction is necessary for change to occur. But without the friction of conflict, there is no change. And without change, there is no story. A body at rest remains at rest unless it enters into conflict.

Stephen Fischer

## "NO" DIALOGUE

The Munro passage above also illustrates an essential element of conflict in dialogue: Tension and drama are heightened when characters are constantly (in one form or another) saying no to each other. In the following exchange from Ernest Hemingway's *The Old Man and the Sea*, the old man feels only love for his young protégé, and their conversation is a pledge of affection. Nevertheless, it is the old man's steady denial that lends the scene tension.

"Can I go out and get sardines for you tomorrow?"
"No. Go and play baseball. I can still row and Rogelio will throw the net."
"I would like to go. If I cannot fish with you, I would like to serve in some way."
"You brought me a beer," the old man said. "You are already a man."

"How old was I when you first took me in a boat?"

"Five and you were nearly killed when I brought the fish in too green and he nearly tore the boat to pieces. Can you remember?"

"I can remember the tail slapping and banging and the thwart breaking and the noise of the clubbing. I can remember you throwing me into the bow where the wet coiled lines were and feeling the whole boat shiver and the noise of you clubbing him like chopping a tree down and the sweet blood smell all over me."

"Can you really remember that or did I just tell it to you?"

"I remember everything from when we first went together."

The old man looked at him with his sunburned, confident loving eyes.

"If you were my boy I'd take you out and gamble," he said. "But you are your father's and mother's and you are in a lucky boat."

Neither of these characters is consciously eloquent, and the dialogue is extremely simple. But look how much more it does than "one thing at a time"! It provides exposition on the beginning of the relationship, and it conveys the mutual affection of the two and the conflict within the old man between his love for the boy and his loyalty to the parents. It conveys the boy's eagerness to persuade and carries him into the emotion he had as a small child while the fish was clubbed. The dialogue represents a constant shift of power back and forth between the boy and the old man, as the boy, whatever else he is saying, continues to say *please*, and the old man, whatever else he is saying, continues to say *no*.

Another Hemingway story, "Hills Like White Elephants," as well as the chapter 2 story "Where Are You Going, Where Have You Been?" also offer clear examples of "no" dialogue. Notice, however, that the conflict does not simply get stuck in a rut, because the characters continue to find new ways to ask and answer the questions as each tries to find the other's vulnerable points.

## SPECIFICITY

In dialogue, just as in narrative, we will tend to believe a character who speaks in concrete details and to be skeptical of one who generalizes or who delivers judgments unsupported by example. When the boy in the Hemingway passage protests, "I remember everything," we believe him because of the vivid details in his memory of the fish. If one character says, "It's perfectly clear from all his actions that he adores me and would do anything for me," and another says, "I had my hands all covered with the clay slick, and he just reached over to lift a lock of hair out of my eyes and tuck it behind my ear," which character do you believe is the more loved?

Similarly, in conflict dialogue, "details are the rocks characters throw at each other," says Stephen Fischer. Our memories for hurts and slights are sadly long, and an accusation that begins as a general blame—"You never think of my feelings"—is likely to be backed up with specific proof as the argument escalates—"You said you'd pick me up at seven New Year's Eve, but you left me waiting for an hour in the snow." "There's nothing generic in our lives," Fischer explains, "and the sparks given off in conflict may reveal all the facts we need to know about the characters."

It's interesting to observe that whereas in narrative you will demonstrate control if you state the facts and let the emotional value rise off of them, in dialogue you will convey information more naturally if the emphasis is on the speaker's feelings. "My brother is due to arrive at midafternoon and is bringing his four children with him" reads as bald exposition; whereas, "That idiot brother of mine thinks he can walk in in the middle of the afternoon and plunk his four kids in my lap!" or, "I can't wait till my brother gets here at three! You'll see—those are the four sweetest kids this side of the planet"—will sound like talk and will slip us the information sideways.

Examine your dialogue to see if it does more than one thing at a time. Do the sound and syntax characterize by region, education, attitude? Do the choice of words and their syntax reveal that the character is stiff, outgoing, stifling anger, ignorant of the facts, perceptive, bigoted, afraid? Is the conflict advanced by "no" dialogue, in which the characters say no to each other in different ways? Is the drama heightened by the characters' inability or unwillingness to tell the whole truth?

Once you are comfortable with the voice of your character, it is well to acknowledge that everyone has many voices and that what that character says will be, within his or her verbal range, determined by the character *to whom* it is said. All of us have one sort of speech for the vicar and another for the man who pumps the gas. Huck Finn, whose voice is idiosyncratically his own, says, "Yes, sir" to the judge and "Maybe I am, maybe I ain't" to his degenerate dad.

## FORMAT AND STYLE

The *format and style of dialogue*, like punctuation, has as its goal to be invisible; and though there may be occasions when departing from the rules is justified by some special effect, it's best to consider such occasions rare. Here are some basic guidelines:

What a character says aloud should be in quotation marks; thoughts should not. This helps clearly differentiate between the spoken and the internal, especially by acknowledging that speech is more deliberately formulated. If you feel that thoughts need to be set apart from narrative, use italics instead of quotation marks.

Begin the dialogue of each new speaker as a new paragraph. This helps orient the reader and keep clear who is speaking. If an action is described between the dialogue lines of two speakers, put that action in the paragraph of the speaker it describes:

"I wish I'd taken that picture." Larry traced the horizon with his index finger.

Janice snatched the portfolio away. "You've got chicken grease on your hands," she said, "and this is the only copy!"

Notice that the punctuation goes inside the quotation marks.

A dialogue tag tells us who has spoken—*John said, Mary said, Tim announced.* When a tag is used, it is connected to the dialogue line with a comma, even though the dialogue line may sound like a full sentence: *"I'm paying tonight," Mary said.* (Misusing a period in place of the comma with a tag is one of the most common mistakes in dialogue format.)

Like a luggage tag or a name tag, a dialogue tag is for the purpose of identification, and *said* is usually adequate to the task. People also *ask* and *reply* and occasionally *add*, *recall*, *remember*, or *remind*. But sometimes an unsure writer will strain for emphatic synonyms: *She gasped, he whined, they chorused, John snarled, Mary spat.* This is unnecessary and obtrusive, because although unintentional repetition usually makes for awkward style, the word *said* is as invisible as punctuation. When reading we're scarcely aware of it, whereas we are forced to be aware of *she wailed*. If it's clear who is speaking without any dialogue tag at all, don't use one. Usually an identification at the beginning of a dialogue passage and an occasional reminder are sufficient. If the speaker is inherently identified in the speech pattern, so much the better.

Similarly, tonal dialogue tags should be used sparingly: *he said with relish; she added limply*. Such phrases are blatant "telling," and the chances are that good dialogue will convey its own tone. *"Get off my case!" she said angrily.* We do not need to be told that she said this angrily. If she said it sweetly, then we would probably need to be told. If the dialogue does not give us a clue to the manner in which it is said, an action will often do so better than an adverb. *"I'll have a word with Mr. Ritter about it," he said with finality* is weaker than *"I'll have a word with Mr. Ritter about it," he said, and picked up his hat.*

It helps to make the dialogue tag unobtrusive if it comes within the spoken line: *"Don't give it a second thought," he said. "I was just going anyway."* (A midline tag has the added benefit of helping readers hear a slight pause or change in the speaker's inflection.) A tag that comes at the beginning of the line may look too much like a play script: *He said, "Don't give it a second thought . . ."* whereas a tag that comes after too much speech becomes confusing or superfluous: *"Don't give it a second thought. I was going anyway, and I'll just take these and drop them at the copy shop on the way," he said.* If we didn't know who was speaking long before this tag appears, it's too late to be of use and simply calls attention to itself.

## VERNACULAR

*Vernacular* is a tempting, and can be an excellent, means of characterizing, but it is difficult to do well and easy to overdo. Dialect, regionality, and childhood should be achieved by word choice and syntax. Misspellings should be kept to a minimum because they distract and slow the reader, and worse, they tend to make the character seem stupid. There is no point in spelling phonetically any word as it is ordinarily pronounced: Almost all of us say things like "fur" for *for*, "uv" for *of*, "wuz" for *was*, "an" for *and*, and "sez" for *says*. It's common to drop the *g* in words ending in *ing*. When you misspell these words in dialogue, you indicate that the speaker is ignorant enough to spell them that way when writing. Even if you want to indicate ignorance, you may alienate the reader by the means you choose to do so. John Updike puts this point well when he complains of a Tom Wolfe character:

> "(his) pronunciations are steadfastly spelled out—'sump'm' for 'something,' 'far fat' for 'fire fight'—in a way that a Faulkner character would be spared. For Faulkner, Southern life was life; for Wolfe it is a provincial curiosity . . ."

It is largely to avoid the charge of creating "provincial curiosities" that most fiction writers now avoid misspellings.

It can be even trickier catching the voice of a foreigner with imperfect English, because everyone has a native language, and when someone whose native language is French or Ibu starts to learn English, the grammatical mistakes they make will be based on the grammatical structure of the native language. Unless you know French or Ibu, you will make mistaken mistakes, and your dialogue is likely to sound as if it came from second-rate sitcoms.

In vernacular or standard English, the bottom-line rule is that dialogue must be speakable. If it isn't speakable, it isn't dialogue.

> "Certainly I had had a fright I wouldn't soon forget," Reese would say later, "and as I slipped into bed fully dressed except for my shoes, which I flung God-knows-where, I wondered why I had subjected myself to a danger only a fool would fail to foresee for the dubious pleasure of spending one evening in the company of a somewhat less than brilliant coed."

Nobody would say this because it can't be said. It is not only convoluted beyond reason but it also stumbles over its alliteration, "only a fool would fail to foresee for," and takes more breath than the human lungs can hold. Read your dialogue aloud and make sure it is comfortable to the mouth, the breath, and the ear. If not, then it won't ring true as talk.

## *Thought*

Fiction has a flexibility denied to film and drama, where everything the spectator knows must be shown. In fiction you have the privilege of entering a character's mind, sharing at its source internal conflict, reflection, and the crucial processes of decision and discovery. Like speech, a character's thought can be offered in summary (*He hated the way she ate*), or as indirect thought (*Why did she hold her fork straight up like that?*), or directly, as if we are overhearing the character's own mind (*My God, she's going to drop the yolk!*). As with speech, the three methods can be alternated in the same paragraph to achieve at once immediacy and pace.

Methods of presenting a character's thought will be more fully discussed in chapter 8 on point of view. What's most important to characterization is that thought, like speech, reveals more than information. It can also set mood, reveal or betray desires, develop theme, and so forth.

The territory of a character's mind is above all likely to be the center of the action. Aristotle says, that a man "is his desire," that is, his character is defined by his ultimate purpose, good or bad. *Thought*, says Aristotle, is the process by which a person works backward in his mind from his goal to determine what action he can take toward that goal at a given moment.

It is not, for example, your ultimate desire to read this book. Very likely you don't even "want" to read it; you'd rather be sleeping or jogging or making love. But your ultimate goal is, say, to be a rich, respected, and famous writer. In order to attain this goal, you reason, you must know as much about the craft as you can learn. To do this, you would like to take a graduate degree at the Writer's Workshop in Iowa. To do that, you must take an undergraduate degree in _____, where you now find yourself, and must get an A in Ms. or Mr. _____'s creative writing course. To do that, you must produce a character sketch from one of the assignments at the end of this chapter by a week from Tuesday. To do so, you must sit here reading this chapter now instead of sleeping, jogging, or making love. Your ultimate motive has led you logically backward to a deliberate "moral" decision on the action you can take at this minor crossroad. In fact, it turns out that you want to be reading after all.

The relation that Aristotle perceives among desire, thought, and action seems to me a very useful one for an author, both in structuring plot and in creating character. What does this protagonist want to happen in the last paragraph of this story? What is the particular thought process by which this person works backward to determine what she or he will do now, in the situation that presents itself on page one?

> I was on my way to what I hoped would be *the* romantic vacation of my life, off to Door County for a whole week of sweet sane rest. More rest. I needed more rest.
>
> David Haynes, *All American Girls*

The action, of course, may be the wrong one. Thought thwarts us, because it leads to a wrong choice, or because thought is full of conflicting desires and consistent inconsistencies, or because there is enormous human tension between suppressed thought and expressed thought:

> When he shuts off the shower, the phone is ringing. A sense that it has been ringing for a long time—can a mechanical noise have a quality of desperation?—propels him naked and dripping into the living room. He picks up the phone and his caller, as he has suspected, is Mieko . . . He is already annoyed after the first hello. Mieko's voice is sharp, high, very Japanese, although she speaks superb English. He says, "Hello, Mieko," and he sounds annoyed.
>
> Jane Smiley, "Long Distance"

In "Where Are You Going, Where Have You Been?" at the end of chapter 2, Connie wants to get away every chance she can from a family she despises. From the opening paragraphs, she devises a number of schemes and subterfuges to avoid their company. At the end of the story her success is probably permanent, at a cost she had not figured into her plan. Through the story she is richly characterized, inventing two personalities in order single-mindedly to pursue her freedom, finally caught between conflicting and paralyzing desires.

A person, a character, can't do much about what he or she wants; it just is (which is another way of saying that character is desire). What we can deliberately choose is our behavior, the action we take in a given situation. Achievement of our desire would be easy if the thought process between desire and act were not so faulty and so wayward, or if there were not such an abyss between the thoughts we think and those that we are willing and able to express.

The four methods of direct characterization are forms of "showing" that bring character vividly alive. But there may also be times that you wish to shape our knowledge of and reaction to your characters by "telling" us about them, judging and interpreting for the reader. The indirect methods of characterization will be taken up in the next chapter.

## *Gryphon*

### CHARLES BAXTER

On Wednesday afternoon, between the geography lesson on ancient Egypt's hand-operated irrigation system and an art project that involved drawing a model city next to a mountain, our fourth-grade teacher, Mr. Hibler, developed a cough. This cough began with a series of muffled throat clearings and progressed to propulsive noises contained within Mr. Hibler's closed mouth. "Listen to him," Carol Peterson whispered to me. "He's gonna blow up." Mr. Hibler's laughter—dazed and infrequent—sounded a bit like his cough, but as we worked on our model cities we would look up, thinking he was enjoying a joke, and see Mr. Hibler's face turning red, his cheeks puffed out. This was not laughter. Twice he bent over, and his loose tie, like a plumb line, hung down straight from his neck as he exploded himself into a Kleenex. He would excuse himself, then go on coughing. "I'll bet you a dime," Carol Peterson whispered, "we get a substitute tomorrow."

Carol sat at the desk in front of mine and was a bad person—when she thought no one was looking she would blow her nose on notebook paper, then crumble it up and throw it into the wastebasket—but at times of crisis she spoke the truth. I knew I'd lose the dime.

"No deal," I said.

When Mr. Hibler stood us up in formation at the door just prior to the final bell, he was almost incapable of speech. "I'm sorry, boys and girls," he said. "I seem to be coming down with something."

"I hope you feel better tomorrow, Mr. Hibler," Bobby Kryzanowicz, the faultless brown-noser said, and I heard Carol Peterson's evil giggle. Then Mr. Hibler opened the door and we walked out to the buses, a clique of us starting noisily to hawk and cough as soon as we thought we were a few feet beyond Mr. Hibler's earshot.

Five Oaks being a rural community, and in Michigan, the supply of substitute teachers was limited to the town's unemployed community college graduates, a pool of about four mothers. These ladies fluttered, provided easeful class days, and nervously covered material we had mastered weeks earlier. Therefore it was a surprise when a woman we had never seen came into the class the next day, carrying a purple purse, a checkerboard lunchbox, and a few books. She put the books on one side of Mr. Hibler's desk and the lunchbox on the other, next to the Voice of Music phonograph. Three of us in the back of the room were playing with Heever, the chameleon that lived in the terrarium and on one of the plastic drapes, when she walked in.

She clapped her hands at us. "Little boys," she said, "why are you bent over together like that?" She didn't wait for us to answer. "Are you tormenting an animal? Put it back. Please sit down at your desks. I want no cabals this time of the day." We just stared at her. "Boys," she repeated, "I asked you to sit down."

I put the chameleon in his terrarium and felt my way to my desk, never taking my eyes off the woman. With white and green chalk, she had started to draw a tree on the left side of the blackboard. She didn't look usual. Furthermore, her tree was outsized, disproportionate, for some reason.

"This room needs a tree," she said, with one line drawing the suggestion of a leaf. "A large, leafy, shady, deciduous . . . oak."

Her fine, light hair had been done up in what I would learn years later was called a chignon, and she wore gold-rimmed glasses whose lenses seemed to have the faintest blue tint. Harold Knardahl, who sat across from me, whispered "Mars," and I nodded slowly, savoring the imminent weirdness of the day. The substitute drew another branch with an extravagant arm gesture, then turned around and said, "Good morning. I don't believe I said good morning to all you yet."

Facing us, she was no special age—an adult is an adult—but her face had two prominent lines, descending vertically from the sides of her mouth to her chin. I knew where I had seen those lines before: *Pinocchio*. They were marionette lines. "You may stare at me," she said to us, as a few more kids from the last bus came into the room, their eyes fixed on her, "for a few more seconds, until the bell rings. Then I will permit no more staring. Looking I will permit. Staring, no. It is impolite to stare, and a sign of bad breeding. You cannot make a social effort while staring."

Harold Knardahl did not glance at me, or nudge, but I heard him whisper "Mars" again, trying to get more mileage out of his single joke with the kids who had just come in.

When everyone was seated, the substitute teacher finished her tree, put down her chalk fastidiously on the phonograph, brushed her hands, and faced us. "Good morning," she said. "I am Miss Ferenczi, your teacher for the day. I am fairly new to your community, and I don't believe any of you know me. I will therefore start by telling you a story about myself."

While we settled back, she launched into her tale. She said her grandfather had been a Hungarian prince; her mother had been born in some place called Flanders, had been a pianist, and had played concerts for people Miss Ferenczi referred to as "crowned heads." She gave us a knowing look. "Grieg," she said, "the Norwegian master, wrote a concerto for piano that was," she paused, "my mother's triumph at her debut concert in London." Her eyes searched the ceiling. Our eyes followed. Nothing up there but ceiling tile. "For reasons that I shall not go into, my family's fortunes took us to Detroit, then north to dreadful Saginaw, and now here I am in Five Oaks, as your substitute teacher, for today, Thursday, October the eleventh. I believe it will be a good day: All the forecasts coincide. We shall start with your reading lesson. Take out your reading book. I believe it is called *Broad Horizons*, or something along those lines."

Jeannie Vermeesch raised her hand. Miss Ferenczi nodded at her. "Mr. Hibler always starts the day with the Pledge of Allegiance," Jeannie whined.

"Oh, does he? In that case," Miss Ferenczi said, "you must know it *very* well by now, and we certainly need not spend our time on it. No, no allegiance pledging on the premises today, by my reckoning. Not with so much sunlight coming into the room. A pledge does not suit my mood." She glanced at her watch. "Time is flying. Take out *Broad Horizons*."

She disappointed us by giving us an ordinary lesson, complete with vocabulary word drills, comprehension questions, and recitation. She didn't seem to care for the material, however. She sighed every few minutes and rubbed her glasses with a frilly perfumed handkerchief that she withdrew, magician style, from her left sleeve.

After reading we moved on to arithmetic. It was my favorite time of the morning, when the lazy autumn sunlight dazzled its way through ribbons of clouds past the windows on the east side of the classroom, and crept across the linoleum floor. On the playground the first group of children, the kindergartners, were running on the quack grass just beyond the monkey bars. We were doing multiplication tables. Miss Ferenczi had made John Wazny stand up at his desk in the front row. He was supposed to go through the tables of six. From where I was sitting, I could smell the Vitalis soaked into John's plastered hair. He was doing fine until he came to six times eleven and six times twelve. "Six times eleven," he said, "is sixty-eight. Six times twelve is . . ." He put his fingers to his head, quickly and secretly sniffed his fingertips, and said, "seventy-two." Then he sat down.

"Fine," Miss Ferenczi said. "Well now. That was very good."

"Miss Ferenczi!" One of the Eddy twins was waving her hand desperately in the air. "Miss Ferenczi! Miss Ferenczi!"

"Yes?"

"John said that six times eleven is sixty-eight and you said he was right!"

"*Did* I?" She gazed at the class with a jolly look breaking across her marionette's face. "Did I say that? Well, what *is* six times eleven?"

"It's sixty-six!"

She nodded. "Yes. So it is. But, and I know some people will not entirely agree with me, at some times it is sixty-eight."

"When? When is it sixty-eight?"

We were all waiting.

"In higher mathematics, which you children do not yet understand, six times eleven can be considered to be sixty-eight." She laughed through her nose. "In higher mathematics numbers are . . . more fluid. The only thing a number does is contain a certain amount of something. Think of water. A cup is not the only way to measure a certain amount of water, is it?" We were staring, shaking our heads. "You could use saucepans or thimbles. In either case, the water *would be the same*. Perhaps," she started again, "it would be better for you to think that six times eleven is sixty-eight only when I am in the room."

"Why is it sixty-eight," Mark Poole asked, "when you're in the room?"

"Because it's more interesting that way," she said, smiling very rapidly behind her blue-tinted glasses. "Besides, I'm your substitute teacher, am I not?" We all nodded. "Well, then, think of six times eleven equals sixty-eight as a substitute fact."

"A substitute fact?"

"Yes." Then she looked at us carefully. "Do you think," she asked, "that anyone is going to be hurt by a substitute fact?"

We looked back at her.

"Will the plants on the windowsill be hurt?" We glanced at them. There were sensitive plants thriving in a green plastic tray, and several wilted ferns in small clay pots. "Your dogs and cats, or your moms and dads?" She waited. "So," she concluded, "what's the problem?"

"But it's wrong," Janice Weber said, "isn't it?"

"What's your name, young lady?"

"Janice Weber."

"And you think it's wrong, Janice?"

"I was just asking."

"Well, all right. You were just asking. I think we've spent enough time on this matter by now, don't you, class? You are free to think what you like. When your teacher, Mr. Hibler, returns, six times eleven will be sixty-six again, you can rest assured. And it will be that for the rest of your lives in Five Oaks. Too bad, eh?" She raised her eyebrows and glinted herself at us. "But for now, it wasn't. So much for that. Let us go to your assigned problems for today, as painstakingly outlined, I see, in Mr. Hibler's lesson plan. Take out a sheet of paper and write your names in the upper left-hand corner."

For the next half hour we did the rest of our arithmetic problems. We handed them in and went on to spelling, my worst subject. Spelling always came before lunch. We were taking spelling dictation and looking at the clock. "Thorough," Miss Ferenczi said. "Boundary." She walked in the aisles between the desks, holding the spelling book open and looking down at our papers. "Balcony." I clutched my pencil. Somehow, the way she said those words, they seemed foreign, Hungarian, mis-voweled and mis-consonanted. I stared down at what I had spelled. *Balconie.* I turned my pencil upside down and erased my mistake. *Balconey.* That looked better, but still incorrect. I cursed the world of spelling and tried erasing it again and saw the paper beginning to wear away. *Balkony.* Suddenly I felt a hand on my shoulder.

"I don't like that word either," Miss Ferenczi whispered, bent over, her mouth near my ear. "It's ugly. My feeling is, if you don't like a word, you don't have to use it." She straightened up, leaving behind a slight odor of Clorets.

At lunchtime we went out to get our trays of sloppy joes, peaches in heavy syrup, coconut cookies, and milk, and brought them back to the classroom, where Miss Ferenczi was sitting at the desk, eating a brown sticky thing she had unwrapped from tightly rubber-banded wax paper. "Miss Ferenczi," I said, raising my hand. "You don't have to eat with us. You can eat with the other teachers. There's a teachers' lounge," I ended up, "next to the principal's office."

"No, thank you," she said. "I prefer it here."

"We've got a room monitor," I said. "Mrs. Eddy." I pointed to where Mrs. Eddy, Joyce and Judy's mother, sat silently at the back of the room, doing her knitting.

"That's fine," Miss Ferenczi said. "But I shall continue to eat here, with you children. I prefer it," she repeated.

"How come?" Wayne Razmer asked without raising his hand.

"I talked with the other teachers before class this morning," Miss Ferenczi said, biting into her brown food. "There was a great rattling of the words for the fewness of ideas. I didn't care for their brand of hilarity. I don't like ditto machine jokes."

"Oh," Wayne said.

"What's that you're eating?" Maxine Sylvester asked, twitching her nose. "Is it food?"

"It most certainly *is* food. It's a stuffed fig. I had to drive almost down to Detroit to get it. I also bought some smoked sturgeon. And this," she said, lifting some green leaves out of her lunchbox, "is raw spinach, cleaned this morning before I came out here to the Garfield-Murry School."

"Why're you eating raw spinach?" Maxine asked.

"It's good for you," Miss Ferenczi said. "More stimulating than soda pop or smelling salts." I bit into my sloppy joe and stared blankly out the window. An almost invisible moon was faintly silvered in the daytime autumn sky. "As far as food is concerned," Miss Ferenczi was saying, "you have to shuffle the pack. Mix it up. Too many people eat . . . well, never mind."

"Miss Ferenczi," Carol Peterson said, "what are we going to do this afternoon?"

"Well," she said, looking down at Mr. Hibler's lesson plan, "I see that your teacher, Mr. Hibler, has you scheduled for a unit on the Egyptians." Carol groaned. "Yessss," Miss Ferenczi continued, "that is what we will do: the Egyptians. A remarkable people. Almost as remarkable as the Americans. But not quite." She lowered her head, did her quick smile, and went back to eating her spinach.

After noon recess we came back into the classroom and saw that Miss Ferenczi had drawn a pyramid on the blackboard, close to her oak tree. Some of us who had been playing baseball were messing around in the back of the room, dropping the bats and the gloves into the playground box, and I think that Ray Schontzeler had just slugged me when I heard Miss Ferenczi's high-pitched voice quavering with emotion. "Boys," she said, "come to order right this minute and take your seats. I do not wish to waste a minute of class time. Take out your geography books." We trudged to our desks and, still sweating, pulled out *Distant Lands and Their People.* "Turn to page forty-two." She waited for thirty seconds, then looked over at Kelly Munger. "Young man," she said, "why are you still fossicking in your desk?"

Kelly looked as if his foot had been stepped on. "Why am I what?"

"Why are you . . . burrowing in your desk like that?"

"I'm lookin' for the book, Miss Ferenczi."

Bobby Kryzanowicz, the faultless brown-noser who sat in the first row by choice, softly said, "His name is Kelly Munger. He can't ever find his stuff. He always does that."

"I don't care what his name is, especially after lunch," Miss Ferenczi said. "*Where is your book?*"

"I just found it." Kelly was peering into his desk and with both hands pulled at the book, shoveling along in front of it several pencils and crayons, which fell into his lap and then to the floor.

"I hate a mess," Miss Ferenczi said. "I hate a mess in a desk or a mind. It's . . . unsanitary. You wouldn't want your house at home to look like your desk at school, now, would you?" She didn't wait for an answer. "I should think not. A house at home should be as neat as human hands can make it. What were we talking about? Egypt. Page forty-two. I note from Mr. Hibler's lesson plan that you have been discussing the modes of Egyptian irrigation. Interesting, in my view, but not so interesting as what we are about to cover. The pyramids and Egyptian slave labor. A plus on one side, a minus on the other." We had our books open to page forty-two, where there was a picture of a pyramid, but Miss Ferenczi wasn't looking at the book. Instead, she was staring at some object just outside the window.

"Pyramids," Miss Ferenczi said, still looking past the window. "I want you to think about the pyramids. And what was inside. The bodies of the pharaohs, of course, and their attendant treasures. Scrolls. Perhaps," Miss Ferenczi said, with something gleeful but unsmiling in her face, "these scrolls were novels for the pharaohs, helping them to pass the time in their long voyage through the centuries. But then, I am joking." I was looking at the lines on Miss Ferenczi's face. "Pyramids," Miss Ferenczi went on, "were the repositories of special cosmic powers. The nature of a pyramid is to guide cosmic energy forces into a concentrated point. The Egyptians knew that; we have generally forgotten it. Did you know," she asked, walking to the side of the room so that she was standing by the coat closet, "that George Washington had Egyptian blood, from his grandmother? Certain features of the Constitution of the United States are notable for their Egyptian ideas."

Without glancing down at the book, she began to talk about the movement of souls in Egyptian religion. She said that when people die, their souls return to Earth in the form of carpenter ants, or walnut trees, depending on how they behaved— "well or ill"—in life. She said that the Egyptians believed that people act the way they do because of magnetism produced by tidal forces in the solar system, forces produced by the sun and by its "planetary ally," Jupiter. Jupiter, she said, was a planet, as we had been told, but had "certain properties of stars." She was speaking very fast. She said that the Egyptians were great explorers and conquerors. She said that the greatest of all the conquerors, Genghis Khan, had had forty horses and forty young women killed on the site of his grave. We listened. No one tried to stop her. "I myself have been in Egypt," she said, "and have witnessed much dust and many brutalities." She said that an old man in Egypt who worked for a circus had personally shown her an animal in a cage, a monster, half bird and half lion. She said that this monster was called a gryphon and that she had heard about them but never seen them until she traveled to the outskirts of Cairo. She said that Egyptian astronomers had discovered the planet Saturn, but had not seen its rings. She said that the Egyptians were the first to discover that dogs, when they are ill, will not drink from rivers, but wait for rain, and hold their jaws open to catch it.

"She lies."

We were on the school bus home. I was sitting next to Carl Whiteside, who had bad breath and a huge collection of marbles. We were arguing. Carl thought she was lying. I said she wasn't, probably.

"I didn't believe that stuff about the bird," Carl said, "and what she told us about the pyramids? I didn't believe that either. She didn't know what she was talking about."

"Oh, yeah?" I had liked her. She was strange. I thought I could nail him. "If she was lying," I said, "what'd she say that was a lie?"

"Six times eleven isn't sixty-eight. It isn't ever. It's sixty-six, I know for a fact."

"She said so. She admitted it. What else did she lie about?"

"I don't know," he said. "Stuff."

"What stuff?"

"Well." He swung his legs back and forth. "You ever see an animal that was half lion and half bird?" He crossed his arms. "It sounded real fakey to me."

"It could happen," I said. I had to improvise, to outrage him. "I read in this newspaper my mom bought in the IGA about this scientist, this mad scientist in the Swiss Alps, and he's been putting genes and chromosomes and stuff together in test tubes, and he combined a human being and a hamster." I waited, for effect. "It's called a humster."

"You never." Carl was staring at me, his mouth open, his terrible bad breath making its way toward me. "What newspaper was it?"

"The *National Enquirer*," I said, "that they sell next to the cash registers." When I saw his look of recognition, I knew I had bested him. "And this mad scientist," I said, "his name was, um, Dr. Frankenbush." I realized belatedly that this name was a mistake and waited for Carl to notice its resemblance to the name of the other famous mad master of permutations, but he only sat there.

"A man and a hamster?" He was staring at me, squinting, his mouth opening in distaste. "Jeez. What'd it look like?"

When the bus reached my stop, I took off down our dirt road and ran up through the back yard, kicking the tire swing for good luck. I dropped my books on the back steps so I could hug and kiss our dog, Mr. Selby. Then I hurried inside. I could smell Brussels sprouts cooking, my unfavorite vegetable. My mother was washing other vegetables in the kitchen sink, and my baby brother was hollering in his yellow playpen on the kitchen floor.

"Hi, Mom," I said, hopping around the playpen to kiss her, "Guess what?"

"I have no idea."

"We had this substitute today, Miss Ferenczi, and I'd never seen her before, and she had all these stories and ideas and stuff."

"Well. That's good." My mother looked out the window behind the sink, her eyes on the pine woods west of our house. Her face and hairstyle always reminded other people of Betty Crocker, whose picture was framed inside a gigantic spoon on the side of the Bisquick box; to me, though, my mother's face just looked white. "Listen, Tommy," she said, "go upstairs and pick your clothes off the bathroom floor, then go outside to the shed and put the shovel and ax away that your father left outside this morning."

"She said that six times eleven was sometimes sixty-eight!" I said. "And she said she once saw a monster that was half lion and half bird." I waited. "In Egypt, she said."

"Did you hear me?" my mother asked, raising her arm to wipe her forehead with the back of her hand. "You have chores to do."

"I know," I said. "I was just telling you about the substitute."

"It's very interesting," my mother said, quickly glancing down at me, "and we can talk about it later when your father gets home. But right now you have some work to do."

"Okay, Mom." I took a cookie out of the jar on the counter and was about to go outside when I had a thought. I ran into the living room, pulled out a dictionary next to the TV stand, and opened it to the G's. *Gryphon:* "variant of griffin." *Griffin:* "a fabulous beast with the head and wings of an eagle and the body of a lion." Fabulous was right. I shouted with triumph and ran outside to put my father's tools back in their place.

Miss Ferenczi was back the next day, slightly altered. She had pulled her hair down and twisted it into pigtails, with red rubber bands holding them tight one inch from the ends. She was wearing a green blouse and pink scarf, making her difficult to look at for a full class day. This time there was no pretense of doing a reading lesson or moving on to arithmetic. As soon as the bell rang, she simply began to talk.

She talked for forty minutes straight. There seemed to be less connection between her ideas, but the ideas themselves were, as the dictionary would say, fabulous. She said she had heard of a huge jewel, in what she called the Antipodes, that was so brilliant that when the light shone into it at a certain angle it would blind whoever was looking at its center. She said that the biggest diamond in the world was cursed and had killed everyone who owned it, and that by a trick of fate it was called the Hope diamond. Diamonds are magic, she said, and this is why women wear them on their fingers, as a sign of the magic of womanhood. Men have strength, Miss Ferenczi said, but no true magic. That is why men fall in love with women but women do not fall in love with men: they just love being loved. George Washington had died because of a mistake he made about a diamond. Washington was not the first *true* President, but she did not say who was. In some places in the world, she said, men and women still live in the trees and eat monkeys for breakfast. Their doctors are magicians. At the bottom of the sea are creatures thin as pancakes which have never been studied by scientists because when you take them up to the air, the fish explode.

There was not a sound in the classroom, except for Miss Ferenczi's voice, and Donna DeShano's coughing. No one even went to the bathroom.

Beethoven, she said, had not been deaf; it was a trick to make himself famous, and it worked. As she talked, Miss Ferenczi's pigtails swung back and forth. There are trees in the world, she said, that eat meat: their leaves are sticky and close up on bugs like hands. She lifted her hands and brought them together, palm to palm. Venus, which most people think is the next closest planet to the sun, is not always closer, and, besides, it is the planet of greatest mystery because of its thick cloud cover. "I know what lies underneath those clouds," Miss Ferenczi said, and waited. After the silence, she said, "Angels. Angels live under those clouds." She said that angels were not invisible to everyone and were in fact smarter than most people. They did not dress in robes as was often claimed but instead wore formal evening clothes, as if they were about to attend a concert. Often angels *do* attend concerts and sit in the aisles where, she said, most people pay no attention to them. She said the most terrible angel had the shape of the Sphinx. "There is no running away from that one," she said. She said that unquenchable fires burn just under the surface of the earth in Ohio, and that the baby Mozart fainted dead away in his cradle when he first heard the sound of a trumpet. She said that someone named Narzim al Harrardim was the greatest writer who ever lived. She said that planets control behavior, and anyone conceived during a solar eclipse would be born with webbed feet.

"I know you children like to hear these things," she said, "these secrets, and that is why I am telling you all this." We nodded. It was better than doing comprehension questions for the readings in *Broad Horizons*.

"I will tell you one more story," she said, "and then we will have to do some arithmetic." She leaned over, and her voice grew soft. "There is no death," she said. "You must never be afraid. Never. That which is, cannot die. It will change into different earthly and unearthly elements, but I know this as sure as I stand here in front of you, and I swear it: you must not be afraid. I have seen this truth with these eyes. I know it because in a dream God kissed me. Here." And she pointed with her right index finger to the side of her head, below the mouth, where the vertical lines were carved into her skin.

Absent-mindedly we all did our arithmetic problems. At recess the class was out on the playground, but no one was playing. We were all standing in small groups, talking about Miss Ferenczi. We didn't know if she was crazy, or what. I looked out beyond the playground, at the rusted cars piled in a small heap behind a clump of sumac, and I wanted to see shapes there, approaching me.

On the way home, Carl sat next to me again. He didn't say much, and I didn't either. At last he turned to me. "You know what she said about the leaves that close up on bugs?"

"Huh?"

"The leaves," Carl insisted. "The meat-eating plants. I know it's true. I saw it on television. The leaves have this icky glue that the plants have got smeared all over them and the insects can't get off 'cause they're stuck. I saw it." He seemed demoralized. "She's tellin' the truth."

"Yeah."

"You think she's seen all those angels?"

I shrugged.

"I don't think she has," Carl informed me. "I think she made that part up."

"There's a tree," I suddenly said. I was looking out the window at the farms along County Road H. I knew every barn, every broken windmill, every fence, every anhydrous ammonia tank, by heart. "There's a tree that's . . . that I've seen . . ."

"Don't you try to do it," Carl said. "You'll just sound like a jerk."

I kissed my mother. She was standing in front of the stove. "How was your day?" she asked.

"Fine."

"Did you have Miss Ferenczi again?"

"Yeah."

"Well?"

"She was fine, Mom," I asked, "can I go to my room?"

"No," she said, "not until you've gone out to the vegetable garden and picked me a few tomatoes." She glanced at the sky. "I think it's going to rain. Skedaddle and do it now. Then you come back inside and watch your brother for a few minutes while I go upstairs. I need to clean up before dinner." She looked down at me. "You're looking a little pale, Tommy." She touched the back of her hand to my forehead and I felt her diamond ring against my skin. "Do you feel all right?"

"I'm fine," I said, and went out to pick the tomatoes.

Coughing mutedly, Mr. Hibler was back the next day, slipping lozenges into his mouth when his back was turned at forty-five minute intervals and asking us how much of the prepared lesson plan Miss Ferenczi had followed. Edith Atwater took the responsibility for the class of explaining to Mr. Hibler that the substitute hadn't always done exactly what he would have done, but we had worked hard even though she talked a lot. About what? he asked. All kinds of things, Edith said. I sort of forgot. To our relief, Mr. Hibler seemed not at all interested in what Miss Ferenczi had said to fill the day. He probably thought it was woman's talk; unserious and not suited for school. It was enough that he had a pile of arithmetic problems from us to correct.

For the next month, the sumac turned a distracting red in the field, and the sun traveled toward the southern sky, so that its rays reached Mr. Hibler's Halloween display on the bulletin board in the back of the room, fading the scarecrow with a pumpkin head from orange to tan. Every three days I measured how much farther the sun had moved toward the southern horizon by making small marks with my black Crayola on the north wall, ant-sized marks only I knew were there, inching west.

And then in early December, four days after the first permanent snowfall, she appeared again in our classroom. The minute she came in the door, I felt my heart begin to pound. Once again, she was different: this time, her hair hung straight down and seemed hardly to have been combed. She hadn't brought her lunchbox with her, but she was carrying what seemed to be a small box. She greeted all of us and talked about the weather. Donna DeShano had to remind her to take her overcoat off.

When the bell to start the day finally rang, Miss Ferenczi looked out at all of us and said, "Children, I have enjoyed your company in the past, and today I am going to reward you." She held up the small box. "Do you know what this is?" She waited. "Of course you don't. It is a tarot pack."

Edith Atwater raised her hand. "What's a tarot pack, Miss Ferenczi?"

"It is used to tell fortunes," she said. "And that is what I shall do this morning. I shall tell your fortunes, as I have been taught to do."

"What's fortune?" Bobby Kryzanowicz asked.

"The future, young man. I shall tell you what your future will be. I can't do your whole future, of course. I shall have to limit myself to the five-card system, the wands, cups, swords, pentacles, and the higher arcanes. Now who wants to be first?"

There was a long silence. Then Carol Peterson raised her hand.

"All right," Miss Ferenczi said. She divided the pack into five smaller packs and walked back to Carol's desk, in front of mine. "Pick one card from each of these packs," she said. I saw that Carol had a four of cups, a six of swords, but I couldn't see the other cards. Miss Ferenczi studied the cards on Carol's desk for a minute. "Not bad," she said.

"I do not see much higher education. Probably an early marriage. Many children. There's something bleak and dreary here, but I can't tell you what. Perhaps just the tasks of a housewife life. I think you'll do very well, for the most part." She smiled at Carol, a smile with a certain lack of interest. "Who wants to be next?"

Carl Whiteside raised his hand slowly.

"Yes," Miss Ferenczi said, "let's do a boy." She walked over to where Carl sat. After he picked his five cards, she gazed at them for a long time. "Travel," she said. "Much distant travel. You might go into the Army. Not too much romantic interest here. A late marriage, if at all. Squabbles. But the Sun is in your major arcana, here, yes, that's a very good card." She giggled. "Maybe a good life."

Next I raised my hand, and she told me my future. She did the same with Bobby Kryzanowicz, Kelly Munger, Edith Atwater, and Kim Foor. Then she came to Wayne Razmer. He picked his five cards, and I could see that the Death card was one of them.

"What's your name?" Miss Ferenczi asked.

"Wayne."

"Well, Wayne," she said, "you will undergo a *great* metamorphosis, the greatest, before you become an adult. Your earthly element will leap away, into thin air, you sweet boy. This card, this nine of swords here, tells of suffering and desolation. And this ten of wands, well, that's certainly a heavy load."

"What about this one?" Wayne pointed to the Death card.

"That one? That one means you will die soon, my dear." She gathered up the cards. We were all looking at Wayne. "But do not fear," she said. "It's not really death, so much as change." She put the cards on Mr. Hibler's desk. "And now, let's do some arithmetic."

At lunchtime Wayne went to Mr. Faegre, the principal, and told him what Miss Ferenczi had done. During the noon recess, we saw Miss Ferenczi drive out of the parking lot in her green Rambler. I stood under the slide, listening to the other kids coasting down and landing in the little depressive bowl at the bottom. I was kicking stones and tugging at my hair right up to the moment when I saw Wayne come out to the playground. He smiled, the dead fool, and with the fingers of his right hand he was showing everyone how he had told on Miss Ferenczi.

I made my way toward Wayne, pushing myself past two girls from another class. He was watching me with his little pinhead eyes.

"You told," I shouted at him. "She was just kidding."

"She shouldn't have," he shouted back. "We were supposed to be doing arithmetic."

"She just scared you," I said. "You're a chicken. You're a chicken, Wayne. You are. Scared of a little card," I singsonged.

Wayne fell at me, his two fists hammering down on my nose. I gave him a good one in the stomach and then I tried for his head. Aiming my fist, I saw that he was crying. I slugged him.

"She was right," I yelled. "She was always right! She told the truth!" Other kids were whooping. "You were just scared, that's all!"

And then large hands pulled at us, and it was my turn to speak to Mr. Faegre.

In the afternoon Miss Ferenczi was gone, and my nose was stuffed with cotton clotted with blood, and my lip had swelled, and our class had been combined with Mrs. Mantei's sixth-grade class for a crowded afternoon science unit on insect life in ditches and swamps. I knew where Mrs. Mantei lived: she had a new house trailer just down the road from us, at the Clearwater Park. She was no mystery. Somehow she and Mr. Bodine, the other fourth-grade teacher, had managed to fit forty-five desks into the room. Kelly Munger asked if Miss Ferenczi had been arrested, and Mrs. Mantei said, no, of course not. All that afternoon, until the buses came to pick us up, we learned about field crickets and two-striped grasshoppers, water bugs, cicadas, mosquitoes, flies, and moths. We learned about insects' hard outer shell, the exoskeleton, and the usual parts of the mouth, including the labrum, mandible, maxilla, and glossa. We learned about compound eyes and the four-stage metamorphosis from egg to larva to pupa to adult. We learned something, but not much, about mating. Mrs. Mantei drew, very skillfully, the internal anatomy of the grasshopper on the blackboard. We learned about the dance of the honeybee, directing other bees in the hive to pollen. We found out about which insects were pests to man, and which were not. On lined white pieces of paper we made lists of insects we might actually see, then a list of insects too small to be clearly visible, such as fleas; Mrs. Mantei said that our assignment would be to memorize these lists for the next day, when Mr. Hibler would certainly return and test us on our knowledge.

---

## Every Tongue Shall Confess

### ZZ PACKER

As Pastor Everett made the announcements that began the service, Clareese Mitchell stood with her choir members, knowing that once again she had to Persevere, put on the Strong Armor of God, the Breastplate of Righteousness, but she was having her monthly womanly troubles and all she wanted to do was curse the Brothers' Church Council of Greater Christ Emmanuel Pentecostal Church of the Fire Baptized, who'd decided that the Sisters had to wear *white* every Missionary Sunday, which was, of course, the day of the month when her womanly troubles were always at their absolute worst! And to think that the Brothers' Church Council of Greater Christ Emmanuel Pentecostal Church of the Fire Baptized had been the first place she'd looked for guidance and companionship nearly ten years ago when her aunt Alma had fallen ill. And why not? They were God-fearing, churchgoing men; men like Deacon Julian Jeffers, now sitting in the first row of pews, closest to the altar, right under the leafy top of the corn plant she'd brought in to make the sanctuary more homey. Two months ago she'd been reading the book of Micah and posed the idea of a Book of Micah discussion group to the Deacon Jeffers and he'd said, "Oh, Sister Clareese! We should make *you* a deacon!" Which of course they didn't. Deacons, like pastors, were men—not that she was complaining. But it still rankled that Jeffers had said he'd get back to her about the Micah discussion group and he never had.

Clareese's cross-eyes roved to the back of the church where Sister Drusella and Sister Maxwell sat, resplendent in their identical wide-brimmed, purple-flowered hats, their unsaved guests sitting next to them. The guests wore frightened smiles, and Clareese tried to shoot them reassuring looks. The gold-lettered banner behind them read: "We Are More Than Conquerors in Christ Our Lord," and she tried to use this as a focal point. But her cross-eyes couldn't help it; they settled, at last, on Deacon McCreedy, making his way down the aisle for the second time. Oh, how she hated him!

She would never forget—never, never, never—the day he came to the hospital where she worked; she was still wearing her white nurse's uniform and he'd said he was concerned about her spiritual well-being—*Liar!*—then drove her to where she lived with her aunt Alma, whose room resounded with perpetual snores and hacking and wheezing—as if Clareese didn't have enough of this at the hospital—and while Alma slept, Clareese poured Deacon McCreedy some fruit punch, which he drank between forkfuls of chicken, plus half their pork roast. No sooner than he'd wiped his hands on the napkin—didn't bother using a fork—he stood and walked behind her, covering her cross-eyes as though she were a child, as though he were about to give her a gift—a Bible with her very own name engraved on it, perhaps—but he didn't give her anything, he'd just covered her wandering eyes and said, "Sing 'On Christ the Solid Rock I Stand.' Make sure to do the Waterfall." And she was happy to do it, happy to please Deacon McCreedy, so she began singing in her best, cleanest voice until she felt his hand slide up the scratchy white pantyhose of her nurse's uniform and up toward the control-top of her pantyhose. Before she could stop him, one finger was wriggling around inside, and by then it was too late to tell him she was having her monthly womanly troubles. He drew back in disgust—no, *hatred*—then rinsed his hand in the kitchen sink and left without saying a word, not a thanks for the chicken or the pork roast or her singing. Not a single word of apology for anything. But she could have forgiven him—if Sisters could even forgive Deacons—for she could have understood that an unmarried man might have *needs,* but what really bothered her was how he ignored her. How a few weeks later she and Aunt Alma had been waiting for the bus after Wednesday-night prayer meeting and he *drove past.* That's right. No offer of a ride, no slowing down, no nothing. Aunt Alma was nearly blind and couldn't even see it was him, but Clareese recognized his car at once.

Yes, she wanted to curse the Brothers' Church Council of Greater Christ Emmanuel Pentecostal Church of the Fire Baptized, but Sisters and Brothers could not curse, could not even swear or take an oath, for *neither shalt thou swear by thy head, because thou canst not make one hair white or black.* So no oath, no swearing, and of course no betting—an extension of swearing—which was why she'd told the other nurses at University Hospital that she would not join their betting pool to predict who would get married first, Patty or Edwina. She told them about the black and white hairs and all Nurse Holloway did was clomp her pumps—as if she was too good for the standard orthopedically correct shoes—down the green tiles of the hall and shout behind her back, "Somebody sure needs to get laid." Oh, how the other RNs tittered in their gossipy way.

Now everyone applauded when Pastor Everett announced that Sister Nina would be getting married to Harold, one of the Brothers from Broadway Tongues of Spirit Church. Then Pastor Everett said, "Sister Nina will be holding a Council so we can get husbands for the rest of the hardworking Sisters." Like Sister Clareese, is what he meant. The congregation laughed at the joke. Ha ha. And perhaps the joke *was* on her. If she'd been married, Deacon McCreedy wouldn't have dared do what he did; if she'd been married perhaps she'd also be working fewer shifts at the hospital, perhaps she would have never met that patient—that man—who'd almost gotten her fired! And at exactly that moment, it hit her, right below the gut, a sharp pain, and she imagined her uterus, that Texas-shaped organ, the Rio Grande of her monthly womanly troubles flushing out to the Gulf.

Pastor Everett had finished the announcements. Now it was time for testimony service. She tried to distract herself by thinking of suitable testimonies. Usually she testified about work. Last week, she'd testified about the poor man with a platelet count of seven, meaning he was a goner, and how Nurse Holloway had told him, "We're bringing you more platelets," and how he'd said, "That's all right. God sent me more." No one at the nurses' station—to say nothing of those atheist doctors—believed him. But when Nurse Holloway checked, sure enough, Glory be to God, he had a count of sixteen. Clareese told the congregation how she knelt on the cold tiled floor of University Hospital's corridor, right then and there, arms outstretched to Glory. And what could the other nurses say to that? Nothing, that's what.

She remembered her testimony from a month ago, how she'd been working the hotline, and a mother had called to say that her son had eaten ants, and Sister Clareese had assured the woman that ants were God's creatures, and though disturbing, they wouldn't harm the boy. But the Lord told Clareese to stay on the line with the mother, not to rush the way other nurses often did, so Clareese stayed on the line. And Glory be to God that she did! Once the mother had calmed down she'd said, "Thank goodness. The insecticide I gave Kevin must have worked." Sister Clareese had stayed after her shift to make sure the woman brought her boy into Emergency. Afterward she told the woman to hold hands with Kevin and give God the Praise he deserved.

But she had told these stories already. As she fidgeted in her choirmistress's chair, she tried to think of new ones. The congregation wouldn't care about how she had to stay on top of codes, or how she had to triple-check patients' charts. The only patients who stuck in her mind were Mrs. Geneva Bosma, whose toe was rotting off, and Mr. Toomey, who had prostate cancer. And, of course, Mr. Cleophus Sanders, the cause of all her current problems. Cleophus was an amputee who liked to turn the volume of his television up so high that his channel-surfing sounded as if someone were being electrocuted, repeatedly. At the nurses' station she'd overheard that Cleophus Sanders was once a musician who in his heyday went by the nickname "Delta Sweetmeat." But he'd gone in and out of the music business, sometimes taking construction jobs. A crane had fallen on his leg and he'd been amputated from the below the knee. No, none of these cases was Edifying in God's sight. Her run-in with Cleophus had been downright un-Edifying.

When Mr. Sanders had been moved into Mr. Toomey's room last Monday, she'd told them both, "I hope everyone has a blessed day!" She'd made sure to say this only after she was safely inside with the door closed behind her. She had to make sure she didn't mention God until the door was closed *behind* her, because Nurse Holloway was always clomping about, trying to say that this was a *university* hospital, as well as a *research* hospital, one at the very *forefront* of medicine, and didn't Registered Nurse Clareese Mitchell recognize and *respect* that not everyone shared her beliefs? That the hospital catered not only to Christians, but to people of the Jewish faith? To Muslims, Hindus, and agnostics? Atheists, even?

This Clareese knew only too well, which was why it was all the more important for her to Spread the Gospel. So she shut the door, and said to Mr. Toomey, louder this time, "I HOPE EVERYONE HAS A BLESSED DAY!"

Mr. Toomey grunted. Heavy and completely white, he reminded Sister Clareese of a walrus: everything about him drooped, his eyes like twin frowns, his nose, perhaps even his mouth, though it was hard to make out because of his frowning blond mustache. Well, Glory be to God, she expected something like a grunt from him, she couldn't say she was surprised: junkies who detox scream and writhe before turning clean; the man with a hangover does not like to wake to the sun. So it was with sinners exposed to the harsh, curing Light of the Lord.

"Hey, sanctified lady!" Cleophus Sanders called from across the room. "He got cancer! Let the man alone."

"I *know* what he *has*," Sister Clareese said. "I'm his *nurse*." This wasn't how she wanted the patient-RN relationship to begin, but Cleophus had gotten the better of her. Yes, that was the problem, wasn't it? *He'd* gotten the better of *her*. This was how Satan worked, throwing you off a little at a time. She would have to Persevere, put on the Strong Armor of God. She tried again.

"My name is Sister Clareese Mitchell, your assigned registered nurse. I can't exactly say that I'm pleased to meet you, because that would be a lie and 'lying lips are an abomination to the Lord.' I will say that I am pleased to do my duty and help you recover."

"*Me oh my!*" Cleophus Sanders said, and he laughed big and long, the kind of laughter that could go on and on, rising and rising, restarting itself if need be, like yeast. He slapped the knee of his amputated leg, the knee that would probably come off if his infection didn't stop eating away at it. But Cleophus Sanders didn't care. He just slapped that infected knee, hooting all the while in an ornery, backwoods kind of way that made Clareese want to hit him. But of course she would never, never do that.

She busied herself by changing Mr. Toomey's catheter, then remaking his bed, rolling the walrus of him this way and that, with little help on his part. As soon as she was done with Mr. Toomey, he turned on the Knicks game. The whole time she'd changed Mr. Toomey's catheter, however, Cleophus had watched her, laughing under his breath, then outright, a waxing and waning of hilarity as if her every gesture were laughably prim and proper.

"Look, Mr. *Cleophus Sanders*," she said, glad for the chance to bite on the ridiculous name, "I am a professional. You may laugh at what I do, but in doing so you laugh at the Almighty who has given me the breath to do it!"

She'd steeled herself for a vulgar reply. But no. Mr. Toomey did the talking.

"I tell *you* what!" Mr. Toomey said, pointing his remote at Sister Clareese, "I'm going to sue this hospital for lack of peace and quiet. All your 'Almighty this' and 'Oh Glory that' is keeping me from watching the game!"

So Sister Clareese murmured her apologies to Mr. Toomey, the whole while Cleophus Sanders put on an act of restraining his amusement, body and bed quaking in seizure-like fits.

Now sunlight filtered through the yellow-tinted windows of Greater Christ Emmanuel Pentecostal Church of the Fire Baptized, lighting Brother Hopkins, the organist, with a halo-like glow. The rest of the congregation had given their testimonies, and it was now time for the choir members to testify, starting with Clareese. Was there any way she could possibly turn her incident with Cleophus Sanders into an edifying testimony experience? Just then, another hit, and she felt a cramping so hard she thought she might double over. It was her turn. Cleophus's laughter and her cramping womb seemed one and the same; he'd inhabited her body like a demon, preventing her from thinking up a proper testimony. As she rose, unsteadily, to her feet, all she managed to say was, "Pray for me."

It was almost time for Pastor Everett to preach his sermon. To introduce it, Sister Clareese had the choir sing "Every Knee Shall Bow, Every Tongue Shall Confess." It was an old-fashioned hymn, unlike the hopped-up gospel songs churches were given to nowadays. And she liked the slow unfolding of its message: how without people uttering a word, all their hearts would be made plain to the Lord; that He would know you not by what you said or did, but by what you'd hoped and intended. The teens, however, mumbled over the verses, and older choir members sang without vigor. The hymn ended up sounding like the national anthem at a school assembly: a stout-hearted song rendered in monotone.

"Thank you, thank you, thank you, Sister Clareese," Pastor Everett said, looking back at her, "for that wonderful tune."

*Tune?* She knew that Pastor Everett thought she was not the kind of person a choirmistress should be; she was quiet, nervous, skinny in all the wrong places, and completely cross-eyed. She knew he thought of her as something worse than a spinster, because she wasn't yet old.

Pastor Everett hunched close to the microphone, as though about to begin a forlorn love song. From the corners of her vision she saw him smile—only for a second but with every single tooth in his mouth. He was yam-colored, and given to wearing epaulets on the shoulders of his robes and gold braiding all down the front. Sister Clareese felt no attraction to him, but she seemed to be the only one who didn't; even the Sisters going on eighty were charmed by Pastor Everett, who, though not entirely handsome, had handsome moments.

"Sister Clareese," he said, turning to where she stood with the choir. "Sister Clareese, I know y'all just sang for us, but I need some *more* help. Satan got these Brothers and Sisters putting m'Lord on hold!"

Sister Clareese knew that everyone expected her and her choir to begin singing again, but she had been alerted to what he was up to; he had called her yesterday. He had thought nothing of asking her to unplug her telephone—her *only* telephone, her *private* line—to bring it to church so that he could use it in some sermon about call-waiting. Hadn't even asked her how she was doing, hadn't bothered to pray over her aunt Alma's sickness. Nevertheless, she'd said, "Why certainly, Pastor Everett. Anything I can do to help."

Now Sister Clareese produced her Princess telephone from under her seat and handed it to the Pastor. Pastor Everett held the telephone aloft, shaking it as if to rid it of demons. "How many of y'all—Brothers and Sisters—got telephones?" the Pastor asked.

One by one, members of the congregation timidly raised their hands.

"All right," Pastor Everett said, as though this grieved him, "almost all of y'all." He flipped through his huge pulpit Bible. "How many of y'all—Brothers and Sisters—got call-waiting?" He turned pages quickly, then stopped, as though he didn't need to search the scripture after all. "Let me tell ya," the Pastor said, nearly kissing the microphone, "there is *Someone!* Who won't *accept* your call-waiting! There is *Someone!* Who won't *wait,* when you put Him on hold!" Sister Nancy Popwell and Sister Drusella Davies now had their eyes closed in concentration, their hands waving slowly in the air in front of them as though they were trying to make their way through a dark room.

The last phone call Sister Clareese had made was on Wednesday, to Mr. Toomey. She knew both he and Cleophus were likely to reject the Lord, but she had a policy of sorts, which was to call patients who'd been in her care for at least a week. She considered it her Christian duty to call—even on her day off—to let them know that Jesus cared, and that she cared. The other RNs resorted to callous catchphrases that they bandied about the nurses' station: "Just because I care *for* them doesn't mean I have to care *about* them," or, "I'm a nurse, not a nursery." Not Clareese. Perhaps she'd been curt with Cleophus Sanders, but she had been so in defense of God. Perhaps Mr. Toomey had been curt with her, but he was going into O.R. soon, and grouchiness was to be expected.

Nurse Patty had been switchboard operator that night and Clareese had had to endure her sighs before the girl finally connected her to Mr. Toomey.

"Praise the Lord, Mr. Toomey!"

"Who's this?"

"This is your nurse, Sister Clareese, and I'm calling to say that Jesus will be with you through your surgery."

"Who?"

"Jesus," she said.

She thought she heard the phone disconnect, then, a voice. Of course. Cleophus Sanders.

"Why ain't you called *me?*" Cleophus said.

Sister Clareese tried to explain her policy, the thing about the week.

"So you care more about some white dude than you care about good ol' Cleophus?"

"It's not that, Mr. Sanders, God cares for white and black alike. Acts 10:34 says, 'God is no respecter of persons.' Black or white. Red, purple, or green—he doesn't care, as long as you accept his salvation and live right." When he was silent on the other end she said, "It's that I've only known you for two days. I'll see you tomorrow."

She tried to hang up, but he said, "Let me play something for you. Something interesting, since all you probably listen to is monks chanting and such."

Before she could respond, there was a noise on the other end that sounded like juke music. Then he came back on the phone and said, "Like that, don't you?"

"I had the phone away from my ear."

"I thought you said 'lying is the abominable.' Do you like or do you don't?" When she said nothing he said, "Truth, now."

She answered yes.

She didn't want to answer yes. But she also didn't want to lie. And what was one to do in that circumstance? If God looked into your heart right then, what would He think? Or would He have to approve because He made your heart that way? Or were you obliged to train it against its wishes? She didn't know what to think, but on the other end Cleophus said, "What you just heard there was the blues. What you just heard there was me."

". . . Let me tell ya!" Pastor Everett shouted, his voice hitting its highest octave, "*Jeeeee-zus*—did not *tell* his *Daddy*—'I'm sorry, Pops, but my girlfriend is on the other line'; *Jeeeee-zus*—never *told* the Omnipotent One, 'Can you wait a sec, I think I got a call from the electric company!' *Jeeeeeeee-zus*—never told Matthew, Mark, Luke, or John, 'I'm *sorry*, but I got to put you on hold; I'm sorry, Brother Luke, but I got some mac and cheese in the oven; I'm *sorry*, but I got to eat this fried chicken'"—and at this, Pastor Everett paused, grinning in anticipation of his own punch line—"'cause it's finger-licking good!'"

Drops of sweat plunked onto his microphone.

Sister Clareese watched as the congregation cheered, the women flagging their Bibles in the air as though the Bibles were as light and yielding as handkerchiefs; their bosoms jouncing as though they were harboring sacks of potatoes in their blouses. They shook tambourines, scores of them all going at once, the sound of something sizzling and frying.

That was it? That was The Message? Of course, she'd only heard part of it, but still. Of course she believed that one's daily life shouldn't outstrip one's spiritual one, but there seemed no place for true belief at Greater Christ Emmanuel Pentecostal Church of the Fire Baptized. Everyone wanted flash and props, no one wanted the Word itself, naked in its fiery glory.

Most of the Brothers and Sisters were up on their feet. "Tell it!" yelled some, while others called out, "Go 'head on!" The organist pounded out the chords to what could have been the theme song of a TV game show.

She looked to see what Sister Drusella's and Sister Maxwell's unsaved guests were doing. Drusella's unsaved guest was her son, which made him easy to bring into the fold: he was living in her shed and had no car. He was busy turning over one of the cardboard fans donated by Hamblin and Sons Funeral Parlor, reading the words intently, then flipping it over again to stare at the picture of a gleaming casket and grieving family. Sister Donna Maxwell's guest was an ex-con she'd written to and tried to save while he was in prison. The ex-con seemed to watch the scene with approval, though one could never really know what was going on in the criminal mind. For all Sister Clareese knew, he could be counting all the pockets he planned to pick.

And they called themselves missionaries. Family members and ex-cons were easy to convince of God's will. As soon as Drusella's son took note of the pretty young Sisters his age, he'd be back. And everyone knew you could convert an ex-con with a few well-timed pecan pies.

Wednesday was her only day off besides Sunday, and though a phone call or two was her policy on days off, she very seldom visited the hospital. And yet, last Wednesday, she'd had to. The more she'd considered Cleophus's situation—his loss of limb, his devil's music, his unsettling laughter—the more she grew convinced that he was her Missionary Challenge. That he was especially in need of Saving.

Minutes after she'd talked with him on the phone, she took the number 42 bus and transferred to the crosstown H, then walked the rest of the way to the hospital.

Edwina had taken over for Patty as nurses' station attendant, and she'd said, "We have an ETOH in—where's your uniform?"

"It's not my shift," she called behind her as she rushed past Edwina and into Room 204.

She opened the door to find Cleophus sitting on the bed, still plucking chords on his unplugged electric guitar that she'd heard him playing over the phone half an hour earlier. Mr. Toomey's bed was empty; one of the nurses must have already taken him to O.R., so Cleophus had the room to himself. The right leg of Cleophus's hospital pants hung down limp and empty, and it was the first time she'd seen his guitar, curvy and shiny as a sportscar. He did not acknowledge her when she entered. He was still picking away at his guitar, singing a song about a man whose woman had left him so high and dry, she'd taken the car, the dog, the furniture. Even the wallpaper. Only when he'd strummed the final chords did Cleophus look up, as if noticing her for the first time.

"Sister *Clare-reeeese!*" He said it as if he were introducing a showgirl.

"It's your soul," Clareese said. "God wants me to help save your soul." The urgency of God's message struck her so hard, she felt the wind knocked out of her. She sat on the bed next to him.

"Really?" he said, cocking his head a little.

"Really and truly," Clareese said, "I know I said I liked your music, but I said it because God gave you that gift for you to use. For Him."

"Uhnn-huh," Cleophus said. "How about this, little lady. How about if God lets me keep this knee, I'll come to church with you. We can go out and get some dinner afterwards. Like a proper couple."

She tried not to be flattered. "The Lord does *not make* deals, Mr. Sanders. But I'm sure the Lord would love to see you in church regardless of what happens to your knee."

"Well, since you seem to be His receptionist, how about you ask the Lord if he can give you the day off. I can take you out on the town. See, if I go to church, I *know* the Lord won't show. But I'm positive you will."

"Believe you me, Mr. Sanders, the Lord is at every service. *Where two or three are gathered together in my name, there am I in the midst of them.*" She sighed, trying to remember what she came to say. "*He is the Way, the Truth and the Life. No man—*"

" . . . *cometh to the father,*" Cleophus said, "*but by me.*"

She looked at him. "You know your Bible."

"Naw. You were speaking and I just heard it." He absently strummed his guitar. "You were talking, saying that verse, and the rest of it came to me. Not even a voice," he said, "more like . . . kind of like music."

She stared. Her hands clapped his, preventing him from playing further. For a moment, she was breathless. He looked at her, suddenly seeming to comprehend what he'd just said, that the Lord had actually spoken to him. For a minute, they sat there, both overjoyed at what the Lord had done, but then he had to go ruin it. He burst out laughing his biggest, most sinful laugh yet.

"Awww!" he cried, doubled over, and then flopped backward onto his hospital bed. Then he closed his eyes, laughing without sound.

She stood up, chest heaving, wondering why she even bothered with him.

"Clareese," he said, trying to clear his voice of any leftover laughter, "don't go." He looked at her with pleading eyes, then patted the space beside him on the bed.

She looked around the room for some cue. Whenever she needed an answer, she relied on some sign from the Lord; a fresh beam of sunlight through the window, the hands of a clock folded in prayer, or the flush of a commode. These were signs that whatever she was thinking of doing was right. If there was a storm cloud, or something in her path, then that was a bad sign. But nothing in the room gave her any indication whether she should stay and witness to Mr. Sanders, or go.

"What, Mr. Sanders, do you want from me? It's my day off. I decided to come by and offer you an invitation to my church because God has given you a gift. A musical gift." She dug into her purse, then pulled out a pocket-sized Bible. "But I'll leave you with this. If you need to find us—our church—the name and number is printed inside."

He took the Bible with a little smile, turning it over, then flipping through it, as if some money might be tucked away inside. "Seriously, though," he'd said, "let me ask you a question that's gonna seem dumb. Childish. Now, I want you to think long and hard about it. Why the hell's there so much suffering in the world if God's doing his job? I mean, look at me. Take old Toomey, too. We done anything *that* bad to deserve all this put on us?"

She sighed. "Because of people, that's why. Not God. It's *people* who allow suffering, people who create it. Perpetrate it."

"Maybe that explains Hitler and all them others, but I'm talking about—" He gestured at the room, the hospital in general.

Clareese tried to see what he saw when he looked at the room. At one time, the white and pale green walls of the hospital rooms had given her solace; the way everything was clean, clean, clean; the many patients that had been in each room, some nice, some dying, some willing to accept the Lord. But most, like Mr. Toomey, cast the Lord aside like wilted lettuce, and now the clean hospital room was just a reminder of the emptiness, the barrenness, of her patients' souls. Cleophus Sanders was just another patient who disrespected the Lord.

"Why does He allow natural disasters to kill people?" Clareese said, knowing that her voice was raised louder than what she meant it to be. "Why are little children born to get some rare blood disease and die? Why," she yelled, waving her arms, "does a crane fall on your leg and smash it? I don't know, Mr. Sanders. And I don't like it. But I'll say this! No one has a *right* to live! The only right we have is to die. That's it! If you get plucked out of the universe and given a chance to become a life, that's more than not having become anything at all, and for that, Mr. Sanders, you should be grateful!"

She had not known where this last bit had come from, and, she could tell, neither had he, but she could hear the other nurses coming down the hall to see who was yelling, and though Cleophus Sanders looked to have more pity on his face than true belief, he had come after her when she turned to leave. She'd heard the clatter of him gathering his crutches, and even when she heard the meaty weight of him slam onto the floor, she did not turn back.

Then there it was. Pastor Everett's silly motion of cupping his hand to his ear, like he was eavesdropping on the choir, his signal that he was waiting for Sister Clareese to sing her solo, waiting to hear the voice that would send the congregation shouting, "Thank you, Jesus, Blessed Savior!"

How could she do it. She thought of Cleophus on the floor and felt ashamed. She hadn't seen him since; her yelling had been brought to the attention of the administrators, and although the hospital was understaffed, the administration had suggested that she not return until next week. They handed her the card of the staff psychiatrist. She had not told anyone at church what had happened. Not even her aunt Alma.

She didn't want to sing. Didn't feel like it, but, she thought, *I will freely sacrifice myself unto Thee: I will praise Thy name, O Lord, for it is good.* Usually thinking of a scripture would give her strength, but this time it just made her realize how much strength she was always needing.

She didn't want to, but she'd do it. She'd sing a stupid solo part—the Waterfall, they called it—not even something she'd *invented* or *planned* to do who knows how many years ago when she'd had to sneeze her brains out, but oh no, she'd tried holding it in, and when she had to sing her solo, those years ago, her near-sneeze had made the words come out tumbling in a series of staccato notes that were almost fluid, and ever since then, she'd had to sing *all* solos that way, it was expected of her, everyone loved it, it was her trademark, she sang: "All-hall other-her her grooouund— is sink-king sand!"

The congregation applauded.

"Saints," the Pastor said, winding down, "you know this world will soon be *over!* Jesus will come back to this tired, sorry Earth in *a moment and a twinkling of an eye! So you can't use call-waiting on the Lord! *Jeeee-zus,* my friends, does not accept conference calls! You are Children of God! You need to PRAY! Put down your phone! Say goodbye to AT&T! You cannot go in God's *direction,* without a little—*genuflection!*"

The congregation went wild, clapping and banging tambourines, whirling in the aisles. But the choir remained standing in case Pastor Everett wanted another song. For the first time, Clareese found that her monthly troubles had settled down. And now that she had the wherewithal to concentrate, she couldn't. Her cross-eyes wouldn't keep steady, they roamed like the wheels of a defective shopping cart, and from one roving eye she saw her aunt Alma, waving her arms as though listening to leftover strains of Clareese's solo.

What would she do? She didn't know if she'd still have her job when she went back on Monday, didn't know what the staff psychiatrist would try to pry out of her. More important, she didn't know what her aunt Alma would do without the special medical referrals Clareese could get her. What was a Sister to do?

Clareese's gaze must have found him just a moment after everyone else's had. A stranger at the far end of the aisle, standing directly opposite Pastor Everett as though about to engage him in a duel. There was Cleophus Sanders with his crutches, the right leg of his pinstriped pants hollow, wagging after him. Over his shoulder was a strap, attached to which was his guitar. Even Deacon McCreedy was looking.

What in heaven's name was Cleophus doing here? To bring his soul to salvation? To ridicule her? For another argument? Perhaps the doctors had told him he did not need the operation after all, and Cleophus was keeping his end of the deal with God. But he didn't seem like the type to keep promises. She saw his eyes search the congregation, and when he saw her, they locked eyes as if he had come to claim her. He did not come to get Saved, didn't care about his soul in that way, all he cared about was—

Now she knew why he'd come. He'd come for her. He'd come *despite* what she'd told him, despite his disbelief. Anyhow, she disapproved. It was God he needed, not her. Nevertheless, she remained standing for a few moments, even after the rest of the choir had already seated themselves, waving their cardboard fans to cool their sweaty faces.

# *Rock Springs*

### RICHARD FORD

Edna and I had started down from Kalispell, heading for Tampa-St. Pete where I still had some friends from the old glory days who wouldn't turn me in to the police. I had managed to scrape with the law in Kalispell over several bad checks—which is a prison crime in Montana. And I knew Edna was already looking at her cards and thinking about a move, since it wasn't the first time I'd been in law scrapes in my life. She herself had already had her own troubles, losing her kids and keeping her ex-husband, Danny, from breaking in her house and stealing her things while she was at work, which was really why I had moved in in the first place, that and needing to give my little daughter, Cheryl, a better shake in things.

I don't know what was between Edna and me, just beached by the same tides when you got down to it. Though love has been built on frailer ground than that, as I well know. And when I came in the house that afternoon, I just asked her if she wanted to go to Florida with me, leave things where they sat, and she said, "Why not? My datebook's not that full."

Edna and I had been a pair eight months, more or less man and wife, some of which time I had been out of work, and some when I'd worked at the dog track as a lead-out and could help with the rent and talk sense to Danny when he came around. Danny was afraid of me because Edna had told him I'd been in prison in Florida for killing a man, though that wasn't true. I had once been in jail in Tallahassee for stealing tires and had gotten into a fight on the county farm where a man had lost his eye. But I hadn't done the hurting, and Edna just wanted the story worse than it was so Danny wouldn't act crazy and make her have to take her kids back, since she had made a good adjustment to not having them, and I already had Cheryl with me. I'm not a violent person and would never put a man's eye out, much less kill someone. My former wife, Helen, would come all the way from Waikiki Beach to testify to that. We never had violence, and I believe in crossing the street to stay out of trouble's way. Though Danny didn't know that.

But we were half down through Wyoming, going toward I-80 and feeling good about things, when the oil light flashed on in the car I'd stolen, a sign I knew to be a bad one.

I'd gotten us a good car, a cranberry Mercedes I'd stolen out of an ophthalmologist's lot in Whitefish, Montana. I stole it because I thought it would be comfortable over a long haul, because I thought it got good mileage, which it didn't, and because I'd never had a good car in my life, just old Chevy junkers and used trucks back from when I was a kid swamping citrus with Cubans.

The car made us all high that day. I ran the windows up and down, and Edna told us some jokes and made faces. She could be lively. Her features would light up like a beacon and you could see her beauty, which wasn't ordinary. It all made me giddy, and I drove clear down to Bozeman, then straight on through the park to Jackson Hole. I rented us the bridal suite in the Quality Court in Jackson and left Cheryl and her little dog, Duke, sleeping while Edna and I drove to a rib barn and drank beer and laughed till after midnight.

It felt like a whole new beginning for us, bad memories left behind and a new horizon to build on. I got so worked up, I had a tattoo done on my arm that said FAMOUS TIMES, and Edna bought a Bailey hat with an Indian feather band and a little turquoise-and-silver bracelet for Cheryl, and we made love on the seat of the car in the Quality Court parking lot just as the sun was burning up on the Snake River, and everything seemed then like the end of the rainbow.

It was that very enthusiasm, in fact, that made me keep the car one day longer instead of driving it into the river and stealing another one, like I should've done and *had* done before.

Where the car went bad there wasn't a town in sight or even a house, just some low mountains maybe fifty miles away or maybe a hundred, a barbed-wire fence in both directions, hardpan prairie, and some hawks riding the evening air seizing insects.

I got out to look at the motor, and Edna got out with Cheryl and the dog to let them have a pee by the car. I checked the water and checked the oil stick, and both of them said perfect.

"What's that light mean, Earl?" Edna said. She had come and stood by the car with her hat on. She was just sizing things up for herself.

"We shouldn't run it," I said. "Something's not right in the oil."

She looked around at Cheryl and Little Duke, who were peeing on the hardtop side-by-side like two little dolls, then out at the mountains, which were becoming black and lost in the distance. "What're we doing?" she said. She wasn't worried yet, but she wanted to know what I was thinking about.

"Let me try it again."

"That's a good idea," she said, and we all got back in the car.

When I turned the motor over, it started right away and the red light stayed off and there weren't any noises to make you think something was wrong. I let it idle a minute, then pushed the accelerator down and watched the red bulb. But there wasn't any light on, and I started wondering if maybe I hadn't dreamed I saw it, or that it had been the sun catching an angle off the window chrome, or maybe I was scared of something and didn't know it.

"What's the matter with it, Daddy?" Cheryl said from the backseat. I looked back at her, and she had on her turquoise bracelet and Edna's hat set back on the back of her head and that little black-and-white Heinz dog on her lap. She looked like a little cowgirl in the movies.

"Nothing, honey, everything's fine now," I said.

"Little Duke tinkled where I tinkled," Cheryl said, and laughed.

"You're two of a kind," Edna said, not looking back. Edna was usually good with Cheryl, but I knew she was tired now. We hadn't had much sleep, and she had a tendency to get cranky when she didn't sleep. "We oughta ditch this damn car first chance we get," she said.

"What's the first chance we got?" I asked, because I knew she'd been at the map.

"Rock Springs, Wyoming," Edna said with conviction. "Thirty miles down this road." She pointed out ahead.

I had wanted all along to drive the car into Florida like a big success story. But I knew Edna was right about it, that we shouldn't take crazy chances. I had kept thinking of it as my car and not the ophthalmologist's, and that was how you got caught in these things.

"Then my belief is we ought to go to Rock Springs and negotiate ourselves a new car," I said. I wanted to stay upbeat, like everything was panning out right.

"That's a great idea," Edna said, and she leaned over and kissed me hard on the mouth.

"That's a great idea," Cheryl said. "Let's pull on out of here right now."

The sunset that day I remember as being the prettiest I'd ever seen. Just as it touched the rim of the horizon, it all at once fired the air into jewels and red sequins the precise likes of which I had never seen before and haven't seen since. The West has it all over everywhere for sunsets, even Florida, where it's supposedly flat but where half the time trees block your view.

"It's cocktail hour," Edna said after we'd driven awhile. "We ought to have a drink and celebrate something." She felt better thinking we were going to get rid of the car. It certainly had dark troubles and was something you'd want to put behind you.

Edna had out a whiskey bottle and some plastic cups and was measuring levels on the glove-box lid. She liked drinking, and she liked drinking in the car, which was something you got used to in Montana, where it wasn't against the law, but where, strangely enough, a bad check would land you in Deer Lodge Prison for a year.

"Did I ever tell you I once had a monkey?" Edna said, setting my drink on the dashboard where I could reach it when I was ready. Her spirits were already picked up. She was like that, up one minute and down the next.

"I don't think you ever did tell me that," I said. "Where were you then?"

"Missoula," she said. She put her bare feet on the dash and rested the cup on her breasts. "I was waitressing at the AmVets. This was before I met you. Some guy came in one day with a monkey. A spider monkey. And I said, just to be joking, 'I'll roll you for that monkey.' And the guy said, 'Just one roll?' And I said, 'Sure.' He put the monkey down on the bar, picked up the cup, and rolled out boxcars. I picked it up and rolled out three fives. And I just stood there looking at the guy. He was just some guy passing through, I guess a vet. He got a strange look on his face—I'm sure not as strange as the one I had—but he looked kind of sad and surprised and satisfied all at once. I said, 'We can roll again.' But he said, 'No, I never roll twice for anything.' And he sat and drank a beer and talked about one thing and another for a while, about nuclear war and building a stronghold somewhere up in the Bitterroot, whatever it was, while I just watched the monkey, wondering what I was going to do with it when the guy left. And pretty soon he got up and said, 'Well, good-bye, Chipper'—that was this monkey's name, of course. And then he left before I could say anything. And the monkey just sat on the bar all that night. I don't know what made me think of that, Earl. Just something weird. I'm letting my mind wander."

"That's perfectly fine," I said. I took a drink of my drink. "I'd never own a monkey," I said after a minute. "They're too nasty. I'm sure Cheryl would like a monkey, though, wouldn't you, honey?" Cheryl was down on the seat playing with Little Duke. She used to talk about monkeys all the time then. "What'd you ever do with that monkey?" I said, watching the speedometer. We were having to go slower now because the red light kept fluttering on. And all I could do to keep it off was go slower. We were going maybe thirty-five and it was an hour before dark, and I was hoping Rock Springs wasn't far away.

"You really want to know?" Edna said. She gave me a quick glance, then looked back at the empty desert as if she was brooding over it.

"Sure," I said. I was still upbeat. I figured I could worry about breaking down and let other people be happy for a change.

"I kept it a week." And she seemed gloomy all of a sudden, as if she saw some aspect of the story she had never seen before. "I took it home and back and forth to the AmVets on my shifts. And it didn't cause any trouble. I fixed a chair up for it to sit on, back of the bar, and people liked it. It made a nice little clicking noise. We changed its name to Mary because the bartender figured out it was a girl. Though I was never really comfortable with it at home. I felt like it watched me too much. Then one day a guy came in, some guy who'd been in Vietnam, still wore a fatigue coat. And he said to me, 'Don't you know that a monkey'll kill you? It's got more strength in its fingers than you got in your whole body.' He said people had been killed in Vietnam by monkeys, bunches of them marauding while you were asleep, killing you and covering you with leaves. I didn't believe a word of it, except that when I got home and got undressed I started looking over across the room at Mary on her chair in the dark watching me. And I got the creeps. And after a while I got up and went out to the car, got a length of clothesline wire, and came back in and wired her to the doorknob through her little silver collar, then went back and tried to sleep. And I guess I must've slept the sleep of the dead—though I don't remember it—because when I got up I found Mary had tipped off her chair-back and hanged herself on the wire line. I'd made it too short."

Edna seemed badly affected by that story and slid low in the seat so she couldn't see out over the dash. Isn't that a shameful story, Earl, what happened to that poor little monkey?"

"I see a town! I see a town!" Cheryl started yelling from the back seat, and right up Little Duke started yapping and the whole car fell into a racket. And sure enough she had seen something I hadn't, which was Rock Springs, Wyoming, at the bottom of a long hill, a little glowing jewel in the desert with I-80 running on the north side and the black desert spread out behind.

"That's it, honey," I said. "That's where we're going. You saw it first."

"We're hungry," Cheryl said. "Little Duke wants some fish, and I want spaghetti." She put her arms around my neck and hugged me.

"Then you'll just get it," I said. "You can have anything you want. And so can Edna and so can Little Duke." I looked over at Edna, smiling, but she was staring at me with eyes that were fierce with anger. "What's wrong?" I said.

"Don't you care anything about that awful thing that happened to me?" Her mouth was drawn tight, and her eyes kept cutting back at Cheryl and Little Duke, as if they had been tormenting her.

"Of course I do," I said. "I thought that was an awful thing." I didn't want her to be unhappy. We were almost there, and pretty soon we could sit down and have a real meal without thinking somebody might be hurting us.

"You want to know what I did with that monkey?" Edna said.

"Sure I do," I said.

"I put her in a green garbage bag, put it in the trunk of my car, drove to the dump, and threw her in the trash." She was staring at me darkly, as if the story meant something to her that was real important but that only she could see and that the rest of the world was a fool for.

"Well, that's horrible," I said. "But I don't see what else you could do. You didn't mean to kill it. You'd have done it differently if you had. And then you had to get rid of it, and I don't know what else you could have done. Throwing it away might seem unsympathetic to somebody, probably, but not to me. Sometimes that's all you can do, and you can't worry about what somebody else thinks." I tried to smile at her, but the red light was staying on if I pushed the accelerator at all, and I was trying to gauge if we could coast to Rock Springs before the car gave out completely. I looked at Edna again. "What else can I say?" I said.

"Nothing," she said, and stared back at the dark highway. "I should've known that's what you'd think. You've got a character that leaves something out, Earl. I've known that a long time."

"And yet here you are," I said. "And you're not doing so bad. Things could be a lot worse. At least we're all together here."

"Things could always be worse," Edna said. "You could go to the electric chair tomorrow."

"That's right," I said. "And somewhere somebody probably will. Only it won't be you."

"I'm hungry," said Cheryl. "When're we gonna eat? Let's find a motel. I'm tired of this. Little Duke's tired of it too."

Where the car stopped rolling was some distance from the town, though you could see the clear outline of the interstate in the dark with Rock Springs lighting up the sky behind. You could hear the big tractors hitting the spacers in the overpass, revving up for the climb to the mountains.

I shut off the lights.

"What're we going to do now?" Edna said irritably, giving me a bitter look.

"I'm figuring it," I said. "It won't be hard, whatever it is. You won't have to do anything."

"I'd hope not," she said and looked the other way.

Across the road and across a dry wash a hundred yards was what looked like a huge mobile-home town, with a factory or a refinery of some kind lit up behind it and in full swing. There were lights on in a lot of the mobile homes, and there were cars moving along an access road that ended near the freeway overpass a mile the other way. The lights in the mobile homes seemed friendly to me, and I knew right then what I should do.

"Get out," I said, opening my door.

"Are we walking?" Edna said.

"We're pushing."

"I'm not pushing." Edna reached up and locked her door.

"All right," I said. "Then you just steer."

"You're pushing us to Rock Springs, are you, Earl? It doesn't look like it's more than about three miles."

"I'll push," Cheryl said from the back.

"No, hon. Daddy'll push. You just get out with Little Duke and move out of the way."

Edna gave me a threatening look, just as if I'd tried to hit her. But when I got out she slid into my seat and took the wheel, staring angrily ahead straight into the cottonwood scrub.

"Edna can't drive that car," Cheryl said from out in the dark. "She'll run it in the ditch."

"Yes, she can, hon. Edna can drive it as good as I can. Probably better."

"No she can't," Cheryl said. "No she can't either." And I thought she was about to cry, but she didn't.

I told Edna to keep the ignition on so it wouldn't lock up and to steer into the cottonwoods with the parking lights on so she could see. And when I started, she steered it straight off into the trees, and I kept pushing until we were twenty yards into the cover and the tires sank in the soft sand and nothing at all could be seen from the road.

"Now where are we?" she said, sitting at the wheel. Her voice was tired and hard, and I knew she could have put a good meal to use. She had a sweet nature, and I recognized that this wasn't her fault but mine. Only I whished she could be more hopeful.

"You stay right here, and I'll go over to that trailer park and call us a cab," I said.

"What cab?" Edna said, her mouth wrinkled as if she'd never heard anything like that in her life.

"There'll be cabs," I said, and tried to smile at her "There's cabs everywhere."

"What're you going to tell him when he gets here? Our stolen car broke down and we need a ride to where we can steal another one? That'll be a big hit, Earl."

"I'll talk," I said. "You just listen to the radio for ten minutes and then walk on out to the shoulder like nothing was suspicious. And you and Cheryl act nice. She doesn't need to know about this car."

"Like we're not suspicious enough already, right?" Edna looked up at me out of the lighted car. "You don't think right, did you know that, Earl? You think the world's stupid and you're smart. But that's not how it is. I feel sorry for you. You might've *been* something, but things just went crazy someplace."

I had a thought about poor Danny. He was a vet and crazy as a shit-house mouse, and I was glad he wasn't in for all this. "Just get the baby in the car," I said, trying to be patient. "I'm hungry like you are."

"I'm tired of this," Edna said. "I wish I'd stayed in Montana."

"Then you can go back in the morning," I said. "I'll buy the ticket and put you on the bus. But not till then."

"Just get on with it, Earl." She slumped down in the seat, turning off the parking lights with one foot and the radio on with the other.

The mobile-home community was as big as any I'd ever seen. It was attached in some way to the plant that was lighted up behind it, because I could see a car once in a while leave one of the trailer streets, turn in the direction of the plant, then go slowly into it. Everything in the plant was white, and you could see that all the trailers were painted white and looked exactly alike. A deep hum came out of the plant, and I thought as I got closer that it wouldn't be a location I'd ever want to work in.

I went right to the first trailer where there was a light, and knocked on the metal door. Kids' toys were lying in the gravel around the little wood steps, and I could hear talking on TV that suddenly went off. I heard a woman's voice talking, and then the door opened wide.

A large Negro woman with a wide, friendly face stood in the doorway. She smiled at me and moved forward as if she was going to come out, but she stopped at the top step. There was a little Negro boy behind her peeping out from behind her legs, watching me with his eyes half closed. The trailer had that feeling that no one else was inside, which was a feeling I knew something about.

"I'm sorry to intrude," I said. "But I've run up on a little bad luck tonight. My name's Earl Middleton."

The woman looked at me, then out into the night toward the freeway as if what I had said was something she was going to be able to see. "What kind of bad luck?" she said, looking down at me again.

"My car broke down out on the highway," I said. "I can't fix it myself, and I wondered if I could use your phone to call for help."

The woman smiled down at me knowingly. "We can't live without cars, can we?"

"That's the honest truth," I said.

"They're like out hearts," she said, her face shining in the little bulb light that burned beside the door. "Where's your car situated?"

I turned and looked over into the dark, but I couldn't see anything because of where we'd put it. "It's over there," I said. "You can't see it in the dark."

"Who all's with you now?" the woman said. "Have you got your wife with you?"

"She's with my little girl and our dog in the car," I said. "My daughter's asleep or I would have brought them."

"They shouldn't be left in the dark by themselves," the woman said and frowned. "There's too much unsavoriness out there."

"The best I can do is hurry back." I tried to look sincere, since everything except Cheryl being asleep and Edna being my wife was the truth. The truth is meant to serve you if you'll let it, and I wanted it to serve me. "I'll pay for the phone call," I said. "If you'll bring the phone to the door I'll call from right here."

The woman looked at me again as if she was searching for a truth of her own, then back out into the night. She was maybe in her sixties, but I couldn't say for sure. "You're not going to rob me, are you, Mr. Middleton?" She smiled like it was a joke between us.

"Not tonight," I said, and smiled a genuine smile. "I'm not up to it tonight. Maybe another time."

"Then I guess Terrel and I can let you use our phone with Daddy not here, can't we, Terrel? This is my grandson, Terrel Junior, Mr. Middleton." She put her hand on the boy's head and looked down at him. "Terrel won't talk. Though if he did he'd tell you to use our phone. He's a sweet boy." She opened the screen for me to come in.

The trailer was a big one with a new rug and a new couch and a living room that expanded to give the space of a real house. Something good and sweet was cooking in the kitchen, and the trailer felt like it was somebody's comfortable new home instead of just temporary. I've lived in trailers, but they were just snailbacks with one room and no toilet, and they always felt cramped and unhappy—though I've thought maybe it might've been me that was unhappy in them.

There was a big Sony TV and a lot of kids' toys scattered on the floor. I recognized a Greyhound bus I'd gotten for Cheryl. The phone was beside a new leather recliner, and the Negro woman pointed for me to sit down and call and gave me the phone book. Terrel began fingering his toys and the woman sat on the couch while I called, watching me and smiling.

There were three listings for cab companies, all with one number different. I called the numbers in order and didn't get an answer until the last one, which answered with the name of the second company. I said I was on the highway beyond the inter-state and that my wife and family needed to be taken to town and I would arrange for a tow later. While I was giving the location, I looked up the name of a tow service to tell the driver in case he asked.

When I hung up, the Negro woman was sitting looking at me with the same look she had been staring with into the dark, a look that seemed to want truth. She was smiling, though. Something pleased her and I reminded her of it.

"This is a very nice home," I said, resting in the recliner, which felt like the dri-ver's seat of the Mercedes, and where I'd have been happy to stay.

"This isn't *our* house, Mr. Middleton," the Negro woman said. "The company owns these. They give them to us for nothing. We have our own home in Rockford, Illinois."

"That's wonderful," I said.

"It's never wonderful when you have to be away from home, Mr. Middleton, though we're only here three months, and it'll be easier when Terrel Junior begins his special school. You see, our son was killed in the war, and his wife ran off without Terrel Junior. Though you shouldn't worry. He can't understand us. His little feelings can't be hurt." The woman folded her hands in her lap and smiled in a satisfied way. She was an attrac-tive woman, and had on a blue-and-pink floral dress that made her seem bigger than she could've been, just the right woman to sit on the couch she was sitting on. She was good nature's picture, and I was glad she could be, with her little brain-damaged boy, living in a place where no one in his right mind would want to live a minute. "Where do *you* live, Mr. Middleton?" she said politely, smiling in the same sympathetic way.

"My family and I are in transit," I said. "I'm an ophthalmologist, and we're mov-ing back to Florida, where I'm from. I'm setting up practice in some little town where it's warm year-round. I haven't decided where."

"Florida's a wonderful place," the woman said. "I think Terrel would like it there."

"Could I ask you something?" I said.

"You certainly may," the woman said. Terrel had begun pushing his Greyhound across the front of the TV screen, making a scratch that no one watching the set could miss. "Stop that, Terrel Junior," the woman said quietly. But Terrel kept push-ing his bus on the glass, and she smiled at me again as if we both understood some-thing sad. Except I knew Cheryl would never damage a television set. She had respect for nice things, and I was sorry for the lady that Terrel didn't. "What did you want to ask?" the woman said.

"What goes on in that plant or whatever it is back there beyond these trailers, where all the lights are on?"

"Gold," the woman said and smiled.

"It's what?" I said.

"Gold," the Negro woman said, smiling as she had for almost all the time I'd been there. "It's a gold mine."

"They're mining gold back there?" I said, pointing.

"Every night and every day." She smiled in a pleased way.

"Does your husband work there?" I said.

"He's the assayer," she said. "He controls the quality. He works three months a year, and we live the rest of the time at home in Rockford. We've waited a long time for this. We've been happy to have our grandson, but I won't say I'll be sorry to have him go. We're ready to start our lives over." She smiled broadly at me and then at Terrel, who was giving her a spiteful look from the floor. "You said you had a daughter," the Negro woman said. "And what's her name?"

"Irma Cheryl," I said. "She's named for my mother."

"That's nice. And she's healthy, too. I can see it in your face." She looked at Terrel Junior with pity.

"I guess I'm lucky," I said.

"So far you are. But children bring you grief, the same way they bring you joy. We were unhappy for a long time before my husband got his job in the gold mine. Now, when Terrel starts to school, we'll be kids again." She stood up. "You might miss your cab, Mr. Middleton," she said, walking toward the door, though not to be forcing me out. She was too polite. "If *we* can't see your car, the cab surely won't be able to."

"That's true." I got up off the recliner, where I'd been so comfortable. "None of us have eaten yet, and your food makes me know how hungry we probably all are."

"There are fine restaurants in town, and you'll find them," the Negro woman said. "I'm sorry you didn't meet my husband. He's a wonderful man. He's everything to me."

"Tell him I appreciate the phone," I said. "You saved me."

"You weren't hard to save," the woman said. "Saving people is what we were all put on earth to do. I just passed you on to whatever's coming to you."

"Let's hope it's good," I said, stepping back into the dark.

"I'll be hoping, Mr. Middleton. Terrel and I will both be hoping."

I waved to her as I walked out into the darkness toward the car where it was hidden in the night.

The cab had already arrived when I got there. I could see its little red-and-green roof lights all the way across the dry wash, and it made me worry that Edna was already saying something to get us in trouble, something about the car or where we'd come from, something that would cast suspicion on us. I thought, then, how I never planned things well enough. There was always a gap between my plan and what happened, and I only responded to things as they came along and hoped I wouldn't get in trouble. I was an offender in the law's eyes. But I always *thought* differently, as if I weren't an offender and had no intention of being one, which was the truth. But as I read on a napkin once, between the idea and the act a whole kingdom lies. And I had a hard time with my acts, which were oftentimes offender's acts, and my ideas, which were as good as the gold they mined there where the bright lights were blazing.

"We're waiting for you, Daddy," Cheryl said when I crossed the road. "The taxicab's already here."

"I see, hon," I said, and gave Cheryl a big hug. The cabdriver was sitting in the driver's seat having a smoke with the lights on inside. Edna was leaning against the back of the cab between the taillights, wearing her Bailey hat. "What'd you tell him?" I said when I got close.

"Nothing," she said. "What's there to tell?"

"Did he see the car?"

She glanced over in the direction of the trees where we had hid the Mercedes. Nothing was visible in the darkness, though I could hear Little Duke combing around in the underbrush tracking something, his little collar tinkling. "Where're we going?" she said. "I'm so hungry I could pass out."

"Edna's in a terrible mood," Cheryl said. "She already snapped at me."

"We're tired, honey," I said. "So try to be nicer."

"She's never nice," Cheryl said.

"Run go get Little Duke," I said. "And hurry back."

"I guess my questions come last here, right?" Edna said.

I put my arm around her. "That's not true."

"Did you find somebody over there in the trailers you'd rather stay with? You were gone long enough."

"That's not a thing to say," I said. "I was just trying to make things look right, so we don't get put in jail."

"So you don't, you mean." Edna laughed a little laugh I didn't like hearing.

"That's right. So I don't," I said. "I'd be the one in Dutch." I stared out at the big, lighted assemblage of white buildings and white lights beyond the trailer community, plumes of white smoke escaping up into the heartless Wyoming sky, the whole company of buildings looking like some unbelievable castle, humming away in a distorted dream. "You know what all those buildings are there?" I said to Edna, who hadn't moved and who didn't really seem to care if she ever moved anymore ever.

"No. But I can't say it matters, because it isn't a motel and it isn't a restaurant."

"It's a gold mine," I said, staring at the gold mine, which, I knew now, was a greater distance from us than it seemed, though it seemed huge and near, up against the cold sky. I thought there should've been a wall around it with guards instead of just the lights and no fence. It seemed as if anyone could go in and take what they wanted, just the way I had gone up to that woman's trailer and used the telephone, though that obviously wasn't true.

Edna began to laugh then. Not the mean laugh I didn't like, but a laugh that had something caring behind it, a full laugh that enjoyed a joke, a laugh she was laughing the first time I laid eyes on her, in Missoula in the East Gate Bar in 1979, a laugh we used to laugh together when Cheryl was still with her mother and I was working steady at the track and not stealing cars or passing bogus checks to merchants. A better time all around. And for some reason it made me laugh just hearing her, and we both stood there behind the cab in the dark, laughing at the gold mine in the desert, me with my arm around her and Cheryl out rustling up Little Duke and the cabdriver smoking in the cab and our stolen Mercedes-Benz, which I'd had such hopes for in Florida, stuck up to its axle in sand, where I'd never get to see it again.

"I always wondered what a gold mine would look like when I saw it," Edna said, still laughing, wiping a tear from her eye.

"Me too," I said. "I was always curious about it."

"We're a couple of fools, aren't we, Earl?" she said, unable to quit laughing completely. "We're two of a kind."

"It might be a good sign, though," I said.

"How could it be? It's not our gold mine. There aren't any drive-up windows." She was still laughing.

"We've seen it," I said, pointing. "That's it right there. It may mean we're getting closer. Some people never see it at all."

"In a pig's eye, Earl," she said. "You and me see it in a pig's eye."

And she turned and got in the cab to go.

The cabdriver didn't ask anything about our car or where it was, to mean he'd noticed something queer. All of which made me feel like we had made a clean break from the car and couldn't be connected with it until it was too late, if ever. The driver told us a lot about Rock Springs while he drove, that because of the gold mine a lot of people had moved there in just six months, people from all over, including New York, and that most of them lived out in the trailers. Prostitutes from New York City, who he called "B-girls," had come into town, he said, on the prosperity tide, and Cadillacs with New York plates cruised the little streets every night, full of Negroes with big hats who ran the women. He told us that everybody who got in his cab now wanted to know where the women were, and when he got our call he almost didn't come because some of the trailers were brothels operated by the mine for engineers and computer people away from home. He said he got tired of running back and forth out there just for vile business. He said that *60 Minutes* had even done a program about Rock Springs and that a blow-up had resulted in Cheyenne, though nothing could be done unless the boom left town. "It's prosperity's fruit," the driver said. "I'd rather be poor, which is lucky for me."

He said all the motels were sky-high, but since we were a family he could show us a nice one that was affordable. But I told him we wanted a first-rate place where they took animals, and the money didn't matter because we had had a hard day and wanted to finish on a high note. I also knew that it was in the little nowhere places that the police look for you and find you. People I'd known were always being arrested in cheap hotels and tourist courts with names you'd never heard of before. Never in Holiday Inns or TraveLodges.

I asked him to drive us to the middle of town and back out again so Cheryl could see the train station, and while we were there I saw a pink Cadillac with New York plates and a TV aerial being driven slowly by a Negro in a big hat down a narrow street where there were just bars and a Chinese restaurant. It was an odd sight, nothing you could ever expect.

"There's your pure criminal element," the cabdriver said and seemed sad. "I'm sorry for people like you to see a thing like that. We've got a nice town here, but there're some that want to ruin it for everybody. There used to be a way to deal with trash and criminals, but those days are gone forever."

"You said it," Edna said.

"You shouldn't let it get *you* down," I said to him. "There's more of you than them. And there always will be. You're the best advertisement this town has. I know Cheryl will remember you and not *that* man, won't you, honey?" But Cheryl was asleep by then, holding Little Duke in her arms on the taxi seat.

The driver took us to the Ramada Inn on the interstate, not far from where we'd broken down. I had a small pain of regret as we drove under the Ramada awning that we hadn't driven up in a cranberry-colored Mercedes but instead in a beat-up old Chrysler taxi driven by an old man full of complaints. Though I knew it was for the best. We were better off without that car; better, really, in any other car but that one, where the signs had turned bad.

I registered under another name and paid for the room in cash so there wouldn't be any questions. On the line where it said "Representing" I wrote "Ophthalmologist" and put "M.D." after the name. It had a nice look to it, even though it wasn't my name.

When we got to the room, which was in the back where I'd asked for it, I put Cheryl on one of the beds and Little Duke beside her so they'd sleep. She'd missed dinner, but it only meant she'd be hungry in the morning, when she could have anything she wanted. A few missed meals don't make a kid bad. I'd missed a lot of them myself and haven't turned out completely bad.

"Let's have some fried chicken," I said to Edna when she came out of the bathroom. "They have good fried chicken at Ramadas, and I noticed the buffet was still up. Cheryl can stay right here, where it's safe, till we're back."

"I guess I'm not hungry anymore," Edna said. She stood at the window staring out into the dark. I could see out the window past her some yellowish foggy glow in the sky. For a moment I thought it was the gold mine out in the distance lighting the night, though it was only the interstate.

"We could order up," I said. "Whatever you want. There's a menu on the phone book. You could just have a salad."

"You go ahead," she said. "I've lost my hungry spirit." She sat on the bed beside Cheryl and Little Duke and looked at them in a sweet way and put her hand on Cheryl's cheek just as if she'd had a fever. "Sweet little girl," she said. "Everybody loves you."

"What do you want to do?" I said. "I'd like to eat. Maybe I'll order up some chicken."

"Why don't you do that?" she said. "It's your favorite." And she smiled at me from the bed.

I sat on the other bed and dialed room service. I asked for chicken, garden salad, potato and a roll, plus a piece of hot apple pie and iced tea. I realized I hadn't eaten all day. When I put down the phone I saw that Edna was watching me, not in a hateful way or a loving way, just in a way that seemed to say she didn't understand something and was going to ask me about it.

"When did watching me get so entertaining?" I said and smiled at her. I was trying to be friendly. I knew how tired she must be. It was after nine o'clock.

"I was just thinking how much I hated being in a motel without a car that was mine to drive. Isn't that funny? I started feeling like that last night when that purple car wasn't mine. That purple car just gave me the willies, I guess, Earl."

"One of those cars *outside* is yours," I said. "Just stand right there and pick it out."

"I know," she said. "But that's different, isn't it?" She reached and got her blue Bailey hat, put it or her head, and set it way back like Dale Evans. She looked sweet. "I used to like to go to motels, you know," she said. "There's something secret about them and free—I was never paying, of course. But you felt safe from everything and free to do what you wanted because you'd made the decision to be there and paid that price, and all the rest was the good part. Fucking and everything, you know." She smiled at me in a good-natured way.

"Isn't that the way this is?" I was sitting on the bed, watching her, not knowing what to expect her to say next.

"I don't guess it is, Earl," she said and stared out the window. "I'm thirty-two and I'm going to have to give up on motels. I can't keep that fantasy going anymore."

"Don't you like this place?" I said and looked around at the room. I appreciated the modern paintings and the lowboy bureau and the big TV. I seemed like a plenty nice enough place to me, considering where we'd been.

"No, I don't," Edna said with real conviction. "There's no use in my getting mad at you about it. It isn't your fault. You do the best you can for everybody. But every trip teaches you something. And I've learned I need to give up on motels before some bad thing happens to me. I'm sorry."

"What does that mean?" I said, because I really didn't know what she had in mind to do, though I should've guessed.

"I guess I'll take that ticket you mentioned," she said, and got up and faced the window. "Tomorrow's soon enough. We haven't got a car to take me anyhow."

"Well, that's a fine thing," I said, sitting on the bed, feeling like I was in shock. I wanted to say something to her, to argue with her, but I couldn't think what to say that seemed right. I didn't want to be mad at her, but it made me mad.

"You've got a right to be mad at me, Earl," she said, "but I don't think you can really blame me." She turned around and faced me and sat on the windowsill, her hands on her knees. Someone knocked on the door, and I just yelled for them to set the tray down and put it on the bill.

"I guess I *do* blame you," I said, and I was angry. I thought about how I could've disappeared into that trailer community and hadn't, had come back to keep things going, had tried to take control of things for everybody when they looked bad.

"Don't. I wish you wouldn't," Edna said and smiled at me like she wanted me to hug her. "Anybody ought to have their choice in things if they can. Don't you believe that, Earl? Here I am out here in the desert where I don't know anything, in a stolen car, in a motel room under an assumed name, with no money of my own, a kid that's not mine, and the law after me. And I have a choice to get out of all of it by getting on a bus. What would you do? I know exactly what you'd do."

"You think you do," I said. But I didn't want to get into an argument about it and tell her all I could've done and didn't do. Because it wouldn't have done any good. When you get to the point of arguing, you're past the point of changing anybody's mind, even though it's supposed to be the other way, and maybe for some classes of people it is, just never mine.

Edna smiled at me and came across the room and put her arms around me where I was sitting on the bed. Cheryl rolled over and looked at us and smiled, then closed her eyes, and the room was quiet. I was beginning to think of Rock Springs in a way I knew I would always think of it, a lowdown city full of crimes and whores and disappointments, a place where a woman left me, instead of a place where I got things on the straight track once and for all, a place I saw a gold mine.

"Eat your chicken, Earl," Edna said. "Then we can go to bed. I'm tired, but I'd like to make love to you anyway. None of this is a matter of not loving you, you know that."

Sometime late in the night, after Edna was asleep, I got up and walked outside into the parking lot. It could've been anytime because there was still the light from the interstate frosting the low sky and the big red Ramada sign humming motionlessly in the night and no light at all in the east to indicate it might be morning. The lot was full of cars all nosed in, a couple of them with suitcases strapped to their roofs and their trunks weighed down with belongings the people were taking someplace, to a new home or a vacation resort in the mountains. I had laid in bed a long time after Edna was asleep, watching the Atlanta Braves on television, trying to get my mind off how I'd feel when I saw that bus pull away the next day, and how I'd feel when I turned around and there stood Cheryl and Little Duke and no one to see about them but me alone, and that the first thing I had to do was get hold of some automobile and get the plates switched, then get them some breakfast and get us all on the road to Florida, all in the space of probably two hours, since that Mercedes would certainly look less hid in the daytime than the night, and word travels fast. I've always taken care of Cheryl myself as long as I've had her with me. None of the women ever did. Most of them didn't even seem to like her, though they took care of me in a way so that I could take care of her. And I knew that once Edna left, all that was going to get harder. Though what I wanted most to do was not think about it just for a little while, try to let my mind go limp so it could be strong for the rest of what there was. I thought that the difference between a successful life and an unsuccessful one, between me at that moment and all the people who owned the cars that were nosed into their proper places in the lot, maybe between me and that woman out in the trailers by the gold mine, was how well you were able to put things like this out of your mind and not be bothered by them, and maybe, too, by how many troubles like this one you had to face in a lifetime. Through luck or design they had all faced fewer troubles, and by their own characters, they forgot them faster. And that's what I wanted for me. Fewer troubles, fewer memories of trouble.

I walked over to a car, a Pontiac with Ohio tags, one of the ones with bundles and suitcases strapped to the top and a lot more in the trunk, by the way it was riding. I looked inside the driver's window. There were maps and paperback books and sunglasses and the little plastic holders for cans that hang on the window wells. And in the back there were kids' toys and some pillows and a cat box with a cat sitting in it staring up at me like I was the face of the moon. It all looked familiar to me, the very same things I would have in my car if I had a car. Nothing seemed surprising, nothing different. Though I had a funny sensation at that moment and turned and looked up at the windows along the back of the motel. All were dark except two. Mine and another one. And I wondered, because it seemed funny, what would you think a man was doing if you saw him in the middle of the night looking in the windows of cars in the parking lot of the Ramada Inn? Would you think he was trying to get his head cleared? Would you think he was trying to get ready for a day when trouble would come down on him? Would you think his girlfriend was leaving him? Would you think he had a daughter? Would you think he was anybody like you?

🐬 🐬 🐬

## *Writing Exercises*

### INDIVIDUAL

1. Every family has one—a black sheep, an eccentric, somebody who is, well, a little different. For a page or two describe that person in your own family. It may well be someone others talk about and disapprove of, but whom you find intriguing. It could be that notorious aunt who used to party with Janis Joplin, or your nerdy uncle who also happens to be a self-made millionaire. Is there the germ of a story in the rumors, the envy, and the half-told tales? Or, perhaps the story grows out of the actual encounters you have had with this person.

2. Describe a character's bedroom using the setting to reveal the character. What does the furniture look like? What's on the walls? In the drawers? Underneath the bed? In the closet? Try to use all five senses. Finish your survey of the room by arriving at a single, especially important object that is connected to a secret your character has hidden from almost everyone. Tell us about the secret.

   (You may want to use this exercise as an extension of exercise #7 in chapter 2—the exercise based on Tim O'Brien's "The Things They Carried." Perhaps the object in the room is the one that one of those characters was carrying.)

3. Have you ever worked as a Bible salesman or waitress? Do you have a neighbor who is a postal worker? An aunt who is a stockbroker? A cousin who rides in rodeos? Make a list of the jobs you've had and about which you have second-hand knowledge—(much as you did in exercise 5, chapter 1).

   Now choose one of these jobs and assign it to a character. Using dialogue, description, action, and the main character's thoughts, write a scene that takes place when your character is at work. With whom does she work? What problems might come up that are job-related? Or, alternately, how might she go about talking through personal issues while on the job?

4. Write a scene in which two characters are having a hard time talking to each other. Perhaps one person is trying to teach someone else how to do something, but it's not going very well—there's some resistance on the part of the student, the teacher isn't a very good one, or the student doesn't want to let on that she already knows how to do this task. Maybe one character has to convey some news that is hard to convey. This news might be bad, even tragic, or just difficult ("I'd like to start seeing other people, but I hope we can still be friends."). Maybe your two characters just find themselves at odds—one just got a raise, the other just got fired. Maybe they're arguing, maybe they're flirting. In any case, let them talk.

5. Have a character write a letter to someone with whom she's had a misunderstanding or disagreement, but have her do this *without addressing the problem directly*. Perhaps she's being polite, perhaps she's trying to protect herself, but in any case, she dances around the main issue in the letter, which is not to say that she does not scold, warn, set straight, dress down, or otherwise tell the second character off.

   In the course of this letter, she will be telling us something about the second character, the one with whom she has the problem, but inadvertently, she will be telling us even more about herself—about her own prejudices, biases, insecurities, jealousies, and fears.

### COLLABORATIVE

6. Look through the want ads in a newspaper or at an online auction site such as eBay. Find a listing that intrigues you and bring it to class. Divide up into small groups. As a group, choose one of the ads the members of your group brought in and collectively imagine the story behind this ad. Who is the person selling this object and why is he getting rid of it? Have financial setbacks forced him to sell a prized possession? Or, is he just trying to clean out his deceased grandmother's house? Perhaps he's fencing stolen goods. Try as well to imagine the whole history (or what is sometimes called the provenance) of the object—not just how the seller came by it, but also who made it or found it originally, who has owned it along the way, where it has traveled, and so on. Someone will need to take notes.

   Now, exchange ads with a second group. Each group should now brainstorm a character who wants to buy this item. In fact, it should be a character who absolutely *must* buy it. Why does he need this item so desperately? Why must he outbid all others? What is he willing to spend? What will be the personal cost of bidding that high? What will he do with the object if he gets it? What might he be willing to do if someone outbids him?

# 4

# THE FLESH MADE WORD
## *Characterization, Part II*

## The Indirect Methods of Character Presentation

There are two methods of indirect characterization—indirect in the sense that, rather than being presented directly to our sight and hearing, the character is described in summarized, abstract, or judgmental terms by either the author or another speaker. Both of these methods are forms of "telling," and both may shape our overall view.

### AUTHORIAL INTERPRETATION

The first indirect method of presenting a character is authorial interpretation— "telling" us the character's background, motives, values, virtues, and the like.

The advantages of this indirect method are enormous, for its use leaves you free to move in time and space; to know anything you choose to know whether the character knows it or not; and, godlike, to tell us what we are to feel. The indirect method allows you to convey a great deal of information in a short time.

> The most excellent Marquis of Lumbria lived with his two daughters, Caroline, the elder, and Luisa; and his second wife, Doa Vicenta, a woman with a dull brain, who, when she was not sleeping, was complaining of everything, especially the noise . . .
> The Marquis of Lumbria had no male children, and this was the most painful thorn in his existence. Shortly after having become a widower, he had married Doa Vicenta, his present wife, in order to have a son, but she proved sterile.
> The Marquis' life was as monotonous and as quotidian, as unchanging and regular, as the murmur of the river below the cliff or as the liturgic services in the cathedral.
>
> Miguel De Unamuno, *The Marquis of Lumbria*

The disadvantage of this indirect method is that it distances the reader as all generalizations and abstractions tend to do. Indeed, in the passage above, it may well be part of Unamuno's purpose to convey the "monotonous" and "quotidian" quality of the Marquis's life by this summarized and distanced rehearsal of facts, motives, and judgments. Nearly every author will use the indirect method occasionally, and you may find it useful when you want to cover the exposition quickly. However, direct presentation of the characters—showing them in action and allowing readers to draw their own conclusions—is much more likely to please a modern audience.

### INTERPRETATION BY ANOTHER CHARACTER

A character may also be presented through the opinions of other characters, which may be considered a second indirect method. When this method is employed, however, the second character must give his or her opinions in speech, action, or thought. In the process, the observing character is inevitably also characterized. Whether we accept the opinion depends on what we think of that character as he or she is thus directly characterized. In this scene from Jane Austen's *Mansfield Park*, for example, the busybody Mrs. Norris gives her opinion of the heroine.

> ". . . there is something about Fanny, I have often observed it before,—she likes to go her own way to work; she does not like to be dictated to; she takes her own independent walk whenever she can; she certainly has a little spirit of secrecy, and independence, and nonsense, about her, which I would advise her to get the better of."
> As a general reflection on Fanny, Sir Thomas thought nothing could be more unjust, though he had been so lately expressing the same sentiments himself, and he tried to turn the conversation, tried repeatedly before he could succeed.

Here Mrs. Norris's opinion is directly presented in her speech and Sir Thomas's in his thoughts, each of them being characterized in the process. It is left to the reader to decide (without much difficulty) whose view of Fanny is the more reliable.

Similarly, in Clyde Edgerton's contemporary novel *Raney*, the opposing outlooks of a newlywed "odd couple" are dramatized through their contradictory characterizations of a lonely and preoccupied neighbor.

> "Charles," I said, "you'd rather sit down back there in the bedroom and read a book than talk to a live human being like Mrs. Moss."
>
> "I'm not so sure I agree with your assessment of Mrs. Moss," he says.
>
> "What do you mean by that?"
>
> "It means I have had one conversation with Mrs. Moss and one conversation with Mrs. Moss is enough. I am not interested in her falling off the commode and having a hairline rib fracture. I am not interested in her cataract operation. Mrs. Moss is unable to comprehend anything beyond her own problems and you know it."
>
> . . . . Mrs. Moss does talk about herself right much. She'll come over in her apron to borrow a cup of something. One Sunday she borrowed a cup of flour after I saw a bag of Red Band in her shopping cart—on top—at the Piggly Wiggly on Saturday. But the way I figure it is this: Mrs. Moss has had a lifetime of things happening to her and all along she's had these other people—her husband and children—to watch these things happen. So she didn't ever have to *tell* anybody. Then her husband died and her children left and there was nobody around to watch these things happen anymore, so she don't have any way to share *except* to tell. So the thing to do is listen. It's easy to cut her off when she just goes on and on. You just start talking about something else. She follows right along.
>
> "She's given me several pints of preserves and one quart of chow-chow," I said. "She can comprehend that."
>
> "Raney, that has nothing to do with the fact that she is senile and self-centered. There are old people who aren't self-centered, you know."
>
> "Charles, she also showed me how to keep applesauce from turning brown in the jar, and she's going to give me some cactus seeds and she said she'd help me dig up a circle and plant them. And give me some big rocks to go around that. If she's so self-centered, why is she giving me preserves and chow-chow and seeds?"
>
> "Because it's a habit. A life-long habit. If you were Atilla the Hun she'd give you preserves and chow-chow and seeds."
>
> "Charles. Sometimes I wonder about your heart."

Set halfway through the novel, this argument confirms the reader's view of Charles as an urban liberal who is broad-minded in abstract principles yet impatient with actual people, while Raney, the small-town narrator, tends to be narrow-minded in the abstract but compassionate with individuals, at least those long-familiar to her. What is crystallized about this couple through their argument is even more important than what is learned about the incidental character of the neighbor.

## Conflict Between Methods of Presentation

The conflict that is the essence of character can be effectively (and, if it doesn't come automatically, quite consciously) achieved in fiction by producing a conflict between methods of presentation. A character can be directly revealed to us through *appearance*, *dialogue*, *action*, and *thought*. If you set one of these methods (most frequently *thought*) at odds with the others, then dramatic tension will be produced. Imagine, for example, a character who is impeccably and expensively dressed, who speaks eloquently, who acts decisively, and whose mind is revealed to us as full of order and determination. He is inevitably a flat character. But suppose that he is impeccable, eloquent, decisive, and that his mind is a mess of wounds and panic. He is at once interesting.

Here is the opening passage of Saul Bellow's *Seize the Day*, in which appearance and action are blatantly at odds with thought. Notice that it is the tension between suppressed thought and what is expressed through appearance and action that produces the rich character conflict.

> When it came to concealing his troubles, Tommy Wilhelm was not less capable than the next fellow. So at least he thought, and there was a certain amount of evidence to back him up. He had once been an actor—no, not quite, an extra—and he knew what acting should be. Also, he was smoking a cigar, and when a man is smoking a cigar, wearing a hat, he has an advantage: it is harder to find out how he feels. He came from the twenty-third floor down to the lobby on the mezzanine to collect his mail before breakfast, and he believed—he hoped—he looked passably well: doing all right.

Tommy Wilhelm is externally composed but mentally anxious, mainly anxious about looking externally composed. By contrast, in the next passage, from Samuel Beckett's *Murphy*, the landlady, Miss Carridge, who has just discovered a suicide in one of her rooms, is anxious in speech and action but is mentally composed.

> She came speeding down the stairs one step at a time, her feet going so fast that she seemed on little caterpillar wheels, her forefinger sawing horribly at her craw for Celia's benefit. She slithered to a stop on the steps of the house and screeched for the police. She capered in the street like a consternated ostrich, with strangled distracted rushes towards the York and Caledonian Roads in turn, embarrassingly equidistant from the tragedy, tossing up her arms, undoing the good work of the samples, screeching for police aid. Her mind was so collected that she saw clearly the impropriety of letting it appear so.

In this third example, from Zora Neale Hurston's "The Gilded Six-Bits," it is the very intensity of the internal that both prevents and dictates action:

> Missie May was sobbing. Wails of weeping without words. Joe stood, and after a while he found out that he had something in his hand. And then he stood and

felt without thinking and without seeing with his natural eyes. Missie May kept on crying and Joe kept on feeling so much, and not knowing what to do with all his feelings, he put Slemmon's watch charm in his pants pocket and took a good laugh and went to bed.

I have said that thought is most frequently at odds with one or more of the other three methods of direct presentation—reflecting the difficulty we have expressing ourselves openly or accurately—but this is by no means always the case. A character may be successfully, calmly, even eloquently expressing fine opinions while betraying himself by pulling at his ear, or herself by crushing her skirt. Captain Queeg of Herman Wouk's *The Caine Mutiny* is a memorable example of this, maniacally clicking the steel balls in his hand as he defends his disciplinary code.

Often we are not privy to the thoughts of a character at all, so that the conflicts must be expressed in a contradiction between the external methods of direct presentation, appearance, speech, and action. Character A may be speaking floods of friendly welcome, betraying his real feeling by backing steadily away. Character B, dressed in taffeta ruffles and ostrich plumes, may wail pityingly over the miseries of the poor. Notice that the notion of "betraying oneself" is important here: We're more likely to believe the evidence unintentionally given than deliberate expression.

A classic example of such self-betrayal is found in Leo Tolstoy's *The Death of Ivan Ilyich,* where the widow confronts her husband's colleague at the funeral.

> . . . Noticing that the table was endangered by his cigarette ash, she immediately passed him an ashtray, saying as she did so: "I consider it an affectation to say that my grief prevents my attending to practical affairs. On the contrary, if anything can—I won't say console me, but—distract me, it is seeing to everything concerning him." She again took out her handkerchief as if preparing to cry, but suddenly, as if mastering her feeling, she shook herself and began to speak calmly. "But there is something I want to talk to you about."

It is no surprise either to the colleague or to us that Praskovya Federovna wants to talk about getting money.

Finally, character conflict can be expressed by creating a tension between the direct and the indirect methods of presentation, and this is a source of much irony. We are presented with a judgment of the character, who then speaks, appears, acts, or thinks in contradiction of this judgment, as in the opening of this story by Tobias Wolff:

> . . . Riley was flashy, so flashy that even his bright red hair seemed an affectation, and it was said that he'd had affairs with some of his students. Brooke did not as a rule give credit to those rumors, but in Riley's case he was willing to make an exception. He had once seen a very pretty girl leaving Riley's office in tears. Students did at times cry over bad grades, but this girl's misery was something else: it looked more like a broken heart than a C–.

They belonged to the same parish, and Brooke, who liked to sit in the back of the church, often saw Riley at Mass with his wife and their four red-haired children. Seeing the children and their father together, like a row of burning candles, always made Brooke feel more kindly toward Riley. Then Riley would turn to his wife or look around, and the handlebars of his unnecessarily large moustache would come into view, and Brooke would dislike him again.

"An Episode in the Life of Professor Brooke"

Given the behavior observed by Brooke, we may begin to share his suspicions, only to see the evidence of Riley at church with his seemingly unified family. When Brooke's dislike returns with a glimpse of the flamboyant moustache, we may well doubt Brooke's objectivity in judging his colleague, whom he dislikes even for the natural color of his hair and later for his "powder-blue suits." In fact, as the story progresses, it is the judgmental Brooke who betrays his own wife, while Riley does nothing more incriminating than rating the faces of women they pass on the road.

## THE CHARACTER JOURNAL

Whether indirect, direct, or, most commonly, both direct and indirect methods are used, a full and rich fictional character will need to be both credible and complex, will show purpose (and that purpose will reveal something about his or her morality), and in the course of the story will undergo some, perhaps small but nonetheless significant, change. In order to explore these elements of character, your journal can be an invaluable help.

As a writer you may have the lucky, facile sort of imagination to which characters spring full-blown, complete with gestures, histories, and passions. Or it may be that you need to explore in order to exploit, to draw your characters out gradually and coax them into being. That can be lucky, too.

For either kind of writer, but especially the latter, the journal lets you coax and explore without committing yourself to anything or anyone. It allows you to know everything about your character whether you use it or not. Before you put a character in a story, know how well that character sleeps. Know what the character eats for lunch and how much it matters, what he buys and how the bills get paid, how she spends what we call working hours. Know how your character would prefer to spend evenings and weekends and why such plans get thwarted. Know what memories the character has of pets and parents, cities, snow, or school. You may end up using none of this information in the brief segment of your character's life that is your plot, but knowing it may teach you how your bookperson taps a pencil or twists a lock of hair, and when and why. When you know these things, you will have taken a step past invention toward the moment of imagination in which you become your character, live in his or her skin, and produce an action that, for the reader, rings universally true.

Use the journal to note your observations of people. Try writing down your impressions of the library assistant who annoys you or the loner at the bar who intrigues you. Try to capture a gesture or the messages that physical features and clothing send. Invent a reason for that harshness or that loneliness; invent a past.

Then try taking the character out of context and setting her or him in another. Get your character in trouble, and you may be on your way to a short story.

It is interesting and relevant that actors schooled in the Stanislavski Method write biographies of the characters they must play. Adherents of "The Method" believe that in the process of inventing a dramatic character's past, the actor will find points of emotional contact with that role and so know how to make the motives and actions prescribed by the script natural and genuine. As a writer you can also use "The Method," imagining much that you will not bring specifically to "the script" but that will enrich your sense of that character until you know with absolute certainty how he or she will move, act, react, and speak.

THE OLDER WE GET, THE MORE . . . you realize there's a whole range of things that you will never do, of things and people you will never be. As life becomes more and more limiting, there is something wonderful about being able to get inside the skin of people unlike yourself.

Lee Smith

### THE UNIVERSAL PARADOX

Though critics often praise literature for exhibiting characteristics of the *individual*, the *typical*, and the *universal* all at the same time, I don't think this is of much use to the practicing writer. For though you may labor to create an individual character, and you may make that character a credible example of type, I don't think you can *set out to be* "universal."

It is true, I believe, that if literature has any social justification or use it is that readers can identify the common humanity in, and can therefore identify with, characters vastly different from themselves in century, geography, gender, culture, and beliefs; and that this enhances the scope of the reader's sympathy. It is also true that if the fiction does not have this universal quality—if a middle-class American male author creates as protagonist a middle-class American male with whom only middle-class American male readers can sympathize—then the fiction is thin and small. William Sloane voices the "frightening" demand of the reader in his book *The Craft of Writing*: "Tell me about me. I want to be more alive. Give me me." Yet, paradoxically, if you aim for the universal, you're likely to achieve the pompous, whereas if you aim for the individual, you're more apt to create a character in whom a reader can see aspects of himself or herself.

Imagine this scene: The child chases a ball into the street. The tires screech, the bumper thuds, the blood geysers into the air, the pulp of the small body lies inert on the asphalt. How would a bystander react? (Is it universal?) How would a passing doctor react? (Is it typical?) How would Dr. Henry Lowes, just coming from the maternity ward of his own hospital, where his wife has had her fourth miscarriage, react? (Is it individual?) Each question narrows the range of convincing reaction, and as a writer you want to convince in each range. If you succeed in the third, you are likely to have succeeded in the other two.

My advice then is to labor in the range of the particular. If you aim for a universal character you may end up with a vague or dull or windy one. On the other hand, if you set out to write a typical character you're likely to produce a caricature, because people are typical only in the generalized qualities that lump them together. *Typical* is the most provincial adjective in a writer's vocabulary, signaling that you're writing only for those who share your assumptions. A "typical" schoolgirl in Dar es Salaam is a very different type from one in San Francisco. Furthermore, every person is typical of many things successively or simultaneously. She may be in turn a "typical" school-girl, bride, divorcée, and feminist. He may be at one and the same time a "typical" New Yorker, math professor, doting father, and adulterer. It is in the confrontation and convolution of types that much of our individuality is produced.

Writing in generalities and typicalities is akin to bigotry—we see only what's alike about people, not what's unique. When effective, a description of type blames the charac-ter for the failure to individualize, and if an author sets out deliberately to produce types rather than individuals, then that author invariably wants to condemn or ridicule those types. Joyce Carol Oates illustrates the technique in "How I Contemplated the World from the Detroit House of Corrections and Began My Life Over Again":

> George, Clyde G. 240 Sioux. A manufacturer's representative; children, a dog, a wife. Georgian with the usual columns. You think of the White House, then of Thomas Jefferson, then your mind goes blank on the white pillars and you think of nothing.

Mark Helprin, in "The Schreuderspitze," takes the ridicule of type to comic extreme:

> In Munich are many men who look like weasels. Whether by genetic accident, meticulous crossbreeding, an early and puzzling migration, coincidence, or a reason that we do not know, they exist in great numbers. Remarkably, they accentuate this unfortunate tendency by wearing mustaches, Alpine hats, and tweed. A man who resembles a rodent should never wear tweed.

This is not to say that all characters must be fully drawn or *"round."* Flat characters—who exist only to exhibit a function or a single characteristic—are use-ful and necessary. Eric Bentley suggests in *The Life of the Drama* that if a messenger's function in a play is to deliver his message, it would be very tedious to stop and learn about his psychology. The same is true in fiction: in Margaret Atwood's "Happy Endings" (near the end of chapter 7), the character of James, "who has a motorcycle and a fabulous record collection" exists for no purpose other than to make Mary's adulterous lover John jealous, and we do not want to hear about his adventures "away on his motorcycle, being free." Nevertheless, onstage even a flat character has a face and a costume, and in fiction detail can give even a flat character a few angles and contours. The servant classes in the novels of Henry James are notoriously absent as individuals because they exist only in their functions (*that excellent creature had already assembled the baggage*, etc.), whereas Charles Dickens, who peoples his novels with dozens of flat characters, brings even these alive in detail.

> And Mrs. Miff, the wheezy little pew opener—a mighty dry old lady, sparely dressed, with not an inch of fullness anywhere about her—is also here.

> *Dombey and Son*

To borrow a notion from George Orwell's *Animal Farm*, all good characters are created round, but some are created rounder than others.

## Credibility

Though you aim at individuality and not typicality in characters, your characters will exhibit typicality in the sense of "appropriateness." A Baptist Texan behaves differently from an Italian nun; a rural schoolboy behaves differently from a professor emeritus at Harvard. If you are to succeed in creating an individual character, particular and alive, you will also inevitably know what is appropriate to that sort of person and will let us know as much as we need to know to feel the appropriateness of the behavior.

For instance, we need to know soon, preferably in the first paragraph, the character's gender, age, and race or nationality. We need to know something of his or her class, period, and region. A profession (or the clear lack of it) and a marital status help, too. *Almost any reader can identify with almost any character; what no reader can identify with is confusion.* When some or several of the fundamentals of type are withheld from us—when we don't know whether we're dealing with a man or a woman, an adult or a child—the process of identifying cannot begin, and the story is slow to move us.

None of the information need come as information; it can be implied by appearance, tone, action, or detail. In the next example Barbara Kingsolver plunges the character of Leah Price and her family into a new life for which they are clearly ill-prepared, practically and politically. Although they are focused on their destination, by the end of the first two paragraphs, we know a lot about the family and the culture they carry with them.

> We came from Bethlehem, Georgia, bearing Betty Crocker cake mixes into the jungle. My sisters and I were all counting on having one birthday apiece during our twelve-month mission. "And heaven knows," our mother predicted, "they won't have Betty Crocker in the Congo."
>
> "Where we are headed, there will *be* no buyers and sellers at all," my father corrected. His tone implied that Mother failed to grasp our mission, and that her concern with Betty Crocker confederated her with the coin-jingling sinners who vexed Jesus till he pitched a fit and threw them out of the church. "Where we are headed," he said, to make things perfectly clear, "not so much as a Piggly Wiggly." Evidently Father saw this as a point in the Congo's favor. I got the most spectacular chills, just from trying to imagine.

> *The Poisonwood Bible*

We know that the family is Southern, not only because their town of origin is named, but also from expressions such as "vexed" and "pitched a fit," as well as from mention of the Piggly Wiggly grocery chain. Not only do we know that they are missionaries, but further, we hear the father's sermonizing voice through his repetition of the phrase "where we are headed," preaching that is echoed in the implication that the mother is "confederated" with "the coin-jingling sinners." We also hear hints of the harsh pleasure the father will take in the family's hardship. The Betty Crocker mixes tell us that the women are trying to hang on to a little bit of home comfort, yet at the same time they are taking all-American '50s culture to a place where it is irrelevant and ultimately destructive—indeed, the cake mixes are quickly ruined by jungle humidity. And although we don't know the exact age of the narrator, she seems to be a teenager old enough to hear the subtext of her father's reprovals and to relish the false sophistication of phrases like "the most spectacular chills" and "imagine." In a very short space, Kingsolver has sketched the family, their dangerous ignorance, and the father's divisive, single-minded determination.

The following passage is an even more striking example of implied information.

> Every time the same story. Your Barbie is roommates with my Barbie, and my Barbie's boyfriend comes over and your Barbie steals him, okay? Kiss kiss kiss. Then the two Barbies fight. You dumbbell! He's mine. Oh no he's not, you stinky! Only Ken's invisible, right? Because we don't have money for a stupid-looking boy doll when we'd both rather ask for a new Barbie outfit next Christmas. We have to make do with your mean-eyed Barbie and my bubblehead Barbie and our one outfit apiece not including the sock dress.
>
> Sandra Cisneros, "Barbie-Q"

Here there is no description whatever of the characters, and no direct reference to them except for the designations *you* and *I*. What do we nevertheless know about their gender, their age, their financial status, the period in which they live, their personalities, their attitudes, their relationship, the narrator's emotions?

Students of writing are sometimes daunted by the need to give so much information immediately. The thing to remember is that credibility consists in the combination of appropriateness and specificity. The trick is to find telling details that will convey the information while our attention remains on the desire or emotion of the character. Nobody wants to read a story that begins:

> She was a twenty-eight-year-old suburban American woman, relatively affluent, who was extremely distressed when her husband, Peter, left her.

But most of that, and much more besides, could be contained in a few details.

> After Peter left with the VCR, the microwave, and the key to the garage, she went down to the kitchen and ate three jars of peanut butter without tasting a single spoonful.

I don't mean to imply that it is necessarily easy to signal the essentials of type immediately. It would be truer to say that it is necessary and hard. The opening paragraph of a story is its second strongest statement (the final paragraph is the strongest) and sets the tone for all that follows. If the right words don't come to you as a gift, you may have to sit sifting and discarding the inadequate ones for a long time before you achieve both clarity and interest.

## Purpose

Your character's purpose—that is, the desire that impels her or him to action—will determine our degree of identification and sympathy on the one hand, or judgment on the other.

Aristotle, in *The Poetics,* says that "there will be an element of character if what a person says or does reveals a certain moral purpose; and a good element of character, if the purpose so revealed is good." It might seem that the antiheroes, brutes, hoods, whores, perverts, and bums who people modern literature do very little in the way of revealing good moral purpose. The history of Western literature shows a movement downward and inward: downward through society from royalty to gentry to the middle classes to the lower classes to the dropouts; inward from heroic action to social drama to individual consciousness to the subconscious to the unconscious. What has remained consistent is that, for the time spent in an author's world, we understand and identify with the protagonist or protagonists, we "see their point of view"; and the fiction succeeds largely because we are willing to grant them a goodness that we would not grant them in life. While you read, you expand your mental scope by identifying with, temporarily "becoming," a character, borrowing a different mind. Fiction, as critic Laurence Gonzales says of rock music, "lets you wander around in someone else's hell for a while and see how similar it is to your own."

Obviously we don't identify with all characters, and those whose purpose is revealed as ambiguous or evil will invite varying degrees of judgment. When the Joyce Carol Oates' story "Where Are You Going, Where Have You Been?" from chapter 2 Arnold Friend is described as "stiffly relaxed," with a "slippery friendly smile" and a series of familiar styles that "did not come together," we are immediately skeptical of him; because we suspect his purpose toward Connie, we pass judgment on his fundamental character.

## Complexity

If the characters of your story are credible through being appropriate and individual, and if they invite identification or judgment through a sense of their purpose, they also need to be complex. They need to exhibit enough conflict and contradiction that we can recognize them as belonging to the contradictory human race; and they should exhibit a range of possibility so that a shift of power in the plot can also produce a shift of purpose or morality. That is, they need to be capable of change.

Conflict is at the core of character as it is of plot. If plot begins with trouble, then character begins with a person in trouble; and trouble most dramatically occurs because we all have traits, tendencies, and desires that are at war, not simply with the world and other people, but with other traits, tendencies, and desires of our own. All of us probably know a woman of the strong, striding, independent sort, attractive only to men who like a strong and striding woman. And when she falls in love? She becomes a clinging sentimentalist. All of us know a father who is generous, patient, and dependable. And when the children cross the line? He smashes crockery and wields a strap. All of us are gentle, violent; logical, schmaltzy; tough, squeamish; lusty, prudish; sloppy, meticulous; energetic, apathetic; manic, depressive. Perhaps you don't fit that particular list of contradictions, but you are sufficiently in conflict with yourself that as an author you have characters enough in your own psyche to people the work of a lifetime if you will identify, heighten, and dramatize these conflicts within character, which Aristotle called "consistent inconsistencies."

UNLIKE EVEN THOSE CLOSEST TO US IN REAL LIFE—our spouses, our lovers, our kin, whom we can never know completely—fictional people retain only as much privacy and secrecy as those who create them decide to let them keep.

Doug Bauer

If you think of the great characters of literature, you can see how inner contradiction—consistent inconsistency—brings each to a crucial dilemma. Hamlet is a strong and decisive man who procrastinates. Dorothea Brooke of *Middlemarch* is an idealistic and intellectual young woman, a total fool in matters of the heart. Ernest Hemingway's Francis Macomber wants to test his manhood against a lion and cannot face the test. Here, in a moment of crisis from *Mom Kills Self and Kids*, Alan Saperstein reveals with great economy the consistent inconsistency of his protagonist, a man who hadn't much time for his family until their absence makes clear how dependent he has been on them.

When I arrived home from work I found my wife had killed our two sons and taken her own life.
    I uncovered a blast of foul, black steam from the pot on the stove and said, "Hi, hon, what's for dinner?" But she did not laugh. She did not bounce to her feet and pirouette into the kitchen to greet me. My little one didn't race into my legs and ask what I brought him. The seven-year-old didn't automatically beg me to play a game knowing my answer would be a tired, "Maybe later."

In "The Self as Source," Cheryl Moskowitz proposes a fiction technique that relies specifically on identifying conflicting parts of the writer's personality. She points to Robert Louis Stevenson's *The Strange Case of Dr. Jekyll and Mr. Hyde* as a fairly blatant model for such fiction, and quotes from Dr. Jekyll:

. . . I thus drew steadily nearer to that truth . . . that man is not truly one, but two. I say two, because the state of my own knowledge does not pass beyond that point. . . . I hazard the guess that man will ultimately be known for a mere polity of multifarious, incongruous and independent denizens.

Moskowitz suggests "character imaging," making lists of the qualities, images, and actions that describe such incongruities in the writer's personality. Here is a sample list from a student exercise:

| Elegant | Vulgar |
|---|---|
| silk scarf to the knees | sequins on a fringed cowhide vest |
| still | laughing |
| frowns at library noise | hands out candy |
| startled gazelle | slobbering puppy |
| Waterford crystal | souvenir plate made in Mexico |
| a single white rosebud | two dozen overblown red roses |
| walks alone into the woods | throws a costume party |

At this point the contradictory lists could be transformed into two separate, named characters. Then, where might they meet? In what situation might they find themselves? How would a confrontation between these two play out?

It is, of course, impossible to know to what degree Shakespeare, Eliot, Hemingway, or Saperstein self-consciously used their own inner contradictions to build and dramatize their characters. An author works not only from his or her own personality but also from observation and imagination, and I fully believe that you are working at full stretch only when all three are involved. The question of autobiography is a complicated one, and as writer you frequently won't know yourself how much you have experienced, how much you have observed, and how much you have invented. Actress Mildred Dunnock once observed that drama is possible "because people can feel what they haven't experienced," an observation that surely extends to the writing and reading of fiction. If you push yourself to write at the outer edge of your emotional experience—what you can imagine yourself doing, even if you might not risk such actions in life—then all your writing is autobiographical in the sense that it must have passed through your mind.

## Change

In a story, as opposed to a sketch or anecdote, says poet and novelist Al Young, "stuff happens, people *change*, situations *change*, there is no standing still." Certainly the easiest way to check the plot of your story is to ask, "Does my character change from opening to end? Do I give the sense that his or her life will never be quite the same again?"

Often the notion of change is mistaken by new writers to mean change that is abrupt and contrived, from Scrooge to St. Nick—yet this rarely happens in life or in realistic fiction. Rather, change can be as subtle as a step in a new direction, a slight shift in belief, or a willingness to question a rigid view or recognize unseen value in a person or situation. Our society's belief in the power of change is reaffirmed each New Year's Day, and one of the vicarious pleasures fiction offers is the chance to experience the workings of change within a character's consciousness.

John L'Heureux offers a psychological framework for viewing change: "A story is about a single moment in a character's life when a definitive choice is made, after which nothing is the same." The moment in "Where Are You Going, Where Have You Been?" when Connie hears the implied threat to her family and goes out to the waiting Arnold Friend is a moment of choice that leads to life-or-death change.

The "integrity" of fiction is a concept John L'Heureux emphasizes, for in good fiction incidents lead to a single moment when the main character makes a decision that regards—and determines—his or her essential integrity, after which nothing will ever be the same. He uses integrity in its primal sense of "wholeness," since at the moment of choice the character elects to live either more in harmony or more at odds with his or her best self. The decision made in that moment affects the character's relationship with the self forever.

"What we do determines what we become," fiction writer Nancy Huddleston Packer affirms. "Because character and event are interlocked, stories don't end in accident; rather, the consequences of the story come from the character who determines events. Our decisions make us who we are forever afterward."

## Reinventing Character

Here are a few others ways you can try to make a character fresh and forceful in your mind before you start writing.

If the character is based on you or on someone you know, drastically alter the model in some external way: Change blond hair to dark or thin to thick; imagine the character as the opposite gender or radically alter the setting in which the character must act. Part of the trouble with writing directly from experience is that you know too much about it—what "they" did, how you felt. Under such circumstances it's hard to know whether everything in your mind is getting onto the page. An external alteration forces you to re-see, and so to see more clearly, and so to convey more clearly what you see.

On the other hand, if the character is created primarily out of your observation or invention and is unlike yourself, try to find an internal area that you have in common with the character. If you are a blond, slender young woman and the character is a fat, balding man, do you nevertheless have in common a love of French *haute cuisine*? Are you haunted by the same sort of dream? Do you share a fear of public performance or a susceptibility to fine weather?

I can illustrate these techniques only from my own writing, because I am the only author whose self I can identify with any certainty in fictional characters. In one novel, I wanted to open with a scene in which the heroine buries a dog in her backyard.

I had recently buried a dog in my backyard. I wanted to capture the look and feel of red Georgia earth at sunrise, the tangle of roots, and the smell of decay. But I knew that I was likely to make the experience too much my own, too little my character's. I set about to make her not-me. I have long dark hair and an ordinary figure, and I tend to live in Levi's. I made Shaara Soole

> . . . big boned, lanky, melon-breasted, her best feature was a head of rusty barbed-wire hair that she tried to control with a wardrobe of scarves and head-band things. Like most costume designers, she dressed with more originality than taste, usually on the Oriental or Polynesian side, sometimes with voluminous loops of thong and matte metal over an ordinary shirt. This was somewhat eccentric in Hubbard, Georgia, but Shaara may have been oblivious to her eccentricity, being so concerned to keep her essential foolishness in check.

Having thus separated Shaara from myself, I was able to bury the dog with her arms and through her eyes rather than my own. On the other hand, a few pages later I was faced with the problem of introducing her ex-husband, Boyd Soole. I had voluminous notes on this character, and I knew that he was almost totally unlike me. A man, to begin with, and a huge man, a theater director with a natural air of power and author-ity and very little interest in domestic affairs. I sat at my desk for several days, unable to make him move convincingly. My desk oppressed me, and I felt trapped and uncom-fortable, my work thwarted, it seemed, by the very chair and typewriter. Then it oc-curred to me that Boyd was *also* sitting at a desk trying to work.

> The dresser at the Travelodge was some four inches too narrow and three inches too low. If he set his feet on the floor his knees would sit free of the drawer but would be awkwardly constricted left and right. If he crossed his legs, he could hook his right foot comfortably outside the left of the kneehole but would bruise his thigh at the drawer. If he shifted back he was placed at an awkward distance from his script. And in this position he could not work.

This passage did not instantly allow me to live inside Boyd Soole's skin, nor did it solve all my problems with his characterization. But it did let me get on with the story, and it gave me a flash of sympathy for him that later grew much more pro-found than I had foreseen.

Often, identifying what you have in common with the feelings of your character will also clarify what is important about her or him to the story—why, in fact, you chose to write about such a person at all. Even if the character is presented as a vil-lain, you have something in common, and I don't mean something forgivable. If he or she is intolerably vain, watch your own private gestures in front of the mirror and borrow them. If he or she is cruel, remember how you enjoyed hooking the worm.

There is no absolute requirement that a writer need behave honestly in life; there is absolutely no such requirement. Great writers have been public hams, domestic dictators, emotional con artists, and Nazis. What is required for fine writing is hon-esty on the page—not how the characters *should* react at the funeral, the surprise party, in bed, but how they *would*. In order to develop such honesty of observation on the page, you must begin with a willing honesty of observation (though mercifully not of behavior) in yourself.

## Creating a Group or Crowd

Sometimes it is necessary to introduce several or many people in the same scene, and this needn't present a problem, because the principle is pretty much the same in every case, and is the same as in film: pan, then close-up. In other words, give us a sense of the larger scene first, then a few details to characterize individuals. If you begin by concentrating too long on one character only, we will tend to see that person as being alone.

> Herm peered through the windshield and eased his foot up off the gas. Damn, he thought, it's not going to let up. The yellow lights made slick pools along the shoulder. He fiddled with the dial, but all he could get was blabber-radio and somebody selling vinyl siding. His back ached. His eyes itched. A hundred and forty miles to go.

At this point, if you introduce a wife, two children, and a dog to the scene, we will have to make rapid and uncomfortable adjustments in our mental picture. Better to begin with the whole carful and then narrow it down to Herm:

> Herm peered through the windshield and glanced over at Inga, who was snoring lightly against the window. The kids hadn't made a sound for about half an hour either, and only Cheza was wheezing dogbreath now and then on the back of his neck. He eased his foot up off the gas. Damn, he thought . . .

If the action involves several characters who therefore need to be seen right away, introduce them as a group and then give us a few characterizing details:

> All the same there were four guns on him before he'd focused enough to count. "Peace," he said again. There were three old ones, one of them barely bigger than a midget, and the young one was fat. One of the old ones had on a uniform jacket much too big for him, hanging open on his slack chest. The young one spun a string of their language at him.

If the need is to create a crowd, it is still important, having established that there *is* a crowd, to give us a few details. We will believe more thoroughly in large numbers of people if you offer example images for us. Here, for example, is a passage from *Underworld* in which Don LeLillo introduces two parts of a crowd, the boys who are waiting to sneak into the ballpark and the last legitimate arrivals:

> . . . they have found one another by means of slidy looks that detect the fellow foolhard and here they stand, black kids and white kids up from the subways or

off the local Harlem streets, bandidos, fifteen in all, and according to topical legends maybe four will get through for every one that's caught.

They are waiting nervously for the ticket holders to clear the turnstiles, the last loose cluster of fans, the stragglers and loiterers. They watch the late-arriving taxis from downtown and the brilliantined men stepping dapper to the windows, policy bankers and supper club swells and Broadway hotshots, high aura'd, picking lint off their sleeves.

## *Character: A Summary*

It may be helpful to summarize the practical advice on character that this chapter and the previous chapter contain.

1. Be aware of the four methods of direct character presentation–appearance, speech, action, and thought—and of the indirect methods, authorial interpretation and the presentation by another character.

2. Reveal the character's conflicts by presenting attributes in at least one of these methods that contrast with attributes you present in the others.

3. Focus sharply on how the character looks, on what she or he wears and owns, and on how she or he moves. Let us focus on it, too.

4. Examine the character's speech to make sure it does more than convey information. Does it characterize, accomplish exposition, and reveal emotion, intent, or change? Does it advance the conflict through "no" dialogue? Speak it aloud: Does it "say"?

5. Build action by making your characters discover and decide. Make sure that what happens is action and not mere event or movement, that is, that it contains the possibility for human change.

6. Use your journal to explore and build ideas for characters.

7. Know the details of your character's life: what he or she does during every part of the day, thinks about, remembers, wants, likes and dislikes, eats, says, means.

8. Know all the influences that go into the making of your character's type: age, gender, race, nationality, marital status, region, education, religion, profession.

9. Know what your character wants, both generally out of life, and specifically in the context of the story. Keeping that desire in mind, "think backward" with the character to decide what he or she would do in any situation presented.

10. Identify, heighten, and dramatize consistent inconsistencies. What does your character want that is at odds with whatever else the character wants? What patterns of thought and behavior work against the primary goal?

11. If the character is based on a real model, including yourself, make a dramatic external alteration.

12. If the character is imaginary or alien to you, identify a mental or emotional point of contact.

# A Visit of Charity

## EUDORA WELTY

It was mid-morning—a very cold, bright day. Holding a potted plant before her, a girl of fourteen jumped off the bus in front of the Old Ladies' Home, on the outskirts of town. She wore a red coat, and her straight yellow hair was hanging down loose from the pointed white cap all the little girls were wearing that year. She stopped for a moment beside one of the prickly dark shrubs with which the city had beautified the Home, and then proceeded slowly toward the building, which was of whitewashed brick and reflected the winter sunlight like a block of ice. As she walked vaguely up the steps she shifted the small pot from hand to hand; then she had to set it down and remove her mittens before she could open the heavy door.

"I'm a Campfire Girl . . . I have to pay a visit to some old lady," she told the nurse at the desk. This was a woman in a white uniform who looked as if she were cold; she had close-cut hair which stood up on the very top of her head exactly like a sea wave. Marian, the little girl, did not tell her that this visit would give her a minimum of only three points in her score.

"Acquainted with any of our residents?" asked the nurse. She lifted one eyebrow and spoke like a man.

"With any old ladies? No—but—that is, any of them will do," Marian stammered. With her free hand she pushed her hair behind her ears, as she did when it was time to study Science.

The nurse shrugged and rose. "You have a nice *multiflora cineraria* there," she remarked as she walked ahead down the hall of closed doors to pick out an old lady.

There was loose, bulging linoleum on the floor. Marian felt as if she were walking on the waves, but the nurse paid no attention to it. There was a smell in the hall like the interior of a clock. Everything was silent until, behind one of the doors, an old lady of some kind cleared her throat like a sheep bleating. This decided the nurse. Stopping in her tracks, she first extended her arm, bent her elbow, and leaned forward from the hips—all to examine the watch strapped to her wrist; then she gave a loud double-rap on the door.

"There are two in each room," the nurse remarked over her shoulder.

"Two what?" asked Marian without thinking. The sound like a sheep's bleating almost made her turn around and run back.

One old woman was pulling the door open in short, gradual jerks, and when she saw the nurse a strange smile forced her old face dangerously awry. Marian, suddenly propelled by the strong, impatient arm of the nurse, saw next the side-face of another old woman, even older, who was lying flat in bed with a cap on and a counterpane drawn up to her chin.

"Visitor," said the nurse, and after one more shove she was off up the hall.

Marian stood tongue-tied; both hands held the potted plant. The old woman, still with that terrible, square smile (which was a smile of welcome) stamped on her bony face, was waiting. . . . Perhaps she said something. The old woman in bed said nothing at all, and she did not look around.

Suddenly Marian saw a hand, quick as a bird claw, reach up in the air and pluck the white cap off her head. At the same time, another claw to match drew her all the way into the room, and the next moment the door closed behind her.

"My, my, my," said the old lady at her side.

Marian stood enclosed by a bed, a washstand and a chair; the tiny room had altogether too much furniture. Everything smelled wet—even the bare floor. She held on to the back of the chair, which was wicker and felt soft and damp. Her heart beat more and more slowly, her hands got colder and colder, and she could not hear whether the old women were saying anything or not. She could not see them very clearly. How dark it was! The window shade was down, and the only door was shut. Marian looked at the ceiling. . . . It was like being caught in a robbers' cave, just before one was murdered.

"Did you come to be our little girl for a while?" the first robber asked.

Then something was snatched from Marian's hand—the little potted plant.

"Flowers!" screamed the old woman. She stood holding the pot in an undecided way. "Pretty flowers," she added.

Then the old woman in bed cleared her throat and spoke. "They are not pretty," she said, still without looking around, but very distinctly.

Marian suddenly pitched against the chair and sat down in it.

"Pretty flowers," she first old woman insisted. "Pretty—pretty . . ."

Marian wished she had the little pot back for just a moment—she had forgotten to look at the plant herself before giving it away. What did it look like?

"Stinkweeds," said the other old woman sharply. She had a bunchy white forehead and red eyes like a sheep. Now she turned them toward Marian. The fogginess seemed to rise in her throat again, and she bleated, "Who—are—you?"

To her surprise, Marian could not remember her name. "I'm a Campfire Girl," she said finally.

"Watch out for the germs," said the old woman like a sheep, not addressing anyone.

"One came out last month to see us," said the first old woman.

A sheep or a germ? wondered Marian dreamily, holding on to the chair.

"Did not!" cried the other old woman.

"Did so! Read to us out of the Bible, and we enjoyed it!" screamed the first.

"Who enjoyed it!" said the woman in bed. Her mouth was unexpectedly small and sorrowful, like a pet's.

"We enjoyed it," insisted the other. "You enjoyed it—I enjoyed it."

"We all enjoyed it," said Marian, without realizing that she had said a word.

The first old woman had just finished putting the potted plant high, high on the top of the wardrobe, where it could hardly be seen from below. Marian wondered how she had ever succeeded in placing it there, how she could ever have reached so high.

"You mustn't pay any attention to old Addie," she now said to the little girl. "She's ailing today."

"Will you shut your mouth?" said the woman in bed. "I am not."

"You're a story."

"I can't stay but a minute—really, I can't," said Marian suddenly. She looked down at the wet floor and thought that if she were sick in here they would have to let her go.

With much to-do the first old woman sat down in a rocking chair—still another piece of furniture!—and began to rock. With the fingers of one hand she touched a very dirty cameo pin on her chest. "What do you do at school?" she asked.

"I don't know . . ." said Marian. She tried to think but she could not.

"Oh, but the flowers are beautiful," the old woman whispered. She seemed to rock faster and faster; Marian did not see how anyone could rock so fast.

"Ugly," said the woman in bed.

"If we bring flowers—" Marian began, and then fell silent. She had almost said that if Campfire Girls brought flowers to the Old Ladies' Home, the visit would count one extra point, and if they took a Bible with them on the bus and read it to the old ladies, it counted double. But the old woman had not listened, anyway; she was rocking and watching the other one, who watched back from the bed.

"Poor Addie is ailing. She has to take medicine—see?" she said, pointing a horny finger at a row of bottles on the table, and rocking so high that her black comfort shoes lifted off the floor like a little child's.

"I am no more sick than you are," said the woman in bed.

"Oh, yes you are!"

"I just got more sense than you have, that's all," said the other old woman, nodding her head.

"That's only the contrary way she talks when *you all* come," said the first old lady with sudden intimacy. She stopped the rocker with a neat pat of her feet and leaned toward Marian. Her hand reached over—it felt like a petunia leaf, clinging and just a little sticky.

"Will you hush! Will you hush!" cried the other one.

Marian leaned back rigidly in her chair.

"When I was a little girl like you, I went to school and all," said the old woman in the same intimate, menacing voice. "Not here—another town . . ."

"Hush!" said the sick woman. "You never went to school. You never came and you never went. You never were anything—only here. You never were born! You don't know anything. Your head is empty, your heart and hands and your old black purse are all empty, even that little old box that you brought with you you brought empty—you showed it to me. And yet you talk, talk, talk, talk, talk all the time until I think I'm losing my mind! Who are you? You're a stranger—a perfect stranger! Don't you know you're stranger? Is it possible that they have actually done a thing like this to anyone—sent them in a stranger to talk, and rock, and tell away her whole long rigmarole? Do they seriously suppose that I'll be able to keep it up, day in, day out, night in, night out, living in the same room with a terrible old woman—forever?"

Marian saw the old woman's eyes grow bright and turn toward her. This old woman was looking at her with despair and calculation in her face. Her small lips suddenly dropped apart, and exposed a half circle of false teeth with tan gums.

"Come here, I want to tell you something," she whispered. "Come here!"

Marian was trembling, and her heart nearly stopped beating altogether for a moment.

"Now, now, Addie," said the first old woman. "That's not polite. Do you know what's really the matter with old Addie today?" She, too, looked at Marian; one of her eyelids dropped low.

"The matter?" the child repeated stupidly. "What's the matter with her?"

"Why, she's mad because it's her birthday!" said the first old woman, beginning to rock again and giving a little crow as though she had answered her own riddle.

"It is not, it is not!" screamed the old woman in bed. "It is not my birthday, no one knows when that is but myself, and will you please be quiet and say nothing more, or I'll go straight out of my mind!" She turned her eyes toward Marian again, and presently she said in the soft, foggy voice, "When the worst comes to the worst, I ring this bell, and the nurse comes." One of her hands was drawn out from under the patched counterpane—a thin little hand with enormous black freckles. With a finger which would not hold still she pointed to a little bell on the table among the bottles.

"How old are you?" Marian breathed. Now she could see the old woman in bed very closely and plainly, and very abruptly, from all sides, as in dreams. She wondered about her—she wondered for a moment as though there was nothing else in the world to wonder about. It was the first time such a thing had happened to Marian.

"I won't tell!"

The old face on the pillow, where Marian was bending over it, slowly gathered and collapsed. Soft whimpers came out of the small open mouth. It was a sheep that she sounded like—a little lamb. Marian's face drew very close, the yellow hair hung forward.

"She's crying!" She turned a bright, burning face up to the first old woman.

"That's Addie for you," the old woman said spitefully.

Marian jumped up and moved toward the door. For the second time, the claw almost touched her hair, but it was not quick enough. The little girl put her cap on.

"Well, it was a real visit," said the old woman, following Marian through the doorway and all the way out into the hall. Then from behind she suddenly clutched the child with her sharp little fingers. In an affected, high-pitched whine she cried, "Oh, little girl, have you a penny to spare for a poor old woman that's not got anything of her own? We don't have a thing in the world—not a penny for candy—not a thing! Little girl, just a nickel—a penny—"

Marian pulled violently against the old hands for a moment before she was free. Then she ran down the hall, without looking behind her and without looking at the nurse, who was reading *Field & Stream* at her desk. The nurse, after another triple motion to consult her wrist watch, asked automatically the question put to visitors in all institutions: "Won't you stay and have dinner with *us?*"

Marian never replied. She pushed the heavy door open into the cold air and ran down the steps.

Under the prickly shrub she stooped and quickly, without being seen, retrieved a red apple she had hidden there.

Her yellow hair under the white cap, her scarlet coat, her bare knees all flashed in the sunlight as she ran to meet the big bus rocketing through the street.

"Wait for me!" she shouted. As though at an imperial command, the bus ground to a stop.

She jumped on and took a big bite out of the apple.

## *Bullet in the Brain*

### TOBIAS WOLFF

Anders couldn't get to the bank until just before it closed, so of course the line was endless and he got stuck behind two women whose loud, stupid conversation put him in a murderous temper. He was never in the best of tempers anyway, Anders—a book critic known for the weary, elegant savagery with which he dispatched almost everything he reviewed.

With the line still doubled around the rope, one of the tellers stuck a "POSITION CLOSED" sign in her window and walked to the back of the bank, where she learned against a desk and began to pass the time with a man shuffling papers. The women in front of Anders broke off their conversation and watched the teller with hatred. "Oh, that's nice," one of them said. She turned to Anders and added, confident of his accord, "One of those little human touches that keep us coming back for more."

Anders had conceived his own towering hatred of the teller, but he immediately turned it on the presumptuous crybaby in front of him. "Damned unfair," he said, "Tragic, really. If they're not chopping off the wrong leg, or bombing your ancestral village, they're closing their positions."

She stood her ground. "I didn't say it was tragic," she said, "I just think it's a pretty lousy way to treat your customers."

"Unforgivable," Anders said. "Heaven will take note."

She sucked in her cheeks but stared past him and said nothing. Anders saw that the other woman, her friend, was looking in the same direction. And then the tellers stopped what they were doing, and the customers slowly turned, and silence came over the bank. Two men wearing black ski masks and blue business suits were standing to the side of the door. One of them had a pistol pressed against the guard's neck. The guard's eyes were closed, and his lips were moving. The other man had a sawed-off shotgun. "Keep your big mouth shut!" the man with the pistol said, though no one had spoken a word. "One of you tellers hits the alarm, you're all dead meat. Got it?"

The tellers nodded.

"Oh, bravo," Anders said. "*Dead meat.*" He turned to the woman in front of him. "Great script, eh? The stern, brass-knuckled poetry of the dangerous classes."

She looked at him with drowning eyes.

The man with the shotgun pushed the guard to his knees. He handed the shotgun to his partner and yanked the guard's wrists up behind his back and locked them together with a pair of handcuffs. He toppled him onto the floor with a kick between the shoulder blades. Then he took his shotgun back and went over to the security gate at the end of the counter. He was short and heavy and moved with peculiar slowness, even torpor. "Buzz him in," his partner said. The man with the shotgun opened the gate and sauntered along the line of tellers, handing each of them a Hefty bag. When he came to the empty position he looked over at the man with the pistol, who said, "Whose slot is that?"

Anders watched the teller. She put her hand to her throat and turned to the man she'd been talking to. He nodded. "Mine," she said.

"Then get your ugly ass in gear and fill that bag."

"There you go," Anders said to the woman in front of him. "Justice is done."

"Hey! Bright boy! Did I tell you to talk?"

"No," Anders said.

"Then shut your trap."

"Did you hear that?" Anders said. "'Bright boy.' Right out of 'The Killers.'"

"Please be quiet," the woman said.

"Hey, you deaf or what?" The man with the pistol walked over to Anders. He poked the weapon into Anders' gut. "You think I'm playing games?"

"No," Anders said, but the barrel tickled like a stiff finger and he had to fight back the titters. He did this by making himself stare into the man's eyes, which were clearly visible behind the holes in the mask: pale blue and rawly red-rimmed. The man's left eyelid kept twitching. He breathed out a piercing, ammoniac smell that shocked Anders more than anything that had happened, and he was beginning to develop a sense of unease when the man prodded him again with the pistol.

"You like me, bright boy!" he said. "You want to suck my dick!"

"No," Anders said.

"Then stop looking at me."

Anders fixed his gaze on the man's shiny wing-tip shoes.

"Not down there. Up there." He stuck the pistol under Anders' chin and pushed it upward until Anders was looking at the ceiling.

Anders had never paid much attention to that part of the bank, a pompous old building with marble floors and counters and pillars, and gilt scrollwork over the tellers' cages. The domed ceiling had been decorated with mythological figures whose fleshy, toga-draped ugliness Anders had taken in at a glance many years earlier and afterward declined to notice. Now he had no choice but to scrutinize the painter's work. It was even worse than he remembered, and all of it executed with the utmost gravity. The artist had a few tricks up his sleeve and used them again and again—a certain rosy blush on the underside of the clouds, a coy backward glance on the faces of the cupids and fauns. The ceiling was crowded with various dramas, but the one that caught Anders' eye was Zeus and Europa—portrayed, in this rendition, as a bull ogling a cow from behind a haystack. To make the cow sexy, the painter had canted her hips suggestively and given her long, droopy eyelashes through which she gazed back at the bull with sultry welcome. The bull wore a smirk and his eyebrows were arched. If there'd been a bubble coming out of his mouth, it would have said, "Hubba hubba."

"What's so funny, bright boy?"

"Nothing."

"You think I'm comical? You think I'm some kind of clown?"

"No."

"You think you can fuck with me?"

"No."

"Fuck with me again, you're history. *Capiche?*"

Anders burst out laughing. He covered his mouth with both hands and said, "I'm sorry, I'm sorry," then snorted helplessly through his fingers and said, "*Capiche*—oh, God, *capiche*," and at that the man with the pistol raised the pistol and shot Anders right in the head.

The bullet smashed Anders' skull and ploughed through his brain and exited behind his right ear, scattering shards of bone into the cerebral cortex, the corpus callosum, back toward the basal ganglia, and down into the thalamus. But before all this occurred, the first appearance of the bullet in the cerebrum set off a crackling chain of iron transports and neuro-transmissions. Because of their peculiar origin these traced a peculiar pattern, flukishly calling to life a summer afternoon some forty years past, and long since lost to memory. After striking the cranium the bullet was moving at 900 feet per second, a pathetically sluggish, glacial pace compared to the synaptic lightning that flashed around it. Once in the brain, that is, the bullet came under the mediation of brain time, which gave Anders plenty of leisure to contemplate the scene that, in a phrase he would have abhorred, "passed before his eyes."

It is worth noting what Anders did not remember, given what he did remember. He did not remember his first lover, Sherry, or what he had most madly loved about her, before it came to irritate him—her unembarrassed carnality, and especially the cordial way she had with his unit, which she called Mr. Mole, as in, "Uh-oh, looks like Mr. Mole wants to play," and, "let's hide Mr. Mole!" Anders did not remember his wife, whom he had also loved before she exhausted him with her predictability, or his daughter, now a sullen professor of economics at Dartmouth. He did not remember standing just outside his daughter's door as she lectured her bear about his naughtiness and described the truly appalling punishments Paws would receive unless he changed his ways. He did not remember a single line of the hundreds of poems he had committed to memory in his youth so that he could give himself the shivers at will—not "Silent, upon a peak in Darien," or "My God, I heard this day," or "All my pretty ones? Did you say all? O hell-kite! All?" None of these did he remember; not one. Anders did not remember his dying mother saying of his father, "I should have stabbed him in his sleep."

He did not remember Professor Josephs telling his class how Athenian prisoners in Sicily had been released if they could recite Aeschylus, and then reciting Aeschylus himself, right there, in the Greek. Anders did not remember how his eyes had burned at those sounds. He did not remember the surprise of seeing a college classmate's name on the jacket of a novel not long after they graduated, or the respect he had felt after reading the book. He did not remember the pleasure of giving respect.

Nor did Anders remember seeing a woman leap to her death from the building opposite his own just days after his daughter was born. He did not remember shouting, "Lord have mercy!" He did not remember deliberately crashing his father's car into a tree, or having his ribs kicked in by three policemen at an anti-war rally, or waking himself up with laughter. He did not remember when he began to regard the heap of books on his desk with boredom and dread, or when he grew angry at writers for writing them. He did not remember when everything began to remind him of something else.

This is what he remembered. Heat. A baseball field. Yellow grass, the whirr of insects, himself leaning against a tree as the boys of the neighborhood gather for a pickup game. He looks on as the others argue the relative genius of Mantle and Mays. They have been worrying this subject all summer, and it has become tedious to Anders; an oppression, like the heat.

Then the last two boys arrive, Coyle and a cousin of his from Mississippi. Anders has never met Coyle's cousin before and will never see him again. He says hi with the rest but takes no further notice of him until they've chosen sides and someone asks the cousin what position he wants to play. "Shortstop," the boy says. "Short's the best position they is." Anders turns and looks at him. He wants to hear Coyle's cousin repeat what he's just said, but he knows better than to ask. The others will think he's being a jerk, ragging the kid for his grammar. But that isn't it, not at all— it's that Anders is strangely roused, elated, by those final two words, their pure unexpectedness and their music. He takes the field in a trance, repeating them to himself.

The bullet is already in the brain; it won't be outrun forever, or charmed to a halt. In the end it will do its work and leave the troubled skull behind, dragging its comet's tail of memory and hope and talent and love into the marble hall of commerce. That can't be helped. But for now Anders can still make time. Time for the shadows to lengthen on the grass, time for the tethered dog to bark at the flying ball, time for the boy in right field to smack his sweat-blackened mitt and softly chant, *They is, they is, they is*.

# Tandolfo the Great

### RICHARD BAUSCH

"Tandolfo," he says to his own image in the mirror over the bathroom sink. "She loves you not, you goddam fool."

He's put the makeup on, packed the bag of tricks—including the rabbit, whom he calls Chi-Chi; and the bird, attention-getter, which he calls Witch. He's to do a birthday party on the other side of the river. Some five-year-old, and so this is going to be one of those tough ones, a crowd of babies, and all the adults waiting around for him to screw up.

He has fortified himself with something, and he feels ready. He isn't particularly worried about it. But there's a little something else he has to do, first. Something on the order of the embarrassingly ridiculous: he has to make a small delivery.

This morning, at the local bakery, he picked up a big pink wedding cake, with its six tiers and its scalloped edges and its little bride and groom on top. He'd ordered it on his own: he'd taken the initiative, planning to offer it to a young woman of his acquaintance. He managed somehow to set the thing on the back-seat of the car and when he got home he found a note from her announcing, all excited and happy, that she's engaged. The man she'd had such trouble with has had a change of heart; he wants to get married after all. She's going to Houston to live. She loves her dear old Tandolfo with a big kiss and a hug always, and she knows he'll have every happiness. She's so thankful for his friendship. Her magic man. He's her sweet clown. She has actually driven over here and, finding him gone, left the note for him, folded under the door knocker—her pink notepaper, with the little tangle of flowers at the top. She wants him to call her, come by as soon as he can to help celebrate. *Please*, she says. *I want to give you a big hug.* He read this and then walked out to stand on the sidewalk and look at the cake in its place on the backseat of the car.

"Good God," he said. He'd thought he would put the clown outfit on, deliver the cake in person in the evening; an elaborate proposal to a girl he's never even kissed. He's a little unbalanced, and he knows it. Over the months of their working to-gether for the county government, he's built up tremendous feelings of loyalty and yearning toward her. He thought she felt something, too. He interpreted gestures—her hand lingering on his shoulder when he made her laugh; her endearments to him, tinged as they seemed to be with a kind of sadness, as if she were afraid for what the world might do to someone so romantic.

"You sweet clown," she said. And she said it a lot. And she talked to him about her ongoing trouble, the guy she'd been in love with who kept waffling about getting married. He wanted no commitments. Tandolfo, aka Rodney Wilbury, told her that he hated men who weren't willing to run the risks of love. Why, he personally was the type who'd always believed in marriage and children, lifelong commitments. He had caused difficulties for himself and life was a disappointment so far, but he be-lieved in falling in love and starting a family. She didn't hear him. It all went right through her like white noise on the radio. For weeks he had come around to visit her, had invited her to watch him perform. She confided in him, and he thought of movies where the friend sticks around and is a good listener, and eventually gets the girl. They fall in love. He put his hope in that. He was optimistic; he'd ordered and bought the cake. Apparently the whole time, all through the listening and being noble with her, she thought of it as nothing more than friendship, accepting it from him because she was accustomed to being offered friendship.

Now he leans close to the mirror to look at his own eyes through the makeup. They look clear enough. "Loves you absolutely not. You must be crazy. You must be the great Tandolfo."

Yes.

Twenty-six-year-old, out-of-luck Tandolfo. In love. With a great oversized cake in the backseat of his car. It's Sunday, a cool April day. He's a little inebriated. That's the word he prefers. It's polite; it suggests something faintly silly. Nothing could be sillier than to be dressed like this in the broad daylight, and to go driving across the bridge into Virginia to put on a magic show. Nothing, could be sillier than to have spent all that money on a completely useless purchase—a cake six tiers high. Maybe fifteen pounds of sugar.

When he has made his last check of the clown face in the mirror, and the bag of tricks and props, he goes to his front door and stands at the screen looking out at the architectural shadow of it in the backseat. The inside of the car will smell like icing for days. He'll have to keep the windows open even if it rains; he'll go to work smelling like confectionery delights. The whole thing makes him laugh. A wedding cake. He steps out of the house and makes his way in the late-afternoon sun down the sidewalk to the car. As if they have been waiting for him, three boys come skating down from the top of the hill. He has the feeling that if he tried to sneak out like this at two in the morning, someone would come by and see him anyway. "Hey, Rodney," one boy says. "I mean Tandolfo."

Tandolfo recognizes him. A neighborhood boy, a tough. Just the kind to make trouble, just the kind with no sensitivity to the suffering of others. "Leave me alone or I'll turn you into spaghetti," he says.

"Hey, guys—it's Tandolfo the Great." The boy's hair is a bright blond color, and you can see through it to his scalp.

"Scram," Tandolfo says. "Really."

"Aw, what's your hurry, man?"

"I've just set off a nuclear device," Tandolfo says with grave seriousness. "It's on a timer. Proof."

"Do a trick for us," the blond one says. "Where's that scurvy rabbit of yours?"

"I gave it the week off." Someone, last winter, poisoned the first Chi-Chi. He keeps the cage indoors now. "I'm in a hurry. No rabbit to help with the driving."

But they're interested in the cake now. "Hey, what's that in your car? Is that what I think it is?"

"Just stay back."

"Is that a cake, man? Is that real?"

Tandolfo gets his cases into the trunk, and hurries to the driver's side door. The three boys are peering into the backseat.

"Hey, man. A cake. Can we have a piece of cake?"

"Back off," Tandolfo says.

The white-haired one says, "Come on, Tandolfo."

"Hey, Tandolfo, I saw some guys looking for you, man. They said you owed them money."

He gets in, ignoring them. He starts the car.

"You sucker," one of them says.

"Hey, man. Who's the cake for?"

He drives away, thinks of himself leaving them in a cloud of exhaust. Riding through the green shade, he glances in the rear-view mirror and sees the clown face, the painted smile. It makes him want to laugh. He tells himself he's his own cliché— a clown with a broken heart. Looming behind him is the cake, like a passenger in the backseat.

He drives slow. He has always believed viscerally that gestures mean everything. When he moves his hands and brings about the effects that amaze little children, he feels larger than life, unforgettable. He learned the magic while in high school, as a way of making friends, and though it didn't really make him any friends, he's been practicing it ever since. It's an extra source of income, and lately income has had a way of disappearing too quickly. He's been in some trouble—betting the horses; betting the sports events. He's hungover all the time. There have been several polite warnings at work. He's managed so far to tease everyone out of the serious looks, the cool evaluative study of his face. The fact is, people like him in an abstract way, the way they like distant clownish figures: the comedian whose name they can't remember. He can see it in their eyes. Even the rough characters after his loose change have a certain sense of humor about it. He's a phenomenon, a subject of conversation.

There's traffic on Key Bridge, and he's stuck for a while. It becomes clear that he'll have to go straight to the birthday party. Sitting behind the wheel of the car with his cake on the backseat, he becomes aware of people in other cars noticing him. In the car to his left, a girl stares, chewing gum. She waves, rolls her window down. Two others are with her, one in the backseat. "Hey," she says. He nods. Smiles inside what he knows is the painted smile. His teeth will look dark against the makeup.

"Where's the party?" she says.

But the traffic moves again. He concentrates. The snarl is on the other side of the bridge—construction of some kind. He can see the cars lined up, waiting to go up the hill into Rosslyn and beyond. Time is beginning to be a consideration. In his glove box, he has a flask of bourbon. He reaches over and takes it out, looks around himself. No police anywhere. Just the idling cars and people tuning their radios or arguing or simply staring out as if at some distressing event. The smell of the cake is making him woozy. He takes a swallow of the bourbon, then puts it back. The car with the girls in it goes by him in the left lane, and they are not even looking at him. He watches them go on ahead. He's in the wrong lane again; he can't remember a time when his lane was the only one moving. He told her once that he considered himself in the race of people who gravitate to the nonmoving lanes of highways, and who cause traffic lights to turn yellow by approaching them. She took the idea and carried it out a little—saying she was of the race of people who emitted enzymes which instilled a sense of impending doom in marriageable young men, and made them wary of long-term relationships.

"No," Tandolfo/Rodney said. "I'm living proof that isn't so. I have no such fear, and I'm with you."

"But you're of the race of people who make mine relax all the enzymes."

"You're not emitting the enzymes now, I see."

"No," she said. "It's only with marriageable young men."

"I emit enzymes that prevent people like you from seeing that I'm a marriageable young man."

"I'm too relaxed to tell," she said, and touched his shoulder. A plain affectionate moment that gave him tossing nights and fever.

Because of the traffic, he arrives late at the birthday party. He gets out of the car and two men come down from the house to greet him. He keeps his face turned away, remembering too late the breath mints in his pocket.

"Jesus," one of the men says. "Look at this. Hey—who comes out of the cake? This is a kid's birthday party."

"The cake stays."

"What does he mean, it stays? Is that a trick?"

They're both looking at him. The one spoken to must be the birthday boy's father—he's wearing a party cap that says DAD. He has long dirty-looking strands of blond hair jutting out from the cap, and there are streaks of sweaty grit on the sides of his face. "So you're the Great Tandolfo," he says, extending a meaty red hand. "Isn't it hot in that makeup?"

"No, sir."

"We've been playing volleyball."

"You've exerted yourselves."

They look at him. "What do you do with the cake?" the one in the DAD cap asks.

"Cake's not part of the show, actually."

"You just carrying it around with you?"

The other man laughs. He's wearing a T-shirt with a smile face on the chest. "This ought to be some show," he says.

They all make their way across the street and the lawn, to the porch of the house. It's a big party—bunting everywhere and children gathering quickly to see the clown.

"Ladies and gentlemen," says the man in the DAD cap. "I give you Tandolfo the Great."

Tandolfo isn't ready yet. He's got his cases open, but he needs a table to put everything on. The first trick is where he releases the bird. He'll finish with the best trick, in which the rabbit appears as if from a pan of flames: it always draws a gasp, even from the adults; the fire blooms in the pan, down goes the "lid"—it's the rabbit's tight container—the latch is tripped, and the skin of the "lid" lifts off. *Voilà!* Rabbit. The fire is put out by the fireproof cage bottom. He's gotten pretty good at making the switch, and if the crowd isn't too attentive—as children often are not—he can perform certain hand tricks with some style. But he needs a table, and he needs time to set up.

The whole crowd of children is seated in front of the door into the house. He's standing here on the porch, his back to the stairs, and he's been introduced.

"Hello, boys and girls," he says, and bows. "Tandolfo needs a table."

"A table," one of the women says. All the adults are ranged against the porch wall, behind the children. He sees light sweaters, shapely hips, and wild tresses; he sees beer cans in tight fists and heavy jowls, bright ice-blue eyes. A little row of faces, and one elderly face. He feels more inebriated than he likes now, and he tries to concentrate.

"Mommy, I want to touch him," one child says.

"Look at the cake," says another, who's sitting on the railing to Tandolfo's right, with a new pair of shiny binoculars trained on the car. "Do we get some cake?"

"There's cake," says the man in the DAD cap. "But not that cake. Get down, Ethan."

"I want that cake."

"Get down. This is Teddy's birthday."

"Mommy, I want to touch him."

"I need a table, folks. I told somebody that over the telephone."

"He did say he needed a table. I'm sorry," says a woman who is probably the birthday boy's mother. She's quite pretty, leaning in the doorframe with a sweater tied to her waist.

"A table," says another woman. Tandolfo sees the birthmark on her mouth, which looks like a stain. He thinks of this woman as a child in school, with this difference from other children, and his heart goes out to her.

"I need a table," he says to her, his voice as gentle as he can make it.

"What's he going to do, perform an operation?" says DAD.

It amazes Tandolfo how easily people fall into talking about him as though he were an inanimate object, or something on a television screen. "The Great Tandolfo can do nothing until he gets a table," he says, with as much mysteriousness and drama as he can muster under the circumstances.

"I want that cake out there," says Ethan, still perched atop the porch railing. The other children start talking about cake and ice cream, and the big cake Ethan has spotted; there's a lot of confusion, and restlessness. One of the smaller children, a girl in a blue dress, comes forward and stands gazing at Tandolfo. "What's your name?" she says, swaying slightly, her hands behind her back.

"Go sit down," he says to her. "We have to sit down or Tandolfo can't do his magic."

In the doorway, two of the men are struggling with a folding card table. It's one of those rickety ones with the skinny legs, and it won't do.

"That's kind of rickety, isn't it?" says the woman with the birthmark.

"I said Tandolfo needs a sturdy table, boys and girls."

There's more confusion. The little girl has come forward and taken hold of his pant leg. she's just standing there holding it, looking at him. "We have to go sit down," he says, bending to her, speaking sweetly, clownlike. "We have to do what Tandolfo wants."

Her small mouth opens wide, as if she's trying to yawn, and with pale blue eyes quite calm and staring she emits a screech, an ear-piercing, nonhuman shriek that brings everything to a stop. Tandolfo/Rodney steps back, with his amazement and his inebriate heart, and now everyone's gathering around the girl, who continues to scream, less piercing now, her hands fisted at her sides, those blue eyes closed tight.

"What happened?" the man in the DAD cap wants to know. "Where the hell's the magic tricks?"

"I told you all I needed a *table*."

"Whud you say to her to make her cry?" He indicates the little girl, who is not merely crying but is giving forth a series of broken, grief-stricken howls.

"I want magic tricks," the birthday boy says, loud. "Where's the magic tricks?"

"Perhaps if we moved the whole thing inside," the woman with the birthmark says, fingering her left ear and making a face.

The card table has somehow made its way to Tandolfo, through the confusion and grief. The man in the DAD cap sets it down and opens it.

"There," he says, as if his point is made.

In the next moment, Tandolfo realizes that someone's removed the little girl. Everything's relatively quiet again, though her cries are coming through the walls of one of the rooms inside the house. There are perhaps fifteen children, mostly seated before him; five or six men and women behind them, or kneeling with them. "Okay, now," DAD says. "Tandolfo the Great."

"Hello, little boys and girls," Tandolfo/Rodney says. "I'm happy to be here. Are you glad to see me?" A general uproar goes up. "Well, good," he says. "Because just look what I have in my magic bag." And with a flourish, he brings out the hat from which he will release Witch. The bird is encased inside a fold of shiny cloth, pulsing there. He can feel it. He rambles on, talking fast, or trying to, and when the time comes to reveal the bird, he almost flubs it. But Witch flaps his wings and makes enough of a commotion to distract even the adults, who applaud now, and get the children to applaud. "Isn't that wonderful," Tandolfo hears. "Where did that bird come from?"

"He had it hidden away," says the birthday boy.

"Now," Tandolfo says, "for my next spell, I need a little friend from the audience." He looks right at the birthday boy—round face; short nose; freckles. Bright red hair. Little green eyes. The whole countenance speaks of glutted appetites and sloth. This kid could be on Roman coins, an emperor. He's not used to being compelled to do anything, but he seems eager for a chance to get into the act. "How about you?" Tandolfo says to him.

The others, led by their parents, cheer.

The birthday boy gets to his feet and makes his way over the bodies of the other children to stand with Tandolfo. In order for the trick to work, Tandolfo must get everyone watching the birthday boy, and there's a funny hat he keeps in the bag for this purpose. "Now," he says to the boy, "since you're part of the show, you have to wear a costume." He produces the hat as if from behind the boy's ear. Another cheer goes up. He puts the hat on his head and adjusts it, crouching down. The green eyes stare impassively at him; there's no hint of awe or fascination in them. "There we are," he says. "What a handsome fellow."

But the birthday boy takes the hat off.

"No, no. We have to wear the hat to be onstage."

"Ain't a stage," the boy says.

"Well, but hey," Tandolfo says for the benefit of the adults. "Didn't you know that all the world's a stage?" He tries to put the hat on again, but the boy moves from under his reach and slaps his hand away. "We have to wear the hat," Tandolfo says, trying to control his anger. "We can't do the magic without our magic hats." He tries once more, and the boy waits until the hat is on, then simply removes it and holds it behind him, shying away when Tandolfo tries to retrieve it. The noise of the others now sounds like the crowd at a prizefight; there's a contest going on, and they're enjoying it. "Give Tandolfo the hat now. We want magic, don't we?"

"Do the magic," the boy demands.

"I'll do the magic if you give me the hat."

"I won't."

Nothing. No support from the adults. Perhaps if he weren't a little tipsy, perhaps if he didn't feel ridiculous and sick at heart and forlorn, with his wedding cake and his odd mistaken romance, his loneliness, which he has always borne gracefully and in humor, and his general dismay; perhaps if he were to find it in himself to deny the sudden, overwhelming sense of the unearned affection given this little slovenly version of stupid complacent spoiled satiation standing before him—he might've simply gone on to the next trick.

Instead, he leans down and in the noise of the moment, says to the boy, "Give me the hat, you little prick."

The green eyes widen slightly.

It grows quiet. Even the small children can tell that something's happened to change everything.

"Tandolfo has another trick," Rodney says, "where he makes the birthday boy pop like a balloon. Especially if he's a fat birthday boy."

A stirring among the adults.

"Especially if he's an ugly little slab of flesh like this one here."

"Now just a minute," says DAD.

"Pop," Rodney says to the birthday boy, who drops the hat and then, seeming to remember that defiance is expected, makes a face. Sticks out his tongue. Rodney/ Tandolfo is quick with his hands by training, and he grabs the tongue.

"Awk," the boy says. "Aw-aw-aw."

"Abracadabra." Rodney lets go, and the boy falls backward into the lap of one of the older children. "Whoops, time to sit down," says Rodney.

Very quickly, he's being forcibly removed. They're rougher than gangsters. They lift him, punch him, tear at his costume—even the women. Someone hits him with a spoon. The whole scene boils out onto the lawn, where someone has released the case that Chi-Chi was in. Chi-Chi moves about wide-eyed, hopping between running children, evading them, as Tandolfo the Great cannot evade the adults. He's being pummeled, because he keeps trying to return for his rabbit. And the adults won't let him off the curb.

"Okay," he says finally, collecting himself. He wants to let them know he's not like this all the time; wants to say it's circumstances, grief, personal pain hidden inside seeming brightness and cleverness; he's a man in love, humiliated, wrong about everything. He wants to tell them, but he can't speak for a moment, can't even quite catch his breath. He stands in the middle of the street, his funny clothes torn, his face bleeding, all his magic strewn everywhere. "I would at least like to collect my rabbit," he says, and is appalled at the absurd sound of it—its huge difference from what he intended to say. He straightens, pushes the hair out of his eyes, adjusts the clown nose, and looks at them. "I would say that even though I wasn't as patient as I could've been, the adults have not comported themselves well here," he says.

"Drunk," one of the women says.

Almost everyone's chasing Chi-Chi now. One of the older boys approaches him, carrying Witch's case. Witch looks out the air hole, impervious, quiet as an idea. And now one of the men, someone Tandolfo hasn't noticed before, an older man clearly wearing a hairpiece, brings Chi-Chi to him. "Bless you," Rodney says, staring into the man's sleepy, deploring gaze.

"I don't think we'll pay you," the man says. The others are all filing back into the house, herding the children before them.

Rodney speaks to the man. "The rabbit appears out of fire."

The man nods. "Go home and sleep it off, kid."

"Right, thank you."

He puts Chi-Chi in his compartment, stuffs everything in its place in the trunk. Then he gets in and drives away. Around the corner he stops, wipes off what he can of the makeup; it's as if he's trying to remove the grime of bad opinion and disapproval. Nothing feels any different. He drives to the little suburban street where she lives with her parents, and by the time he gets there it's almost dark. The houses are set back in the trees; he sees lighted windows, hears music, the sound of children playing in the yards. He parks the car and gets out. A breezy April dusk.

"I am Tandolfo the soft-hearted," he says. "Hearken to me." Then he sobs. He can't believe it. "Jeez," he says. "Goddam."

He opens the back door of the car, leans in to get the cake. He'd forgotten how heavy it is. Staggering with it, making his way along the sidewalk, intending to leave it on her doorstep, he has an inspiration. Hesitating only for the moment it takes to make sure there are no cars coming, he goes out and sets it down in the middle of the street.

Part of the top sags slightly, from having bumped his shoulder as he pulled it off the backseat of the car. The bride and groom are almost supine, one on top of the other. He straightens them, steps back, and looks at it. In the dusky light, it looks blue. It sags just right, with just the right angle, expressing disappointment and sorrow.

Yes, he thinks. This is the place for it. The aptness of it, sitting out like this, where anyone might come by and splatter it all over creation, actually makes him feel some faint sense of release, as if he were at the end of a story. Everything will be all right if he can think of it that way. He's wiping his eyes, thinking of moving to another town. There are money troubles and troubles at work, and failures beginning to catch up to him, and he's still aching in love. He thinks how he has suffered the pangs of failure and misadventure, but in this painful instance there's symmetry, and he will make the one eloquent gesture—leaving a wedding cake in the middle of the road, like a sugar-icinged pylon. Yes.

He walks back to the car, gets in, pulls it around, and backs into the driveway of the house across the street. Leaving the engine idling, he rolls the window down and rests his arm on the sill, gazing at the incongruous shape of it there in the falling dark. He feels almost glad, almost—in some strange inexpressible way—vindicated, and he imagines what she might do if she saw him here. In a moment he's fantasizing that she comes running from her house, calling his name, looking at the cake and admiring it. This fantasy gives way to something else: images of destruction, flying sugar and candy debris. He's quite surprised to find that he wants her to stay where she is, doing whatever she's doing. He realizes with a feeling akin to elation that what he really wants—and for the moment all he really wants—is what he now has: a perfect vantage point from which to watch oncoming cars.

Turning the engine off, he waits, concentrating on the one thing, full of anticipation—dried blood and grime on his face, his hair all on end, his eyes glazed with rage and humiliation—a man imbued with interest, and happily awaiting the results of his labor.

## Writing Exercises

### INDIVIDUAL

1. All of our skin cells are shed and replaced every month or so, which means we go through maybe a 1,000 new skins in a lifetime. Most of the rest of our cells are replaced as well. We're constantly in transition, never the same person, and most of these kinds of changes are gradual and so not too scary. But is beauty only skin deep? What about those bodily changes that are more sudden and so, more noticeable?

    Imagine a character whose appearance has recently changed, perhaps dramatically. Maybe it was a car accident or plastic surgery, maybe just a diet, a haircut, or some new contact lenses. But remember, even a subtle change may seem huge to your character.

    First, write a description of your character *before* the change. How does he feel about himself? What does he wear and how does he carry himself? How does his self-image affect the kinds of details you choose to focus on?

    Next, describe the character's *new* appearance. Explore the change. Does he pay more attention to his appearance now? How so? New clothes? Does the new look mean a "new you," or is the old self still lurking inside? Character is always a problem of appearance and reality.

2. Sometimes, our characters are too closely based on real-life people or parts of ourselves. We identify so closely with them that we are unwilling to let them get into any serious trouble, and trouble is what a story is all about.

    Write a scene in which your character gets into trouble. How might you have her mess up? Perhaps it's just a little mistake with big repercussions. She makes a fool of herself by saying or doing the wrong thing, or is stubborn, sticking to her guns, even though she is dead wrong about something. Maybe someone else is at fault, but she is the one who feels hurt or humiliated. But just maybe she's chosen to do something downright bad. An indiscretion? An "experiment"? An immoral act?

3. Write two versions of an opening paragraph of a story that introduces a character indirectly—one in which you (as the author) describe her and a second in which another character in the story does the describing.

    In your first version tell the reader what he needs to know about your character: some of the basics (gender, age, race/nationality, class, region, period, etc.), but go further as well, revealing some details about her personality and desires, her values and emotions.

    In your second version, let another character introduce the character. Here, you will have to decide what this second character's attitude toward the first character might be, as well as what he or she does and does not know about her.

4. Have a character *imagine* a conversation with another character. The conversation he is anticipating (and, in some sense, rehearsing for) should be unavoidable. It could, however, be one of two types: a conversation your character is dreading (a shameful admission, breaking the bad news of breakup, etc.) or one your character is looking forward to (revealing his new promotion or raise, a declaration of love, etc.). This first character's imagined version of the conversation should ideally reveal several things: what he *thinks* of the other character and what the other character may actually be like, but more especially, something important and revealing about the character himself, the one who is doing the anticipating.

## COLLABORATIVE

5. Go to a mall, park, restaurant, or some other public place and eavesdrop. In your notebook, write down some lines of dialogue you overhear—anything that captures your attention. Bring your notebook to class, pick your favorite line or two, and write them on the board. From among all the lines of dialogue on the board, each student will choose one to begin a scene. Somewhere along the line, incorporate at least three more lines of dialogue from the board into the scene. Write quickly, and have fun!

6. Divide up into small groups of at least three people each. Each member of the group should brainstorm a list of character names: first and last names, even nicknames if you want. One or two of the names may be blatantly symbolic, but most should be more subtly evocative: compelling but plausible, ordinary but suggestive. Everyone should come up with six to eight names.

   Now, switch lists. Pick a name from this new list, write it on the back of the list (or a separate sheet of paper), and let it help you imagine a character. Write out some basic information about the character (age, race, religion, education, class, marital status, profession), and add a few interesting details about the character (hobbies, bad habits, fears, personality quirks, desires, aspirations, past experiences). Do this for three or four of the character names.

   Finally, switch papers again (making sure no one ends up with their original list of names). Take this cast of characters home and use it to begin a story.

7. Pair up. With your partner, decide on some kind of situation in which two characters are at odds. The more at stake, the better.

   Now, each of you should take the point of view of one or the other of the characters. Flip a coin if you have to. On your own, write a monologue in your character's voice. Let your character speak freely, without restraint, expressing why he feels as strongly as he does.

   Read your monologues aloud to each other. Now, putting the monologues aside, but letting them inform your understanding of the characters, each of you should write a scene in which the two characters talk to each other. They might argue with each other directly, or perhaps the disagreement just colors the way they relate to each other. Maybe one or both of them make verbal digs, act preoccupied, or somehow hint at what's wrong. You might give them something to do together—maybe they're decorating a Christmas tree, going somewhere in a car, preparing for a garage sale, playing Monopoly, or just trying to wolf down breakfast before heading out the door.

Read each other's scenes and compare how each of you used the same material in different ways.

8. Pair up. With your partner, decide on a situation where one character is rambling on about something and a second character is forced to listen. Perhaps the first character is fed up with a shiftless son, just had a fight with her husband, was stuck in a traffic jam, or received a scolding from an unreasonable teacher or boss. Now, each of you should freewrite a monologue for this character, letting her go on and on.

   Exchange monologues, read them silently, and then, individually, rewrite the scene from the point of view of the *listener*, using the three methods of conveying speech. Use the monologue your partner gave you, but *summarize* some of it, present some of it as *indirect speech*, and finally, for use as *direct quotation*, select a few of the choicest, juiciest, most revealing lines.

# 5

# FAR, FAR AWAY
## *Fictional Place*

- *Place and Atmosphere*
- *Harmony and Conflict Between Character and Place*
- *Place and Character*
- *Place and Emotion*
- *Symbolic and Suggestive Place*
- *Alien and Familiar Place*
- *An Exercise in Place*

"It's the job of the writer to create a world that entices you in and shows you what's at stake there," says fiction writer Nancy Huddleston Packer. For some writers, that world itself may inspire the story, while others will tend to focus on setting and atmosphere during the revision process. Still, even from the first, raw draft, it is important to remember Elizabeth Bowen's maxim that "nothing happens nowhere" and Jerome Stern's further admonition that a scene that seems to happen nowhere often seems not to happen at all. The failure to create an atmosphere, to establish a sense of where or when the story takes place, will leave readers bored or confused. And just as the rhythm of your prose must work with and not against your intention, so the use of place must work with and not against your ultimate meaning. Setting helps define a story's dimensions. Setting grounds a story in place.

Like dialogue, setting must do more than one thing at once, from illuminating the story's symbolic underpinnings to such practical kinds of "showing" as reflecting emotion or revealing subtle aspects of a character's life. Yet just as character and plot are interlinked, so character itself is a product of place and culture. We need not only know a character's gender, race, and age, but also in what atmosphere she or he operates to understand the significance of the action. For instance, could you imagine Scarlett O'Hara, from *Gone with the Wind*, without her plantation? Scarlett O'Hara acts as she does because she's a product of the Old South. The setting in which she's always lived defines and helps to explain her.

Sister Clareese in ZZ Packer's story "Every Tongue Shall Confess" doesn't challenge the hypocritical and sexist deacons of the Greater Christ Emanuel Church of the Fire Baptized, because her church, with its familiar roles and expectations, is comforting and the most important thing in her life. The two bickering old women in Eudora Welty's story "A Visit of Charity" behave the way they do because they've been forgotten by the outside world, forced to live out their last days together in the cold, dark nursing home. The main character in Dan Chaon's story "Big Me" reacts against the unpleasant reality of his small town life by imagining an alternative small town in which good and evil are well defined and he's the one in control. His overinvolvement in this imaginary world is what causes him to take the risks that are essential to the story. And finally, setting itself may give rise to an external conflict—one as big as the Vietnam war in "The Things They Carried" or as small as the disrupted birthday party in "Tandolfo the Great." The setting need not seem scary or even problematic to us as readers—a child's birthday party seems harmless enough—but if the character—in this case a drunk, enraged, humiliated clown—finds the setting to be hostile, then a conflict is born.

WHEN I WAS WRITING *Searches and Seizure,* I was living in London, and I needed to describe a hotel room. I've been in lots of hotel rooms, of course, but I didn't want to depend upon my memory. And so I went to the Royal Garden Hotel in Kensington and rented a room, simply to study the furniture there, to feel the glossy top of the wood that is almost not wood, to get the smell of the shower, the textures in the bath, to look at the rhetoric on the cards on top of the television set. This is stuff that I could not invent, and it was important to me to have it down very, very accurately. So I took notes. Somebody watching me would have thought I was a madman.

Stanley Elkin

But realistic settings constructed from memory or research are only part of the challenge, for an intensely created fantasy world makes new boundaries for the mind. *Once upon a time, long ago and far away, a dream, hell, heaven, a garbage shaft, Middle Earth, Hogwarts boarding school,* and *the subconscious* all have been the settings of excellent fiction. Even Utopian fiction, set *Nowhere* with a capital N (or *nowhere* spelled backward, as Samuel Butler had it in *Erehwon*), happens in a nowhere with distinct physical characteristics. Outer space is an exciting setting precisely because its physical boundary is the outer edge of our familiar world. Obviously this does not absolve the writer from the necessity of giving outer space its own characteristics, atmosphere, and logic. If anything, these must be more intensely realized within the fiction, since we have less to borrow from in our own experience.

> The westering sun shining in on his face woke Shevek as the dirigible, clearing the last high pass of the Ne Theras, turned south . . . He pressed his face to the dusty window, and sure enough, down there between two low rusty ridges was a great walled field, the Port. He gazed eagerly, trying to see if there was a space-ship on the pad. Despicable as Urras was, still it was another world; he wanted to see a ship from another world, a voyager across the dry and terrible abyss, a thing made by alien hands. But there was no ship in the Port.
>
> Ursula K. Le Guin, *The Dispossessed*

We may be in outer space, but we are on a planet that shares certain aspects with our own—a westering sun, a mountain pass, and a walled field with two low rusty ridges—disappointingly empty. We've gone some place specific and real, and it is that reality and specificity that allow us to get lost in the story.

But what ingredients, when mixed together, make a setting? Is setting simply a description of the current weather conditions and the sights and smells and sounds immediately in the foreground of your story? Not necessarily. Fiction writer Michael Martone says that a truly effective evocation of fictional setting might resemble those old painted murals in post offices from the 1930s and early '40s. Any one of the figures in the mural has his or her own story, while at the same time those stories are embedded in the larger story of the whole painting. As we stand there observing the figures, we may see the social interactions be-tween them but at the same time, we also observe the layers of history and social forces around these characters as evidenced in their buildings, their inventions, their appliances, their transportation, their agriculture, their efforts to tame and control nature.

"These murals attempt," says Martone, " by the design of hundreds of details, to convey the simultaneous presence of history and social life of the greater community along with the personal specific struggle of a protagonist. Purely as a practical mat-ter, placing stories in such a fertile media will make it easy for things to happen [in a story], for characters to do things."

To illustrate this, Martone refers to a story by Rick DeMarinis entitled "Under the Wheat," about a construction worker who is building nuclear silos in a nearly deserted North Dakota town. As Martone points out, the character in this story is always looking up or down through various membranes of time and space. He is dwarfed by the constructed and the natural features of the place. Here he is fishing on the still surface of the lake created by a nearby dam:

Something takes my hook and strips off ten yards of line and then stops dead. Snag. I reel it in. The pole is bent double and the line is singing. Then something lets go but it isn't the line because I'm still snagged. It breaks the surface, a lady's shoe. It's brown and white with a short heel. I toss it into the bottom of the boat. The water is shallow here, and clear. There's something dark and wide under me like a shadow on the water. An old farmhouse, submerged when the dam filled. There's a deep current around the structure. I can see fence, tires, an old truck, feed pens. There is a fat farmer in the yard looking up at me, checking the weather, and I jump away from him, almost tipping the boat. My heart feels tangled in my ribs. But it is only a stump with arms. The current takes my boat in easy circles. A swimmer would be in serious trouble. I crank up the engine and head back. No fish today. So be it. Sometimes you come home empty-handed. The shoe is new, stylish and was made in Spain.

Setting can be rich and layered with many relics from the past—the barn, the fence, the truck. And it can be ominous—where did that lady's shoe come from?

## Place and Atmosphere

Your fiction must have an *atmosphere* because without it your characters will be unable to breathe.

Part of the atmosphere of a scene or story is its setting, including the locale, period, weather, and time of day. Part of the atmosphere is its *tone*, an attitude taken by the narrative voice that can be described in terms of a quality—sinister, facetious, formal, solemn, wry. The two facets of atmosphere, setting and tone, are often inextricably mixed in the ultimate effect. A sinister atmosphere might be achieved partly by syntax, rhythm, and word choice; partly by darkness, dampness, and a desolated landscape, as is shown in the first line of Edgar Allan Poe's "The Fall of the House of Usher":

During the whole of a dull, dark, and soundless day in the autumn of the year, when the clouds hung oppressively low in the heavens, I had been passing alone, on horseback, through a singularly dreary tract of country; and at length found myself, as the shades of the evening drew on, within view of the melancholy House of Usher.

In Annie Proulx's story "What Kind of Furniture Would Jesus Pick?" we can feel the extent of a beleaguered housewife's oppression when we read this description of the wind attacking her Wyoming ranch:

The house lay directly in line with a gap in the encircling hills to the northwest, and through this notch the prevailing winds poured, falling on the house with ferocity. The house shuddered as the wind punched it and slid along its sides like a released torrent from a broken dam. Week after week in winter it sank and rose, attacked and feinted. When she put her head down and went out to the truck it yanked at her clothing, shot up her sleeves, whisked her hair into a raveled fright wig.

The words *encircling hills, prevailing winds, falling, ferocity, shuddered, punched, released torrent, broken dam, week after week, sank and rose, attacked and feinted, put her head down, yanked, shot, whisked,* and *raveled fright wig* leave no doubt as to how she's feeling, not only about the wind, but about her life in general.

You can orient your reader in a place with straight information (*On the southern bank of the Bayou Teche . . .*), but as with the revelation of character, you may more effectively reveal place through concrete detail (*The bugs hung over the black water in clusters of a steady hum*). Stuart Dybeck offers another set of evocative details in his story "Breasts": *Joe's bedroom window was open too, and a breeze that tingled the blinds they hadn't bothered to draw seemed tinted with the glow of the new arc lights the city had erected.* In both of these examples the information is indirect. We aren't sure yet what to make of the clusters of bugs or the open blinds, but they reveal an attitude toward the setting, and we seem to experience it firsthand.

## Harmony and Conflict Between Character and Place

If character is the foreground of fiction, setting is the background, and as in a painting's composition, the foreground may be in harmony or in conflict with the background. If we think of the Impressionist paintings of the late nineteenth century, we think of the harmony of, say, women with light-scattering parasols strolling against summer landscapes of light-scattering trees. By contrast, the Spanish painter Jose Cortijo has a portrait of a girl on her Communion day; she sits curled and ruffled, in a lace mantilla, on an ornately carved Mediterranean throne against a backdrop of stark, harshly lit, poverty-stricken shacks.

Likewise, the setting and characters of a story may be in harmony:

> The Bus to St. James's—a Protestant Episcopal school for boys and girls—started its round at eight o'clock in the morning, from a corner of Park Avenue in the Sixties. The earliness of the hour meant that some of the parents who took their children there were sleepy and still without coffee, but with a clear sky the light struck the city at an extreme angle, the air was fresh, and it was an exceptionally cheerful time of day. It was the hour when cooks and door men walk dogs, and when porters scrub the lobby floor mats with soap and water.
>
> John Cheever, "The Bus to St. James's"

Contentment, regularity, and peace are suggested by this passage. For the parents and the students of St. James, all is right with the world.

Or there can be an inherent conflict between the background and foreground:

> . . . He opened the door himself and started down the walk to get her going. The sky was a dying violet and the houses stood out darkly against it, bulbous liver-colored monstrosities of a uniform ugliness though no two were alike. Since this had been a fashionable neighborhood forty years ago, his mother persisted in thinking they did well to have an apartment in it. Each house had a narrow collar of dirt around it in which sat, usually, a grubby child. Julian walked with his hands in his pockets, his head down and thrust forward and his eyes glazed with the determination to make himself completely numb during the time he would be sacrificed to her pleasure.
>
> Flannery O'Connor, "Everything That Rises Must Converge"

Notice how images of the time of day work with concrete details of place to create very different atmospheres—on the one hand *morning, Park Avenue, earliness, clear sky, light, extreme angle, air, fresh, cheerful, dogs, scrub, soap, water;* and on the other *dying violet, darkly, bulbous liver-colored monstrosities, uniform ugliness, narrow, dirt, grubby child.* Notice also that where conflict occurs, there is already "narrative content," or the makings of a story. We might reasonably expect that in the Cheever story, where the characters are in apparent harmony with their background, there is or will be conflict in the foreground between or among those children, parents, and perhaps the servitors who keep their lives so well scrubbed. It won't surprise us when the peace and quiet of this world shatters, and the weather gets downright dangerous by the end of the story.

## Place and Character

One of the most economical means of sketching a character is simply to show readers a personal space that the character has created, be it a bedroom, locker, kitchen, hideout, office cubicle, or even the interior of a car. This technique is illustrated in Elizabeth Tallent's story "Prowler," as Dennis, a divorced father, surveys his thirteen-year-old son's bedroom.

> Dennis believes it tells everything about Kenny: photo-realist motorcycles, chrome and highly evolved threat, grace the walls, along with a frail Kafka razor-bladed from a library book, a sin so small and so unprecedented that Dennis uncharacteristically forgot to mention it to him. If Kenny's motorcycle paintings are depressing, surely jug-eared Kafka promises complexity, contradiction, hope?

Through the description of Kenny's room, we see that the boy is making a transition to the rocky years of adolescence, showing both a typical interest in fast, powerful, rebellious vehicles and also signs of more private teenage angst (and what is he doing with razor blades anyway?). Not every parent would interpret a Kafka portrait, much less a stolen one, as a sign of hope—in this case, the reflection may reveal as much about the observing father as about the indirectly observed son, adding a further layer of complexity.

Doug Coupland uses an even more self-conscious version of the same technique to create a quick portrait of the household of fanatical young Microsoft employees featured in his novel *Microserfs*:

> More details about our group house—Our House of Wayward Mobility.
>
> Because the house receives almost no sun, moss and algae tend to colonize what surfaces they can. There is a cherry tree, crippled by a fungus. The rear verandah, built of untreated 2×4's, has quietly rotted away, and the sliding door in the kitchen has been braced shut with a hockey stick to prevent the unwary from straying into the suburban abyss. . . .
>
> Inside, each of us has a bedroom. Because of the McDonald's-like turnover in the house, the public rooms—the living room, kitchen, dining room, and basement—are bleak to say the least. The dormlike atmosphere precludes heavy-duty interior design ideas. In the living room are two velveteen sofas that were too big and too ugly for some long-gone tenants to take with them. Littered about the Tiki Green shag carpet are:
>
> + Two Microsoft Works PC inflatable beach cushions
> + One Mitsubishi 27-inch color TV
> + Various vitamin bottles
> + Several weight-gaining system cartons (mine)
> + 86 copies of MacWEEK arranged in chronological order by Bug Barbecue, who will go berserk if you so much as move one issue out of date
> + Bone-shaped chew toys for when Mishka visits
> + Two PowerBooks
> + Three IKEA mugs encrusted with last month's blender drink sensation
> + Two 12.5 pound dumbbells (Susan's)
> + A Windows NT box
> + Three baseball caps (two Mariners, one A's)
> + Abe's Battlestar Galactica trading card album
> + Todd's pile of books on how to change your life to win! (*Getting Past OK, 7 Habits of Highly Effective People* . . .)
>
> The kitchen is stocked with ramshackle 1970s avocado green appliances. You can almost hear the ghost of Emily Hartley yelling "Hi, Bob!" every time you open the fridge door (a sea of magnets and 4×6-inch photos of last year's house parties). Our mail is in little piles by the front door: bills, Star Trek junk mail, and the heap-o-catalogues next to the phone.
>
> I think we'd order our lives via 1-800 numbers if we could.

Like their mold-ravaged house, the Microserfs also receive almost no sun as they pursue their project shipping deadlines round the clock; the litter of objects listed gives clues to whatever thin slices of personality remain.

What generalizations might you make about the Microserfs after reading this passage? Are they self-absorbed? Driven? Wealthy? Immature? Focused? Sloppy? All these descriptions may apply, but they seem bland and inadequate when juxtaposed with the list of specific details that bring them to life in a way that mere adjectives never could.

Here is Michael Martone again: "The reader is to be pulled in by the preponderance of the evidence that he or she has been sifting through. As you read, the details fall like snow that suddenly is ash. The character is clearly visible once he is coated, like a statue in the town square after such a storm, with a film of detail."

SUPPOSE WE THINK OF A SCENE IN YOUR NOVEL as a scene in a play. Any scene in any play takes place on some sort of set. I feel that the sets in your play are quite wonderful, but you never let us see them. A spotlight follows every move the characters make and throws an almost blinding radiance on them, but it is a little like the spotlight a burglar uses when he is cracking a safe; it illuminates a small circle and the rest of the stage is in darkness most of the time . . . . It would be better, I think, if you occasionally used a spotlight large enough to illuminate the corners of the room, for those corners have gone on existing all through the most dramatic moments.

Caroline Gordon to Flannery O'Connor

## Place and Emotion

Our relation to place, time, and weather, like our relation to clothes and other objects, is charged with emotion more or less subtle, more or less profound. It is filled with judgment mellow or harsh. And it alters according to what happens to us. In some rooms you are always trapped; you enter them with grim purpose and escape them as soon as you can. Others invite you to settle in, to nestle or carouse. Some landscapes lift your spirits; others depress you. Cold weather gives you energy and bounce, or else it clogs your head and makes you huddle, struggling. You describe yourself as a night person or a morning person. The house you loved as a child now makes you, precisely because you were once happy there, think of loss and death. It is central to fiction that all such emotion be used or heightened (or invented) to dramatic effect.

Imagine experiencing a thunderstorm when in the throes of a new love: the rain might seem to glitter, the lightning to sizzle, the thunder to rumble with anticipation. The downpour would refresh and exhilarate, nourishing the newly budding violets. Then imagine how the very same storm would feel in the midst of a lousy romantic breakup: the raindrops would be thick and cold, almost greasy; the lightning would slash at the clouds; the thunder would growl. Torrents of rain would beat the delicate tulips to the ground.

Because we have all had the experience of seeing our inner emotional states reflected by the outer world, we instinctively understand that setting can serve as a mirror of emotion. Seen through the eyes of a character, setting is never neutral.

In Frederick Busch's story "Ralph the Duck," the narrator thinks back on a troubling incident that had taken place during his rounds at the local college that evening. He sits with a "king-sized drink composed of sour mash whiskey and ice" and

> In our back room, which is on the northern end of the house, and cold for sitting in that close to dawn, I sat and watched the texture of the sky change. It was going to snow, and I wanted to see the storm come up the valley.

He seems to sense that there is worse trouble to come, and in fact it later arrives in the middle of an ice storm. Yet by the story's end, when he is feeling some relief and hope (to which the laconic narrator himself would never admit), we see these feelings mirrored in a very different view of the same landscape.

> I was at the northern windows, looking through the mullions down the valley to the faint red line along the mounds and little peaks of the ridge beyond the valley. The sun was going to come up, and I was looking for it.

Setting can help to portray a swirl of emotion, as in this moment from "Where Are You Going, Where Have You Been?" in which Arnold Friend's attempts to disorient and terrorize Connie are succeeding, and she is losing her grasp on all that is familiar, even as she feels nostalgic for the home she is leaving:

> The kitchen looked like a place she had never seen before, some room she had run inside but which wasn't good enough, wasn't going to help her. The kitchen window had never had a curtain, after three years, and there were dishes in the sink for her to do—probably—and if you ran your hand across the table you'd probably feel something sticky there.

Emotion is conveyed in these and similar passages, even as the story is being anchored in place. When a reader senses that setting is being used to reveal something important, there is no danger of its being what one student calls "the stuff you skip."

What do we skip? Self-indulgent description of setting that seems to exist only as an excuse for flowery, inflated language: "The majestic mountains rose like great behemoths above the grassy plains, and the plains themselves rolled away like a great and endless ocean." Description of setting that feels forced—an overly fastidious catalog of details, often awkwardly placed: "The dead man's pantry was stocked with canisters of oatmeal, Cream of Wheat, corn meal, flour (white and whole wheat), rice (brown and white), couscous, instant grits, and Wheatena, and bottles of various cooking oils—corn, olive, canola, sunflower and vegetable." Description that is generic and perfunctory, lacking in emotional significance or authorial judgment: "Robert's farm consisted of 1276 acres of land, most of which was tillable, but seventy-seven acres of which was made up of woodlots and inaccessible bottomland along three different creeks."

Michael Martone, in a lecture on setting, noted: "In many stories I read, [household] appliances are often deployed neutrally used mainly . . . as a way to fill up space, background things merely to run or handle, props, business for the character to perform when the real action is happening between people."

When we read any nonessential description, our eyes and minds will glaze over and we'll either skip ahead to the good parts or stop reading altogether.

"SWALLOWS, FLITTING OVER THE SURFACE OF THE WATER, twittered gaily"— eliminate such commonplaces. You have to choose small details in describing nature, grouping them in such a way that if you close your eyes after reading it you can picture the whole thing. For example, you'll get a picture of a moonlit night if you write that on the dam of the mill a piece of broken bottle flashed like a bright star and the black shadow of a dog or a wolf rolled by like a ball, etc.

Anton Chekhov to his brother Alexander

## Symbolic and Suggestive Place

Ever since the rosy-fingered dawn came over the battlefield of Homer's *Iliad* (and no doubt well before that), poets and writers have used the context of history, night, storm, stars, sea, city, and plain to give their stories a sense of reaching out toward the universe. Sometimes the universe resonates with an answer, and in his plays Shakespeare consistently drew parallels between the conflicts of the heavenly bodies and the conflicts of nations and characters.

In "The Life You Save May Be Your Own," Flannery O'Connor uses the elements in a conscious Shakespearian way, letting the setting reflect and affect the theme.

The old woman and her daughter were sitting on their own porch when Mr. Shiflet came up their road for the first time. The old woman slid to the edge of her chair and leaned forward, shading her eyes from the piercing sunset with her hand. The daughter could not see far in front of her and continued to play with her fingers. Although the old woman lived in this desolate spot with only her daughter, and she had never seen Mr. Shiflet before, she could tell, even from a distance, that he was a tramp and no one to be afraid of. His left coat sleeve was folded up to show there was only half an arm in it and his gaunt figure listed lightly to the side as if the breeze were pushing him. He had on a black town suit and a brown felt hat that was turned up in the front and down in the back and he carried a tin tool box by a handle. He came on at an amble, up her road, his face turned toward the sun which appeared to be balancing itself on the peak of a small mountain.

The focus in this opening paragraph of the story is on the characters and their actions, and the setting is economically, almost incidentally, established: *porch, road, sunset, breeze, peak, small mountain.* What the passage gives us is a type of landscape, rural and harsh; the only adjectives in the description of the setting are *piercing, desolate,* and *small.* But this general background works together with details of action, thought, and appearance to establish a great deal more that is both informational and emotional. The old woman's peering suggests that people on the road are not only unusual but suspicious. On the other hand, that she is reassured to see a tramp suggests both a period and a set of assumptions about country life. That Mr. Shiflet wears a town suit establishes him as a stranger to this set of assumptions. That the sun appears to be balancing itself (we are not sure whether it is the old woman's observation or the author's) leaves us, at the end of the paragraph, with a sense of anticipation and tension.

Now, what happens in the story is this: Mr. Shiflet repairs the old woman's car and (in order to get the car) marries her retarded daughter. He abandons the daughter on their honeymoon and picks up a hitchhiker who insults both Mr. Shiflet and the memory of his mother. The hitchhiker jumps out. Mr. Shiflet curses and drives on.

Throughout the story, as in the first paragraph, the focus remains on the characters and their actions. Yet the landscape and the weather make their presence felt, subtly commenting on attitudes and actions. As Mr. Shiflet's fortunes wax promising and he expresses satisfaction with his own morality, "A fat yellow moon appeared in the branches of the fig tree as if it were going to roost there with the chickens." When, hatching his plot, he sits on the steps with the mother and daughter, "The old woman's three mountains were black against the sky." Once he has abandoned the girl, the weather grows "hot and sultry, and the country had flattened out. Deep in the sky a storm was preparing very slowly and without thunder." Once more there is a sunset, but this time the sun "was a reddening ball that through his windshield was slightly flat on the bottom and top," and this deflated sun reminds us of the "balanced" one about to be punctured by the peak in its inevitable decline. When the hitchhiker has left him, a cloud covers the sun, and Mr. Shiflet in his fury prays for the Lord to "break forth and wash the slime from this earth!" His prayer is apparently answered.

After a few minutes there was a guffawing peal of thunder from behind and fantastic raindrops, like tin-can tops, crashed over the rear of Mr. Shiflet's car. Very quickly he stepped on the gas and with his stump sticking out the window he raced the galloping shower to Mobile.

The setting in this story, as this bald summary emphasizes, is deliberately used as a comment on the actions. The behavior of the weather, in ironic juxtaposition to the title, "The Life You Save May Be Your Own," makes clear that the "slime" Mr. Shiflet has damned may be himself. Yet the reader is never aware of this as a symbolic intrusion. The setting remains natural and realistically convincing, an incidental backdrop, until the heavens are ready to make their guffawing comment.

Robert Coover's settings rarely present a symbolic or sentient universe, but they produce in us an emotionally charged expectation of what is likely to happen here. The following passages are the opening paragraphs of three short stories from a single collection, *Pricksongs and Descants*. Notice how the three different settings are achieved not only by imagery and content, but also by the very different rhythms of the sentence structure.

A pine forest in the midafternoon. Two children follow an old man, dropping breadcrumbs, singing nursery tunes. Dense earthy greens seep into the darkening distance, flecked and streaked with filtered sunlight. Spots of red, violet, pale blue, gold, burnt orange. The girl carries a basket for gathering flowers. The boy is occupied with the crumbs. Their song tells of God's care for little ones.

"The Gingerbread House"

*Situation:* television panel game, live audience. Stage strobelit and cameras insecting about. Moderator, bag shape corseted and black suited behind desk/rostrum, blinking mockmodesty at lens and lamps, practised pucker on his soft mouth and brows arched in mild goodguy astonishment. Opposite him, the panel: Aged Clown, Lovely Lady and Mr. America, fat as the continent and bald as an eagle. There is an empty chair between Lady and Mr. A, which is now filled, to the delighted squeals of all, by a spectator dragged protesting from the Audience, nondescript introduced as Unwilling Participant, or more simply, Bad Sport. Audience: same as ever, docile, responsive, good-natured, terrifying. And the Bad Sport, you ask, who is he? fool! thou art!

"Panel Game"

She arrives at 7:40, ten minutes late, but the children, Jimmy and Bitsy, are still eating supper, and their parents are not ready to go yet. From the other rooms come the sounds of a baby screaming, water running, a television musical (no words: probably a dance number—patterns of gliding figures come to mind). Mrs. Tucker sweeps into the kitchen, fussing with her hair, and snatches a baby bottle full of milk out of a pan of warm water, rushes out again. Harry! she calls. The babysitter's here already!

"The Babysitter"

Here are three quite familiar places: a fairy-tale forest, a television studio, and a suburban house. In at least the first two selections, the locale is more consciously and insistently set than in the O'Connor opening, yet all three remain suggestive backdrops rather than active participants—no guffawing or galloping here. Coover directs our attitude toward these places through imagery and tone.

In "The Gingerbread House," the forest is a neverland, and the time is once upon a time, though there are grimmer-than-Grimm hints of violence about it. Simple sentence structure helps establish the childlike quality appropriate to a fairy tale. But a more complex sentence intervenes, with surprising intensity of imagery: *dense, earthy, seep, darkening, flecked, streaked, filtered*. Because of this, the innocence of the tone is set askew, so that by the time we hear of God's care for little ones, we fully and accurately expect a brutal disillusionment.

Setting can often, and in a variety of ways, arouse reader expectation and foreshadow events to come. In "The Gingerbread House," there is an implied conflict between character and setting, between the sentimentality of the children's flowers and nursery tunes and the threatening forest, so that we are immediately aware of the central conflict of the story: innocence versus violence. As in the Cheever story "The Bus to St. James's," anticipation can also be aroused by an insistent single attitude toward setting, and in this case the reader, being a contrary sort of person, is likely to anticipate a change or paradox.

Where conflict between character and setting is immediately introduced, as it is in both "The Gingerbread House" and "Panel Game," it is usually because the character is unfamiliar with, or uncomfortable in, the setting. In "Panel Game" it's both. The television studio is a place of hysteria, chaos, and hypocrisy (as evidenced by the moderator's mockmodesty and practiced pucker). The television studio, which is in fact a familiar and unthreatening place to most of us, has been made mad. This is achieved partly by violating expected grammar. The sentences are not sentences. They are missing vital verbs and logical connectives, so that the images are squashed against each other. The prose is cluttered, effortful, negative; as a result, as reader you know "the delighted squeals of all" do not include your own, and you're ready to sympathize with the unwilling central character (you!).

In "The Babysitter," notice that the setting is ordinary and is presented as ordinary. The sentences have standard and rather leisurely syntax; neither form nor image startles. Details are generic, not specific: the house is presented without a style; the children are named but not seen; Mrs. Tucker behaves in a way predictable and familiar to most anyone in contemporary America. What Coover has in fact done is to present us with a setting so usual, so "typical," that we begin to suspect that something unusual is afoot.

Indeed, the Tuckers, their house, their children, their car, their night out, and their babysitter remain unvaryingly typical throughout all the external actions in the course of the evening. Against this relentlessly wholesome backdrop play the individual fantasies of the characters—brilliant, brutal, sexual, dangerous, and violent—that provide the conflict of the story.

## Alien and Familiar Place

Many poets and novelists have observed that the function of literature is to make the ordinary fresh and strange. F. Scott Fitzgerald, on the other hand, advised a young writer that reporting extreme things as if they were ordinary was the starting point of fiction. Both of these views are true, and they are particularly true of setting. Whether a place is familiar or unfamiliar, comfortable or discomfiting in fiction has nothing to do with whether the reader actually knows the place and feels good there. It is an attitude taken, an assumption made. In his detective novels, Ross Macdonald assumes a familiarity toward California that is perfectly translatable into any language ("I turned left off the highway and down an old switchback blacktop to a dead end"), whereas even the natives of North Hollywood must feel alien on Tom Wolfe's version of their streets.

> . . . endless scorched boulevards lined with one-story stores, shops, bowling alleys, skating rinks, taco drive-ins, all of them shaped not like rectangles but like trapezoids, from the way the roofs slant up from the back and the plate-glass fronts slant out as if they're going to pitch forward on the sidewalk and throw up.
>
> *The Kandy-Kolored Tangerine-Flake Streamline Baby*

The prose of Tom Wolfe, whether about rural North Carolina, Fifth Avenue, or Cape Kennedy, lives in a tone of constant breathless astonishment. By contrast, Ray Bradbury's outer space is pure down-home.

> It was quiet in the deep morning of Mars, as quiet as a cool black well, with stars shining in the canal waters, and, breathing in every room, the children curled with their spiders in closed hands.
>
> *The Martian Chronicles*

One great advantage of being a writer is that you may create the world. Places and the elements have the significance and the emotional effect you give them in language. As a person you may be depressed by rain, but as an author you are free to make rain mean freshness, growth, bounty, and God. You may choose; the only thing you are not free to do is not to choose.

As with character, the first requisite of effective setting is to know it fully, to experience it mentally, and the second is to create it through significant detail. What sort of place is this, and what are its peculiarities? What is the weather like, the light, the season, the time of day? What are the contours of the land and architecture? What are the social assumptions of the inhabitants, and how familiar and comfortable are the characters with this place and its lifestyle? These things are not less important in fiction than in life, but more so, since their selection inevitably takes on significance. And as in the stories at the end of this chapter, "The English Pupil," "Wickedness," and "Love and Hydrogen," setting may become a character itself.

## An Exercise in Place

Here are a series of passages about war, set in different periods and places. The first is in Russia during the campaign of Napoleon, the second on the island of Pianosa during World War II, and the third in a post-holocaust future.

Several tens of thousands of the slain lay in diverse postures and various uniforms. Over the whole field, previously so gaily beautiful with the glitter of bayonets and cloudlets of smoke in the morning sun, there now spread a mist of damp and smoke and a strange acid smell of saltpeter and blood. Clouds gathered and drops of rain began to fall on the dead and wounded, on the frightened, exhausted, and hesitating men, as if to say: Enough, men! Enough! Cease! Bethink yourselves! What are you doing?

Leo Tolstoy, *War and Peace*

Their only hope was that it would never stop raining, and they had no hope because they all knew it would. When it did stop raining in Pianosa, it rained in Bologna. When it stopped raining in Bologna, it began again in Pianosa. If there was no rain at all, there were freakish, inexplicable phenomena like the epidemic of diarrhea or the bomb line that moved. Four times during the first six days they were assembled and briefed and then sent back. Once, they took off and were flying in formation when the control tower summoned them down. The more it rained, the worse they suffered. The worse they suffered, the more they prayed that it would continue raining.

Joseph Heller, *Catch-22*

She liked the wild, quatrosyllabic lilt of the word, Barbarian. Then, looking beyond the wooden fence, she saw a trace of movement in the fields beyond. It was not the wind among the young corn; or, if it was wind among the young corn, it carried her the whinny of a raucous horse. It was too early for poppies but she saw a flare of scarlet. She ceased to watch the Soldiers; instead she watched the movement flow to the fences and crash through them and across the tender wheat. Bursting from the undergrowth came horseman after horseman. They flashed with curious curved plates of metal dredged up from the ruins. Their horses were bizarrely caparisoned with rags, small knives, bells and chains dangling from manes and tails, and man and horse together, unholy centaurs crudely daubed with paint, looked twice as large as life. They fired long guns. Confronted with the terrors of the night in the freshest hours of the morning, the gentle crowd scattered, wailing.

Angela Carter, *Heroes and Villains*

Compare the settings. How do climate, period, imagery, and language contribute to each? To what degree is setting a sentient force? Is there conflict between character and setting? How does setting affect and/or reveal the attitude taken toward the war? What mood, what emotions are implied?

# The English Pupil

### ANDREA BARRETT

Outside Uppsala, on a late December afternoon in 1777, a figure tucked in a small sleigh ordered his coachman to keep driving.

"Hammarby," he said. "Please."

The words were cracked, almost unintelligible. The coachman was afraid. At home he had a wife, two daughters, and a mother-in-law, all dependent on him; his employers had strictly forbidden him to take the sleigh beyond the city limits, and he feared for his job. But his master was dying and these afternoon drives were his only remaining pleasure. He was weak and depressed and it had been months since he'd voiced even such a modest wish.

How could the coachman say no? He grumbled a bit and then drove the few miles across the plain without further complaint.

It was very cold. The air was crisp and dry. The sun, already low in the sky, made the fields glitter. Beneath the sleigh the snow was so smooth that the runners seemed to float. Carl Linnaeus, wrapped in sheepskins, watched the landscape speeding by and thought of Lappland, which he'd explored when he was young. Aspens and alders and birches budding, geese with their tiny yellow goslings. Gadflies longing to lay their eggs chased frantic herds of reindeer. In Jokkmokk, near the Gulf of Bothnia, the local pastor had tried to convince him that the clouds sweeping over the mountains carried off trees and animals. He had learned how to trap ptarmigan, how to shoot wolves with a bow, how to make thread with reindeer tendons, and how to cure chilblains with the fat that exuded from toasted reindeer cheese. At night, under the polar star, the sheer beauty of the natural world had knocked him to the ground. He had been twenty-five then, and wildly energetic. Now he was seventy.

His once-famous memory was nearly gone, eroded by a series of strokes—he forgot where he was and what he was doing; he forgot the names of plants and animals; he forgot faces, places, dates. Sometimes he forgot his own name. His mind, which had once seemed to hold the whole world, had been occupied by a great dark lake that spread farther every day and around which he tiptoed gingerly. When he reached for facts they darted like minnows across the water and could only be captured by cunning and indirection. Pehr Artedi, the friend of his youth, had brought order to the study of fishes, the minnows included. In Amsterdam Artedi had fallen into a canal after a night of beer and conversation and had been found the next morning, drowned.

The sleigh flew through the snowy landscape. His legs were paralyzed, along with one arm and his bladder and part of his face; he could not dress or wash or feed himself. At home, when he tried to rise from his armchair unaided, he fell and lay helpless on the floor until his wife, Sara Lisa, retrieved him. Sara Lisa was busy with other tasks and often he lay there for some time.

But Sara Lisa was back at their house in Uppsala, and he was beyond her reach. The horses pulling him might have been reindeer; the coachman a Lapp dressed in fur and skins. Hammarby, the estate he'd bought as a country retreat years ago, at the height of his fame, was waiting for him. The door leading into the kitchen was wide and the sleigh was small. Linnaeus gestured for the coachman to push the sleigh inside.

The coachman was called Pehr; a common name. There had been Artedi, of course, and then after him all the students named Pehr: Pehr Lofling, Pehr Forskal, Pehr Osbeck, Pehr Kalm. Half of them were dead. This Pehr, the coachman Pehr, lifted Linnaeus out of the sleigh and carried him carefully into the house. The kitchen was clean and almost bare: a rough table, a few straight chairs.

Pehr set Linnaeus on the floor, propped against the wall, and then he went back outside and unhitched the horses and shoved the sleigh through the door and in front of the stone fireplace. He was very worried and feared he had made a mistake. His master's face was white and drawn and his hand, gesturing from the sleigh to the door again and again, had been curled like a claw.

"Fire?" Linnaeus said, or thought he said. At certain moments, when the lake receded a bit and left a wider path around the shore, he was aware that the words coming out of his mouth bore little resemblance to the words he meant. Often he could only produce a syllable at a time. But he said something and gestured toward the fireplace, and Pehr had a good deal of sense. Pehr lifted Linnaeus back into the sleigh, tucked the sheepskins around his legs and his torso, and then built a fire. Soon the flames began to warm the room. The sky darkened outside; the room was dark except for the glow from the logs. Pehr went out to tend to the horses and Linnaeus, staring into the flames, felt his beloved place around him.

He'd rebuilt this house and added several wings; on the hill he'd built a small museum for his herbarium and his insect collection and his rocks and zoological specimens. In his study and bedroom the walls were papered from ceiling to floor with botanical etchings and prints, and outside, among the elms and beyond the Siberian garden, the glass bells he'd hung sang in the wind. In his youth he had heard the cries of ptarmigan, which had sounded like a kind of laughter. The fire was warm on his face and his hands, and when Pehr returned from the horses Linnaeus gestured toward his tobacco and his pipe.

Pehr filled the pipe, lit it, and placed it in his master's mouth. "We should go back," he said. "Your family will be worried." Worried was a kind word, Pehr knew; his master's wife would be raging, possibly blaming him. They were an hour late already and the sun was gone.

Linnaeus puffed on his pipe and said nothing. He was very pleased with himself. The fire was warm, his pipe drew well, no one knew where he was but Pehr and Pehr had the rare gift of silence. A dog lying near the hearth would have completed his happiness. Across the dark lake in his mind he saw Pompey, the best of all his dogs, barking at the water. Pompey had walked with him each summer Sunday from here to the parish church and sat in the pew beside him. They'd stayed for an hour, ample time for a sermon; if the parson spoke longer they rose and left anyway. Pompey, so smart and funny, had learned the pattern if not the meaning. When Linnaeus was ill, Pompey left for church at the appropriate time, hopped into the appropriate bench, stayed for an hour and then scampered out. The neighbors had learned to watch for his antics. Now he was dead.

"Sir?" the coachman said.

His name was Pehr, Linnaeus remembered. Like Osbeck and Forskal, Lofling and Kalm. There had been others, too: those he had taught at the university in Uppsala and those he had taught privately here at Hammarby. Germans and Danes, Russians and Swiss, Finns and a few Norwegians; a Frenchman, who had not worked out, and an American, who had; one Englishman, still around. And then there were those he had hardly known, who had come by the hundreds to the great botanic excursions he'd organized around the city. Dressed in loose linen suits, their arms full of nets and jars, they had trailed him in a huge parade, gathering plants and insects and herding around him at resting places to listen to him lecture on the treasures they'd found. They were young, and when he was young he had often kept them out for twelve or thirteen hours at a stretch. On their return to the Botanic Gardens they had sometimes been hailed by a kettledrum and French horns. Outside the garden the band had stopped and cheered: *Vivat scientia! Vivat Linnaeus!* Lately there were those who attacked his work.

The coachman was worried, Linnaeus could see. He crouched to the right of the sleigh, tapping a bit of kindling on the floor. "They will be looking for you," he said.

And of course it was true; his family was always looking for him. Always looking, wanting, needing, demanding. He had written and taught and lectured and tutored, traveled and scrabbled and scrambled; and always Sara Lisa said there was not enough money, they needed more, she was worried about Carl Junior and the girls. Carl Junior was lazy, he needed more schooling. The girls needed frocks, the girls needed shoes. The girls needed earrings to wear to a dance where they might meet appropriate husbands.

The three oldest looked and acted like their mother: large-boned, coarse-featured, practical. Sophia seemed to belong to another genus entirely. He thought of her fine straight nose, her beautiful eyes. When she was small he used to take her with him to his lectures, where she would stand between his knees and listen. Now she was engaged. On his tour of Lappland, with the whole world still waiting to be named, he'd believed that he and everyone he loved would live forever.

Now he had named almost everything and everyone knew his name. How clear and simple was the system of his nomenclature! Two names, like human names: a generic name common to all the species of one genus; a specific name distinguishing differences. He liked names that clearly described a feature of the genus: *Potamogeton*, by the river; *Drosera*, like a dew. Names that honored botanists also pleased him. In England the King had built a huge garden called Kew, in which wooden labels named each plant according to his system. The King of France had done the same thing at the Trianon. In Spain and Russia and South America plants bore names that he'd devised, and on his coat he wore the ribbon that named him a Knight of the Polar Star. But his monkey Grinn, a present from the Queen, was dead; and also Sjup the raccoon and the parrot who had sat on his shoulder at meals and the weasel who wore a bell on his neck and hunted rats among the rocks.

There was a noise outside. Pehr leapt up and a woman and a man walked through the door. Pehr was all apologies, blushing, shuffling, nervous. The woman touched his arm and said, "It wasn't your fault." Then she said, "Papa?"

One of his daughters, Linnaeus thought. She was pretty, she was smiling; she was almost surely Sophia. The man by her side looked familiar, and from the way he held Sophia's elbow Linnaeus wondered if it might be her husband. Had she married? He remembered no wedding. Her fiancé? Her fiancé, then. Or not: the man bent low, bringing his face down to Linnaeus's like the moon falling from the sky.

"Sir?" he said. "Sir?"

One of those moments in which no words were possible was upon him. He gazed at the open, handsome face of the young man, aware that this was someone he knew. The man said, "It's Rotheram, sir."

Rotheram. Rotheram. The sound was like the wind moving over the Lappland hills. Rotheram, one of his pupils, not a fiancé at all. Human beings had two names, like plants, by which they might be recalled. Nature was a cryptogram and the scientific method a key; nature was a labyrinth and this method the thread of Ariadne. Or the world was an alphabet written in God's hand, which he, Carl Linnaeus, had been called to decipher. One of his pupils had come to see him, one of the pupils he'd sent to all the corners of the world and called, half-jokingly, his apostles. This one straightened now, a few feet away, most considerately not blocking the fire. What was his name? He was young, vigorous, strongly built. Was he Lofling, then? Or Ternström, Hasselquist, Falck?

The woman frowned. "Papa," she said. "Can we just sit you up? We've been looking everywhere for you."

Sophia. The man bent over again, sliding his hands beneath Linnaeus's armpits and gently raising him to a sitting position. He was Hasselquist or Ternström, Lofling or Forskal or Falck. Or he was none of them, because all of them were dead.

Linnaeus's mind left his body, rose and traveled along the paths his apostles had taken. He was young again, as they had been: twenty-five, thirty, thirty-five, the years he had done his best work. He was Christopher Ternström, that married pastor who'd been such a passionate botanist. Sailing to the East Indies in search of a tea plant and some living goldfish to give to the Queen, mailing letters back to his teacher from Cádiz. On a group of islands off Cambodia he had succumbed to a tropical fever. His wife had berated Linnaeus for luring her husband to his death.

But he was not Linnaeus. He was Fredrik Hasselquist, modest and poor, who had landed in Smyrna and traveled through Palestine and Syria and Cyprus and Rhodes, gathering plants and animals and keeping a diary so precise that it had broken Linnaeus's heart to edit it. Twice he had performed this task, once for Hasselquist, once for Artedi. After the drowning, he had edited Artedi's book on the fish. Hasselquist died in a village outside Smyrna, when he was thirty.

Of course there were those who had made it back: Pehr Osbeck, who had returned from China with a huge collection of new plants and a china tea-set decorated with Linnaeus's own flower; Marten Kahler, who'd returned with nothing. Kahler's health had been broken by the shipwreck in the North Sea, by the fever that followed the attack in Marseilles, by his endless, grinding poverty. The chest containing his collections had been captured by pirates long before it reached Sweden. Then there was Rolander, Daniel Rolander—was that the man who was with him now?

But he had said Ro . . ., Ro . . ., *Rotheram, that's who it was, the English pupil.* Nomenclature is a mnemonic art. In Surinam the heat had crumpled Rolander's body and melted his mind. All he brought home was a lone pot of Indian fig covered with cochineal insects, which Linnaeus's gardener had mistakenly washed away. Lost insects and a handful of gray seeds, which Rolander claimed to be pearls. When Linnaeus gently pointed out the error, Rolander had left in a huff for Denmark, where he was reportedly living on charity. The others were dead: Lofling, Forskal, and Falck.

Sophia said, "Papa, we looked all over—why didn't you come back?"

Pehr the coachman said, "I'm sorry, he begged me."

The pupil—*Lofling?*—said, "How long has he been weeping like this?"

But Pehr wasn't weeping, Pehr was fine. Someone, not Pehr or Sophia, was laughing. Linnaeus remembered how Lofling had taken dictation from him when his hands were crippled by gout. Lofling was twenty-one, he was only a boy; he had tutored Carl Junior, the lazy son. In Spain Lofling had made a name for himself and had sent letters and plants to Linnaeus; then he'd gone to South America with a Spanish expedition. Venezuela; another place Linnaeus had never been. But he had seen it, through Lofling's letters and specimens. Birds so brightly colored they seemed to be jeweled and rivers that pulsed, foamy and brown, through ferns the height of a man. The letter from Spain announcing Lofling's death from fever had come only months after little Johannes had died.

There he sat, in his sleigh in the kitchen, surrounded by the dead. "Are you laughing, Papa?" Sophia said. "Are you happy?"

His apostles had gone out into the world like his own organs: extra eyes and hands and feet, observing, gathering, naming. Someone was stroking his hands. Pehr Forskal, after visiting Marseilles and Malta and Constantinople, reached Alexandria one October and dressed as a peasant to conceal himself from marauding Bedouins. In Cairo he roamed the streets in his disguise and made a fine collection of new plants; then he traveled by Suez and Jedda to Arabia, where he was stricken by plague and died. Months later, a letter arrived containing a stalk and a flower from a tree that Linnaeus had always wanted to see: the evergreen from which the Balm of Gilead was obtained. The smell was spicy and sweet but Forskal, who had also tutored Carl Junior, was gone. And Falck, who had meant to accompany Forskal on his Arabian journey, was gone as well—he had gone to St. Petersburg instead, and then traveled through Turkestan and Mongolia. Lonely and lost and sad in Kazan, he had shot himself in the head.

Outside the weather had changed and now it was raining. The pupil: Falck or Forskal, Osbeck or Rolander—*Rotheram, who had fallen ill several years ago, whom Sophia had nursed, who came and went from his house like family*—said, "I hate to move you, sir: I know you're enjoying it here. But the rain is ruining the track. We'll have a hard time if we don't leave soon."

Rolander? There was a story about Rolander, which he had used as the basis for a lecture on medicine and, later, in a paper. Where had it come from? A letter, perhaps. Or maybe Rolander had related it himself, before his mind disintegrated completely. On the ship, on the way to Surinam, he had fallen ill with dysentery. Ever the scientist, trained by his teacher, he'd examined his feces and found thousands of mites in them. He held his magnifying glass to the wooden beaker he'd sipped from in the night, and found a dense white line of flour mites down near the base.

Kahler lashed himself to the mast of his boat, where he remained two days and two nights without food.

Hasselquist died in the village of Bagda.

Pehr Kalm crossed the Great Lakes and walked into Canada.

In Denmark, someone stole Rolander's gray seeds, almost as if they'd been truly pearls.

Generic names, he had taught these pupils, must be clear and stable and expressive. They should not be vague or confusing; neither should they be primitive, barbarous, lengthy, or difficult to pronounce. They should have significant metaphorical or historical associations with the character of the genus. Another botanist had named the thyme-leaved bell-flower after him: *Linnaea borealis*. One June, in Lappland, he had seen it flourishing. His apostles had died in this order: Ternström, Hasselquist, Lofling, Forskal, Falck, and then finally Kahler, at home. His second son, Johannes, had died at the age of two, between Hasselquist and Lofling; but that was also the year of Sophia's birth. Once, when Sophia had dropped a tray full of dishes, he had secretly bought a new set to replace them, to spare her from her mother's wrath.

His apostles had taken wing like swallows, but they had failed to return. Swallows wintered beneath the lakes, or so he had always believed. During the autumn, he had written, they gather in large groups in the weeds and then dive, resting beneath the ice until spring. An English friend—Collinson, Peter in his own tongue but truly Pehr, and also dead—had argued with him over this and begged him to hold some swallows under water to see if they could live there. Was it so strange to think they might sleep beneath the water above which they hovered in summer? Was it not stranger to think they flew for thousands of miles? He knew another naturalist who believed that swallows wintered on the moon. But always there had been people, like his wife, who criticized his every word.

He had fought off all of them. The Queen had ennobled him: he was Carl von Linné now. But the pupils he'd sent out as his eyes and ears were dead. During his years in Uppsala he had written and lectured about the mud iguana of Carolina and Siberian buckwheat and bearberries; about lemmings and ants and a phosphorescent Chinese grasshopper. Fossils, crystals, the causes of leprosy and intermittent fever— all these things he had known about because of his pupils' travels. Over his bedroom door he'd inscribed this motto: "Live blamelessly; God is present."

A group of men had appeared to the left of the fire. Lofling, Forskal, Falck he saw, and also Ternström and Hasselquist. And another, whom he'd forgotten about: Carl Thunberg, his fellow Smalander.

Thunberg was back, then? Thunberg, the last he had heard, was still alive. From Paris Thunberg had gone to Holland. From Holland he had gone to the Cape of Good Hope, and then to Java and finally to Japan. In Japan he had been confined to the tiny island of Deshima, isolated like all the foreigners. So desperate had he been to learn about the Japanese flora that he had picked daily through the fodder the servants brought to feed the swine and cattle. He had begged the Japanese servants to bring him samples from their gardens.

Of all his pupils, Thunberg had been the most faithful about sending letters and herbarium specimens home. He had been scrupulous about spreading his teacher's methods. "I have met some Japanese doctors," he'd written. "I have been teaching them botany and Linnaean taxonomy. They welcome your method and sing your praises." He had also, Linnaeus remembered, introduced into Japan the treatment of syphilis by quicksilver. He had left Japan with crates of specimens; he'd been headed for Ceylon. But here he was, sharp-featured and elegant, leaning on the mantelpiece and trading tales with his predecessors.

"The people are small and dark and suspicious of us," he was saying. "They find us coarse. But their gardens are magnificent, and they have ways of stunting trees that I have never seen before."

"In Palestine," Hasselquist replied, "the land is so dry that the smallest plants send roots down for many feet, searching for buried water."

"The tropics cannot be described," Lofling said. "The astonishing fertility, the way the vegetation is layered from the ground to the sky, the epiphytes clumped in the highest branches like lace . . ."

"Alexandria," Forskal said. "Everything there is so ancient, so layered with history."

"My health is broken," Falck said; and Kahler said, "I walked from Rome almost all the way to Sweden."

*In Lappland,* Linnaeus said silently, *a gray gnat with striated wings and black legs cruelly tormented me and my most miserable horse.* His apostles did not seem to hear him. *A very bright and calm day,* he said. *The great Myrgiolingen was flying in the marshes.*

"We'll go home now, Papa," the tall woman said. "We'll put you to bed. Won't you like that?"

Her face was as radiant as a star. What was her name? Beside her, his apostles held leaves and twigs and scraps of blossoms, all new and named by them with their teacher's advice. They were trading these among themselves. A leaf from a new succulent for a spray from a never-seen orchid. Two fronds of a miniature fern for a twig from a dwarf evergreen. They were so excited that their voices were rising; they might have been playing cards, laying down plants for bets instead of gold. But the woman and the other pupil didn't seem to notice them. The woman and the other pupil were wholly focused on helping Pehr the coachman push the sleigh back outside.

The woman opened the doors and held them. Pehr and the pupil pushed and pulled. The crisp, winy air of the afternoon had turned dank and raw, and a light rain was turning the snow to slush. Linnaeus said nothing, but he turned and gazed over his shoulder. The group gathered by the fireplace stepped back, displeased, when Pehr returned and doused the fire. Thunberg looked at Linnaeus and raised an eyebrow. Linnaeus nodded.

In the hands of his lost ones were the plants he had named for them: *Artedia,* an umbelliferous plant, and *Osbeckia,* tall and handsome; *Loeflingia,* a small plant from Spain; *Thunbergia* with its black eye centered in yellow petals, and the tropical *Ternstroemia.* There were more, he couldn't remember them all. He'd named thousands of plants in his life.

Outside, the woman and the pupil separated. *Sophia? Sophia, my favorite.* Sophia bundled herself into the borrowed sleigh in which she'd arrived; the pupil wedged himself into Pehr's sleigh, next to Linnaeus. In the dark damp air they formed a line that could hardly be seen: Pehr's sleigh, and then Sophia's, and behind them, following the cunning signal Linnaeus had given, the last sleigh filled with his apostles. Pehr huddled into his coat and gave the signal to depart. It was late and he was weary. To their left, the rain and melting snow had turned the low field into a lake. Linnaeus looked up at his pupil—*Rotheram? Of course it was him: the English pupil, the last one, the one who would survive him*—and tried to say, "The death of many whom I have induced to travel has turned my hair gray, and what have I gained? A few dried plants, accompanied by great anxiety, unrest, and care."

Rotheram said, "Rest your head on my arm. We will be home before you know it."

# *Wickedness*

### RON HANSEN

At the end of the nineteenth century a girl from Delaware got on a milk train in Omaha and took a green wool seat in the second-class car. August was outside the window, and sunlight was a yellow glare on the trees. Up front, a railway conductor in a navy-blue uniform was gingerly backing down the aisle with a heavy package in a gunnysack that a boy was helping him with. They were talking about an agreeable seat away from the hot Nebraska day that was persistent outside, and then they were setting their cargo across the runnered aisle from the girl and tilting it against the shellacked wooden wall of the railway car before walking back up the aisle and elsewhere into August.

She was sixteen years old and an Easterner just recently hired as a county schoolteacher, but she knew enough about prairie farming to think the heavy package was a crank-and-piston washing machine or a boxed plowshare and coulter, something no higher than the bloody stump where the poultry were chopped with a hatchet and then wildly high-stepped around the yard. Soon, however, there was a juggling movement and the gunnysack slipped aside, and she saw an old man sitting there, his limbs hacked away, and dark holes where his ears ought to have been, the skin pursed at his jaw hinge like pink lips in a kiss. The milk train jerked into a roll through the railway yard, and the old man was jounced so that his gray cheek pressed against the hot window glass. Although he didn't complain, it seemed an uneasy position, and the girl wished she had the courage to get up from her seat and tug the jolting body upright. She instead got to her page in *Quo Vadis* and pretended to be so rapt by the book that she didn't look up again until Columbus, where a doctor with liquorice on his breath sat heavily beside her and openly stared over his newspaper before whispering that the poor man was a carpenter in Genoa who'd been caught out in the great blizzard of 1888. Had she heard of that one?

The girl shook her head.

She ought to look out for their winters, the doctor said. Weather in Nebraska could be the wickedest thing she ever saw.

She didn't know what to say, so she said nothing. And at Genoa a young teamster got on in order to carry out the old man, whose half body was heavy enough that the boy had to yank the gunnysack up the aisle like sixty pounds of mail.

In the year 1888, on the twelfth day of January, a pink sun was up just after seven and southeastern zephyrs of such soft temperature were sailing over the Great Plains that squatters walked their properties in high rubber boots and April jackets and some farmhands took off their Civil War greatcoats to rake silage into the cattle troughs. However, sheep that ate whatever they could the night before raised their heads away from food and sniffed the salt tang in the air. And all that morning streetcar mules were reported to be acting up, nipping each other, jingling the hitch rings, foolishly waggling their dark manes and necks as though beset by gnats and horseflies.

A Danish cattleman named Axel Hansen later said he was near the Snake River and tipping a teaspoon of saleratus into a yearling's mouth when he heard a faint groaning in the north that was like the noise of a high waterfall at a fair distance. Axel looked toward Dakota, and there half the sky was suddenly gray and black and indigo blue with great storm clouds that were seething up high as the sun and wrangling toward him at horse speed. Weeds were being uprooted, sapling trees were bullwhipping, and the top inches of snow and prairie soil were being sucked up and stirred like the dirty flour that was called red dog. And then the onslaught hit him hard as furniture, flying him onto his back so that when Axel looked up, he seemed to be deep undersea and in icehouse cold. Eddying snow made it hard to breathe any way but sideways, and getting up to just his knees and hands seemed a great attainment. Although his sod house was but a quarter-mile away, it took Axel four hours to get there. Half his face was frozen gray and hard as weatherboarding so the cattleman was speechless until nightfall, and then Axel Hansen simply told his wife, That was not pleasant.

Cow tails stuck out sideways when the wind caught them. Sparrows and crows whumped hard against the windowpanes, their jerking eyes seeking out an escape, their wings fanned out and flattened as though pinned up in an ornithologist's display. Cats died, dogs died, pigeons died. Entire farms of cattle and pigs and geese and chickens were wiped out in a single night. Horizontal snow that was hard and dry as salt dashed and seethed over everything, sloped up like rooftops, tricked its way across creek beds and ditches, milkily purled down city streets, stole shanties and coops and pens from a bleak landscape that was even then called the Great American Desert. Everything about the blizzard seemed to have personality and hateful intention. Especially the cold. At six a.m., the temperature at Valentine, Nebraska, was thirty degrees above zero. Half a day later the temperature was fourteen below, a drop of forty-four degrees and the difference between having toes and not, between staying alive overnight and not, between ordinary concerns and one overriding idea.

Ainslie Classen was hopelessly lost in the whiteness and tilting low under the jamming gale when his right elbow jarred against a joist of his pigsty. He walked around the sty by skating his sore red hands along the upright shiplap and then squeezed inside through the slops trough. The pigs scampered over to him, seeking his protection, and Ainslie put himself among them, getting down in their stink and their body heat, socking them away only when they ganged up or when two or three presumed he was food. Hurt was nailing into his finger joints until he thought to work his hands into the pigs' hot wastes, then smeared some onto his skin. The pigs grunted around him and intelligently snuffled at his body with their pink and tender noses, and Ainslie thought, *You are not me but I am you,* and Ainslie Classen got through the night without shame or injury.

Whereas a Hartington woman took two steps out her door and disappeared until the snow sank away in April and raised her body up from her garden patch.

An Omaha cigar maker got off the Leavenworth Street trolley that night, fifty yards from his own home and five yards from another's. The completeness of the blizzard so puzzled him that the cigar maker tramped up and down the block more than twenty times and then slept against a lamppost and died.

A cattle inspector froze to death getting up on his quarter horse. The next morning he was still tilting the saddle with his upright weight, one cowboy boot just inside the iced stirrup, one bear-paw mitten over the horn and reins. His quarter horse apparently kept waiting for him to complete his mount, and then the quarter horse died too.

A Chicago boy visiting his brother for the holidays was going to a neighbor's farm to borrow a scoop shovel when the night train of blizzard raged in and overwhelmed him. His tracks showed the boy mistakenly slanted past the sod house he'd just come from, and then tilted forward with perhaps the vain hope of running into some shop or shed or railway depot. His body was found four days later and twenty-seven miles from home.

A forty-year-old wife sought out her husband in the open range land near O'Neill and days later was found standing up in her muskrat coat and black bandanna, her scarf-wrapped hands tightly clenching the top strand of rabbit wire that was keeping her upright, her blue eyes still open but cloudily bottled by a half inch of ice, her jaw unhinged as though she'd died yelling out a name.

The one a.m. report from the Chief Signal Officer in Washington, D.C., had said Kansas and Nebraska could expect "fair weather, followed by snow, brisk to high southerly winds gradually diminishing in force, becoming westerly and warmer, followed by colder."

Sin Thomas undertook the job of taking Emily Flint home from their Holt County schoolhouse just before noon. Sin's age was sixteen, and Emily was not only six years younger but also practically kin to him, since her stepfather was Sin's older brother. Sin took the girl's hand and they haltingly tilted against the uprighting gale on their walk to a dark horse, gray-maned and gray-tailed with ice. Sin cracked the reins loose of the crowbar tie-up and helped Emily up onto his horse, jumping up onto the croup from a soapbox and clinging the girl to him as though she were groceries he couldn't let spill.

Everything she knew was no longer there. She was in a book without descriptions. She could put her hand out and her hand would disappear. Although Sin knew the general direction to Emily's house, the geography was so duned and drunk with snow that Sin gave up trying to nudge his horse one way or another and permitted its slight adjustments away from the wind. Hours passed and the horse strayed southeast into Wheeler County, and then in misery and pneumonia it stopped, planting its overworked legs like four parts of an argument and slinging its head away from Sin's yanks and then hanging its nose in anguish. Emily hopped down into the snow and held on the boy's coat pocket at Sin uncinched the saddle and jerked off a green horse blanket and slapped it against his iron leggings in order to crack the ice from it. And then Sin scooped out a deep nook in a snow slope that was as high and steep as the roof of a New Hampshire house. Emily tightly wrapped herself in the green horse blanket and slumped inside the nook in the snow, and the boy crept on top of her and stayed like that, trying not to press into her.

Emily would never say what was said or was cautiously not said that night. She may have been hysterical. In spite of the fact that Emily was out of the wind, she later said that the January night's temperature was like wire-cutting pliers that snipped at her ears and toes and fingertips until the horrible pain became only a nettling and then a kind of sleep and her feet seemed as dead as her shoes. Emily wept, but her tears froze cold as penny nails and her upper lip seemed candlewaxed by her nose and she couldn't stop herself from feeling the difference in the body on top of her. She thought Sin Thomas was responsible, that the night suited his secret purpose, and she so complained of the bitter cold that Sin finally took off his Newmarket overcoat and tailored it around the girl; but sixty years later, when Emily wrote her own account of the ordeal, she forgot to say anything about him giving her his over-coat and only said in an ordinary way that they spent the night inside a snowdrift and that "by morning the storm had subsided."

With daybreak Sin told Emily to stay there and, with or without his Newmarket overcoat, the boy walked away with the forlorn hope of chancing upon his horse. Winds were still high, the temperature was thirty-five degrees below zero, and the snow was deep enough that Sin pulled lopsidedly with every step and then toppled over just a few yards away. And then it was impossible for him to get to his knees, and Sin only sank deeper when he attempted to swim up into the high wave of snow hanging over him. Sin told himself that he would try again to get out, but first he'd build up his strength by napping for just a little while. He arranged his body in the snow gully so that the sunlight angled onto it, and then Sin Thomas gave in to sleep and within twenty minutes died.

His body was discovered at noon by a Wheeler County search party, and shortly after that they came upon Emily. She was carried to a nearby house where she slumped in a kitchen chair while girls her own age dipped Emily's hands and feet into pans of ice water. She could look up over a windowsill and see Sin Thomas's body standing up-right on the porch, his hands woodenly crossed at his chest, so Emily kept her brown eyes on the pinewood floor and slept that night with jars of hot water against her skin. She could not walk for two months. Even scissoring tired her hands. She took a cashier's job with the Nebraska Farm Implements Company and kept it for forty-five years, staying all her life in Holt County. She died in a wheelchair on a hospital porch in the month of April. She was wearing a glamorous sable coat. She never married.

The T.E.D. Schusters' only child was a seven-year-old boy named Cleo who rode his Shetland pony to the Westpoint school that day and had not shown up on the doorstep by two p.m., when Mr. Schuster went down into the root cellar, dumped purple sugar beets onto the earthen floor, and upended the bushel basket over his head as he slung himself against the onslaught in his second try for Westpoint. Hours later Mrs. Schuster was tapping powdered salt onto the night candles in order to preserve the wax when the door abruptly blew open and Mr. Schuster stood there without Cleo and utterly white and petrified with cold. She warmed him up with okra soup and tenderly wrapped his frozen feet and hands in strips of gauze that she'd dipped in kerosene, and they were sitting on milking stools by a red-hot stove, their ankles just touching, only the usual sentiments being expressed, when they heard a clopping on the wooden stoop and looked out to see the dark Shetland pony turned gray and shaggy-bearded with ice, his legs as wobbly as if he'd just been born. Jammed under the saddle skirt was a damp, rolled-up note from the Scottish school-teacher that said, Cleo is safe. The Schusters invited the pony into the house and bewildered him with praises as Cleo's mother scraped ice from the pony's shag with her own ivory comb, and Cleo's father gave him sugar from the Dresden bowl as steam rose up from the pony's back.

Even at six o'clock that evening, there was no heat in Mathias Aachen's house, and the seven Aachen children were in whatever stockings and clothing they owned as they put their hands on a Hay-burner stove that was no warmer then soap. When a jar of apricots burst open that night and the iced orange syrup did not ooze out, Aachen's wife told the children, You ought now to get under your covers. While the seven were crying and crowding onto their dirty floor mattresses, she rang the green tent cloth along the iron wire dividing the house and slid underneath horse blankets in Mathias Aachen's gray wool trousers and her own gray dress and a ghastly muskrat coat that in hot weather gave birth to insects.

Aachen said, Every one of us will be dying of cold before morning. Freezing here. In Nebraska.

His wife just lay there, saying nothing.

Aachen later said he sat up bodingly until shortly after one a.m., when the house temperature was so exceedingly cold that a gray suede of ice was on the teapot and his pretty girls were whimpering in their sleep. You are not meant to stay here, Aachen thought, and tilted hot candle wax into his right ear and then his left, until he could only hear his body drumming blood. And then Aachen got his Navy Colt and kissed his wife and killed her. And then walked under the green tent cloth and killed his seven children, stopping twice to capture a scuttling boy and stopping once more to reload.

Hattie Benedict was in her Antelope County schoolyard overseeing the noon recess in a black cardigan sweater and gray wool dress when the January blizzard caught her unaware. She had been impatiently watching four girls in flying coats playing Ante I Over by tossing a spindle of chartreuse yarn over the one-room school-house, and then a sharp cold petted her neck and Hattie turned toward the open fields of hoarfrosted scraggle and yellow grass. Just a half mile away was a gray blur of snow underneath a dark sky that was all hurry and calamity, like a nighttime city of sin-black buildings and havoc in the streets. Wind tortured a creekside cotton-wood until it cracked apart. A tin water pail rang in a skipping roll to the horse path. One quarter of the tar-paper roof was torn from the schoolhouse and sailed southeast forty feet. And only then did Hattie yell for the older boys with their ciga-rettes and clay pipes to hurry in from the prairie twenty rods away, and she was hus-tling a dallying girl inside just as the snowstorm socked into her Antelope County schoolhouse, shipping the building awry off its timber skids so that the southwest side heavily dropped six inches and the oak-plank floor became a slope that Hattie ascended unsteadily while ordering the children to open their *Webster Franklin Fourth Reader* to the Lord's Prayer in verse and to say it aloud. And then Hattie stood by her desk with her pink hands held theatrically to her cheeks as she looked up at the walking noise of bricks being jarred from the chimney and down the roof. Every window view was as white as if butchers' paper had been tacked up. Winds pounded into the windowpanes and dry window putty trickled onto the unpainted sills. Even the slough grass fire in the Hay-burner stove was sucked high into the tin stack pipe so that the soot on it reddened and snapped. Hattie could only stare. Four of the boys were just about Hattie's age, so she didn't say anything when they ignored the reading assignment and earnestly got up from the wooden benches in order to argue *oughts* and *ought nots* in the cloakroom. She heard the girls saying Amen and then she saw Janusz Vasko, who was fifteen years old and had grown up in Nebraska weather, gravely exiting the cloakroom with a cigarette behind one ear and his right hand raised high overhead. Hattie called on him, and Janusz said the older boys agreed that they could get the littler ones home, but only if they went out right away. And before she could even give it thought, Janusz tied his red handkerchief over his nose and mouth and jabbed his orange corduroy trousers inside his antelope boots with a pencil.

Yes, Hattie said, please go, and Janusz got the boys and girls to link themselves together with jump ropes and twine and piano wire, and twelve of Hattie Benedict's pupils walked out into a nothingness that the boys knew from their shoes up and dully worked their way across as though each crooked stump and tilted fence post was a word they could spell in a plainspoken sentence in a book of practical knowledge. Hours later the children showed up at their homes, aching and crying in raw pain. Each was given cocoa or the green tea of the elder flower and hot bricks were put next to their feet while they napped and newspapers printed their names incorrectly. And then, one by one, the children disappeared from history.

Except for Johan and Alma Lindquist, aged nine and six, who stayed behind in the schoolhouse, owing to the greater distance to their ranch. Hattie opened a week-old Omaha newspaper on her desktop and with caution peeled a spotted yellow apple on it, eating tan slices from her scissor blade as she peered out at children who seemed irritatingly sad and pathetic. She said, You wish you were home.

The Lindquists stared.

Me too, she said. She dropped the apple core onto the newspaper page and watched it ripple with the juice stain. Have you any idea where Pennsylvania is?

East, the boy said. Johan was eating pepper cheese and day-old rye bread from a tin lunch box that sparked with electricity whenever he touched it. And his sister nudged him to show how her yellow hair was beguiled toward her green rubber comb whenever she brought it near.

Hattie was talking in such quick English that she could tell the Lindquists couldn't quite understand it. She kept hearing the snow pinging and pattering against the windowpanes, and the storm howling like clarinets down the stack pipe, but she perceived the increasing cold in the room only when she looked to the Lindquists and saw their Danish sentences grayly blossoming as they spoke. Hattie went into the cloakroom and skidded out the poorhouse box, rummaging from it a Scotch plaid scarf that she wrapped twice around her skull and ears just as a squaw would, and snipping off the fingertips of some red knitted gloves that were only slightly too small. She put them on and then she got into her secondhand coat and Alma whispered to her brother but Hattie said she'd have no whispering, she hated that, she couldn't wait for their kin to show up for them, she had too many responsibilities, and nothing interesting ever happened in the country. Everything was stupid. Everything was work. She didn't even have a girlfriend. She said she'd once been sick for four days, and two by two practically every woman in Neligh mistrustfully visited her rooming house to squint at Hattie and palm her forehead and talk about her symptoms. And then they'd snail out into the hallway and prattle and whisper in the hawk and spit of the German language.

Alma looked at Johan with misunderstanding and terror, and Hattie told them to get out paper and pencils; she was going to say some necessary things and the children were going to write them down. She slowly paced as she constructed a paragraph, one knuckle darkly striping the blackboard, but she couldn't properly express herself. She had forgotten herself so absolutely that she thought forgetting was a yeast in the air; or that the onslaught's only point was to say over and over again that she was next to nothing. Easily bewildered. Easily dismayed. The Lindquists were shying from the crazy woman and concentrating their shame on a nickel pad of Wisconsin paper. And Hattie thought, *You'll give me an ugly name and there will be cartoons and snickering and the older girls will idly slay me with jokes and imitations.*

She explained she was taking them to her rooming house, and she strode purposefully out into the great blizzard as if she were going out to a garden to fetch some strawberries, and Johan dutifully followed, but Alma stayed inside the schoolhouse with her purple scarf up over her mouth and nose and her own dark sandwich of pepper cheese and rye bread clutched to her breast like a prayer book. And then Johan stepped out of the utter whiteness to say Alma had to hurry up, that Miss Benedict was angrily asking him if his sister had forgotten how to use her legs. So Alma stepped out of the one-room schoolhouse, sinking deep in the snow and sloshing ahead in it as she would in a pond until she caught up with Hattie Benedict, who took the Lindquists' hands in her own and walked them into the utter whiteness and night of the afternoon. Seeking to blindly go north to her rooming house, Hattie put her high button shoes in the deep tracks that Janusz and the schoolchildren had made, but she misstepped twice, and that was enough to get her on a screw-tape path over snow humps and hillocks that took her south and west and very nearly into a great wilderness that was like a sea in high gale.

Hattie imagined herself reaching the Elkhorn River and discovering her rooming house standing high and honorable under the sky's insanity. And then she and the Lindquist children would duck over their teaspoons of tomato soup and soda crackers as the town's brooms and scarecrows teetered over them, hooking their green hands on the boy and girl and saying, Tell us about it. She therefore created a heroine's part for herself and tried to keep to it as she floundered through drifts as high as a four-poster bed in a white room of piety and weeping. Hattie pretended gaiety by saying once, See how it swirls! but she saw that the Lindquists were tucking deep inside themselves as they trudged forward and fell and got up again, the wind drawing tears from their squinting eyes, the hard, dry snow hitting their skin like wildly flying pencils. Hours passed as Hattie tipped away from the press of the wind into country that was a puzzle to her, but she kept saying, Just a little farther, until she saw Alma playing Gretel by secretly trailing her right hand along a high wave of snow in order to secretly let go yet another crumb of her rye bread. And then, just ahead of her, she saw some pepper cheese that the girl dropped some time ago. Hissing spindrifts tore away from the snow swells and spiked her face like sharp pins, but then a door seemed to inch ajar and Hattie saw the slight, dark change of a haystack and she cut toward it, announcing that they'd stay there for the night.

She slashed away an access into the haystack and ordered Alma to crawl inside, but the girl hesitated as if she were still thinking of the gingerbread house and the witch's oven, and Hattie acidly whispered, You'll be a dainty mouthful. She meant it as a joke but her green eyes must have seemed crazy, because the little girl was crying when Hattie got inside the haystack next to her, and then Johan was crying, too, and Hattie hugged the Lindquists to her body and tried to shush them with a hymn by Dr. Watts, gently singing, Hush, my dears, lie still and slumber. She couldn't get her feet inside the haystack, but she couldn't feel them anyway just then, and the haystack was making everything else seem right and possible. She talked to the children about hot pastries and taffy and Christmas presents, and that night she made up a story about the horrible storm being a wicked old man whose only thought was to eat them up, but he couldn't find them in the haystack even though he looked and looked. The old man was howling, she said, because he was so hungry.

At daybreak a party of farmers from Neligh rode out on their high plowhorses to the Antelope County schoolhouse in order to get Hattie and the Lindquist children, but the room was empty and the bluetick hound that was with them kept scratching up rye bread until the party walked along behind it on footpaths that wreathed around the schoolyard and into a haystack twenty rods away where the older boys smoked and spit tobacco juice at recess. The Lindquist girl and the boy were killed by the cold, but Hattie Benedict had stayed alive inside the hay, and she wouldn't come out again until the party of men yanked her by the ankles. Even then she kept the girl's body hugged against one side and the boy's body hugged to the other, and when she was put up on one horse, she stared down at them with green eyes that were empty of thought or understanding and inquired if they'd be okay. Yes, one man said. You took good care of them.

Bent Lindquist ripped down his kitchen cupboards and carpentered his own triangular caskets, blacking them with shoe polish, and then swaddled Alma and

Johan in black alpaca that was kindly provided by an elder in the Church of Jesus Christ of Latter-Day Saints. And all that night Danish women sat up with the bodies, sopping the Lindquists' skin with vinegar so as to impede putrefaction.

Hattie Benedict woke up in a Lincoln hospital with sweet oil of spermaceti on her hands and lips, and weeks later a Kansas City surgeon amputated her feet with a polished silver hacksaw in the presence of his anatomy class. She was walking again by June, but she was attached to cork-and-iron shoes and she sighed and grunted with every step. Within a year she grew so overweight that she gave up her crutches for a wicker-backed wheelchair and stayed in Antelope County on a pension of forty dollars per month, letting her dark hair grow dirty and leafy, reading one popular romance per day. And yet she complained so much about her helplessness, especially in winter, that the Protestant churches took up a collection and Hattie Benedict was shipped by train to Oakland, California, whence she sent postcards saying she'd married a trolley repairman and she hated Nebraska, hated their horrible weather, hated their petty lives.

On Friday the thirteenth some pioneers went to the upper stories of their houses to jack up the windows and crawl out onto snow that was like a jeweled ceiling over their properties. Everything was sloped and planed and caped and whitely furbelowed. One man couldn't get over his boyish delight in tramping about on deer-hide snowshoes at the height of his roof gutters, or that his dogwood tree was forgotten but for twigs sticking out of the snow like a skeleton's fingers. His name was Eldad Alderman, and he jabbed a bamboo fishing pole in four likely spots a couple of feet below his snowshoes before the bamboo finally thumped against the plank roof of his chicken coop. He spent two hours spading down to the coop and then squeezed in through the one window in order to walk among the fowl and count up. Half his sixty hens were alive; the other half were still nesting, their orange beaks lying against their white hackles, sitting there like a dress shop's hats, their pure white eggs not yet cold underneath them. In gratitude to those thirty chickens that withstood the ordeal, Eldad gave them Dutch whey and curds and eventually wrote a letter praising their constitutions in the *American Poultry Yard*.

Anna Shevschenko managed to get oxen inside a shelter sturdily constructed of oak scantling and a high stack of barley straw, but the snow powder was so fine and fiercely penetrating that it sifted through and slowly accumulated on the floor. The oxen tamped it down and inchingly rose toward the oak scantling rafters, where they were stopped as the snow flooded up, and by daybreak were overcome and finally asphyxiated. Widow Shevschenko decided then that an old woman could not keep a Nebraska farm alone, and she left for the East in February.

One man lost three hundred Rhode Island Red chickens; another lost two hundred sixty Hereford cattle and sold their hides for two dollars apiece. Hours after the Hubenka boy permitted twenty-one hogs to get out of the snowstorm and join their forty Holsteins in the upper barn, the planked floor in the cattle linter collapsed under the extra weight and the livestock perished. Since even coal picks could no more than chip the earth, the iron-hard bodies were hauled aside until they could be put underground in April, and just about then some Pawnee Indians showed up outside David City. Knowing their manner of living, Mr. Hubenka told them where the carcasses were rotting in the sea wrack of weed tangles and thaw-water jetsam, and the Pawnee rode their ponies onto the property one night and hauled the carrion away.

And there were stories about a Union Pacific train being arrested by snow on a railway siding near Lincoln, and the merchandisers in the smoking car playing euchre, high five, and flinch until sunup; about cowboys staying inside a Hazard bunkhouse for three days and getting bellyaches from eating so many tins of anchovies and saltine crackers; about the Omaha YMCA where shop clerks paged through inspirational pamphlets or played checkers and cribbage or napped in green leather Chesterfield chairs until the great blizzard petered out.

Half a century later, in Atkinson, there was a cranky talker named Bates, who maintained he was the fellow who first thought of attaching the word *blizzard* to the onslaught of high winds and slashing dry snow and ought to be given credit for it. And later, too, a Lincoln woman remembered herself as a little girl peering out through yellowed window paper at a yard and countryside that were as white as the first day of God's creation. And then a great white Brahma bull with street-wide horns trotted up to the house, the night's snow puffing up from his heavy footsteps like soap flakes, gray funnels of air flaring from his nostrils and wisping away in the horrible cold. With a tilt of his head the great bull sought out the hiding girl under a Chesterfield table and, having seen her, sighed and trotted back toward Oklahoma.

Wild turkey were sighted over the next few weeks, their wattled heads and necks just above the snow like dark sticks, some of them petrified that way but others simply waiting for happier times to come. The onslaught also killed prairie dogs, jackrabbits, and crows, and the coyotes that relied upon them for food got so hungry that skulks of them would loiter like juveniles in the yards at night and yearn for scraps and castaways in old songs of agony that were always misunderstood.

Addie Dillingham was seventeen and irresistible that January day of the great blizzard, a beautiful English girl in an hourglass dress and an ankle-length otter-skin coat that was sculpted brazenly to display a womanly bosom and bustle. She had gently agreed to join an upperclassman at the Nebraska School of Medicine on a journey across the green ice of the Missouri River to Iowa, where there was a party at the Masonic Temple in order to celebrate the final linking of Omaha and Council Bluffs. The medical student was Repler Hitchcock of Council Bluffs—a good companion, a Republican, and an Episcopalian—who yearned to practice electro-therapeutics in Cuernavaca, Mexico. He paid for their three-course luncheon at the Paxton Hotel and then the couple strolled down Douglas Street with four hundred other partygoers, who got into cutters and one-horse open sleighs just underneath the iron legs and girders of what would eventually be called the Ak-Sar-Ben Bridge. At a cap-pistol shot the party jerked away from Nebraska and there were champagne toasts and cheers and yahooing, but gradually the party scattered and Addie could only hear the iron shoes of the plowhorse and the racing sleigh hushing across the shaded window glass of river, like those tropical flowers shaped like saucers and cups that slide across the green silk of a pond of their own accord.

At the Masonic Temple there were coconut macaroons and hot syllabub made with cider and brandy, and quadrille dancing on a puncheon floor to songs like the

"Butterfly Whirl" and "Cheater Swing" and "The Girl I Left Behind Me." Although the day was getting dark and there was talk about a great snowstorm roistering outside, Addie insisted on staying out on the dance floor until only twenty people remained and the quadrille caller had put away his violin and his sister's cello. Addie smiled and said, Oh what fun! as Repler tidily helped her into her mother's otterskin coat and then escorted her out into a grand empire of snow that Addie thought was thrilling. And then, although the world by then was wrathfully meaning everything it said, she walked alone to the railroad depot at Ninth and Broadway so she could take the one-stop train called The Dummy across to Omaha.

Addie sipped hot cocoa as she passed sixty minutes up close to the railroad depot's coal stoker oven and some other partygoers sang of Good King Wenceslaus over a parlor organ. And then an old yardman who was sheeped in snow trudged through the high drifts by the door and announced that no more trains would be going out until morning.

Half the couples stranded there had family in Council Bluffs and decided to stay overnight, but the idea of traipsing back to Repler's house and sleeping in his sister's trundle bed seemed squalid to Addie, and she decided to walk the iron railway trestle across to Omaha.

Addie was a half hour away from the Iowa railway yard and up on the tracks over the great Missouri before she had second thoughts. White hatchings and tracings of snow flew at her horizontally. Wind had rippled snow up against the southern girders so that the high white skin was pleated and patterned like oyster shell. Every creosote tie was tented with snow that angled down into dark troughs that Addie could fit a leg through. Everything else was night sky and mystery, and the world she knew had disappeared. And yet she walked out onto the trestle, teetering over to a catwalk and side-stepping along it in high-button shoes, forty feet above the ice, her left hand taking the yield from one guy wire as her right hand sought out another. Yelling winds were yanking at her, and the iron trestle was swaying enough to tilt her over into nothingness, as though Addie Dillingham were a playground game it was just inventing. Halfway across, her gray tam-o'-shanter was snagged out just far enough into space that she could follow its spider-drop into the night, but she only stared at the great river that was lying there moon-white with snow and intractable. Wishing for her jump.

Years later Addie thought that she got to Nebraska and did not give up and was not overfrightened because she was seventeen and could do no wrong, and accidents and dying seemed a government you could vote against, a mother you could ignore. She said she panicked at one jolt of wind and sank down to her knees up there and briefly touched her forehead to iron that hurt her skin like teeth, but when she got up again, she could see the ink-black stitching of the woods just east of Omaha and the shanties on timber piers just above the Missouri River's jagged stacks of ice. And she grinned as she thought how she would look to a vagrant down there plying his way along a rope in order to assay his trotlines for gar and catfish and then, perhaps, appraising the night as if he'd heard a crazy woman screaming in a faraway hospital room. And she'd be jauntily up there on the iron trestle like a new star you could wish on, and as joyous as the last high notes of "The Girl I Left Behind Me."

# *Love and Hydrogen*

## JIM SHEPARD

Imagine five or six city blocks could lift, with a bump, and float away. The impression the 804-foot-long *Hindenburg* gives on the ground is that of an airship built by giants and excessive even to their purposes. The fabric hull and mainframe curve upward sixteen stories high.

Meinert and Gnüss are out on the gangway ladder down to the starboard #1 engine car. They're helping out the machinists, in a pinch. Gnüss is afraid of heights, which amuses everyone. It's an open aluminum ladder with a single handrail extending eighteen feet down into the car's hatchway. They're at 2,000 feet. The clouds below strand by and dissipate. It's early in a mild May in 1937.

Their leather caps are buckled around their chins, but they have no goggles. The air buffets by at eighty-five miles per hour. Meinert shows him how to hook his arm around the leading edge of the ladder to keep from being blown off as he leaves the hull. Even through the sheepskin gloves the metal is shockingly cold from the slipstream. The outer suede of the grip doesn't provide quite the purchase they would wish when hanging their keisters out over the open Atlantic. Every raised foot is wrenched from the rung and flung into space.

Servicing the engines inside the cupola, they're out of the blast, but not the cold. Raising a head out of the shielded area is like being cuffed by a bear. It's a pusher arrangement, thank God. The back ends of the cupolas are open to facilitate maintenance on the blocks and engine mounts. The engines are 1,100-horsepower diesels four feet high. The propellers are twenty-two feet long. When they're down on their hands and knees adjusting the vibration dampers, those props are a foot and a half away. The sound is like God losing his temper, kettledrums in the sinuses, fists in the face.

Meinert and Gnüss are both Regensburgers. Meinert was in his twenties and Gnüss a child during the absolute worst years of the inflation. They lived on mustard sandwiches, boiled kale, and turnip mash. Gnüss's most cherished toy for a year and a half was a clothespin on which his father had painted a face. They're ecstatic to have found positions like this. Their work fills them with elation, and the kind of spuriously proprietary pride that mortal tour guides might feel on Olympus. Meals that seem giddily baronial—plates crowded with sausages, tureens of soups, platters of venison or trout or buttered potatoes—appear daily, once the passengers have been served, courtesy of Luftschiffbau Zeppelin. Their sleeping berths, aboard and ashore, are more luxurious than any other place they've previously laid their heads.

Meinert and Gnüss are in love. This complicates just about everything. They steal moments when they can—on the last Frankfurt to Rio run, they exchanged an intense and acrobatic series of caresses 135 feet up inside the superstructure, when Meinert was supposed to have been checking a seam on one of the gasbags for wear, their glue pots clacking and clocking together—but mostly their ardor is channeled so smoothly into underground streams that even their siblings, watching them work, would be satisfied with their rectitude.

Meinert loves Gnüss's fussiness with detail, his loving solicitude with all schedules and plans, the way he seems to husband good feeling and pass it around among his shipmates. He loves the celebratory delight Gnüss takes in all meals, and watches him with the anticipatory excitement that an enthusiast might bring to a sublime stretch of *Aïda*. Gnüss has a shy and diffident sense of humor that's particularly effective in groups. At the base of his neck, so it's hidden by a collar, he has a tattoo of a figure eight of rope: an infinity sign. He's exceedingly well proportioned.

Gnüss loves Meinert's shoulders, his way of making every physical act worthy of a Johnny Weissmuller, and the way he can play the irresponsible daredevil and still erode others' disapproval or righteous indignation. He's openmouthed at the way Meinert flaunts the sort of insidious and disreputable charm that all mothers warn against. In his bunk at night, Gnüss sometimes thinks, *I refuse to list all his other qualities*, for fear of agitating himself too completely. He calls Meinert *Old Shatterhand*. They joke about the age difference.

It goes without saying that the penalty for exposed homosexuality in this case would begin at the loss of one's position. Captain Pruss, a fair man and an excellent captain, a month ago remarked in Gnüss's presence that he'd throw any fairy he came across bodily out of the control car.

Meinert bunks with Egk; Gnüss with Thoolen. It couldn't be helped. Gnüss had wanted to petition for their reassignment as bunkmates—what was so untoward about friends wanting to spend more time together?—but Meinert the daredevil had refused to risk it. Each night Meinert lies in his bunk wishing they'd risked it. As a consolation, he passed along to Gnüss his grandfather's antique silver pocket watch. It had already been engraved *To My Dearest Boy*.

Egk is a fat little man with boils. Meinert considers him to have been well named. He whistles the same thirteen-note motif each night before lights out.

How much happiness is someone entitled to? This is the question that Gnüss turns this way and that in his aluminum bunk in the darkness. The ship betrays no tremor or sense of movement as it slips through the sky like a fish.

He is proud of his feelings for Meinert. He can count on one hand the number of people he's known he believes to be capable of feelings as exalted as his.

Meinert, meanwhile, has developed a flirtation with one of the passengers: perhaps the only relationship possible that would be more forbidden than his relationship with Gnüss. The flirtation alternately irritates and frightens Gnüss.

The passenger is one of those languid teenagers who own the world. She has a boy's haircut. She has a boy's chest. She paints her lips but otherwise wears no makeup. Her parents are briskly polite with the crew and clearly excited by their first adventure on an airship; she is not. She has an Eastern name: Tereska.

Gnüss had to endure their exchange of looks when the girl's family first came aboard. Passengers had formed a docile line at the base of the main gangway. Gnüss and Meinert had been shanghaied to help the chief steward inspect luggage and personal valises for matches, lighters, camera flashbulbs, flashlights, even a child's sparking toy pistol: anything that might mix apocalyptically with their ship's seven million cubic feet of hydrogen. Two hundred stevedores in the ground crew were arrayed every ten feet or so around their perimeter, dragging slightly back and forth on their ropes with each shift in the wind. Meinert made a joke about drones pulling a queen. The late afternoon was blue with rain and fog. A small, soaked Hitler Youth contingent with two bedraggled Party pennants stood at attention to see them off.

Meinert was handed Tereska's valise, and Tereska wrestled it back, rummaging through it shoulder to shoulder with him. They'd given one another playful bumps.

The two friends finished their inspections and waited at attention until all the passengers were up the gangway. "Isn't she the charming little rogue," Gnüss remarked.

"Don't scold, Auntie," Meinert answered.

The first signal bell sounded. Loved ones who came to see the travelers off waved and shouted. A passenger unbuckled his wrist-watch and tossed it from one of the observation windows as a farewell present. Meinert and Gnüss were the last ones aboard and secured the gangway. Two thousand pounds of water ballast was dropped. The splash routed the ranks of the Hitler Youth contingent. At 150 feet the signal bells of the engine telegraphs jangled, and the engines one by one roared to life. At 300 feet the bells rang again, calling for higher revolutions.

On the way to their subsequent duties, the two friends took a moment at a free spot at an observation window, watching the ground recede. The passengers were oohing and aahing the mountains of Switzerland and Austria as they fell away to the south, inverted in the mirrorlike expanse of the lake. The ship lifted with the smoothness of planetary motion.

Aloft, their lives had really become a pair of stupefying narratives. Frankfurt to Rio in three and a half days. Frankfurt to New York in two. The twenty-five passenger cabins on A deck slept two in state-room comfort and featured featherlight and whisper-quiet sliding doors. On B deck passengers could lather up in the world's first airborne shower. The smoking room, off the bar and double-sealed all the way round, stayed open until the last guests said good night. The fabric-covered walls in the lounge and public areas were decorated with hand-painted artwork. Each room had its own theme: the main salon, a map of the world crosshatched by the routes of famous explorers; the reading room, scenes of the history of postal delivery. An aluminum bust of General von Hindenberg sat in a halo of light on an ebony base in a niche at the top of the main gangway. A place setting for two for dinner involved fifty-eight pieces of Dresden china and silver. The butter knives' handles were themselves minizeppelins. Complimentary sleeping caps were bordered with the legend *An Bord Des Luftschiffes Hindenburg*. Luggage tags were stamped *Im Zeppelin Über Den Ozean* and featured an image of the *Hindenburg* bearing down, midocean, on what looked like the Santa Maria.

When he can put Tereska out of his head, Gnüss is giddy with the danger and improbability of it all. The axial catwalk is 10 inches wide at its base and 782 feet long and 110 feet above the passenger and crew compartments below. Crew members require the nimbleness of structural steelworkers. The top of the gas cells can only be inspected from the vertical ringed ladders running along the inflation pipes: sixteen stories up into the radial and spiraling bracing wires and mainframe. Up that high, the airship's interior seems to have its own weather. Mists form. The vast cell walls holding the seven million cubic feet of hydrogen billow and flex.

At the very top of Ladder #4 on the second morning out, Meinert hangs from one hand. He spins slowly above Gnüss, down below with the glue pots, like a high-wire act seen at such a distance that all the spectacle is gone. He sings one of his songs from the war, when as a seventeen-year-old he served on the LZ-98 and bombed London when the winds let them reach it. His voice is a floating echo from above:

*In Paris people shake all over*
*In terror as they wait.*
*The Count prefers to come at night,*
*Expect us at half past eight!*

Gnüss nestles in and listens. On either side of the catwalk, great tanks carry 143,000 pounds of diesel oil and water. Alongside the tanks, bays hold food supplies, freight, and mail. This is one of his favorite places to steal time. They sometimes linger here for the privacy and the ready excuses—inspection or errands—that all this storage space affords.

Good news: Meinert signals that he's located a worn patch, necessitating help. Gnüss climbs to him with another glue pot and a pot of the gelatin latex used to render the heavy-duty sailmaker's cotton gas-tight. His erection grows as he climbs.

Their repairs complete, they're both strapped in on the ladder near the top, mostly hidden in the gloom and curtaining folds of the gas cell. Gnüss, in a reverie after their lovemaking, asks Meinert if he can locate the most ecstatic feeling he's ever experienced. Meinert can. It was when he'd served as an observer on a night attack on Calais.

Gnüss still has Meinert's warm sex in his hand. This had been the LZ-98, captained by Lehmann, Meinert reminds him. They'd gotten nowhere on a hunt for fogbound targets in England, but conditions over Calais had been ideal for the observation basket: thick cloud at 4,000 feet, but the air beneath crystalline. The big airships were much safer when operating above cloud. But then: how to see their targets?

The solution was exhilarating: on their approach they throttled the motors as far back as they could while retaining the power to maneuver. The zeppelin was leveled out at 500 feet above the cloud layer, and then, with a winch and a cable, Meinert, as Air Observer, was lowered 2,000 feet in the observation basket, a hollow metal capsule scalloped open at the top. He had a clear view downward, and his gondola, so relatively tiny, was invisible from the ground.

Dropping into space in that little bucket had been the most frightening and electric thing he'd ever done. He'd been swept along alone under the cloud ceiling and over the lights of the city, like the messenger of the gods.

The garrison of the fort had heard the sound of their motors, and the light artillery had begun firing in that direction. But only once had a salvo come close enough to have startled him with its crash.

His cable extended above his head into the darkness and murk. It bowed forward. The capsule canted from the pull. The wind streamed past him. The lights rolled by below. From his wicker seat he directed the immense invisible ship above by telephone, and set and reset their courses by eye and by compass. He crisscrossed them over the fort for forty-five minutes, signaling when to drop their small bombs and phosphorus incendiaries. The experience was that of a sorcerer's, hurling thunderbolts on his own. That night he'd been a regular Regensburg Zeus. The bombs and incendiaries detonated on the railroad station, the warehouses, and the munitions dumps. When they fell they spiraled silently out of the darkness above and plummeted past his capsule, the explosions carried away behind him. Every so often luminous ovals from the fort's searchlights rippled the bottoms of the clouds like a hand lamp beneath a tablecloth.

Gnüss, still hanging in his harness, is disconcerted by the story. He tucks Meinert's sex back into the opened pants.

"That feeling comes back to me when I'm my happiest: hiking or alone," Meinert muses. "And when I'm with you, as well," he adds, after having seen Gnüss's face.

Gnüss buckles his own pants, unhooks his harness, and begins his careful descent. "I don't think I make you feel like Zeus," he says, a little sadly.

"Well, like Pan, anyway," Meinert calls out from above him.

That evening darkness falls on the ocean below while the sun is still a glare on the frames of the observation windows. Meinert and Gnüss have their evening duties, as waiters. Their stations are across the room from one another. The dining room is the very picture of a fine hotel restaurant, without the candles. After dinner, they continue to ferry drinks from the bar on B deck to thirsty guests in the lounge and reading rooms. Through the windows, the upper surfaces of the clouds in the moonlight are as brilliant as breaking surf. Tereska is nowhere to be found.

Upon retiring, passengers leave their shoes in the corridor, as on shipboard. Newspaper correspondents stay up late in the salon, typing bulletins to send by wireless ahead to America. In the darkness and quiet before they themselves turn in, Gnüss leads Meinert halfway up Ladder #4 yet again, to reward him for having had no contact whatsoever with that teenager. Their continuing recklessness feels like Love itself.

Like their airship, their new home when not flying is Friedrichshafen, beside the flatly placid Lake Constance. The Company's presence has transformed the little town. In gratitude the town fathers have erected a Zeppelin fountain in the courtyard of the Rathaus, the centerpiece of which is the Count bestride a globe, holding a log-sized airship in his arms.

Friedrichshafen is on the north side of the lake, with the Swiss mountains across the water to the south, including the snowcapped Säntis, rising some 8,000 feet. Meinert has tutored Gnüss in mountain hiking, and Gnüss has tutored Meinert in oral sex above the tree line. They've taken chances as though cultivating a death wish: in a lift in the famous Insel Hotel, in rented rooms in the wood-carving town of Überlingen and Meersburg with its old castle dating back to the seventh century. In vineyards on the southern exposures of hillsides. Even, once in a lavatory in the Maybach engine plant, near the gear manufacturing works.

When not perversely risking everything they had for no real reason, they lived like the locals, with their coffee and cake on Sunday afternoon and their raw smoked ham as the ubiquitous appetizer for every meal. They maintained their privacy as weekend hikers and developed the southerner's endless capacity for arguing the merits of various mountain trails. By their third year in Friedrichshafen their motto was "A mountain each weekend." They spent nights in mountain huts, and in winter they might go entire days skiing without seeing other adventurers. If Meinert had asked his friend which experience had been the most ecstatic of *his* young life, Gnüss would have cited the week they spent alone in a hut over one Christmas holiday.

Neither has been back to Regensburg for years. Gnüss's most vivid memory of it, for reason he can't locate, is of the scrape and desolation of his dentist's tooth-cleaning instruments one rainy March morning. Meinert usually refers to their hometown as Vitality's Graveyard. His younger brother still writes to him twice a week. Gnüss still sends a portion of his pay home to his parents and sisters.

Gnüss knows that he's being the young and foolish one but nevertheless can't resist comparing the invincible intensity of his feelings for Meinert with his pride at serving on this airship—this machine that conquers two oceans at once, the one above and the one below—this machine that brought their country supremacy in passenger, mail, and freight service to the North and South American continents only seventeen years after the Treaty of Versailles.

Even calm, cold, practical minds that worked on logarithms or carburetors felt the strange joy, the uncanny fascination, the radiance of atmospheric and gravitational freedom. They'd watched the *Graf Zeppelin*, their sister ship, take off one beautiful morning, the sun dazzling on its aluminum dope as if it were levitating on light, and it was like watching Juggernaut float free of the earth. One night they'd gone down almost to touch the waves and scared a fishing boat in the fog, and had joked afterward about what the boat's crew must have experienced: looking back to see a great dark, whirring thing rise like a monster upon them out of the murky air.

They're both party members. They were over Aachen during the national referendum on the annexation of the Rhineland, and helped the chief steward rig up a polling booth on the port promenade deck. The Yes vote had carried among the passengers and crew by a count of 103 to 1.

Meals in flight are so relaxed that some guests arrive for breakfast in their pajamas. Tereska is one such guest, and Gnüss from his station watches Meinert chatting and flirting with her. *She's only an annoyance,* he reminds himself, but his brain seizes and charges around enough to make him dizzy.

The great mass of the airship is off-limits to passengers except for those on guided tours. Soon after the breakfast service is cleared, Meinert informs him, with insufficient contrition, that Tereska's family has requested him as their guide. An hour later, when it's time for the tour to begin, there's Tereska alone, in her boyish shirt and sailor pants. She jokes with Meinert and lays a hand on his forearm. He jokes with her.

Gnüss, beside himself, contrives to approach her parents, sunning themselves by a port observation window. He asks if they'd missed the tour. It transpires that the bitch has forewarned them that it would involve a good deal of uncomfortable climbing and claustrophobic poking about.

He stumbles about below decks, only half-remembering his current task. What's happened to his autonomy? What's happened to his ability to generate contentment for himself independent of Meinert's behavior? Before all this he saw himself in the long term as First Officer, or at least Chief Sailmaker: a solitary and much admired figure of cool judgments and sober self-mastery. Instead, now he feels overheated and coursed through with kineticism, like an agitated and kenneled dog.

He delivers the status report on the ongoing inspection of the gas cells. "Why are you *weeping*?" Sauter, the Chief Engineer, asks.

Responsibility has flown out the window. He takes to carrying Meinert's grandfather's watch inside his pants. His briefs barely hold the weight. It bumps and sidles against his genitals. Does it show? Who cares?

He sees Meinert only once all afternoon, and then from a distance. He searches for him as much as he dares during free moments. During lunch the Chief Steward slaps him on the back of the head for gathering wool.

Three hours are spent in a solitary and melancholy inspection of the rearmost gas cell. In the end he can't say for sure what he's seen. If the cell had disappeared entirely, it's not clear he would have noticed.

Rhine salmon for the final dinner. Fresh trout from the Black Forest. There's an all-night party among the passengers to celebrate their arrival in America. At the bar the man who'd thrown away his wristwatch on departure amuses himself by balancing a fountain pen on its flat end.

They continue to be separated for most of the evening, which creeps along glacially. Gnüss sorts glassware for storage upon landing, and Meinert lends a hand back at the engine gondolas, helping record fuel consumption. The time seems out of joint, and Gnüss finally figures out why: a prankster has set the clock in the bar back, to extend the length of the celebration.

On third watch he takes a break. He goes below and stops by the crew's quarters. No luck. He listens in on a discussion of suitable first names for children conceived aloft in a zeppelin. The consensus favors Shelium, if a girl.

Someone asks if he's seen Meinert. Startled, he eyes the questioner. Apparently the captain's looking for him. Two machinists exchange looks.

Has Gnüss seen him or not? the questioner wants to know. He realizes he hasn't answered. The whole room has taken note of his paralysis. He says he hasn't, and excuses himself.

He finds Meinert on the catwalk heading aft. Relief and anger and frustration swarm the cockleshell of his head. His frontal lobe is in tumult. Before he can speak Meinert tells him to keep his voice down, and that the party may be over. What does *that* mean? Gnüss wants to know. His friend doesn't answer.

They go hunting for privacy without success. A crossbrace near the bottom of the tail supports a card game.

On the way back forward, they're confronted by their two room-mates, Egk and Thoolen, who block the catwalk as though they've formed an alliance. Perhaps they feel neglected. "Do you two *ever* separate?" Egk asks. "Night and day I see you together." Thoolen nods unpleasantly. One is Hamburg at its most insolent, the other Bremerhaven at its foggiest. "Shut up, you fat bellhop," Meinert says.

They roughly squeeze past, and Egk and Thoolen watch them go. *"I'm so in love!"* Egk sings out. Thoolen laughs.

Gnüss follows his friend in silence until they reach the ladder down to B deck. It's a busy hub. Crew members come and go briskly. Meinert hesitates. He seems absorbed in a recessed light fixture. It breaks Gnüss's heart to see that much sadness in the contours of his preoccupation.

"What do you mean: the party may be over?" Gnüss demands quietly.

"Pruss wants to see me. He says for disciplinary matters. After that, you know as much as I," Meinert says.

The radio officer and the ship's doctor pass through the corridor at the bottom of the stairs, glancing up as they go, without stopping their quiet conversation.

When Gnüss is unable to respond, Meinert adds, "Maybe he just wants me to police up my uniform."

At a loss, Gnüss finally puts a hand on Meinert's arm. Meinert smiles, and whispers, *"You are the most important thing in the world right now."*

The unexpectedness of it brings tears to Gnüss's eyes. Meinert murmurs that he needs to get into his dining room whites. It's nearly time to serve the third breakfast. They've served two luncheons, two dinners, and now three breakfasts.

They descend the stairs together. Gnüss is already dressed and so gives his friend another squeeze on the arm and tells him not to worry, and then goes straight to the galley. His eyes still bleary with tears, he loads linen napkins into the dumbwaiter. Anxiety is like a whirling pillar in his chest. He remembers another of Meinert's war stories, one whispered to him in the early morning after they'd first spent the night together. They'd soaked each other and the bed linens with love and then had collapsed. He woke to words in his ear, and at first thought his bedmate was talking in his sleep. The story concerned Meinert's captain after a disastrous raid one moonless night over the Channel. Meinert had been at his post in the control car. The captain had started talking to himself. He'd said that both radios were smashed, not that it mattered, both radiomen being dead. And that both outboard engines were beyond repair, not that *that* mattered, since they had no fuel.

Around four A.M., the passengers start exclaiming at the lights of Long Island. The all-night party has petered out into knots of people waiting and chatting along the promenade. Gnüss and Meinert set out the china, sick with worry. Once the place settings are all correct, they allow themselves a look out an open window. They see below that they've overtaken the liner *Staatendam*, coming into New York Harbor. She salutes them with blasts of her siren. Passengers crowd her decks waving handkerchiefs.

They're diverted north to avoid a front of thunderstorms. All morning, they drift over New England, gradually working their way back to Long Island Sound.

At lunch Captain Pruss appears in the doorway for a moment, and then is gone. They bus tables. The passengers all abandon their seats to look out on New York City. From the exclamations they make, it's apparently some sight. Steam whistles sound from boats on the Hudson and East Rivers. Someone at the window points out the *Bremen* just before it bellows a greeting. The *Hindenburg's* passengers wave back with a kind of patriotic madness.

The tables cleared, the waiters drift back to the windows. Gnüss puts an arm around Meinert's shoulders, despair making him courageous. Through patchy cloud they can see shoal water, or tiderips, beneath them.

Pelicans flock in their wake. What looks like a whale races to keep pace with their shadow.

In New Jersey they circle over miles of stunted pines and bogs, their shadow running along the ground like a big fish on the surface.

It's time for them to take their landing stations.

Sauter passes them on their way to the catwalk and says that they should give the bracing wires near Ladder #4 another check and that he'd noticed a bit of hum.

By the time they reach the base of #4, it's more than a bit of a hum. Gnüss volunteers to go, anxious to do something concrete for his disconsolate beloved. He wipes his eyes and climbs swiftly while Meinert waits below on the catwalk.

Meinert's grandfather's pocket watch bumps and tumbles about his testicles while he climbs. Once or twice he has to stop to rearrange himself. The hum is near the top, hard to locate. At their favorite perch, he stops and hooks on his harness. His weight supported, he turns his head slightly to try and make his ears direction finders. He runs a thumb and forefinger along nearby cables to test for vibration. The cables are covered in graphite to suppress sparks. The slickness seems sexual to him. He's dismayed by his single-mindedness.

On impulse, he takes the watch, pleasingly warm, from his pants. He loops it around one of the cable bolts just so he can look at it. The short chain keeps slipping from the weight. He wraps it once around the nut on the other side of the beam. The nut feels loose to him. He removes and pockets the watch, finds the spanner on his tool belt, fits it snugly over the nut, and tightens it, and then, uncertain, tightens it again. There's a short, high-pitched sound of metal under stress or tearing.

Below him, his lover, tremendously resourceful in all sorts of chameleon-like self-renovations, and suffused with what he understands to be an unprecedented feeling for his young young boy, has been thinking to himself, *Imagine instead that you were perfectly happy.* Shivering, with his coat collar turned up as though he was sitting around a big cold aerodrome, he leans against a cradle of wires and stays and reexperiences unimaginable views, unearthly lightness, the hull starlit at altitude, electrical storms and the incandescence of clouds, and Gnüss's lips on his throat. He remembers his younger brother's iridescent fingers after having blown soap bubbles as a child.

Below the ship, frightened horses spook like flying fish discharged from seas of yellow grass. Miles away, necklaces of lightning drop and fork.

Inside the hangarlike hull, they can feel the gravitational forces as Captain Pruss brings the ship up to the docking mast in a tight turn. The sharpness of the turn overstresses the after-hull structure, and the bracing wire bolt that Gnüss overtightened snaps like a rifle shot. The recoiling wire slashes open the gas cell opposite. Seven or eight feet above Gnüss's alarmed head, the escaping hydrogen encounters the prevailing St. Elmo's fire playing atop the ship.

From the ground, in Lakehurst, New Jersey, the *Hindenburg* malingers in a last wide circle, uneasy in the uneasy air.

The fireball explodes outward and upward, annihilating Gnüss at its center. More than 100 feet below on the axial catwalk, as the blinding light envelops everything below it, Meinert knows that whatever time has come is theirs, and won't be like anything else.

Four hundred and eighty feet away, loitering on the windblown and sandy flats weedy with dune grass, Gerhard Fichte, chief American representative of Luftschiffbau Zeppelin and senior liaison to Goodyear, hears a sound like surf in a cavern and sees the hull interior blooming orange, lit from within like a Japanese lantern, and understands the catastrophe to his company even before the ship fully explodes. He thinks: *Life, motion, everything was untrammeled and without limitation, pathless, ours.*

## Writing Exercises

### INDIVIDUAL

1. This exercise involves two steps. First, describe a public place from your own childhood that continues to evoke powerful, emotional memories. It could be a movie theater, shopping mall, ballpark, the parking lot at your high school, or even the town dump.

   Now set a scene in this location. Use dialogue, description, action, and the thoughts of at least one of your characters. The scene should involve at least two characters, both of whom are uncomfortable in this setting. One is trying to break through the other's denial in some way. The setting somehow makes this difficult or colors the way in which the two of them must talk. Make the issue both specific and dramatic.

2. Think of a place that most people know from the way it's depicted on television or in the movies—a courthouse, movie set, police station, hospital, or the like. Such places are usually presented in clichés that bear little relation to reality. Pick such a place and do your own research on it; visit it if you can. Keep an eye out for persuasive details. Then write a description (perhaps from a character's point of view) that goes beyond or contradicts the usual clichés.

3. Have your character accept a ride from someone she doesn't know well. Describe the ride and the car, particularly its interior. Instead of naming or generalizing about your character's feelings, focus on the details and let them reveal her emotional state and comfort level. Let the details tell us whether the car is luxurious, pristine, a family runabout, a mess. What is that odor? Is that a child's sippy cup? Pet hair? Running shoes? You're the author and so may know the future. Will the character's impressions of the owner, based on the car's condition, prove accurate?

4. Put a character in conflict with a setting. Imagine a character who misunderstands the nature of the place, or overlooks something important, or is oblivious of the danger suggested by certain details.

    Or imagine a character whose reaction to a place is the opposite of what we would expect: she is carefree in a dark urban alley; he is tranquil and reflective at the shooting range; she is fearful in the church; he is contented in the funeral home.

5. Describe a place where a character feels trapped. It could be obvious—a jail cell, dentist's chair, elevator, or orphanage—but it might be less obvious—an RV, an amusement park, a wedding rehearsal, or a library. Use sensory details to suggest your character's discomfort, claustrophobia, and dread.

6. Photographers and filmmakers use a technique called depth of field. So do fiction writers. Write a scene in which you move back and forth between two "fields of action." Have two things going at once—one involving your characters in the foreground and a second having to do with the background. For instance, you might give us some dialogue among the characters on a picnic, then a paragraph about that storm brewing on the horizon, then back to the picnic, and so on. Don't worry too much about making explicit connections or creating transitions between paragraphs. In time, the two strands will figure out their own way of interweaving.

### COLLABORATIVE

7. As a class, create a "virtual" dorm room on the blackboard. Going around the room, have everyone name an object in the room. Be as specific as possible: is the stereo top of the line and brand new, or is it an obscure brand, fifteen years old, with a broken tape deck? List some CDs, books, and magazines. Describe the condition of things, how they are organized (or disorganized). Use brand names. What's in the closet? The drawers?

Important: before starting this exercise, no one should suggest anything about the person who lives in the room; instead, let the character emerge as the room comes into focus, as individuals build on the suggestions of those who spoke before them. You may not even want to specify gender; let the room tell you!

When everyone has added something, discuss the room you have created and the person who lives there. Are there any especially surprising elements? Are there details that seem contradictory? Which objects are the most revealing and intriguing? What story or stories might emerge from the details? What is going to happen to this character?

# 6

# LONG AGO
## *Fictional Time*

- *Summary and Scene*

- *Revising Summary and Scene*

- *Flashback*

- *Slow Motion*

Literature is, by virtue of its nature and subject matter, tied to time in a way the other arts are not. A painting represents a frozen instant of time that viewers experience at a time of their own choosing. Music bridges a span of time, which also dictates tempo and rhythm, but the time scheme is self-enclosed and makes no reference to time in the world outside itself. In fiction, the concern is *content time*, the period covered in the story. It is quite possible to write a story that takes about twenty minutes to read and covers about twenty minutes of action (Jean-Paul Sartre performed experiments in this *durational realism*), but no one has suggested such a correspondence as a fictional requirement. Sometimes the time period covered is telescoped, sometimes stretched. The history of the world up until now can be covered in a sentence; four seconds of crisis may take a chapter. It's even possible to do both at once: William Golding's entire novel *Pincher Martin* takes place between the time the drowning protagonist begins to take off his boots and the moment he dies with his boots still on. But when asked by a student, "How long does it really take?" Golding replied, "Eternity."

## *Summary and Scene*

*Summary* and *scene* are methods of treating time in fiction. A summary covers a relatively long period of time in relatively short compass; a scene deals at length with a relatively short period of time.

Summary narration is a useful and often necessary device: it may give information, fill in a character's background, let us understand a motive, alter pace, create a transition, leap moments or years. For example, early in *The Poisonwood Bible*, summary is used both to fast-forward through time to the story's present moment and to set the political context:

> In the year of our Lord 1960 a monkey barreled through space in an American rocket; a Kennedy boy took the chair out from under a fatherly general named Ike; and the whole world turned on an axis called the Congo. The monkey sailed right overhead, and on a more earthly plane men in locked rooms bargained for the Congo's treasure. But I was there. Right on the head of that pin.

In the following example from Ian McEwan's *Enduring Love*, the narrator is preparing to pick up his wife at the airport. The summary leading up to their reunion doesn't tell us every single thing he did that morning (information we don't really need) but gives us enough description of his preparations to let us know how eagerly he's looking forward to his wife's return:

> On the way out to Heathrow I had made a detour into Convent Garden and found a semilegal place to park, near Carluccio's. I went in and put together a picnic whose centerpiece was a great ball of mozzarella, which the assistant fished out of an earthenware vat with a wooden claw. I also bought black olives, mixed salad, and focaccia. Then I hurried up Long Acre to Rota's to take delivery of Clarissa's birthday present. Apart from the flat and our car, it was the most expensive single item I had ever bought. The rarity of this little book seemed to give off a heat I could feel through the thick brown wrapping paper as I walked back up the street. Forty minutes later I was scanning the screens for arrival information.

Short bits of summary often come in the middle of a scene, as in this excerpt from Alice Munro's story "Hateship, Friendship, Courtship, Loveship, Marriage." The main character, Johanna, is trying on potential wedding dresses in a clothing store, and the summary explores her reasons for having blurted out her secret to the saleswoman:

> "It's likely what I'll get married in," said Johanna.
> She was surprised at that coming out of her mouth. It wasn't a major error—the woman didn't know who she was and would probably not be talking to anybody who did know. Still, she had meant to keep absolutely quiet. She must

have felt she owed this person something—that they'd been through the disaster of the green suit and the discovery of the brown dress together and that was a bond. Which was nonsense. The woman was in the business of selling clothes, and she'd succeeded in doing just that.

"Oh!" the woman cried out. "How wonderful!"

Even the history of a relationship can be given in summary, as seen in this paragraph from Munro's "What is Remembered":

Pierre and Jonas had grown up together in West Vancouver—they could remember it before the Lion's Gate Bridge was built, when it seemed like a small town. Their parents were friends. When they were eleven or twelve years old they had built a rowboat and launched it at Dundarave Pier. At the university they had parted company for awhile—Jonas was studying to be an engineer, while Pierre was enrolled in the Classics, and the Arts and Engineering students traditionally despised each other. But in the years since then the friendship had to some extent been revived. Jonas, who was not married, came to visit Pierre and Meriel, and sometimes stayed with them for a week at a time.

All four of these summaries use concrete details to engage the reader—the monkey barreling through space, a giant ball of mozzarella, the disaster of the green suit, launching a rowboat. Vivid and specific summary is enlightening and enjoyable to read. On the other hand, a general, perfunctory summary—"They met a few years ago and fell in love. He thought she was beautiful, she thought he was cute. They had many lively dates together before they got engaged"—is likely to be one of those passages that readers skip.

Summary can be called the mortar of the story, but scenes are the building blocks. Scene is the crucial means of allowing your reader to experience the story with the characters. Basically defined, a scene is dialogue and action that take place between two or more characters over a set period of "real" time. Like a story, on its own small scale, a scene has a turning point or mini-crisis that propels the story forward toward its conclusion. Scene is *always* necessary to fiction, for it allows readers to see, hear, and sense the story's drama moment-to-moment. Jerome Stern, in *Making Shapely Fiction*, astutely observes that like a child in a tantrum, when you want everyone's full attention you "make a scene," using the writer's full complement of "dialogue, physical reactions, gestures, smells, sounds, and thoughts." A confrontation, a turning point, or a crisis occurs at given moments that take on significance as moments and cannot be summarized. The form of a story requires confrontations, turning points, and crises, and therefore requires scenes.

It is quite possible to write a short story in a single scene, without hardly any summary at all, as demonstrated by "The Use of Force" and "A Visit of Charity." It is nearly impossible, however, to write a successful story entirely in summary. One of the most common errors beginning fiction writers make is to summarize events rather than to realize them as moments.

Here is a moment in the story "Tandolfo the Great," which I've summarized to show the limitations of summary. The clown, Rodney, has just called the birthday boy a name: "Then Rodney decides to go further and tells the spoiled little birthday boy that he is ugly and fat. When the rude boy sticks out his tongue, Rodney grabs it and then quickly lets go, causing the boy to sit down hard. The boy's parents and their friends forcibly and roughly remove Rodney, take him outside, drop him onto the curb and prevent him from rescuing his rabbit. He tries to stick up for himself, but nobody takes him seriously."

This summary keeps us at a distance from the action and characters, just when we expect, and need, to be up close. This particular moment is a turning point, and in the scene, as Richard Bausch actually wrote it, we are right there, experiencing everything along with Rodney, delighting in his attack on the birthday boy, suffering his humiliation when he's manhandled, feeling his need to rescue Chi-Chi the rabbit, squirming in discomfort when he reveals his drunken state:

It grows quiet. Even the small children can tell that something's happened to change everything.

"Tandolfo has another trick," Rodney says, "where he makes the birthday boy pop like a balloon. Especially if he's a fat birthday boy."

A stirring among the adults.

"Especially if he's an ugly little slab of flesh like this one here."

"Now just a minute," says DAD.

"Pop," Rodney says to the birthday boy, who drops the hat and then, seeming to remember that defiance is expected, makes a face. Sticks out his tongue. Rodney/Tandolfo is quick with his hands by training, and he grabs the tongue.

"Awk," the boy says. "Aw-aw-aw."

"Abracadabra." Rodney lets go, and the boy falls backward into the lap of one of the older children. "Whoops, time to sit down," says Rodney.

Very quickly, he's being forcibly removed. They're rougher than gangsters. They lift him, punch him, tear at his costume, even the women. Someone hits him with a spoon. The whole scene boils out onto the lawn, where someone has released the cage that Chi-Chi was in. Chi-Chi moves about wide-eyed, hopping between running children, evading them, as Tandolfo the Great cannot evade the adults. He's being pummeled, because he keeps trying to return for his rabbit. And the adults won't let him off the curb . . .

He straightens, pushes the hair out of his eyes, adjusts the clown nose, and looks at them. "I would say that even though I wasn't as patient as I could've been, the adults have not comported themselves well here," he says.

"Drunk," one of the women says.

Transitions between summary and scene must also be carefully crafted. In the following paragraph from Margaret Atwood's *Lady Oracle*, the narrator has been walking home from her Brownie troop with older girls who tease and terrify her with threats of a bad man. The first paragraph of this quotation summarizes the way things were over a period of a few months and then makes a transition to one of the afternoons:

> The snow finally changed to slush and then to water, which trickled down the hill of the bridge in two rivulets, one on either side of the path; the path itself turned to mud. The bridge was damp, it smelled rotten, the willow branches turned yellow, the skipping ropes came out. It was light again in the afternoons, and on one of them, when for a change Elizabeth hadn't run off but was merely discussing the possibilities with the others, a real man actually appeared.

The second paragraph, the beginning of a scene, specifies a particular moment:

> He was standing at the far side of the bridge, a little off the path, holding a bunch of daffodils in front of him. He was a nice-looking man, neither old nor young, wearing a good tweed coat, not at all shabby or disreputable. He didn't have a hat on, his taffy-colored hair was receding and the sunlight gleamed on his high forehead.

Notice that the scene is introduced when an element of conflict and confrontation occurs. That the threatened bad man does appear and that he is surprisingly innocuous promises a turn of events and a change in the relationship among the girls. We need to see the moment when this change occurs.

Throughout *Lady Oracle*, a typical pattern recurs: a summary leading up to, and followed by, a scene that represents a turning point. Here is another example—one with a different setting and characters—from later in the novel:

> My own job was fairly simple. I stood at the back of the archery range, wearing a red leather change apron, and rented out the arrows. When the barrels of arrows were almost used up, I'd go down to the straw targets. The difficulty was that we couldn't make sure all the arrows had actually been shot before we went down to clear the targets. Rob would shout, Bows DOWN, please, arrows OFF the string, but occasionally someone would let an arrow go, on purpose or by accident. This was how I got shot. We'd pulled the arrows and the men were carrying the barrels back to the line; I was replacing a target face, and I'd just bent over.

To get comfortable with this pattern of storytelling, it may help to think of your own past as a movement through time: *I was born in Arizona and lived there with my parents until I was eighteen; then I spent three years in New York before going on to England.* Or you might instead remember the way things were during a period of that time: *In New York we used to go down Broadway for a midnight snack, and Judy would always dare us to do some nonsense or other before we got back.* But when you think of the events that significantly altered your life, your mind will present you with a scene: *Then one afternoon Professor Bovie stopped me in the hall after class and wagged his glasses at me. "Have you thought about studying in England?"*

The moments that altered your life you remember at length and in detail; your memory tells you your story, and it is a great natural storyteller.

A STORY ISN'T ABOUT A MOMENT IN TIME, a story is about *the* moment in time.

W. D. Wetherell

Scene and summary are often intermixed, of course, and summary may serve precisely to heighten scene.

As we saw in a previous example from the Munro story about the woman in the clothing store, summary used within a scene can suggest contrast with the past, intensify mood, or delay while creating suspense about what will happen next. This example from Rosellen Brown's *Before and After*—in which a father, disturbed by reports of a young girl's murder, is checking out his son's car in a dark garage—does all three.

> The snow was lavender where the light came down on it, like the weird illumination you see in planetariums that changes every color and makes white electric blue. Jacob and I loved to go to the science museum in Boston—not that long ago he had been at that age when the noisy saga of whirling planets and inexplicable anti-gravitational feats, narrated by a man with a deep official-facts voice, was thrilling. He was easily, unstintingly thrilled, or used to be. Not now, though.

Notice how Brown uses brief summaries both of the way things used to be and the way things have changed over time, as well as images of time, weather, and even the whirling cosmos to rouse our fear toward the "instant" in which major change occurs:

> At the last instant I thought I'd look at the trunk. I was beginning to feel relief wash over me like that moon-white air outside—a mystery still, where he might be, but nothing suspicious. The trunk snapped open and rose with the slow deliberation of a drawbridge, and then I thought I'd fall over for lack of breath. Because I knew I was looking at blood.

In this excerpt from *Saturday* by Ian McEwan, a novel that takes place on one Saturday, the main character, a neurosurgeon, has awakened in the middle of the night and is staring out the window at the street below. A bit of summary in this scene lets us know how things appear outside his window right now as opposed to how they usually look. Notice the smooth transitions between the time periods and how the sensory descriptions ground us in both:

> He leans forward, pressing his weight onto his palms against the sill, exulting in the emptiness and clarity of the scene. His vision—always good—seems to have sharpened. He sees the paving stone mica glistening in the pedestrianised square,

pigeon excrement hardened by distance and cold into something almost beauti-ful, like a scattering of snow. He likes the symmetry of black cast-iron posts and their even darker shadows, and the lattice of cobbled gutters. The overfull litter baskets suggest abundance rather than squalor; the vacant benches set around the circular gardens look benignly expectant of their daily traffic—cheerful lunchtime office crowds, the solemn, studious boys from the Indian hostel, lovers in quiet raptures or crisis, the crepuscular drug dealers, the ruined old lady with her wild haunting calls. Go away! She'll shout for hours at a time, and squawk harshly, sounding like some marsh bird or zoo creature.

Standing here, as immune to the cold as a marble statue, gazing towards Charlotte Street, towards a foreshortened jumble of facades, scaffolding and pitched roofs, Henry thinks the city is a success . . .

The movements between scene and summary can be quite fluid—you can easily move in and out and back and forth between them quite easily as long as the reader is not confused, and as long as both scene and summary seem relevant and engaging.

It is crucial that a fiction writer understand the difference between the two and know when and how to best use both of them.

---

ONE SIMPLE TRICK TO HELP YOU CONCENTRATE ON writing a scene at a specific time in a specific location is to state, right away, something like this: 10 A.M., NYC Athletic Club, Jim and John. If you know when, where, and how, you could probably jump in, and if not, add one more element: what. What are they competing for? What are they in conflict about?

Josip Novakovich

## Revising Summary and Scene

Some writers have a tendency to oversummarize, racing through more time and more events than are necessary to tell the story. The danger there is lack of depth. Other writers undersummarize, finding it difficult to deal with quick leaps and tran-sitions, dwelling at excessive length on every scene, including the scenes of the past. The danger of such writing is that readers may not sense which scenes are more im-portant than others. The writer seems not to have made this decision himself or her-self. Reluctant to do the writer's job, a reader may lose patience.

After you have written (and especially workshopped) a few stories, you will know which sort of writer you are, and in which direction you need to work.

Following are some comments you may hear in workshop—and suggestions for revising your story accordingly:

- If people say *you have enough material for a novel*, then you have probably not distilled your material down to the very few scenes that contain the significance you seek.
- Pick one event of all those you have included that contains a moment of crucial change in your character. Write *that* scene in detail, moment by moment. Take time to create the place and the period. Make us see, taste, smell. Let characters speak. Is there a way to indicate, sketch, contain—or simply omit—all that earlier life you raced through in summary? If this proves too difficult, have you really found out yet what your story is about? Explore the scene, rather than the summary, for clues.
- Try condensing an unnecessary scene to a sentence. Every scene should feel necessary to the story. Each one should build on the one before, and in each scene something surprising should happen—the conflict should escalate. Scenes in which nothing important happens can be summarized. For instance, this exchange of information between the characters does not merit a scene: "Suzie stopped by her parents' house to talk to her mother about the missing money, but her father told her that her mother had gone to visit a sick friend. She said she'd call later and went back to her apartment."
- Try fusing two or even three such scenes into one. Ask yourself what is being accomplished in each scene, and try to determine whether or not one scene could do the work for all of them. For instance, in the previous example, you might have a scene following the one where Suzie visits her parent's house in which, back at her apartment, Suzie's boyfriend tells her that her mother has called and wants to speak to her right away. Another scene might include a telephone call between Suzie and her mother, in which her mother asks her to come to the casino and bring her credit card, and then, finally, you may have a scene where Suzie enters the casino and finds her mother standing, zombie-like, in front of the slot machines. This final scene is likely to be the only one really necessary. There might be some summary of the visit with her father and the telephone call with her mother, or Suzie might mention some or all of these things to her mother when she sees her in the casino—perhaps this is the third time in a week that her mother has called in a panic, which upsets not only Suzie but her boyfriend too. And why is her mother continuing to lie to Suzie's father? Sick friend, indeed.

  This scene-combining may seem impossible at first, and it may involve sacrificing a delicious phrase or a nifty nuance, but it is simply the necessary work of plotting

- If your critics say *you write long* or *your story really begins on page three* (or *six*, or *eleven*), have you indulged yourself in setting things up, or dwelt on the story's past at the expense of its present? Where the writer begins writing the story is not necessarily where the final version of the story will begin. Look through your story for a better place to begin.

Chekhov advised his fellow writers to tear the story in half and begin in the middle; in fact, most stories begin as close to the end as possible. Nancy Huddleston Packer says: "The first line of a story should hook readers' attention and pull them into the middle of the action. You want readers to feel like the train is leaving without them, so they'd better get on board and keep reading as fast as they can."

John Gardner described a story as being a "vivid and continuous dream" that the writer creates in the mind of the reader. John L'Heureux applies this notion to the opening of a story, saying that the first paragraph should be designed to help readers "sink into the dream of the story." Like the opening frame of a movie, the opening paragraph entices readers into the story-dream, economically setting the tone; establishing the world, level of reality, and point of view; indirectly conveying information; and "promising" that certain concerns will be dealt with over the course of the story. Often the possible ground for some change or reversal is established in the opening as well.

- If your readers are *confused by what happens at the end*, it may very well be that you have summarized the crisis instead of realizing it in a scene. The crisis moment in a story *must always be presented as a scene*. This is the moment we have been waiting for. This is the payoff when the slipper fits. We want to be there. We want to feel the moment that change happens, hear it, taste it, see it in color in close-up on the wide screen of our minds. This is also a hard job, sometimes the hardest a writer has to do—it's draining to summon up all that emotion in all its intensity. And there isn't always a glass slipper handy when you need one; it may be difficult enough to identify the moment when you need that scene.

Many writers avoid writing crisis scenes in early drafts, perhaps because in fiction, as in our lives, we often try to avoid intense conflict. In order to write a vivid close up scene for the reader, a writer must first fully imagine that scene, must place him or herself in it and emotionally experience it, moment by moment. Many writers find it necessary to take it a step further, as Dan Chaon did when he wrote "Big Me":

> "I'll also tell you that the hardest part of the story for me—the final confrontation between Andy and Mickleson—was ultimately written as I actually acted out the scene late at night. Imagine our poor neighbor lady glancing over and seeing me prancing around my study, gesticulating and saying things like 'Hold still, I'll whisper,' and then writing wildly on a legal pad. My neighbor closed her curtain discreetly, as I suppose I should have as well."

It is often the case that such scenes, even in the imagination, are uncomfortable places to be. However, your job as a writer is to recognize the need for such a scene and to try to overcome your squeamishness about going there. Failure to create these essential scenes will result in an unsatisfying ending, and ultimately an unsatisfying story.

So when is the right time to end your story? As the following writers suggest, the best place to look for an answer to this question is the story itself.

It will turn out that your first page has a lot to do with your last page. Just as in a poem, the first line has a lot to do with the last line, even though you didn't know what it was going to be.

Doris Betts

An ending that seems unsatisfactory might actually be fine. The trouble with the ending might be that the beginning or the middle doesn't set up the ending. A problem scene may not be a problem because of the way it is written. The revision of the ending might need to be carried out back in the beginning of the story . . . You start writing the ending when you write your first word.

Jerome Stern, *Making Shapely Fiction*

The climax is that major event, usually toward the end, that brings all the tunes you have been playing so far into one major chord, after which at least one of your people is profoundly changed. If someone isn't changed, then what is the point of your story? For the climax, there must be a killing or a healing or a domination. It can be a real killing, a murder, or it can be a killing of the spirit, or of something terrible inside one's soul, or it can be a killing of a deadness within, after which the person becomes alive again. The healing may be about union, reclamation, the rescue of a fragile prize. But whatever happens, we need to feel that it was inevitable, that even though we may be amazed, it feels absolutely right, that of course things would come to this, of course they would shake down in this way.

Anne Lamott, *Bird By Bird*

I don't like endings that feel like they've got a big bow or THE END sign. What I really like in an ending is to feel satisfied that there was completion within the story, and yet, in some way, the story is still open.

Jill McCorkle

## Flashback

*Flashback*—in either scene or summary—is one of the most magical of fiction's contrivances, easier and more effective in this medium than in any other, because the reader's mind is a swifter mechanism for getting into the past than anything that has been devised for stage or even film. In fiction you can give the reader a smoothly worded transition into the past, and the force of the story will be time-warped to whenever and wherever you want it.

Nevertheless, many beginning writers use unnecessary flashbacks. While flashback can be a useful way to provide background to character or the history of events—the information that screenwriters call *backstory*—it isn't the only way. Rather, dialogue, brief summary, a reference, or detail can often tell us all we need to know.

If you are tempted to use flashback to fill in the whole past, try using your journal for exploring background. Write down everything, fast. Then take a hard look at it to decide just how *little* of it you can use, how much of it the reader can infer, how you can sharpen an image to imply a past incident or condense a grief into a line of dialogue. Trust the reader's experience of life to understand events from attitudes. And keep the present of the story moving.

For instance, when thinking about the backstory for the scene involving Suzie and her gambling-addicted mother, you might write in your journal about the escalation of Suzie's mother's problem with money—how it started when Suzie's older sister ran away from home, how her mother began buying gadgets and appliances she saw on TV, how Suzie came home one day to find her mother rearranging brand-new living room furniture, the "old" furniture she'd bought six months ago already sitting out in the yard. Then riverboat casinos came to Davenport, and when her mother's friends decided to go there on a lark, only Suzie's mother stayed all night, Suzie and her father were frantic with worry, etc., etc.

When looking at all this material, you might be tempted to use some of it in flashbacks—a scene when Suzie and her parents discover that their older daughter has run away? Or when Suzie finds her mother rearranging the furniture? Or when the mother stays out all night at the casino and Suzie and her father are calling everyone they know? But should you interrupt the present story for any of these potential flashbacks? Are they worth bringing it to a halt? I'd say no, except for possibly the first example—the aftermath of the older daughter's disappearance. That scene could have deep emotional resonance and help us to better understand the mother's problems. The other examples could appear in the story in summary form, if they need to appear at all.

Writing out all of this background material is never a waste of time. Even if most of it is never mentioned in either scene or summary, it will inform your understanding of the characters and allow you to understand their problems and empathize with them, helping you to create a fuller, richer, more plausible story.

Flashback is effectively used in fiction to *reveal* at the *right point*. It does not so much distract us from, as contribute to, the central action of the story, deepening our understanding of character and theme. If you find that you do need to use a flashback to reveal, at some point, why the character reacts as she does, or how totally he is misunderstood by those around him, or some other point of emotional significance, then there are several ways to help the reader make that leap in time.

- Provide a smooth, clear transition between present and past. A connection between what's happening in the present and what happened in the past will often best transport the reader, just as it does the character. But avoid overly blatant transitions such as, "Henry thought back to the time" and "I drifted back in memory." Assume the reader's intelligence and ability to follow a leap back. For example:

The kid in the Converse high-tops lifted off on the tips of his toes and slam-dunked it in.

Joe'd done that once, in the lot off Seymour Street, when he was still four inches shorter than Ruppert and had already started getting zits. It was early fall, and . . .

♦ A graceful transition to the past allows you to summarize necessary background quickly, as in this example from James W. Hall's *Under Cover of Daylight*.

> Thorn watched as Sugarman made a quick inspection of the gallery. Thorn sat on the couch where he'd done his homework as a boy, the one that looked out across the seawall toward Carysfort light.
>
> That was how his nights had been once, read a little Thoreau, do some algebra, and look up, shifting his body so he could see through the louvers the fragile pulse of that marker light, and let his mind roam, first out the twelve miles to the reef and then pushing farther, out past the shipping lanes into a world he pictured as gaudy and loud, chaotic. Bright colors and horns honking, exotic vegetables and market stalls, and water, clear and deep and shadowy, an ocean of fish, larger and more powerful than those he had hauled to light. Beyond the reef.

♦ If you are writing in the past tense, begin the flashback in the past perfect (*she had driven; he had worked*) and use the construction "had + (verb)" two or three times more. Then switch to the simple past (*he raced; she crept*); the reader will be with you. If you are writing in the present tense, you may want to keep the whole flashback in the past tense.

♦ Try to avoid a flashback within a flashback. If you find yourself tempted by this awkward shape, it probably means you're trying to let flashback carry too much of the story.

♦ When the flashback ends, be very clear that you are catching up to the present again. Repeat an action or image that the reader will remember belonging to the basic time period of the story. For instance, if, in the present time of the story the characters are eating dinner in a fancy restaurant, you could bring us back into the present by mentioning some of the sights and smells of the place—the sight of the annoying waiter coming toward them again, the delicious smell of the coffee in the cup your character is savoring. Or you could have the character set down his fork and glance at the other character across the table. However you decide to do it, you must place the reader firmly where he or she belongs. Often simply beginning the paragraph with "Now . . ." will accomplish the reorientation.

## Slow Motion

*Flashback* is a term borrowed from film, and I want to borrow another—*slow motion*—to point out a correlation between narrative time and significant detail.

When people experience moments of great intensity, their senses become especially alert and they register, literally, more than usual. In extreme crisis people have the odd sensation that time is slowing down, and they see, hear, smell, and remember ordinary sensations with extraordinary clarity. This psychological fact can work artistically in reverse: you can create the intensity by using detail with special focus and precision. The phenomenon is so universal that it has become a standard film technique to register a physical blow, gunshot, sexual passion, or extreme fear in slow motion. The technique works forcefully in fiction as well. Note in the quotation from Rosellen Brown above how the trunk "snapped open and rose with the slow deliberation of a drawbridge."

Ian McEwan, in *A Child in Time*, demonstrates the technique:

> . . . He was preparing to overtake when something happened—he did not quite see what—in the region of the lorry's wheels, a hiatus, a cloud of dust, and then something black and long snaked through a hundred feet towards him. It slapped the windscreen, clung there a moment and was whisked away before he had time to understand what it was. And then—or did this happen in the same moment?—the rear of the lorry made a complicated set of movements, a bouncing and swaying, and slewed in a wide spray of sparks, bright even in sunshine. Something curved and metallic flew off to one side. So far Stephen had had time to move his foot towards the brake, time to notice a padlock swinging on a loose flange, and 'Wash me please' scrawled in grime. There was a whinnying of scraped metal and new sparks, dense enough to form a white flame which seemed to propel the rear of the lorry into the air.

Anyone who has faced some sort of accident can identify with the experience of sensuous slowdown McEwan records. But the slow-motion technique works also with experiences most of us have not had and to which we must submit in imagination:

> Blood was spurting from an artery in my left leg. I could not see it, and I do not recall how I knew it . . . for a short time I was alone with Patrick. I told myself I was in good hands, but I did not do this with words; I surrendered myself. I focused on breathing. I slowed my breathing, and tried to remain absolutely in the present, in each moment . . . waiting to die or stay alive was like getting an injection as a child, when you first learned not to think, but to gather yourself into the present, to breathe slowly, to relax your muscles, even your arm as the nurse swabbed it with alcohol, to feel the cool alcohol, to smell it, to feel your feet on the floor and see the color of the wall, and nothing else as your slow breathing opened you up to the incredible length and breadth and depth of one second.
>
> Andre Dubus, "Breathing"

And the technique will work when the intensity or trauma of the moment is not physical but emotional:

> They were in the deep sleep of midnight when Pauline came quietly into her son's room and saw that there were two in his bed. She turned on the light. The room was cold and stuffy; warm in the core of it was the smell of a body she had known since she gave birth to him, unmistakable to her as the scent that leads a bitch to

her puppy, and it was mingled with the scents of sexuality caressed from the female nectary. The cat was a rolled fur glove in an angle made by Sasha's bent knees. The two in the bed opened their eyes; they focussed out of sleep and saw Pauline. She was looking at them, at their naked shoulders above the covers . . .

Nadine Gordimer, A Sport of Nature

Central to this technique are the alert but matter-of-fact acceptance of the event and the observation of small, sometimes apparently random, details. The characters do not say, "Oh my God, we're going to die!" or "What an outrage!" Instead they record a padlock swinging, the cool feel of an alcohol swab, a cat rolled into the angle of bent knees.

Beginning writers often overuse summary in their fiction because it seems to be the fastest and most direct way of getting information across. Often, however, we want the reader to linger awhile and experience certain moments along with the characters. Once you become adept at the skill of manipulating time in fiction, you will find that the necessity of setting your story at some specific time is a liberating opportunity.

---

IN OUR EFFORT TO KEEP THE ACTION FROM lagging, we hurry the reader over crucial moments. But anything that is very exciting can't be taken in hurriedly. If somebody is killed in an automobile accident, people who were involved in the accident or who merely witnessed it will be busy for days afterwards piecing together a picture of what happened. They simply couldn't take it all in at that time. When we are writing fiction, we have to give the reader ample time to take in what is happening, particularly if it is very important.

Caroline Gordon to Flannery O'Conner

---

# *The Swimmer*

### JOHN CHEEVER

It was one of those midsummer Sundays when everyone sits around saying, "I *drank* too much last night." You might have heard it whispered by the parishioners leaving the church, heard it from the lips of the priest himself, struggling with his cassock in the *vestiarium*, heard it from the golf links and the tennis courts, heard it from the wildlife preserve where the leader of the Audubon group was suffering from a terrible hangover.

"I *drank* too much," said Donald Westerhazy. "We all *drank* too much," said Lucinda Merrill. "It must have been the wine," said Helen Westerhazy. "I *drank* too much of that claret."

This was at the edge of the Westerhazys' pool. The pool, fed by an artesian well with a high iron content, was a pale shade of green. It was a fine day. In the west there was a massive stand of cumulus cloud so like a city seen from a distance—from the bow of an approaching ship—that it might have had a name. Lisbon. Hackensack. The sun was hot. Neddy Merrill sat by the green water, one hand in it, one around a glass of gin. He was a slender man—he seemed to have the especial slenderness of youth— and while he was far from young he had slid down his banister that morning and given the bronze backside of Aphrodite on the hall table a smack, as he jogged down toward the smell of coffee in his dining room. He might have been compared to a summer's day, particularly the last hours of one, and while he lacked a tennis racket or a sail bag the impression was definitely one of youth, sport, and clement weather. He had been swimming and now he was breathing deeply, stertorously as if he could gulp into his lungs the components of that moment, the heat of the sun, the in-tenseness of his pleasure. It all seemed to flow into his chest. His own house stood in Bullet Park, eight miles to the south, where his four beautiful daughters would have had their lunch and might be playing tennis. Then it occurred to him that by taking a dogleg to the southwest he could reach his home by water.

His life was not confining and the delight he took in this observation could not be explained by its suggestion of escape. He seemed to see, with a cartographer's eye, that string of swimming pools, that quasi-subterranean stream that curved across the county. He had made a discovery, a contribution to modern geography; he would name the stream Lucinda after his wife. He was not a practical joker nor was he a fool but he was determinedly original and had a vague and modest idea of himself as a legendary figure. The day was beautiful and it seemed to him that a long swim might enlarge and celebrate its beauty.

He took off a sweater that was hung over his shoulders and dove in. He had an inexplicable contempt for men who did not hurl themselves into pools. He swam a choppy crawl, breathing either with every stroke or every fourth stroke and counting somewhere well in the back of his mind the one-two one-two of a flutter kick. It was not a serviceable stroke for long distances but the domestication of swimming had saddled the sport with some customs and in his part of the world a crawl was custom-ary. To be embraced and sustained by the light green water was less a pleasure, it seemed, than the resumption of a natural condition, and he would have liked to swim without trunks, but this was not possible, considering his project. He hoisted himself up on the far curb—he never used the ladder—and started across the lawn. When Lucinda asked where he was going he said he was going to swim home.

The only maps and charts he had to go by were remembered or imaginary but these were clear enough. First there were the Grahams, the Hammers, the Lears, the Howlands, and the Crosscups. He would cross Ditmar Street to the Bunkers and come, after a short portage, to the Levys, the Welchers, and the public pool in Lan-caster. Then there were the Hallorans, the Sachses, the Biswangers, Shirley Adams, the Gilmartins, and the Clydes. The day was lovely, and that he lived in a world so generously supplied with water seemed like a clemency, a beneficence. His heart was high and he ran across the grass. Making his way home by an uncommon route gave him the feeling that he was a pilgrim, an explorer, a man with a destiny, and he knew that he would find friends all along the way; friends would line the banks of the Lucinda River.

He went through a hedge that separated the Westerhazys' land from the Grahams', walked under some flowering apple trees, passed the shed that housed their pump and filter, and came out at the Grahams' pool. "Why, Neddy," Mrs. Graham said, "what a marvelous surprise. I've been trying to get you on the phone all morning. Here, let me get you a drink." He saw then, like any explorer, that the hospitable customs and traditions of the natives would have to be handled with diplomacy if he was ever going to reach his destination. He did not want to mystify or seem rude to the Grahams nor did he have the time to linger there. He swam the length of their pool and joined them in the sun and was rescued, a few minutes later, by the arrival of two carloads of friends from Connecticut. During the uproarious reunions he was able to slip away. He went down by the front of the Grahams' house, stepped over a thorny hedge, and crossed a vacant lot to the Hammers'. Mrs. Hammer, looking up from her roses, saw him swim by although she wasn't quite sure who it was. The Lears heard him splashing past the open windows of their living room. The Howlands and the Crosscups were away. After leaving the Howlands' he crossed Ditmar Street and started for the Bunkers', where he could hear, even at that distance, the noise of a party.

The water refracted the sound of voices and laughter and seemed to suspend it in midair. The Bunkers' pool was on a rise and he climbed some stairs to a terrace where twenty-five or thirty men and women were drinking. The only person in the water was Rusty Towers, who floated there on a rubber raft. Oh, how bonny and lush were the banks of the Lucinda River! Prosperous men and women gathered by the sapphire-colored waters while caterer's men in white coats passed them cold gin. Overhead a red de Haviland trainer was circling around and around and around in the sky with something like the glee of a child in a swing. Ned felt a passing affection for the scene, a tenderness for the gathering, as if it was something he might touch. In the distance he heard thunder. As soon as Enid Bunker saw him she began to scream: "Oh, look who's here! What a marvelous surprise! When Lucinda said that you wouldn't come I thought I'd *die*." She made her way to him through the crowd, and when they had finished kissing she led him to the bar, a progress that was slowed by the fact that he stopped to kiss eight or ten other women and shake the hands of as many men. A smiling bartender he had seen at a hundred parties gave him a gin and tonic and he stood by the bar for a moment, anxious not to get struck in any conversation that would delay his voyage. When he seemed about to be surrounded he dove in and swam close to the side to avoid colliding with Rusty's raft. At the far end of the pool he bypassed the Tomlinsons with a broad smile and jogged up the garden path. The gravel cut his feet but this was the only unpleasantness. The party was confined to the pool, and as he went toward the house he heard the brilliant, watery sound of voices fade, heard the noise of a radio from the Bunkers' kitchen, where someone was listening to a ballgame. Sunday afternoon. He made his way through the parked cars and down the grassy border of their driveway to Alewives Lane. He did not want to be seen on the road in his bathing trunks but there was no traffic and he made the short distance to the Levys' driveway, marked with a PRIVATE PROPERTY sign and a green tube for *The New York Times*. All the doors and windows of the big house were open but there were no signs of life; not even a dog barked. He went around the side of the house to the pool and saw that the Levys had only recently left. Glasses and bottles and dishes of nuts were on a table at the deep end, where there was a bathhouse or gazebo, hung with Japanese lanterns. After swimming the pool he got himself a glass and poured a drink. It was his fourth or fifth drink and he had swum nearly half the length of the Lucinda River. He felt tired, clean, and pleased at that moment to be alone; pleased with everything.

It would storm. The stand of cumulus cloud—that city—had risen and darkened, and while he sat there he heard the percussiveness of thunder again. The de Haviland trainer was still circling overhead and it seemed to Ned that he could almost hear the pilot laugh with pleasure in the afternoon; but when there was another peal of thunder he took off for home. A train whistle blew and he wondered what time it had gotten to be. Four? Five? He thought of the provincial station at that hour, where a waiter, his tuxedo concealed by a raincoat, a dwarf with some flowers wrapped in newspaper, and a woman who had been crying would be waiting for the local. It was suddenly growing dark; it was that moment when the pinheaded birds seem to organize their song into some acute and knowledgeable recognition of the storm's approach. Then there was a fine noise of rushing water from the crown of an oak at his back, as if a spigot there had been turned. Then the noise of fountains came from the crowns of all the tall trees. Why did he love storms, what was the meaning of his excitement when the door sprang open and the rain wind fled rudely up the stairs, why had the simple task of shutting the windows of an old house seemed fitting and urgent, why did the first watery notes of a storm wind have for him the unmistakable sound of good news, cheer, glad tidings? Then there was an explosion, a smell of cordite, and rain lashed the Japanese lanterns that Mrs. Levy had bought in Kyoto the year before last, or was it the year before that?

He stayed in the Levys' gazebo until the storm had passed. The rain had cooled the air and he shivered. The force of the wind had stripped a maple of its red and yellow leaves and scattered them over the grass and the water. Since it was midsummer the tree must be blighted, and yet he felt a peculiar sadness at this sign of autumn. He braced his shoulders, emptied his glass, and started for the Welchers' pool. This meant crossing the Lindleys' riding ring and he was surprised to find it overgrown with grass and all the jumps dismantled. He wondered if the Lindleys had sold their horses or gone away for the summer and put them out to board. He seemed to remember having heard something about the Lindleys and their horses but the memory was unclear. On he went, barefoot through the wet grass, to the Welchers', where he found their pool was dry.

This breach in his chain of water disappointed him absurdly, and he felt like some explorer who seeks a torrential headwater and finds a dead stream. He was disappointed and mystified. It was common enough to go away for the summer but no one ever drained his pool. The Welchers had definitely gone away. The pool furniture was folded, stacked, and covered with a tarpaulin. The bathhouse was locked. All the windows of the house were shut, and when he went around to the driveway in front he saw a FOR SALE sign nailed to a tree. When had he last heard from the Welchers—when, that is, had he and Lucinda last regretted an invitation to dine with them? It seemed only a week or so ago. Was his memory failing or had he so disciplined it in the repression of unpleasant facts that he had damaged his sense of the truth? Then in the distance he heard the sound of a tennis game. This cheered him, cleared away all his apprehensions and let him regard the overcast sky and the cold air with indifference. This was the day that Neddy Merrill swam across the county. That was the day! He started off then for his most difficult portage.

Had you gone for a Sunday afternoon ride that day you might have seen him, close to naked, standing on the shoulders of Route 424, waiting for a chance to cross. You might have wondered if he was the victim of foul play, had his car broken down, or was he merely a fool. Standing barefoot in the deposits of the highway—beer cans, rags, and blowout patches—exposed to all kinds of ridicule, he seemed pitiful. He had known when he started that this was a part of his journey—it had been on his maps—but confronted with the lines of traffic, worming through the summery light, he found himself unprepared. He was laughed at, jeered at, a beer can was thrown at him, and he had no dignity or humor to bring to the situation. He could have gone back, back to the Westerhazys', where Lucinda would still be sitting in the sun. He had signed nothing, vowed nothing, pledged nothing, not even to himself. Why, believing as he did, that all human obduracy was susceptible to common sense, was he unable to turn back? Why was he determined to complete his journey even if it meant putting his life in danger? At what point had this prank, this joke, this piece of horseplay become serious? He could not go back, he could not even recall with any clearness the green water at the Westerhazys', the sense of inhaling the day's components, the friendly and relaxed voices saying that they had *drunk* too much. In the space of an hour, more or less, he had covered a distance that made his return impossible.

An old man, tooling down the highway at fifteen miles an hour, let him get to the middle of the road, where there was a grass divider. Here he was exposed to the ridicule of the northbound traffic, but after ten or fifteen minutes he was able to cross. From here he had only a short walk to the Recreation Center at the edge of the Village of Lancaster, where there were some handball courts and a public pool.

The effect of the water on voices, the illusion of brilliance and suspense, was the same here as it had been at the Bunkers' but the sounds here were louder, harsher, and more shrill, and as soon as he entered the crowded enclosure he was confronted with regimentation. "ALL SWIMMERS MUST TAKE A SHOWER BEFORE USING THE POOL. ALL SWIMMERS MUST USE THE FOOTBATH. ALL SWIMMERS MUST WEAR THEIR IDENTIFICATION DISKS." He took a shower, washed his feet in a cloudy and bitter solution, and made his way to the edge of the water. It stank of chlorine and looked to him like a sink. A pair of lifeguards in a pair of towers blew police whistles at what seemed to be regular intervals and abused the swimmers through a public address system. Neddy remembered the sapphire water at the Bunkers' with longing and thought that he might contaminate himself—damage his own prosperousness and charm—by swimming in this murk, but he reminded himself that he was an explorer, a pilgrim, and that this was merely a stagnant bend in the Lucinda River. He dove, scowling with distaste, into the chlorine and had to swim with his head above water to avoid collisions, but even so he was bumped into, splashed, and jostled. When he got to the shallow end both lifeguards were shouting at him: "Hey, you, you without the identification disk, get outa the water." He did, but they had no way of pursuing him and he went through the reek of suntan oil and chlorine out through the hurricane fence and passed the handball courts. By crossing the road he entered the wooded part of the Halloran estate. The woods were not cleared and the footing was treacherous and difficult until he reached the lawn and the clipped beech hedge that encircled their pool.

The Hallorans were friends, an elderly couple of enormous wealth who seemed to bask in the suspicion that they might be Communists. They were zealous reformers but they were not Communists, and yet when they were accused, as they sometimes were, of subversion, it seemed to gratify and excite them. Their beech hedge was yellow and he guessed this had been blighted like the Levys' maple. He called hullo, hullo, to warn the Hallorans of his approach, to palliate his invasion of their privacy. The Hallorans, for reasons that had never been explained to him, did not wear bathing suits. No explanations were in order, really. Their nakedness was a detail in their uncompromising zeal for reform and he stepped politely out of his trunks before he went through the opening in the hedge.

Mrs. Halloran, a stout woman with white hair and a serene face, was reading the *Times*. Mr. Halloran was taking beech leaves out of the water with a scoop. They seemed not surprised or displeased to see him. Their pool was perhaps the oldest in the county, a fieldstone rectangle, fed by a brook. It had no filter or pump and its waters were the opaque gold of the stream.

"I'm swimming across the county," Ned said.

"Why, I didn't know one could," exclaimed Mrs. Halloran.

"Well, I've made it from the Westerhazys'," Ned said. "That must be about four miles."

He left his trunks at the deep end, walked to the shallow end, and swam this stretch. As he was pulling himself out of the water he heard Mrs. Halloran say, "We've been *terribly* sorry to hear about all your misfortunes, Neddy."

"My misfortunes?" Ned asked. "I don't know what you mean."

"Why, we heard that you'd sold the house and that your poor children . . ."

"I don't recall having sold the house," Ned said, "and the girls are at home."

"Yes," Mrs. Halloran sighed. "Yes . . ." Her voice filled the air with an unseasonable melancholy and Ned spoke briskly. "Thank you for the swim."

"Well, have a nice trip," said Mrs. Halloran.

Beyond the hedge he pulled on his trunks and fastened them. They were loose and he wondered if, during the space of an afternoon, he could have lost some weight. He was cold and he was tired and the naked Hallorans and their dark water had depressed him. The swim was too much for his strength but how could he have guessed this, sliding down the banister that morning and sitting in the Westerhazys' sun? His arms were lame. His legs felt rubbery and ached at the joints. The worst of it was the cold in his bones and the feeling that he might never be warm again.

Leaves were falling down around him and he smelled woodsmoke on the wind. Who would be burning wood at this time of year?

He needed a drink. Whiskey would warm him, pick him up, carry him through the last of his journey, refresh his feeling that it was original and valorous to swim across the county. Channel swimmers took brandy. He needed a stimulant. He crossed the lawn in front of the Hallorans' house and went down a little path to where they had built a house for their only daughter, Helen, and her husband, Eric Sachs. The Sachses' pool was small and he found Helen and her husband there.

"Oh, *Neddy*," Helen said. "Did you lunch at Mother's?"

"Not *really*," Ned said. "I *did* stop to see your parents." This seemed to be explanation enough. "I'm terribly sorry to break in on you like this but I've taken a chill and I wonder if you'd give me a drink."

"Why, I'd *love* to," Helen said, "but there hasn't been anything in this house to drink since Eric's operation. That was three years ago."

Was he losing his memory, had his gift for concealing painful facts let him forget that he had sold his house, that his children were in trouble, and that his friend had been ill? His eyes slipped from Eric's face to his abdomen, where he saw three pale sutured scars, two of them at least a foot long. Gone was his navel, and what, Neddy thought, would the roving hand, bed-checking one's gifts at 3 A.M. make of a belly with no navel, no link to birth, this breach in the succession?

"I'm sure you can get a drink at the Biswangers'," Helen said. "They're having an enormous do. You can hear it from here. Listen!"

She raised her head and from across the road, the lawns, the gardens, the woods, the fields, he heard again the brilliant noise of voices over water. "Well, I'll get wet," he said, still feeling that he had no freedom of choice about his means of travel. He dove into the Sachses' cold water and, gasping, close to drowning, made his way from one end of the pool to the other. "Lucinda and I want *terribly* to see you," he said over his shoulder, his face set toward the Biswangers'. "We're sorry it's been so long and we'll call you *very* soon."

He crossed some fields to the Biswangers' and the sounds of revelry there. They would be honored to give him a drink, they would be happy to give him a drink. The Biswangers invited him and Lucinda for dinner four times a year, six weeks in advance. They were always rebuffed and yet they continued to send out their invitations, unwilling to comprehend the rigid and undemocratic realities of their society. They were the sort of people who discussed the price of things at cocktails, exchanged market tips during dinner, and after dinner told dirty stories to mixed company. They did not belong to Neddy's set—they were not even on Lucinda's Christmas card list. He went toward their pool with feelings of indifference, charity, and some unease, since it seemed to be getting dark and these were the longest days of the year. The party when he joined it was noisy and large. Grace Biswanger was the kind of hostess who asked the optometrist, the veterinarian, the real-estate dealer, and the dentist. No one was swimming and the twilight, reflected on the water of the pool, had a wintry gleam. There was a bar and he started for this. When Grace Biswanger saw him she came toward him, not affectionately as he had every right to expect, but bellicosely.

"Why, this party has everything," she said loudly, "including a gate crasher."

She could not deal him a social blow—there was no question about this and he did not flinch. "As a gate crasher," he asked politely, "do I rate a drink?"

"Suit yourself," she said. "You don't seem to pay much attention to invitations."

She turned her back on him and joined some guests, and he went to the bar and ordered a whiskey. The bartender served him but he served him rudely. His was a world in which the caterer's men kept the social score, and to be rebuffed by a part-time barkeep meant that he had suffered some loss of social esteem. Or perhaps the man was new and uninformed. Then he heard Grace at his back say: "They went for broke overnight—nothing but income—and he showed up drunk one Sunday and asked us to loan him five thousand dollars. . . ." She was always talking about money. It was worse than eating your peas off a knife. He dove into the pool, swam its length and went away.

The next pool on his list, the last but two, belonged to his old mistress, Shirley Adams. If he had suffered any injuries at the Biswangers' they would be cured here. Love—sexual roughhouse in fact—was the supreme elixir, the pain killer, the brightly colored pill that would put the spring back into his step, the joy of life in his heart. They had had an affair last week, last month, last year. He couldn't remember. It was he who had broken it off, his was the upper hand, and he stepped through the gate of the wall that surrounded her pool with nothing so considered as self-confidence. It seemed in a way to be his pool, as the lover, particularly the illicit lover, enjoys the possessions of his mistress with an authority unknown to holy matrimony. She was there, her hair the color of brass, but her figure, at the edge of the lighted, cerulean water, excited in him no profound memories. It had been, he thought, a lighthearted affair, although she had wept when he broke it off. She seemed confused to see him and he wondered if she was still wounded. Would she, God forbid, weep again?

"What do you want?" she asked.

"I'm swimming across the county."

"Good Christ. Will you ever grow up?"

"What's the matter?"

"If you've come here for money," she said, "I won't give you another cent."

"You could give me a drink."

"I could but I won't. I'm not alone."

"Well, I'm on my way."

He dove in and swam the pool, but when he tried to haul himself up onto the curb he found that the strength in his arms and shoulders had gone, and he paddled to the ladder and climbed out. Looking over his shoulder he saw, in the lighted bath-house, a young man. Going out onto the dark lawn he smelled chrysanthemums or marigolds—some stubborn autumnal fragrance—on the night air, strong as gas. Looking overhead he saw that the stars had come out, but why should he seem to see Andromeda, Cepheus, and Cassiopeia? What had become of the constellations of midsummer? He began to cry.

It was probably the first time in his adult life that he had ever cried, certainly the first time in his life that he had ever felt so miserable, cold, tired, and bewildered. He could not understand the rudeness of the caterer's barkeep or the rudeness of a mistress who had come to him on her knees and showered his trousers with tears. He had swum too long, he had been immersed too long, and his nose and his throat were sore from the water. What he needed then was a drink, some company, and some clean, dry clothes, and while he could have cut directly across the road to his home he went on to the Gilmartins' pool. Here, for the first time in his life, he did not dive but went down the steps into the icy water and swam a hobbled sidestroke that he might have learned as a youth. He staggered with fatigue on his way to the Clydes' and paddled the length of their pool, stopping again and again with his hand on the curb to rest. He climbed up the ladder and wondered if he had the strength to get home. He had done what he wanted, he had swum the county, but he was so stupefied with exhaustion that his triumph seemed vague. Stooped, holding on to the gateposts for support, he turned up the driveway of his own house.

The place was dark. Was it so late that they had all gone to bed? Had Lucinda stayed at the Westerhazys' for supper? Had the girls joined her there or gone someplace else? Hadn't they agreed, as they usually did on Sunday, to regret all their invitations and stay at home? He tried the garage doors to see what cars were in but the doors were locked and rust came off the handles onto his hands. Going toward the house, he saw that the force of the thunderstorm had knocked one of the rain gutters loose. It hung down over the front door like an umbrella rib, but it could be fixed in the morning. The house was locked, and he thought that the stupid cook or the stupid maid must have locked the place up until he remembered that it had been some time since they had employed a maid or a cook. He shouted, pounded on the door, tried to force it with his shoulder, and then, looking in at the windows, saw that the place was empty.

---

## Mrs. Dutta Writes a Letter

### CHITRA BANERJEE DIVAKARUNI

When the alarm goes off at 5:00 A.M., buzzing like a trapped wasp, Mrs. Dutta has been lying awake for quite a while. Though it has now been two months, she still has difficulty sleeping on the Perma Rest mattress Sagar and Shyamoli, her son and daughter-in-law, have bought specially for her. It is too American-soft, unlike the reassuringly solid copra ticking she is used to at home. *Except this is home now*, she reminds herself. She reaches hurriedly to turn off the alarm, but in the dark her fingers get confused among the knobs, and the electric clock falls with a thud to the floor. Its insistent metallic call vibrates out through the walls of her room until she is sure it will wake everyone. She yanks frantically at the wire until she feels it give, and in the abrupt silence that follows she hears herself breathing, a sound harsh and uneven and full of guilt.

Mrs. Dutta knows, of course, that this turmoil is her own fault. She should just not set the alarm. There is no need for her to get up early here in Sunnyvale, in her son's house. But the habit, taught to her by her mother-in-law when she was a bride of seventeen, *a good wife wakes before the rest of the household*, is one she finds impossible to break. How hard it was then to pull her unwilling body away from her husband's sleep-warm clasp, Sagar's father whom she had just learned to love. To stumble to the kitchen that smelled of stale garam masala and light the coal unoon so she could make morning tea for them all—her parents-in-law, her husband, his two younger brothers, the widow aunt who lived with them.

After dinner, when the family sits in front of the TV, she attempts to tell her grandchildren about those days. "I was never good at starting that unoon—the smoke stung my eyes, making me cough and cough. Breakfast was never ready on time, and my mother-in-law—oh, how she scolded me until I was in tears. Every night I would pray to Goddess Durga, please let me sleep late, just one morning!"

"Mmmm," Pradeep says, bent over a model plane.

"Oooh, how awful," says Mrinalini, wrinkling her nose politely before she turns back to a show filled with jokes that Mrs. Dutta does not understand.

"That's why you should sleep in now, Mother," says Shyamoli, smiling from the recliner where she sits looking through the *Wall Street Journal*. With her legs crossed so elegantly under the shimmery blue skirt she has changed into after work, and her unusually fair skin, she could pass for an American, thinks Mrs. Dutta, whose own skin is brown as roasted cumin. The thought fills her with an uneasy pride.

From the floor where he leans against Shyamoli's knee, Sagar adds, "We want you to be comfortable, Ma. To rest. That's why we brought you to America."

In spite of his thinning hair and the gold-rimmed glasses which he has recently taken to wearing, Sagar's face seems to Mrs. Dutta still that of the boy she used to send off to primary school with his metal tiffin box. She remembers how he crawled into her bed on stormy monsoon nights, how when he was ill no one else could make him drink his barley water. Her heart balloons in sudden gladness because she is really here, with him and his children in America. "Oh, Sagar"—she smiles—"now you're talking like this! But did you give me a moment's rest while you were growing up?" And she launches into a description of childhood pranks that has him shaking his head indulgently while disembodied TV laughter echoes through the room.

But later he comes into her bedroom and says, a little shamefaced, "Mother, please, don't get up so early in the morning. All that noise in the bathroom, it wakes us up, and Molli has such a long day at work . . ."

And she, turning a little so he shouldn't see her foolish eyes filling with tears as though she were a teenage bride again and not a woman well over sixty, nods her head, *yes, yes*.

Waiting for the sounds of the stirring household to release her from the embrace of her Perma Rest mattress, Mrs. Dutta repeats the 108 holy names of God. *Om Keshavaya Namah, Om Narayanaya Namah, Om Madhavaya Namah.* But underneath she is thinking of the bleached-blue aerogram from Mrs. Basu that has been waiting unanswered on her bedside table all week, filled with news from home. There was a robbery at Sandhya Jewelry Store, the bandits had guns but luckily no one was hurt. Mr. Joshi's daughter, that sweet-faced child, has run away with her singing teacher, who would've thought it. Mrs. Barucha's daughter-in-law had one more baby girl, yes, their fourth, you'd think they'd know better than to keep trying for a boy. Last Tuesday was Bangla Bandh, another labor strike, everything closed down, even the buses not running, but you can't really blame them, can you, after all factory workers have to eat, too. Mrs. Basu's tenants, whom she'd been trying to evict forever, had finally moved out, good riddance, but you should see the state of the flat.

At the very bottom Mrs. Basu wrote, *Are you happy in America?*

Mrs. Dutta knows that Mrs. Basu, who has been her closest friend since they both came to Ghoshpara Lane as young brides, cannot be fobbed off with descriptions of Fisherman's Wharf and the Golden Gate Bridge, or even anecdotes involving grandchildren. And so she has been putting off her reply while in her heart family loyalty battles with insidious feelings of—but she turns from them quickly and will not name them even to herself.

Now Sagar is knocking on the children's doors—a curious custom, this, children being allowed to close their doors against their parents—and with relief Mrs. Dutta gathers up her bathroom things. She has plenty of time. It will take a second rapping from their mother before Pradeep and Mrinalini open their doors and stumble out. Still, she is not one to waste the precious morning. She splashes cold water on her face and neck (she does not believe in pampering herself), scrapes the night's gumminess from her tongue with her metal tongue cleaner, and brushes vigorously, though the minty toothpaste does not leave her mouth feeling as clean as did the bittersweet neem stick she'd been using all her life. She combs the knots out of her hair. Even at her age, it is thicker and silkier than her daughter-in-law's permed curls. *Such vanity*, she scolds her reflection, *and you a grandmother and a widow besides*. Still, as she deftly fashions her hair into a neat coil, she remembers how her husband would always compare it to night rain.

She hears a commotion outside.

"Pat! Minnie! What d'you mean you still haven't washed up? I'm late every morning to work nowadays because of you kids."

"But, Mom, *she's* in there. She's been there forever . . ." says Mrinalini.

Pause. Then, "So go to the downstairs bathroom."

"But all our stuff is here," says Pradeep, and Mrinalini adds, "It's not fair. Why can't *she* go downstairs?"

A longer pause. Inside the bathroom Mrs. Dutta hopes Shyamoli will not be too harsh on the girl. But a child who refers to elders in that disrespectful way ought to be punished. How many times had she slapped Sagar for something far less, though he was her only one, the jewel of her eye, come to her after she had been married for seven years and everyone had given up hope already? Whenever she lifted her hand to him it was as though her heart was being put through a masala grinder. Such is a mother's duty.

But Shyamoli only says, in a tired voice, "That's enough! Go put on your clothes, hurry."

The grumblings recede. Footsteps clatter down the stairs. Inside the bathroom Mrs. Dutta bends over the sink, gripping the folds of her sari. Hard to think through the pounding in her head to what it is she feels most—anger at the children for their rudeness, or at Shyamoli for letting them go unrebuked. Or is it shame that clogs her throat, stinging, sulfuric, indigestible?

It is 9.00 A.M. and the house, after the flurry of departures, of frantic "I can't find my socks," and "Mom, he took my lunch money," and "I swear I'll leave you kids behind if you're not in the car in exactly one minute," has settled into its placid daytime rhythms.

Busy in the kitchen, Mrs. Dutta has recovered her spirits. It is too exhausting to hold on to grudges, and, besides, the kitchen—sunlight sliding across its countertops while the refrigerator hums reassuringly—is her favorite place.

Mrs. Dutta hums too as she fries potatoes for alu dum. Her voice is rusty and slightly off-key. In India she would never have ventured to sing, but with everyone gone, the house is too quiet, all that silence pressing down on her like the heel of a giant hand, and the TV voices, with their unreal accents, are no help at all. As the potatoes turn golden-brown, she permits herself a moment of nostalgia for her Calcutta kitchen—the new gas stove bought with the birthday money Sagar sent, the scoured brass pots stacked by the meat safe, the window with the lotus-pattern grille through which she could look down on children playing cricket after school. The mouth-watering smell of ginger and chili paste, ground fresh by Reba the maid, and, in the evening, strong black Assam cha brewing in the kettle when Mrs. Basu came by to visit. In her mind she writes to Mrs. Basu, *Oh, Roma, I miss it all so much, sometimes I feel that someone has reached in and torn out a handful of my chest.*

But only fools indulge in nostalgia, so Mrs. Dutta shakes her head clear of images and straightens up the kitchen. She pours the half-drunk glasses of milk down the sink, though Shyamoli has told her to save them in the refrigerator. But surely Shyamoli, a girl from a good Hindu family, doesn't expect her to put contaminated jutha things in with the rest of the food? She washes the breakfast dishes by hand instead of letting them wait inside the dishwater till night, breeding germs. With practiced fingers she throws an assortment of spices into the blender: coriander, cumin, cloves, black pepper, a few red chilies for vigor. No stale bottled curry powder for *her!* *At least the family's eating well since I arrived,* she writes in her mind, *proper Indian food, rotis that puff up the way they should, fish curry in mustard sauce, and real pulao with raisins and cashews and ghee—the way you taught me, Roma—instead of Rice-a-roni.* She would like to add, *They love it,* but thinking of Shyamoli she hesitates.

At first Shyamoli had been happy enough to have someone take over the cooking. It's wonderful to come home to a hot dinner, she'd say, or, Mother, what crispy papads, and your fish gravy is out of this world. But recently she's taken to picking at her food, and once or twice from the kitchen Mrs. Dutta has caught wisps of words, intensely whispered: *cholesterol, all putting on weight, she's spoiling you.* And though Shyamoli always refuses when the children ask if they can have burritos from the freezer instead, Mrs. Dutta suspects that she would really like to say yes.

The children. A heaviness pulls at Mrs. Dutta's entire body when she thinks of them. Like so much in this country they have turned out to be—yes, she might as well admit it—a disappointment.

For this she blames, in part, the Olan Mills portrait. Perhaps it had been imprac-tical of her to set so much store on a photograph, especially one taken years ago. But it was such a charming scene—Mrinalini in a ruffled white dress with her arm around her brother, Pradeep chubby and dimpled in a suit and bow tie, a glorious au-tumn forest blazing red and yellow behind them. (Later Mrs. Dutta would learn, with a sense of having been betrayed, that the forest was merely a backdrop in a stu-dio in California, where real trees did not turn such colors.)

The picture had arrived, silver-framed and wrapped in a plastic sheet filled with bubbles, with a note from Shyamoli explaining that it was a Mother's Day gift. (A strange concept, a day set aside to honor mothers. Did the sahebs not honor their mothers the rest of the year, then?) For a week Mrs. Dutta could not decide where it should be hung. If she put it in the drawing room, visitors would be able to admire her grandchildren, but if she put it on the bedroom wall, she would be able to see the photo, last thing, before she fell asleep. She had finally opted for the bedroom, and later, when she was too ill with pneumonia to leave her bed for a month, she'd been glad of it.

Mrs. Dutta was not unused to living on her own. She had done it for the last three years, since Sagar's father died, politely but stubbornly declining the offers of various relatives, well-meaning and otherwise, to come and stay with her. In this she had surprised herself as well as others, who thought of her as a shy, sheltered woman, one who would surely fall apart without her husband to handle things for her. But she managed quite well. She missed Sagar's father, of course, especially in the evenings, when it had been his habit to read to her the more amusing parts of the newspaper while she rolled out rotis. But once the grief receded, she found it rather pleasant to be mistress of her own life, as she confided to Mrs. Basu. She liked being able, for the first time ever, to lie in bed all evening and read a new novel of Shankar's straight through if she wanted, or to send out for hot brinjal pakoras on a rainy day without feeling guilty that she wasn't serving up a balanced meal.

When the pneumonia hit, everything changed.

Mrs. Dutta had been ill before, but those illnesses had been different. Even in bed she'd been at the center of the household, with Reba coming to find out what should be cooked, Sagar's father bringing her shirts with missing buttons, her mother-in-law, now old and tamed, complaining that the cook didn't brew her tea strong enough, and Sagar running in crying because he'd had a fight with the neighbor boy. But now there was no one to ask her, querulously, *Just how long do you plan to remain sick,* no one waiting in impatient exasperation for her to take on her duties again, no one whose life was inconvenienced the least bit by her illness.

There was, therefore, no reason for her to get well.

When this thought occurred to Mrs. Dutta, she was so frightened that her body grew numb. The walls of the room spun into blackness, the bed on which she lay, a vast four-poster she had shared with Sagar's father since her marriage, rocked like a mastless dinghy caught in a storm, and a great, muted roar reverberated in the cavi-ties of her skull. For a moment, unable to move or see, she thought, *I'm dead.* Then her vision, desperate and blurry, caught on the portrait. *My grandchildren.* She fo-cused, with some difficulty, on the bright, oblivious sheen of their child faces, the eyes so like Sagar's that for a moment she could feel heartsickness cramping her joints like arthritis. She drew in a shuddering breath; the roaring seemed to recede. When the afternoon post brought another letter from Sagar, *Mother, you really should come and live with us, we worry about you all alone in India, especially when you're sick like this,* she wrote back the same day, with fingers that still shook a little, *You're right, my place is with you, with my grandchildren.*

But now that she is here on the other side of the world, she is wrenched by doubt. She knows the grandchildren love her—how can it be otherwise among family? And she loves them, she reminds herself, though they have put away, somewhere in the back of a closet, the vellum-bound *Ramayana for Young Readers* that she carried all the way from India in her hand luggage. Though their bodies twitch with impatience when she tries to tell them stories of her girlhood. Though they offer the most transparent excuses when she asks them to sit with her while she chants the evening arati. *They're flesh of my flesh, blood of my blood,* she reminds herself. But sometimes when she listens, from the other room, to them speaking on the phone, their American voices rising in excitement as they discuss a glittering alien world of Power Rangers, Spice Girls, and Spirit Week at school, she almost cannot believe it.

Stepping into the backyard with a bucket of newly washed clothes, Mrs. Dutta views the sky with some anxiety. The butter-gold sunlight is gone, black-bellied clouds have taken over the horizon, and the air feels still and heavy on her face, as before a Bengal storm. What if her clothes don't dry by the time the others return home?

Washing clothes has been a problem for Mrs. Dutta ever since she arrived in California.

"We can't, Mother," Shyamoli had said with a sigh when Mrs. Dutta asked Sagar to put up a clothesline for her in the backyard. (Shyamoli sighed often nowadays. Perhaps it was an American habit? Mrs. Dutta did not remember the Indian Shyamoli, the docile bride she'd mothered for a month before putting her on a Pan Am flight to join her husband, pursing her lips in quite this way to let out a breath at once patient and vexed.) "It's just not *done*, not in a nice neighborhood like this one. And being the only Indian family on the street, we have to be extra careful. People here, sometimes—." She'd broken off with a shake of her head. "Why don't you just keep your dirty clothes in the hamper I've put in your room, and I'll wash them on Sunday along with everyone else's."

Afraid of causing another sigh, Mrs. Dutta had agreed reluctantly. But she knew she should not store unclean clothes in the same room where she kept the pictures of her gods. That brought bad luck; and the odor. Lying in bed at night she could smell it distinctly, even though Shyamoli claimed the hamper was airtight. The sour, starchy old-woman smell embarrassed her.

What embarrassed her more was when, Sunday afternoons, Shyamoli brought the laundry into the family room to fold. Mrs. Dutta would bend intensely over her knitting, face tingling with shame, as her daughter-in-law nonchalantly shook out the wisps of lace, magenta and sea-green and black, that were her panties, laying them next to a stack of Sagar's briefs. And when, right in front of everyone, Shyamoli pulled out Mrs. Dutta's own crumpled, baggy bras from the clothes heap, she wished the ground would open up and swallow her, like the Sita of mythology.

Then one day Shyamoli set the clothes basket down in front of Sagar.

"Can you do them today, Sagar?" (Mrs. Dutta, who had never, through the forty-two years of her marriage, addressed Sagar's father by name, tried not to wince.) "I've got to get that sales report into the computer by tonight."

Before Sagar could respond, Mrs. Dutta was out of her chair, knitting needles dropping to the floor.

"No no no, clothes and all is no work for the man of the house. I'll do it." The thought of her son's hands searching through the basket and lifting up his wife's— and her own—underclothes filled her with horror.

"Mother!" Shyamoli said. "This is why Indian men are so useless around the house. Here in America we don't believe in men's work and women's work. Don't I work outside all day, just like Sagar? How'll I manage if he doesn't help me at home?"

"I'll help you instead," Mrs. Dutta ventured.

"You don't understand, do you, Mother?" Shyamoli said with a shaky smile. Then she went into the study.

Mrs. Dutta sat down in her chair and tried to understand. But after a while she gave up and whispered to Sagar that she wanted him to teach her how to run the washer and dryer.

"Why, Mother? Molli's quite happy to . . ."

"I've got to learn it. . . ." Her voice warped with distress as she rummaged through the tangled heap for her clothes.

Her son began to object, then shrugged. "Oh very well. If that's what you really want."

But later, when she faced them alone, the machines with their cryptic symbols and rows of gleaming knobs terrified her. What if she pressed the wrong button and flooded the entire floor with soapsuds? What if she couldn't turn the machines off and they kept going, whirring maniacally, until they exploded? (This had happened to a woman on a TV show just the other day, and she had jumped up and down, screaming. Everyone else found it hilarious, but Mrs. Dutta sat stiff-spined, gripping the armrest of her chair.) So she took to washing her clothes in the bathtub when she was alone. She had never done such a chore before, but she remembered how the village washerwomen of her childhood would beat their saris clean against river rocks. And a curious satisfaction filled her as her clothes hit the porcelain with the same solid wet *thunk*.

*My small victory, my secret.*

This is why everything must be dried and put safely away before Shyamoli returns. Ignorance, as Mrs. Dutta knows well from years of managing a household, is a great promoter of harmony. So she keeps an eye on the menacing advance of the clouds as she hangs up her blouse and underwear. As she drapes her sari along the redwood fence that separates her son's property from the neighbor's, first wiping it clean with a dish towel she has secretly taken from the bottom drawer of the kitchen. But she isn't too worried. Hasn't she managed every time, even after that-freak hailstorm last month when she had to use the iron from the laundry closet to press everything dry?

The memory pleases her. In her mind she writes to Mrs. Basu, *I'm fitting in so well here, you'd never guess I came only two months back. I've found new ways of doing things, of solving problems creatively. You would be most proud if you saw me.*

When Mrs. Dutta decided to give up her home of forty-five years, her relatives showed far less surprise than she had expected.

"Oh, we all knew you'd end up in America sooner or later," they said. "It was a foolishness to stay on alone so long after Sagar's father, may he find eternal peace, passed away. Good thing that boy of yours came to his senses and called you to join him. Everyone knows a wife's place is with her husband, and a widow's with her son."

Mrs. Dutta had nodded meek agreement, ashamed to let anyone know that the night before she had awakened weeping.

"Well, now that you're going, what'll happen to all your things?"

Mrs. Dutta, still troubled over those treacherous tears, had offered up her household effects in propitiation. "Here, Didi, you take this cutwork bedspread. Mashima, for a long time I meant for you to have these Corning Ware dishes, I know how much you admire them. And, Boudi, this tape recorder that Sagar sent a year back is for you. Yes yes, I'm quite sure. I can always tell Sagar to buy me another one when I get there."

Mrs. Basu, coming in just as a cousin made off triumphantly with a bone china tea set, had protested. "Prameela, have you gone crazy? That tea set used to belong to your mother-in-law."

"But what'll I do with it in America? Shyamoli has her own set—"

A look that Mrs. Dutta couldn't read flitted across Mrs. Basu's face. "But do you want to drink from it for the rest of your life?"

"What do you mean?"

Mrs. Basu hesitated. Then she said, "What if you don't like it there?"

"How can I not like it, Roma?" Mrs. Dutta's voice was strident, even to her own ears. With an effort she controlled it and continued, "I'll miss my friends, I know— and you most of all. The things we do together—evening tea, our walk around Rabindra Sarobar Lake, Thursday night Bhagavat Geeta class. But Sagar—they're my only family. And blood is blood after all."

"I wonder," Mrs. Basu said dryly, and Mrs. Dutta recalled that though both of Mrs. Basu's children lived just a day's journey away, they came to see her only on occasions when common decency demanded their presence. Perhaps they were tightfisted in money matters too. Perhaps that was why Mrs. Basu had started renting out her downstairs a few years ago, even though, as anyone in Calcutta knew, tenants were more trouble than they were worth. Such filial neglect must be hard to take, though Mrs. Basu, loyal to her children as indeed a mother should be, never complained. In a way Mrs. Dutta had been better off, with Sagar too far away for her to put his love to the test.

"At least don't give up the house," Mrs. Basu was saying. "It'll be impossible to find another place in case—"

"In case what?" Mrs. Dutta asked, her words like stone chips. She was surprised to find that she was angrier with Mrs. Basu than she'd ever been. Or was it fear?

*My son isn't like yours,* she'd been on the verge of spitting out. She took a deep breath and made herself smile, made herself remember that she might never see her friend again.

"Ah, Roma," she said, putting her arm around Mrs. Basu, "you think I'm such an old witch that my Sagar and my Shyamoli will be unable to live with me?"

Mrs. Dutta hums a popular Rabindra Sangeet as she pulls her sari from the fence. It's been a good day, as good as it can be in a country where you might stare out the window for hours and not see one living soul. No vegetable vendors with wicker baskets balanced on their heads, no knife-sharpeners calling *scissors-knives-choppers, scissors-knives-choppers* to bring the children running. No dehati women with tattoos on their arms to sell you cookware in exchange for your old silk saris. Why, even the animals that frequented Ghoshpara Lane had personality. Stray dogs that knew to line up outside the kitchen door just when leftovers were likely to be thrown out, the goat who maneuvered its head through the garden grille hoping to get at her dahlias, cows who planted themselves majestically in the center of the road, ignoring honking drivers. And right across the street was Mrs. Basu's two-story house, which Mrs. Dutta knew as well as her own. How many times had she walked up the stairs to that airy room painted sea-green and filled with plants where her friend would be waiting for her.

*What took you so long today, Prameela? Your tea is cold already.*

*Wait till you hear what happened, Roma. Then you won't scold me for being late. . . .*

Stop it, you silly woman, Mrs. Dutta tells herself severely. Every single one of your relatives would give an arm and a leg to be in your place, you know that. After lunch you're going to write a nice, long letter to Roma, telling her exactly how delighted you are to be here.

From where Mrs. Dutta stands, gathering up petticoats and blouses, she can look into the next yard. Not that there's much to see, just tidy grass and a few pale-blue-flowers whose name she doesn't know. There are two wooden chairs under a tree, but Mrs. Dutta has never seen anyone using them. What's the point of having such a big yard if you're not even going to sit in it? she thinks. Calcutta pushes itself into her mind again, Calcutta with its narrow, blackened flats where families of six and eight and ten squeeze themselves into two tiny rooms, and her heart fills with a sense of loss she knows to be illogical.

When she first arrived in Sagar's home, Mrs. Dutta wanted to go over and meet her next-door neighbors, maybe take them some of her special rose-water rasogollahs, as she'd often done with Mrs. Basu. But Shyamoli said she shouldn't. Such things were not the custom in California, she explained earnestly. You didn't just drop in on people without calling ahead. Here everyone was busy, they didn't sit around chatting, drinking endless cups of sugar tea. Why, they might even say something unpleasant to her.

"For what?" Mrs. Dutta had asked disbelievingly, and Shyamoli had said, "Because Americans don't like neighbors to"—here she used an English phrase—"invade their privacy." Mrs. Dutta, who didn't fully understand the word *privacy* because there was no such term in Bengali, had gazed at her daughter-in-law in some bewilderment.

But she understood enough to not ask again. In the following months, though, she often looked over the fence, hoping to make contact. People were people, whether in India or America, and everyone appreciated a friendly face. When Shyamoli was as old as Mrs. Dutta, she would know that, too.

Today, just as she is about to turn away, out of the corner of her eye Mrs. Dutta notices a movement. At one of the windows a woman is standing, her hair a sleek gold like that of the TV heroines whose exploits baffle Mrs. Dutta when sometimes she tunes in to an afternoon serial. She is smoking a cigarette, and a curl of gray rises lazily, elegantly from her fingers. Mrs. Dutta is so happy to see another human being in the middle of her solitary day that she forgets how much she disapproves of smoking, especially in women. She lifts her hand in the gesture she has seen her grandchildren use to wave an eager hello.

The woman stares back at Mrs. Dutta. Her lips are a perfect-painted red, and when she raises her cigarette to her mouth, its tip glows like an animal's eye. She does not wave back or smile. Perhaps she is not well? Mrs. Dutta feels sorry for her, alone in her illness in a silent house with only cigarettes for solace, and she wishes the etiquette of America had not prevented her from walking over with a word of cheer and a bowl of her fresh-cooked alu dum.

Mrs. Dutta rarely gets a chance to be alone with her son. In the morning he is in too much of a hurry even to drink the fragrant cardamom tea which she (remembering how as a child he would always beg for a sip from her cup) offers to make him. He doesn't return until dinnertime, and afterward he must help the children with their homework, read the paper, hear the details of Shyamoli's day, watch his favorite TV crime show in order to unwind, and take out the garbage. In between, for he is a solicitous son, he converses with Mrs. Dutta. In response to his questions she assures him that her arthritis is much better now; no, no, she's not growing bored being at home all the time; she has everything she needs—Shyamoli has been so kind—but perhaps he could pick up a few aerograms on his way back tomorrow? She recites obediently for him an edited list of her day's activities and smiles when he praises her cooking. But when he says, "Oh, well, time to turn in, another working day tomorrow," she is racked by a vague pain, like hunger, in the region of her heart.

So it is with the delighted air of a child who has been offered an unexpected gift that she leaves her half-written letter to greet Sagar at the door today, a good hour before Shyamoli is due back. The children are busy in the family room doing homework and watching cartoons (mostly the latter, Mrs. Dutta suspects). But for once she doesn't mind because they race in to give their father hurried hugs and then race back again. And she has him, her son, all to herself in a kitchen filled with the familiar, pungent odors of tamarind sauce and chopped coriander leaves.

"Khoka," she says, calling him by the childhood name she hasn't used in years, "I could fry you two-three hot-hot luchis, if you like." As she waits for his reply she can feel, in the hollow of her throat, the rapid beat of her blood. And when he says yes, that would be very nice, she shuts her eyes and takes a deep breath, and it is as though merciful time has given her back her youth, that sweet, aching urgency of being needed again.

Mrs. Dutta is telling Sagar a story.

"When you were a child, how scared you were of injections! One time, when the government doctor came to give us compulsory typhoid shots, you locked yourself in the bathroom and refused to come out. Do you remember what your father finally did? He went into the garden and caught a lizard and threw it in the bathroom window, because you were even more scared of lizards than of shots. And in exactly one second you ran out screaming—right into the waiting doctor's arms."

Sagar laughs so hard that he almost upsets his tea (made with real sugar, because Mrs. Dutta knows it is better for her son than that chemical powder Shyamoli likes to use). There are tears in his eyes, and Mrs. Dutta, who had not dared to hope he would find her story so amusing, feels gratified. When he takes off his glasses to wipe them, his face is oddly young, not like a father's at all, or even a husband's, and she has to suppress an impulse to put out her hand and rub away the indentations the glasses have left on his nose.

"I'd totally forgotten," says Sagar. "How can you keep track of those old, old things?"

Because it is the lot of mothers to remember what no one else cares to, Mrs. Dutta thinks. To tell them over and over until they are lodged, perforce, in family lore. We are the keepers of the heart's dusty corners.

But as she starts to say this, the front door creaks open, and she hears the faint click of Shyamoli's high heels. Mrs. Dutta rises, collecting the dirty dishes.

"Call me fifteen minutes before you're ready to eat so I can fry fresh luchis for everyone," she tells Sagar.

"You don't have to leave, Mother," he says.

Mrs. Dutta smiles her pleasure but doesn't stop. She knows Shyamoli likes to be alone with her husband at this time, and today in her happiness she does not grudge her this.

"You think I've nothing to do, only sit and gossip with you?" she mock-scolds. "I want you to know I have a very important letter to finish."

Somewhere behind her she hears a thud, a briefcase falling over. This surprises her. Shyamoli is always so careful with her case because it was a gift from Sagar when she was finally made a manager in her company.

"Hi!" Sagar calls, and when there's no answer, "Hey, Molli, you okay?"

Shyamoli comes into the room slowly, her hair disheveled as though she's been running her fingers through it. A hectic color blotches her cheeks.

"What's the matter, Molli?" Sagar walks over to give her a kiss. "Bad day at work?" Mrs. Dutta, embarrassed as always by this display of marital affection, turns toward the window, but not before she sees Shyamoli move her face away.

"Leave me alone." Her voice is wobbly. "Just leave me alone."

"But what is it?" Sagar says in concern.

"I don't want to talk about it right now." Shyamoli lowers herself into a kitchen chair and puts her face in her hands. Sagar stands in the middle of the room, looking helpless. He raises his hand and lets it fall, as though he wants to comfort his wife but is afraid of what she might do.

A protective anger for her son surges inside Mrs. Dutta, but she leaves the room silently. In her mind-letter she writes, *Women need to be strong, not react to every little thing like this. You and I, Roma, we had far worse to cry about, but we shed our tears in-visibly. We were good wives and daughters-in-law, good mothers, Dutiful, uncomplaining. Never putting ourselves first.*

A sudden memory comes to her, one she hasn't thought of in years, a day when she scorched a special kheer dessert. Her mother-in-law had shouted at her, "Didn't your mother teach you anything, you useless girl?" As punishment she refused to let Mrs. Dutta go with Mrs. Basu to the cinema, even though *Sahib, Bibi aur Ghulam,* which all Calcutta was crazy about, was playing, and their tickets were bought already. Mrs. Dutta had wept the entire afternoon, but before Sagar's father came home she washed her face carefully with cold water and applied kajal to her eyes so he wouldn't know.

But everything is getting mixed up, and her own young, trying-not-to-cry face blurs into another—why, it's Shyamoli's—and a thought hits her so sharply in the chest she has to hold on to the bedroom wall. *And what good did it do? The more we bent, the more people pushed us, until one day we'd forgotten that we could stand up straight. Maybe Shyamoli's doing the right thing, after all. . . .*

Mrs. Dutta lowers herself heavily on to her bed, trying to erase such an insidious idea from her mind. Oh, this new country where all the rules are upside down, it's confusing her. Her mind feels muddy, like a pond in which too many water buffaloes have been wading. Maybe things will settle down if she can focus on the letter to Roma.

Then she remembers that she has left the half-written aerogram on the kitchen table. She knows she should wait until after dinner, after her son and his wife have sorted things out. But a restlessness—or is it defiance?—has taken hold of her. She's sorry Shyamoli's upset, but why should she have to waste her evening because of that? She'll go get her letter—it's no crime, is it? She'll march right in and pick it up, and even if Shyamoli stops in midsentence with another one of those sighs, she'll refuse to feel apologetic. Besides, by now they're probably in the family room, watching TV.

*Really, Roma,* she writes in her head as she feels her way along the unlighted corridor, *the amount of TV they watch here is quite scandalous. The children too, sitting for hours in front of that box like they've been turned into painted Kesto Nagar dolls, and then talking back when I tell them to turn it off.* Of course, she will never put such blasphemy into a real letter. Still, it makes her feel better to say it, if only to herself.

In the family room the TV is on, but for once no one is paying it any attention. Shyamoli and Sagar sit on the sofa, conversing. From where she stands in the corridor, Mrs. Dutta cannot see them, but their shadows—enormous against the wall where the table lamp has cast them—seem to flicker and leap at her.

She is about to slip unseen into the kitchen when Shyamoli's rising voice arrests her. In its raw, shaking unhappiness it is so unlike her daughter-in-law's assured tones that Mrs. Dutta is no more able to move away from it than if she had heard the call of the nishi, the lost souls of the dead on whose tales she grew up.

"It's easy for you to say 'Calm down.' I'd like to see how calm *you'd* be if she came up to you and said, 'Kindly tell the old lady not to hang her clothes over the fence into my yard.' She said it twice, like I didn't understand English, like I was an idiot.

All these years I've been so careful not to give these Americans a chance to say something like this, and now—"

"Shhh Shyamoli, I *said* I'd talk to Mother about it."

"You always say that, but you never *do* anything. You're too busy being the perfect son, tiptoeing around her feelings. But how about mine?"

"Hush, Molli, the children . . ."

"Let them hear. I don't care anymore. They're not stupid. They already know what a hard time I've been having with her. You're the only one who refuses to see it."

In the passage Mrs. Dutta shrinks against the wall. She wants to move away, to not hear anything else, but her feet are formed of cement, impossible to lift, and Shyamoli's words pour into her ears like smoking oil.

"I've explained over and over, and she still keeps on doing what I've asked her not to—throwing away perfectly good food, leaving dishes to drip all over the countertops. Ordering my children to stop doing things I've given them permission for. She's taken over the entire kitchen, cooking whatever she likes. You come in the door and the smell of grease is everywhere, in all our clothes. I feel like this isn't my house anymore."

"Be patient, Molli, she's an old woman, after all."

"I know. That's why I tried so hard. I know having her here is important to you. But I can't do it any longer. I just can't. Some days I feel like taking the kids and leaving." Shyamoli's voice disappears into a sob.

A shadow stumbles across the wall to her, and then another. Behind the weatherman's nasal tones announcing a week of sunny days, Mrs. Dutta can hear a high, frightened weeping. The children, she thinks. It's probably the first time they've seen their mother cry.

"Don't talk like that, sweetheart." Sagar leans forward, his voice, too, miserable. All the shadows on the wall shiver and merge into a single dark silhouette.

Mrs. Dutta stares at that silhouette, the solidarity of it. Sagar and Shyamoli's murmurs are lost beneath a noise—is it in her veins, this dry humming, the way the taps in Calcutta used to hum when the municipality turned the water off? After a while she discovers that she has reached her room. In darkness she lowers herself on to her bed very gently, as though her body is made of the thinnest glass. Or perhaps ice, she is so cold. She sits for a long time with her eyes closed, while inside her head thoughts whirl faster and faster until they disappear in a gray dust storm.

When Pradeep finally comes to call her for dinner, Mrs. Dutta follows him to the kitchen where she fries luchis for everyone, the perfect circles of dough puffing up crisp and golden as always. Sagar and Shyamoli have reached a truce of some kind: she gives him a small smile, and he puts out a casual hand to massage the back of her neck. Mrs. Dutta demonstrates no embarrassment at this. She eats her dinner. She answers questions put to her. She smiles when someone makes a joke. If her face is still, as though she has been given a shot of Novocain, no one notices. When the table is cleared, she excuses herself, saying she has to finish her letter.

Now Mrs. Dutta sits on her bed, reading over what she wrote in the innocent afternoon.

*Dear Roma,*

*Although I miss you, I know you will be pleased to hear how happy I am in America. There is much here that needs getting used to, but we are no strangers to adjusting, we old women. After all, haven't we been doing it all our lives?*

*Today I'm cooking one of Sagar's favorite dishes, alu-dum. . . . It gives me such pleasure to see my family gathered around the table, eating my food. The children are still a little shy of me, but I am hopeful that we'll soon be friends. And Shyamoli, so confident and successful—you should see her when she's all dressed for work. I can't believe she's the same timid bride I sent off to America just a few years ago. But, Sagar, most of all, is the joy of my old age. . . .*

With the edge of her sari Mrs. Dutta carefully wipes a tear that has fallen on the aerogram. She blows on the damp spot until it is completely dry, so the pen will not leave an incriminating smudge. Even though Roma would not tell a soul, she cannot risk it. She can already hear them, the avid relatives in India who have been waiting for something just like this to happen. *That Dutta-ginni, so set in her ways, we knew she'd never get along with her daughter-in-law.* Or worse, *Did you hear about poor Prameela, how her family treated her, yes, even her son, can you imagine?*

This much surely she owes to Sagar.

And what does she owe herself, Mrs. Dutta, falling through black night with all the certainties she trusted in collapsed upon themselves like imploded stars, and only an image inside her eyelids for company? A silhouette—man, wife, children—joined on a wall, showing her how alone she is in this land of young people. And how unnecessary.

She is not sure how long she sits under the glare of the overhead light, how long her hands clench themselves in her lap. When she opens them, nail marks line the soft flesh of her palms, red hieroglyphs—her body's language, telling her what to do.

*Dear Roma,* Mrs. Dutta writes,

*I cannot answer your question about whether I am happy, for I am no longer sure I know what happiness is. All I know is that it isn't what I thought it to be. It isn't about being needed. It isn't about being with family either. It has something to do with love, I still think that, but in a different way than I believed earlier, a way I don't have the words to explain. Perhaps we can figure it out together, two old women drinking cha in your downstairs-flat (for I do hope you will rent it to me on my return), while around us gossip falls—but lightly, like summer rain, for that is all we will allow it to be. If I'm lucky—and perhaps, in spite of all that has happened, I am—the happiness will be in the figuring out.*

Pausing to read over what she has written, Mrs. Dutta is surprised to discover this: Now that she no longer cares whether tears blotch her letter, she feels no need to weep.

# A Serious Talk

### RAYMOND CARVER

Vera's car was there, no others, and Burt gave thanks for that. He pulled into the drive and stopped beside the pie he'd dropped the night before. It was still there, the aluminum pan upside down, a halo of pumpkin filling on the pavement. It was the day after Christmas.

He'd come on Christmas day to visit his wife and children. Vera had warned him beforehand. She'd told him the score. She'd said he had to be out by six o'clock because her friend and his children were coming for dinner.

They had sat in the living room and solemnly opened the presents Burt had brought over. They had opened his packages while other packages wrapped in festive paper lay piled under the tree waiting for after six o'clock.

He had watched the children open their gifts, waited while Vera undid the ribbon on hers. He saw her slip off the paper, lift the lid, take out the cashmere sweater.

"It's nice," she said. "Thank you, Burt."

"Try it on," his daughter said.

"Put it on," his son said.

Burt looked at his son, grateful for his backing him up.

She did try it on. Vera went into the bedroom and came out with it on.

"It's nice," she said.

"It's nice on *you*," Burt said, and felt a welling in his chest.

He opened his gifts. From Vera, a gift certificate at Sondheim's men's store. From his daughter, a matching comb and brush. From his son, a ballpoint pen.

Vera served sodas, and they did a little talking. But mostly they looked at the tree. Then his daughter got up and began setting the dining-room table, and his son went off to his room.

But Burt liked it where he was. He liked it in front of the fireplace, a glass in his hand, his house, his home.

Then Vera went into the kitchen.

From time to time his daughter walked into the dining room with something for the table. Burt watched her. He watched her fold the linen napkins into the wine glasses. He watched her put a slender vase in the middle of the table. He watched her lower a flower into the vase, doing it ever so carefully.

A small wax and sawdust log burned on the grate. A carton of five more sat ready on the hearth. He got up from the sofa and put them all in the fireplace. He watched until they flamed. Then he finished his soda and made for the patio door. On the way, he saw the pies lined up on the sideboard. He stacked them in his arms, all six, one for every ten times she had ever betrayed him.

In the driveway in the dark, he'd let one fall as he fumbled with the door.

The front door was permanently locked since the night his key had broken off inside it. He went around to the back. There was a wreath on the patio door. He rapped on the glass. Vera was in her bathrobe. She looked out at him and frowned. She opened the door a little.

Burt said, "I want to apologize to you for last night. I want to apologize to the kids, too."

Vera said, "They're not here."

She stood in the doorway and he stood on the patio next to the philodendron plant. He pulled at some lint on his sleeve.

She said, "I can't take any more. You tried to burn the house down."

"I did not."

"You did. Everybody here was a witness."

He said, "Can I come in and talk about it?"

She drew the robe together at her throat and moved back inside.

She said, "I have to go somewhere in an hour."

He looked around. The tree blinked on and off. There was a pile of colored tissue paper and shiny boxes at one end of the sofa. A turkey carcass sat on a platter in the center of the dining-room table, the leathery remains in a bed of parsley as if in a horrible nest. A cone of ash filled the fireplace. There were some empty Shasta cola cans in there too. A trail of smoke stains rose up the bricks to the mantel, where the wood that stopped them was scorched black.

He turned around and went back to the kitchen.

He said, "What time did your friend leave last night?"

She said, "If you're going to start that, you can go right now."

He pulled a chair out and sat down at the kitchen table in front of the big ashtray. He closed his eyes and opened them. He moved the curtain aside and looked out at the backyard. He saw a bicycle without a front wheel standing upside down. He saw weeds growing along the redwood fence.

She ran water into a saucepan. "Do you remember Thanksgiving?" she said. "I said then that was the last holiday you were going to wreck for us. Eating bacon and eggs instead of turkey at ten o'clock at night."

"I know it," he said. "I said I'm sorry."

"Sorry isn't good enough."

The pilot light was out again. She was at the stove trying to get the gas going under the pan of water.

"Don't burn yourself," he said. "Don't catch yourself on fire."

He considered her robe catching fire, him jumping up from the table, throwing her down onto the floor and rolling her over and over into the living room, where he would cover her with his body. Or should he run to the bedroom for a blanket?

"Vera?"

She looked at him.

"Do you have anything to drink? I could use a drink this morning."

"There's some vodka in the freezer."

"When did you start keeping vodka in the freezer?"

"Don't ask."

"Okay," he said, "I won't ask."

He got out the vodka and poured some into a cup he found on the counter.

She said, "Are you just going to drink it like that, out of a cup?" She said, "Jesus, Burt. What'd you want to talk about, anyway? I told you I have someplace to go. I have a flute lesson at one o'clock."

"Are you still taking flute?"

"I just said so. What is it? Tell me what's on your mind, and then I have to get ready."

"I wanted to say I was sorry."

She said, "You said that."

He said, "If you have any juice, I'll mix it with this vodka."

She opened the refrigerator and moved things around.

"There's cranapple juice," she said.

"That's fine," he said.

"I'm going to the bathroom," she said.

He drank the cup of cranapple juice and vodka. He lit a cigarette and tossed the match into the big ashtray that always sat on the kitchen table. He studied the butts in it. Some of them were Vera's brand, and some of them weren't. Some even were lavender-colored. He got up and dumped it all under the sink.

The ashtray was not really an ashtray. It was a big dish of stoneware they'd bought from a bearded potter on the mall in Santa Clara. He rinsed it out and dried it. He put it back on the table. And then he ground out his cigarette in it.

The water on the stove began to bubble just as the phone began to ring.

He heard her open the bathroom door and call to him through the living room. "Answer that! I'm about to get into the shower."

The kitchen phone was on the counter in a corner behind the roasting pan. He moved the roasting pan and picked up the receiver.

"Is Charlie there?" the voice said.

"No," Burt said.

"Okay," the voice said.

While he was seeing to the coffee, the phone rang again.

"Charlie?"

"Not here," Burt said.

This time he left the receiver off the hook.

Vera came back into the kitchen wearing jeans and a sweater and brushing her hair.

He spooned the instant into the cups of hot water and then spilled some vodka into his. He carried the cups over to the table.

She picked up the receiver, listened. She said, "What's this? Who was on the phone?"

"Nobody," he said. "Who smokes colored cigarettes?"

"I do."

"I didn't know you did that."

"Well, I do."

She sat across from him and drank her coffee. They smoked and used the ashtray.

There were things he wanted to say, grieving things, consoling things, things like that.

"I'm smoking three packs a day," Vera said. "I mean, if you really want to know what goes on around here."

"God almighty," Burt said.

Vera nodded.

"I didn't come over here to hear that," he said.

"What did you come over here to hear, then? You want to hear the house burned down?"

"Vera," he said. "It's Christmas. That's why I came."

"It's the day after Christmas," she said. "Christmas has come and gone," she said. "I don't ever want to see another one."

"What about me?" he said. "You think I look forward to holidays?"

The phone rang again. Burt picked it up.

"It's someone wanting Charlie," he said.

"What?"

"Charlie," Burt said.

Vera took the phone. She kept her back to him as she talked. Then she turned to him and said, "I'll take this call in the bedroom. So would you please hang up after I've picked it up in there? I can tell, so hang it up when I say."

He took the receiver. She left the kitchen. He held the receiver to his ear and listened. He heard nothing. Then he heard a man clear his throat. Then he heard Vera pick up the other phone. She shouted, "Okay, Burt! I have it now, Burt!"

He put down the receiver and stood looking at it. He opened the silverware drawer and pushed things around inside. He opened another drawer. He looked in the sink. He went into the dining room and got the carving knife. He held it under hot water until the grease broke and ran off. He wiped the blade on his sleeve. He moved to the phone, doubled the cord, and sawed through without any trouble at all. He examined the ends of the cord. Then he shoved the phone back into its corner behind the roasting pan.

She came in. She said, "The phone went dead. Did you do anything to the telephone?" She looked at the phone and then picked it up from the counter.

"Son of a bitch!" she screamed. She screamed, "Out, out, where you belong!" She was shaking the phone at him. "That's it! I'm going to get a restraining order, that's what I'm going to get!"

The phone made a *ding* when she banged it down on the counter.

"I'm going next door to call the police if you don't get out of here now!"

He picked up the ashtray. He held it by its edge. He posed with it like a man preparing to hurl the discus.

"Please," she said. "That's our ashtray."

He left through the patio door. He was not certain, but he thought he had proved something. He hoped he had made something clear. The thing was, they had to have a serious talk soon. There were things that needed talking about, important things that had to be discussed. They'd talk again. Maybe after the holidays were over and things got back to normal. He'd tell her the goddamn ashtray was a goddamn dish, for example.

He stepped around the pie in the driveway and got back into his car. He started the car and put it into reverse. It was hard managing until he put the ashtray down.

🐚 🐚 🐚

## *Writing Exercises*

### INDIVIDUAL

1. This exercise is meant to help you remember a period of time and then find a scene within it. First, think of a time you remember well and can write about with authority. The memory could have to do with an occupation (summer job, internship, summer school), an activity (music lessons, sports practice, play rehearsal), a routine (what you always did after school, family traditions, what you and a certain boyfriend always did on Sunday mornings), or a condition (pregnancy, illness, addiction).

   Now, write a summary of a typical day during this period. Your summary should be generalized and habitual, yet specific and detailed. For instance, "The summer I worked at Camp Itchy-Itchy, we counselors would get the campers up at 6:45 A.M. for our morning "stretch-n-tone" on the tennis courts. Then it was off to a breakfast of . . ." Or, "The year before my parents finally divorced I would often listen to them arguing in the next room about . . ."

   Finally, move to a specific moment. "One time . . ." Select this moment with care. It should be significant, introducing a conflict or representing a turning point. Create the scene. Use dialogue, significant details.

2. Make a list of activities that take place over a brief period of time, a few hours at most. Here are some ideas, but come up with your own: a dinner date, changing a flat tire, birthday party, a drive home from school, a basketball game, or cleaning your room. Try to write a short (five-page) story confined to that period of time.

3. Imagine an accident. It might be minor—a finger cut while slicing vegetables, a knocked-over vase—or it might be major—a car wreck, a gallery of paintings destroyed by a fire sprinkler. Now, write several versions of the accident: a one-sentence summary, a one-paragraph summary, a full scene, and finally, a slo-o-o-o-wed down version of the scene. It may help to think of filmmaking. Begin with a panoramic establishing shot and let the camera keep zooming in, closer and closer, to an extreme close-up.

4. Even if the action of your story takes place mainly in 2001, your character might at some point remember in vivid detail an important event that happened in 1968. Most stories include at least a short flashback.

   Write a flashback, a scene involving one of your characters that took place before the opening of the story. Your goal is to reveal who that character used to be. The flashback should help explain or illuminate the main story. You might want to base this flashback on something that actually happened to you, or to someone you know, in order to give the flashback an air of authority.

5. Invent a story that takes place over a fairly long period of time (at least six months, perhaps several years). It might involve a school year abroad, a lengthy

illness, or an entire childhood. Make a list of possible events in the story; you may even want to draw a time line. Sketch out your story, bearing in mind that you will have to cover great stretches of time. What will you show in scenes? What can be summarized? For common or everyday experiences, can one scene or summary suggest the rest? (A single scene of newlyweds fighting can convey the nature of all their arguments. Likewise, a summary of a specific/generalized day at the office can give a sense of a character's everyday life.)

6. Write a very short (two- to three-page) story in which you use (in miniature) scene, summary, flashback, and slow motion.

### COLLABORATIVE

7. With a partner, choose a photograph of a distinctive character from a magazine advertisement.
   a. Invent a name and some background for the character. Then choose a dominant trait. Is the character cynical? Devoutly religious? Naïve? Obsessive?
   b. One partner writes a scene that reveals this character trait, i.e., the day the character collected his first bottle cap.
   c. The other partner should write a summary covering several years, which reveals the development of the same character trait.

Compare your two approaches to the same character.

8. With a partner, rewrite a fairy tale. First, each of you should outline the story on your own. Just list the events of the story. Next (and again, individually), think about how you might write your own fleshed-out version: which aspects of the story would you emphasize? Which would you de-emphasize? Looking at your list, decide what parts should be shown in scene: the crisis or climactic scene certainly (Red Riding Hood's encounter with the disguised wolf), but what else? What can be summarized? Red Riding Hood's mother packing her picnic basket? The walk through the woods? Red's relationship with her grandmother? What you choose to emphasize; this will help you determine what to show in scene and what to summarize.

   Once you've looked over your list and reimagined the story on your own terms, write a flashback scene for your fairy tale (a previous visit to her grandmother's house, a fight with her own mother, etc.). Where might you put this flashback? What does it reveal about the characters? Where in the story would it have the most impact?

   Now, compare your outlines and flashbacks. How did your choices differ?

# 7

# THE TOWER AND THE NET
## Story Form, Plot, and Structure

- *Conflict, Crisis, and Resolution*

- *The Arc of the Story*

- *Patterns of Power*

- *Connection and Disconnection*

- *Story Form as a Check Mark*

- *Story and Plot*

- *The Short Story and the Novel*

- *Reading as Writers*

What makes you want to write?

It seems likely that the earliest storytellers—in the tent or the harem, around the campfire or on the Viking ship—told stories out of an impulse to tell stories. They made themselves popular by distracting their listeners from a dull or dangerous evening with heroic exploits and a skill at creating suspense: What happened next? And after that? And then what happened?

Natural storytellers are still around, and a few of them are very rich. Some are on the best-seller list; more are in television and film. But it's probable that your impulse to write has little to do with the desire or the skill to work out a plot. On the contrary, you want to write because you are a sensitive observer. You have something to say that does not answer the question *What happened next?* You share with most—and the best—contemporary fiction writers a sense of the injustice, the absurdity, and the beauty of the world; and you want to register your protest, your laughter, and your affirmation.

Yet readers still want to wonder what happened next, and unless you make them wonder, they will not turn the page. You must master plot, because no matter how profound or illuminating your vision of the world may be, you cannot convey it to those who do not read you.

When editors take the trouble to write a rejection letter to a young author (and they do so only when they think the author talented), the gist of the letter most frequently is: "This piece is sensitive (perceptive, vivid, original, brilliant, funny, moving), but it is not a *story.*"

How do you know when you have written a story? And if you're not a natural-born wandering minstrel, can you go about learning to write one?

S TRUCTURE IS THE ART THAT CONCEALS ITSELF—you only *see* the structure in a badly structured story, and call it formula.

Stephen Fischer

It's interesting that we react with such different attitudes to the words "formula" and "form" as they apply to a story. A formula story is hackwork: to write one, you read three dozen copies of *Cosmopolitan* or *Amazing Stories*, make a list of what kinds of characters and situations the editors buy, shuffle nearly identical characters around in slightly altered situations, and sit back to hope for a check. Whereas form is a term of the highest artistic approbation, even reverence, with overtones of *order, harmony, model, archetype.*

And "story" is a "form" of literature. Like a face, it has necessary features in a necessary harmony. We're aware of the infinite variety of human faces, aware of their unique individuality, which is so powerful that once you know a face you can recognize it twenty years after you last saw it despite the changes it has undergone. We're aware that minute alterations in the features can express grief, anger, or joy. If you place side by side two photographs of, say, Julia Roberts and Geronimo, you are instantly aware of the fundamental differences of age, race, sex, class, and century; yet these two faces are more like each other than either is like a foot or a fern, both of which have their own distinctive forms. Every face has two eyes, a nose between them, a mouth below, a forehead, two cheeks, two ears, and a jaw. If a face is missing one of these features, you may say, "I love this face in spite of its lacking a nose," but you must acknowledge the *in spite of*. You can't simply say, "This is a wonderful face."

The same is true of a story. You might say, "I love this piece even though there's no crisis action in it." You can't simply say, "This is a wonderful *story.*"

## Conflict, Crisis, and Resolution

One of the useful ways of describing the necessary features of story form is to speak of *conflict*, *crisis*, and *resolution*.

Conflict is a fundamental element of fiction. Playwright Elia Kazan describes it simply as "two dogs fighting over a bone"; William Faulkner reminds us that in addition to a conflict of wills, fiction also shows "the heart in conflict with itself," so that conflict seethes both within and between characters. In life, "conflict" often carries negative connotations, yet in fiction, be it comic or tragic, dramatic conflict is fundamental because in literature only trouble is interesting.

*Only* trouble is interesting. This is not so in life. Life offers periods of comfortable communication, peaceful pleasure, and productive work, all of which are extremely interesting to those involved. But passages about such times by themselves make for dull reading; they can be used as lulls in an otherwise tense situation, as a resolution, even as a hint that something awful is about to happen. They cannot be used as a whole plot, as Margaret Atwood sardonically illustrates in her story "Happy Endings," which appears at the end of this chapter.

> ALMOST ALL GOOD STORIES ARE SAD because it is the human struggle that engages us readers and listeners the most. To watch characters confront their hardships and uncertainties makes us feel better about our own conflicts and confusions and fears. We have a sense of community, of sympathy, a cleansing sympathy, as Aristotle said, and relief that we are safe in our room only reading the story. A story of sadness, even tragedy, makes us feel, paradoxically, better, as though we are confronting our own conflicts and fears, and have endured.
>
> Robert Morgan

Suppose, for example, you go on a picnic. You find a beautiful deserted meadow with a lake nearby. The weather is splendid and so is the company. The food's delicious, the water's fine, and the insects have taken the day off. Afterward, someone asks you how your picnic was. "Terrific," you reply, "really perfect." No story.

But suppose the next week you go back for a rerun. You set your picnic blanket on an anthill. You all race for the lake to get cold water on the bites, and one of your friends goes too far out on the plastic raft, which deflates. He can't swim and you have to save him. On the way in you gash your foot on a broken bottle. When you get back to the picnic, the ants have taken over the cake and a possum has demolished the chicken. Just then the sky opens up. When you gather your things to race for the car, you notice an irritated bull has broken through the fence. The others run for it, but because of your bleeding heel the best you can do is hobble. You have two choices: try to outrun him or stand perfectly still and hope he's interested only in a moving target. At this point, you don't know if your friends can be counted on for help, even the nerd whose life you saved. You don't know if it's true that a bull is attracted by the smell of blood.

A year later, assuming you're around to tell about it, you are still saying, "Let me *tell* you what happened last year." And your listeners are saying, "What a story!"

As Charles Baxter, in *Burning Down the House*, more vividly puts it:

> Say what you will about it, Hell is story-friendly. If you want a compelling story, put your protagonist among the damned. The mechanisms of hell are nicely attuned to the mechanisms of narrative. Not so the pleasures of Paradise. Paradise is not a story. It's about what happens when the stories are over.

If it takes trouble to make a picnic into a story, this is equally true of the great themes of life: birth, love, sex, work, and death. Here is a very interesting love story to live: Jan and Jon meet in college. Both are beautiful, intelligent, talented, popular, and well adjusted. They're of the same race, class, religion, and political persuasion. They are sexually compatible. Their parents become fast friends. They marry on graduating, and both get rewarding work in the same city. They have three children, all of whom are healthy, happy, beautiful, intelligent, and popular; the children love and respect their parents to a degree that is the envy of everyone. All the children succeed in work and marriage. Jan and Jon die peacefully, of natural causes, at the same moment, at the age of eighty-two, and are buried in the same grave.

No doubt this love story is very interesting to Jan and Jon, but you can't make a novel of it. Great love stories involve intense passion and a monumental impediment to that passion's fulfillment. So: They love each other passionately, but their parents are sworn enemies (*Romeo and Juliet*). Or: They love each other passionately, but he's black and she's white, and he has an enemy who wants to punish him (*Othello*). Or: They love each other passionately, but she's married (*Anna Karenina*). Or: He loves her passionately, but she falls in love with him only when she has worn out his passion ("Frankly, my dear, I don't give a damn.")

In each of these plots, there is both intense desire and great danger to the achievement of that desire; generally speaking, this shape holds good for all plots. It can be called 3-D: *Drama* equals *desire* plus *danger*. One common fault of talented young writers is to create a main character who is essentially passive. This is an understandable fault; as a writer you are an observer of human nature and activity, and so you identify easily with a character who observes, reflects, and suffers. But such a character's passivity transmits itself to the page, and the story also becomes passive. Charles Baxter regrets that "In writing workshops, this kind of story is often the rule rather than the exception." He calls it:

> the fiction of finger-pointing . . . In such fiction, people and events are often accused of turning the protagonist into the kind of person the protagonist is, usually an unhappy person. That's the whole story. When blame has been assigned, the story is over.

In such flawed stories, the central character (and by implication, the story's author) seems to take no responsibility for what that character wants to have happen. This is quite different from Aristotle's rather startling claim that a man *is* his desire.

> FICTION IS THE ART FORM OF HUMAN YEARNING. That is absolutely essential to any work of fictional narrative art—a character who yearns. And that is not the same as a character who simply has problems. . . . The yearning is also the thing that generates what we call plot, because the elements of the plot come from thwarted or blocked or challenged attempts to fulfill that yearning.
>
> Robert Olen Butler

In fiction, in order to engage our attention and sympathy, the protagonist must *want*, and want intensely. The thing that the character wants need not be violent or spectacular; it is the intensity of the wanting that introduces an element of danger. She may want, like the protagonist in David Madden's *The Suicide's Wife,* no more than to get her driver's license, but if so, she must feel that her identity and her future depend on her getting a driver's license, while a corrupt highway patrolman tries to manipulate her. He may want, like Samuel Beckett's Murphy, only to tie himself to his rocking chair and rock, but if so, he will also want a woman who nags him to get up and get a job. She may want, like the heroine of Margaret Atwood's *Bodily Harm,* only to get away from it all for a rest, but if so, she must need rest for her survival, while tourists and terrorists involve her in machinations that begin in discomfort and end in mortal danger.

It's important to realize that the great dangers in life and in literature are not necessarily the most spectacular. Another mistake frequently made by young writers is to think that they can best introduce drama into their stories by way of murderers, chase scenes, crashes, and vampires, the external stock dangers of pulp and TV. In fact, all of us know that the most profound impediments to our desire usually lie close to home, in our own bodies, personalities, friends, lovers, and families. Fewer people have cause to panic at the approach of a stranger with a gun than at the approach of Mama with the curling iron. More passion is destroyed at the breakfast table than in a time warp.

A frequently used critical tool divides possible conflicts into several basic categories: man against man, man against nature, man against society, man against machine, man against God, man against himself. Most stories fall into these categories, and in a literature class they can provide a useful way of discussing and comparing works. But the employment of categories can be misleading to new writers, insofar as it suggests that literary conflicts take place in these abstract, cosmic dimensions. A writer needs a specific story to tell, and if you sit down to pit "man" against "nature," you will have less of a story than if you pit seventeen-year-old James Tucker of Weehawken, New Jersey, against a two-and-a-half-foot bigmouth bass in the backwoods of Toomsuba, Mississippi. (The value of specificity is a point to which we return again and again.)

Once conflict is established and developed in a story, the conflict must come to a crisis—the final turning point—and a resolution. Order is a major value that literature offers us, and order implies that the subject has been brought to closure. In life this never quite happens, but whether or not the lives of fictional characters end, the story does, and we are left with a satisfying sense of completion.

What I want to do now is to present several ways—they are all essentially metaphors—of seeing this pattern of *conflict-crisis-resolution* in order to make the shape and its variations clearer, and particularly to indicate what a crisis action is.

## The Arc of the Story

Novelist John L'Heureux says that a story is about a single moment in a character's life that culminates in a defining choice after which nothing will be the same again. Such a moment is Connie's decision to go off with Arnold Friend in "Where Are You Going, Where Have You Been?" or Lavendar's death in "The Things They Carried." Plotting is a matter of finding the decision points that lead to this final choice and choosing the best scenes through which to dramatize them.

The editor and teacher Mel McKee states flatly that "a story is a war. It is sustained and immediate combat." He offers four imperatives for the writing of this "war" story.

> (1) get your fighters fighting, (2) have something—the stake—worth their fighting over, (3) have the fight dive into a series of battles with the last battle in the series the biggest and most dangerous of all, (4) have a walking away from the fight.

The stake over which wars are fought is usually a territory, and it's important that this "territory" in a story be as tangible and specific as the Gaza Strip. For example, in William Carlos Williams's story "The Use of Force," found at the end of this chapter, the war is fought over the territory of the little girl's mouth, and the fight begins narrowing to that territory from the first paragraph. As with warring nations, the story territory itself can come to represent all sorts of serious abstractions—self-determination, domination, freedom, dignity, identity—but the soldiers fight yard by yard over a particular piece of grass or sand.

Just as a minor "police action" may gradually escalate into a holocaust, story form follows its most natural order of "complications" when each battle is bigger than the last. It begins with a ground skirmish, which does not decide the war. Then one side brings in spies, and the other, guerrillas; these actions do not decide the war. So one side brings in the air force, and the other answers with antiaircraft. One side takes to missiles, and the other answers with rockets. One side has poison gas, and the other has a hand on the nuclear button. Metaphorically, this is what happens in a story. As long as one antagonist can recoup enough power to counterattack, the conflict goes on. But, at some point in the story, one of the antagonists will produce a weapon from which the other cannot recover. *The crisis action is the last battle and makes the outcome inevitable;* there can no longer be any doubt who wins the particular territory—though there can be much doubt about moral victory. When this has happened the conflict ends with a significant and permanent *change*—which is the definition, in fiction, of a resolution.

Notice that although a plot involves a desire and a danger to that desire, it does not necessarily end happily if the desire is achieved, nor unhappily if it is not. The more morally complex the story, the less straightforward the idea of winning and losing becomes. In *Hamlet*, Hamlet's desire is to kill King Claudius, and he is prevented from doing so for most of the play by other characters, intrigues, and his own mental state. When he finally succeeds, it is at the cost of every significant life in the play, including his own. Although the hero "wins" his particular "territory," the play is a tragedy. In Margaret Atwood's *Bodily Harm*, on the other hand, the heroine ends up in a political prison. Yet the discovery of her own strength and commitment is such that we know she has achieved salvation. *What does my character win by losing his struggle, or lose by winning?* John L'Heureux suggests the writer ask himself or herself.

## *Patterns of Power*

Novelist Michael Shaara described a story as a power struggle between equal forces. It is imperative, he argued, that each antagonist have sufficient power that the reader is left in doubt about the outcome. We may be wholly in sympathy with one character and even reasonably confident that she or he will triumph. But the antagonist must represent a real and potent danger, and the pattern of the story's complications will be achieved by *shifting the power back and forth from one antagonist to the other*. Finally, an action will occur that will shift the power irretrievably in one direction.

"Power" takes many forms—physical strength, charm, knowledge, moral power, wealth, ownership, rank, and so on. Most obvious is the power of brute force, as wielded by mobster Max Blue in Leslie Marmon Silko's epic novel *Almanac of the Dead:*

> . . . Max thinks of himself as an executive producer of one-night-only performances, dramas played out in the warm California night breezes, in a phone booth in downtown Long Beach. All Max had done was dial a phone number and listen while the pigeon repeats, "Hello? Hello? Hello? Hello?" until .22-pistol shots snap *pop!pop!* and Max hangs up.

A character who blends several types of power—good looks, artistic talent, social privilege, and the self-assurance that stems from it—is Zavier Chalfant, son of a furniture factory owner in Donald Secreast's story "Summer Help." Zavier is seen through the eyes of Wanda, a longtime employee assigned the coveted job of painting designs on the most expensive pieces. As the plant supervisor introduces them:

> . . . Zavier Chalfant was letting his gaze rest lightly on Wanda. Most boys—and that's what Zavier was, after all, a boy of about twenty-one—were very embarrassed their first day on the job. Zavier, in contrast, seemed more amused than embarrassed . . . His thick blond hair covered the collar of his jacket but was clean and expertly cut so he looked more like a knight than a hippie . . . his face looked like a Viking's face; she'd always been partial to Vikings. Of course, Zavier was too thin to be a Viking all the way down, but he had the face of an adventurer. Of an artist.

Wanda's awe of Zavier's power is confirmed when he easily paints a design she must labor over.

> "Color is my specialty." Zavier deftly added the highlights to the woman's face and hands. "It's everything." He finished the flesh parts in a matter of minutes. He took another brush from Wanda and in six or seven strokes had filled in the woman's robe.

Yet if power is entirely one-sided, suspense will be lost, so it is important to identify a source of power for each character surrounding the story's conflict. Remember that "power" takes many forms, some of which have the external appearance of weakness. Anyone who has ever been tied to the demands of an invalid can understand this: sickness can be great strength. Weakness, need, passivity, an ostensible desire not to be any trouble to anybody—all these can be used as manipulative tools to prevent the protagonist from achieving his or her desire. Martyrdom is immensely powerful, whether we sympathize with it or not; a dying man absorbs all our energies.

The power of weakness has generated the central conflict in many stories and in such plays as *Uncle Vanya* and *The Glass Menagerie*. Here is a passage in which it is swiftly and deftly sketched:

> This sepulchral atmosphere owed a lot to the presence of Mrs. Taylor herself. She was a tall, stooped woman with deep-set eyes. She sat in her living room all day long and chain-smoked cigarettes and stared out the picture window with an air of unutterable sadness, as if she knew things beyond mortal bearing. Sometimes she would call Taylor over and wrap her arms around him, then close her eyes and hoarsely whisper, "Terence, Terence!" Eyes still closed, she would turn her head and resolutely push him away.
>
> Tobias Wolff, *This Boy's Life*

## Connection and Disconnection

Some students, as well as critics, object to the description of narrative as a war or power struggle. Seeing the world in terms of conflict and crisis, of enemies and warring factions, not only constricts the possibilities of literature, they argue, but also promulgates an aggressive and antagonistic view of our own lives.

Speaking of the "gladiatorial view of fiction," Ursula Le Guin writes:

> People are cross-grained, aggressive, and full of trouble, the storytellers tell us; people fight themselves and one another, and their stories are full of their struggles. But to say that that *is* the story is to use one aspect of existence, conflict, to subsume all other aspects, many of which it does not include and does not comprehend.
>
> *Romeo and Juliet* is a story of the conflict between two families, and its plot involves the conflict of two individuals with those families. Is that all it involves? Isn't *Romeo and Juliet* about something else, and isn't it the something else that makes the otherwise trivial tale of a feud into a tragedy?

I'm indebted to dramatist Claudia Johnson for this further—and, it seems to me, crucial—insight about that "something else": whereas the dynamic of the power struggle has long been acknowledged, narrative is also driven by a pattern of connection and disconnection between characters that is the main source of its emotional effect. Over the course of a story, and within the smaller scale of a scene, characters make and break emotional bonds of trust, love, understanding, or compassion with one another. A connection may be as obvious as a kiss or as subtle as a glimpse; a connection may be broken with an action as obvious as a slap or as subtle as an arched eyebrow.

In *Romeo and Juliet*, for example, the Montague and Capulet families are fiercely disconnected, but the young lovers manage to connect in spite of that. Throughout the play they meet and part, disconnect from their families in order to connect with each other, finally part from life in order to be with each other eternally. Their ultimate departure in death reconnects the feuding families.

Johnson puts it this way:

> . . . underlying any good story, fictitious or true—is a deeper pattern of change, a pattern of connection and disconnection. The conflict and the surface events are like waves, but underneath is an emotional tide, the ebb and flow of human connection. . . .

Patterns of conflict and connection occur in every story, and sometimes they are evident in much smaller compass, as in this scene from Leslee Becker's story "The Personals." The story takes place shortly after the Loma Prieta earthquake, a catastrophe that has united the community, in the eyes of bookshop owner Alice, while reminding her how cut off from others she actually is. The story centers around her nervous first date with Warren, a shoe salesman and widower still grieving his wife Doris. Described by one reviewer as "factory irregulars," the lonely couple end their date with an after-hours visit to Warren's shoe store.

Suddenly, music began, and Warren emerged from the back room, holding liquor, glasses, shoe boxes, and stockings. "For you," he said, spreading the things at her feet. He opened a box and removed shoes with dramatic high heels. "I've got hand bags, too," he said. "For you, Doris."

She knew he had not realized his mistake, and she said nothing as he sat on the floor in front of her. She felt his hand on her heel, her shoe sliding off effort-lessly. She watched the back of him in the mirror and did not want to look at herself as he lifted her foot and pressed it against his chest.

"I don't want to be alone anymore," he said.

She felt her foot slipping out of his hand, the stocking rasping under his fingers. He got to his feet immediately and sat next to her. She looked to the mirror and saw him touch his toupee and wince.

"It's all right," she said. "Warren . . ."

"I'll take you home," he said.

The moment she reached for his hand he got up and began replacing the shoes in the box. "Please," she said. "I know what you're feeling."

"How can you? I don't even know. I'll take you back."

He went into the back room, and the music stopped. While she slipped her shoe on, she felt small and dishonest.

As soon as they returned to the car, she told him what she had done after the earthquake. "I was in a huge department store. Nobody was paying attention to me. I stole things."

"Promise me," he said, "you won't tell anyone about tonight."

"But nothing happened."

"Yeah," he said.

In this short excerpt, Warren tries to connect with Alice through a generous dis-play of shoes, only to blunder and break the fragile connection by calling her by his dead wife's name. When he presses further, Alice withdraws, then tries to ease his humiliation by first offering common emotional experience and then admitting a secret. But it is too late, at least for the present, and Warren refuses to reconnect, perhaps ashamed of the neediness he has revealed.

While the pattern of either conflict or connection may dominate in a given work, "stories are about *both* conflict and connection," says novelist and poet Robert Morgan.

A story which is only about conflict will be shallow. There must be some deep-ening of our understanding of the characters. Stories are rarely just about con-flicts between good and bad. They are more often about conflicts of loyalty, one good versus another: does a man join up to serve his country, or stay home to help protect and raise his children? The writer strives to bring art to a level where a story is not so much a plot as about human connection, and not just about the conflict of good versus bad, but about the conflict of loyalty with loyalty.

Human wills clash; human belonging is necessary. In discussing human behavior, psychologists speak in terms of "tower" and "network" patterns, the need to climb (which implies conflict) and the need for community, the need to win out over others and the need to belong to others; and these two forces also drive fiction. Like conflict and its complications, connection and its complications can produce a pattern of change, and both inform the process of change recorded in scene and story.

## Story Form as a Check Mark

The nineteenth-century German critic Gustav Freitag analyzed plot in terms of a pyramid of five actions: an exposition, followed by a complication (or *nouement*, "knotting up," of the situation), leading to a crisis, which is followed by a "falling action" or anticlimax, resulting in a resolution (or *dénouement*, "unknotting").

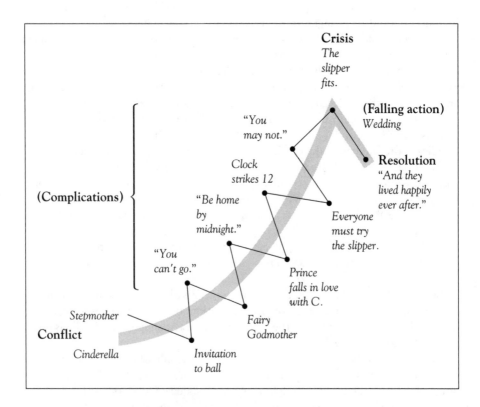

In the compact short-story form, the falling action is likely to be very brief or nonexistent, and often the crisis action itself implies the resolution, which is not necessarily stated but exists as an idea established in the reader's mind.

So for our purposes it is probably more useful to think of story shape not as a pyramid with sides of equal length but as an inverted check mark. If we take the familiar tale of Cinderella and diagram its power struggle using this model, we can see how the various elements reveal themselves even in this simple children's story.

At the opening of the tale we're given the basic conflict: Cinderella's mother has died, and her father has married a brutal woman with two waspish daughters. Cinderella is made to do all the dirtiest and most menial work, and she weeps among the cinders. The Stepmother has on her side the strength of ugliness and evil (two very powerful qualities in literature as in life). With her daughters she also has the strength of numbers, and she has parental authority. Cinderella has only beauty and goodness, but (in literature and life) these are also very powerful.

At the beginning of the struggle in "Cinderella," the power is very clearly on the Stepmother's side. But the first event (action, battle) of the story is that an invitation arrives from the Prince, which explicitly states that *all* the ladies of the land are invited to a ball. Notice that Cinderella's desire is not to triumph over her Stepmother (though she eventually will, much to our satisfaction); such a desire would diminish her goodness. She simply wants to be relieved of her mistreatment. She wants equality, so that the Prince's invitation, which specifically gives her a right equal to the Stepmother's and Stepdaughters' rights, shifts the power to her.

The Stepmother takes the power back by blunt force: you may not go; you must get us ready to go. Cinderella does so, and the three leave for the ball.

Then what happens? The Fairy Godmother appears. It is *very* powerful to have magic on your side. The Fairy Godmother offers Cinderella a gown, glass slippers, and a coach with horses and footmen, giving her more force than she has yet had.

But the magic is not all-potent. It has a qualification that portends bad luck. It will last only until midnight (unlike the Stepmother's authority), and Cinderella must leave the ball before the clock strikes twelve or risk exposure and defeat.

What happens next? She goes to the ball and the Prince falls in love with her—and love is an even more powerful weapon than magic in a literary war. In some versions of the tale, the Stepmother and Stepsisters are made to marvel at the beauty of the Princess they don't recognize, pointing to the irony of Cinderella's new power.

And then? The magic quits. The clock strikes twelve, and Cinderella runs down the steps in her rags to her rats and pumpkin, losing a slipper, bereft of her power in every way.

But after that, the Prince sends out a messenger with the glass slipper and a dictum (a dramatic repetition of the original invitation in which all ladies were invited to the ball) that every female in the land is to try on the slipper. Cinderella is given her rights again by royal decree.

What happens then? In most good retellings of the tale, the Stepmother also repeats her assumption of brute authority by hiding Cinderella away, while our expectation of triumph is tantalizingly delayed with grotesque comedy: one sister cuts off a toe, the other a heel, trying to fit into the heroine's rightful slipper.

After that, Cinderella tries on the slipper and it fits. *This is the crisis action.* Magic, love, and royalty join to recognize the heroine's true self; evil, numbers, and authority are powerless against them. At this point, the power struggle has been decided; the outcome is inevitable. When the slipper fits, no further action can occur that will deprive Cinderella of her desire. Nothing will be the same again: the change in the lives of all concerned is significant and permanent.

The tale has a brief "falling action" or "walking away from the fight": the Prince sweeps Cinderella up on his white horse and gallops away to their wedding. The story comes to closure with the classic resolution of all comedy: they lived happily ever after.

If we also look at "Cinderella" in terms of connection/disconnection, we see a pattern as clear as that represented by the power struggle. The first painful disconnection is that Cinderella's mother has died; her father has married (connected with) a woman who spurns (disconnects from) her; the Prince's invitation offers connection; the Stepmother's cruelty alienates again. The Fairy Godmother connects as a magical friend, but the disappearance of the coach and gown disconnect Cinderella temporarily from that grand and glorious fairy-tale union, marriage to the Prince. If we consult the emotions that this tale engenders—pity, anger, hope, fear, romance, anticipation, disappointment, triumph—we see that both the struggle between antagonist/protagonist and the pattern of alienation/connectedness is necessary to ensure, not only that there is an action, but also that we care about its outcome. The traditional happy ending is the grand connection, marriage; the traditional tragic outcome is the final disconnection, death.

> ART IS PLEASING YOURSELF . . . But you can please yourself and it won't be art. Art is having the mastery to take your experience, whether it's visual or mental, and make meaningful shapes that convey a reality to others.
>
> Gail Godwin

In the *Poetics*, the first extensive work of extant Western literary criticism, Aristotle referred to the crisis action of a tragedy as a *peripeteia*, or reversal of the protagonist's fortunes. Critics and editors agree that a reversal of some sort is necessary to all story structure, comic as well as tragic. Although the protagonist need not lose power, land, or life, he or she must in some significant way be changed or moved by the action. Aristotle specified that this reversal came about because of *hamartia*, which has for centuries been translated as a "tragic flaw" in the protagonist's character, usually assumed to be, or defined as, pride. But more recent critics have defined and translated *hamartia* much more narrowly as a "mistake in identity" with the reversal coming about in a "recognition."

It is true that recognition scenes have played a disproportionately large role in the crisis actions of plots both comic and tragic, and that these scenes frequently stretch credibility. In real life, you are unlikely to mistake the face of your mother, son, uncle, or even friend, and yet such mistakes have provided the turning point of many traditional plots. If, however, the notion of "recognition" is extended to more abstract and subtle realms, it becomes a powerful metaphor for moments of "realization." In other words, the "recognition scene" in literature may stand for that moment in life when we "recognize" that the man we have considered good is evil, the event we have considered insignificant is crucial, the woman we have thought out of touch with reality is a genius, the object we have thought desirable is poison. There is in this symbolic way a recognition in "Cinderella." We knew that she was essentially a princess, but until the Prince recognizes her as one, our knowledge must be frustrated.

James Joyce developed a similar idea when he spoke of, and recorded both in his notebooks and in his stories, moments of what he called *epiphany*. As Joyce saw it, epiphany is a crisis action in the mind, a moment when a person, an event, or a thing is seen in a light so new that it is as if it has never been seen before. At this recognition, the mental landscape of the viewer is permanently changed.

In many of the finest modern short stories and novels, the true territory of struggle is the main character's mind, and so the real crisis action must occur there. Yet it is important to grasp that Joyce chose the word *epiphany* to represent this moment of reversal, and that the word means "a *manifestation* of a supernatural being"; specifically, in Christian doctrine, "the manifestation of Christ to the gentiles." By extension, then, in a short story any mental reversal that takes place in the crisis of a story must be *manifested*; it must be triggered or shown by an action. The slipper must fit. It would not do if the Stepmother just happened to change her mind and give up the struggle; it would not do if the Prince just happened to notice that Cinderella looked like his love. The moment of recognition must be manifested in an action.

This point, that the crisis must be manifested or externalized in an action, is absolutely central, although sometimes difficult to grasp when the struggle of the story takes place in a character's mind. In "The Things They Carried" in chapter 2, for example, the young lieutenant's mental determination to change himself into a hardened leader is manifested in the action of burning photographs, letters, and finally a village.

In a revenge story, it is easy to see how the conflict must come to crisis. The common revenge plot, from *Hamlet* to *Kill Bill*, takes this form: someone important to the hero (father, sister, lover, friend) is killed, and for some reason the authorities who ought to be in charge of justice can't or won't avenge the death. The hero must do so, then, and the crisis action is manifested in the swing of the dagger, the blast of the gun, the swallowing of the poison, whatever.

But suppose the story is about a struggle between two brothers on a fishing trip, and the change that takes place is that the protagonist, believing for most of the action that he holds his older brother in contempt, discovers at the end of the story that they are deeply bound by love and family history. Clearly this change is an epiphany, a mental reversal. A writer insufficiently aware of the nature of crisis action might signal the change in a paragraph that begins "Suddenly Larry remembered their father and realized that Jeff was very much like him." Well, unless that memory and that realization are manifested in an action, the reader is unable to share them, and therefore cannot be moved with the character.

Jeff reached for the old net and neatly bagged the trout, swinging round to offer it with a triumphant, "Got it! We got it, didn't we?" The trout flipped and struggled, giving off a smell of weed and water and fecund mud. Jeff's knuckles were lined with grime. The knuckles and the rich river smell filled him with a memory of their first fishing trip together, the sight of their father's hands on the same scarred net. . . .

Here the epiphany, a memory leading to a realization, is triggered by an action and sensory details that the reader can share; the reader now has a good chance of also being able to share the epiphany. Less commonly, a story may offer readers an epiphany that the main character neglects to see, as in the short story "Everything That Rises Must Converge," which appears at the end of this chapter. Such characters are often on the verge of great change, yet lack the maturity or courage to take that difficult leap to recognition.

Much great fiction, and the preponderance of serious modern fiction, echoes life in its suggestion that there are no clear or permanent solutions, that the conflicts of character, relationship, and the cosmos cannot be permanently resolved. Most of the stories in this volume end, in Vladimir Nabokov's words, "with no definite full-stop, but with the natural motion of life." None could end "they lived happily ever after" or even "they lived unhappily ever after."

Yet the story form demands a resolution. Is there such a thing as a no-resolution resolution? Yes, and it has a very specific form. Go back to the metaphor that "a story is a war." After the skirmish, after the guerrillas, after the air strike, after the poison gas and the nuclear holocaust, imagine that the two surviving combatants, one on each side, emerge from their fallout shelters. They crawl, then stumble to the fence that marks the border. Each possessively grasps the barbed wire with a bloodied fist. The "resolution" of this battle is that neither side will ever give up and that no one will ever win; *there will never be a resolution.* This is a distinct reversal (the recognition takes place in the reader's mind) of the opening scene, in which it seemed eminently worthwhile to open a ground skirmish. In the statement of the conflict was an inherent possibility that one side or the other could win. Inherent in the resolution is a statement that no one can ever win. That is a distinct reversal and a powerful change.

## Story and Plot

So far, I have used the words "story" and "plot" interchangeably. The equation of the two terms is so common that they are often comfortably understood as synonyms. When an editor says, "This is not a story," the implication is not that it lacks characters, theme, setting, or even incident, but that it has no plot.

Yet there is a distinction frequently drawn between the two terms, a distinction that although simple in itself, gives rise to manifold subtleties in the craft of narrative and that also represents a vital decision that you as a writer must make: Where should your narrative begin?

The distinction is easily made. A *story* is a series of events recorded in their chronological order. A *plot* is a series of events deliberately arranged so as to reveal their dramatic, thematic, and emotional significance. A story gives us only "what happened next," whereas plot's concern is "what, how, and why," with scenes ordered to highlight the workings of cause and effect.

Here, for example, is a fairly standard story: A sober, industrious, and rather dull young man meets the woman of his dreams. She is beautiful, brilliant, passionate, and compassionate; more wonderful still, she loves him. They plan to marry, and on the eve of their wedding his friends give him a stag party in the course of which they tease him, ply him with liquor, and drag him off to a whorehouse for a last fling. There he stumbles into a cubicle . . . to find himself facing his bride-to-be.

Where does this story become interesting? Where does the *plot* begin?

You may start, if you like, with the young man's *Mayflower* ancestry. But if you do, it's going to be a very long story, and we're likely to close the book about the middle of the nineteenth century. You may begin with the first time he meets the extraordinary woman, but even then you must cover at least weeks, probably months, in a few pages; and that means you must summarize, skip, and generalize, and you'll have a hard time both maintaining your credibility and holding our attention. Begin at the stag party? Better. If you do so, you will somehow have to let us know all that has gone before, either through dialogue or through the young man's memory, but you have only one evening of action to cover, and we'll get to the conflict quickly. Suppose you begin instead the next morning, when the man wakes with a hangover in bed in a brothel with his bride on his wedding day. Is that, perhaps, the best of all? An immediate conflict that must lead to a quick and striking crisis?

E. M. Forster distinguishes between plot and story by describing story as:

> the chopped off length of the tape worm of time . . . a narrative of events arranged in their time sequence. A plot is also a narrative of events, the emphasis falling on causality. "The king died, and then the queen died," is a story. "The king died, and then the queen died of grief," is a plot. The time sequence is preserved, but the sense of causality overshadows it. Or again: "The queen died, no one knew why, until it was discovered that it was through grief at the death of the king." This is a plot with a mystery in it, a form capable of high development. It suspends the time sequence, it moves as far away from the story as its limitations will allow. Consider the death of the queen. If it is in a story we say, "and then?" If it is in a plot we ask, "why?"

The human desire to know *why* is as powerful as the desire to know what happened next, and it is a desire of a higher order. Once we have the facts, we inevitably look for the links between them, and only when we find such links are we satisfied that we "understand." Rote memorization in a science class bores almost everyone. Grasp and a sense of discovery begin only when we perceive *why* "a body in motion tends to remain in motion" and what an immense effect this actuality has on the phenomena of our lives.

A STORY HAS TO BE A GOOD DATE, because the reader can stop at any time. . . . Remember, readers are selfish and have no compulsion to be decent about anything.

Kurt Vonnegut

The same is true of the events of a story. Random incidents neither move nor illuminate; we want to know why one thing leads to another and to feel the inevitability of cause and effect.

Here is a series of uninteresting events chronologically arranged.

> Ariadne had a bad dream.
> She woke up tired and cross.
> She ate breakfast
> She headed for class.
> She saw Leroy.
> She fell on the steps and broke her ankle.
> Leroy offered to take notes for her.
> She went to a hospital.

This series of events does not constitute a plot, and if you wish to fashion it into a plot, you can do so only by letting us know the meaningful relations among the events. We first assume that Ariadne woke in a temper because of her bad dream, and that Leroy offered to take notes for her because she broke her ankle. But why did she fall? Perhaps because she saw Leroy? Does that suggest that her bad dream was about him? Was she, then, thinking about his dream-rejection as she broke her egg irritably on the edge of the frying pan? What is the effect of his offer? Is it a triumph or just another polite form of rejection when, really, he could have missed class once to drive her to the x-ray lab? The emotional and dramatic significance of these ordinary events emerges in the relation of cause to effect, and where such relation can be shown, a possible plot comes into existence. Notice also that in this brief attempt to form the events into a plot, I have introduced both conflict and a pattern of connection/disconnection.

Ariadne's is a story you might very well choose to tell chronologically: it needs to cover only an hour or two, and that much can be handled in the compressed form of the short story. But such a choice of plot is not inevitable even in this short compass. Might it be more gripping to begin with the wince of pain as she stumbles? Leroy comes to help her up and the yolk yellow of his T-shirt fills her field of vision. In the shock of pain she is immediately back in her dream. . . .

When "nothing happens" in a story, it is because we fail to sense the causal relation between what happens first and what happens next. When something does "happen," it is because the resolution of a short story or a novel describes a change in the character's life, an effect of the events that have gone before. This is why Aristotle insisted with such apparent simplicity on "a beginning, a middle, and an end." A story is capable of many meanings, and it is first of all in the choice of structure—which portion of the story forms the plot—that you offer us the gratifying sense that we "understand."

## The Short Story and the Novel

Many editors and writers insist that the short story and the novel are vastly different creatures. It is my belief, however, that, like the distinction between story and plot, the distinction between the two forms is very simple, and the many and profound possibilities of difference proceed from that simple source: A short story is short, and a novel is long.

Because of this, a short story can waste no words. It usually features the perspective of one or a very few characters. It may recount only one central action and one major change in the life of the central character or characters. It can afford no digression that does not directly affect the action. A short story strives to create what Edgar Allan Poe called "the single effect"—a single emotional impact that imparts a flash of understanding, though both impact and understanding may be complex. The virtue of a short story is its density, for it raises a single "what if" question, while a novel may raise many. If it is tight, sharp, economic, well knit, and charged, then it is a good short story because it has exploited a central attribute of the form—that it is short.

Occasionally in workshops, a new writer struggling to craft the shape of conflict-crisis-resolution may wonder if a story's lack of one of these elements means the work "must be a novel." Tempting as this hope may be, it only sidesteps the inevitable challenge of plotting, for not only must a novel have a large-scale plot structure, but individual chapters or episodes frequently are shaped around a pattern of conflict-crisis-incremental change that impels the novel onward.

Further, while no literary form is superior to another, few novelists achieve publication without first having crafted any number of short stories. The greater the limitation of space, the greater the necessity for pace, sharpness, and density. Short stories ask the writer to rise to the challenges of shaping, "showing," and making significance again and again, experiences that later may save that writer countless hours and pages when the time to tackle a novel comes along.

The form of the novel is an expanded story form. It asks for a conflict, a crisis, and a resolution, and no technique described in this book is irrelevant to its effectiveness.

## *Reading as Writers*

Learning to read as a writer involves focusing on craft, the choices and the techniques of the author. In *On Becoming a Novelist*, John Gardner urges young writers to read "the way a young architect looks at a building, or a medical student watches an operation, both devotedly, hoping to learn from a master, and critically alert for any possible mistake." "Bad poets imitate; good poets steal," was T. S. Eliot's advice.

Ask yourself as you read: what is memorable, effective, moving? Reread, if possible, watching for the techniques that produced those reactions in you. *Why did the author choose to begin at this point? Why did s/he make this choice of imagery, setting, ending? What gives this scene its tension; what makes me feel sympathetic?* You can also learn from stories that don't personally move you—how would you have handled the same material, and what would have changed with that approach? Be greedy from your own viewpoint as an author: *What, from this story, can I learn/ imitate/steal?*

# The Use of Force

### WILLIAM CARLOS WILLIAMS

They were new patients to me, all I had was the name, Olson. Please come down as soon as you can, my daughter is very sick.

When I arrived I was met by the mother, a big startled looking woman, very clean and apologetic who merely said, Is this the doctor? and let me in. In the back, she added. You must excuse us, doctor, we have her in the kitchen where it is warm. It is very damp here sometimes.

The child was fully dressed and sitting on her father's lap near the kitchen table. He tried to get up, but I motioned for him not to bother, took off my overcoat and started to look things over. I could see that they were all very nervous, eyeing me up and down distrustfully. As often, in such cases, they weren't telling me more than they had to, it was up to me to tell them; that's why they were spending three dollars on me.

The child was fairly eating me up with her cold, steady eyes, and no expression to her face whatever. She did not move and seemed, inwardly, quiet; an unusually attractive little thing, and as strong as a heifer in appearance. But her face was flushed, she was breathing rapidly, and I realized that she had a high fever. She had magnificent blonde hair, in profusion. One of those picture children often reproduced in advertising leaflets and the photogravure sections of the Sunday papers.

She's had a fever for three days, began the father, and we don't know what it comes from. My wife has given her things, you know, like people do, but it don't do no good. And there's been a lot of sickness around. So we tho't you'd better look her over and tell us what is the matter.

As doctors often do I took a trial shot at it as a point of departure. Has she had a sore throat?

Both parents answered me together, No . . . No, she says her throat don't hurt her.

Does your throat hurt you? added the mother to the child. But the little girl's expression didn't change, nor did she move her eyes from my face.

Have you looked?

I tried to, said the mother, but I couldn't see.

As it happens, we had been having a number of cases of diphtheria in the school to which this child went during that month and we were all, quite apparently, thinking of that, though no one had as yet spoken of the thing.

Well, I said, suppose we take a look at the throat first. I smiled in my best professional manner and asking for the child's first name I said, come on, Mathilda, open your mouth and let's take a look at your throat.

Nothing doing.

Aw, come on, I coaxed, just open your mouth wide and let me take a look. Look, I said opening both hands wide, I haven't anything in my hands. Just open up and let me see.

Such a nice man, put in the mother. Look how kind he is to you. Come on, do what he tells you to. He won't hurt you.

At that I ground my teeth in disgust. If only they wouldn't use the word "hurt" I might be able to get somewhere. But I did not allow myself to be hurried or disturbed, but speaking quietly and slowly I approached the child again.

As I moved my chair a little nearer, suddenly with one catlike movement both her hands clawed instinctively for my eyes and she almost reached them too. In fact she knocked my glasses flying and they fell, though unbroken, several feet away from me on the kitchen floor.

Both the mother and father almost turned themselves inside out in embarrassment and apology. You bad girl, said the mother, taking her and shaking her by one arm. Look what you've done. The nice man.

For heaven's sake, I broke in. Don't call me a nice man to her. I'm here to look at her throat on the chance that she might have diphtheria and possibly die of it. But that's nothing to her. Look here, I said to the child, we're going to look at your throat. You're old enough to understand what I'm saying. Will you open it now by yourself or shall we have to open it for you?

Not a move. Even her expression hadn't changed. Her breaths however were coming faster and faster. Then the battle began. I had to do it. I had to have a throat culture for her own protection. But first I told the parents that it was entirely up to them. I explained the danger but said that I would not insist on a throat examination so long as they would take the responsibility.

If you don't do what the doctor says you'll have to go to the hospital, the mother admonished her severely.

Oh yeah? I had to smile to myself. After all, I had already fallen in love with the savage brat, the parents were contemptible to me. In the ensuing struggle they grew more and more abject, crushed, exhausted while she surely rose to magnificent heights of insane fury of effort bred of her terror of me.

The father tried his best, and he was a big man but the fact that she was his daughter, his shame at her behavior and his dread of hurting her made him release her just at the critical moment several times when I had almost achieved success, till I wanted to kill him. But his dread also that she might have diphtheria made him tell me to go on, go on though he himself was almost fainting, while the mother moved back and forth behind us raising and lowering her hands in an agony of apprehension.

Put her in front of you on your lap, I ordered, and hold both her wrists.

But as soon as he did the child let out a scream. Don't, you're hurting me. Let go of my hands. Let them go I tell you. Then she shrieked terrifyingly, hysterically. Stop it! Stop it! You're killing me!

Do you think she can stand it, doctor! said the mother.

You get out, said the husband to his wife. Do you want her to die of diphtheria? Come on now, hold her, I said.

Then I grasped the child's head with my left hand and tried to get the wooden tongue depressor between her teeth. She fought, with clenched teeth, desperately! But now I also had grown furious—at a child. I tried to hold myself down but I couldn't. I know how to expose a throat for inspection. And I did my best. When finally I got the wooden spatula behind the last teeth and just the point of it into the mouth cavity, she opened up for an instant but before I could see anything she came down again and gripping the wooden blade between her molars she reduced it to splinters before I could get it out again.

Aren't you ashamed, the mother yelled at her. Aren't you ashamed to act like that in front of the doctor?

Get me a smooth-handled spoon of some sort, I told the mother. We're going through with this. The child's mouth was already bleeding. Her tongue was cut and she was screaming in wild hysterical shrieks. Perhaps I should have desisted and come back in an hour or more. No doubt it would have been better. But I have seen at least two children lying dead in bed of neglect in such cases, and feeling that I must get a diagnosis now or never I went at it again. But the worst of it was that I too had got beyond reason. I could have torn the child apart in my own fury and enjoyed it. It was a pleasure to attack her. My face was burning with it.

The damned little brat must be protected against her own idiocy, one says to one's self at such times. Others must be protected against her. It is social necessity. And all these things are true. But a blind fury, a feeling of adult shame, bred of a longing for muscular release are the operatives. One goes on to the end.

In a final unreasoning assault I overpowered the child's neck and jaws. I forced the heavy silver spoon back of her teeth and down her throat till she gagged. And there it was—both tonsils covered with membrane. She had fought valiantly to keep me from knowing her secret. She had been hiding that sore throat for three days at least and lying to her parents in order to escape just such an outcome as this.

Now truly she was furious. She had been on the defensive before but now she attacked. Tried to get off her father's lap and fly at me while tears of defeat blinded her eyes.

## *Happy Endings*

### MARGARET ATWOOD

John and Mary meet.
What happens next?
If you want a happy ending, try A.

**A**

John and Mary fall in love and get married. They both have worthwhile and remunerative jobs which they find stimulating and challenging. They buy a charming house. Real estate values go up. Eventually, when they can afford live-in help, they have two children, to whom they are devoted. The children turn out well. John and Mary have a stimulating and challenging sex life and worthwhile friends. They go on fun vacations together. They retire. They both have hobbies which they find stimulating and challenging. Eventually they die. This is the end of the story.

## B

Mary falls in love with John but John doesn't fall in love with Mary. He merely uses her body for selfish pleasure and ego gratification of a tepid kind. He comes to her apartment twice a week and she cooks him dinner, you'll notice that he doesn't even consider her worth the price of a dinner out, and after he's eaten the dinner he fucks her and after that he falls asleep, while she does the dishes so he won't think she's untidy, having all those dirty dishes lying around, and puts on fresh lipstick so she'll look good when he wakes up, but when he wakes up he doesn't even notice, he puts on his socks and his shorts and his pants and his shirt and his tie and his shoes, the reverse order from the one in which he took them off. He doesn't take off Mary's clothes, she takes them off herself, she acts as if she's dying for it every time, not because she likes sex exactly, she doesn't, but she wants John to think she does because if they do it often enough surely he'll get used to her, he'll come to depend on her and they will get married, but John goes out the door with hardly so much as a good-night and three days later he turns up at six o'clock and they do the whole thing over again.

Mary gets run-down. Crying is bad for your face, everyone knows that and so does Mary but she can't stop. People at work notice. Her friends tell her John is a rat, a pig, a dog, he isn't good enough for her, but she can't believe it. Inside John, she thinks, is another John who is much nicer. This other John will emerge like a butterfly from a cocoon, a Jack from a box, a pit from a prune, if the first John is only squeezed enough.

One evening John complains about the food. He has never complained about the food before. Mary is hurt.

Her friends tell her they've seen him in a restaurant with another woman, whose name is Madge. It's not even Madge that finally gets to Mary: it's the restaurant. John has never taken Mary to a restaurant. Mary collects all the sleeping pills and aspirins she can find, and takes them and a half a bottle of sherry. You can see what kind of a woman she is by the fact that it's not even whiskey. She leaves a note for John. She hopes he'll discover her and get her to the hospital in time and repent and then they can get married, but this fails to happen and she dies.

John marries Madge and everything continues as in A.

## C

John, who is an older man, falls in love with Mary, and Mary, who is only twenty-two, feels sorry for him because he's worried about his hair falling out. She sleeps with him even though she's not in love with him. She met him at work. She's in love with someone called James, who is twenty-two also and not yet ready to settle down.

John on the contrary settled down long ago: this is what is bothering him. John has a steady, respectable job and is getting ahead in his field, but Mary isn't impressed by him, she's impressed by James, who has a motorcycle and a fabulous record collection. But James is often away on his motorcycle, being free. Freedom isn't the same for girls, so in the meantime Mary spends Thursday evenings with John. Thursdays are the only days John can get away.

John is married to a woman called Madge and they have two children, a charming house which they bought just before the real estate values went up, and hobbies which they find stimulating and challenging, when they have the time. John tells Mary how important she is to him, but of course he can't leave his wife because a commitment is a commitment. He goes on about this more than is necessary and Mary finds it boring, but older men can keep it up longer so on the whole she has a fairly good time.

One day James breezes in on his motorcycle with some top-grade California hybrid and James and Mary get higher than you'd believe possible and they climb into bed. Everything becomes very underwater, but along comes John, who has a key to Mary's apartment. He finds them stoned and entwined. He's hardly in any position to be jealous, considering Madge, but nevertheless he's overcome with despair. Finally he's middle-aged, in two years he'll be bald as an egg and he can't stand it. He purchases a handgun, saying he needs it for target practice—this is the thin part of the plot, but it can be dealt with later—and shoots the two of them and himself.

Madge, after a suitable period of mourning, marries an understanding man called Fred and everything continues as in A, but under different names.

**D**

Fred and Madge have no problems. They get along exceptionally well and are good at working out any little difficulties that may arise. But their charming house is by the seashore and one day a giant tidal wave approaches. Real estate values go down. The rest of the story is about what caused the tidal wave and how they escape from it. They do, though thousands drown, but Fred and Madge are virtuous and lucky. Finally on high ground they clasp each other, wet and dripping and grateful, and continue as in A.

**E**

Yes, but Fred has a bad heart. The rest of the story is about how kind and understanding they both are until Fred dies. Then Madge devotes herself to charity work until the end of A. If you like, it can be "Madge," "cancer," "guilty and confused," and "bird watching."

**F**

If you think this is all too bourgeois, make John a revolutionary and Mary a counterespionage agent and see how far that gets you. Remember, this is Canada. You'll still end up with A, though in between you may get a lustful brawling saga of passionate involvement, a chronicle of our times, sort of.

You'll have to face it, the endings are the same however you slice it. Don't be deluded by any other endings, they're all fake, either deliberately fake, with malicious intent to deceive, or just motivated by excessive optimism if not by downright sentimentality.

The only authentic ending is the one provided here:

*John and Mary die. John and Mary die. John and Mary die.*

So much for endings. Beginnings are always more fun. True connoisseurs, however, are known to favor the stretch in between, since it's the hardest to do anything with.

That's about all that can be said for plots, which anyway are just one thing after another, a what and a what and a what.

Now try How and Why.

# Everything That Rises Must Converge

### FLANNERY O'CONNOR

Her doctor had told Julian's mother that she must lose twenty pounds on account of her blood pressure, so on Wednesday nights Julian had to take her downtown on the bus for a reducing class at the Y. The reducing class was designed for working girls over fifty, who weighed from 165 to 200 pounds. His mother was one of the slimmer ones, but she said ladies did not tell their age or weight. She would not ride the buses by herself at night since they had been integrated, and because the reducing class was one of her few pleasures, necessary for her health, and *free*, she said Julian could at least put himself out to take her, considering all she did for him. Julian did not like to consider all she did for him, but every Wednesday night he braced himself and took her.

She was almost ready to go, standing before the hall mirror, putting on her hat, while he, his hands behind him, appeared pinned to the door frame, waiting like Saint Sebastian for the arrows to begin piercing him. The hat was new and had cost her seven dollars and a half. She kept saying, "Maybe I shouldn't have paid that for it. No, I shouldn't have. I'll take it off and return it tomorrow. I shouldn't have bought it."

Julian raised his eyes to heaven. "Yes, you should have bought it," he said. "Put it on and let's go." It was a hideous hat. A purple velvet flap came down on one side of it and stood up on the other; the rest of it was green and looked like a cushion with the stuffing out. He decided it was less comical than jaunty and pathetic. Everything that gave her pleasure was small and depressed him.

She lifted the hat one more time and set it down slowly on top of her head. Two wings of gray hair protruded on either side of her florid face, but her eyes, sky-blue, were as innocent and untouched by experience as they must have been when she was ten. Were it not that she was a widow who had struggled fiercely to feed and clothe and put him through school and who was supporting him still, "until he got on his feet," she might have been a little girl that he had to take to town.

"It's all right, it's all right," he said. "Let's go." He opened the door himself and started down the walk to get her going. The sky was a dying violet and the houses stood out darkly against it, bulbous liver-colored monstrosities of a uniform ugliness though no two were alike. Since this had been a fashionable neighborhood forty years ago, his mother persisted in thinking they did well to have an apartment in it. Each house had a narrow collar of dirt around it in which sat, usually, a grubby child. Julian walked with his hands in his pockets, his head down and thrust forward and his eyes glazed with the determination to make himself completely numb during the time he would be sacrificed to her pleasure.

The door closed and he turned to find the dumpy figure, surmounted by the atrocious hat, coming toward him. "Well," she said, "you only live once and paying a little more for it, I at least won't meet myself coming and going."

"Some day I'll start making money," Julian said gloomily—he knew he never would—"and you can have one of those jokes whenever you take the fit." But first they would move. He visualized a place where the nearest neighbors would be three miles away on either side.

"I think you're doing fine," she said, drawing on her gloves. "You've only been out of school a year. Rome wasn't built in a day."

She was one of the few members of the Y reducing class who arrived in hat and gloves and who had a son who had been to college. "It takes time," she said, "and the world is in such a mess. This hat looked better on me than any of the others, though when she brought it out I said, 'Take that thing back. I wouldn't have it on my head,' and she said, 'Now wait till you see it on,' and when she put it on me, I said, 'We-ull,' and she said, 'If you ask me, that hat does something for you and you do something for the hat, and besides,' she said, 'with that hat, you won't meet yourself coming and going.'"

Julian thought he could have stood his lot better if she had been selfish, if she had been an old hag who drank and screamed at him. He walked along, saturated in depression, as if in the midst of his martyrdom he had lost his faith. Catching sight of his long, hopeless, irritated face, she stopped suddenly with a grief-stricken look, and pulled back on his arm. "Wait on me," she said. "I'm going back to the house and take this thing off and tomorrow I'm going to return it, I was out of my head. I can pay the gas bill with the seven-fifty."

He caught her arm in a vicious grip. "You are not going to take it back," he said. "I like it."

"Well," she said, "I don't think I ought . . ."

"Shut up and enjoy it," he muttered, more depressed than ever.

"With the world in the mess it's in," she said, "it's a wonder we can enjoy anything. I tell you, the bottom rail is on the top."

Julian sighed.

"Of course," she said, "if you know who you are, you can go anywhere." She said this every time he took her to the reducing class. "Most of them in it are not our kind of people," she said, "but I can be gracious to anybody. I know who I am."

"They don't give a damn for your graciousness," Julian said savagely. "Knowing who you are is good for one generation only. You haven't the foggiest idea where you stand now or who you are."

She stopped and allowed her eyes to flash at him. "I most certainly do know who I am," she said, "and if you don't know who you are, I'm ashamed of you."

"Oh hell," Julian said.

"Your great-grandfather was a former governor of this state," she said. "Your grandfather was a prosperous landowner. Your grandmother was a Godhigh."

"Will you look around you," he said tensely, "and see where you are now?" and he swept his arm jerkily out to indicate the neighborhood, which the growing darkness at least made less dingy.

"You remain what you are," she said, "Your great-grandfather had a plantation and two hundred slaves."

"There are no more slaves," he said irritably.

"They were better off when they were," she said. He groaned to see that she was off on that topic. She rolled onto it every few days like a train on an open track.

He knew every stop, every junction, every swamp along the way, and knew the exact point at which her conclusion would roll majestically into the station: "It's ridiculous. It's simply not realistic. They should rise, yes, but on their own side of the fence."

"Let's skip it," Julian said.

"The ones I feel sorry for," she said, "are the ones that are half white. They're tragic."

"Will you skip it?"

"Suppose we were half white. We would certainly have mixed feelings."

"I have mixed feelings now," he groaned.

"Well let's talk about something pleasant," she said. "I remember going to Grandpa's when I was a little girl. Then the house had double stairways that went up to what was really the second floor—all the cooking was done on the first. I used to like to stay down in the kitchen on account of the way the walls smelled. I would sit with my nose pressed against the plaster and take deep breaths. Actually the place belonged to the Godhighs but your grandfather Chestny paid the mortgage and saved it for them. They were in reduced circumstances," she said, "but reduced or not, they never forgot who they were."

"Doubtless that decayed mansion reminded them," Julian muttered. He never spoke of it without contempt or thought of it without longing. He had seen it once when he was a child before it had been sold. The double stairways had rotted and been torn down. Negroes were living in it. But it remained in his mind as his mother had known it. It appeared in his dreams regularly. He would stand on the wide porch, listening to the rustle of oak leaves, then wander through the high-ceilinged hall into the parlor that opened onto it and gaze at the worn rugs and faded draperies. It occurred to him that it was he, not she, who could have appreciated it. He preferred its threadbare elegance to anything he could name and it was because of it that all the neighborhoods they had lived in had been a torment to him—whereas she had hardly known the difference. She called her insensitivity "being adjustable."

"And I remember the old darky who was my nurse, Caroline. There was no better person in the world. I've always had a great respect for my colored friends," she said. "I'd do anything in the world for them and they'd . . ."

"Will you for God's sake get off that subject?" Julian said. When he got on a bus by himself, he made it a point to sit down beside a Negro, in reparation as it were for his mother's sins.

"You're mighty touchy tonight," she said. "Do you feel all right?"

"Yes I feel all right," he said. "Now lay off."

She pursed her lips. "Well, you certainly are in a vile humor," she observed. "I just won't speak to you at all."

They had reached the bus stop. There was no bus in sight and Julian, his hands still jammed in his pockets and his head thrust forward, scowled down the empty street. The frustration of having to wait on the bus as well as ride on it began to creep up his neck like a hot hand. The presence of his mother was borne in upon him as she gave a pained sigh. He looked at her bleakly. She was holding herself very erect under the preposterous hat, wearing it like a banner of her imaginary dignity.

There was in him an evil urge to break her spirit. He suddenly unloosened his tie and pulled it off and put it in his pocket.

She stiffened. "Why must you look like *that* when you take me to town?" she said. "Why must you deliberately embarrass me?"

"If you'll never learn where you are," he said, "you can at least learn where I am."

"You look like a—thug," she said.

"Then I must be one," he murmured.

"I'll just go home," she said. "I will not bother you. If you can't do a little thing like that for me . . ."

Rolling his eyes upward, he put his tie back on. "Restored to my class," he muttered. He thrust his face toward her and hissed, "True culture is in the mind, the *mind*," he said, and tapped his head, "the mind."

"It's in the heart," she said, "and in how you do things and how you do things is because of who you *are*."

"Nobody in the damn bus cares who you are."

"I care who I am," she said icily.

The lighted bus appeared on top of the next hill and as it approached, they moved out into the street to meet it. He put his hand under her elbow and hoisted her up on the creaking step. She entered with a little smile, as if she were going into a drawing room where everyone had been waiting for her. While he put in the tokens, she sat down on one of the broad front seats for three which faced the aisle. A thin woman with protruding teeth and long yellow hair was sitting on the end of it. His mother moved up beside her and left room for Julian beside herself. He sat down and looked at the floor across the aisle where a pair of thin feet in red and white canvas sandals were planted.

His mother immediately began a general conversation meant to attract anyone who felt like talking, "Can it get any hotter?" she said and removed from her purse a folding fan, black with a Japanese scene on it, which she began to flutter before her.

"I reckon it might could," the woman with the protruding teeth said, "but I know for a fact my apartment couldn't get no hotter."

"It must get the afternoon sun," his mother said. She sat forward and looked up and down the bus. It was half filled. Everybody was white. "I see we have the bus to ourselves," she said. Julian cringed.

"For a change," said the woman across the aisle, the owner of the red and white canvas sandals. "I come on one the other day and they were thick as fleas—up front and all through."

"The world is in a mess everywhere," his mother said. "I don't know how we've let it get in this fix."

"What gets my goat is all those boys from good families stealing automobile tires," the woman with the protruding teeth said. "I told my boy, I said you may not be rich but you been raised right and if I ever catch you in any such mess, they can send you on to the reformatory. Be exactly where you belong."

"Training tells," his mother said. "Is your boy in high school?"

"Ninth grade," the woman said.

"My son just finished college last year. He wants to write but he's selling typewriters until he gets started," his mother said.

The woman leaned forward and peered at Julian. He threw her such a malevolent look that she subsided against the seat. On the floor across the aisle there was an abandoned newspaper. He got up and got it and opened it out in front of him. His mother discreetly continued the conversation in a lower tone but the woman across the aisle said in a loud voice, "Well that's nice. Selling typewriters is close to writing. He can go right from one to the other."

"I tell him," his mother said, "that Rome wasn't built in a day."

Behind the newspaper Julian was withdrawing into the inner compartment of his mind where he spent most of his time. This was a kind of mental bubble in which he established himself when he could not bear to be a part of what was going on around him. From it he could see out and judge but in it he was safe from any kind of penetration from without. It was the only place where he felt free of the general idiocy of his fellows. His mother had never entered it but from it he could see her with absolute clarity.

The old lady was clever enough and he thought that if she had started from any of the right premises, more might have been expected of her. She lived according to the laws of her own fantasy world, outside of which he had never seen her set foot. The law of it was to sacrifice herself for him after she had first created the necessity to do so by making a mess of things. If he had permitted her sacrifices, it was only because her lack of foresight had made them necessary. All of her life had been a struggle to act like a Chestny without the Chestny goods, and to give him everything she thought a Chestny ought to have; but since, said she, it was fun to struggle, why complain? And when you had won, as she had won, what fun to look back on the hard times? He could not forgive her that she had enjoyed the struggle and that she thought *she* had won.

What she meant when she said she had won was that she had brought him up successfully and had sent him to college and that he had turned out so well—good looking (her teeth had gone unfilled so that his could be straightened), intelligent (he realized he was too intelligent to be a success), and with a future ahead of him (there was of course no future ahead of him). She excused his gloominess on the grounds that he was still growing up and his radical ideas on his lack of practical experience. She said he didn't yet know a thing about "life," that he hadn't even entered the real world—when already he was as disenchanted with it as a man of fifty.

The further irony of all this was that in spite of her, he had turned out so well. In spite of going to only a third-rate college, he had, on his own initiative, come out with a first-rate education; in spite of growing up dominated by a small mind, he had ended up with a large one; in spite of all her foolish views, he was free of prejudice and unafraid to face facts. Most miraculous of all, instead of being blinded by love for her as she was for him, he had cut himself emotionally free of her and could see her with complete objectivity. He was not dominated by his mother.

The bus stopped with a sudden jerk and shook him from his meditation. A woman from the back lurched forward with little steps and barely escaped falling in his newspaper as she righted herself. She got off and a large Negro got on. Julian kept his paper lowered to watch. It gave him a certain satisfaction to see injustice in daily operation. It confirmed his view that with a few exceptions there was no one worth knowing within a radius of three hundred miles. The Negro was well dressed and carried a briefcase. He looked around and then sat down on the other end of the seat where the woman with the red and white canvas sandals was sitting. He immediately unfolded a newspaper and obscured himself behind it. Julian's mother's elbow at once prodded insistently into his ribs. "Now you see why I won't ride on these buses by myself," she whispered.

The woman with the red and white canvas sandals had risen at the same time the Negro sat down and had gone further back in the bus and taken the seat of the woman who had got off. His mother leaned forward and cast her an approving look.

Julian rose, crossed the aisle, and sat down in the place of the woman with the canvas sandals. From this position, he looked serenely across at his mother. Her face had turned an angry red. He stared at her, making his eyes the eyes of a stranger. He felt his tension suddenly lift as if he had openly declared war on her.

He would have liked to get in conversation with the Negro and to talk with him about art or politics or any subject that would be above the comprehension of those around them, but the man remained entrenched behind his paper. He was either ignoring the change of seating or had never noticed it. There was no way for Julian to convey his sympathy.

His mother kept her eyes fixed reproachfully on his face. The woman with the protruding teeth was looking at him avidly as if he were a type of monster new to her.

"Do you have a light?" he asked the Negro.

Without looking away from his paper, the man reached in his pocket and handed him a packet of matches.

"Thanks," Julian said. For a moment he held the matches foolishly. A NO SMOKING sign looked down upon him from over the door. This alone would not have deterred him; he had no cigarettes. He had quit smoking some months before because he could not afford it. "Sorry," he muttered and handed back the matches. The Negro lowered the paper and gave him an annoyed look. He took the matches and raised the paper again.

His mother continued to gaze at him but she did not take advantage of his momentary discomfort. Her eyes retained their battered look. Her face seemed to be unnaturally red, as if her blood pressure had risen. Julian allowed no glimmer of sympathy to show on his face. Having got the advantage, he wanted desperately to keep it and carry it through. He would have liked to teach her a lesson that would last her a while, but there seemed no way to continue the point. The Negro refused to come out from behind his paper.

Julian folded his arms and looked stolidly before him, facing her but as if he did not see her, as if he had ceased to recognize her existence. He visualized a scene in which, the bus having reached their stop, he would remain in his seat and when she said, "Aren't you going to get off?" he would look at her as at a stranger who had rashly addressed him. The corner they got off on was usually deserted, but it was well lighted and it would not hurt her to walk by herself the four blocks to the Y. He decided to wait until the time came and then decide whether or not he would let her get off by herself. He would have to be at the Y at ten to bring her back, but he could leave her wondering if he was going to show up. There was no reason for her to think she could always depend on him.

He retired again into the high-ceilinged room sparsely settled with large pieces of antique furniture. His soul expanded momentarily but then he became aware of his mother across from him and the vision shriveled. He studied her coldly. Her feet in little pumps dangled like a child's and did not quite reach the floor. She was training on him an exaggerated look of reproach. He felt completely detached from her. At that moment he could with pleasure have slapped her as he would have slapped a particularly obnoxious child in his charge.

He began to imagine various unlikely ways by which he could teach her a lesson. He might make friends with some distinguished Negro professor or lawyer and bring him home to spend the evening. He would be entirely justified but her blood pressure would rise to 300. He could not push her to the extent of making her have a stroke, and moreover, he had never been successful at making any Negro friends. He had tried to strike up an acquaintance on the bus with some of the better types, with ones that looked like professors or ministers or lawyers. One morning he had sat down next to a distinguished-looking dark brown man who had answered his questions with a sonorous solemnity but who had turned out to be an undertaker. Another day he had sat down beside a cigar-smoking Negro with a diamond ring on his finger, but after a few stilted pleasantries, the Negro had rung the buzzer and risen, slipping two lottery tickets into Julian's hand as he climbed over him to leave.

He imagined his mother lying desperately ill and his being able to secure only a Negro doctor for her. He toyed with that idea for a few minutes and then dropped it for a momentary vision of himself participating as a sympathizer in a sit-in demonstration. This was possible but he did not linger with it. Instead, he approached the ultimate horror. He brought home a beautiful suspiciously Negroid woman. Prepare yourself, he said. There is nothing you can do about it. This is the woman I've chosen. She's intelligent, dignified, even good, and she's suffered and she hasn't thought it *fun*. Now persecute us, go ahead and persecute us. Drive her out of here, but remember, you're driving me too. His eyes were narrowed and through the indignation he had generated, he saw his mother across the aisle, purple-faced, shrunken to the dwarf-like proportions of her moral nature, sitting like a mummy beneath the ridiculous banner of her hat.

He was tilted out of his fantasy again as the bus stopped. The door opened with a sucking hiss and out of the dark a large, gaily dressed, sullen-looking colored woman got on with a little boy. The child, who might have been four, had on a short plaid suit and a Tyrolean hat with a blue feather in it. Julian hoped that he would sit down beside him and that the woman would push in beside his mother. He could think of no better arrangement.

As she waited for her tokens, the woman was surveying the seating possibilities— he hoped with the idea of sitting where she was least wanted. There was something familiar-looking about her but Julian could not place what it was. She was a giant of a woman. Her face was set not only to meet opposition but to seek it out. The downward tilt of her large lower lip was like a warning sign: DON'T TAMPER WITH ME. Her bulging figure was encased in a green crepe dress and her feet overflowed in red shoes. She had on a hideous hat. A purple velvet flap came down on one side of it and stood up on the other; the rest of it was green and looked like a cushion with the stuffing out. She carried a mammoth red pocketbook that bulged throughout as if it were stuffed with rocks.

To Julian's disappointment, the little boy climbed up on the empty seat beside his mother. His mother lumped all children, black and white, into the common category, "cute," and she thought little Negroes were on the whole cuter than little white children. She smiled at the little boy as he climbed on the seat.

Meanwhile the woman was bearing down upon the empty seat beside Julian. To his annoyance, she squeezed herself into it. He saw his mother's face change as the woman settled herself next to him and he realized with satisfaction that this was more objectionable to her than it was to him. Her face seemed almost gray and there was a look of dull recognition in her eyes, as if suddenly she had sickened at some awful confrontation. Julian saw that it was because she and the woman had, in a sense, swapped sons. Though his mother would not realize the symbolic significance of this, she would feel it. His amusement showed plainly on his face.

The woman next to him muttered something unintelligible to herself. He was conscious of a kind of bristling next to him, muted growling like that of an angry cat. He could not see anything but the red pocketbook upright on the bulging green thighs. He visualized the woman as she had stood waiting for her tokens—the ponderous figure, rising from the red shoes upward over the solid hips, the mammoth bosom, the haughty face, to the green and purple hat.

His eyes widened.

The vision of the two hats, identical, broke upon him with the radiance of a brilliant sunrise. His face was suddenly lit with joy. He could not believe that Fate had thrust upon his mother such a lesson. He gave a loud chuckle so that she would look at him and see that he saw. She turned her eyes on him slowly. The blue in them seemed to have turned a bruised purple. For a moment he had an uncomfortable sense of her innocence, but it lasted only a second before principle rescued him. Justice entitled him to laugh. His grin hardened until it said to her as plainly as if he were saying aloud: Your punishment exactly fits your pettiness. This should teach you a permanent lesson.

Her eyes shifted to the woman. She seemed unable to bear looking at him and to find the woman preferable. He became conscious again of the bristling presence at his side. The woman was rumbling like a volcano about to become active. His mother's mouth began to twitch slightly at one corner. With a sinking heart, he saw incipient signs of recovery on her face and realized that this was going to strike her suddenly as funny and was going to be no lesson at all. She kept her eyes on the woman and an amused smile came over her face as if the woman were a monkey that had stolen her hat. The little Negro was looking up at her with large fascinated eyes. He had been trying to attract her attention for some time.

"Carver!" the woman said suddenly. "Come heah!"

When he saw that the spotlight was on him at last, Carver drew his feet up and turned himself toward Julian's mother and giggled.

"Carver!" the woman said. "You heah me? Come heah!"

Carver slid down from the seat but remained squatting with his back against the base of it, his head turned slyly around toward Julian's mother, who was smiling at him. The woman reached a hand across the aisle and snatched him to her. He righted himself and hung backwards on her knees, grinning at Julian's mother. "Isn't he cute?" Julian's mother said to the woman with the protruding teeth.

"I reckon he is," the woman said without conviction.

The Negress yanked him upright but he eased out of her grip and shot across the aisle and scrambled, giggling wildly, onto the seat beside his love.

"I think he likes me," Julian's mother said, and smiled at the woman. It was the smile she used when she was being particularly gracious to an inferior. Julian saw everything lost. The lesson had rolled off her like rain on a roof.

The woman stood up and yanked the little boy off the seat as if she were snatching him from contagion. Julian could feel the rage in her at having no weapon like his mother's smile. She gave the child a sharp slap across his leg. He howled once and then thrust his head into her stomach and kicked his feet against her shins. "Behave," she said vehemently.

The bus stopped and the Negro who had been reading the newspaper got off. The woman moved over and set the little boy down with a thump between herself and Julian. She held him firmly by the knee. In a moment he put his hands in front of his face and peeped at Julian's mother through his fingers.

"I see yoooooooo!" she said and put her hand in front of her face and peeped at him.

The woman slapped his hand down. "Quit yo' foolishness," she said, "before I knock the living Jesus out of you!"

Julian was thankful that the next stop was theirs. He reached up and pulled the cord. The woman reached up and pulled it at the same time. Oh my God, he thought. He had the terrible intuition that when they got off the bus together, his mother would open her purse and give the little boy a nickel. The gesture would be as natural to her as breathing. The bus stopped and the woman got up and lunged to the front, dragging the child, who wished to stay on, after her. Julian and his mother got up and followed. As they neared the door, Julian tried to relieve her of her pocketbook.

"No," she murmured, "I want to give the little boy a nickel."

"No!" Julian hissed. "No!"

She smiled down at the child and opened her bag. The bus door opened and the woman picked him up by the arm and descended with him, hanging at her hip. Once in the street she set him down and shook him.

Julian's mother had to close her purse while she got down the bus step but as soon as her feet were on the ground, she opened it again and began to rummage inside. "I can't find but a penny," she whispered, "but it looks like a new one."

"Don't do it!" Julian said fiercely between his teeth. There was a streetlight on the corner and she hurried to get under it so that she could better see into her pocketbook. The woman was heading off rapidly down the street with the child still hanging backward on her hand.

"Oh little boy!" Julian's mother called and took a few quick steps and caught up with them just beyond the lamppost. "Here's a bright new penny for you," and she held out the coin, which shone bronze in the dim light.

The huge woman turned and for a moment stood, her shoulders lifted and her face frozen with frustrated rage, and stared at Julian's mother. Then all at once she seemed to explode like a piece of machinery that had been given one ounce of pressure too much. Julian saw the black fist swing out with the red pocketbook. He shut his eyes and cringed as he heard the woman shout, "He don't take nobody's pennies!" When he opened his eyes; the woman was disappearing down the street with the little boy staring wide-eyed over her shoulder. Julian's mother was sitting on the sidewalk.

"I told you not to do that," Julian said angrily. "I told you not to do that!"

He stood over her for a minute, gritting his teeth. Her legs were stretched out in front of her and her hat was on her lap. He squatted down and looked her in the face. It was totally expressionless. "You got exactly what you deserved," he said. "Now get up."

He picked up her pocketbook and put what had fallen out back in it. He picked the hat up off her lap. The penny caught his eye on the sidewalk and he picked that up and let it drop before her eyes into the purse. Then he stood up and leaned over and held his hands out to pull her up. She remained immobile. He sighed. Rising above them on either side were black apartment buildings, marked with irregular rectangles of light. At the end of the block a man came out of a door and walked off in the opposite direction. "All right," he said, "suppose somebody happens by and wants to know why you're sitting on the sidewalk?"

She took the hand and, breathing hard, pulled heavily up on it and then stood for a moment, swaying slightly as if the spots of light in the darkness were circling around her. Her eyes, shadowed and confused, finally settled on his face. He did not try to conceal his irritation. "I hope this teaches you a lesson," he said. She leaned forward and her eyes raked his face. She seemed trying to determine his identity. Then, as if she found nothing familiar about him, she started off with a headlong movement in the wrong direction.

"Aren't you going on to the Y?" he asked.

"Home," she muttered.

"Well, are we walking?"

For answer she kept going. Julian followed along, his hands behind him. He saw no reason to let the lesson she had had go without backing it up with an explanation of its meaning. She might as well be made to understand what had happened to her. "Don't think that was just an uppity Negro woman," he said. "That was the whole colored race which will no longer take your condescending pennies. That was your black double. She can wear the same hat as you, and to be sure," he added gratuitously (because he thought it was funny), "it looked better on her than it did on you, What all this means," he said, "is that the old world is gone. The old manners are obsolete and your graciousness is not worth a damn." He thought bitterly of the house that had been lost for him. "You aren't who you think you are," he said.

She continued to plow ahead, paying no attention to him. Her hair had come undone on one side. She dropped her pocketbook and took no notice. He stooped and picked it up and handed it to her but she did not take it.

"You needn't act as if the world had come to an end," he said, "because it hasn't. From now on you've got to live in a new world and face a few realities for a change. Buck up," he said, "it won't kill you."

She was breathing fast.

"Let's wait on the bus," he said.

"Home," she said thickly.

"I hate to see you behave like this," he said. "Just like a child. I should be able to expect more of you." He decided to stop where he was and make her stop and wait for a bus. "I'm not going any farther," he said, stopping. "We're going on the bus."

She continued to go on as if she had not heard him. He took a few steps and caught her arm and stopped her. He looked into her face and caught his breath. He was looking into a face he had never seen before. "Tell Grandpa to come get me," she said.

He stared, stricken.

"Tell Caroline to come get me," she said.

Stunned, he let her go and she lurched forward again, walking as if one leg were shorter than the other. A tide of darkness seemed to be sweeping her from him. "Mother!" he cried. "Darling, sweetheart, wait!" Crumpling, she fell to the pavement. He dashed forward and fell at her side, crying, "Mamma, Mamma!" He turned her over. Her face was fiercely distorted. One eye, large and staring, moved slightly to the left as if it had become unmoored. The other remained fixed on him, raked his face again, found nothing and closed.

"Wait here, wait here!" he cried and jumped up and began to run for help toward a cluster of lights he saw in the distance ahead of him. "Help, help!" he shouted, but his voice was thin, scarcely a thread of sound. The lights drifted farther away the faster he ran and his feet moved numbly as if they carried him nowhere. The tide of darkness seemed to sweep him back to her, postponing from moment to moment his entry into the world of guilt and sorrow.

᠎᠎᠎ 🔆 🔆 🔆

## Writing Exercises

### INDIVIDUAL

1. Write a short story on a three by five card or the back of a postcard. Notice that if you're going to manage a conflict, crisis, and resolution in this small space, you'll have to introduce the conflict immediately.

2. For this exercise, you will create what Jerome Stern calls the "Bear at the Door" scene. In this scene, your character must have an external problem. ("Honey, there's a bear at the door.") The problem should be significant. ("Honey, it's huge.") The problem should be pressing. ("Honey, I think it's trying to get in.") And the problem should force your character to act. ("Honey, do something!") Your character should have an internal conflict that affects her/his ability to deal with this problem—the bear within him/herself.
   a. Come up with a list of external conflicts, avoiding the overly dramatic or overly mundane. Choose the most intriguing one.
   b. Write a scene that places a character in the middle of the external conflict. Complicate the situation with the character's internal needs and desires.

3. Write a scene placing two characters in this very fundamental conflict: one wants something that the other does not want to give. The something may be anything—money, respect, jewelry, sex, information, a match—but be sure to focus on that one desire and how it puts the two characters at odds.

4. For each character in one of your stories-in-progress, list all the predictable actions each could take to keep the plot moving. Now try mixing up the characters and the actions and see if you come up with a more interesting and surprising plot.

5. Write a very short story (no longer than three pages) in which the protagonist does *not* get what s/he wants, but which, for the reader at least, ends in a satisfying way.

6. Robert Olen Butler wrote a collection of short stories, *Tabloid Dreams*, that was inspired by headlines and articles in supermarket tabloids (e.g., "Jealous Husband Returns in Form of Parrot"). Buy a tabloid magazine of your own. Find the silliest story in it. Use it as the jumping off point for a short, serious story.

7. Imagine an intriguing circumstance: either make something up, or think of something you witnessed, heard, or read about in the newspaper. The circumstance should be puzzling, with no obvious explanation. (See page 11, "The Incongruity," about three women, one with a baby stroller, at a supermarket pay phone very late at night.) Other examples might be a man and a woman arguing outside in a violent rainstorm; a young woman at the bus station late at night wearing a wig; a man in a soaked tuxedo walking along the beach on a sunny day.

   Write three very brief stories (two hundred words), each offering a different explanation for the **same** circumstance. Each story should have different characters and a different plot. Consider that in each story this same circumstance may function within the story in different ways: in one story, it may be the opening scene; in another, it might appear at the end.

8. Imagine some deceit growing out of control. Your character "borrowed" something without asking, and now it's lost or broken; the babysitter was distracted on the phone, and now one of the kids is missing; a character told a lie that seemed harmless (the dog ate the homework, etc.). The little lie is now big; it has come back to haunt him.

   Now crank things up another notch: the lost item is irreplaceable, and the owner had promised to get the borrower a job at the local TV station; the missing child has a medical condition and cannot go long without medication, etc. How might this trouble be related to the character's desire? She was desperate to impress others, he was fixated on getting into medical school. Take the situation and go with it.

9. Create a tempting situation, one with universal appeal, or one that is specific to a certain character. Whatever the case, make the situation as tempting as possible, low risk, with almost no chance of discovery. Now, sketch out three versions of the story: (1) The character resists temptation; (2) She gives in and gets away with it; and (3) She gives in but either doesn't get away with it, doesn't like the results of her deed, or is tormented by a guilty conscience.

10. Think of a specific goal a character might have. Use your own experience or that of someone close to you (e.g., your ex-boyfriend's rock star dreams). Was the goal achieved or not? If so, was it easy or an uphill struggle? What obstacles would have made it a lot more difficult? If the goal was achieved, imagine it wasn't. If not, imagine what success would have been like.

### COLLABORATIVE

11. Most writers create stories intuitively, without a "game plan." Nonetheless, at some point you may get an idea for a story from its crisis, which will require plotting backward to find out how the character reached such an extreme point. This group exercise, adapted from John Gardner's *The Art of Fiction*, asks you to plot backward:

    A man (or woman) sets his house on fire, but insurance money is not the motive. Working in a small group, plot the story that led him to this point. Then choose three scenes that should be dramatized, in addition to the crisis scene in which the fire is set.

    Compare your stories and scenes with those of the other groups.

12. Every student should come to class with what he or she considers to be a good first line for a story—either invented or lifted from somewhere. Students can write these lines on the board, discuss them, and then vote on one line for the entire class to use. Everyone will begin a story using the same line. After writing for a short period of time, students may stop and read their exercises aloud in order to see how different people have used the line differently and in what various directions the stories have gone and might go.

13. In front of the class, try an improvisation. Two women or two men play roommates and best friends. Friend One has just decided to break up with a long-term boyfriend or girlfriend. In the first improvisation, Friend Two thinks this is a great idea and agrees with every reason that Friend One mentions. Let this run for a few minutes and see what happens. Then repeat the situation, but this time Friend Two thinks breaking up is the worst possible thing Friend One could do and argues with every justification offered.

    Afterward, have the actors and class audience discuss the differences. Which scene was more interesting? Which was harder to act and might therefore be harder to write?

14. This exercise derives from one called "The Story Machine" in *What If? Writing Exercises for Fiction Writers*, edited by Anne Bernays and Pamela Painter. Everyone gets ten index cards. On five of them write down an occupation or character label (e.g., mall Santa, kleptomaniac, surrogate mother, etc.). On the other five, write down an interesting, mildly unusual behavior or action. For the action, avoid the commonplace (reading a book, shopping) and the

outrageous (curing cancer, murder). Examples might include stockpiling appliances, punching someone in the nose, taking a pregnancy test, or shoplifting something worthless.

Collect all the cards of each category, shuffle the two piles, and pass them out so that everyone has five of each kind. Flip over one of each type of card, and then, looking at the pair, imagine the possible story behind it. Why did the mall Santa punch someone in the nose? Continue flipping pairs of cards until you find a combination that really sparks your imagination. (Reshuffle if necessary.) Once you've found the combination you like, write the story. What brought your character to this moment? What are the consequences of this action?

# 8

# CALL ME ISHMAEL
## *Point of View*

- *Who Speaks?*

- *To Whom?*

- *In What Form?*

- *At What Distance?*

- *Consistency: A Final Caution*

*Point of view* is the most complex element of fiction. We can label and analyze it in a number of different ways, but however we describe it, point of view ultimately concerns the relationship among writer, characters, and reader.

The first thing to do is to set aside the common use of the phrase "point of view" as synonymous with "opinion," as in *It's my point of view that they all ought to be shot.* Rather than thinking of point of view as an opinion or belief, begin instead with the more literal synonym of "vantage point." *Who* is standing *where* to watch the scene?

Since we are dealing with words on a page, these questions might be better translated as: *Who speaks? To whom? In what form? At what distance from the action?*

## Who Speaks?

The primary point-of-view decision that you as author must make before you can set down the first sentence of the story is *person.* This is the simplest and crudest subdivision that must be made in deciding who speaks. The story can be told . . .

- *in the third person* (she walked out into the harsh sunlight),
- *the second person* (you walked out into the harsh sunlight),
- *or the first person* (I walked out into the harsh sunlight).

From the reader's perspective, third- and second-person stories are told by an author; first-person stories, by the character acting as "I."

## THIRD PERSON

*Third person,* in which the author is telling the story, can be subdivided again according to the degree of knowledge the author assumes.

**Omniscience**    The *omniscient author* has total knowledge and tells us directly what we are supposed to think. As omniscient author you are God. You can:

1. Objectively report the action of the story;
2. Go into the mind of any character;
3. Interpret for us that character's appearance, speech, actions, and thoughts, even if the character cannot do so;
4. Move freely in time or space to give us a panoramic, telescopic, microscopic, or historical view; tell us what has happened elsewhere or in the past or what will happen in the future; and
5. Provide general reflections, judgments, and truths.

In all these aspects, we will accept what the omniscient author tells us. If you tell us that Ruth is a good woman, that Jeremy doesn't really understand his own motives, that the moon is going to explode in four hours, and that everybody will be better off for it, we will believe you. Here is a paragraph that blatantly exhibits all five of these areas of knowledge.

(1) Joe glared at the screaming baby. (2) Frightened by his scowl, the baby gulped and screamed louder. I hate that thing, Joe thought. (3) But it was not really hatred that he felt. (4) Only two years ago he himself had screamed like that. (5) Children can't tell hatred from fear.

This illustration is awkwardly compressed, but authors well in control of their craft can move easily from one area of knowledge to another. In the first scene of *War and Peace,* Tolstoy describes Anna Scherer.

To be an enthusiast had become her social vocation, and sometimes even when she did not feel like it, she became enthusiastic in order not to disappoint the expectations of those who knew her. The subdued smile which, though it did not suit her faded features, always played around her lips, expressed as in a spoiled child, a continual consciousness of her charming defect, which she neither wished, nor could, nor considered it necessary to correct.

In two sentences Tolstoy tells us what is in Anna's mind, what the expectations of her acquaintances are, what she looks like, what suits her, what she can and cannot do; and he offers a general reflection on spoiled children.

The omniscient voice is the voice of the classical epic ("And Meleager, far-off, knew nothing of this, but felt his vitals burning with fever"), of the Bible ("So the Lord sent a pestilence upon Israel; and there fell seventy thousand men"), and of most nineteenth-century novels ("Tito put out his hand to help him, and so strangely quick are men's souls that in this moment, when he began to feel that his atonement was accepted, he had a darting thought of the irksome efforts it entailed"). But it is one of the manifestations of modern literature's movement downward in class from heroic to common characters, from external action to the psychological action of the mind, that authors of realistic fiction have largely avoided the godlike stance of the omniscient author and have chosen to restrict themselves to fewer areas of knowledge.

**Limited Omniscience**   The *limited omniscient* viewpoint is one in which the author may move with some, but not all, of the omniscient author's freedom. The most commonly used form of the limited omniscient point of view is one in which the author can see events objectively and also grants himself or herself access to the mind of one character, but *not* to the minds of the others, nor to any explicit powers of judgment. Limited omniscience is particularly useful for the short story because it very quickly establishes the point-of-view character or *means of perception*. The short story is so compressed a form that there is rarely time or space to develop more than one consciousness. Staying with external observation and one character's thoughts helps control the focus and avoid awkward point-of-view shifts. A further advantage of limited omniscience is that it mimics our individual experience of life, that is, our own inability to penetrate the minds and motivations of others, which can lead to the kinds of conflicts or struggles for connection that inspire much fiction.

Limited omniscience is also frequently used for the novel, as in Gail Godwin's *The Odd Woman*.

> It was ten o'clock on the evening of the same day, and the permanent residents of the household on the mountain were restored to routines and sobriety. Jane, on the other hand, sat by herself in the kitchen, a glass of Scotch before her on the cleanly wiped table, going deeper and deeper into a mood she could recognize only as unfamiliar. She could not describe it; it was both frightening and satisfying. It was like letting go and being taken somewhere. She tried to trace it back. When, exactly, had it started?

It is clear here that the author has limited her omniscience. She is not going to tell us the ultimate truth about Jane's soul, nor is she going to define for us the unfamiliar mood that the character herself cannot define. The author has the facts at her disposal, and she has Jane's thoughts, and that is all.

The advantage of the limited omniscient voice is immediacy. Here, because we are not allowed to know more than Jane does about her own thoughts and feelings, we grope *with* her toward understanding. In the process, a contract has been made between the author and the reader, and this contract must not now be broken. If at this point the author should step in and answer Jane's question "When, exactly, had it started?" with "Jane was never to remember this, but in fact it had started one afternoon when she was two years old," we would feel it as an abrupt and uncalled-for *authorial intrusion*. Nevertheless, within the limits the author has set herself, there is fluidity and a range of possibilities.

**The Objective Author**    As an objective author, you restrict your knowledge to the external facts that might be observed by a human witness; to the senses of sight, sound, smell, taste, and touch. In the story "Hills Like White Elephants," Ernest Hemingway reports what is said and done by a quarreling couple, both without any direct revelation of the characters' thoughts and without comment.

> The American and the girl with him sat at a table in the shade, outside the building. It was very hot and the express from Barcelona would come in forty minutes. It stopped at this junction for two minutes and went on to Madrid.
> "What should we drink?" the girl asked. She had taken off her hat and put it on the table.
> "It's pretty hot," the man said.
> "Let's drink beer."
> "Dos cervezas," the man said into the curtain.
> "Big ones?" a woman asked from the doorway.
> "Yes. Two big ones."
> The woman brought two glasses of beer and two felt pads. She put the felt pads and the beer glasses on the table and looked at the man and the girl. The girl was looking off at the line of hills. They were white in the sun and the country was brown and dry.

In the course of this story we learn, entirely by inference, that the girl is pregnant and that she feels herself coerced by the man into having an abortion. Neither pregnancy nor abortion is ever mentioned. The narrative remains clipped, austere, and external. What does Hemingway gain by this pretense of objective reporting? The reader is allowed to discover what is really happening. The characters avoid the subject, prevaricate, and pretend, but they betray their real meanings and feelings through gestures, repetitions, and slips of the tongue. The reader, focus directed by the author, learns by inference, as in life, so that we finally have the pleasure of knowing the characters better than they know themselves.

## SECOND PERSON

First and third persons are most common in literature; the second person remains an idiosyncratic and experimental form, but it is worth mentioning because several contemporary authors have been attracted to its possibilities.

Lorrie Moore's story "How to Become a Writer" illustrates how a reader is made into a character through second person.

First, try to be something, anything, else. A movie star/astronaut. A movie star/missionary. A movie star/kindergarten teacher. President of the World. Fail miserably. It is best if you fail at an early age—say, fourteen. Early, critical disillusionment is necessary so that at fifteen you can write long haiku sentences about thwarted desire. It is a pond, a cherry blossom, a wind brushing against sparrow wing leaving for mountain. Count the syllables. Show it to your mom.

Here the author assigns you, the reader, specific characteristics and reactions, and thereby—assuming that you go along with her characterization of you—pulls you deeper and more intimately into the story.

Some writers choose second person to depict trauma, as its slight sense of detachment mutes possible melodrama and mirrors the sense of shock; others may use it to make a highly individual experience feel more universal.

The second person is the basic mode of the story *only when a character* is referred to as *you*. When one character addresses "you" in letter or monologue, that narrative is still told by the "I" character. When an omniscient author addresses the reader as *you* (*You will remember that John Doderring was left dangling on the cliff at Dover*), this is called "direct address" and does not alter the basic third-person mode of the piece. Only when "you" becomes an actor in the drama, so designated by the author, is the story or novel written in second person.

Unlike third or first person, second person draws attention to itself, and it can also be difficult to maintain—it's easy to slip back into third or first person. Also, some readers may resist second person because they don't identify with the character they are supposed to be in the story. (*You go into a bar. You get very, very drunk.*) It is unlikely that the second person will ever become a major mode of narration as the first and third person are, but for precisely that reason you may find it an attractive experiment.

### FIRST PERSON

A story is told in the first person when one of its characters relates the story's action and events. The term "narrator" is sometimes loosely used to refer to any teller of a tale, but strictly speaking a story has a narrator only when it is told in the first person by one of the characters. This character may be the protagonist, the *I* telling *my* story, in which case that character is a *central narrator* (as in "Who's Irish?" at the end of this chapter); or the character may be telling a story about someone else, in which case he or she is a *peripheral narrator*.

In either case it's important to indicate early which kind of narrator we have so that we know who the story's protagonist is, as in the first paragraph of Alan Sillitoe's "The Loneliness of the Long-Distance Runner."

As soon as I got to Borstal they made me a long-distance cross-country runner. I suppose they thought I was just the build for it because I was long and skinny for my age (and still am) and in any case I didn't mind it much, to tell you the truth, because running had always been made much of in our family, especially running away from the police.

The focus here is immediately thrown on the *I* of the story, and we expect that *I* to be the central character whose desires and decisions impel the action.

But from the opening lines of Amy Bloom's "Silver Water," it is the sister, Rose, who is brought alive through the description of her marvelous singing voice, while the narrator, Violet, is established as an observer and protector of her subject.

> My sister's voice was like mountain water in a silver pitcher; the clear, blue beauty of it cools you and lifts you up beyond your heat, beyond your body. After we went to see *La Traviata*, when she was fourteen and I was twelve, she elbowed me in the parking lot and said, "Check this out." And she opened her mouth unnaturally wide and her voice came out, so crystalline and bright, that all the departing operagoers stood frozen by their cars, unable to take out their keys or open their doors until she had finished and then they cheered like hell.
>
> That's what I like to remember and that's the story I told to all of her therapists. I wanted them to know her, to know that who they saw was not all there was to see.

The central narrator is always, as the term implies, at the center of the action; the peripheral narrator may be in virtually any position that is not the center. He or she may be the second most important character in the story ("Gryphon"), or may appear to be a bystander for much of the story. It is even possible to make the first-person narrator plural, as William Faulkner does in "A Rose for Emily," where the story is told by a narrator identified only as one of "us," the people of the town in which the action has taken place.

That a narrator may be either central or peripheral, that a character may tell either his or her own story or someone else's, is both commonly assumed and obviously logical. But the author and editor Rust Hills, in his book *Writing in General and the Short Story in Particular*, takes interesting and persuasive exception to this idea. When point of view fails, Hills argues, it is always because the perception we are using for the course of the story is different from that of the character who is moved or changed by the action. Even when a narrator seems to be a peripheral observer and the story is "about" someone else, in fact it is the narrator who is changed, and must be, in order for us to be satisfied by our emotional identification with him or her.

> This, I believe, is what will always be the case in successful fiction: that either the character moved by the action will be the point-of-view character, or else the point-of-view character will *become* the character moved by the action. Call it Hills' Law.

Obviously, this view does not mean that we have to throw out the useful fictional device of the peripheral narrator. Hills uses the familiar example of *The Great Gatsby* to illustrate his meaning. Nick Carroway as a peripheral narrator observes and tells the story of Jay Gatsby, but by the end of the book it is Nick's life that has been changed by what he has observed.

Anton Chekhov (as paraphrased by Tobias Wolff) cautioned, "The narrator cannot escape the *consequences* of the story he is telling. If he does, it's not a story. It's an anecdote, a tale, or something else."

Central or peripheral, a first-person narrator is a character, so it's vital to remember that she or he has all the limitations of a human being and cannot be omniscient. The narrator is confined to reporting what she or he could realistically know. More than that, although the narrator may certainly interpret actions, deliver dictums, and predict the future, these remain the fallible opinions of a human being; we are not bound to accept them as we are bound to accept the interpretations, truths, and predictions of the omniscient author. You may want us to accept the narrator's word, and then the most difficult part of your task, and the touchstone of your story's success, will be to convince us to trust and believe the narrator. On the other hand, it may be an important part of your purpose that we should reject the narrator's opinions and form our own. If the answer to *Who speaks?* is *a child, a bigot, a jealous lover, an animal, a schizophrenic, a murderer, a liar*, the implications may be that the narrator speaks with limitations we do not necessarily share. To the extent that the narrator displays and betrays such limitations, she or he is an *unreliable narrator*.

Here is a woman, imperious and sour, who tells her own story.

I have always, always, tried to do right and help people. It's a part of my community duty and my duty to God. But I can tell you right now, you don't never gets no thanks for it! . . .

Use to be a big ole fat sloppy woman live cross the street went to my church. She had a different man in her house with her every month! She got mad at me for tellin the minister on her about all them men! Now, I'm doin my duty and she got mad! I told her somebody had to be the pillar of the community and if it had to be me, so be it! She said I was the pill of the community and a lotta other things, but I told the minister that too and pretty soon she was movin away. Good! I like a clean community!

J. California Cooper, "The Watcher"

We mistrust every judgment this woman makes, but we are also aware of an author we do trust, manipulating the narrator's tone to expose her. The outburst is fraught with ironies, but because the narrator is unaware of them, they are directed against herself. We can hear that interference is being dressed up as duty. When she brags in cliché, we agree that she's more of a pill than a pillar. When she appropriates biblical language—"so be it!"—we suspect that even the minister might agree. Punctuation itself, the self-righteous overuse of the exclamation point, suggests her inappropriate intensity. It occurs to us we'd probably like the look of that "big ole fat sloppy" neighbor; and we know for certain why that neighbor moved away.

In this case the narrator is wholly unreliable, and we're unlikely to accept any judgment she could make. But it is also possible for a narrator to be reliable in some areas of value and unreliable in others. Mark Twain's Huckleberry Finn is a famous case in point. Here Huck has decided to free his friend Jim, and he is astonished that Tom Sawyer is going along with the plan.

> Here was a boy that was respectable, and well brung up; and had a character to lose; and folks at home that had characters; and he was bright and not leather-headed; and knowing and not ignorant; and not mean, but kind; and yet here he was, without any more pride, or rightness, or feeling, than to stoop to this business, and make himself a shame, and his family a shame, before everybody. I couldn't understand it, no way at all.

The extended irony in this excerpt is that slavery should be defended by the respectable, the bright, the knowing, the kind, and those of character. We reject Huck's assessment of Tom as well as the implied assessment of himself as worth so little that he has nothing to lose by freeing a slave. Huck's moral instincts are better than he himself can understand. (Notice, incidentally, how Huck's lack of education is communicated by word choice and syntax and how sparse the misspellings are.) So author and reader are in intellectual opposition to Huck the narrator, but morally identify with him. Similarly reliable "unreliable" narrators, whose distorted views reveal a strangely accurate portrait of the social institutions that confine them, include Chief Bromden, the narrator of Ken Kesey's *One Flew Over the Cuckoo's Nest*, and the "hysterical" wife and patient, forbidden to write, who relates Charlotte Perkins Gilman's 1892 story "The Yellow Wallpaper."

THE TRUTH IS NOT DISTORTED HERE, but rather a certain distortion is used to get at the truth.

Flannery O'Connor

The unreliable narrator—who has become one of the most popular characters in modern fiction—is far from a newcomer to literature and in fact predates fiction. Every drama contains characters who speak for themselves and present their own cases, and from whom we are partly or wholly distanced in one area of value or another. So we admire Oedipus's intellect but are exasperated by his lack of intuition, we identify with Othello's morality but mistrust his logic, we trust Mr. Spock's brain but not his heart, we count on Bridget Jones's wit, as revealed in her diary, but not her judgment. As these examples suggest, the unreliable narrator often presents us with an example of consistent inconsistency and always presents us with dramatic irony, because we always "know" more than he or she does about the characters, the events, and the significance of both.

THERE SHOULD BE THE ILLUSION that it's the character's point of view, when in fact it isn't; it's really the narrator who is there but who doesn't make herself . . . known in that role. . . . What I really want is that intimacy in which the reader is under the impression that he isn't really reading this; that he is participating in it as he goes along.

Toni Morrison

## To Whom?

In choosing a point of view, the author implies an identity not only for the teller of the tale, but also for the intended audience. To whom is the story being told?

### THE READER

Most fiction is addressed to a literary convention, "the reader." When we open a book, we tacitly accept our role as a member of this unspecified audience. After all, the most common assumption of the tale-teller, whether omniscient author or narrating character, is that the reader is an open and amenable Everyman, and that the telling needs no justification.

### ANOTHER CHARACTER

More specifically, the story may be told to *another character*, or *characters*, in which case we as readers "overhear" it; the teller of the tale does not acknowledge us even by implication.

In the *epistolary* novel or story, the narrative consists entirely of letters written from one character to another, or between characters. The recipient of the letter may be a stranger or a close friend or relative, like the near-annual readers of *The Christmas Letters*, by Lee Smith.

First, my apologies for not writing a Christmas letter last year (for not returning calls, for not returning letters, etc.). The fact is, for a long time I couldn't do anything. Not a damn thing. Nothing. I was shell-shocked, immobilized. This was followed by a period when I did *too many things*. Marybeth, who has been through it, wrote to me about this time, saying, "Don't make any big decisions"— very good advice, and I wish I'd followed it. Instead, I agreed to a separation agreement, then to a quick no-fault divorce, then to Sandy's plan of selling the house P.D.Q. I just wanted everything *over with*—the way you feel that sudden irresistible urge to clean out your closet sometimes.

Or the convention of the story may be that of a monologue, spoken aloud by one character to another.

May I, *monsieur,* offer my services without running the risk of intruding? I fear you may not be able to make yourself understood by the worthy ape who presides over the fate of this establishment. In fact, he speaks nothing but Dutch. Unless you authorize me to plead your case, he will not guess that you want gin.

Albert Camus, *The Fall*

Again, the possible variations are infinite: the narrator may speak in intimate confessional to a friend or lover, or may present his case to a jury or a mob; she may be writing a highly technical report of the welfare situation, designed to hide her emotions; he may be pouring out his heart in a love letter he knows (and we know) he will never send.

In any of these cases, the convention employed is the opposite of that employed in a story told to "the reader." The listener as well as the teller is involved in the action; the assumption is not that we readers are there but that we are not. We are eavesdroppers, with all the ambiguous intimacy that position implies.

### THE SELF

An even greater intimacy is implied if the character's story is as secret as a diary or as private as a mind, addressed to *the self* and not intended to be heard by anyone inside or outside the action.

In a *diary* or *journal,* the convention is that the thoughts are written but not expected to be read by anyone except the writer.

Tuesday 3 January

9 A.M. Ugh. Cannot face thought of going to work. Only thing which makes it tolerable is thought of seeing Daniel again, but even that is inadvisable since I am fat, have spot on chin, and desire only to sit on cushion eating chocolate and watching Xmas specials. It seems wrong and unfair that Christmas, with its stressful and unmanageable financial and emotional challenges, should first be forced upon one wholly against one's will, then rudely snatched away just when one is starting to get into it.

Helen Fielding, *Bridget Jones's Diary*

The protagonist here is clearly using her diary to vent her feelings and does not intend it to be read by anyone else. Still, she has deliberately externalized her secret thoughts in a journal.

### INTERIOR MONOLOGUE

Because the author has the power to enter a character's mind, the reader also has the power to eavesdrop on that character's thoughts. Overheard thoughts are generally of two kinds, of which the more common is *interior monologue,* the convention being that we follow that character's thoughts in their sequence.

I must organize myself. I must, as they say, pull myself together, dump this cat from my lap, stir—yes, resolve, move, do. But do what? My will is like the rosy dustlike light in this room: soft, diffuse, and gently comforting. It lets me do . . . anything . . . nothing. My ears hear what they happen to; I eat what's put before me; my eyes see what blunders into them; my thoughts are not thoughts, they are dreams. I'm empty or I'm full . . . depending; and I cannot choose. I sink my claws in Tick's fur and scratch the bones of his back until his rear rises amorously. Mr. Tick, I murmur, I must organize myself, I must pull myself together. And Mr. Tick rolls over on his belly, all ooze.

William H. Gass, "In the Heart of the Heart of the Country"

This interior monologue ranges, as human thoughts do, from sense impression to self-admonishment, from cat to light to eyes and ears, from specific to general and back again. But the logical connections between these things are all provided; the mind "thinks" logically and grammatically as if the character were trying to express himself.

## STREAM OF CONSCIOUSNESS

*Stream of consciousness* acknowledges the fact that the human mind does not operate with the order and clarity of the monologue just quoted. Even what little we know of its operations makes clear that it skips, elides, makes and breaks images, leaps faster and further than any mere sentence can suggest. Any mind at any moment is simultaneously accomplishing dozens of tasks that cannot be conveyed simultaneously. As you read this sentence, part of your mind is following the sense of it; part of your mind is directing your hand to hold the book open; part of it is twisting your spine into a more comfortable position; part of it is still lingering on the last interesting image of this text, Mr. Tick rolling over on his belly, which reminds you of a cat you had once that was also *all ooze*, which reminds you that you're nearly out of milk and have to finish this chapter before the store closes—and so forth.

In *Ulysses*, James Joyce tried to catch the speed and multiplicity of the mind with the technique that has come to be known as stream of consciousness. The device is difficult and in many ways thankless: since the speed of thought is so much faster than that of writing or speaking, and stream of consciousness tries to suggest the process as well as the content of the mind, *it requires a much more—not less—rigorous selection and arrangement* than ordinary grammar requires. But Joyce and a very few other writers have handled stream of consciousness as an ebullient and exciting way of capturing the mind.

Yes because he never did a thing like that before as ask to get his breakfast in bed with a couple of eggs since the City Arms hotel when he used to be pretending to be laid up with a sick voice doing his highness to make himself interesting to that old faggot Mrs. Riordan that he thought he had a great leg of and she never left us a farthing all for masses for herself . . .

James Joyce, *Ulysses*

The preceding two examples, of interior monologue and stream of consciousness, respectively, are written in the first person, so that we overhear the minds of narrator characters. We may also overhear the thoughts of the characters through the third-person omniscient and limited omniscient authors, as in John Edgar Wideman's *tour de force* story "The Tambourine Lady." Here, Wideman succeeds in the challenging fusion of third-person narrative and stream of consciousness, so that although the answer to the question "who speaks?" is technically "the author," nevertheless we are aware of the point-of-view character speaking to herself in rapid-fire associative thought:

> . . . She thinks about how long it takes to get to the end of your prayers, how the world might be over and gone while you are still saying the words to yourself. Words her mama taught her, words her mama said her mother had taught her so somebody would always be saying them world without end amen. So God would not forget his children . . .

## In What Form?

The form of the story also contributes to the overall point of view. That form may announce itself as a generalized *story*, either *written* or *spoken;* or it may suggest *reportage, confessional, interior monologue,* or *stream of consciousness;* or it may be overtly identified as *monologue, oratory, journal,* or *diary.* This list is not exhaustive; you can tell your story in the form of a catalog or a television commercial as long as you can also contrive to give it the form of a story.

Form is important to point of view because the form in which a story is told indicates the degree of self-consciousness on the part of the teller; this will in turn affect the language chosen, the intimacy of the relationship, and the honesty of the telling. A written account will imply less spontaneity, on the whole, than one that appears to be spoken aloud, which suggests less spontaneity than thought. A narrator writing a letter to his grandmother may be less honest than he is when he tells the same facts aloud to his friend.

Certain relationships established by the narrative between teller and audience make certain forms more likely than others, but almost any combination of answers is possible to the questions: *Who speaks? To whom? In what form?* If you are speaking as an omniscient author to the literary convention of "the reader," we may assume that you are using the convention of "written story" as your form. But you might say:

> Wait, step over here a minute. What's this in the corner, stuffed down between the bedpost and the wall?

If you do this, you slip at least momentarily into the different convention of the spoken word—the effect is that we are drawn more immediately into the scene—and the point of view of the whole is slightly altered. A central narrator might be thinking, and therefore "talking to herself," while actually angrily addressing her thoughts to another character. Conversely, one character might be writing a letter to another but letting the conscious act of writing deteriorate into a betrayal of his own secret thoughts. Any complexities such as these will alter and inform the total point of view.

## At What Distance?

As with the chemist at her microscope and the lookout in his tower, fictional point of view always involves the *distance*, close or far, of the perceiver from the thing perceived. *Authorial distance*, sometimes called *psychic distance*, is the degree to which we as readers feel on the one hand intimacy and identification with, or on the other hand detachment and alienation from, the characters.

When desired, a sense of distance may be increased through the use of abstract nouns, summary, typicality, and apparent objectivity. Such techniques, which in other contexts might be seen as writing flaws, are employed in the following passage purposely to detach readers from characters.

> It started in the backyards. At first the men concentrated on heat and smoke, and on dangerous thrusts with long forks. Their wives gave them aprons in railroad stripes, with slogans on the front—Hot Stuff, The Boss—to spur them on. Then it began to get mixed up who should do the dishes, and you can't fall back on paper plates forever, and around that time the wives got tired of making butterscotch brownies and jello salads with grated carrots in them and wanted to make money instead, and one thing led to another.
>
> Margaret Atwood, "Simmering"

Conversely, closeness and sympathy can be achieved by concrete detail, scene, a character's thoughts, and so forth.

> She dreams she does not already have three children. A squeeze around the flowers in her hands chokes off three and four and five years of breath. Instantly she is ashamed and frightened in her superstition. She looks for the first time at the preacher, forces humility into her eyes, as if she believes he is, in fact, a man of God. She can imagine God, a small black boy, timidly pulling the preacher's coattail.
>
> Alice Walker, "Roselily"

Or a combination of techniques may make us feel simultaneously sympathetic and detached—a frequent effect of comedy—as in this example:

> I'm a dishwasher in a restaurant. I'm not trying to impress anybody. I'm not bragging. It's just what I do. It's not the glamorous job people make it out to be. Sure, you make a lot of dough and everybody looks up to you and respects you, but then again there's a lot of responsibility. It weighs on you. It wears on you. Everybody wants to be a dishwasher these days, I guess, but they've got an idealistic view of it.
>
> Robert McBrearty, "The Dishwasher"

As author you may ask us to identify completely with one character and totally condemn another. One character may judge another harshly while you as author suggest that we should qualify that judgment. If there is also a narrator, that narrator may think himself morally superior while behind his back you make sure that we will think him morally deficient.

The one relationship in which there must not be any distance, however, is between author and reader.

It is a frustrating experience for many beginning (and established) authors to find that, whereas they meant the protagonist to appear sensitive, their readers find him self-pitying; whereas the author meant her to be witty, the readers find her vulgar. When this happens there is a failure of authorial or psychic distance: The author did not have sufficient perspective on the character to convince us to share his or her judgment. I recall one class in which a student author had written, with excellent use of image and scene, the story of a young man who fell in love with an exceptionally beautiful young woman, and whose feelings turned to revulsion when he found out she had had a mastectomy. The most vocal feminist in the class loved this story, which she described as "the exposé of a skuzzwort." This was not, from the author's point of view, a successful reading of his story. He had meant for the young man in the story to be seen as a sympathetic character.

WHEN WRITERS ARE SELF-CONSCIOUS about themselves as writers they often keep a great distance from their characters, sounding as if they were writing encyclopedia entries instead of stories. Their hesitancy about physical and psychological intimacy can be a barrier to vital fiction.

Conversely, a narration that makes readers hear the characters' heavy breathing and smell their emotional anguish diminishes distance. Readers feel so close to the characters that, for those magical moments, they *become* those characters.

Jerome Stern

A writer may also create either distance or closeness through the use of time, space, tone, and irony. A story that happened long ago in a far away land, told by a detached narrator, won't feel the same as one happening in present tense, told by one of the characters. A story's tone and use of irony are also indications of how the reader should view the characters and their situations. For example, in the story "Orientation," which appears at the end of this chapter, we can't help but view the office workers from a distance because of the narrator's tone. He describes the serial killer in the next cubicle—and the way he kills people—in the same flat, casual way he describes another worker's love of penguins.

POINT OF VIEW

### Who Speaks?

| *The Author* | *The Author* | *A Character* |
|---|---|---|
| In: Third Person | In: Second Person | In: First Person |
| Editorial Omniscient | "You" as Character | Central Narrator |
| Limited Omniscient | "You" as Reader- | Peripheral Narrator |
| Objective | Turned-Character | |

### To Whom?

| The Reader | Another Character or Characters | The Self |
|---|---|---|

### In What Form?

Story, Monologue, Letter, Journal, Interior Monologue,
Stream of Consciousness, etc.

### At What Distance?

Complete Identification          Complete Opposition

Choosing and *controlling* the psychic distance that best suits a given story is one of the most elusive challenges a writer faces. The good news for novice writers feeling overwhelmed by all these considerations is that point-of-view choices, like plot and theme, are seldom calculated and preplanned. Rather, point of view tends to evolve organically as a story develops, and you can usually trust intuition to guide you through several drafts. It is when a story is well underway that analysis of its specific point-of-view issues becomes most useful, and the feedback of other workshop members may be of particular value.

## Consistency: A Final Caution

In establishing the story's point of view, you make your own rules, but having made them, you must stick to them. Your position as a writer is analogous to that of a poet who may choose whether to write free verse or a ballad stanza. If the poet chooses the stanza, then he or she is obliged to rhyme. Beginning writers of prose fiction are often tempted to shift viewpoint when it is both unnecessary and disruptive for readers.

Leo's neck flushed against the prickly weave of his uniform collar. He concentrated on his buttons and tried not to look into the face of the bandmaster, who, however, was more amused than angry.

This is an awkward point-of-view shift because, having felt Leo's embarrassment with him, we are suddenly asked to leap into the bandmaster's feelings. The shift can be corrected by moving instead from Leo's mind to an observation that he might make.

> Leo's neck flushed against the prickly weave of his uniform collar. He concentrated on his buttons and tried not to look into the face of the bandmaster, who, however, was astonishingly smiling.

The rewrite is easier to follow because we remain with Leo's mind as he observes that the bandmaster is not angry. It further serves the purpose of implying that Leo fails to concentrate on his buttons, and so intensifies his confusion.

Apart from the use of significant detail, there is no more important skill for a writer of fiction to grasp than this, the control of point of view. Sometimes it may be hard simply to recognize that your narrative has leapt from one point of view to another—often, in workshop, students are troubled by a point-of-view shift in someone else's story but can't spot one in their own. In other cases there's a healthy desire to explore every possibility in a scene, and a mistaken sense that this can't be done without changing point of view. Indeed, no writing rule is so frequently broken to such original and inventive effect as *consistency in point of view*, as several stories in this volume attest. Yet the general rule of consistency holds, and a writer shows his amateurism in the failure to stick to a single point of view. Once established, point of view constitutes a contract between author and reader, and it will be difficult to break the contract gracefully. If you have restricted yourself to the mind of James Lordly for five pages, as he observes the actions of Mrs. Grumms and her cats, you will violate the contract by suddenly dipping into Mrs. Grumms's mind to let us know what she thinks of James Lordly. We are likely to feel misused, and likely to cancel the contract altogether, if you then suddenly give us the thoughts of the cats.

# Orientation

### DANIEL OROZCO

Those are the offices and these are the cubicles. That's my cubicle there, and this is your cubicle. This is your phone. Never answer your phone. Let the Voicemail System answer it. This is your Voicemail System Manual. There are no personal phone calls allowed. We do, however, allow for emergencies. If you must make an emergency phone call, ask your supervisor first. If you can't find your supervisor, ask Phillip Spiers, who sits over there. He'll check with Clarissa Nicks, who sits over there. If you make an emergency phone call without asking, you may be let go.

These are your IN and OUT boxes. All the forms in your IN box must be logged in by the date shown in the upper left-hand corner, initialed by you in the upper right-hand corner, and distributed to the Processing Analyst whose name is numerically coded in the lower left-hand corner. The lower right-hand corner is left blank. Here's your Processing Analyst Numerical Code Index. And here's your Forms Processing Procedures Manual.

You must pace your work. What do I mean? I'm glad you asked that. We pace our work according to the eight-hour workday. If you have twelve hours of work in your IN box, for example, you must compress that work into the eight-hour day. If you have one hour of work in your IN box, you must expand that work to fill the eight-hour day. That was a good question. Feel free to ask questions. Ask too many questions, however, and you may be let go.

That is our receptionist. She is a temp. We go through receptionists here. They quit with alarming frequency. Be polite and civil to the temps. Learn their names, and invite them to lunch occasionally. But don't get close to them, as it only makes it more difficult when they leave. And they always leave. You can be sure of that.

The men's room is over there. The women's room is over there. John LaFountaine, who sits over there, uses the women's room occasionally. He says it is accidental. We know better, but we let it pass. John LaFountaine is harmless, his forays into the forbidden territory of the women's room simply a benign thrill, a faint blip on the dull flat line of his life.

Russell Nash, who sits in the cubicle to your left, is in love with Amanda Pierce, who sits in the cubicle to your right. They ride the same bus together after work. For Amanda Pierce, it is just a tedious bus ride made less tedious by the idle nattering of Russell Nash. But for Russell Nash, it is the highlight of his day. It is the highlight of his life. Russell Nash has put on forty pounds, and grows fatter with each passing month, nibbling on chips and cookies while peeking glumly over the partitions at Amanda Pierce, and gorging himself at home on cold pizza and ice cream while watching adult videos on TV.

Amanda Pierce, in the cubicle to your right, has a six-year-old son named Jamie, who is autistic. Her cubicle is plastered from top to bottom with the boy's crayon artwork—sheet after sheet of precisely drawn concentric circles and ellipses, in black and yellow. She rotates them every other Friday. Be sure to comment on them. Amanda Pierce also has a husband, who is a lawyer. He subjects her to an escalating array of painful and humiliating sex games, to which Amanda Pierce reluctantly submits. She comes to work exhausted and freshly wounded each morning, wincing from the abrasions to her breasts, or the bruises on her abdomen, or the second-degree burns on the backs of her thighs.

But we're not supposed to know any of this. Do not let on. If you let on, you may be let go.

Amanda Pierce, who tolerates Russell Nash, is in love with Albert Bosch, whose office is over there. Albert Bosch, who only dimly registers Amanda Pierce's existence, has eyes only for Ellie Tapper, who sits over there. Ellie Tapper, who hates Albert Bosch, would walk through fire for Curtis Lance. But Curtis Lance hates Ellie Tapper. Isn't the world a funny place? Not in the ha-ha sense, of course.

Anika Bloom sits in that cubicle. Last year, while reviewing quarterly reports in a meeting with Barry Hacker, Anika Bloom's left palm began to bleed. She fell into a trance, stared into her hand, and told Barry Hacker when and how his wife would die. We laughed it off. She was, after all, a new employee. But Barry Hacker's wife is dead. So unless you want to know exactly when and how you'll die, never talk to Anika Bloom.

Colin Heavey sits in that cubicle over there. He was new once, just like you. We warned him about Anika Bloom. But at last year's Christmas Potluck, he felt sorry for her when he saw that no one was talking to her. Colin Heavey brought her a drink. He hasn't been himself since. Colin Heavey is doomed. There's nothing he can do about it, and we are powerless to help him. Stay away from Colin Heavey. Never give any of your work to him. If he asks to do something, tell him you have to check with me. If he asks again, tell him I haven't gotten back to you.

This is the Fire Exit. There are several on this floor, and they are marked accordingly. We have a Floor Evacuation Review every three months, and an Escape Route Quiz once a month. We have our Biannual Fire Drill twice a year, and our Annual Earthquake Drill once a year. These are precautions only. These things never happen.

For your information, we have a comprehensive health plan. Any catastrophic illness, any unforeseen tragedy is completely covered. All dependents are completely covered. Larry Bagdikian, who sits over there, has six daughters. If anything were to happen to any of his girls, or to all of them, if all six were to simultaneously fall victim to illness or injury—stricken with a hideous degenerative muscle disease or some rare toxic blood disorder, sprayed with semiautomatic gunfire while on a class field trip, or attacked in their bunk beds by some prowling nocturnal lunatic—if any of this were to pass, Larry's girls would all be taken care of. Larry Bagdikian would not have to pay one dime. He would have nothing to worry about.

We also have a generous vacation and sick leave policy. We have an excellent disability insurance plan. We have a stable and profitable pension fund. We get group discounts for the symphony, and block seating at the ballpark. We get commuter ticket books for the bridge. We have Direct Deposit. We are all members of Costco.

This is our kitchenette. And this, this is our Mr. Coffee. We have a coffee pool, into which we each pay two dollars a week for coffee, filters, sugar, and CoffeeMate. If you prefer Cremora or half-and-half to CoffeeMate, there is a special pool for three dollars per week. If you prefer Sweet'n Low to sugar, there is a special pool for two-fifty a week. We do not do decaf. You are allowed to join the coffee pool of your choice, but you are not allowed to touch the Mr. Coffee.

This is the microwave oven. You are allowed to *heat* food in the microwave oven. You are not, however, allowed to *cook* food in the microwave oven.

We get one hour for lunch. We also get one fifteen-minute break in the morning, and one fifteen-minute break in the afternoon. Always take your breaks. If you skip a break, it is gone forever. For your information, your break is a privilege, not a right. If you abuse the break policy, we are authorized to rescind your breaks. Lunch, however, is a right, not a privilege. If you abuse the lunch policy, our hands will be tied, and we will be forced to look the other way. We will not enjoy that.

This is the refrigerator. You may put your lunch in it. Barry Hacker, who sits over there, steals food from this refrigerator. His petty theft is an outlet for his grief. Last New Year's Eve, while kissing his wife, a blood vessel burst in her brain.

Barry Hacker's wife was two months pregnant at the time, and lingered in a coma for half a year before dying. It was a tragic loss for Barry Hacker. He hasn't been himself since. Barry Hacker's wife was a beautiful woman. She was also completely covered. Barry Hacker did not have to pay one dime. But his dead wife haunts him. She haunts all of us. We have seen her, reflected in the monitors of our computers, moving past our cubicles. We have seen the dim shadow of her face in our photocopies. She pencils herself in in the receptionist's appointment book with the notation: To see Barry Hacker. She has left messages in the receptionist's Voicemail box, messages garbled by the electronic chirrups and buzzes in the phone line, her voice echoing from an immense distance within the ambient hum. But the voice is hers. And beneath her voice, beneath the tidal *whoosh* of static and hiss, the gurgling and crying of a baby can be heard.

In any case, if you bring a lunch, put a little something extra in the bag for Barry Hacker. We have four Barrys in this office. Isn't that a coincidence?

This is Matthew Payne's office. He is our Unit Manager, and his door is always closed. We have never seen him, and you will never see him. But he is here. You can be sure of that. He is all around us.

This is the Custodian's Closet. You have no business in the Custodian's Closet.

And this, this is our Supplies Cabinet. If you need supplies see Curtis Lance. He will log you in on the Supplies Cabinet Authorization Log, then give you a Supplies Authorization Slip. Present your pink copy of the Supplies Authorization Slip to Ellie Tapper. She will log you in on the Supplies Cabinet Key Log, then give you the key. Because the Supplies Cabinet is located outside the Unit Manager's office, you must be very quiet. Gather your supplies quietly. The Supplies Cabinet is divided into four sections. Section One contains letterhead stationery, blank paper and envelopes, memo and note pads, and so on. Section Two contains pens and pencils and typewriter and printer ribbons, and the like. In Section Three we have erasers, correction fluids, transparent tapes, glue sticks, et cetera. And in Section Four we have paper clips and push pins and scissors and razor blades. And here are the spare blades for the shredder. Do not touch the shredder, which is located over there. The shredder is of no concern to you.

Gwendolyn Stich sits in that office there. She is crazy about penguins, and collects penguin knickknacks: penguin posters and coffee mugs and stationery, penguin stuffed animals, penguin jewelry, penguin sweaters and T-shirts and socks. She has a pair of penguin fuzzy slippers she wears when working late at the office. She has a tape cassette of penguin sounds which she listens to for relaxation. Her favorite colors are black and white. She has personalized license plates that read PEN GWEN. Every morning she passes through all the cubicles to wish each of us a *good morning*. She brings Danish on Wednesdays for Hump Day morning break, and doughnuts on Fridays for TGIF afternoon break. She organizes the Annual Christmas Potluck, and is in charge of the Birthday List. Gwendolyn Stich's door is always open to all of us. She will always lend an ear, and put in a good word for you; she will always give you a hand, or the shirt off her back, or a shoulder to cry on. Because her door is always open, she hides and cries in a stall in the women's room. And John LaFountaine—who, enthralled when a woman enters, sites quietly in his stall with his knees to his chest—John LaFountaine has heard her vomiting in there. We have come upon Gwendolyn Stich huddled in the stairwell, shivering in the updraft, sipping a Diet Mr. Pibb and hugging her knees. She does not let any of this interfere with her work. If it interfered with her work, she might have to be let go.

Kevin Howard sits in that cubicle over there. He is a serial killer, the one they call the Carpet Cutter, responsible for the mutilations across town. We're not sup-posed to know that, so do not let on. Don't worry. His compulsion inflicts itself on strangers only, and the routine established is elaborate and unwavering. The victim must be a white male, a young adult no older than thirty, heavyset, with dark hair and eyes, and the like. The victim must be chosen at random, before sunset, from a public place; the victim is followed home, and must put up a struggle; et cetera. The carnage inflicted is precise: the angle and direction of the incisions; the layering of skin and muscle tissue; the rearrangement of the visceral organs; and so on. Kevin Howard does not let any of this interfere with his work. He is, in fact, our fastest typ-ist. He types as if he were on fire. He has a secret crush on Gwendolyn Stich, and leaves a red-foil-wrapped Hershey's Kiss on her desk every afternoon. But he hates Anika Bloom, and keeps well away from her. In his presence, she has uncontrollable fits of shaking and trembling. Her left palm does not stop bleeding.

In any case, when Kevin Howard gets caught, act surprised. Say that he seemed like a nice person, a bit of a loner, perhaps, but always quiet and polite.

This is the photocopier room. And this, this is our view. It faces southwest. West is down there, toward the water. North is back there. Because we are on the seven-teenth floor, we are afforded a magnificent view. Isn't it beautiful? It overlooks the park, where the tops of those trees are. You can see a segment of the bay between those two buildings over there. You can see this building reflected in the glass panels of that building across the way. There. See? That's you, waving. And look there. There's Anika Bloom in the kitchenette, waving back.

Enjoy this view while photocopying. If you have problems with the photocopier, see Russell Nash. If you have any questions, ask your supervisor. If you can't find your supervisor, ask Phillip Spiers. He sits over there. He'll check with Clarissa Nicks. She sits over there. If you can't find them, feel free to ask me. That's my cubicle. I sit in there.

# Who's Irish

### GISH JEN

In China, people say mixed children are supposed to be smart, and definitely my granddaughter Sophie is smart. But Sophie is wild, Sophie is not like my daugh-ter Natalie, or like me. I am work hard my whole life, and fierce besides. My hus-band always used to say he is afraid of me, and in our restaurant, busboys and cooks all afraid of me too. Even the gang members come for protection money, they try to talk to my husband. When I am there, they stay away. If they come by mistake, they pretend they are come to eat. They hide behind the menu, they order a lot of food. They talk about their mothers. Oh, my mother have some arthritis, need to take herbal medicine, they say. Oh, my mother getting old, her hair all white now.

I say, Your mother's hair used to be white, but since she dye it, it become black again. Why don't you go home once in a while and take a look? I tell them, Confucius say a filial son knows what color his mother's hair is.

My daughter is fierce too, she is vice president in the bank now. Her new house is big enough for everybody to have their own room, including me. But Sophie take after Natalie's husband's family, their name is Shea, Irish. I always thought Irish people are like Chinese people, work so hard on the railroad, but now I know why the Chinese beat the Irish. Of course, not all Irish are like the Shea family, of course not. My daughter tell me I should not say Irish this, Irish that.

How do you like it when people say the Chinese this, the Chinese that, she say.

You know, the British call the Irish heathen, just like they call the Chinese, she say.

You think the Opium War was bad, how would you like to live right next door to the British, she say.

And that is that. My daughter have a funny habit when she win an argument, she take a sip of something and look away, so the other person is not embarrassed. So I am not embarrassed. I do not call anybody anything either. I just happen to mention about the Shea family, an interesting fact: four brothers in the family, and not one of them work. The mother, Bess, have a job before she got sick, she was executive secretary in a big company. She is handle everything for a big shot, you would be surprised how complicated her job is, not just type this, type that. Now she is a nice woman with a clean house. But her boys, every one of them is on welfare, or so-called severance pay, or so-called disability pay. Something. They say they cannot find work, this is not the economy of the fifties, but I say, Even the black people doing better these days, some of them live so fancy, you'd be surprised. Why the Shea family have so much trouble? They are white people, they speak English. When I come to this country, I have no money and do not speak English. But my husband and I own our restaurant before he die. Free and clear, no mortgage. Of course. I understand I am just lucky, come from a country where the food is popular all over the world. I understand it is not the Shea family's fault they come from a country where everything is boiled. Still, I say.

She's right, we should broaden our horizons, say one brother, Jim, at Thanksgiving. Forget about the car business. Think about egg rolls.

Pad thai, say another brother, Mike. I'm going to make my fortune in pad thai. It's going to be the new pizza.

I say, You people too picky about what you sell. Selling egg rolls not good enough for you, but at least my husband and I can say, We made it. What can you say? Tell me. What can you say?

Everybody chew their tough turkey.

I especially cannot understand my daughter's husband John, who has no job but cannot take care of Sophie either. Because he is a man, he say, and that's the end of the sentence.

Plain boiled food, plain boiled thinking. Even his name is plain boiled: John. Maybe because I grew up with black bean sauce and hoisin sauce and garlic sauce, I always feel something is missing when my son-in-law talk.

But, okay: so my son-in-law can be man, I am baby-sitter. Six hours a day, same as the old sitter, crazy Amy, who quit. This is not so easy, now that I am sixty-eight, Chinese age almost seventy. Still, I try. In China, daughter take care of mother. Here it is the other way around. Mother help daughter, mother ask, Anything else I can do? Otherwise daughter complain mother is not supportive. I tell daughter, We do not have this word in Chinese, *supportive*. But my daughter too busy to listen, she has to go to meeting, she has to write memo while her husband go to the gym to be a man. My daughter say otherwise he will be depressed. Seems like all his life he has this trouble, depression.

No one wants to hire someone who is depressed, she say. It is important for him to keep his spirits up.

Beautiful wife, beautiful daughter, beautiful house, oven can clean itself automatically. No money left over, because only one income, but lucky enough, got the baby-sitter for free. If John lived in China, he would be very happy. But he is not happy. Even at the gym things go wrong. One day, he pull a muscle. Another day, weight room too crowded. Always something.

Until finally, hooray, he has a job. Then he feel pressure.

I need to concentrate, he say. I need to focus.

He is going to work for insurance company. Salesman job. A paycheck, he say, and at least he will wear clothes instead of gym shorts. My daughter buy him some special candy bars from the health-food store. They say THINK! on them, and are supposed to help John think.

John is a good-looking boy, you have to say that, especially now that he shave so you can see his face.

I am an old man in a young man's game, say John.

I will need a new suit, say John.

This time I am not going to shoot myself in the foot, say John.

Good, I say.

She means to be supportive, my daughter say. Don't start the send her back to China thing, because we can't.

Sophie is three years old American age, but already I see her nice Chinese side swallowed up by her wild Shea side. She looks like mostly Chinese. Beautiful black hair, beautiful black eyes. Nose perfect size, not so flat looks like something fell down, not so large looks like some big deal got stuck in wrong face. Everything just right, only her skin is a brown surprise to John's family. So brown, they say. Even John say it. She never goes in the sun, still she is that color, he say. Brown. They say. Nothing the matter with brown. They are just surprised. So brown. Nattie is not that brown, they say. They say, It seems like Sophie should be a color in between Nattie and John. Seems funny, a girl named Sophie Shea be brown. But she is brown, maybe her name should be Sophie Brown. She never go in the sun, still she is that color, they say. Nothing the matter with brown. They are just surprised.

The Shea family talk is like this sometimes, going around and around like a Christmas-tree train.

Maybe John is not her father, I say one day, to stop the train. And sure enough, train wreck. None of the brothers ever say the word *brown* to me again.

Instead, John's mother, Bess, say, I hope you are not offended.

She say, I did my best on those boys. But raising four boys with no father is no picnic.

You have a beautiful family, I say.

I'm getting old, she say.

You deserve a rest, I say. Too many boys make you old.

I never had a daughter, she say. You have a daughter.

I have a daughter, I say. Chinese people don't think a daughter is so great, but you're right. I have a daughter.

I was never against the marriage, you know, she say. I never thought John was marrying down. I always thought Nattie was just as good as white.

I was never against the marriage either, I say. I just wonder if they look at the whole problem.

Of course you pointed out the problem, you are a mother, she say. And now we both have a granddaughter. A little brown granddaughter, she is so precious to me.

I laugh. A little brown granddaughter, I say. To tell you the truth, I don't know how she came out so brown.

We laugh some more. These days Bess need a walker to walk. She take so many pills, she need two glasses of water to get them all down. Her favorite TV show is about bloopers, and she love her bird feeder. All day long, she can watch that bird feeder, like a cat.

I can't wait for her to grow up, Bess say. I could use some female company.

Too many boys, I say.

Boys are fine, she say. But they do surround you after a while.

You should take a break, come live with us, I say. Lots of girls at our house.

Be careful what you offer, say Bess with a wink. Where I come from, people mean for you to move in when they say a thing like that.

Nothing the matter with Sophie's outside, that's the truth. It is inside that she is like not any Chinese girl I ever see. We go to the park, and this is what she does. She stand up in the stroller. She take off all her clothes and throw them in the fountain.

Sophie! I say. Stop!

But she just laugh like a crazy person. Before I take over as baby-sitter, Sophie has that crazy-person sitter, Amy the guitar player. My daughter thought this Amy very creative—another word we do not talk about in China. In China, we talk about whether we have difficulty or no difficulty. We talk about whether life is bitter or not bitter. In America, all day long, people talk about creative. Never mind that I cannot even look at this Amy, with her shirt so short that her belly button showing. This Amy think Sophie should love her body. So when Sophie take off her diaper, Amy laugh. When Sophie run around naked, Amy say she wouldn't want to wear a diaper either. When Sophie go *shu-shu* in her lap,

Amy laugh and say there are no germs in pee. When Sophie take off her shoes, Amy say bare feet is best, even the pediatrician say so. That is why Sophie now walk around with no shoes like a beggar child. Also why Sophie love to take off her clothes.

Turn around! say the boys in the park. Let's see that ass!

Of course, Sophie does not understand. Sophie clap her hands, I am the only one to say, No! This is not a game.

It has nothing to do with John's family, my daughter say. Amy was too permissive, that's all.

But I think if Sophie was not wild inside, she would not take off her shoes and clothes to begin with.

You never take off your clothes when you were little. I say, All my Chinese friends had babies, I never saw one of them act wild like that.

Look, my daughter say. I have a big presentation tomorrow.

John and my daughter agree Sophie is a problem, but they don't know what to do.

You spank her, she'll stop, I say another day.

But they say, Oh no.

In America, parents not supposed to spank the child.

It gives them low self-esteem, my daughter say. And that leads to problems later, as I happen to know.

My daughter never have big presentation the next day when the subject of spanking come up.

I don't want you to touch Sophie, she say. No spanking, period.

Don't tell me what to do, I say.

I'm not telling you what to do, say my daughter. I'm telling you how I feel.

I am not your servant, I say. Don't you dare talk to me like that.

My daughter have another funny habit when she lose an argument. She spread out all her fingers and look at them, as if she like to make sure they are still there.

My daughter is fierce like me, but she and John think it is better to explain to Sophie that clothes are a good idea. This is not so hard in the cold weather. In the warm weather, it is very hard.

Use your words, my daughter say. That's what we tell Sophie. How about if you set a good example.

As if good example mean anything to Sophie. I am so fierce, the gang members who used to come to the restaurant all afraid of me, but Sophie is not afraid.

I say, Sophie, if you take off your clothes, no snack.

I say, Sophie, if you take off your clothes, no lunch.

I say, Sophie, if you take off your clothes, no park.

Pretty soon we are stay home all day, and by the end of six hours she still did not have one thing to eat. You never saw a child stubborn like that.

I'm hungry! She cry when my daughter come home.

What's the matter, doesn't your grandmother feed you? My daughter laugh.

No! Sophie say. She doesn't feed me anything!

My daughter laugh again. Here you go, she say.

She say to John, Sophie must be growing.

Growing like a weed, I say.

Still Sophie take off her clothes, until one day I spank her. Not too hard, but she cry, and when I tell her if she doesn't put her clothes back on I'll spank her again, she put her clothes back on. Then I tell her she is good girl, and give her some food to eat. The next day we go to the park and, like a nice Chinese girl, she does not take off her clothes.

She stop taking off her clothes, I report. Finally!

How did you do it? my daughter ask.

After twenty-eight years experience with you, I guess I learn something, I say.

It must have been a phase, John say, and his voice is suddenly like an expert.

His voice is like an expert about everything these days, now that he carry a leather briefcase, and wear shiny shoes, and can go shopping for a new car. On the company, he say. The company will pay for it, but he will be able to drive it whenever he want.

A free car, he say. How do you like that.

It's good to see you in the saddle again, my daughter say. Some of your family patterns are scary.

At least I don't drink, he say. He say, and I'm not the only one with scary family patterns.

That's for sure, say my daughter.

Everyone is happy. Even I am happy, because there is more trouble with Sophie, but now I think I can help her Chinese side fight against her wild side. I teach her to eat food with fork or spoon or chopsticks, she cannot just grab into the middle of a bowl of noodles. I teach her not to play with garbage cans. Sometimes I spank her, but not too often, and not too hard.

Still, there are problems. Sophie like to climb everything. If there is a railing, she is never next to it. Always she is on top of it. Also, Sophie like to hit the mommies of her friends. She learn this from her playground best friend, Sinbad, who is four. Sinbad wear army clothes every day and like to ambush his mommy. He is the one who dug a big hole under the play structure, a foxhole he call it, all by himself. Very hardworking. Now he wait in the foxhole with a shovel full of wet sand. When his mommy come, he throw it right at her.

Oh, it's all right, his mommy say. You can't get rid of war games, it's part of their imaginative play. All the boys go through it.

Also, he like to kick his mommy, and one day he tell Sophie to kick his mommy too.

I wish this story is not true.

Kick her, kick her! Sinbad say.

Sophie kick her. A little kick, as if she just so happened was swinging her little leg and didn't realize that big mommy leg was in the way. Still I spank Sophie and make Sophie say sorry, and what does the mommy say?

Really, it's all right, she say. It didn't hurt.

After that, Sophie learn she can attack mommies in the playground, and some will say, Stop, but others will say, Oh, she didn't mean it, especially if they realize Sophie will be punished.

This is how, one day, bigger trouble come. The bigger trouble start when Sophie hide in the foxhole with that shovel full of sand. She wait, and when I come look for her, she throw it at me. All over my nice clean clothes.

Did you ever see a Chinese girl act this way!

Sophie! I say. Come out of there, say you're sorry.

But she does not come out. Instead, she laugh. Naaah, naah-na, naaa-naaa, she say.

I am not exaggerate: millions of children in China, not one act like this.

Sophie! I say. Now! Come out now!

But she know she is in big trouble. She know if she come out, what will happen next. So she does not come out. I am sixty-eight, Chinese age almost seventy, how can I crawl under there to catch her? Impossible. So I yell, yell, yell, and what happen? Nothing. A Chinese mother would help, but American mothers, they look at you, they shake their head, they go home. And, of course, a Chinese child would give up, but not Sophie.

I hate you! she yell. I hate you, Meanie!

Meanie is my new name these days.

Long time this goes on, long long time. The foxhole is deep, you cannot see too much, you don't know where is the bottom. You cannot hear too much either. If she does not yell, you cannot even know she is still there or not. After a while, getting cold out, getting dark out. No one left in the playground, only us.

Sophie, I say. How did you become stubborn like this? I am go home without you now.

I try to use a stick, chase her out of there, and once or twice I hit her, but still she does not come out. So finally I leave. I go outside the gate.

Bye-bye! I say. I'm go home now.

But still she does not come out and does not come out. Now it is dinnertime, the sky is black. I think I should maybe go get help, but how can I leave a little girl by herself in the playground? A bad man could come. A rat could come. I go back in to see what is happen to Sophie. What if she have a shovel and is making a tunnel to escape?

Sophie! I say.

No answer.

Sophie!

I don't know if she is alive. I don't know if she is fall asleep down there. If she is crying, I cannot hear her.

So I take the stick and poke.

Sophie! I say. I promise I no hit you. If you come out, I give you a lollipop.

No answer. By now I worried. What to do, what to do, what to do? I poke some more, even harder, so that I am poking and poking when my daughter and John suddenly appear.

What are you doing? What is going on? say my daughter.

Put down that stick! say my daughter.

You are crazy! say my daughter.

John wiggle under the structure, into the foxhole, to rescue Sophie.

She fell asleep, say John the expert. She's okay. That is one big hole.

Now Sophie is crying and crying.

Sophie, my daughter say, hugging her. Are you okay, peanut? Are you okay?

She's just scared, say John.

Are you okay? I say too. I don't know what happen, I say.

She's okay, say John. He is not like my daughter, full of questions. He is full of answers until we get home and can see by the lamplight.

Will you look at her? he yell then. What the hell happened?

Bruises all over her brown skin, and a swollen-up eye.

You are crazy! say my daughter. Look at what you did! You are crazy!

I try very hard, I say.

How could you use a stick? I told you to use your words!

She is hard to handle, I say.

She's three years old! You cannot use a stick! say my daughter.

She is not like any Chinese girl I ever saw, I say.

I brush some sand off my clothes. Sophie's clothes are dirty too, but at least she has her clothes on.

Has she done this before? ask my daughter. Has she hit you before?

She hits me all the time, Sophie say, eating ice cream.

Your family, say John.

Believe me, say my daughter.

A daughter I have, a beautiful daughter. I took care of her when she could not hold her head up. I took care of her before she could argue with me, when she was a little girl with two pigtails, one of them always crooked. I took care of her when we have to escape from China, I took care of her when suddenly we live in a country with cars everywhere, if you are not careful your little girl get run over. When my husband die, I promise him I will keep the family together, even though it was just two of us, hardly a family at all.

But now my daughter take me around to look at apartments. After all, I can cook, I can clean, there's no reason I cannot live by myself, all I need is a telephone. Of course, she is sorry. Sometimes she cry, I am the one to say everything will be okay. She say she have no choice, she doesn't want to end up divorced. I say divorce is terrible, I don't know who invented this terrible idea. Instead of live with a telephone, though, surprise, I come to live with Bess. Imagine that. Bess make an offer and, sure enough, where she come from, people mean for you to move in when they say things like that. A crazy idea, go to live with someone else's family, but she like to have some female company, not like my daughter, who does not believe in company. These days when my daughter visit, she does not bring Sophie. Bess say we should give Nattie time, we will see Sophie again soon. But seems like my daughter have more presentation than ever before, every time she come she have to leave.

I have a family to support, she say, and her voice is heavy, as if soaking wet. I have a young daughter and a depressed husband and no one to turn to.

When she say no one to turn to, she mean me.

These days my beautiful daughter is so tired she can just sit there in a chair and fall asleep. John lost his job again, already, but still they rather hire a baby-sitter than ask me to help, even they can't afford it. Of course, the new baby-sitter is much younger, can run around. I don't know if Sophie these days is wild or not wild. She call me Meanie, but she like to kiss me too, sometimes. I remember that every time I see a child on TV. Sophie like to grab my hair, a fistful in each hand, and then kiss me smack on the nose. I never see any other child kiss that way.

The satellite TV has so many channels, more channels than I can count, including a Chinese channel from the Mainland and a Chinese channel from Taiwan, but most of the time I watch bloopers with Bess. Also, I watch the bird feeder—so many, many kinds of birds come. The Shea sons hang around all the time, asking when will I go home, but Bess tell them, Get lost.

She's permanent resident, say Bess. She isn't going anywhere.

Then she wink at me, and switch the channel with the remote control.

Of course, I shouldn't say Irish this, Irish that, especially now I am become honorary Irish myself, according to Bess. Me! Who's Irish? I say, and she laugh. All the same, if I could mention one thing about some of the Irish, not all of them of course, I like to mention this: Their talk just stick. I don't know how Bess Shea learn to use her words, but sometimes I hear what she say a long time later. *Permanent resident. Not going anywhere.* Over and over I hear it, the voice of Bess.

# Gusev

## ANTON CHEKHOV

### I

It was getting dark; it would soon be night.

Gusev, a discharged soldier, sat up in his hammock and said in an undertone:

"I say, Pavel Ivanitch. A soldier at Sutchan told me: while they were sailing a big fish came into collision with their ship and stove a hole in it."

The nondescript individual whom he was addressing, and whom everyone in the ship's hospital called Pavel Ivanitch, was silent, as though he had not heard.

And again a stillness followed . . . The wind frolicked with the rigging, the screw throbbed, the waves lashed, the hammocks creaked, but the ear had long ago become accustomed to these sounds, and it seemed that everything around was asleep and silent. It was dreary. The three invalids—two soldiers and a sailor—who had been playing cards all the day were asleep and talking in their dreams.

It seemed as though the ship were beginning to rock. The hammock slowly rose and fell under Gusev, as though it were heaving a sigh, and this was repeated once, twice, three times. . . . Something crashed on to the floor with a clang: it must have been a jug falling down.

"The wind has broken loose from its chain . . ." said Gusev, listening.

This time Pavel Ivanitch cleared his throat and answered irritably:

"One minute a vessel's running into a fish, the next, the wind's breaking loose from its chain. Is the wind a beast that it can break loose from its chain?"

"That's how christened folk talk."

"They are as ignorant as you are then. They say all sorts of things. One must keep a head on one's shoulders and use one's reason. You are a senseless creature."

Pavel Ivanitch was subject to sea-sickness. When the sea was rough he was usually ill-humoured, and the merest trifle would make him irritable. And in Gusev's opinion there was absolutely nothing to be vexed about. What was there strange or wonderful, for instance, in the fish or in the wind's breaking loose from its chain? Suppose the fish were as big as a mountain and its back were as hard as a sturgeon: and in the same way, supposing that away yonder at the end of the world there stood great stone walls and the fierce winds were chained up to the walls. . . . if they had not broken loose, why did they tear about all over the sea like maniacs, and struggle to escape like dogs? If they were not chained up, what did become of them when it was calm?

Gusev pondered for a long time about fishes as big as a mountain and stout, rusty chains, then he began to feel dull and thought of his native place to which he was returning after five years' service in the East. He pictured an immense pond covered with snow. . . . On one side of the pond the red-brick building of the potteries with a tall chimney and clouds of black smoke; on the other side—a village. . . . His brother Alexey comes out in a sledge from the fifth yard from the end; behind him sits his little son Vanka in big felt over-boots, and his little girl Akulka, also in big felt boots. Alexey has been drinking, Vanka is laughing, Akulka's face he could not see, she had muffled herself up.

"You never know, he'll get the children frozen . . ." thought Gusev. "Lord send them sense and judgment that they may honour their father and mother and not be wiser than their parents."

"They want re-soleing," a delirious sailor says in a bass voice. "Yes, yes!"

Gusev's thoughts break off, and instead of a pond there suddenly appears apropos of nothing a huge bull's head without eyes, and the horse and sledge are not driving along, but are whirling round and round in a cloud of smoke. But still he was glad he had seen his own folks. He held his breath from delight, shudders ran all over him, and his fingers twitched.

"The Lord let us meet again," he muttered feverishly, but he at once opened his eyes and sought in the darkness for water.

He drank and lay back, and again the sledge was moving, then again the bull's head without eyes, smoke, clouds. . . . And so on till daybreak.

## II

The first outline visible in the darkness was a blue circle—the little round window; then little by little Gusev could distinguish his neighbour in the next hammock, Pavel Ivanitch. The man slept sitting up, as he could not breathe lying down. His face was grey, his nose was long and sharp, his eyes looked huge from the terrible thinness of his face, his temples were sunken, his beard was skimpy, his hair was long. . . . Looking at him you could not make out of what class he was, whether he were a gentleman, a merchant, or a peasant. Judging from his expression and his long hair he might have been a hermit or a lay brother in a monastery—but if one listened to what he said it seemed that he could not be a monk. He was worn out by his cough and his illness and by the stifling heat, and breathed with difficulty, moving his parched lips. Noticing that Gusev was looking at him he turned his face towards him and said:

"I begin to guess. . . . Yes. . . . I understand it all perfectly now."

"What do you understand, Pavel Ivanitch?"

"I'll tell you. . . . It has always seemed to me strange that terribly ill as you are you should be here in a steamer where it is so hot and stifling and we are always being tossed up and down, where, in fact, everything threatens you with death; now it is all clear to me. . . . Yes. . . . Your doctors put you on the steamer to get rid of you. They get sick of looking after poor brutes like you. . . . You don't pay them anything, they have a bother with you, and you damage their records with your deaths—so, of course, you are brutes! It's not difficult to get rid of you. . . . All that is necessary is, in the first place, to have no conscience or humanity, and, secondly, to deceive the steamer authorities. The first condition need hardly be considered, in that respect we are artists; and one can always succeed in the second with a little practice. In a crowd of four hundred healthy soldiers and sailors half a dozen sick ones are not conspicuous; well, they drove you all on to the steamer, mixed you with the healthy ones, hurriedly counted you over, and in the confusion nothing amiss was noticed, and when the steamer had started they saw that there were paralytics and consumptives in the last stage lying about on the deck. . . ."

Gusev did not understand Pavel Ivanitch; but supposing he was being blamed, he said in self-defence:

"I lay on the deck because I had not the strength to stand; when we were unloaded form the barge on to the ship I caught a fearful chill."

"It's revolting," Pavel Ivanitch went on. "The worst of it is they know perfectly well that you can't last out the long journey, and yet they put you here. Supposing you get as far as the Indian Ocean, what then? It's horrible to think of it. . . . And that's their gratitude for your faithful, irreproachable service!"

Pavel Ivanitch's eyes looked angry; he frowned contemptuously and said, gasping:

"Those are the people who ought to be plucked in the newspapers till the feathers fly in all directions."

The two sick soldiers and the sailor were awake and already playing cards. The sailor was half reclining in his hammock, the soldiers were sitting near him on the floor in the most uncomfortable attitudes. One of the soldiers had his right arm in a sling, and the hand was swathed up in a regular bundle so that he held his cards under his right arm or in the crook of his elbow while he played with the left. The ship was rolling heavily. They could not stand up, nor drink tea, nor take their medicines.

"Were you an officer's servant?" Pavel Ivanitch asked Gusev.

"Yes, an officer's servant."

"My God, my God!" said Pavel Ivanitch, and he shook his head mournfully. "To tear a man out of his home, drag him twelve thousand miles away, then to drive him into consumption and . . . and what is it all for, one wonders? To turn him into a servant for some Captain Kopeikin or midshipman Dirka! How logical!"

"It's not hard work, Pavel Ivanitch. You get up in the morning and clean the boots, get the samovar, sweep the rooms, and then you have nothing more to do. The lieutenant is all the day drawing plans, and if you like you can say your prayers, if you like you can read a book or go out into the street. God grant everyone such a life."

"Yes, very nice, the lieutenant draws plans all the day and you sit in the kitchen and pine for home. . . . Plans indeed! . . . It is not plans that matter, but a human life. Life is not given twice, it must be treated mercifully."

"Of course, Pavel Ivanitch, a bad man gets no mercy anywhere, neither at home nor in the army, but if you live as you ought and obey orders, who has any need to insult you? The officers are educated gentlemen, they understand. . . . In five years I was never once in prison, and I was never struck a blow, so help me God, but once."

"What for?"

"For fighting. I have a heavy hand, Pavel Ivanitch. Four Chinamen came into our yard; they were bringing firewood or something, I don't remember. Well, I was bored and I knocked them about a bit, one's nose began bleeding, damn the fellow. . . . The lieutenant saw it through the little window, he was angry and gave me a box on the ear."

"Foolish, pitiful man . . ." whispered Pavel Ivanitch. "You don't understand anything."

He was utterly exhausted by the tossing of the ship and closed his eyes; his head alternately fell back and dropped forward on his breast. Several times he tried to lie down but nothing came of it; his difficulty in breathing prevented it.

"And what did you hit the four Chinamen for?" he asked a little while afterwards.

"Oh, nothing. They came into the yard and I hit them."

And a stillness followed. . . . The card-players had been playing for two hours with enthusiasm and loud abuse of one another, but the motion of the ship overcame them, too; they threw aside the cards and lay down. Again Gusev saw the big pond, the brick building, the village. . . . Again the sledge was coming along, again Vanka was laughing and Akulka, silly little thing, threw open her fur coat and stuck her feet out, as much as to say: "Look, good people, my snowboots are not like Vanka's, they are new ones."

"Five years old, and she has no sense yet," Gusev muttered in delirium. "Instead of kicking your legs you had better come and get your soldier uncle a drink. I will give you something nice."

Then Andron with a flintlock gun on his shoulder was carrying a hare he had killed, and he was followed by the decrepit old Jew Isaitchik, who offers to barter the hare for a piece of soap; then the black calf in the shed, then Domma sewing at a shirt and crying about something, and then again the bull's head without eyes, black smoke. . . .

Overhead someone gave a loud shout, several sailors ran by, they seemed to be dragging something bulky over the deck, something fell with a crash. Again they ran by. . . . Had something gone wrong? Gusev raised his head, listened, and saw that the two soldiers and the sailor were playing cards again; Pavel Ivanitch was sitting up moving his lips. It was stifling, one hadn't strength to breathe, one was thirsty, the water was warm, disgusting. The ship heaved as much as ever.

Suddenly something strange happened to one of the soldiers playing cards. . . . He called hearts diamonds, got muddled in his score, and dropped his cards, then with a frightened, foolish smile looked round at all of them.

"I shan't be a minute, mates, I'll . . ." he said, and lay down on the floor.

Everybody was amazed. They called to him, he did not answer.

"Stephan, maybe you are feeling bad, eh?" the soldier with his arm in a sling asked him. "Perhaps we had better bring the priest, eh?"

"Have a drink of water, Stephan . . ." said the sailor. "Here, lad, drink."

"Why are you knocking the jug against his teeth?" said Gusev angrily. "Don't you see, turnip head?"

"What?"

"What?" Gusev repeated, mimicking him. "There is no breath in him, he is dead! That's what! What nonsensical people, Lord have mercy on us. . . !"

## III

The ship was not rocking and Pavel Ivanitch was more cheerful. He was no longer ill-humoured. His face had a boastful, defiant, mocking expression. He looked as though he wanted to say: "Yes, in a minute I will tell you something that will make you split your sides with laughing." The little round window was open and a soft breeze was blowing on Pavel Ivanitch. There was a sound of voices, of the plash of oars in the water. . . . Just under the little window someone began droning in a high, unpleasant voice: no doubt it was a Chinaman singing.

"Here we are in the harbour," said Pavel Ivanitch, smiling ironically. "Only another month and we shall be in Russia. Well, worthy gentlemen and warriors! I shall arrive at Odessa and from there go straight to Harkov. In Harkov I have a friend, a literary man. I shall go to him and say, 'Come, old man, put aside your horrid subjects, ladies' amours and the beauties of nature, and show up human depravity.'"

For a minute he pondered, then said:

"Gusev, do you know how I took them in?"

"Took in whom, Pavel Ivanitch?"

"Why, these fellows. . . . You know that on this steamer there is only a first-class and a third-class, and they only allow peasants—that is the rift-raft—to go in the third. If you have got on a reefer jacket and have the faintest resemblance to a gentleman or a bourgeois you must go first-class, if you please. You must fork out five hundred roubles if you die for it. Why, I ask, have you made such a rule? Do you want to raise the prestige of educated Russians thereby? Not a bit of it. We don't let you go third-class simply because a decent person can't go third-class; it is very horrible and disgusting. Yes, indeed. I am very grateful for such solicitude for decent people's welfare. But in any case, whether it is nasty there or nice, five hundred roubles I haven't got. I haven't pilfered government money. I haven't exploited the natives, I haven't trafficked in contraband, I have flogged no one to death, so judge whether I have the right to travel first-class and even less to reckon myself of the educated class? But you won't catch them with logic. . . . One has to resort to deception. I put on a workman's coat and high boots, I assumed a drunken, servile mug and went to the agents: 'Give us a little ticket, your honour,' said I. . . ."

"Why, what class do you belong to?" asked a sailor.

"Clerical. My father was an honest priest, he always told the great ones of the world the truth to their faces; and he had a great deal to put up with in consequence."

Pavel Ivanitch was exhausted with talking and gasped for breath, but still went on:

"Yes, I always tell people the truth to their faces. I am not afraid of anyone or anything. There is a vast difference between me and all of you in that respect. You are in darkness, you are blind, crushed; you see nothing and what you do see you don't understand. . . . You are told the wind breaks loose from its chain, that you are beasts, Petchenyegs, and you believe it; they punch you in the neck, you kiss their hands; some animal in a sable-lined coat robs you and then tips you fifteen kopecks and you: 'Let me kiss your hand, sir.' You are pariahs, pitiful people. . . . I am a different sort. My eyes are open, I see it all as clearly as a hawk or an eagle when it floats over the earth, and I understand it all. I am a living protest. I see irresponsible tyranny— I protest. I see cant and hypocrisy—I protest. I see swine triumphant—I protest. And I cannot be suppressed, no Spanish Inquisition can make me hold my tongue. No. . . . Cut out my tongue and I would protest in dumb show; shut me up in a cellar—I will shout from it to be heard half a mile away, or I will starve myself to death that they may have another weight on their black consciences. Kill me and I will haunt them with my ghost. All my acquaintances say to me: 'You are a most insufferable person, Pavel Ivanitch.' I am proud of such a reputation. I have served three years in the far East, and I shall be remembered there for a hundred years: I had rows with everyone. My friends write to me from Russia, 'Don't come back,' but here I am going back to spite them . . . yes. . . . That is life as I understand it. That is what one can call life."

Gusev was looking at the little window and was not listening. A boat was swaying on the transparent, soft, turquoise water all bathed in hot, dazzling sunshine. In it there were naked Chinamen holding up cages with canaries and calling out:

"It sings, it sings!"

Another boat knocked against the first; the steam cutter darted by. And then there came another boat with a fat Chinaman sitting in it, eating rice with little sticks.

Languidly the water heaved, languidly the white seagulls floated over it.

"I should like to give that fat fellow one in the neck," thought Gusev, gazing at the stout Chinaman, with a yawn.

He dozed off, and it seemed to him that all nature was dozing, too. Time flew swiftly by; imperceptibly the day passed, imperceptibly the darkness came on. . . . The steamer was no longer standing still, but moving on further.

## IV

Two days passed, Pavel Ivanitch lay down instead of sitting up; his eyes were closed, his nose seemed to have grown sharper.

"Pavel Ivanitch," Gusev called to him. "Hey, Pavel Ivanitch."

Pavel Ivanitch opened his eyes and moved his lips.

"Are you feeling bad?"

"No . . . it's nothing . . ." answered Pavel Ivanitch, gasping. "Nothing; on the contrary—I am rather better. . . . You see I can lie down. I am a little easier. . . ."

"Well, thank God for that, Pavel Ivanitch."

"When I compare myself with you I am sorry for you . . . poor fellow. My lungs are all right, it is only a stomach cough. . . . I can stand hell, let alone the Red Sea. Besides I take a critical attitude to my illness and to the medicines they give me for it. While you . . . you are in darkness. . . . It's hard for you, very, very hard!"

The ship was not rolling, it was calm, but as hot and stifling as a bath-house; it was not only hard to speak but even hard to listen. Gusev hugged his knees, laid his head on them and thought of his home. Good heavens, what a relief it was to think of snow and cold in that stifling heat! You drive in a sledge, all at once the horses take fright at something and bolt. . . . Regardless of the road, the ditches, the ravines, they dash like mad things, right through the village, over the pond by the pottery works, out across the open fields. "Hold on," the pottery hands and the peasants shout, meeting them. "Hold on." But why? Let the keen, cold wind beat in one's face and bite one's hands; let the lumps of snow, kicked up by the horses' hoofs, fall on one's cap, on one's back, down one's collar, on one's chest; let the runners ring on the snow, and the traces and the sledge be smashed, deuce take them one and all! And how delightful when the sledge upsets and you go flying full tilt into a drift, face downwards in the snow, and then you get up white all over with icicles on your moustaches; no cap, no gloves, your belt undone. . . . People laugh, the dogs bark. . . .

Pavel Ivanitch half opened one eye, looked at Gusev with it, and asked softly:

"Gusev, did your commanding officer steal?"

"Who can tell, Pavel Ivanitch! We can't say, it didn't reach us."

And after that a long time passed in silence. Gusev brooded, muttered something in delirium, and kept drinking water; it was hard for him to talk and hard to listen, and he was afraid of being talked to. An hour passed, a second, a third; evening came on, then night, but he did not notice it. He still sat dreaming of the frost.

There was a sound as though someone came into the hospital, and voices were audible, but a few minutes passed and all was still again.

"The Kingdom of Heaven and eternal peace," said the soldier with his arm in a sling. "He was an uncomfortable man."

"What?" asked Gusev. "Who?"

"He is dead, they have just carried him up."

"Oh, well," muttered Gusev, yawning, "the Kingdom of Heaven be his."

"What do you think?" the soldier with his arm in a sling asked Gusev. "Will he be in the Kingdom of Heaven or not?"

"Who is it you are talking about?"

"Pavel Ivanitch."

"He will be . . . he suffered so long. And there is another thing, he belonged to the clergy, and the priests always have a lot of relations. Their prayers will save him."

The soldier with the sling sat down on a hammock near Gusev and said in an undertone:

"And you, Gusev, are not long for this world. You will never get to Russia."

"Did the doctor or his assistant say so?" asked Gusev.

"It isn't that they said so, but one can see it. . . . One can see directly when a man's going to die. You don't eat, you don't drink; it's dreadful to see how thin you've got. It's consumption, in fact. I say it, not to upset you, but because maybe you would like to have the sacrament and extreme unction. And if you have any money you had better give it to the senior officer."

"I haven't written home . . ." Gusev sighed. "I shall die and they won't know."

"They'll hear of it," the sick sailor brought out in a bass voice. "When you die they will put it down in the *Gazette*, at Odessa they will send in a report to the commanding officer there and he will send it to the parish or somewhere.

Gusev began to be uneasy after such a conversation and to feel a vague yearning. He drank water—it was not that; he dragged himself to the window and breathed the hot, moist air—it was not that; he tried to think of home, of the frost—it was not that. . . . At last it seemed to him one minute longer in the ward and he would certainly expire.

"It's stifling, mates . . ." he said. "I'll go on deck. Help me up, for Christ's sake."

"All right," assented the soldier with the sling. "I'll carry you, you can't walk, hold on to my neck."

Gusev put his arm round the soldier's neck, the latter put his unhurt arm round him and carried him up. On the deck sailors and time-expired soldiers were lying asleep side by side; there were so many of them it was difficult to pass.

"Stand down," the soldier with the sling said softly. "Follow me quietly, hold on to my shirt. . . ."

It was dark. There was no light on deck, nor on the masts, nor anywhere on the sea around. At the furthest end of the ship the man on watch was standing perfectly still like a statue, and it looked as though he were asleep. It seemed as though the steamer were abandoned to itself and were going at its own will.

"Now they will throw Pavel Ivanitch into the sea," said the soldier with the sling. "In a sack and then into the water."

"Yes, that's the rule."

"But it's better to lie at home in the earth. Anyway, your mother comes to the grave and weeps."

"Of course."

There was a smell of hay and of dung. There were oxen standing with drooping heads by the ships' rail. One, two, three; eight of them! And there was a little horse. Gusev put out his hand to stroke it, but it shook its head, showed its teeth, and tried to bite his sleeve.

"Damned brute . . ." said Gusev angrily.

The two of them, he and the soldier, threaded their way to the head of the ship, then stood at the rail and looked up and down. Overhead deep sky, bright stars, peace and stillness, exactly as at home in the village, below darkness and disorder. The tall waves were resounding, no one could tell why. Whichever wave you looked at each one was trying to rise higher than all the rest and to chase and crush the next one; after it a third as fierce and hideous flew noisily, with a glint of light on its white crest.

The sea has no sense and no pity. If the steamer had been smaller and not made of thick iron, the waves would have crushed it to pieces without the slightest compunction, and would have devoured all the people in it with no distinction of saints or sinners. The steamer had the same cruel and meaningless expression. This monster with its huge beak was dashing onwards, cutting millions of waves in its path; it had no fear of the darkness nor the wind, nor of space, nor of solitude, caring for nothing, and if the ocean had its people, this monster would have crushed them, too, without distinction of saints or sinners.

"Where are we now?" asked Gusev.

"I don't know. We must be in the ocean."

"There is no sight of land. . ."

"No indeed! They say we shan't see it for seven days."

The two soldiers watched the white foam with the phosphorus light on it and were silent, thinking. Gusev was the first to break the silence.

"There is nothing to be afraid of," he said, "only one is full of dread as though one were sitting in a dark forest; but if, for instance, they let a boat down on to the water this minute and an officer ordered me to go a hundred miles over the sea to catch fish, I'd go. Or, let's say, if a Christian were to fall into the water this minute, I'd go in after him. A German or a Chinaman I wouldn't save, but I'd go in after a Christian."

"And are you afraid to die?"

"Yes. I am sorry for the folks at home. My brother at home, you know, isn't steady; he drinks, he beats his wife for nothing, he does not honour his parents. Everything will go to ruin without me, and father and my old mother will be begging their bread, I shouldn't wonder. But my legs won't bear me, brother, and it's hot here. Let's go to sleep."

## V

Gusev went back to the ward and got into his hammock. He was again tormented by a vague craving, and he could not make out what he wanted. There was an oppression on his chest, a throbbing in his head, his mouth was so dry that it was difficult for him to move his tongue. He dozed, and murmured in his sleep, and, worn out with nightmares, his cough, and the stifling heat, towards morning he fell into a sound sleep. He dreamed that they were just taking the bread out of the oven in the barracks and he climbed into the stove and had a steam bath in it, lashing himself with a bunch of birch twigs. He slept for two days, and at midday on the third two sailors came down and carried him out.

He was sewn up in sailcloth and to make him heavier they put with him two iron weights. Sewn up in the sailcloth he looked like a carrot or a radish: broad at the head and narrow at the feet. . . . Before sunset they brought him up to the deck and put him on a plank; one end of the plank lay on the side of the ship, the other on a box, placed on a stool. Round him stood the soldiers and the officers with their caps off.

"Blessed be the Name of the Lord . . ." the priest began. "As it was in the beginning, is now, and ever shall be."

"Amen," chanted three sailors.

The soldiers and the officers crossed themselves and looked away at the waves. It was strange that a man should be sewn up in sailcloth and should soon be flying into the sea. Was it possible that such a thing might happen to anyone?

The priest strewed earth upon Gusev and bowed down. They sang "Eternal Memory."

The man on watch duty tilted up the end of the plank, Gusev slid off and flew head foremost, turned a somersault in the air and splashed into the sea. He was covered with foam and for a moment looked as though he were wrapped in lace, but the minute passed and he disappeared in the waves.

He went rapidly towards the bottom. Did he reach it? It was said to be three miles to the bottom. After sinking sixty or seventy feet, he began moving more and more slowly, swaying rhythmically, as though he were hesitating and, carried along by the current, moved more rapidly sideways than downwards.

Then he was met by a shoal of the fish called harbour pilots. Seeing the dark body the fish stopped as though petrified, and suddenly turned round and disappeared. In less than a minute they flew back swift as an arrow to Gusev, and began zig-zagging round him in the water.

After that another dark body appeared. It was a shark. It swam under Gusev with dignity and no show of interest, as though it did not notice him, and sank down upon its back, then it turned belly upwards, basking in the warm, transparent water and languidly opened its jaws with two rows of teeth. The harbour pilots are delighted, they stop to see what will come next. After playing a little with the body the shark nonchalantly puts its jaws under it, cautiously touches it with its teeth, and the sailcloth is rent its full length from head to foot; one of the weights falls out and frightens the harbour pilots, and striking the shark on the ribs goes rapidly to the bottom.

Overhead at this time the clouds are massed together on the side where the sun is setting; one cloud like a triumphal arch, another like a lion, a third like a pair of scissors. . . . From behind the clouds a broad, green shaft of light pierces through and stretches to the middle of the sky; a little later another, violet-coloured, lies beside it; next that, one of gold, then one rose-coloured. . . . The sky turns a soft lilac. Looking at this gorgeous, enchanted sky, at first the ocean scowls, but soon it, too, takes tender, joyous, passionate colours for which it is hard to find a name in human speech.

🐋 🐋 🐋

## *Writing Exercises*

### INDIVIDUAL

1. Write a scene where the two main characters are keeping secrets from each other. Write the scene from each perspective. In each version we will have access to the secret of the point-of-view character, but not the secret of the other. Even so, the non-point-of-view character's behavior and dialogue may hint at his/her secret, regardless of whether or not the main character perceives it.

2. In the first-person or third-person limited omniscient, write a scene where your character hears the sound of someone trying to break into the house. Your character is home alone (although it may not be her house), vulnerable in some way: in the bath, or in bed, or trapped in a windowless room. The scene should begin with the first hint of danger and it should end the moment before your narrator actually sees the intruder. Your goal here is to imagine in a convincing way your narrator's emotions and perceptions, and to create as much suspense as possible.

   Part 2: Write the same scene from the perspective of the intruder. This might be a random break-in by a common burglar, or maybe the intruder's story is more complex. Consider your intruder's expectations: does he expect the home to be empty? If not, who does he think might be there? Consider whether or not your intruder knows (or thinks he knows) the occupant of the house. In this scene, the reader should identify with the intruder, and again, your goal is to create suspense.

3. Have a character write two versions of the same event for different audiences. Examples: A prisoner writing about the crime he's been convicted of—one letter to his mother, the other to a partner in crime. A man, engaged to be married, sends two e-mails about his bachelor party—one to his old fraternity brother, another to his future brother-in-law. A college student puffs up his summer job in his resume, and then fires off a frustrated e-mail to his friend about that same summer job.

4. Write five openings to a story, each from a different authorial distance. The first version should be written from a great distance. With each version you should lessen the authorial distance, so that by the fifth version we immediately feel close to the character. It may help to use filmmaking as an analogy: your first version should be like a panoramic establishing shot, and your fifth version an extreme close-up. For instance:
   a. It was the blizzard of 1972, the worst storm Boston had experienced in a decade. A young woman, holding her coat closed over her pregnant stomach, struggled down Broad Street.
   b. Jennifer Meyers clutched her coat and prayed she wouldn't slip on a patch of ice.
   c. Jenny waddled down the snowy sidewalk and imagined how silly she must look; a pregnant woman staggering around in a blizzard.
   d. How Jenny wished she was back inside her little apartment, at one with her futon couch, an afghan pulled up to her chin, watching *Days of Our Lives*.
   e. What was she thinking? Trudging through a blinding storm to the Circle K just for a pint of Chunky Monkey? Pregnancy cravings were one thing, but this was ridiculous.

   Now write the opening paragraph of your story. Start at a great distance, but steadily reduce the psychic distance with each sentence, so that by the final sentence of the paragraph the reader feels extremely close to the character.

5. Select a tense situation such as an auto accident, a potentially violent encounter, or a disintegrating love affair, and describe it four times from four different points of view:
   a. first person
   b. third-person *limited* omniscient
   c. third-person objective
   d. third-person omniscient
   Which point of view works best for this material, and why?

6. Choose a significant incident from a child's life (your own or invented). First, write a scene from the point of view of the child in first-person present tense. Try to capture a child's perceptions, vocabulary, and syntax. Now rewrite the scene in first-person past tense from the perspective of the same character as an adult. In this version, your character will not only possess an adult's perception of the event, but will also be able to recall his own childish reaction to it. Try to convey how your character feels about his child-self through his tone (affectionate, amused, nostalgic, embarrassed, mocking, ironic and detached, etc.). What do you gain/lose with the two different points of view?

7. Write a gossipy letter from the point of view of one family member who passes scathing judgments on another, but let readers know that the speaker really loves or envies the other (an unreliable narrator). Alternatively, have the speaker loudly praise the other family member, but let readers hear harsh criticism implied.

8. Write down a false statement about yourself, such as "I have a pet snake." Keep going, elaborating on the false statement, allowing the "I" character to develop. You are beginning to create a narrator who is not like you, which will give you more imaginative freedom than you might feel when writing about yourself as the "I" narrator.

9. Imagine a character who is your complete opposite in some specific way. For example, if you hate country music, take on the "I" voice of someone who is, among other things, a country music fan. Now choose an action (walking to school, eating in a cafe, making a sale to a customer), and write a scene in which your "opposite I" character is performing that action. Make the character sympathetic and intriguing. Don't announce that he or she is a country music lover, but allow the detail and dialogue in the scene to gradually reveal this to the reader.

## COLLABORATIVE

10. Brainstorm a list of characters who might be receiving instructions (a new waiter, a band member, a bride, a mother-to-be, a dog, a baby). These instructions should come *from* another character who thinks the recipient is sure to be incompetent (a boss, bandleader, mother-in-law, etc.).
    a. Write one set of instructions.
    b. Read the pieces back to the class, identifying the speaker and implied listener. Discuss whether or not class members would classify each piece as a short-short story and why.

11. In groups of five, choose a Bible story (for example, Lazarus raised from the dead), a well-known historical or news event (the Kennedy assassination), or a fairy tale (Hansel and Gretel).

   a. List five characters who have some role in the story, including minor characters and perhaps even inanimate objects (the gingerbread house) or animals (the birds that eat Hansel's scattered crumbs).

   b. The group should choose one central event to depict, and then each group member should write about that moment from one of the five character's points of view. Try to exaggerate that character's concerns or private agenda so that we see how his or her view colors the story.

   c. Decide on the most dramatic order in which to present the monologues.

   d. Read the series of monologues back to the class.

   e. *Class Feedback:* How does each character's perspective alter the commonly known story?

# 9

# *IS* AND *IS NOT*
## Comparison

- *Types of Metaphor and Simile*

- *Metaphoric Faults to Avoid*

- *Allegory*

- *Symbol*

Every reader reading is a self-deceiver: We simultaneously "believe" a story and know that it is a fiction, a fabrication. Our belief in the reality of the story may be so strong that it produces physical reactions—tears, trembling, sighs, gasps, a headache. At the same time, as long as the fiction is working for us, we know that our submission is voluntary; that we have, as Samuel Taylor Coleridge pointed out, suspended disbelief. "It's just a movie," says the exasperated father as he takes his shrieking six-year-old out to the lobby. For the father the fiction is working; for the child it is not.

Simultaneous belief and awareness of illusion are present in both the content and the craft of literature, and what is properly called artistic pleasure derives from the tension of this *is* and *is not*. The content of a plot, for instance, tells us that something happens that does not happen, that people who do not exist behave in such a way, and that the events of life—which we know to be random, unrelated, and unfinished—are necessary, patterned, and come to closure. Pleasure in artistry comes precisely when the illusion rings true without destroying the knowledge that it is an illusion.

In the same way, the techniques of every art offer us the tension of things that are and are not alike. This is true of poetry, in which rhyme is interesting because *tend* sounds like *mend* but not exactly like; it is also true of music, whose interest lies in variations on a theme. And it is the fundamental nature of metaphor, from which literature derives.

Metaphor is the literary device by which we are told that something is, or is like, something that it clearly is not, or is not exactly, like. What a good metaphor does is surprise us with the unlikeness of the two things compared while at the same time convincing us of the truth of the likeness. In the process it may also illuminate the meaning of the story and its theme. A bad metaphor fails to surprise or convince or both—and so fails to illuminate.

## Types of Metaphor and Simile

The simplest distinction between kinds of comparison, and usually the first one grasped by beginning students of literature, is between *metaphor* and *simile*. A simile makes a comparison with the use of *like* or *as*, a metaphor without. Though this distinction is technical, it is not entirely trivial, for a metaphor demands a more literal acceptance. If you say, "A woman is a rose," you ask for an extreme suspension of disbelief, whereas "A woman is like a rose" acknowledges the artifice in the statement.

In both metaphor and simile, the resonance of comparison is in the essential or abstract quality that the two objects share. When a writer speaks of "the eyes of the houses" or "the windows of the soul," the comparison of eyes to windows contains the idea of transmitting vision between the inner and the outer. When we speak of "the king of beasts," we don't mean that a lion wears a crown or sits on a throne (although in children's stories the lion often does precisely that, in order to suggest a primitive physical likeness); we mean that king and lion share abstract qualities of power, position, pride, and bearing.

In both metaphor and simile a physical similarity can yield up a characterizing abstraction. So if "a woman" is either "a rose" or "like a rose," the significance lies not in the physical similarity but in the essential qualities that such similarity implies: slenderness, suppleness, fragrance, beauty, color—and perhaps the hidden threat of thorns.

Every metaphor and simile I have used so far is either a cliché or a dead metaphor (a metaphor so familiar that it has lost its original meaning). Each of them may at one time have surprised by their aptness, but by now each has been used so often that the surprise is gone. I wished to use familiar examples in order to clarify that *resonance of comparison depends on the abstractions conveyed in the likeness of the things compared*. A good metaphor reverberates with the essential; this is the writer's principle of choice.

So Flannery O'Connor, in "A Good Man Is Hard to Find," describes the mother as having "a face as broad and innocent as a cabbage." A soccer ball is roughly the same size and shape as a cabbage; so is a schoolroom globe; so is a street lamp. But if the mother's face had been as broad and innocent as any of these things, she would be a different woman altogether. A cabbage is also rural, heavy, dense, and cheap, and so it conveys a whole complex of abstractions about the woman's class and mentality. There is, on the other hand, no innocence in the face of Shrike, in Nathanael West's *Miss Lonelyhearts*, who "buried his triangular face like a hatchet in her neck."

Sometimes the aptness of a comparison is achieved by taking it from an area of reference relevant to the thing compared. In *Dombey and Son*, Charles Dickens describes the ships' instrument maker, Solomon Gills, as having "eyes as red as if they had been small suns looking at you through a fog." The simile suggests a seascape, whereas in *One Flew Over the Cuckoo's Nest*, Ken Kesey's Ruckly, rendered inert by shock therapy, has eyes "all smoked up and gray and deserted inside like blown fuses." But the metaphor may range further from its original, in which case the abstraction conveyed must strike us as strongly and essentially appropriate. William Faulkner's Emily Grierson in "A Rose for Emily" has "haughty black eyes in a face the flesh of which was strained across the temple and about the eyesockets as you imagine a lighthouse-keeper's face ought to look." Miss Emily has no connection with the sea, but the metaphor reminds us not only of her sternness and self-sufficiency, but also that she has isolated herself in a locked house. The same character as an old woman has eyes that "looked like two pieces of coal pressed into a lump of dough," and the image domesticates her, robs her of her light.

Both metaphors and similes can be *extended*, meaning that the writer continues to present aspects of likeness in the things compared.

> There was a white fog . . . standing all around you like something solid. At eight or nine, perhaps, it lifted as a shutter lifts. We had a glimpse of the towering multitude of trees, of the immense matted jungle, with the blazing little ball of sun hanging over it—all perfectly still—and then the shutter came down again, smoothly, as if sliding in greased grooves.
>
> Joseph Conrad, *Heart of Darkness*

Notice that Conrad moves from a generalized image of "something solid" to the specific simile "as a shutter lifts"; reasserts the simile as a metaphor, "then the shutter came down again"; and becomes still more specific in the extension "as if sliding in greased grooves."

Also note that Conrad emphasizes the dumb solidity of the fog by comparing the larger natural image with the smaller manufactured object. This is a technique that contemporary writers have used to effects both comic and profound, as when Frederick Barthelme in *The Brothers* describes a young woman "with a life stretching out in front of her like so many unrented videos" or a man's head "bobbing like an enormous Q-Tip against the little black sky."

In a more usual metaphoric technique, the smaller or more ordinary image is compared with one more significant or intense, as in this example from Louise Erdrich's "Machimanito," where the narrator invokes the names of Anishinabe Indians dead of tuberculosis:

> Their names grew within us, swelled to the brink of our lips, forced our eyes open in the middle of the night. We were filled with the water of the drowned, cold and black—airless water that lapped against the seal of our tongues or leaked slowly from the corners of our eyes. Within us, like ice shards, their names bobbed and shifted.

A *conceit*, which can be either metaphor or simile, is a comparison of two things radically and startlingly unlike—in Samuel Johnson's words, "yoked by violence together." A conceit is as far removed as possible from the purely sensuous comparison of "the eyes of the potato." It compares two things that have very little or no immediately apprehensible similarity; and so it is the nature of the conceit to be long. The author must explain to us, sometimes at great length, why these things can be said to be alike. When John Donne compares a flea to the Holy Trinity, the two images have no areas of reference in common, and we don't understand. He must explain to us that the flea, having bitten both the poet and his lover, now has the blood of three souls in its body.

The conceit is more common to poetry than to prose because of the density of its imagery, but it can be used to good effect in fiction. In *The Day of the Locust*, Nathanael West uses a conceit in an insistent devaluation of love. The screenwriter Claude Estee says:

> Love is like a vending machine, eh? Not bad. You insert a coin and press home the lever. There's some mechanical activity inside the bowels of the device. You receive a small sweet, frown at yourself in the dirty mirror, adjust your hat, take a firm grip on your umbrella and walk away, trying to look as though nothing had happened.

"Love is like a vending machine" is a conceit; if the writer didn't explain to us in what way love is like a vending machine, we'd founder trying to figure it out. So he goes on to develop the vending machine in images that suggest not "love" but seamy sex. The last image—"trying to look as though nothing had happened"—has nothing to do with the vending machine; we accept it because by this time we've fused the two ideas in our minds.

Deborah Galyan employs conceit in "The Incredible Appearing Man," in a playfully self-conscious description of the overpowering effect of a new baby's presence.

> A baby transforms you, body and soul. The moment you give birth, your mind is instantaneously filled with Styrofoam peanuts. Your past is trash-compacted to make room for all the peanuts. As the baby grows, you add more peanuts, and the little tin can of your past gets more compressed. But it is still there, underneath all the peanuts. The smashed cans of your past never entirely disappear.

The comparison of a mind and a trash compactor is a conceit because their physical or sensuous similarity is not the point. Rather, the similarity is in the abstract idea of material (metal cans or memories) that once loomed large being crushed and all but crowded out by the volume of daily experience.

## Metaphoric Faults to Avoid

Comparison is not a frivolity. It is, on the contrary, the primary business of the brain. Some eighteenth-century philosophers spoke of the human mind as a "*tabula rasa*," a blank slate on which sense impressions were recorded, compared, and grouped.

Now we're more likely to speak of the mind as a "computer" "storing" and "processing" "data." What both metaphors acknowledge is that comparison is the basis of all learning and all reasoning. When a child burns his hand on the stove and hears his mother say, "It's hot," and then goes toward the radiator and again hears her say, "It's hot," the child learns not to burn his fingers. The implicit real-life comparison is meant to convey a fact, and it teaches a mode of behavior. By contrast, the goal of literary comparison is to convey not a fact but a perception, and thereby to enlarge our scope of understanding. When we speak of "the flames of torment," our impulse is comprehension and compassion.

Nevertheless, metaphor is a dirty word in some critical circles, because of the strain of the pursuit. Clichés, mixed metaphors, and similes that are inept, unapt, obscure, or done to death mar good prose and tax the patience of the most willing reader. After eyes have been red suns, burnt-out fuses, lighthouse keepers, and lumps of coal, what else can they be?

The answer is, always something. But because by definition metaphor introduces an alien image into the flow of the story, metaphor is to some degree always self-conscious. Badly handled, it calls attention to the writer rather than to the meaning and produces a sort of hiccup in the reader's involvement. A good metaphor fits so neatly that it fuses to and illuminates the meaning. Generally speaking, where metaphors are concerned, less is more and, if in doubt, don't.

Certainly, there are more *don'ts* than *dos* to list for the writing of metaphor and simile, because every good comparison is its own justification by virtue of being apt and original.

To study good metaphor, read. In the meantime, avoid the following:

*Cliché* metaphors are metaphors so familiar that they have lost the force of their original meaning. They are inevitably apt comparisons; if they were not, they wouldn't have been repeated often enough to become clichés. But such images fail to surprise, and we blame the writer for this expenditure of energy without a payoff. Or, to put it a worse way:

Clichés are *the last word* in bad writing, and *it's a crying shame* to see all you *bright young things* spoiling your *deathless prose* with phrases as *old as the hills*. You must *keep your nose to the grindstone*, because *the sweet smell of success* only comes to those who *march to the tune of a different drummer*.

It's a sad fact that at this stage of literary history, you may not say that eyes are like pools or stars, and you should be very wary of saying that they flood with tears. These have been so often repeated that they've become shorthand for emotions (attractions in the first and second instances, grief in the third) without the felt force of those emotions. Anytime you as writer record an emotion without convincing us to feel that emotion, you introduce a fatal distance between author and reader. Therefore, neither may your characters be hawk-eyed nor eagle-eyed; nor may they have ruby lips or pearly teeth or peaches-and-cream complexions or necks like swans or thighs like hams. Let them not shed single tears or freeze like deer caught in headlights. If you sense—and you may—that the moment calls for the special intensity of metaphor, you may have to sift through a whole stock of clichés that come readily to mind. Or it may be time for freewriting and giving the mind room to play. Sometimes your internal critic may reject as fantastic the comparison that, on second look, proves fresh and apt.

In any case, *pools* and *stars* have become clichés for *eyes* because they capture and manifest something essential about the nature of eyes. As long as eyes continue to contain liquid and light, there will be a new way of saying so.

Cliché can be useful as a device, however, for establishing authorial distance from a character or narrator. If the author tells us that Rome wasn't built in a day, we're likely to think the author has little to contribute to human insight; but if a character says so, in speech or thought, the judgment attaches to the character rather than to the author.

> The door closed and he turned to find the dumpy figure, surmounted by the atrocious hat, coming toward him. "Well," she said, "*you only live once* and paying a little more for it, I at least won't *meet myself coming and going.*"
>
> "Some day I'll start making money . . ."
>
> "I think you're doing fine," she said, drawing on her gloves. "You've only been out of school a year. *Rome wasn't built in a day.*"

> Flannery O'Connor, "Everything That Rises Must Converge" (italics added)

*Far-fetched metaphors* are the opposite of clichés: They surprise but are not apt. As the dead metaphor *far-fetched* suggests, the mind must travel too far to carry back the likeness, and too much is lost on the way. When such a comparison does work, we speak laudatorily of a "leap of the imagination." But when it does not, what we face is in effect a failed conceit: The explanation of what is alike about these two things does not convince. Very good writers in the search for originality sometimes fetch too far. Ernest Hemingway's talent was not for metaphor, and on the rare occasions that he used a metaphor, he was likely to strain. In this passage from A *Farewell to Arms,* the protagonist has escaped a firing squad and is fleeing the war.

> You had lost your cars and your men as a floorwalker loses the stock of his department in a fire. There was, however, no insurance. You were out of it now. You had no more obligation. If they shot floorwalkers after a fire in the department store because they spoke with an accent they had always had, then certainly the floorwalkers would not be expected to return when the store opened again for business. They might seek other employment; if there was any other employment and the police did not get them.

Well, this doesn't work. We may be willing to see the likeness between stock lost in a department store fire and men and cars lost in a military retreat; but "they" *don't* shoot floorwalkers as the Italian military shot defeated line officers. And although a foreign accent might be a disadvantage in a foreign war, it's hard to see how a floorwalker could be killed because of one, although it might make it hard for him to get hired in the first place, if. . . . The mind twists trying to find any illuminating or essential logic in the comparison of a soldier to a floorwalker, and fails, so that the protagonist's situation is trivialized in the attempt.

*Mixed metaphors* are so called because they ask us to compare the original image with things from two or more different areas of reference: *As you walk the path of life, don't founder on the reefs of ignorance.* Life can be a path or a sea, but it cannot be both at the same time. The point of the metaphor is to fuse two images in a single tension. The mind is adamantly unwilling to fuse three.

Separate metaphors or similes too close together, especially if they come from areas of reference very different in value or tone, disturb in the same way the mixed metaphor does. The mind doesn't leap; it staggers.

> They fought like rats in a Brooklyn sewer. Nevertheless her presence was the axiom of his heart's geometry, and when she was away you would see him walking up and down the street dragging his cane along the picket fence like an idle boy's stick.

Any of these metaphors or similes might be acceptable by itself, but rats, axioms, and boys' sticks connote three different areas and tones, and two sentences cannot contain them all. Pointed in too many directions, a reader's attention follows none.

*Obscure* and *overdone metaphors* falter because the author has misjudged the difficulty of the comparison. The result is either confusion or an insult to the reader's intelligence. In the case of obscurity, a similarity in the author's mind isn't getting onto the page. One student described the spines on a prickly pear cactus as being "slender as a fat man's fingers." I was completely confused by this. Was it ironic, that the spines weren't slender at all? Ah no, he said, hadn't I noticed how startling it was when someone with a fleshy body had bony fingers and toes? The trouble here was that the author knew what he meant but had left out the essential abstraction in the comparison, the startling quality of the contrast: "the spines of the fleshy prickly pear, like slender fingers on a fat man."

In this case, the simile was underexplained. It's probably a more common impulse—we're so anxious to make sure the reader gets it—to explain the obvious. In the novel *Raw Silk,* I had the narrator describe quarrels with her husband, "which I used to face with my dukes up in high confidence that we'd soon clear the air. The air can't be cleared now. We live in marital Los Angeles. This is the air—polluted, poisoned." A critic friend pointed out to me that anybody who didn't know about L.A. smog wouldn't get it anyway, and that all the last two words did was ram the comparison down the reader's throat. He was right. "The air can't be cleared now. We live in marital Los Angeles. This is the air." The rewrite is much stronger because it neither explains nor exaggerates; and the reader enjoys supplying the metaphoric link.

Metaphors using *topical references,* including brand names, esoteric objects, or celebrity names, can work as long as a sense of the connection is given; don't rely for effect on knowledge that the reader may not have. To write, "The sisters looked like the Dixie Chicks" is to make the trio do your job; and if the reader happens to be a

Beethoven buff, or Hungarian, or reading your story twenty years from now, there may be no way of knowing what the reference refers to. "They had the blindingly blond, in-your-face exuberance of the Dixie Chicks" will convey the sense even for someone who doesn't watch country music cable. Likewise, "She was as beautiful as Theda Bara" may not mean much to you, whereas if I say, "She had the saucer eyes and satin hair of Theda Bara," you'll get it, close enough.

## Allegory

*Allegory* is a fictional form in which the action of the story represents a different action or a philosophical idea. The simplest illustration of an allegory is a fable, in which, for example, the race between the tortoise and the hare is used to illustrate the philosophical notion that "the race is not always to the swift." Such a story can be seen as an extended simile, with the original figure of the comparison suppressed: The tortoise and the hare represent types of human beings, but people are never mentioned and the comparison takes place in the reader's mind. George Orwell's *Animal Farm* is a less naïve animal allegory, exploring ideas about corruption in a socialist society. Children may read *The Lion, the Witch, and the Wardrobe* without seeing the Christian allegory clear to adults; *The Lord of the Flies* has long been taught to adolescents to illustrate how impulses toward evil and goodness become manifest in groups. The plots of such stories are self-contained, but their significance lies in the reference to outside events or ideas.

In the hands of Dante, John Bunyan, Franz Kafka, Samuel Beckett, and such contemporary authors as John Edgar Wideman and Ursula K. Le Guin, the allegory has yielded works of serious philosophical and political insight. But it is a tricky form and can seem to smirk. A naïve philosophical fable leads to a simpleminded idea that can be stated in a single phrase; a social satire rests on our familiarity with the latest Washington sex scandal, sports lockout, or celebrity brouhaha, and so appeals to a limited and insular readership.

## Symbol

A *symbol* is an object or event that represents something beyond itself. Unlike metaphor and simile, it need not contain a comparison. Sometimes an object is invested arbitrarily with such meaning, as a flag represents a nation and patriotism. Sometimes a single event stands for a whole complex of events, as the crucifixion of Christ stands as well for resurrection and redemption. Such events and attendant qualities in turn may become invested in an object like the cross. These symbols are not metaphor: the cross represents redemption but is not similar to redemption, which cannot be said to be wooden or T-shaped. In Flannery O'Connor's 1965 story "Everything That Rises Must Converge," the protagonist's mother encounters a black woman wearing the same absurd hat of which she has been so proud. The hat can in no way be said to "resemble" desegregation, but in the course of the story it comes to represent the tenacious nostalgia of gentility and the aspirations of the new black middle class, and therefore the unacknowledged "converging" of equality.

Nevertheless, most literary symbols, including this one, do in the course of the action derive their extra meaning from some sort of likeness on the level of emotional or ideological abstraction. The hat is not "like" desegregation, but the action of the story reveals that both women are able to buy such a hat and choose it; this is a concrete example of equality, and so represents the larger concept of equality.

> THE TRUER THE SYMBOL, THE DEEPER it leads you, the more meaning it opens up.
>
> Flannery O'Connor

Margaret Drabble's novel *The Garrick Year* recounts the disillusionment of a young wife and mother who finds no escape from her situation. The book ends with a family picnic in an English meadow and the return home.

> On the way back to the car, Flora dashed at a sheep that was lying in the path, but unlike all the others it did not get up and move: it stared at us instead with a sick and stricken indignation. Flora passed quickly on, pretending for pride's sake that she had not noticed its recalcitrance; but as I passed, walking slowly, supported by David, I looked more closely and I saw curled up and clutching at the sheep's belly a real snake. I did not say anything to David: I did not want to admit that I had seen it, but I did see it, I can see it still. It is the only wild snake that I have ever seen. In my book on Herefordshire it says that that part of the country is notorious for its snakes. But "Oh, well, so what," is all that one can say, the Garden of Eden was crawling with them too, and David and I managed to lie amongst them for one whole pleasant afternoon. One just has to keep on and to pretend, for the sake of the children, not to notice. Otherwise one might just as well stay at home.

The sheep is a symbol of the young woman's emotional situation. It does resemble her, but only on the level of the abstractions: sickness, indignation, and yet resignation at the fatal dangers of the human condition. There is here a metaphor that could be expressed as such (*she was as sick and resigned as the sheep*), but the strength of the symbol is that such literal expression does not take place: we let the sheep stand in the place of the young woman while we reach out to the larger significance.

A symbol may also begin as and grow from a metaphor, so that it finally contains more qualities than the original comparison. In John Irving's novel *The World According to Garp*, the young Garp mishears the word "undertow" as "under toad" and compares the danger of the sea to the lurking fantasies of his childish imagination.

Throughout the novel the "under toad" persists, and it comes symbolically to represent all the submerged dangers of ordinary life, ready to drag Garp under just when he thinks he is swimming under his own power.

Fiction is better experienced than interpreted. . . . To fully understand a symbol is to kill it.

Ron Hansen

One important distinction in the use of literary symbols is between those symbols of which the character is aware, and therefore "belong" to him or her, and those symbols of which only writer and reader are aware, and therefore belong to the work. This distinction is often important to characterization, theme, and distance. In the passage quoted from *The Garrick Year,* the narrator is clearly aware of the import of the sheep, and her awareness suggests her intelligence and the final acceptance of her situation, so that we identify with her in recognizing the symbol. In "Everything That Rises Must Converge," the adult son recognizes the symbolism implied as

the vision of the two hats, identical, broke upon him with the radiance of a brilliant sunrise. His face was suddenly lit with joy. He could not believe that Fate had thrust upon his mother such a lesson.

His mother, on the other hand, does not recognize the hat as a symbol of equality, and this distances us from her perception.

Symbols are subject to all the same faults as metaphor: cliché, strain, obscurity, obviousness, and overwriting. For these reasons (and because the word "Symbolism" also describes a particular late-nineteenth-century movement in French poetry, with connotations of obscurity, dream, and magical incantation), *symbolism* as a method has sometimes been treated with scorn in the hard-nosed postmodern world. Flannery O'Connor attributed this attitude in part to a reductive manner of reading.

. . . the word *symbol* scares a good many people off, just as the word *art* does. They seem to feel that a symbol is some mysterious thing put in arbitrarily by the writer to frighten the common reader—sort of a literary Masonic grip that is only for the initiated . . . they approach it as if it were a problem in algebra. Find *x.* And when they do find or think they find this abstraction, *x,* then they go off with an elaborate sense of satisfaction and the notion that they have "understood" the story. Many students confuse the *process* of understanding a thing with understanding it.

*Mystery and Manners*

## THE SYMBOLIC MIND

It seems to me incontrovertible that the writing process is inherently and by definition symbolic. In the structuring of plot, the creation of character and atmosphere, the choice of object, detail, and language, you are selecting and arranging elements to signify more than their literal existence. If this were not so, then you would have no unifying principle of choice and might just as well write about any other sets of events, characters, and objects.

People constantly function symbolically. By night our dreaming minds fuse their own symbols, merging the eternally missed exam or public nakedness with the current anxieties of the dreamer's life. By day, in speaking, we leap past unwieldy words with intuition, body language, tone, and symbol. "Is the oven supposed to be on?" he asks. He is only peripherally curious about whether the oven is supposed to be on. He is really complaining: *You're scatterbrained and extravagant with the money I go out and earn.* "If I don't preheat it, the muffins won't crest," she says, meaning: *You didn't catch me this time! You're always complaining about the food, and God knows I wear myself out trying to please you.* "We used to have salade niçoise in the summertime," he recalls, meaning: *Don't be so damn triumphant. You're still extravagant, and you haven't got the class you used to have when we were young.* "We used to keep a garden," she says, meaning: *You're always away on weekends and never have time to do anything with me because you don't love me anymore; I think you have a mistress.* "What do you expect of me!" he explodes, and neither of them is surprised that ovens, muffins, salads, and gardens have erupted. When people say "we quarreled over nothing," this is what they mean—through the subtext of their dialogue, they quarreled over symbols.

When a literary symbol fails, it is most often because it has not been integrated into the texture of the story. As Bonnie Friedman puts it in *Writing Past Dark*: "Before a thing can be a symbol it must be a thing. It must do its job as a thing in the world before and during and after you have projected all your meaning all over it." In a typical example, we begin the story in a room of a dying woman alone with her collection of perfume bottles. The story ranges back over her rich and sensuous life, and at the end we focus on an empty perfume bottle. It is meant to move us at her death, but it does not. Yet the fault is not in the perfume bottle itself. Presumably a perfume bottle may express mortality as well as a hat may express racial equality. The fault is rather that we need to be convinced of the importance this woman placed on scent as essence, need to know how the collection has played a part in the conflicts of her life, need to see her fumbling now toward her favorite, so that we can emotionally equate the spilling or evaporation of the scent with the death of her own spirit.

GOOD DESCRIPTION IS SYMBOLIC NOT BECAUSE THE writer plants symbols in it but because . . . he forces symbols still largely mysterious to him up into his conscious mind where, little by little as his fiction progresses, he can work with them and finally understand them.

John Gardner

A symbolic object, situation, or event may err because it seems to have been imposed upon the story, existing for its own sake rather than emanating naturally from the characters' lives. Or it may err because it is too heavy or heavy-handed; that is, the author keeps pushing the symbol at us, nudging us in the ribs to say: Get it? In any of these cases we will say that the symbol is *artificial*—a curious word in the critical vocabulary, analogous to the charge of a *formula* plot, since *art*, like *form*, is a word of praise. All writing is "artificial," and when we charge it with being so, we mean that it isn't artificial enough, that the artifice has not concealed itself so as to give the illusion of the natural, and that the artificer must go back to work.

# *The First Day*

### EDWARD P. JONES

On an otherwise unremarkable September morning, long before I learned to be ashamed of my mother, she takes my hand and we set off down New Jersey Avenue to begin my very first day of school. I am wearing a checkeredlike blue-and-green cotton dress, and scattered about these colors are bits of yellow and white and brown. My mother has uncharacteristically spent nearly an hour on my hair that morning, plaiting and replaiting so that now my scalp tingles. Whenever I turn my head quickly, my nose fills with the faint smell of Dixie Peach hair grease. The smell is somehow a soothing one now and I will reach for it time and time again before the morning ends. All the plaits, each with a blue barrette near the tip and each twisted into an uncommon sturdiness, will last until I go to bed that night, something that has never happened before. My stomach is full of milk and oatmeal sweetened with brown sugar. Like everything else I have on, my pale green slip and underwear are new, the underwear having come three to a plastic package with a little girl on the front who appears to be dancing. Behind my ears, my mother, to stop my whining, has dabbed the stingiest bit of her gardenia perfume, the last present my father gave her before he disappeared into memory. Because I cannot smell it, I have only her word that the perfume is there. I am also wearing yellow socks trimmed with thin lines of black and white around the tops. My shoes are my greatest joy, black patent-leather miracles, and when one is nicked at the toe later that morning in class, my heart will break.

I am carrying a pencil, a pencil sharpener, and a small ten-cent tablet with a black-and-white speckled cover. My mother does not believe that a girl in kindergarten needs such things, so I am taking them only because of my insistent whining and because they are presents from our neighbors, Mary Keith and Blondelle Harris. Miss Mary and Miss Blondelle are watching my two younger sisters until my mother returns. The women are as precious to me as my mother and sisters. Out playing one day, I have overheard an older child, speaking to another child, call Miss Mary and Miss Blondelle a word that is brand new to me. This is my mother: When I say the word in fun to one of my sisters, my mother slaps me across the mouth and the word is lost for years and years.

All the way down New Jersey Avenue, the sidewalks are teeming with children. In my neighborhood, I have many friends, but I see none of them as my mother and I walk. We cross New York Avenue, we cross Pierce Street, and we cross L and K, and still I see no one who knows my name. At I Street, between New Jersey Avenue and Third Street, we enter Seaton Elementary School, a timeworn, sad-faced building across the street from my mother's church, Mt. Carmel Baptist.

Just inside the front door, women out of the advertisements in *Ebony* are greeting other parents and children. The woman who greets us has pearls thick as jumbo marbles that come down almost to her navel, and she acts as if she had known me all my life, touching my shoulder, cupping her hand under my chin. She is enveloped in a perfume that I only know is not gardenia. When, in answer to her question, my mother tells her that we live at 1227 New Jersey Avenue, the woman first seems to be picturing in her head where we live. Then she shakes her head and says that we are at the wrong school, that we should be at Walker-Jones.

My mother shakes her head vigorously. "I want her to go here," my mother says. "If I'da wanted her someplace else, I'da took her there." The woman continues to act as if she has known me all my life, but she tells my mother that we live beyond the area that Seaton serves. My mother is not convinced and for several more minutes she questions the woman about why I cannot attend Seaton. For as many Sundays as I can remember, perhaps even Sundays when I was in her womb, my mother has pointed across I Street to Seaton as we come and go to Mt. Carmel. "You gonna go there and learn about the whole world." But one of the guardians of that place is saying no, and no again. I am learning this about my mother: The higher up on the scale of respectability a person is—and teachers are rather high up in her eyes—the less she is liable to let them push her around. But finally, I see in her eyes the closing gate, and she takes my hand and we leave the building. On the steps, she stops as people move past us on either side.

"Mama, I can't go to school?"

She says nothing at first, then takes my hand again and we are down the steps quickly and nearing New Jersey Avenue before I can blink. This is my mother: She says, "One monkey don't stop no show."

Walker-Jones is a larger, newer school and I immediately like it because of that. But it is not across the street from my mother's church, her rock, one of her connections to God, and I sense her doubts as she absently rubs her thumb over the back of her hand. We find our way to the crowded auditorium where gray metal chairs are set up in the middle of the room. Along the wall to the left are tables and other chairs. Every chair seems occupied by a child or adult. Somewhere in the room a child is crying, a cry that rises above the buzz-talk of so many people. Strewn about the floor are dozens and dozens of pieces of white paper, and people are walking over them without any thought of picking them up. And seeing this lack of concern, I am all of a sudden afraid.

"Is this where they register for school?" my mother asks a woman at one of the tables.

The woman looks up slowly as if she has heard this question once too often. She nods. She is tiny, almost as small as the girl standing beside her. The woman's hair is set in a mass of curlers and all of those curlers are made of paper money, here a dollar bill, there a five-dollar bill. The girl's hair is arrayed in curls, but some of them are beginning to droop and this makes me happy. On the table beside the woman's pocketbook is a large notebook, worthy of someone in high school, and looking at me looking at the notebook, the girl places her hand possessively on it. In her other hand she holds several pencils with thick crowns of additional erasers.

"These the forms you gotta use?" my mother asks the woman, picking up a few pieces of the paper from the table. "Is this what you have to fill out?"

The woman tells her yes, but that she need fill out only one.

"I see," my mother says, looking about the room. Then: "Would you help me with this form? That is, if you don't mind."

The woman asks my mother what she means.

"This form. Would you mind helpin me fill it out?"

The woman still seems not to understand.

"I can't read it. I don't know how to read or write, and I'm askin you to help me." My mother looks at me, then looks away. I know almost all of her looks, but this one is brand new to me. "Would you help me, then?"

The woman says Why sure, and suddenly she appears happier, so much more satis-fied with everything. She finishes the form for her daughter and my mother and I step aside to wait for her. We find two chairs nearby and sit. My mother is now diseased, according to the girl's eyes, and until the moment her mother takes her and the form to the front of the auditorium, the girl never stops looking at my mother. I stare back at her. "Don't stare," my mother says to me. "You know better than that."

Another woman out of the *Ebony* ads takes the woman's child away. Now, the woman says upon returning, let's see what we can do for you two.

My mother answers the questions the woman reads off the form. They start with my last name, and then on to the first and middle names. This is school, I think. This is going to school. My mother slowly enunciates each word of my name. This is my mother: As the questions go on, she takes from her pocketbook document after docu-ment, as if they will support my right to attend school, as if she has been saving them up for just this moment. Indeed, she takes out more papers than I have ever seen her do in other places: my birth certificate, my baptismal record, a doctor's letter concerning my bout with chicken pox, rent receipts, records of immunization, a letter about our public assistance payments, even her marriage license—every single paper that has anything even remotely to do with my five-year-old life. Few of the papers are needed here, but it does not matter and my mother continues to pull out the documents with the purpose-fulness of a magician pulling out a long string of scarves. She has learned that money is the beginning and end of everything in this world, and when the woman finishes, my mother offers her fifty cents, and the woman accepts it without hesitation. My mother and I are just about the last parent and child in the room.

My mother presents the form to a woman sitting in front of the stage, and the woman looks at it and writes something on a white card, which she gives to my mother. Before long, the woman who has taken the girl with the drooping curls appears from behind us, speaks to the sitting woman, and introduces herself to my mother and me. She's to be my teacher, she tells my mother. My mother stares.

We go into the hall, where my mother kneels down to me. Her lips are quivering. "I'll be back to pick you up at twelve o'clock. I don't want you to go nowhere. You just wait right here. And listen to every word she say." I touch her lips and press them together. It is an old, old game between us. She puts my hand down at my side, which is not part of the game. She stands and looks a second at the teacher, then she turns and walks away. I see where she has darned one of her socks the night before. Her shoes make loud sounds in the hall. She passes through the doors and I can still hear the loud sounds of her shoes. And even when the teacher turns me toward the classrooms and I hear what must be the singing and talking of all the children in the world, I can still hear my mother's footsteps above it all.

# Hotel Touraine

### ROBERT OLEN BUTLER

*This is where the people who have more money than brains put up. They pay about $100 per month for 2 rooms furnished when they could afford to have a nice home of their own. I had a job in this hotel last year. Worked there for a week. Saw lots of style, but don't see as the people were any happier.*
—Message on the back of a postcard illustrated with a picture of the Hotel Touraine, Boston, Massachusetts

My fifth day at the hotel I pretty near ran down John Stanford Barnhill in the corridor past the second-floor library. I was making time with a pitcher of water to a public room along the way, where some other swell was receiving guests like the whole place was his mansion and he was doing an at-home in his own parlor. The Oriental rugs are thick underfoot all over the Touraine and I was making no sound and Barnhill bolts out of the library door and I pull up sharp, tucking the pitcher into me so I'll take the splash instead of him. Which I do, down my bellboy jacket with the brass buttons, and he says, "Whoa, Dobbin," like I'm a spooked dray horse. I just keep my mouth shut. No *Sorry, sir* or *Excuse me, sir* like I know I'm supposed to do, but this guy's about my age, not much into his twenties, and he's in a serge suit with cigars sticking out of his pocket and he gets my goat in an instant. I'm still figuring out what to think about this job and I decide right off not to play the lackey to guys like this. This is even before I know who he is, exactly, heir to millions by being born the only grandnephew of somebody else who was born to millions and so on. I just take the splash and sashay around him and head on down to where I'm supposed to go. He could yell something after me, about my being a rude working-class bumpkin or some such, but he doesn't. I figure it's running through his head, though.

Then later that day I'm going out of the place in my own clothes, my uniform hanging in a wire locker in the changing room, and you'd think he'd never recognize me, but you'd think wrong. I'm going out of the hotel and he says, "You one of those bare-headed anarchists to boot?" To *boot* meaning bomb-throwing anarchist in addition to water-spilling bellboy, and the whole thing has been set off by my going without a hat, which has always been my way, unlike the vast herds of men in the world. But I don't like a thing to bind me in around my head. All of which sounds grand and free on my part, but I guess that'd be wrong too, because in response to his cheek I say, "No, sir," and I keep on going and I like to bite my tongue off.

I've picked up the habit of servant talk already, after just five days, and I shoot him a hard look over my shoulder and he's already turned away, wearing a Prince Albert coat and a high-crowned bowler, which he's just starting to tip to a woman in a veil going by. So I dash across Tremont, dodging a streetcar and a couple of galloping horses and the express wagon they're pulling, and I cut into the Common.

This is *my* parlor, the Common, and I take a winding way through, slowing down, putting Barnhill out of my mind, though a bunch of guys like him are always floating through this place as well, usually squiring young women in big straw hats full of ostrich feathers. But I swing over to the open fields and the fellows there are playing baseball and one of them who thinks he's Tris Speaker makes a headlong dive for a hit into the outfield and he almost has it but not quite. Then he's in for it to get back to his feet and chase the ball down while the batter's making for third base. I don't blame him for trying, even if he'll never play for the Red Sox.

I turn away and move on and dig into my pocket for the pack of Meccas I bought in the lobby shop before I left the hotel. I open it and stick a smoke into my mouth and light it up and I'm starting to think about Barnhill again. Also there's some fat cigar of a guy in a bowler putting the mash on a sweet-faced girl on the path ahead of me. I go around them and I blow smoke at his right ear and I dig out my free card from the cigarette pack. They're still giving away Champion Athletes and I've got a guy with aviator goggles strapped on his head and a biplane up in the sky over his shoulder and the clouds are streaked with sunset and he's ready to go, this guy Arch Hoxsey. I stick him in my shirt pocket with the cigarettes and hustle up, moving smartly away from my fifth day of work at the Hotel Touraine.

Twenty minutes later, after skirting the edge of Beacon Hill where Barnhill's money was waiting in a marble-columned mansion for somebody to die, I climbed the steps of our tenement in the West End and there was a great caterwauling of kids and a stink from the third-floor toilet and Mr. Spinetti's voice was filling the stairwell from the top floor down, him being the Caruso of tenement-hollerers. I hesitated at our door and stubbed out a second cigarette I'd let myself have right away, just to get certain people out of my mind, and then I stepped in.

Mama was near the window, hunched over the side table, rolling cigars. Her back was to me. "Eli," she said, but she didn't turn around.

"Mama," I said. The smell of tobacco had thickened the air in the room. I stood for a moment getting up the strength to push through it. Maybe it was mostly not wanting to see her hands at work on these things that made me hesitate, but it felt more like I was struggling against the air being heavy with this smell. Then I did finally cross the room and I was behind Mama. Beside her on the floor on one side was a gunnysack of filler leaf and on the other a wooden box with the wrapper leaves, and her hands were moving, moving. I laid my own hand on her shoulder and I wanted to lift my eyes out the window, like the tenement across the way was some great landscape or something, but I couldn't help watching her hands rolling around and around this fancy man's cigar, the thing shaping up there, the loose leaves tightening as she rolled it and it would end up in John Stanford Barnhill's mouth, or somebody just like him, and Mama would get her eight mills pay. Now I looked out the window. Her sill pillow was there for later when she'd lean out into the night and talk to the women in the windows across the way.

"Just a moment," she said. "Let me finish this one."

I went and sat at the small round oak table where we ate and read and talked, the one piece we'd been able to keep from our plans for a house. Papa died under the hooves and wheels of a wagon hauling bricks, down at the wharf, right when we were going to be okay, when we were boarding in a nice house and Papa had plans to buy a bungalow from Sears and Roebuck and put it up out the streetcar line in some direction or other. I won't count the years it's been since. The night before, he gave me Rube Waddell of the St. Louis Browns from a pack of Sweet Caporals he'd smoked that day. Rube in portrait, no cap, his hair parted neatly down the middle. "This man made himself out of nothing," Papa said.

Mama sat down beside me now. I held her hand on the tabletop. She smelled of tobacco. Her eyes looked gray in the dim light. "How's it at your job?" she said.

"Okay," I said.

"You're doing right?"

"Sure."

"They'll take to you."

"I don't know," I said.

She took her hand from under mine and patted at me there, to reassure me. "I did a hundred twenty today," she said.

I looked away from her, landing on the wall where she had a chromo hung of the woman at the well and Jesus asking her for water.

"Nearly a dollar," she said.

That night I lay on my pallet propped up against the wall with a candle burning beside me. I was trying to read a Zane Grey but the cowboys with their horses and ten-gallon hats were steaming me up tonight for some reason. They think all you have to do is plug it or throw a rope around it or ride it to the ground and that solves everything. I could hear Mama breathing heavy in her sleep across the room. Somewhere on another floor some guy was yelling and somewhere else a baby was crying, but these sounds were dim, coming through all the walls in between. I reached into the pocket of my shirt hanging on a chair near me to get my cigarettes and I found Arch Hoxsey. He had a fur collar around his neck. It was cold high up in the air, I guess, no matter what the season. I turned the card over, and it said he started out working in a factory before he became a champion athlete automobile driver and then aeroplane flyer. He set a record and he rose to 11,000 feet. And then he died. He crashed trying to come back to earth on the last day of 1910. I turned his card over and looked him in the eyes. My papa would respect him. For myself, I couldn't figure if he was a fool to leave the ground.

The next morning I was sent to John Stanford Barnhill's rooms on the eighth floor. On the silver tray balanced on my palm was a bottle of whiskey. This was about ten in the morning, though I shouldn't sneer because even Papa started early some days. So I knock on his door, which is slightly open, and he calls for me to come in. I push the door and step into the place, a regular cut-velvet and leather sitting room. It smells strong of cigar smoke. He's left one lit on a saucer on the reading table. The gentleman himself is hanging out the open lower sash like the women in the tenements.

"Your whiskey," I say, and he draws his body in from the window.

"On the table," he says, and I put the tray down next to his cigar. I stare hard at the thing and I guess he sees me doing that.

"There hasn't been a good Cuban crop since 1908," he says, as if he knows I'd know something about cigars.

I look at him.

"They're charging seventy cents for the good ones downstairs," he says.

Now I understand. Let the anarchist bellboy know how much money you've got, that you can spend better than a worker's daily wage on a couple of cigars.

"My mother does that," I say.

"What's that?"

"Hangs out the window. She talks to her friends and watches the street." I regret this at once. Trying to show him he's not so different from us, I've just made Mama look bad.

Barnhill flips his head to the side a little to acknowledge the window and he doesn't even crack a smile, much less a sneer. Instead, he says, "There's elms out there on the Common that John Hancock planted."

"You related to him, are you?"

Now I get a little sneery smile. "John Hancock is . . ."

"I know who he is."

Barnhill laughs. "Of course. No. I'm not related to him."

"So you like looking at trees."

"You want a drink?" he asks, and I think he's dead serious.

"There's easier ways to get me fired," I say.

Barnhill laughs again. He moves to the reading table and I back off a step. He touches the bottle but goes to thinking about something instead. His hand just stays there holding the neck of the bottle, and he's looking at it, thinking. I back up another step. It's time to get out of the room. I turn, and he says, "Not so fast."

I stop and face him again and he's digging in his vest pocket. He holds out his hand with a dime lifted by the thumb and forefinger. "Your tip," he says.

It's two steps away. It's twelve and a half cigars' worth of work. He's not moving. Neither am I. He gives the dime a little up-flip with his hand, like to say, Come and get it.

I lift my chin just a bit and I say, "Put it toward your next Cuban downstairs," and I'm out of that room in a flash.

Not that John Stanford Barnhill struck me as somebody real different from a dozen other guys I'd seen around the Touraine already, living in a hotel when they could so easily have what Papa had wanted all his life. A few of them even had wives with them, so they weren't all just helpless bachelors gagging on a silver spoon. They lived in a hotel so guys like me could hop for them and they could have a chambermaid come in and take away their soiled linens and they could just stroll downstairs and eat a fancy dinner with a little orchestra playing, but of course they could have that in homes of their own if they wanted, except for maybe the orchestra, so I just couldn't get myself to understand. Still can't.

Anyway, later in my sixth day at the Touraine, a bellhop from the next shift sent word he was sick and the manager asked me to stay on for a few extra hours and I said okay. And I run into Barnhill in the early evening while I'm at the front desk gathering up the bags of a man and his wife in automobile dusters. Barnhill is going out and he sees me just as I stand up straight with my arms and hands full and he tips his bowler at me going by, trying to get my goat. I just keep my face hard and steady and he puts his hat back down on his head and gives it a little tap as he goes out the door and into the night. A few minutes later I forget to talk like a servant to the guy in the duster, I guess—he asks me where the electric call bell is and I say, "Over there," and don't mention anything about sir or madam or let-me-lick-the-dust-off-your-boots—and I get a glare from him that I recognize for what it is right off, and still I don't say anything respectful to try to make it up. I don't get a tip and I don't blame him, I guess, seeing as what he's used to from a guy in my place, but I'm still working up an anger that I hope will stay put till this day is over. Then about ten or so the manager tells me things have slowed down enough, I should go on home, and I haven't popped anybody yet, so I'm glad to change from my bellhop suit fast and get out of there.

I don't cut through the Common but go up the mall along Tremont. There are lots of people around. That's good. I walk along among all these people, some in fancy dress and some in work clothes and some smoking a bummed cigarette and some a Cuban cigar, and we all just go on along together and there's a sharp breeze blowing, the first little whisper of the winter ahead, and then I'm coming up to the subway entrance at Park Street. The one-armed man with his two fox-colored dogs who walk around on their back legs is still selling the late edition. I pay a penny for it and then I see a crowd over by the little building where the steps go down to the train. I fold the paper and put it in my pocket and stroll over.

At the center of the crowd is an old man with a telescope on a tripod and he's got a sign up saying TEN CENTS TO SEE THE MOON. I stand watching for a minute. Some guy makes a big show of pulling out his ten cents for the girl he's with, and she sits on the little stool beneath the telescope, smoothing out her dress and pushing back her hat piled high with muslin roses, and then she looks into the telescope and she cries out like she's seen somebody jump off a bridge. The crowd all goes to muttering in wonder at her shock and somebody else steps forward to pay a dime. For all I know, the guy and the girl in the big hat are confederates of the telescope man and they've been put up to this little show just to get the crowd going. But I find myself wanting to look, all the same.

And then Barnhill is at my elbow. "You ever want to just go to the moon?" he says.

I look at him. I get the feeling he's putting the needle in me again, but if he'd like to have a go at me, I wish he'd just do it straight, more like a man. All I know to do is keep my mouth shut.

Then he says, "I figure I owe you a dime. Go look at the moon, on me. Okay?"

He's got that dime up between us again. I take it.

"Good," he says.

We both square around and wait for some guy to finish with his look, and I'm not even thinking to give the dime back. I'm not sure why this telescope makes it different, about taking money from John Stanford Barnhill, but it does. Then I get my chance. I step forward and give Barnhill's money to the telescope man and I say, "I want to see something different."

The old man holds up a forefinger like he's got just the thing. He crouches behind his telescope and looks in and swivels it around and then moves aside. I step over and bend down and I look. Against the dark is a small white globe, and it's ringed all around. "The planet Saturn," the man says to me. Then he tells the crowd, "This gentleman is now on the planet Saturn, the sixth of our sun's eight planets," and he goes on with his pitch. I just ignore him. I watch this other world moving along out there millions of miles away and I wonder who it is that lives on Saturn and what makes them tick. Then the telescope man's hand is on my shoulder and he says, "Time's up."

I straighten, and it takes a moment to get my bearings. I move off toward the Common, away from where I'd left Barnhill. The ring of gawkers opens for me and I'm into the dark, and then Barnhill is beside me again. "You went farther than the moon," he says.

"I went to your home planet," I say.

He laughs, though it sounds forced. "I've got my ticket back," he says.

He's walking with me now and it seems there's more to this than just trying to show up the bellhop. He smells of whiskey, but he's walking steady. "You don't like me," he says.

"Liking the guests ain't part of my job," I say.

"It doesn't make any difference," he says.

We're into an open part of the Common and the breeze has picked up pretty fierce. It's got a sting to it now.

"I'm finished at the Touraine anyway," Barnhill says.

I'm not paying any real attention to him. I'm just thinking about getting away from him. "I've got to get on home," I say, though the word catches in my throat: *home*. I've never had to call the tenement Mama and me live in by that name, and it makes me angry at Barnhill, his forcing me to say this.

We're both stopped now on the path, the empty field before us, the stars and the planets whirling around overhead. What he says about leaving the Touraine finally sinks in.

"Finished?" I say.

Barnhill kind of shivers. "You should wear a hat in this weather," he says, and I'll be damned if he doesn't take off his bowler and put it on my head.

It settles in perfect. I can feel the soft inner rim of it ringing across just below my hairline and on around my head and the hat's light there and it's even made it like the wind has stopped blowing, though I still can feel the bite of air on my face and hands if I try. But I'm fine inside the hat. I let it stay there. "You buying yourself a house?" I ask.

He runs a hand through his hair and lifts his chin a little. "Not quite," he says. "My aunt's cutting me off. She doesn't think much of me either, as it happens."

I'm not proud of it, but the first thing out of my mouth is, "I can get you on as a bellhop."

He looks at me and his face is white from the moon and I find myself wishing he had the guts to pop me. I deserve it and I won't raise a hand back at him. But he just looks at me and he doesn't say a word. So I reach up to his hat to take it off and he says, "No. Keep it."

That's the last thing I'm about to do. I lift the hat and I put it on his head and he doesn't resist. I feel the wind sharp on me again. We just look at each other and there's no more words. Finally I say, "Good night then."

"Good night," he says.

The next day, my last at the Hotel Touraine, I'm thinking about John Stanford Barnhill all morning. Then I'm hanging around the front desk and you can hear the call bell going over and over in the office and the manager comes out and says Barnhill's room number. "I'll take it," I say, and the bell's still ringing as I walk away and I figure he's drunk and in a bad mood and something in me wants it to go like that, to make things simple again. All the way up in the elevator I'm getting ready for a blowup.

Then I step off on the eighth floor and the chambermaid is hopping around waiting for me and she's saying, "Come quick, come quick, he's gone, right in front of me," and I run down the hall and into Barnhill's rooms and the sash is thrown open where he was yesterday and the curtains are blowing in and I dash through the smell of his cigars and I go halfway out the window myself and I take in the chestnuts and Hancock's elms and the wide-open space with some guys out there playing baseball and people moving around, all this before facing what I know has happened. Then I look down, and Barnhill is there, far below, a crowd gathering around him, his arms open wide as if he leaped expecting an embrace.

I pull back in. I turn. The chambermaid is peeking in at the door. "Go get the manager," I say, and she vanishes.

I stand very still for a long moment, trying to read that moonlit face from last night. But my brain has shut down. There's nothing inside me except a clattering in my chest like horses' hooves. And then my eyes focus. The reading table. Cigar butts, long gone cold, in the saucer. And beside them is John Stanford Barnhill's bowler hat. I find myself panting like a dobbin. The room will be full of people very soon. I press myself to move. I take a step and another and another and I am at the side table and the hat sits there, the color of the night sky, and I put my hand on it, I touch my palm to its high crown, and then I pick it up. I put it on my head and it settles on me right away, like it did last night, like when he put it on me with his own hand. And then I'm out the door, heading by the back stairs to the changing room. There's other things for me to do in this world. Other kinds of people. But he was right about me needing a hat.

🐾 🐾 🐾

## *Writing Exercises*

### INDIVIDUAL

1. Create metaphors as quickly as you can. Write down that one thing is another. Don't censor yourself—have fun. Start with a noun. (For instance, a house is a cake. A house is a flower. A house is the wind. A house is a clock. A house is a salesman.) See how many things one thing can become. Some of your metaphors are bound to be striking and useful.

2. Create similes. What is something like? Come up with a list of nouns as sentence subjects, then finish the sentences. (For example: His hair felt like _____. The dog looked like a _____. The room smelled like _____. The train sounded like _____. Etc.) Ask yourself which comparisons work. There should be some similarity in the things compared, more so than in metaphors, which change one thing into another. Read your likenesses and assess them. Keep whatever works and use it in a story.

3. In an earlier piece you have written, identify a few clichés. Cut them. Replace them with concrete details or more original similes or metaphors.

4. In a story you have drafted, look for potential symbols, or come up with new ones.
   a. Create a symbol that your character is aware of. (See the example about the sheep from Margaret Drabble's *The Garrick Year* earlier in this chapter.) Write a scene in which your character either sees or reflects on the symbol; while she may not explicitly state its symbolic meaning, it should be clear that she recognizes it.
   b. Now, using the same story or a different one, write a scene in which a symbol appears, but, though the reader and writer will recognize it, the character herself will be unaware of it.

5. Construct a tense conversation between two characters about "nothing." This might be a husband and wife arguing about the remote control, roommates arguing about who last cleaned the bathroom, a mother scolding her son for not taking the garbage out. Whatever the argument is, it should be clear to the reader that the tension isn't really about uncapped toothpaste, empty rolls of toilet papers, or drinking straight from the milk carton; these are merely symbolic of deeper issues. It's not really about the remote control; it's about how he's remote and must always be in control. (See Raymond Carver's story *A Serious Talk* in Chapter 6.) As you write the argument, develop the subtext so that even though it is not explicitly stated, the reader will understand what the characters are really fighting about.

6. Use a familiar story as a basis for a story of your own—a fairy tale, parable, fable, biblical tale, or Shakespeare play. Reinvent the story, invert the plot, create a surprising reversal. Develop the story until the original source material is submerged. Your story's relationship to the original should not be overtly obvious, though a careful reader might notice it. Ideally, any echoes of the original source should enrich your story, but your story's success should not depend on the reader making that connection.

### COLLABORATIVE

7. Write a fantastic opening line: whimsical, fabulous, dramatic, provocative, or absurd, in which a concrete object appears to a character in some unlikely way. (For example: It was Saturday morning when the tennis shoe fell from the sky and landed at Norman's feet.) Exchange papers, and, using a classmate's first line, develop it into a story. Using the concrete object mentioned in the first sentence as a reoccurring symbol, try to create a story that, while implausible on its surface, encourages the reader to suspend his disbelief.

# 10

# I GOTTA USE WORDS WHEN I TALK TO YOU

## Theme

+ *Idea and Morality in Theme*

+ *How Fictional Elements Contribute to Theme*

+ *Developing Theme as You Write*

How does fiction convey meaning?

Most literature textbooks begin a discussion of theme by warning that theme is not the *message*, not the *moral*, and that the *meaning* of a piece cannot be paraphrased. Theme contains an idea but cannot be stated as an idea. It suggests a morality but offers no moral. Then what is theme, and how as a writer can you pursue that rich resonance?

First of all, theme is what a story is about. But that is not enough, because a story may be "about" a dying Samurai or a quarreling couple or two kids on a trampoline, and those would not be the themes of those stories. A story is also "about" an abstraction, and if the story is significant, that abstraction may be very large; yet thousands of stories are about love, other thousands about death, and still other thousands about both love and death, and to say this is to say little about the theme of any of them.

We might better understand theme if we ask questions like: *What does the story have to say about the idea or abstraction that seems to be contained in it? What attitudes or judgments does it imply? Above all, how do the elements of fiction contribute to our experience of those ideas and attitudes in the story?*

## Idea and Morality in Theme

Literature is stuck with ideas in a way other arts are not. Music, paradoxically the most abstract of the arts, creates a logical structure that need make no reference to the world outside itself. It may express a mood, but it need not draw any conclusions. Shapes in painting and sculpture may suggest forms in the physical world, but they need not represent the world, and they need not contain a message. But words mean, and the grammatical structure of even the simplest sentence contains a concept.

Yet those who choose to deal in the medium of literature consistently discourage focus on concepts and insist on the value of the particular instance. Here is Flannery O'Connor's advice to writers:

> People have a habit of saying, "What is the theme of your story?" and they expect you to give them a statement: "The theme of my story is the economic pressure of the machine on the middle class"—or some such absurdity. And when they've got a statement like that, they go off happy and feel it is no longer necessary to read the story.
>
> Some people have the notion that you read the story and then climb out of it into the meaning, but for the fiction writer himself the whole story is the meaning, because it is an experience, not an abstraction.

What this passage suggests is that a writer of fiction approaches concepts, abstract ideas, generalizations, and truths through their particular embodiments—showing, not telling. "Literature," says John Ciardi, "is never only about ideas, but about the experience of ideas." T. S. Eliot points out that the creation of this experience is itself an intellectual feat.

> We talk as if thought was precise and emotion was vague. In reality there is precise emotion and there is vague emotion. To express precise emotion requires as great intellectual power as to express precise thought.

The value of the literary experience is that it allows us to judge an idea at two levels of consciousness, the rational and the emotional, simultaneously. The kind of "truth" that can be told through thematic resonance is many-faceted and can acknowledge the competing of many truths, exploring paradox and contradiction.

There is a curious prejudice built into our language that makes us speak of telling *the* truth but telling *a* lie. No one supposes that all conceivable falsehood can be wrapped up in a single statement called "the lie"; lies are manifold, varied, and specific. But truth is supposed to be absolute: the truth, the whole truth, and nothing but the truth. This is, of course, impossible nonsense, and *telling a lie* is a truer phrase than *telling the truth*. Fiction does not have to tell *the* truth, but *a* truth.

Anton Chekov wrote that "the writer of fiction should not try to solve such questions as those of God, pessimism and so forth." What is "obligatory for the artist," he said, is not "solving a problem," but "stating a problem correctly." John Keats went even further, defining genius itself as *negative capability*, "that is when a man is capable of being in uncertainties, mysteries and doubts, without any irritable reaching after fact and reason."

YOUR BELIEFS WILL BE THE LIGHT BY WHICH YOU SEE, but they will not be what you see and they will not be a substitute for seeing.

Flannery O'Connor

A story, then, speculates on a possible truth. It is not an answer or a law but a sup-position, an exploration. Every story reaches in its climax and resolution an interim solution to a specifically realized dilemma. But it offers no ultimate solution.

The idea that is proposed, supposed, or speculated about in a fiction may be sim-ple and idealistic, like the notion in "Cinderella" that the good and beautiful will triumph. Or it may be profound and unprovable, like the theme in *Oedipus Rex* that man cannot escape his destiny but may be ennobled in the attempt. Or it may be deliberately paradoxical and offer no guidelines that can be used in life, as in Jane Austen's *Persuasion,* where the heroine, in order to adhere to her principles, must follow advice given on principles less sound than her own.

In any case, while exploring an idea the writer conveys an attitude toward that idea. Rust Hills puts it this way:

. . . coherence in the world [an author] creates is constituted of two concepts he holds, which may be in conflict: one is his world view, his sense of the way the world is; and the other is his sense of morality, the way the world ought to be.

Literature is a persuasive art, and no writer who fails to convince us of the validity of his or her vision of the world can convince us of his or her greatness. The writer, of course, may be powerfully impelled to impose a limited vision of the world as it ought to be, and even to tie that vision to a political stance, wishing not only to persuade and convince but also to propagandize. But because the emotional force of literary persua-sion is in the realization of the particular, the writer is doomed to fail. The greater the work, the more it refers us to some permanent human impulse rather than an easy slogan or a given institutional embodiment of that impulse. Fine writing expands our scope by continually presenting a new way of seeing, a further possibility of emotional identification; it flatly refuses to become a law. I am not a Roman Catholic like Gerard Manley Hopkins and cannot be persuaded by his poetry to become one; but in a moment near despair I can drive along an Illinois street in a Chevrolet station wagon and take strength from the lines of a Jesuit in the Welsh wasteland. I am not a communist as Bertolt Brecht was and cannot be convinced by his plays to become one; but I can see the hauteur of wealth displayed on the Gulf of Mexico and recognize, from a parable of the German Marxist, the difference between a possession and a belonging.

WHEN WE DREAM WE MAKE CONNECTIONS that astound us later. . . .
The same thing happens on the page when we forget ourselves and as it
were, watch our own waking dream. . . . Later we can make sense of
what we've created and craft it accordingly. That's when we appreciate
the poetry of our unconscious mind.

Tom Batt

In the human experience, emotion, logic, and judgment are inextricably mixed,
and we make continual cross-references between and among them. *You're just sulking.*
(I pass judgment on your emotion.) *What do you think of this idea?* (How do you judge
this logic?) *Why do I feel this way?* (What is the logic of this emotion?) *It makes no
sense to be angry about it.* (I pass judgment on the logic of your emotion.) Literature
attempts to fuse three areas of experience organically, denying the force of none of
them, positing that no one is more real than the others. This is why I have insisted
throughout this book on detail and scene (immediate felt experience), the essential
abstractions conveyed therein (ideas), and the attitude implied thereby (judgment).

Not all experience reveals, but all revelation comes through experience. Books
aspire to become a part of that revelatory experience, and the books that are made in
the form of fiction attempt to do so by re-creating the experience of revelation.

## How Fictional Elements Contribute to Theme

Whatever the idea and attitudes that underlie the theme of a story, that story will
bring them into the realm of experience through its particular and unique pattern.
Theme involves emotion, logic, and judgment, all three—but the pattern that forms
the particular experience of that theme is made up of every element of fiction this
book has discussed: the arrangement, shape, and flow of the action, as performed by
the characters, realized in their details, seen in their atmosphere, from a unique
point of view, through the imagery and the rhythm of the language.

This book, for example, contains at least nine stories that may be said to have
"the generation gap" as a major theme: "Everything That Rises Must Converge," "Big
Me," "A Visit of Charity," "The English Pupil," "Mrs. Dutta Writes a Letter," "The
First Day," "Where Are You Going, Where Have You Been?", "Gryphon," and
"Who's Irish?" Some of these are written from the point of view of a member of the
older generation, some from the point of view of the younger. In some, conflict is resolved by bridging the gap; in others, it is not. The characters are variously poor,
middle-class, rural, urban, male, female, adolescent, middle-aged, old, Asian, black,
white. The imagery variously evokes food, schooling, landscape, religion, gambling,
music, painting, horses, sex, speed, and death. It is in the different uses of the elements of fiction that each story makes unique what it has to say about, and what attitude it takes toward, the idea of "the generation gap."

What follows is as short a story as you are likely to encounter in print. It is spare in the extreme—almost, as its title suggests, an outline. Yet the author has contrived in this minuscule compass to direct every fictional element we have discussed toward the exploration of several large themes.

## A Man Told Me the Story of His Life

### GRACE PALEY

*Vicente said:* I wanted to be a doctor. I wanted to be a doctor with my whole heart.

I learned every bone, every organ in the body. What is it for? Why does it work?

The school said to me: Vicente, be an engineer. That would be good. You understand mathematics.

I said to the school: I want to be a doctor. I already know how the organs connect. When something goes wrong, I'll understand how to make repairs.

The school said: Vicente, you will really be an excellent engineer. You show on all the tests what a good engineer you will be. It doesn't show whether you'll be a good doctor.

I said: Oh, I long to be a doctor. I nearly cried. I was seventeen. I said: But perhaps you're right. You're the teacher. You're the principal. I know I'm young.

The school said: And besides, you're going into the army.

And then I was made a cook. I prepared food for two thousand men.

Now you see me. I have a good job. I have three children. This is my wife, Consuela. Did you know I saved her life?

Look, she suffered pain. The doctor said: What is this? Are you tired? Have you had too much company? How many children? Rest overnight, then tomorrow we'll make tests.

The next morning I called the doctor. I said: She must be operated on immediately. I have looked in the book. I see where her pain is. I understand what the pressure is, where it comes from. I see clearly the organ that is making trouble.

The doctor made a test. He said: She must be operated at once. He said to me: Vicente, how did you know?

I think it would be fair to say that this story is about the waste of Vicente's talent through the bad guidance of authority. I'll start by stating, then, that *waste* and *power* are its central themes. How do the elements of fiction illuminate these themes?

The *conflict* is between Vicente and the figures of authority he encounters: teacher, principal, army, doctor. His desire at the beginning of the story is to become a doctor (in itself a figure of authority), and this desire is thwarted by persons of increasing power. In the *crisis action* what is at stake is his wife's life. In this "last battle" he succeeds as a doctor, so that the *resolution* reveals the *irony* of his having been denied in the first place.

The story is told from the *point of view* of a *first-person central narrator*, but with an important qualification. The title, "A Man Told Me the Story of His Life," and the first two words, "*Vicente said,*" posit a *peripheral narrator* reporting what Vicente said. If the story was titled "My Life" and began, "I wanted to be a doctor," Vicente might be making a public appeal, a boast of how wronged he has been. As it is, he told his story privately to the barely sketched author who now wants it known, and this leaves Vicente's modesty intact.

The modesty is underscored by the simplicity of his *speech,* a *rhythm* and *word choice* that suggest educational *limitations* (perhaps that English is a second language). At the same time, that simplicity helps us *identify* with Vicente morally. Clearly, if he has educational limitations, it is not for want of trying to get an education! His credibility is augmented by *understatement,* both as a youth—"But perhaps you're right. You're the teacher"—and as a man—"I have a good job. I have three children." This apparent acceptance makes us trust him at the same time as it makes us angry on his behalf.

It's consistent with the spareness of the language that we do not have an accumulation of minute or vivid details, but the degree of *specificity* is nevertheless a clue to where to direct our sympathy. In the title Vicente is just "A Man." As soon as he speaks he becomes an individual with a name. "The school," collective and impersonal, speaks to him, but when he speaks it is to single individuals, "the teacher," "the principal," and when he speaks of his wife she is personalized as "Consuela."

Moreover, the *sensory details* are so arranged that they relate to each other in ways that give them *metaphoric* and *symbolic significance.* Notice, for example, how Vicente's desire to become a doctor "with my whole heart" is immediately followed by, "I learned every bone, every organ in the body." Here the factual anatomical study refers us back to the heart that is one of those organs, suggesting by implication that Vicente is somebody who knows what a heart is. He knows how things "connect."

An engineer, of course, has to know how things connect and how to make repairs. But so does a doctor, and the authority figures of the school haven't the imagination to see the connection. The army, by putting him to work in a way that involves both connections and anatomical parts, takes advantage of his by-now clear ability to order and organize things—he feeds two thousand men—but it is too late to repair the misdirection of such talents. We don't know what his job is now; it doesn't matter, it's the wrong one.

As a young man, Vicente asked, "What is it for? Why does it work?", revealing a natural fascination with the sort of question that would, of course, be asked on an anatomy test. But no such test is given, and the tests that are given are irrelevant. His wife's doctor will "make tests," but like the school authorities he knows less than Vicente does, and so asks insultingly personal questions. In fact you could say that all the authorities of the story fail the test.

This analysis, which is about two and a half times as long as the story, doesn't begin to exhaust the possibilities for interpretation, and you may disagree with any of my suggestions. But it does indicate how the techniques of characterization, plot, detail, point of view, image, and metaphor all reinforce the themes of waste and power. The story is so densely conceived and developed that it might fairly be titled "Connections," "Tests," "Repairs," "What Is It For?", or "How Did You Know?"—any one of these could lead us toward the themes of waste and the misguidance of authority.

> Sᴛᴏʀɪᴇꜱ . . . ᴅᴏ ɴᴏᴛ ꜱᴏ ᴍᴜᴄʜ ʀᴇꜱɪꜱᴛ interpretation as survive its scrutiny.
>
> C. Michael Curtis

Not every story is or needs to be as intensely interwoven in its elements as "A Man Told Me the Story of His Life," but the development of theme always involves such interweaving to a degree. It is a standard to work toward.

## Developing Theme as You Write

In an essay, your goal is to say as clearly and directly as possible what you mean. In fiction, your goal is to make people and make them do things, and, ideally, never to "say what you mean" at all. Theoretically, an outline can never harm an essay: This is what I have to say, and I'll say it through points A, B, and C. But if a writer sets out to write a story to illustrate an idea, the fiction will almost inevitably be thin. Even if you begin with an outline, as many writers do, it will be an outline of the action and not of your "points." You may not know the meaning of the story until the characters begin to tell you what it is. You'll begin with an image of a person or a situation that seems vaguely to embody something important, and you'll learn as you go what that something is. Likewise, what you mean will emerge in the reading experience and take place in the reader's mind, "not," as the narrator says of Marlow's tales in *Heart of Darkness*, "inside like a kernel but outside, enveloping the tale which brought it out."

But at some point in the writing process, you may find yourself impelled by, under pressure of, or interested primarily in your theme. It will seem that you have set yourself this lonely, austere, and tortuous task because you do have something to say. At this point you will, and you should, begin to let that sorting-comparing-cataloging neocortex of your brain go to work on the stuff of your story. John Gardner describes the process in *The Art of Fiction*.

> Theme, it should be noticed, is not imposed on the story but evoked from within it—initially an intuitive but finally an intellectual act on the part of the writer. The writer muses on the story idea to determine what it is in it that has attracted him, why it seems to him worth telling. Having determined . . . what interests him—and what chiefly concerns the major character . . . he toys with various ways of telling his story, thinks about what has been said before about (his theme), broods on every image that occurs to him, turning it over and over, puzzling it, hunting for connections, trying to figure out—before he writes, while he writes, and in the process of repeated revisions—what it is he really thinks. . . . Only when he thinks out a story in this way does he achieve not just an alternative reality or, loosely, an imitation of nature, but true, firm art—fiction as serious thought.

This process—worrying a fiction until its theme reveals itself, connections occur, images recur, a pattern emerges—is more conscious than readers know, beginning writers want to accept, or established writers are willing to admit. It has become a popular—cliché—stance for modern writers to claim that they haven't the faintest idea what they meant in their writing. *Don't ask me; read the book. If I knew what it meant, I wouldn't have written it. It means what it says.* When an author makes such a response, it is well to remember that an author is a professional liar. What he or she means is not that there are no themes, ideas, or meanings in the work but that these are not separable from the pattern of fictional experience in which they are embodied. It also means that, having done the difficult writerly job, the writer is now unwilling also to do the critic's work. But beginning critics also resist. Students irritated by the analysis of literature often ask, "How do you know she did that on purpose? How do you know it didn't just happen to come out that way?" The answer is that you don't. But what is on the page is on the page. An author no less than a reader or critic can see an emerging pattern, and the author has both the possibility and the obligation of manipulating it. When you have put something on the page, you have two possibilities, and only two: You may cut it or you are committed to it. Gail Godwin asks:

> But what about the other truths you lost by telling it that way?
> Ah, my friend, this is my question too. The choice is always a killing one. One option must die so that another may live. I do little murders in my workroom every day.

Often the choice to commit yourself to a phrase, an image, a line of dialogue will reveal, in a minor convulsion of understanding, what you mean. I have written no story or novel in which this did not occur in trivial or dramatic ways. I once sat bolt upright at 4 A.M. in a strange town with the realization that my sixty-year-old narrator, in a novel full of images of hands and manipulation, had been lying to me for two hundred pages. Sometimes the realistic objects or actions of a work will begin to take on metaphoric or symbolic associations with your theme, producing a crossing of references, or what Richmond Lattimore calls a "symbol complex." In a novel about a woman who traveled around the world, I employed images of dangerous water and the danger of losing balance, both physically and mentally. At some point I came up with—or, as it felt, was given—the image of a canal, the lock in which water finds its balance. This unforeseen connection gave me the purest moment of pleasure I had in writing that book. Yet I dare say no reader could identify it as a moment of particular intensity; nor, I hope, would any reader be consciously aware that the themes of danger and balance joined there.

Such an unpredictable moment of recognition is what Robert Morgan calls "the point beside the point" of the story—"the surprise that seems inevitable once it occurs. The truest vision of a story is probably the peripheral," Morgan explains. "What is going on off to the side may seem marginal at first, but central as the story comes to a climax and resolution. That curvature, the surprising convergence, is definitive in the really good short story."

The fusion of elements into a unified pattern is the nature of creativity, a word devalued to the extent that it has come to mean a random gush of self-expression. God, perhaps, created out of the void; but in the world as we know it, all creativity, from the sprouting of an onion to the painting of *Guernica,* is a matter of selection and arrangement. At the conception of an embryo or a short story, there occurs a conjunction of two unlike things, whether cells or ideas, that have never been joined before. Around this conjunction other cells, other ideas accumulate in a deliberate pattern. That pattern is the unique personality of the creature, and if the pattern does not cohere, it miscarries or is stillborn.

> BREAK UP THE LARGER STORY INTO ITS COMPONENTS, make sure you understand the exact function of each component (a story is like a machine with numerous gears: it should contain no gear that doesn't turn something), and after each component has been carefully set in place, step back and have a look at the whole. Then rewrite until the story flows as naturally as a river, each element so blending with the rest that no one, not even yourself two years from now, can locate the separate parts.
>
> John Gardner

The organic unity of a work of literature cannot be taught—or, if it can, I have not discovered a way to teach it. I can suggest from time to time that concrete image is not separate from character, which is revealed in dialogue and point of view, which may be illuminated by simile, which may reveal theme, which is contained in plot as water is contained in an apple. But I cannot tell you how to achieve this; nor, if you achieve it, will you be able to explain very clearly how you have done so. Analysis separates in order to focus; it assumes that an understanding of the parts contributes to an understanding of the whole, but it does not produce the whole. Scientists can determine with minute accuracy the elements, in their proportions, contained in a piece of human skin. They can gather these elements, stir and warm them, but the result will not be skin. A good critic can show you where a metaphor does or does not illuminate character, where the character does or does not ring true in an action. But the critic cannot tell you how to make a character breathe; the breath is talent and can be neither explained nor produced. No one can tell you what to mean, and no one can tell you how.

In the unified pattern of a fiction there is something to which the name of "magic" may be given, where one empty word is placed upon another and tapped with a third, and a flaming scarf or a long-eared hope is pulled out of the tall black heart. The most magical thing about this magic is that once the trick is explained, it is not explained, and the better you understand how it works, the better it will work again.

Birth, death, work, and love continue to occur. Their meanings change from time to time and place to place, and new meanings engender new forms, which capture and create new meanings until they tire, while birth, death, work, and love continue to recur. Something to which we give the name of "honor" seems to persist, though in one place and time it is embodied in choosing to die for your country, in another, choosing not to. A notion of "progress" survives, though it is expressed now in technology, now in ecology, now in the survival of the fittest, now in the protection of the weak; "love" takes its form now in tenacious loyalty, now in letting go.

Ideas are not new, but the form in which they are expressed is constantly renewed, and new forms give life to what used to be called (in the old form) the "eternal verities."

# Winky

### GEORGE SAUNDERS

Eighty people waited in a darkened meeting room at the Hyatt, wearing mass-produced paper hats. The White Hats were Beginning to Begin. The Pink Hats were Moving Ahead in Beginning. The Green Hats were Very Firmly Beginning, all the way up to the Gold Hats, who had Mastered Living and were standing in a group around the Snack Table, whispering and conferring and elbowing one another whenever someone in a lesser hat walked by.

Trumpets sounded from a concealed tape deck. An actor in a ripped flannel shirt stumbled across the stage with a sign around his neck that said "You."

"I'm lost!" You cried. "I'm wandering in a sort of wilderness!"

"Hey, You, come on over!" shouted a girl across the stage, labeled "Inner Peace." "I bet you've been looking for me your whole life!"

"Boy, have I!" said You. "I'll be right over!"

But then out from the wings sprinted a number of other actors, labeled "Whiny" and "Self-Absorbed" and "Blames Her Fat on Others" and so on, who draped themselves across You and began poking him in the ribs and giving him noogies.

"Oh, I can't believe you love Inner Peace more than you love me, You!" said Insecure. "That really hurts."

"Frankly, I've never been so disappointed in my life," said Disappointed.

"Oh God, all this arguing is giving me a panic attack," said Too High-Strung to Function.

"I'm waiting, You," said Inner Peace. "Do you want me or not?"

"I do, but I seem to be trapped!" You shouted. "I can't seem to get what I want!"

"You and about a billion other people in this world," said Inner Peace sadly.

"Is there no hope for me?" asked You. "If only someone had made a lifelong study of the roadblocks people encounter on their way to Inner Peace!"

"And yet someone has," said Inner Peace.

Another fanfare sounded from the tape deck, and a masked Gold Hat, whose hat appeared to be made of actual gold, bounded onto the stage, flexed his muscles, and dragged Insecure to a paper jail, on which was written: "Pokey for Those Who Would

Keep Us from Inner Peace." Then the Gold Hat dragged Chronically Depressed and Clingy and Helpless and the rest across the stage and shoved them into the Pokey.

"See what I just did?" said the Gold Hat. "I just liberated You from those who would keep him from Inner Peace. So good for You! Question is, is You going to be able to stay liberated? Maybe what You needs is a repeated internal reminder. A mantra. A mantra can be thought of as a repeated internal reminder, can't it? Does anyone out there have a good snappy mantra they could perhaps share with You?"

The crowd was delighted, because they knew the mantra. Even the lowly White Hats knew the mantra—even Neil Yaniky, who sat spellbound and insecure in the first row, sucking his mustache, knew the mantra, because it was on all the TV commercials and also on the front cover of the Orientation Text in big bold letters.

"Give it to me, folks!" shouted the Gold Hat. "What time is it?"

"Now Is the Time for Me to Win!" the crowd shouted. "You got that right, baby!" said the Gold Hat exultantly, ripping off his mask to reveal what many already suspected: This was not some mere Gold Hat but Tom Rodgers himself, founder of the Seminars.

"What fun!" he shouted. "To have something to give, and people who so badly need what I have to offer. Here's what I have to offer, folks, although it's not much, really, just two simple concepts, and the first one is: oatmeal."

From out of his suit he pulled a bowl and a box of oatmeal, and filled the bowl with the oatmeal and held the bowl up.

"Simple, nourishing, inexpensive," he said. "This represents your soul in its pure state. Your soul on the day you were born. You were perfect. You were happy. You were good.

"Now, enter Concept Number Two: crap. Don't worry, folks, I don't use actual crap up here. Only imaginary crap. You'll have to supply the crap, using your mind. Now, if someone came up and crapped in your nice warm oatmeal, what would you say? Would you say: 'Wow, super, thanks, please continue crapping in my oatmeal'? Am I being silly? I'm being a little silly. But guess what, in real life people come up and crap in your oatmeal all the time—friends, co-workers, loved ones, even your kids, especially your kids!—and that's exactly what you do. You say 'Thanks so much!' You say 'Crap away!' You say, and here my metaphor breaks down a bit, 'Is there some way I can help you crap in my oatmeal?'

"Let me tell you something amazing: I was once exactly like you people. A certain someone, a certain guy who shall remain nameless, was doing quite a bit of crapping in my oatmeal, and simply because he'd had some bad luck, simply because he was in some pain, simply because, actually he was in a wheelchair, this certain someone expected me to put my life on hold while he crapped in my oatmeal by demanding round-the-clock attention, this brother of mine, this Gene, and whoops, there goes that cat out of the bag, but does this maybe sound paradoxical? Wasn't he the one with the crap in his oatmeal, being in a wheelchair? Well, yes and no. Sure, he was hurting. No surprise there. Guy drops a motorcycle on a gravel road and bounces two hundred yards without a helmet, yes, he's going to be somewhat hurting. But how was that my fault? Was I the guy riding the motorcycle too fast, drunk, with no helmet? No, I was home, studying my Tacitus, which is what I was into at that stage of my life, so why did Gene expect me to consign my dreams and plans to the dustbin? I had dreams! I had plans! Finally—and this is all in my book, *People of Power*—I found the inner strength to say to Gene, 'Stop crapping in my oatmeal, Gene, I'm simply not going to participate.' And I found the strength to say to our sister, Ellen, 'Ellen, take the ball that is Gene and run with it, because if I sell myself short by catering to Gene, I'm going to be one very angry puppy, and anger does the mean-and-nasty on a person, and I for one love myself and want the best for me, because I am, after all, a child of God.' And I said to myself, as I describe in the book, 'Tom, now is the time for you to win!' That was the first time I thought that up. And do you know what? I won. I'm winning. Today we're friends, Gene and I, and he acknowledges that I was right all along. And as for Ellen, Ellen still has some issues, she'd take a big old dump in my oatmeal right now if I gave her half a chance, but guess what folks, I'm not giving her that half a chance, because I've installed a protective screen over my oatmeal—not a literal screen, but a metaphorical protective screen. Ellen knows it, Gene knows it, and now they pretty much stay out of my hair and away from my oatmeal, and they've made a nice life together, and who do you think paid for Gene's wheelchair ramp with the money he made from a certain series of Seminars?"

The crowd burst into applause. Tom Rodgers held up his hand.

"Now, what about you folks?" he said softly. "Is now the time for you to win? Are you ready to screen off your metaphorical oatmeal and identify your own personal Gene? Who is it that's screwing you up? Who's keeping you from getting what you want? Somebody is! God doesn't make junk. If you're losing, somebody's doing it to you. Today I'll be guiding you through my Three Essential Steps: Identification, Screening, Confrontation. First, we'll Identify your personal Gene. Second, we'll help you mentally install a metaphorical Screen over your symbolic oatmeal. Finally we'll show you how to Confront your personal Gene and make it clear to him or her that your oatmeal is henceforth off-limits."

Tom Rodgers looked intensely out into the crowd.

"So what do you think, guys?" he asked, very softly. "Are you up for it?"

From the crowd came a nervous murmur of assent.

"All right, then," he said. "Let's line up. Let's line up for a change. A *dramatic* change."

He crisply left the stage, and a spotlight panned across five Personal Change Centers, small white tents set up in a row near the fire door.

Neil Yaniky rose with the rest and checked his Line Assignment and joined his Assigned Line. He was a tiny man, nearly thirty, balding on top and balding on the sides, and was still chewing on his mustache and wondering if anyone or everyone else at the Seminar could tell that he was a big stupid faker, because he had no career, really, and no business, but only soldered little triangular things in his basement, for forty-seven cents a little triangular thing, for CompuParts, although he had high hopes for something better, which was why he was here.

The flap of Personal Change Center 4 flew open and in he went, bending low.

Inside were Tom Rodgers and several assistants, and a dummy in a smock sitting in a chair.

"Welcome, Neil," said Tom Rodgers, glancing at Yaniky's name tag. "I'm honored to have you in my Seminar, Neil. Now. The way we'll start, Neil, is for you to please write across the chest of this dummy the name of your real-life personal Gene.

That is, the name of the person you perceive to be crapping in your oatmeal. Do you understand what I'm saying?"

"Yes," said Yaniky.

Tom Rodgers was talking very fast, as if he had hundreds of people to change in a single day, which of course he did. Yaniky had no problem with that. He was just happy to be one of them.

"Do you need help determining who that person is?" said Tom Rodgers. "Your oatmeal-crapper?"

"No," said Yaniky.

"Excellent," said Tom Rodgers. "Now write the name and under it write the major way in which you perceive this person to be crapping in your oatmeal. Be frank. This is just between you and me."

On an erasable markerboard permanently mounted in the dummy's chest Yaniky wrote, "Winky: Crazy-looking and too religious and needs her own place."

"Super!" said Tom Rodgers. "A great start. Now watch what I do. Let's fine-tune. Can we cut 'crazy-looking'? If this person, this Winky, were to get her own place, would the fact that she looks crazy still be an issue? Less of an issue?"

Yaniky pictured his sister looking crazy but in her own apartment.

"Less of an issue," he said.

"All right!" said Tom Rodgers, erasing "crazy-looking." "It's important to simplify so that we can hone in on exactly what we're trying to change. Okay. At this point, we've determined that if we can get her out of your house, the crazy-looking can be lived with. A big step forward. But why stop there? Let me propose something: if she's out of your hair, what the heck do you care if she's religious?"

Yaniky pictured Winky looking crazy and talking crazy about God but in her own apartment.

"It would definitely be better," he said.

"Yes, it would," said Tom Rodgers, and erased until the dummy was labeled "Winky: needs her own place."

"See?" said Tom Rodgers. "See how we've simplified? We've got it down to one issue. Can you live with this simple, direct statement of the problem?"

"Yes," Yaniky said. "Yes, I can."

Yaniky saw now what it was about Winky that got on his nerves. It wasn't her formerly red curls, which had gone white, so it looked like she had soaked the top of her head in glue and dipped it in a vat of cotton balls; it wasn't the bald spot that every morning she painted with some kind of white substance; it wasn't her shiny-pink face that was always getting weird joyful looks on it at bad times, like during his dinner date with Beverly Amstel, when he'd made his special meatballs to no avail, because Bev kept glancing over at Winky in panic; it wasn't the way she came click-click-clicking in from teaching church school and hugged him for too long a time while smelling like flower water, all pumped up from spreading the word of damn Christ; it was simply that they were too old to be living together and he had things he wanted to accomplish and she was too needy and blurred his focus.

"Have you told this person, this Winky, that her living with you is a stumbling block for your personal development?" said Tom Rodgers.

"No I haven't," Yaniky said.

"I thought not," said Tom Rodgers. "You're kindhearted. You don't want to hurt her. That's nice, but guess what? You are hurting her. You're hurting her by not telling her the truth. Am I saying that you, by your silence, are crapping in her oatmeal? Yes, I am. I'm saying that there's a sort of reciprocal crapping going on here. How can Winky grow on a diet of lies? Isn't it true that the truth will set you free? Didn't someone once say that? Wasn't it God or Christ, which would be ironic, because of her being so religious?"

Tom Rodgers gestured to an assistant, who took a wig out of a box and put it on the dummy's head.

"What we're going to do now is act this out symbolically," Tom Rodgers said. "Primitive cultures do this all the time. They might throw Fertility a big party say, or paint their kids white and let them whack Sickness with palm fronds and so forth. Are we somehow smarter than primitive cultures? I doubt it. I think maybe we're dumber. Do we have fewer hemorrhoids? Were Incas killed on freeways? Here, take this."

He handed Yaniky a baseball bat.

"What time is it, Neil?" said Tom Rodgers.

"Time to win?" said Yaniky. "Time for me to win?"

"Now is the time for you to win," said Tom Rodgers, clarifying, and pointed to the dummy.

Yaniky swung the bat and the dummy toppled over and the wig flew off and the assistant retrieved the wig and tossed it back into the box of wigs, and Tom Rodgers gave Yaniky a big hug.

"What you have just symbolically said," Tom Rodgers said, "is: 'No more, Winky. Grow wings, Winky. I love you, but you're killing me, and I am a good person, a child of God, and don't deserve to die. I deserve to live, I demand to live, and therefore, get your own place, girl! Fly and someday thank me!' This is to be your submantra, Neil, okay? *Out you go!* On your way home today I want you to be muttering, not angrily muttering but sort of joyfully muttering, to center yourself, the following words: 'Now Is the Time for Me to Win! Out you go! Out you go!' Will you do that for me?"

"Yes," said Yaniky, very much moved.

"And now here is Vicki," said Tom Rodgers, "One of my very top Gold Hats, who will walk you through the Confrontation step. Neil! I wish you luck, and peace, and all the success in the world."

Vicki had a face that looked as if it had been smashed against a steering wheel in a crash and then carefully reworked until it somewhat resembled her previous face. Several parallel curved indentations ran from temple to chin. She led Yaniky to a folding table labeled "Confrontation Center" and gave him a sheet of paper on which was written, "Gentle, Firm, Loving."

"These are the characteristics of a good Confrontation," she said, a bit mechanically. "Now flip it over."

On the other side was written, "Angry, Wimpy, Accusatory."

"These are the characteristics of a bad Confrontation," said Vicki. "A destructive Confrontation. Okay. So let's say I'm this person, this Winky person, and you're going to tell me to hit the road. Gentle, Firm, Loving. Now begin."

And he began telling Vicki to her damaged face that she was ruining his life and sucking him dry and that she had to go live somewhere else, and Vicki nodded and patted his hand, and now and then stopped him to tell him he was being too severe.

Neil-Neil was coming home soon and Winky was way way behind.

Some days she took her time while cleaning, smiling at happy thoughts, frowning when she imagined someone being taken advantage of, and sometimes the person being taken advantage of was a frail little boy with a scar on his head and the person taking advantage was a big fat man with a cane, and other times the person being taken advantage of was a kindly friendly British girl with a speech impediment and the person taking advantage was her rich, pushy sister who spoke in perfect diction and always got everything she wanted and went around whining while sucking little pink candies. Sometimes Winky asked the rich sister in her mind how she'd like to have the little pink candies slapped right out of her mouth. But that wasn't right. That wasn't Christ's way! You didn't slap the little pink candies out of her mouth, you let her slap your mouth, seventy times seven times, which was like four hundred times, and after she'd slapped you the last time she suddenly understood it all and begged your forgiveness and gave you some candy, because that was the healing power of love.

For crying out loud! What was she doing? Was she crazy? It was time to get going! Why was she standing in the kitchen thinking?

She dashed up the stairs with a strip of broken molding under her arm and a dirty sock over her shoulder.

Halfway up she paused at a little octagonal window and looked dreamily out, thinking, In a way, we own those trees. Beyond the Thieus' was the same old gap in the leaning elms showing the same old meadow that would soon be ToyTowne. But for now it still reminded her of the kind of field where Christ with his lap full of flowers had suffered with the little children, which was a scene she wanted them to put on the cover of the singing album she was going to make, the singing album about God, which would have a watercolor cover like *Shoulder My Burden*, which was a book though but anyways it had this patient donkey piled high with crates and behind it this mountain, and the point of that book was that if you take on the worries and cares of others, Lord Jesus will take on your cares and worries, so that was why the patient donkey and why the crates, and why she prided herself on keeping house for Neil-Neil and never asked him for help.

Holy cow, what was she doing standing on the landing! Was she crazy? Today she was rushing! She was giving Neil-Neil a tea! She burst from the landing, taking two stairs at once. The molding had to go to the attic and the dirty sock to the hamper. While she was up, she could change her top. Because on it was some crusty soup. The wallpaper at the top of the stairs showed about a million of the same girl whacking a smiling goose with a riding crop. Hello, girls! Hello, girls! Ha ha! Hello, geese! Not to leave you out!

From a drawer in her room she took the green top, which Neil-Neil liked. Once when she was wearing it he'd asked if it was new. When had that been? At the lunch at the Beef Barn, when he paid, when he asked would she like to leave Rustic Village

Apartments and come live with him. Oh, that sweetie. She still had the matchbook. Those had been sad days at Rustic Village, with every friend engaged but Doris, who had a fake arm, and boy those girls could sometimes say mean things, but now it was all behind her, and she needed to send poor Doris a card.

But not today, today she was rushing!

Down the stairs she pounded, still holding the molding, sock still over her shoulder.

In the kitchen she ripped open the cookie bag but there were no clean plates, so she rinsed a plate but there was no towel, so she dried the plate with her top. Hey she still had on the yellow top. What the heck? Where was the green top? Hadn't she just gotten it out of her drawer? Ha ha! That was funny She should send that in to *ChristLife*. They liked cute funny things that happened, even if they had nothing to do with Jesus.

The kitchen was a disaster! But first things first. Her top sucked. Not sucked, sucked was a bad word, her top was yugly Dad used to say that, yugly. Not about her. He always said she was purty. Sometimes he said things were purty yugly But not her. He always said she was purty purty, then lifted her up. Oh Dad, Daddy Poppy-Popp! Was Poppy-Popp one with the Savior? She hoped so. Sometimes he used to swear and sometimes he used to drink, and once he swore when he fell down the stairs when he was drunk, but when she ran to him he hopped up laughing, and oh, when he sang "Peace in the Valley" you could tell he felt things would be better beyond, which had been a super example for a young Christian kid to witness.

She flew back up the stairs to change her top. Here was the green top, on the top step! Bad top! I should spank! She gave the green top a snap to undust it and discipline it and, putting the strip of molding and the dirty sock on the step, changed tops right then and there, picked up the molding, threw the dirty sock over her shoulder, and pounded back down the stairs.

There were so many many things to do! Not only now, for the tea, but in the future! It was time to get going! Now that she was out of that lonely apartment she could finally learn to play the piano, and once she learned to play and write songs, she could write her songs about God, then find out about making a record, her record about God, about how God had been good to her in this life, because look at her! A plain girl in a nice home! Oh, she knew she was plain, her legs were thick and her waist was thick and her hair, oh my God—oh my gosh, rather—her hair, what kind of hair was that to have, yugly white hair, and many was the time she had thought, This is not hair, this is a test. The test of white sparse hair, when so many had gorgeous manes, and that was why, when she looked in a mirror by accident and saw her white horrible hair, she always tried to think to herself, Praise God!

Neil-Neil was the all-time sweetie pie. Those girls were crazy! Did they think because a man was small and bald he had no love? Did they think bad things came in small packages? Neil-Neil was like the good brother in the Bible, the one who stayed home with his dad on the farm and never got even a small party. Except there was no bad brother, it was just the two of them, so no party although she'd get her party, a big party in Heaven, and was sort of even having her party now, on earth, because when she saw that little man all pee-stained at Rexall Drug, not begging but just saying to every person who went in that he or she was looking dapper, she knew that he was truly the least of her brothers. The world was a story Christ was telling her. And when she told the pee-man at the Rexall that he was looking dapper himself and he said loudly that she was too ugly to f—, she had only thought to herself, Okay, praise God, he's only saying that because he's in pain, and had smiled with the lightest light in her eyes she could get there by wishing it there, because even if she was a little yugly she was still beautiful in Christ's sight, so for her it was all a party, a little party before a bigger party, the biggest, but what about Neil-Neil, where was his party?

She would do what she could! This would be his party, one tiny installment on the huge huge party he deserved, her brother, her pal to the end, the only loving soul she had yet found in this world.

The bell rang and she threw open the door, and there was Neil-Neil.

"Welcome home!" she said grandly, and bowed at the waist, and the sock fell off her shoulder.

Yaniky had walked home in a frenzy, gazing into shop windows, knowing that some-day soon, when he came into these shops with his sexy wife, he'd simply point out items with his riding crop and they would be loaded into his waiting Benz, although come to think of it, why a riding crop? Who used a riding crop? Did you use a riding crop on the Benz? Ho, man, he was stoked! He wanted a Jag, not a Benz! Golden stat-ues of geese, classy vases, big porcelain frogs, whatever, when his ship came in he'd have it all, because when he was stoked nothing could stop him.

If Dad could see him now walking home in a suit from a seminar at the freaking Hyatt! Poor Dad, not that he was bashing Dad, but had Dad been a seeker? Well, no, Dad had been no seeker, life had beaten Dad. Dad had spent every evening with a beer on the divan, under a comforter, and he remembered poor Ma in her Sunday dress, which had a rip, which she'd taped because she couldn't sew, and Dad in his too big hat, recently fired again, all of them on the way to church, dragging past a crowd of spick hoods on the corner, and one spick said something about Ma's boobs, which were big, but all of Ma was big, so why did the hood have to say something about her big boobs, as if they were nice? When they all knew they weren't nice, they were just a big woman's boobs in a too tight dress on a rainy Sunday morning, and on her head was a slit-open bread bag to keep her gray hair dry. The hood said what he said because one look at Dad told him he could. Dad, with his hunched shoulders and his constant blinking, just took Ma's arm and mumbled to the hood that a comment like that did more damage to the insulter than to the insulted, etc. etc. blah blah blah. Then the hood made a sound like a cow, at Ma, and Neil, who was nine, tried to break away and take a swing at the hood but Ma had his hand and wouldn't turn him loose and secretly he was glad, because he was scared, and then was ashamed at the relief he felt on entering the dark church, where the thin pan-icked preacher who was losing his congregation exchanged sly biblical quotes with Dad while Winky stood beaming as if none of it outside had happened, the lower half of her body gone psychedelic in the stained-glass light.

Oh man, the world had shit on Dad, but it wasn't going to shit on him. No way. If the world thought he was going to live in a neighborhood where spicks insulted his wife's boobs, if the world thought he was going to make his family eat bread dragged through bacon grease while calling it Hobo's Delight, the world was just wrong, he was going to succeed, like the men described in *People of Power*, who had gardens bigger than entire towns and owned whole ships and believed in power and power only. Were thirty horse-drawn carts needed to save the roses? The call went out to the surrounding towns and at dusk lanterns from the carts could be seen approaching on the rocky, bumpy roads. Was a serving girl found attractive? Her husband was sent away to war. Those guys knew how to find and occupy their Power Places, and he did too, like when he sometimes had to solder a thousand triangular things in a night to make the rent, and drink coffee till dawn and crank WMDX full blast to stay psyched. On those nights, when Winky came up making small talk, he boldly waved her away, and when he waved her away, away she went, because she sensed in his body language that he was king, that what he was doing was essential, and when she went away he felt good, he felt strong, and he soldered faster, which was the phenomenon the book called the Power Boost, and the book said that Major Successes tended to be people who could string together Power Boost after Power Boost, which was accomplished by doing exactly what you felt like doing at any given time, with certainty and joy, which was what, he realized, he was about to do, by kicking out Winky!

Now was the time for him to win! Why the heck couldn't he cook his special meatballs for Beverly and afterward make love to her on the couch and tell her his dreams and plans and see if she was the one meant to be his life's helpmate, like Mrs. Thomas Alva Edison, who had once stayed up all night applying labels to a shipment of chemicals essential for the next day's work? But no. Bev was dating someone else now, some kind of guard at the mall, and he remembered the meatball dinner, Winky's pink face periodically thrusting into the steam from the broccoli as she trotted out her usual B.S. on stigmata and the amount of time necessary for an actual physical body to rot. No wonder her roommates had kicked her out, calling him in secret, no wonder her preacher had demanded she stop volunteering so much—another secret call, people had apparently been quitting the church because of her. She was a nut, a real energy sink, it had been a huge mistake inviting her to live with him, and now she simply had to go.

It was sad, yes, a little sad, but if greatness were easy everyone would be doing it.

Yes, she'd been a cute kid and, yes, they'd shared some nice moments, yes yes yes, yes she'd brought him crackers and his little radio that time he'd hid under the steps for five straight hours after Dad started weeping during dinner, and yes, he remembered the scared look in her eyes when she'd come running up to him after taking a hook in the temple while fishing with the big boys, and yes, he'd carried her home as the big boys cackled, yes, it was sad that she sang so bad and thought it was good and sad that her panties were huge now when he found them in the wash, but like it said in the book, a person couldn't throw himself across someone else's funeral pyre without getting pretty goddamned hot.

She had his key so he rang the bell.

She appeared at the door, looking crazy as ever.

"Welcome home!" she said, and bowed at the waist, and a sock fell off her shoulder, and as she bent to pick it up she banged her head against the storm window, the poor dorky thing.

Oh shit, oh shit, he was weakening, he could feel it, the speech he'd practiced on the way home seemed now to have nothing to do with the girl who stood wet-eyed in the doorway, rubbing her bald spot. He wasn't powerful, he wasn't great, he was just the same as everybody else, less than everybody else, other people got married and had real jobs, other people didn't live with their fat, clinging sisters, he was a loser who would keep losing for the rest of his life, because he'd never gotten a break, he'd been cursed with a bad dad and a bad ma and a bad sister, and was too weak to change, too weak to make a new start, and as he pushed by her into the tea-smelling house the years ahead stretched out bleak and joyless in his imagination and his chest went suddenly dense with rage.

"Neil-Neil," she said. "Is something wrong?"

And he wanted to smack her, insult her, say something to wake her up, but only kept moving toward his room, calling her terrible names under his breath.

## This Is What It Means to Say Phoenix, Arizona

### SHERMAN ALEXIE

Just after Victor lost his job at the BIA, he also found out that his father had died of a heart attack in Phoenix, Arizona. Victor hadn't seen his father in a few years, only talked to him on the telephone once or twice, but there still was a genetic pain, which was soon to be pain as real and immediate as a broken bone.

Victor didn't have any money. Who does have money on a reservation, except the cigarette and fireworks salespeople? His father had a savings account waiting to be claimed, but Victor needed to find a way to get to Phoenix. Victor's mother was just as poor as he was, and the rest of his family didn't have any use at all for him. So Victor called the Tribal Council.

"Listen," Victor said. "My father just died. I need some money to get to Phoenix to make arrangements."

"Now, Victor," the council said. "You know we're having a difficult time financially."

"But I thought the council had special funds set aside for stuff like this."

"Now, Victor, we have some money available for the proper return of tribal members' bodies. But I don't think we have enough to bring your father all the way back from Phoenix."

"Well," Victor said. "It ain't going to cost all that much. He had to be cremated. Things were kind of ugly. He died of a heart attack in his trailer and nobody found him for a week. It was really hot, too. You get the picture."

"Now, Victor, we're sorry for your loss and the circumstances. But we can really only afford to give you one hundred dollars."

"That's not even enough for a plane ticket."

"Well, you might consider driving down to Phoenix."

"I don't have a car. Besides, I was going to drive my father's pickup back up here."

"Now, Victor," the council said. "We're sure there is somebody who could drive you to Phoenix. Or is there somebody who could lend you the rest of the money?"

"You know there ain't nobody around with that kind of money."

"Well, we're sorry, Victor, but that's the best we can do."

Victor accepted the Tribal Council's offer. What else could he do? So he signed the proper papers, picked up his check, and walked over to the Trading Post to cash it.

While Victor stood in line, he watched Thomas Builds-the-Fire standing near the magazine rack, talking to himself. Like he always did. Thomas was a storyteller that nobody wanted to listen to. That's like being a dentist in a town where everybody has false teeth.

Victor and Thomas Builds-the-Fire were the same age, had grown up and played in the dirt together. Ever since Victor could remember, it was Thomas who always had something to say.

Once, when they were seven years old, when Victor's father still lived with the family, Thomas closed his eyes and told Victor this story: "Your father's heart is weak. He is afraid of his own family. He is afraid of you. Late at night he sits in the dark. Watches the television until there's nothing but that white noise. Sometimes he feels like he wants to buy a motorcycle and ride away. He wants to run and hide. He doesn't want to be found."

Thomas Builds-the-Fire had known that Victor's father was going to leave, knew it before anyone. Now Victor stood in the Trading Post with a one-hundred-dollar check in his hand, wondering if Thomas knew that Victor's father was dead, if he knew what was going to happen next.

Just then Thomas looked at Victor, smiled, and walked over to him.

"Victor, I'm sorry about your father," Thomas said.

"How did you know about it?" Victor asked.

"I heard it on the wind. I heard it from the birds. I felt it in the sunlight. Also, your mother was just in here crying."

"Oh," Victor said and looked around the Trading Post. All the other Indians stared, surprised that Victor was even talking to Thomas. Nobody talked to Thomas anymore because he told the same damn stories over and over again. Victor was embarrassed, but he thought that Thomas might be able to help him. Victor felt a sudden need for tradition.

"I can lend you the money you need," Thomas said suddenly. "But you have to take me with you."

"I can't take your money," Victor said. "I mean, I haven't hardly talked to you in years. We're not really friends anymore."

"I didn't say we were friends. I said you had to take me with you."

"Let me think about it."

Victor went home with his one hundred dollars and sat at the kitchen table. He held his head in his hands and thought about Thomas Builds-the-Fire, remembered little details, tears and scars, the bicycle they shared for a summer, so many stories.

Thomas Builds-the-Fire sat on the bicycle, waited in Victor's yard. He was ten years old and skinny. His hair was dirty because it was the Fourth of July.

"Victor," Thomas yelled. "Hurry up. We're going to miss the fireworks."

After a few minutes, Victor ran out of his house, jumped the porch railing, and landed gracefully on the sidewalk.

"And the judges award him a 9.95, the highest score of the summer," Thomas said, clapped, laughed.

"That was perfect, cousin," Victor said. "And it's my turn to ride the bike."

Thomas gave up the bike and they headed for the fairgrounds. It was nearly dark and the fireworks were about to start.

"You know," Thomas said. "It's strange how us Indians celebrate the Fourth of July. It ain't like it was *our* independence everybody was fighting for."

"You think about things too much," Victor said. "It's just supposed to be fun. Maybe Junior will be there."

"Which Junior? Everybody on this reservation is named Junior."

And they both laughed.

The fireworks were small, hardly more than a few bottle rockets and a fountain. But it was enough for two Indian boys. Years later, they would need much more.

Afterwards, sitting in the dark, fighting off mosquitoes, Victor turned to Thomas Builds-the-Fire.

"Hey," Victor said. "Tell me a story."

Thomas closed his eyes and told this story: "There were these two Indian boys who wanted to be warriors. But it was too late to be warriors in the old way. All the horses were gone. So the two Indian boys stole a car and drove to the city. They parked the stolen car in front of the police station and then hitchhiked back home to the reservation. When they got back, all their friends cheered and their parents' eyes shone with pride. *You were very brave*, everybody said to the two Indian boys. *Very brave*."

"Ya-hey," Victor said. "That's a good one. I wish I could be a warrior."

"Me, too." Thomas said.

They went home together in the dark, Thomas on the bike now, Victor on foot. They walked through shadows and light from streetlamps.

"We've come a long ways," Thomas said. "We have outdoor lighting."

"All I need is the stars," Victor said. "And besides, you still think about things too much."

They separated then, each headed for home, both laughing all the way.

Victor sat at his kitchen table. He counted his one hundred dollars again and again. He knew he needed more to make it to Phoenix and back. He knew he needed Thomas Builds-the-Fire. So he put his money in his wallet and opened the front door to find Thomas on the porch.

"Ya-hey, Victor," Thomas said. "I knew you'd call me."

Thomas walked into the living room and sat down on Victor's favorite chair.

"I've got some money saved up," Thomas said. "It's enough to get us down there, but you have to get us back."

"I've got this hundred dollars," Victor said. "And my dad had a savings account I'm going to claim."

"How much in your dad's account?"

"Enough. A few hundred."

"Sounds good. When we leaving?"

When they were fifteen and had long since stopped being friends, Victor and Thomas got into a fistfight. That is, Victor was really drunk and beat Thomas up for no reason at all. All the other Indian boys stood around and watched it happen. Junior was there and so were Lester, Seymour, and a lot of others. The beating might have gone on until Thomas was dead if Norma Many Horses hadn't come along and stopped it.

"Hey, you boys," Norma yelled and jumped out of her car. "Leave him alone."

If it had been someone else, even another man, the Indian boys would've just ignored the warnings. But Norma was a warrior. She was powerful. She could have picked up any two of the boys and smashed their skulls together. But worse than that, she would have dragged them all over to some tipi and made them listen to some elder tell a dusty old story.

The Indian boys scattered, and Norma walked over to Thomas and picked him up.

"Hey, little man, are you okay?" she asked.

Thomas gave her a thumbs up.

"Why they always picking on you?"

Thomas shook his head, closed his eyes, but no stories came to him, no words or music. He just wanted to go home, to lie in his bed and let his dreams tell his stories for him.

Thomas Builds-the-Fire and Victor sat next to each other in the airplane, coach section. A tiny white woman had the window seat. She was busy twisting her body into pretzels. She was flexible.

"I have to ask," Thomas said, and Victor closed his eyes in embarrassment.

"Don't," Victor said.

"Excuse me, miss," Thomas asked. "Are you a gymnast or something?"

"There's no something about it," she said. "I was first alternate on the 1980 Olympic team."

"Really?" Thomas asked.

"Really."

"I mean, you used to be a world-class athlete?" Thomas asked.

"My husband still thinks I am."

Thomas Builds-the-Fire smiled. She was a mental gymnast, too. She pulled her leg straight up against her body so that she could've kissed her kneecap.

"I wish I could do that," Thomas said.

Victor was ready to jump out of the plane. Thomas, that crazy Indian storyteller with ratty old braids and broken teeth, was flirting with a beautiful Olympic gymnast. Nobody back home on the reservation would ever believe it.

"Well," the gymnast said. "It's easy. Try it."

Thomas grabbed at his leg and tried to pull it up into the same position as the gymnast. He couldn't even come close, which made Victor and the gymnast laugh.

"Hey," she asked. "You two are Indian, right?"

"Full-blood," Victor said.

"Not me," Thomas said. "I'm half magician on my mother's side and half clown on my father's."

They all laughed.

"What are your names?" she asked.

"Victor and Thomas."

"Mine is Cathy. Pleased to meet you all."

The three of them talked for the duration of the flight. Cathy the gymnast complained about the government, how they screwed the 1980 Olympic team by boycotting.

"Sounds like you all got a lot in common with Indians," Thomas said.

Nobody laughed.

After the plane landed in Phoenix and they had all found their way to the terminal, Cathy the gymnast smiled and waved good-bye.

"She was really nice," Thomas said.

"Yeah, but everybody talks to everybody on airplanes," Victor said. "It's too bad we can't always be that way."

"You always used to tell me I think too much," Thomas said. "Now it sounds like you do."

"Maybe I caught it from you."

"Yeah."

Thomas and Victor rode in a taxi to the trailer where Victor's father died.

"Listen," Victor said as they stopped in front of the trailer. "I never told you I was sorry for beating you up that time."

"Oh, it was nothing. We were just kids and you were drunk."

"Yeah, but I'm still sorry."

"That's all right."

Victor paid for the taxi and the two of them stood in the hot Phoenix summer. They could smell the trailer.

"This ain't going to be nice," Victor said. "You don't have to go in."

"You're going to need help."

Victor walked to the front door and opened it. The stink rolled out and made them both gag. Victor's father had lain in that trailer for a week in hundred-degree temperatures before anyone found him. And the only reason anyone found him was because of the smell. They needed dental records to identify him. That's exactly what the coroner said. They needed dental records.

"Oh, man," Victor said. "I don't know if I can do this."

"Well, then don't."

"But there might be something valuable in there."

"I thought his money was in the bank."

"It is. I was talking about pictures and letters and stuff like that."

"Oh," Thomas said as he held his breath and followed Victor into the trailer.

When Victor was twelve, he stepped into an underground wasp nest. His foot was caught in the hole, and no matter how hard he struggled, Victor couldn't pull free. He might have died there, stung a thousand times, if Thomas Builds-the-Fire had not come by.

"Run," Thomas yelled and pulled Victor's foot from the hole. They ran then, hard as they ever had, faster than Billy Mills, faster than Jim Thorpe, faster than the wasps could fly.

Victor and Thomas ran until they couldn't breathe, ran until it was cold and dark outside, ran until they were lost and it took hours to find their way home. All the way back, Victor counted his stings.

"Seven," Victor said. "My lucky number."

Victor didn't find much to keep in the trailer. Only a photo album and a stereo. Everything else had that smell stuck in it or was useless anyway.

"I guess this is all," Victor said. "It ain't much."

"Better than nothing," Thomas said.

"Yeah, and I do have the pickup."

"Yeah," Thomas said. "It's in good shape."

"Dad was good about that stuff."

"Yeah, I remember your dad."

"Really?" Victor asked. "What do you remember?"

Thomas Builds-the-Fire closed his eyes and told this story: "I remember when I had this dream that told me to go to Spokane, to stand by the Falls in the middle of the city and wait for a sign. I knew I had to go there but I didn't have a car. Didn't have a license. I was only thirteen. So I walked all the way, took me all day, and I finally made it to the Falls. I stood there for an hour waiting. Then your dad came walking up. *What the hell are you doing here?* he asked me. I said, *Waiting for a vision.* Then your father said, *All you're going to get here is mugged.* So he drove me over to Denny's, bought me dinner, and then drove me home to the reservation. For a long time I was mad because I thought my dreams had lied to me. But they didn't. Your dad was my vision. *Take care of each other* is what my dreams were saying. *Take care of each other.*"

Victor was quiet for a long time. He searched his mind for memories of his father, found the good ones, found a few bad ones, added it all up, and smiled.

"My father never told me about finding you in Spokane," Victor said.

"He said he wouldn't tell anybody. Didn't want me to get in trouble. But he said I had to watch out for you as part of the deal."

"Really?"

"Really. Your father said you would need the help. He was right."

"That's why you came down here with me, isn't it?" Victor asked.

"I came because of your father."

Victor and Thomas climbed into the pickup, drove over to the bank, and claimed the three hundred dollars in the savings account.

Thomas Builds-the-Fire could fly.

Once, he jumped off the roof of the tribal school and flapped his arms like a crazy eagle. And he flew. For a second, he hovered, suspended above all the other Indian boys who were too smart or too scared to jump.

"He's flying," Junior yelled, and Seymour was busy looking for the trick wires or mirrors. But it was real. As real as the dirt when Thomas lost altitude and crashed to the ground.

He broke his arm in two places.

"He broke his wing," Victor chanted, and the other Indian boys joined in, made it a tribal song.

"He broke his wing, he broke his wing, he broke his wing," all the Indian boys chanted as they ran off, flapping their wings, wishing they could fly, too. They hated Thomas for his courage, his brief moment as a bird. Everybody has dreams about flying. Thomas flew.

One of his dreams came true for just a second, just enough to make it real.

Victor's father, his ashes, fit in one wooden box with enough left over to fill a cardboard box.

"He always was a big man," Thomas said.

Victor carried part of his father and Thomas carried the rest out to the pickup. They set him down carefully behind the seats, put a cowboy hat on the wooden box and a Dodgers cap on the cardboard box. That's the way it was supposed to be.

"Ready to head back home," Victor asked.

"It's going to be a long drive."

"Yeah, take a couple days, maybe."

"We can take turns," Thomas said.

"Okay," Victor said, but they didn't take turns. Victor drove for sixteen hours straight north, made it halfway up Nevada toward home before he finally pulled over.

"Hey, Thomas," Victor said. "You got to drive for a while."

"Okay."

Thomas Builds-the-Fire slid behind the wheel and started off down the road. All through Nevada, Thomas and Victor had been amazed at the lack of animal life, at the absence of water, of movement.

"Where is everything?" Victor had asked more than once.

Now when Thomas was finally driving they saw the first animal, maybe the only animal in Nevada. It was a long-eared jackrabbit.

"Look," Victor yelled. "It's alive."

Thomas and Victor were busy congratulating themselves on their discovery when the jackrabbit darted out into the road and under the wheels of the pickup.

"Stop the goddamn car," Victor yelled, and Thomas did stop, backed the pickup to the dead jackrabbit.

"Oh, man, he's dead," Victor said as he looked at the squashed animal.

"Really dead."

"The only thing alive in this whole state and we just killed it."

"I don't know," Thomas said. "I think it was suicide."

Victor looked around the desert, sniffed the air, felt the emptiness and loneliness, and nodded his head.

"Yeah," Victor said. "It had to be suicide."

"I can't believe this," Thomas said. "You drive for a thousand miles and there ain't even any bugs smashed on the windshield. I drive for ten seconds and kill the only living thing in Nevada."

"Yeah," Victor said. "Maybe I should drive."

"Maybe you should."

Thomas Builds-the-Fire walked through the corridors of the tribal school by himself. Nobody wanted to be anywhere near him because of all those stories. Story after story.

Thomas closed his eyes and this story came to him: "We are all given one thing by which our lives are measured, one determination. Mine are the stories which can change or not change the world. It doesn't matter which as long as I continue to tell the stories. My father, he died on Okinawa in World War II, died fighting for this country, which had tried to kill him for years. My mother, she died giving birth to me, died while I was still inside her. She pushed me out into the world with her last breath. I have no brothers or sisters. I have only my stories which came to me before I even had the words to speak. I learned a thousand stories before I took my first thousand steps. They are all I have. It's all I can do."

Thomas Builds-the-Fire told his stories to all those who would stop and listen. He kept telling them after people had stopped listening.

Victor and Thomas made it back to the reservation just as the sun was rising. It was the beginning of a new day on earth, but the same old shit on the reservation.

"Good morning," Thomas said.

"Good morning."

The tribe was waking up, ready for work, eating breakfast, reading the newspaper, just like everybody else does. Willene LeBret was out in her garden wearing a bathrobe. She waved when Thomas and Victor drove by.

"Crazy Indians made it," she said to herself and went back to her roses.

Victor stopped the pickup in front of Thomas Builds-the-Fire's HUD house. They both yawned, stretched a little, shook dust from their bodies.

"I'm tired," Victor said.

"Of everything," Thomas added.

They both searched for words to end the journey. Victor needed to thank Thomas for his help, for the money, and make the promise to pay it all back.

"Don't worry about the money," Thomas said. "It don't make any difference anyhow."

"Probably not, enit?"

"Nope."

Victor knew that Thomas would remain the crazy storyteller who talked to dogs and cars, who listened to the wind and pine trees. Victor knew that he couldn't really be friends with Thomas, even after all that had happened. It was cruel but it was real. As real as the ashes, as Victor's father, sitting behind the seats.

"I know how it is," Thomas said. "I know you ain't going to treat me any better than you did before. I know your friends would give you too much shit about it."

Victor was ashamed of himself. Whatever happened to the tribal ties, the sense of community? The only real thing he shared with anybody was a bottle and broken dreams. He owed Thomas something, anything.

"Listen," Victor said and handed Thomas the cardboard box which contained half of his father. "I want you to have this."

Thomas took the ashes and smiled, closed his eyes, and told this story: "I'm going to travel to Spokane Falls one last time and toss these ashes into the water. And your father will rise like a salmon, leap over the bridge, over me, and find his way home.

It will be beautiful. His teeth will shine like silver, like a rainbow. He will rise, Victor, he will rise."

Victor smiled.

"I was planning on doing the same thing with my half," Victor said. "But I didn't imagine my father looking anything like a salmon. I thought it'd be like cleaning the attic or something. Like letting things go after they've stopped having any use."

"Nothing stops, cousin," Thomas said. "Nothing stops."

Thomas Builds-the-Fire got out of the pickup and walked up his driveway. Victor started the pickup and began the drive home.

"Wait," Thomas yelled suddenly from his porch. "I just got to ask one favor."

Victor stopped the pickup, leaned out the window, and shouted back. "What do you want?"

"Just one time when I'm telling a story somewhere, why don't you stop and listen?" Thomas asked.

"Just once?"

"Just once."

Victor waved his arms to let Thomas know that the deal was good. It was a fair trade, and that was all Victor had ever wanted from his whole life. So Victor drove his father's pickup toward home while Thomas went into his house, closed the door behind him, and heard a new story come to him in the silence afterwards.

## Writing Exercises

### INDIVIDUAL

1. Start with a personal essay you've already written: a college application or personal experience is ideal. The essay should describe a specific experience, and also reflect on its meaning and effects. If you don't have an essay to work with, think of a personal experience you would like to explore and write a quick draft.

   Now, without looking at your essay, write a fictional scene depicting your experience (or part of it). Don't spell out the meaning; let the reader draw his own conclusions. Focus on concrete details. Your fictional scene *might* suggest the same themes and ideas that your essay explicitly states. On the other hand, you might find that as you write the scene the themes become more ambiguous, contradictory, richer, or just different. If this happens, go with it.

2. Choose a fiction writer whose work you know well. Drawing on several of her stories or novels, look for similarities, listing as many elements as you can. Look for big things like recurring themes, ideas, images, patterns, subjects, situations, and character types, but don't neglect smaller things like specific actions or gestures, metaphors, minor characters. Is the writer drawn to certain subjects or situations again and again? If she does return to the same material or territory, is

she merely recycling it, or does she continue to find new things in old material? Do you see an evolution or progression in her work?

3. Now do the same thing with your own work. Go through all the stories, fragments, and exercises that you've written so far in this course. What elements recur? If someone were to analyze your work, what would he say you were preoccupied with? If you keep a journal of writing ideas, or clip newspaper stories, go through this material too. What kinds of things do you find compelling? What sort of stories and anecdotes interest you? If you are lucky enough to have a reader who has seen several of your stories, you might ask her to explain what she thinks you are trying to explore in your work. You may be surprised.

4. Think of a family anecdote that is particularly meaningful: it might reveal something about the nature of a specific individual or relationship, or perhaps some truth about families or relationships generally. (This doesn't have to be something you experienced or witnessed; it could be a story about your great-grandparents' courtship, or your mother's childhood.)

   a. First, write the story in the form of a letter to someone close to you (if he already knows the story, pretend he doesn't). Explain explicitly what you think the story reveals/means, and why. Try to convey why this story is so compelling to you.

   b. Depict the story in scene. Instead of explicitly explaining your interpretation, try to suggest it through subtle hints.

5. Write down a list of the things that scare you the most. Try to focus on things you're afraid of right now, at this point in your life, rather than things that might've scared you when you were younger. Look at your list. Which item do you dread the most? Write a story in which you visit this calamity on a character.

## COLLABORATIVE

6. With a partner or in a small group, exchange stories with a classmate. The story should be an early draft on which you haven't received any feedback yet. Read each other's stories twice; on your second read look for recurring images, patterns, connections, and ideas. Examine each other's stories in terms of theme: look not only for *present* themes, but also for underdeveloped or potential ones. Make notes on the manuscript and then explain your interpretation to the author. Basically, tell the author what *you* think the story is "about."

   Listen to your peer's interpretation before explaining your intentions in the story. Don't say anything until he's finished.

   When it comes to revision, consider the differences between your view of your story and your classmate's. If some of your themes failed to reach him, you may want to revise with this as a goal; on the other hand, some of your reader's insights may be more interesting than your own original ideas. Rethink your assumptions about the story and its possible meanings. Don't remain prisoner to your first conception of the story.

7. After you've done the second part of exercise #1 above, give a partner your fictional scene to read. Do not comment on your intentions or say anything that might affect her interpretation. Ask your partner to explain what she thinks the scene is "about": themes, ideas, recurring images, connections, etc. Now give her the essay to read. How is your partner's interpretation different than you intended? How is it the same?

# 11

# PLAY IT AGAIN, SAM
## *Revision*

- *Re-Vision*

- *Worry It and Walk Away*

- *Criticism and the Story Workshop*

- *Revision Questions*

- *Further Suggestions for Revision*

- *Examples of the Revision Process*

"Talent is a long patience," Anton Chekhov remarked, an acknowledgment that the creative process is not all inventive, and extends far beyond the first heated rush. Partly corrective, critical, nutritive, and fostering, revision is a matter of rendering a story the best that it can be. William C. Knott, in *The Craft of Fiction*, cogently observes that "anyone can write—and almost everyone you meet these days is writing. However, only the writers know how to rewrite. It is this ability alone that turns the amateur into a pro."

While the focus of this chapter is the overall revision of stories and the best use of readers' feedback, the methods of shaping, enriching, and enlivening stories discussed throughout this book implicitly concern the revision of fiction, element by element. We have already visited the process of revision through the discussion of the story workshop in the preface (a discussion that will continue here); some of the exercises at the end of most chapters; the chapter 4 review "Character: A Summary"; and in the chapter 6 section "Revising Summary and Scene." The preceding chapter on theme invites you to seek the true subject of your story-in-progress, and to direct your revision work toward exploring that understanding.

## Re-Vision

Revising is a process more dreaded than dreadful. The resistance to rewriting is, if anything, greater than the resistance to beginning in the first place. Yet the chances are that once you have committed yourself to a first draft, you'll be unable to leave it in an unfinished and unsatisfying state. You'll be *unhappy* until it's right. Making it right will involve a second commitment, to seeing the story fresh and creating it again with the advantage of this "re-vision." Alice Munro, in the introduction to her *Selected Stories*, describes the risk, the readiness, and the reward.

> . . . The story, in the first draft, has put on rough but adequate clothes, it is "finished" and might be thought to need no more than a lot of technical adjustments, some tightening here and expanding there, and the slipping in of some telling dialogue and chopping away of flabby modifiers. It's then, in fact, that the story is in the greatest danger of losing its life, of appearing so hopelessly misbegotten that my only relief comes from abandoning it. It doesn't do enough. It does what I intended, but it turns out that my intention was all wrong. . . . I go around glum and preoccupied, trying to think of ways to fix the problem. Usually the right way pops up in the middle of this.
> A big relief. Renewed energy. Resurrection.
> Except that it isn't the right way. Maybe a way *to* the right way. Now I write pages and pages I'll have to discard. New angles are introduced, minor characters brought center stage, lively and satisfying scenes are written, and it's all a mistake. Out they go. But by this time I'm on the track, there's no backing out. I know so much more than I did, I know what I want to happen and where I want to end up and I just have to keep trying till I find the best way of getting there.

To find the best way of getting there, you may have to "see again" more than once. The process of revision involves external and internal insight; you'll need your conscious critic, your creative instinct, and readers you trust. You may need each of them several times, not necessarily in that order. A story gets better not just by polishing and refurbishing, not by improving a word choice here and an image there, but by taking risks with the structure, reenvisioning, being open to new meaning itself. "In the first draft is the talent," said French poet Paul Valery, "in the second is the art."

## Worry It and Walk Away

To write your first draft, you banished the internal critic. Now make the critic welcome. Revision is work, but the strange thing is that you may find you can concentrate on the work for much longer than you could play at freedrafting. It has occurred to me that writing a first draft is very like tennis or softball—I have to be psyched for it. Energy level up, alert, on my toes. A few hours is all I can manage, and at the end of it I'm wiped out. Revision is like careful carpentry, and if I'm under a deadline or just determined to get this thing crafted and polished, I can be good for twelve hours of it.

The first round of rewrites is probably a matter of letting your misgivings surface. Focus for a while on what seems awkward, overlong, undeveloped, flat, or flowery. Tinker. Tighten. Sharpen. More important at this stage than finishing any given page or phrase is that you're getting to know your story in order to open it to new possibilities. You will also get tired of it; you may feel stuck.

Then put it away. Don't look at it for a matter of days or weeks—until you feel fresh on the project. In addition to getting some distance on your story, you're mailing it to your unconscious, not consciously working out the flaws but temporarily letting them go. Rollo May, in *The Courage to Create*, describes what frequently happens next:

> Everyone uses from time to time such expressions as, "a thought pops up," an idea comes "from the blue" or "dawns" or "comes as though out of a dream," or "it suddenly hit me." These are various ways of describing a common experience: the breakthrough of ideas from some depth below the level of awareness.

It is my experience that such realizations occur over and over again in the course of writing a short story or novel. Often I will believe that because I know who my characters are and what happens to them, I know what my story is about—and often I find I'm wrong, or that my understanding is shallow or incomplete.

In the first draft of a recent novel, for instance, I opened with the sentence, "It took a hundred and twelve bottles of champagne to see the young Poindexters off to Arizona." A page later one character whispered to another that the young Mr. Poindexter in question had "consumption." I worked on this book for a year (taking my characters off to Arizona where they dealt with the desert heat, lack of water, alcoholism, loss of religion, and the development of mining interests and the building trade) before I saw the connection between "consumption" and "champagne." When I understood that simple link, I understood the overarching theme—surely latent in the idea from the moment it had taken hold of me—between tuberculosis, spiritual thirst, consumerism, and addiction, all issues of "consumption."

---

". . . THE FIRST IMPULSE IN WRITING IS TO FLOOD IT OUT, let as much run freely as you possibly can. Then to take a walk or go to the bank . . . and come back in a day or six months later. To read it with a cold eye and say, "This is good. This is not. That sentence works. This is magical. This is crummy." You have to maintain your critical sensibility and not just assume, because it was an extraordinary dream for you, that it will be a dream for other people. Because people need maps to your dreams.

Alan Gurganus

It might seem dismaying that you should see what your story is about only after you have written it. Try it; you'll like it. Nothing is more exhilarating than the discovery that a complex pattern has lain in your mind ready to unfold.

Note that in the early stages of revision, both the worrying and the walking away are necessary. Perhaps it is bafflement itself that plunges us to the unconscious space where the answer lies.

## Criticism and the Story Workshop

Once you have thought your story through, drafted it, and worked on it to the best of your ability, someone else's eyes can help to refresh the vision of your own. Wise professionals rely on the help of an agent or editor at this juncture (although even the wisest still smart at censure); anyone can rely on the help of friends, family, or classmates in a story workshop. The trick to making good use of criticism is to be utterly selfish about it. Be greedy for it. Take it all in. Ultimately you are the laborer, the arbiter, and the boss in any dispute about your story, so you can afford to consider any problem and any solution. Most of us feel not only committed to what we have put on the page, but also defensive on its behalf—wanting, really, to be told only that it is a work of genius or, failing that, to find out that we have gotten away with it. Therefore, the first exigency of revision is that you learn to hear, absorb, and accept criticism.

"Revising is like cutting your own hair," says novelist Robert Stone, for while you may sense the need for improvement, it's hard to get right what you can never entirely see for yourself. This is the major advantage of a workshop—your fellow writers may not be able to tell you how to style the material in the way that best suits the story, but they can at least hold up the mirror and see from a more distanced perspective. (If you are just beginning the practice of group critiques, you may wish to look back at the description of common workshop procedures in the Preface.)

How to assimilate so many opinions, let alone choose what is useful? First, give special consideration to the comments of those two or three workshop members with whose responses you have generally agreed before. However, the best—or at any rate the most useful—criticism, John L'Heureux suggests, simply points out what you had already sensed for yourself but had hoped to get away with. Or as Flannery O'Connor put it, with typical bluntness, in fiction "you can do anything you can get away with, but nobody has ever gotten away with much."

It used to be popular to speak of "constructive criticism" and "destructive criticism," but these are misleading terms suggesting that positive suggestions are useful and negative criticism useless. In practice the opposite is usually the case. You're likely to find that the most constructive thing a reader can do is say *I don't believe this, I don't like this, I don't understand this*, pointing to precisely the passages that made you uneasy. This kind of laying-the-finger-on-the-trouble-spot produces an inward groan, but it's also satisfying; you know just where to go to work. Often the most destructive thing a reader can do is offer you a positive suggestion—*Why don't you have him crash the car?*—that is irrelevant to your vision of the story. Be suspicious of praise that is too extravagant, of blame that is too general. If your impulse is to defend the story or yourself, still the impulse. Behave as if bad advice were good advice, and give it serious consideration. You can reject it after you have explored it for anything of use it may offer.

> ... THE WRITING WORKSHOP FINALLY IS THE ONE PLACE where you can be sure you and your work are taken seriously, where your writing intentions are honored, where even in a mean-spirited comment you can divine—if you wish—the truth about your writing, its strengths and its weaknesses. It is a place where you are surrounded by people whose chief interest is also yours, where the talk is never anything but writing and writing well and writing better. . . . It is where you somehow pick up the notion that what you're doing is a good and noble thing, and though you may not write as well as you'd like, it is enough and will suffice.
>
> John L'Heureux

Workshop members often voice sharply divided responses to a manuscript, a situation that may confuse and frustrate the author. Algonquin Books of Chapel Hill editor Duncan Murrell advises workshop writers "to pay close attention to the parts of their work that make readers stumble, but to disregard most of the solutions those readers suggest. Give a flawed story to ten good readers and they'll accurately find the flawed passages before offering ten wildly varying explanations and a handful of contradictory solutions. Good readers have a gut level understanding that something's wrong in a story, but they're often unclear about what it is, or what to do about it. Yet once pointed to the weak sections, authors almost always come up with better solutions than anything a reader or an editor can offer; they know the story and the characters better. The trick is to bite your lip when readers tell you how to fix your story, while noting the passages that need repair."

Indeed, while the author may or may not benefit from peer suggestions, everyone else in the workshop does, for the practice of thinking through and articulating responses to a story's challenges eventually makes all participants more objective critics of their own work. You will notice that the more specific the criticism you offer—or receive—the more useful it proves and the less it stings; similarly, the more specific the praise of "what works," the more likely it is to reinforce good habits— and to be believed. After a semester's experience of workshopping, you'll find that you can critique a story within your own imagination, knowing who would say what, with whom you would agree, and telling yourself what you already know to be true.

Within a day or two of the workshop, novelist, playwright, and teacher Michelle Carter advises that the author try to "re-hear criticism," that is, to assess what it is readers are responding to, which may not be apparent from the suggested "fix." For example, if a number of readers suggest changing the story's point of view from third person to first, Carter might reinterpret that to mean that the narrator seems overly remote from the characters—not that first-person narration is literally a better choice, but that readers want a more immediate experience of the main character's emotional dilemma.

A second example would be wanting "to know more about Character X." This doesn't necessarily mean sprinkling on some facts and history; rather, the reader may be desiring a greater understanding of the character's motivations or a closer rendering of crucial moments.

Additionally, Carter cautions, be tough with yourself, even when you realize that criticism is based on a misreading. Rarely is misinterpretation solely the mistake of the reader: ask what awkwardness of writing or false emphasis might have led to that skewed reading. Novelist Wally Lamb reinforces this point: "Often I think we let the writer get away with too much. If the writing is unclear, we'll read it a second time and make it clear to ourselves and then let the writer off the hook, when, in fact, the writing has to stand for itself . . . You want to work on the writing until it is good enough that the writer doesn't have to be in the room explaining and interpreting."

Kenneth Atchity, in *A Writer's Time*, advises compulsory "vacations" at crucial points in the revising process, in order to let the criticism cook until you feel ready, impatient, to get back to writing. So once again, walk away, and when you feel that you have acquired enough distance from the story to see it anew, go back to work. Make notes of your plans, large and small. Talk to yourself in your journal about what you want to accomplish and where you think you have failed. Let your imagination play with new images or passages of dialogue. Always keep a copy (and/or a document on disk) of the story as it is so that you can go back to the original, and then be ruthless with another copy. Eudora Welty advised cutting sections apart and pinning them back together so that they can be easily rearranged. I like to use the whole surface of the kitchen table as a cut-and-paste board. Some people can keep the story in their heads and do their rearranging directly onto the computer screen—which in any case has made the putting-back-together process less tedious than retyping.

## Revision Questions

As you plan the revision and as you rewrite, you will know (and your critics will tell you) what problems are unique to your story. There are also general, almost universal, pitfalls that you can avoid if you ask yourself the following questions:

*What is my story about?* Another way of saying this is *What is the pattern of change?* Once this pattern is clear, you can check your draft to make sure you've included all the crucial moments of discovery and decision. Is there a crisis action?

*Is there unnecessary summary?* Remember that it is a common impulse to try to cover too much ground. Tell your story in the fewest possible scenes; cut down on summary and unnecessary flashback. These dissipate energy and lead you to tell rather than show.

*Why should the reader turn from the first page to the second?* Is the language fresh? Are the characters alive? Does the first sentence, paragraph, page introduce real tension? If it doesn't, you have probably begun at the wrong place. If you are unable to find a way to introduce tension on the first page, you may have to question whether you have a story after all.

*Is it original?* Almost every writer thinks first, in some way or other, of the familiar, the usual, the given. This character is a stereotype, that emotion is too easy, that phrase is a cliché. First-draft laziness is inevitable, but it is also a way of being dishonest. A good writer will comb the work for clichés and labor to find the exact, the honest, and the fresh.

*Is it clear?* Although ambiguity and mystery provide some of our most profound pleasures in literature, beginning writers are often unable to distinguish between mystery and muddle, ambiguity and sloppiness. You may want your character to be rich with contradiction, but we still want to know whether that character is male or female, black or white, old or young. We need to be oriented on the simplest level of reality before we can share your imaginative world. Where are we? When are we? Who are they? How do things look? What time of day or night is it? What's the weather? What's happening?

*Is it self-conscious?* Probably the most famous piece of advice to the rewriter is William Faulkner's "kill all your darlings." When you are carried away with the purple of your prose, the music of your alliteration, the hilarity of your wit, the profundity of your insights, then the chances are that you are having a better time writing than the reader will have reading. No reader will forgive you, and no reader should. Just tell the story. The style will follow of itself if you just tell the story.

*Where is it too long?* Most of us, and even the best of us, write too long. We are so anxious to explain every nuance, cover every possible aspect of character, action, and setting that we forget the necessity of stringent selection. In fiction, and especially in the short story, we want sharpness, economy, and vivid, telling detail. More than necessary is too much. I have been helped in my own tendency to tell all by a friend who went through a copy of one of my novels, drawing a line through the last sentence of about every third paragraph. Then in the margin he wrote, again and again, "Hit it, and get out." That's good advice for anyone.

*Where is it undeveloped in character, action, imagery, theme?* In any first, second, or third draft of a manuscript there are likely to be necessary passages sketched, skipped, or skeletal. What information is missing, what actions are incomplete, what motives obscure, what images inexact? Where does the action occur too abruptly so that it loses its emotional force? Is the crisis presented as a scene?

*Where is it too general?* Originality, economy, and clarity can all be achieved through the judicious use of significant detail. Learn to spot general, vague, and fuzzy terms. Be suspicious of yourself anytime you see nouns like *someone* and *everything*, adjectives like *huge* and *handsome*, adverbs like *very* and *really*. Seek instead a particular thing, a particular size, an exact degree.

Although the dread of "starting over" is a real and understandable one, the chances are that the rewards of revising will startlingly outweigh the pains. Sometimes a character who is dead on the page will come to life through the addition of a few sentences or significant details. Sometimes a turgid or tedious paragraph can become sharp with a few judicious cuts. Sometimes dropping page one and putting page seven where page three used to be can provide the skeleton of an otherwise limp story. And sometimes, often, perhaps always, the difference between an amateur rough cut and a publishable story is in the struggle at the rewriting stage.

# *Further Suggestions for Revision*

♦ If you have been writing your story on a computer, retype at least one full draft, making both planned and spontaneous changes as you go. The computer's abilities can tempt us to a "fix-it" approach to revision, but jumping in and out of the text to correct problems can result in a revision that reads like patchwork. Rather, the effect of even small changes should ripple through the story, and this is more likely to happen if the writer reenters the story as a whole by literally rewriting it from start to finish.

♦ Screenwriter Stephen Fischer emphasizes that "writing is not a monolithic process, just as cooking is not a monolithic process. You don't just go in the kitchen and cook—you do a number of very specific things that you focus on one at a time—you peel garlic, you dice garlic, you saute onions—these are separate processes. You don't go into a kitchen and flap your arms and just cook—and in the same way, you don't 'just write.'"

To put this analogy into practice: Write two or three revisions of a story draft, focusing on a different issue each time. For example, you might zero in on the motivations of a character whose behavior and dialogue don't yet ring true; or you might simply focus on using setting to reflect emotion or threading physical activity through dialogue scenes. Focusing on a single goal lets you concentrate your efforts—yet other developments will naturally occur in response to the single-focus changes.

♦ In an interview in *Conversations on Writing Fiction*, novelist and teacher Jane Smiley says she asks her student writers to confront their own sets of "evasions," the counterproductive "rituals which don't actually allow them to spend time with or become engaged with their chosen themes or characters." For example, many people find conflict hard to handle in real life and therefore avoid it, often for good reason. Yet many of us sidestep conflict in our fiction too, even knowing its necessity in driving a character toward a defining crisis. If this sounds like an evasion you've experienced, take a look back at places in the story where explosive scenes *should* happen—places where characters ought to confront or defend. Are these, in fact, all-out scenes? Or do your characters neatly sidestep the conflict and retreat to their private thoughts? Does another character too conveniently knock at the door?

Taking refuge in the making of metaphors, however vivid, rather than clearly depicting what *is*, may be another form of evasion, perhaps reflecting a writer's lack of confidence in the interest of his or her material.

Spiraling off into the weird and random may reflect a similar lack of confidence or indecision; overly clever, bantering dialogue that strains to entertain may reflect a desire to dazzle, while avoiding the harder search for dialogue that is both realistic and revealing.

Evasions may be easier to observe in others' work at first, so you might want to ask a trusted workshop friend to help you recognize the evasions in your own stories. As you revise and encounter points of resistance—those places you hesitate to go further or become more specific—ask yourself, Is this right for the story or is it simply my comfortable habit?

> . . . YOU GENERALLY START OUT WITH SOME OVERALL IDEA that you can see
> fairly clearly, as if you were standing on a dock and looking at a ship on the
> ocean. At first you can see the entire ship, but then as you begin work
> you're in the boiler room and you can't see the ship anymore. . . . What you
> really want in an editor is someone who's still on the dock, who can say, Hi,
> I'm looking at your ship, and it's missing a bow, the front mast is crooked,
> and it looks to me as if your propellers are going to have to be fixed.
>
> Michael Crichton

## Examples of the Revision Process

When reading a polished, published story, it can be difficult to imagine that it once
was any other way—difficult to realize that the author made both choices and un-
planned connections, difficult to envision the story's history. After all, by the point
of publication the writer has likely heeded critic Annie Dillard's admonition:
"Process is nothing; erase your tracks. The path is not the work."

Yet a glimpse of these earlier "tracks" may reveal the paths writers forged to final
versions of their stories, and this may in turn inspire you to a more thorough reenvisioning of your own work. What follows are authors' accounts of the revision process.

In her book-length essay "The Writing Life," Annie Dillard uses the metaphor of
knocking out "a bearing wall" for the revising writer's sacrifice of the very aspect of
the story that inspired its writing. Strange as it sounds, this is an experience familiar
to many accomplished writers: "The part you must jettison," says Dillard, "is not
only the best-written part; it is also, oddly, that part which was to have been the very
point. It is the original key passage, the passage on which the rest was to hang, and
from which you yourself drew the courage to begin."

Joyce Carol Oates describes this phenomenon—and more—in her essay "Smooth
Talk: Short Story into Film." Readers of "Where Are You Going, Where Have You
Been?", one of the most famous American stories of the late twentieth century, may
be surprised to learn that the author's initial impulse to write the story disappeared
in the drafting process. Recounts Oates:

> Some years ago in the American Southwest, there surfaced a tabloid psychopath
> known as "The Pied Piper of Tucson." I have forgotten his name, but his specialty
> was the seduction and occasional murder of teen-aged girls. He may or may not have
> had actual accomplices, but his bizarre activities were known among a circle of
> teenagers in the Tucson area; for some reason they kept his secret, deliberately did
> not inform parents or police. It was this fact, not the fact of the mass murderer him-
> self, that struck me at the time. And this was a pre-Manson time, early or mid-1960s.
>
> The Pied Piper mimicked teenagers in their talk, dress, and behavior, but he
> was not a teenager—he was a man in his early thirties. Rather short, he stuffed

rags in his leather boots to give himself height. (And sometimes walked unsteadily as a consequence: did none among his admiring constituency notice?) He charmed his victims as charismatic psychopaths have always charmed their victims, to the bewilderment of others who fancy themselves free of all lunatic attractions. The Pied Piper of Tucson: a trashy dream, a tabloid archetype, sheer artifice, comedy, cartoon—surrounded, however improbably, and finally tragically, by real people. You think that, if you look twice, he won't be there. But there he is.

I don't remember any longer where I first read about this Pied Piper—very likely in *Life* Magazine. I do recall deliberately not reading the full article because I didn't want to be distracted by too much detail. It was not after all the mass murderer himself who intrigued me, but the disturbing fact that a number of teenagers—from "good" families—aided and abetted his crimes. This is the sort of thing authorities and responsible citizens invariably call "inexplicable" because they can't find explanations for it. *They* would not have fallen under this maniac's spell, after all.

An early draft of my short story, "Where Are You Going, Where Have You Been?" —from which the film *Smooth Talk* was adapted by Joyce Chopra and Tom Cole—had the rather too explicit title "Death and the Maiden." It was cast in a mode of fiction to which I am still partial—indeed, every third or fourth story of mine is probably in this mode— "realistic allegory," it might be called. It is Hawthornean, romantic, shading into parable. Like the medieval German engraving from which my title was taken, the story was minutely detailed yet clearly an allegory of the fatal attractions of death (or the devil). An innocent young girl is seduced by way of her own vanity; she mistakes death for erotic romance of a particularly American/trashy sort.

In subsequent drafts the story changed its tone, its focus, its language, its title. It became "Where Are You Going, Where Have You Been?" Written at a time when the author was intrigued by the music of Bob Dylan, particularly the hauntingly elegiac song "It's All Over Now, Baby Blue," it was dedicated to Bob Dylan. The charismatic mass murderer drops into the background and his innocent victim, a fifteen-year-old, moves into the foreground. She becomes the true protagonist of the tale, courting and being courted by her fate, a self-styled 1950s pop figure, alternately absurd and winning. There is no suggestion in the published story that "Arnold Friend" has seduced and murdered other young girls, or even that he necessarily intends to murder Connie. Is his interest "merely" sexual? (Nor is there anything about the complicity of other teenagers. I saved that yet more provocative note for a current story, "Testimony.") Connie is shallow, vain, silly, hopeful, doomed—but capable nonetheless of an unexpected gesture of heroism at the story's end.

Annie Dillard concludes the section of her essay "The Writing Life" by suggesting that a writer may save the abandoned idea for another story: "So it is that a writer writes many books. In each book, he intended several urgent and vivid points, many of which he sacrificed as the book's form hardened . . . The writer returns to these materials, these passionate subjects, as to unfinished business, for they are his life's work."

What follows are an essay by Ron Carlson on the writing of his story "Keith" and the story as it finally appeared.

## *Notes on "Keith"*

### RON CARLSON

The first signal from the real world for the story "Keith": I saw a woman in the hospital. I was in the University of Utah Hospital visiting a friend, and walking along the fifth floor corridor, the glassed part which offers a view of the whole valley below, I passed a young woman who was coming the other way dressed in pajamas and a robe. She was walking very slowly, little stab steps, and she had one hand at the throat of the robe, holding it together. She was very beautiful there moving like that on a floor where only dire things transpired. We were alone for a moment in that strange daylight and then gone and I never saw her again.

But I thought about her, trying to make sense of her youth and her beauty and the implications of her being in that serious place in her bedclothes.

I was teaching in a high school at the time, as a visiting writer, and the hundred people I dealt with every day were young and healthy and full of energy and foolish wisdom, and of course being around such people and reading their stories proves soon enough that their worries are real and that they are young and old at once. My wife and I taught in a boarding school for ten years, long enough to see that high school is a little world with all the allegiances and betrayals any small planet needs. There's a good deal of drama every day in a high school. And it was there I made this odd connection: the young woman I saw wasn't gravely ill, she was simply on a lark. She'd come up to the hospital, changed into her pajamas and was walking around. It was a kind of theater; I saw ten examples of it every day at school. And then—logically—I had the other thought: that would be a great date. You go to the hospital with your girlfriend, change into your pajamas and walk around. It might seem oddly out of context, but to a fiction writer working in a high school who was bothered by a woman he'd seen, it made real good sense. So many times as a writer, you ask "what if?" and then follow the premise as it connects to others.

Many years before I saw the woman in the hospital, while I was teaching high school English in Connecticut, I had taught a story which stayed with me for some reason. The story was "How Beautiful with Shoes," (and I can't find the story or the author's name now) and it was set in the thirties, I think, and it was about the night that an escaped inmate from an insane asylum changes the life of a rural farm girl. Two worlds collide, you could say: he's crazy, incandescent, poetic, doomed. She's stolid, prosaic, asleep. The idea took hold of me. There's a moment in that story when after her rescue from a long night with the lunatic, her fiancé—a sturdy farmhand—comes up and embraces her and she tells him something like: Oh, just go away. Leave me alone. It's the first time she's stood up to him. I loved that and pay tribute to it in "Keith."

When I started writing "Keith," I named the girl Barbara Peterson because I wanted it to be a "standard" name and I wanted her to be a standard success in high school, a type. (Also, Barbara Peterson is the name of one of my friends—one, coincidentally, who definitely breaks type.) I find that many times in my stories

I start with a person who could be a stereotype, a generic character unit, and then work to earn them credibility, personhood. I did it with homeless people in a story called, "The Governor's Ball," and I did it with DeRay who starts as a biker in "DeRay" and proves himself a kind of rocket scientist. All I wanted my Barbara Peterson in the story to be was a person from the "right" world who meets someone who shows her other possibilities.

I pinched the name Zetterstrom from a fine friend of mine in Connecticut, a wonderful photographer, because the name is not typical and it starts with a Z.

The first hint that Keith might be sick emerged with the writing of the story. I was kind of playing with that option until Barbara's friend Dana said, "Bald kids in high school who don't have earrings have got cancer." Then it tipped for me, and that informed the rest of the story with that notion—that he had a life-threatening disease. The idea that he was doomed came from "How Beautiful with Shoes." The madman in that story was also fated for trouble, and I wanted Keith to be speaking from an edge, an extreme time. Being there has caused him to speak out, and it colors what he says and how he says it. There was some ambiguity in early drafts that he might be acting at being sick for the purpose of tricking, seducing Barbara, but that vanished when I found my final scene in the airport. Their frank exchange in this good-bye scene nailed both characters for me. It is an important moment for Barbara because she gets to climb into personhood, take charge, announce an agenda for her own. I knew all along that she wasn't in the story to be a backboard or counterpoint for Keith. If the story was going to be any good, she'd have to be a full person too. What she tells him there by the boarding gate lets me feel that she's arrived, that in fact she's always been in there, measuring things as well as Keith has.

The airport setting was a bit of a surprise and I found it by looking back through the story at the other sets he'd chosen for their "non-dates." The public picnic, the thrift stores, the restaurant, the hospital. The airport as theatre felt simply like a natural extension for Keith, something he would choose.

He was such a pleasure to write. In each moment I simply conjured what would be the thing that would most challenge the expected response and I let him do or say that. He makes that statement about sulfur. He writes her that note. In their discussion about his truck, he tells Barbara to try riding the school bus—as a kind of adventure. No ordinary high school kid would ever associate himself with that kind of remark. And that's what I was after: the non-ordinary.

I have a long personal history with thrift shops, which I won't go into here, except to say I'm always arrested by the bowling balls (most weight for your dollar anywhere) and the trophies, and I've bought more than a few. And there actually used to be a motorcycle hill climbing contest called The Widowmaker Hill Climb in south Salt Lake near where I lived. Having my characters find that big trophy was fun because it felt like a real moment and that's all I'm ever after is a real moment. I didn't see the connection to scooters at the time and I certainly didn't see that the icon of the trophy would become so important in allowing me to close the story quickly in a single paragraph with just the implication I'd hoped for. I didn't see the trophy (big as it was) coming back into the story until I was typing that page.

"Keith" was a story I had in the drawer a long time before I made the final decisions about it and trimmed it up. I'm glad I did. I write from part to whole, staying as specific as I can as I go along in order to create an inventory that might tell me where to go next. "Keith" turned out to be a simple story of moments that speak of a world where wit and a sense of humor might have a chance against the forces of convention.

## Keith

### RON CARLSON

They were lab partners. It was that simple, how they met. She was *the* Barbara Anderson, president of half the school offices and queen of the rest. He was Keith Zetterstrom, a character, an oddball, a Z. His name was called last. The spring of their senior year at their equipment drawer she spoke to him for the first time in all their grades together: "Are you my lab partner?"

He spread the gear on the counter for the inventory and looked at her. "Yes, I am," he said. "I haven't lied to you this far, and I'm not going to start now."

After school Barbara Anderson met her boyfriend, Brian Woodworth, in the parking lot. They had twin red scooters because Brian had given her one at Christmas. "That guy," Barbara said, pointing to where Keith stood in the bus line, "is my lab partner."

"Who is he?" Brian said.

Keith was the window, wallpaper, woodwork. He'd been there for years and they'd never seen him. This was complicated because for years he was short and then he grew tall. And then he grew a long black slash of hair and now he had a crewcut. He was hard to see, hard to fix in one's vision.

The experiments in chemistry that spring concerned states of matter, and Barbara and Keith worked well together, quietly and methodically testing the elements.

"You're Barbara Anderson," he said finally as they waited for a beaker to boil. "We were on the same kickball team in fourth grade and I stood behind you in the sixth-grade Christmas play. I was a Russian soldier."

Barbara Anderson did not know what to say to these things. She couldn't remember the six-grade play . . . and fourth grade? So she said, "What are you doing after graduation?"

"The sky's the limit," he said. "And you are going off to Brown University."

"How did you know that?"

"The list has been posted for weeks."

"Oh, Right. Well, I may go to Brown and I may stay here and go to the university with my boyfriend."

Their mixture boiled and Keith poured some off into a cooling tray. "So what do you do?" he asked her.

Barbara eyed him. She was used to classmates having curiosity about her, and she had developed a pleasant condescension, but Keith had her off guard.

"What do you mean?"

"On a date with Brian, your boyfriend. What do you do?"

"Lots of things. We play miniature golf."

"You go on your scooters and play miniature golf."

"Yes."

"Is there a windmill?"

"Yes, there's a windmill. Why do you ask? What are you getting at?"

"Who wins? The golf."

"Brian," Barbara said. "He does."

Barbara showed the note to Trish, her best friend.

## Reasons You Should Go with Me

A. You are my lab partner.

B. Just to see. (You too, even Barbara Anderson, contain the same restless germ of curiosity that all humanity possesses, a trait that has led us out of the complacency of our dark caves into the bright world where we invented bowling—among other things.)

C. It's not a "date."

"Great," Trish said. "We certainly believe this! But, girl, who wants to graduate without a night out with a bald whatever. And I don't think he's going to ravish you—against your will, that is. Go for it. We'll tell Brian that you're staying at my house."

Keith drove a Chevy pickup, forest-green, and when Barbara climbed in, she asked, "Why don't you drive this to school?"

"There's a bus. I love the bus. Have you ever been on one?"

"Not a school bus."

"Oh, try it," he said. "Try it. It's so big and it doesn't drop you off right at your house."

"You're weird."

"Why? Oh, does the bus go right to your house? Come on, does it? But you've got to admit they're big, and that yellow paint job? Show me that somewhere else, I dare you. Fasten your seat belt, let's go."

The evening went like this: Keith turned onto Bloomfield, the broad business avenue that stretched from near the airport all the way back to the university, and he told her, "I want you to point out your least favorite building on this street."

"So we're not going bowling?"

"No, we're saving that. I thought we'd just get a little something to eat. So, keep your eyes open. Any places you can't stand?" By the time they reached the airport, Barbara had pointed out four she thought were ugly. When they turned around, Keith added: "Now, your final choice, please. And not someplace you just don't like. We're looking for genuine aversion."

Barbara selected a five-story metal building near downtown, with a simple marquee above the main doors that read INSURANCE.

"Excellent," Keith said as he swung the pickup to the curb. He began unloading his truck. "This is truly garish. The architect here is now serving time."

"This is where my father used to work."

Keith paused, his arms full of equipment. "When . . ."

"When he divorced my mom. His office was right up there," She pointed. "I hate driving by this place."

"Good," Keith said with renewed conviction. "Come over here and sit down. Have a Coke."

Barbara sat in a chaise lounge that Keith had set on the floodlit front lawn next to a folding table. He handed her a Coke. "We're eating here?"

"Yes, miss," he said, toting over the cooler and the little propane stove. "It's rustic but traditional: cheese omelets and hash brown potatoes. Sliced tomatoes for a salad with choice of dressing, and—for dessert—ice cream. On the way home, of course." Keith poured some oil into the frying pan. "There is nothing like a meal to alter the chemistry of a place."

On the way home, they did indeed stop for ice cream, and Barbara asked him: "Wasn't your hair long last year, like in your face and down like this?" She swept her hand past his eye.

"It was."

"Why is it so short now?"

Keith ran his hand back over his head. "Seasonal cut. Summer's a coming in. I want to lead the way."

It was an odd week for Barbara. She actually did feel different about the insurance building as she drove her scooter by it on the way to school. When Trish found out about dinner, she said, "That was you! I saw your spread as we headed down to Barney's. You were like camped out, right?"

Wonder spread on Barbara's face as she thought it over. "Yeah, it was cool. He cooked."

"Right. But please, I've known a lot of guys who cook and they were some of the slickest. *High School Confidential* says: 'There are three million seductions and only one goal.'"

"You're a cynic."

"Cynicism is a useful survival skill."

In chemistry, it was sulfur. Liquid, solid, and gas. The hallways of the chemistry annex smelled like rotten eggs and jokes abounded. Barbara winced through the white wispy smoke as Keith stirred the melting sulfur nuggets.

"This is awful," Barbara said.

"This is wonderful," Keith said. "This is the exact smell that greets sinners at the gates of hell. They think it's awful; here we get to enjoy it for free."

Barbara looked at him. "My lab partner is a certifiable . . ."

"Your lab partner will meet you tonight at seven o'clock."

"Keith," she said, taking the stir stick from him and prodding the undissolved sulfur, "I'm dating Brian. Remember?"

"Good for you," he said. "Now tell me something I don't know. Listen: I'll pick you up at seven. This isn't a date. This isn't dinner. This is errands. I'm serious. Necessary errands—for your friends."

Barbara Anderson rolled her eyes.

"You'll be home by nine. Young Mr. Brian can scoot by then. I mean it." Keith leaned toward her, the streams of baking acrid sulfur rising past his face. "I'm not lying to you."

When she got to the truck that night, Keith asked her, "What did you tell Brian?"

"I told him I had errands at my aunt's and to come by at ten for a little while."

"That's awfully late on a school night."

"Keith."

"I mean, why didn't you tell him you'd be with me for two hours?" He looked at her. "I have trouble lending credibility to a relationship that is almost one year old and one in which one of the members has given another an actual full-size, roadworthy motor vehicle, and yet it remains a relationship in which one of the members lies to the other when she plans to spend two hours with her lab partner, a person with whom she has inhaled the very vapors of hell."

"Stop the truck, Keith. I'm getting out."

"And miss bowling? And miss the search for bowling balls?"

Half an hour later they were in Veteran's Thrift, reading the bowling balls. They'd already bought five at Desert Industry Thrift Shops and the Salvation Army store. Keith's rule was it had to be less than two dollars. They already had PATTY for Trish, BETSY and KIM for two more of Barbara's friends, an initialled ball B.R. for Brian even though his last name was Woodworth ("Puzzle him," Keith said. "Make him guess"), and WALT for their chemistry teacher, Mr. Walter Miles. They found three more in the bins in Veteran's Thrift, one marked SKIP, one marked COSMO ("A must," Keith said), and a brilliant green ball, run deeply with hypnotic swirls, which had no name at all.

Barbara was touring the wide shelves of used appliances, toys, and kitchen utensils. "Where do they get all this stuff?"

"You've never been in a secondhand store before, have you?"

"No. Look at all this stuff. This is a quarter?" She held up a large plastic tray with the Beatles' pictures on it.

"That," Keith said, taking it from her and placing it in the cart with their bowling balls, "came from the home of a fan of the first magnitude. Oh, it's a sad story. It's enough to say that this is here tonight because of Yoko Ono." Keith's attention was taken by a large trophy, standing among the dozen other trophies on the top shelf. "Whoa," he said, pulling it down. It was huge, over three feet tall: six golden columns, ascending from a white marble base to a silver obelisk, framed by two embossed silver wreaths, and topped by a silver woman on a rearing motocycle. The inscription on the base read: WIDOWMAKER HILL CLIMB—FIRST PLACE 1987. Keith held it out to show Barbara, like a man holding a huge bottle of aspirin in a television commercial. "But this is another story altogether." He placed it reverently in the basket.

"And that would be?"

"No time. You've got to get back and meet Brian, a person who doesn't know where you are." Keith led her to the checkout. He was quiet all the way to the truck. He placed the balls carefully in the cardboard boxes in the truck bed and then set the huge trophy between them on the seat.

"You don't know where this trophy came from."

Keith put a finger to his lips—"*Shhhh*"—and started the truck and headed to Barbara's house. After several blocks of silence, Barbara folded her arms. "It's a tragic, tragic story," he said in a low voice. "I mean, this girl was a golden girl, an angel, the light in everybody's life."

"Do I want to hear this tragic story?"

"She was a wonder. Straight A's, with an A plus in chemistry. The girl could do no wrong. And then," Keith looked at Barbara, "she got involved with motorcycles."

"Is this her on top of the trophy?"

"The very girl," Keith nodded grimly. "Oh, it started innocently enough with a little red motor scooter, a toy really, and she could be seen running errands for the Ladies' Society and other charities every Saturday and Sunday when she wasn't home studying," Keith turned to Barbara, moving the trophy forward so he could see her. "I should add here that her fine academic standing got her into Brown University, where she was going that fateful fall." Keith laid the trophy back. "When her thirst for speed grew and grew, breaking over her good common sense like a tidal wave, sending her into the arms of a twelve-hundred-cc Harley-Davidson, one of the most powerful two-wheeled vehicles in the history of mankind." They turned onto Barbara's street, and suddenly Barbara ducked, her head against Keith's knee.

"Drive by," she whispered. "Just keep going."

"What?" Keith said. "If I do that Brian won't see you." Keith could see Brian leaning against his scooter in the driveway. "Is that guy always early?"

Keith turned the next corner, and Barbara sat up and opened her door. "I'll go down the alley."

"Cool," Keith said. "So you sneak down the alley to meet your boyfriend? Pretty sexy."

She gave him a look.

"Okay, have fun. But there's one last thing, partner. I'll pick you up at four to deliver these bowling balls."

"Four?"

"Four A.M. Brian will be gone, won't he?"

"Keith."

"It's not a date. We've got to finish this program, right?"

Barbara looked over at Brian and quickly back at Keith as she opened the truck door. "Okay, but meet me at the corner. There," she pointed, "by the postbox."

She was there. The streets of the suburbs were dark and quiet, everything in its place, sleeping, but Barbara Anderson stood in the humming lamplight, hugging her elbows. It was eerily quiet and she could hear Keith coming for two or three blocks before he turned onto her street. He had the heater on in the truck, and when she climbed in he handed her a blue cardigan, which she quickly buttoned up. "Four A.M.," she said, rubbing her hands over the air vent. "Now this is weird out here."

"Yeah," Keith said. "Four o'clock makes it a different planet. I recommend it. But bring a sweater." He looked at her. "You look real sleepy," he said. "You look good. This is the face you ought to bring to school."

Barbara looked at Keith and smiled. "No makeup, okay? It's four A.M." His face looked tired, and in the pale dash lights, with his short, short hair he looked more like a child, a little boy. "What do we do?"

"We give each of these babies," Keith nodded back at the bowling balls in the truck bed, "a new home."

They delivered the balls, placing them carefully on the porches of their friends, including Trish and Brian, and then they spent half an hour finding Mr. Miles's house, which was across town, a tan split-level. Keith handed Barbara the ball marked WALT and made her walk it up to the front porch. When she returned to the truck, Keith said, "Years from now you'll be able to say, 'When I was seventeen I put a bowling ball on my chemistry's teacher's front porch.'"

"His name was Walt," Barbara added.

At five-thirty, as the first gray light rose, Barbara Anderson and Keith walked into Jewel's Café carrying the last two balls: the green beauty and COSMO. Jewel's was the oldest café in the city, an all-night diner full of mailmen. "So," Barbara said, as they slid into one of the huge maroon booths, "who gets these last two?" She was radiant now, fully awake, and energized by the new day.

The waitress appeared and they ordered Round-the-World omelettes, hash browns, juice, milk, coffee, and wheat muffins, and Barbara ate with gusto, looking up halfway through. "So, where next?" She saw his plate. "Hey, you're not eating."

Keith looked odd, his face milky, his eyes gray. "This food is full of the exact amino acids to have a certifiably chemical day," he said. "I'll get around to it."

But he never did. He pushed his plate to the side and turned the place mat over and began to write on it.

"Are you feeling all right?" Barbara said.

"I'm okay."

She tilted her head at him skeptically.

"Hey. I'm okay. I haven't lied to you this far. Why would I start now? You know I'm okay, don't you? Well? Don't you think I'm okay?"

She looked at him and said quietly: "You're okay."

He showed her the note he had written:

Dear Waitress: My girlfriend and I are from rival families—different sides of the tracks, races, creeds, colors, and zip codes, and if they found out we had been out bowling all night, they would banish us to prison schools on separate planets. Please, please find a good home for our only bowling balls. Our enormous sadness is only mitigated by the fact that we know you'll take care of them.

With sweet sorrow—COSMO

In the truck, Barbara said, "Mitigated?"

"Always leave them something to look up."

"You're sick, aren't you?" she said.

"You look good in that sweater," he said. When she started to remove it, he added, "Don't. I'll get it after class, in just," he looked at his watch, "two hours and twenty minutes."

But he wasn't there. He wasn't there all week. The class did experiments with oxidation and Mr. Miles spent two days explaining and diagramming rust. On Friday, Mr. Miles worked with Barbara on the experiments and she asked him what was wrong with Keith. "I'm not sure," her teacher told her. "But I think he's on medication."

Barbara had a tennis match on Tuesday afternoon at school, and Brian picked her up and drove her home. Usually he came in for an hour or so on these school days and they made out a little and raided the fridge, but for the first time she begged off, claiming homework, kissing him on the cheek and running into her house. But on Friday, during her away march at Viewmont, she felt odd again. She knew Brian was in the stands. When she walked off the court after the match it was nearly dark and Brian was waiting. She gave Trish her rackets and Barbara climbed on Brian's scooter without a word. "You weren't that bad," he said. "Viewmont always has a good team."

"Brian, let's just go home."

"You want to stop at Swenson's, get something to eat?"

"No."

So Brian started his scooter and drove them home. Barbara could tell by the way he was driving that he was mad, and it confused her: she felt strangely glad about it. She didn't want to invite him in, let him grope her on the couch. She held on as he took the corners too fast and slipped through the stop signs, but all the way home she didn't put her chin on his shoulder.

At her house, she got the scene she'd been expecting. "Just what is the matter with you?" Brian said. For some reason when he'd gone to kiss her, she'd averted her face. Her heart burned with pleasure and shame. She was going to make up a lie about tennis, but then just said, "Oh Brian. Just leave me alone for a while, will you? Just go home."

Inside, she couldn't settle down. She didn't shower or change clothes. She sat in the dark of her room for a while and then, using only the tiny spot of her desk lamp, she copied her chemistry notes for the week and called Trish.

It was midnight when Trish picked her up quietly by the mailbox on the corner. Trish was smoking one of her Marlboros and blowing smoke into the windshield. She said, "*High School Confidential*, Part Five: Young Barbara Anderson, still in her foxy tennis clothes, and her old friend Trish meet again at midnight, cruise the Strip, pick up two young men with tattoos, and are never seen alive again. Is that it? Count me in."

"Not quite. It goes like this: two sultry babes, one of whom has just been a royal bitch to her boyfriend for no reason, drive to 1147 Fairmont to drop off the week's chemistry notes."

"That would be Keith Zetterstrom's address, I'd guess." Trish said.

"He's my lab partner."

"Of course he is," Trish said.

"He missed all last week. Mr. Miles told me that Keith's on medication."

"Oh my god!" Trish clamped the steering wheel. "He's got cancer. That's that scary hairdo. He's sick."

"No he doesn't. I checked the college lists. He's going to Dickinson."

"Not for long, honey. I should have known this." Trish inhaled and blew smoke thoughtfully out of the side of her mouth. "Bald kids in high school without earrings have got cancer."

Keith was in class the following Monday for the chemistry exam: sulfur and rust. After class, Barbara Anderson took him by the arm and led him to her locker. "Thanks for the notes, partner," he said. "They were absolutely chemical. I aced the quiz."

"You were sick last week."

"Last week." He pondered. "Oh, you mean because I wasn't here. What do you do, come every day? I just couldn't; it would take away the something special I feel for this place. I like to come from time to time and keep the dew on the rose, so to speak."

"I know what's the matter with you."

"Good for you, Barbara Anderson. And I know what's the matter with you too; sounds like a promising relationship."

Barbara pulled his folded sweater from the locker and handed it to him. As she did, Brian came up and said to them both: "Oh, I see." He started to walk away.

"Brian," Keith said, "Listen. You don't see. I'm not a threat to you. How could I be a threat to you? Think about it." Brian stood, his eyes narrowed. Keith went on: "Barbara's not stupid. What am I going to do, trick her? I'm her lab partner in chemistry. Relax." Keith went to Brian and took his hand, shook it. "I'm serious, Woodworth."

Brian stood for a moment longer until Barbara said, "I'll see you at lunch," and then he backed and disappeared down the hall. When he was gone, Barbara said, "Are you tricking me?"

"I don't know. Something's going on. I'm a little confused."

"You're confused. Who are you? Where have you been, Keith Zetterstrom? I've been going to school with you all these years and I've never even seen you and then we're delivering bowling balls together and now you're sick. Where were you last year? What are you doing? What are you going to do next year?"

"Last year I got a C in Spanish with Mrs. Whitehead. It was gruesome. This year is somewhat worse, with a few exceptions, and all in all, I'd say the sky is the limit." Keith took her wrist. "Quote me on that."

Barbara took a sharp breath through her nose and quietly began to cry.

"Oh, let's not," Keith said, pushing a handkerchief into her hand. "Here. Think of this." He moved her back against the wall, out of the way of students passing by. "If I was having a good year, I might never have spoken to you. Extreme times require extreme solutions. I went all those years sitting in the back and then I had to get sick to start talking. Now that's something, isn't it? Besides, I've got a plan. I'll pick you up at nine. Listen: bring your pajamas and a robe."

Barbara looked at him over the handkerchief.

"Hey. Trust me. You were the one who was crying. I'll see you at nine o'clock. This will cheer you up."

The hospital was on the hill, and Keith parked in the farthest corner of the vast parking lot, one hundred yards from the nearest car. Beneath them in the dark night, the city teemed and shimmered, a million lights.

"It looks like a city on another planet," Barbara Anderson said as she stepped out of the truck.

"It does, indeed," Keith said, grabbing his bag. "Now if we only knew if the residents are friendly." He took her arm. "And now I'm going to cheer you up. I'm going to take you in that building," Keith pointed at the huge hospital, lit like an ocean liner in the night, "and buy you a package of gum."

They changed clothes in the fifth-floor restrooms and met in the hallway, in pajamas and robes, and stuffed their street clothes into Barbara's tennis bag.

"Oh, I feel better already," Barbara said.

"Now take my arm like this," Keith moved next to her and placed her hand above his elbow, "and look down like this." He put his chin on his chest. Barbara tried it. "No, not such a sad face, more serious, be strong. Good. Now walk just like this, little stab steps, real slow."

They started down the hallway, creeping along one side. "How far is it?" Barbara said. People passed them walking quietly in groups of two or three. It was the end of visiting hours. "A hundred yards to the elevators and down three floors, then out a hundred more. Keep your face down."

"Are people looking at us?"

"Well, yes. They've never seen a braver couple. And they've never seen such chemical pajamas. What are those little deals, lambs?"

They continued along the windows, through the lobby and down the elevator, in which they stood side by side, their four hands clasped together, while they were looking at their tennis shoes. The other people in the car gave them room out of respect. The main hall was worse, thick with people, everyone going five miles an hour faster than Barbara and Keith, who shuffled along whispering.

In the gift shop, finally, they parted the waters. The small room was crowded, but the people stepped aside and Keith and Barbara stood right at the counter. "A package of chewing gum, please," Keith said.

"Which kind?" said the candy striper.

"Sugarless. My sister and I want our teeth to last forever."

They ran to the truck, leaping and swinging their arms. Keith threw the bag containing their clothes into the truck bed and climbed into the cab. Barbara climbed in, laughing, and Keith said, "Come on, face the facts: you feel better! You're cured!" And she slid across the seat meaning to hug him but it changed for both of them and they kissed. She pulled him to her side and they kissed again, one of her arms around his neck and one of her hands on his face. They fell into a spin there in the truck, eyes closed, holding on to each other in their pajamas, her robe open, their heads against the backseat, kissing. Barbara shifted and Keith sat up; the look they exchanged held.

Below them the city's lights flickered. Barbara cupped her hand carefully on the top of Keith's bald scalp. She pulled him forward and they kissed. When she looked in his eyes again she knew what was going to happen, and it was a powerful feeling that gave her strange new certainty as she went for his mouth again.

There were other moments that surfaced in the truck in the night above the ancient city. Something Keith did, his hand reminded her of Brian, and then that thought vanished as they were beyond Brian in a moment. Later, well beyond even her notions of what to do and what not to do, lathered and breathing as if in toil, she heard herself say, "Yes." She said that several times.

She looked for Keith everywhere, catching glimpses of his head, his shoulder, in the hallways. In chemistry they didn't talk; there were final reports, no need to work together. Finally, three days before graduation, they stood side by side cleaning out their chemistry equipment locker, waiting for Mr. Miles to check them off. Keith's manner was what? Easy, too confident, too neutral. He seemed to take up too much space in the room. She hated the way he kept his face blank and open, as if fishing for the first remark. She held off, feeling the restraint as a physical pang. Mr. Miles inventoried their cupboard and asked for their keys. He had a large ring of thirty or forty of the thin brass keys. Keith handed his to Mr. Miles and then Barbara Anderson found her key in the side of her purse and handed it to the teacher. She hated relinquishing the key; it was the only thing she had that meant she would see Keith, and now with it gone something opened in her and it hurt in a way she'd never hurt before. Keith turned to her and seeing something in her face, shrugged and said, "The end of chemistry as we know it. Which isn't really very well."

"Who are you?" Barbara said, her voice a kind of surprise to her. "You're so glib. Such a little actor." Mr. Miles looked up from his check sheet and several students turned toward them. Barbara was speaking loudly; she couldn't help it. "What are you doing to me? If you ask me this is a pretty chickenshit good-bye." Everyone was looking at her. Then her face would not work at all, the tears coming from some hot place, and Barbara Anderson walked from the room.

Keith hadn't moved. Mr. Miles looked at Keith, alarmed. Keith whispered: "Don't worry, Mr. Miles. She was addressing her remarks to me."

There was one more scene. The night before graduation, while her classmates met in the bright, noisy gym for the yearbook-signing party, Barbara drove out to the airport and met Keith where he said he'd be: at the last gate, H-17. There on an empty stretch of maroon carpet in front of three large banks of seats full of travelers, he was waiting. He handed her a pretty green canvas valise and an empty paper ticket sleeve.

"You can't even talk as yourself," she said. "You always need a setting. Now we're pretending I'm going somewhere?"

He looked serious tonight, weary. There were gray shadows under his eyes. "You wanted a goodbye scene," he said. "I tried not to do this."

"It's all a joke," she said. "You joke all the time."

"You know what my counselor said?" He smiled thinly as if glad to give her this point. "He said that this is a phase, that I'll stop joking soon." Their eyes met and the look held again. "Come here," he said. She stepped close to him. He put his hand on her elbow. "You want a farewell speech. Okay, here you go. You better call Brian and get your scooter back. Tell him I tricked you. Wake up, lady. Get real. I just wanted to see if I could give Barbara Anderson a whirl. And I did. It was selfish, okay? I just screwed you around a little. You said it yourself: it was a joke. That's my speech. How was it?"

"You didn't screw me around, Keith. You didn't give me a whirl." Barbara moved his hand and then put her arms around his neck so she could speak in his ear. She could see some of the people watching them. "You made love to me, Keith. It wasn't a joke. You made love to me and I met you tonight to say—good for you. Extreme times require extreme solutions." She was whispering as they stood alone on that carpet in their embrace. "I wondered how it was going to happen, but you were a surprise. Way to go. What did you think? That I wanted to go off to college an eighteen-year-old virgin? That pajama bit was great; I'll remember it." Now people were de-planing, entering the gate area and streaming around the young couple. Barbara felt Keith begin to tremble, and she closed her eyes. "It wasn't a joke. There's this: I made love to you too. You were there, remember? I'm glad for it." She pulled back slightly and found his lips. For a moment she was keenly aware of the public scene they were making, but that disappeared and they twisted tighter and were just there, kissing. She had dropped the valise and when the mock ticket slipped from her fingers behind his neck, a young woman in a business suit knelt and retrieved it and tapped Barbara on the hand. Barbara clutched the ticket and dropped her head to Keith's chest.

"I remember," he said. "My memory is aces."

"Tell me, Keith," she said. "What are these people thinking? Make something up."

"No need. They've got it right. That's why we came out here. They think we're saying goodbye."

Simply put, that was the last time Barbara Anderson saw Keith Zetterstrom. That fall when she arrived in Providence for her freshman year at Brown, there was one package waiting for her, a large trophy topped by a girl on a motorcycle. She had seen it before. She kept it in her dorm window, where it was visible four stories from the ground, and she told her roommates that it meant a lot to her, that it represented a lot of fun and hard work but her goal had been to win the Widowmaker Hill Climb, and once she had done that, she sold her bikes and gave up her motorcycles forever.

🐾 🐾 🐾

## *Writing Exercises*

### INDIVIDUAL

1. Do a word count of one of your stories. Suppose that it has been accepted for publication, but the magazine has one condition: you must cut it by twenty-five percent. Figure out your word count goal and edit toward it. Be both aggressive and picky.

Cut any expendable scenes or paragraphs, but also wring out every extraneous word and phrase. Cut beyond the twenty-five percent if it feels right to do so.

2. Photocopy a published story you like and highlight the direct dialogue in one color and all indirect discourse or summarized dialogue in another color. Do the same for your most recent story. Compare the two. Are your most important lines in direct dialogue or summarized? (Generally, these should be direct.) Is information or idle chatter direct or summarized? (Generally, these should be summarized.) Revise to make sure that the most important moments are in direct dialogue.

3. For his novel A *Farewell to Arms*, Ernest Hemingway wrote thirty-nine endings before finding the one he decided was best. For one of your stories, write three different endings, each one showing, in some way, how your main character has been changed by the action in the story. Think about what is resolved and what is left unresolved with each ending. Then ask yourself what really needs to happen, emotionally, to your character by the end. In each ending, have the main character's emotional needs truly been addressed, or have you simply tied up some loose ends the reader doesn't care about?

4. Write three new openings to one of your stories. Each one should be at least a few paragraphs long. In each opening, start from a different moment in the story—maybe even at the very end. (Richard Ford's story "Great Falls" opens with these two sentences: "This is not a happy story. I warn you.") What possibilities are created by these new openings?

5. Select one of your stories that is causing you trouble. Print out a hard copy and cut it into scenes, summary, and flashbacks. Number each piece in the order in which it appears. Then lay these pieces out on a table or floor and see what you've got. How many scenes are there? Is every scene necessary? Can some be combined, deleted, or summarized? Are important scenes buried in sections of summary? Are there missing scenes? Is the material from the past in the right places? Try rearranging the sequence of events. Experiment. Move beyond fiddling with sentences to this kind of reenvisioning and rearranging.

6. Choose one of your stories that seems low in tension and try to pump up every conflict you find, and to add new ones. Don't be afraid to be ridiculous; you can always back off later. Throw more and bigger obstacles in your character's way. Let this revision sit for a day or two, then go back and see how much of what you've added does in fact work.

7. Look back through some of the stories you've read in this book and ask what, exactly, the main character wants in each story. Then look at some of your own stories and ask yourself the same question. If you don't have an answer, or if the answer is vague or rambling, you probably don't yet know either your character or his story.

8. Take one of your stories that isn't quite working yet and explore the main character by writing from that character's point of view. You might have her write out a diary entry, e-mail, dream, letter, or even a short autobiography. Don't worry about whether or not what you write will actually fit into the story.

It might, but it might not. In either case, you'll probably learn something important about your character and her story.

9. You may have written a story that is too tidy, one that needs to be messed up a bit. Take a story of yours with a very "final" ending—one in which a relationship ends, someone dies, success is achieved, a moral is revealed, or the like. Now rewrite the opening, briefly announcing the story's final outcome (i.e., "This was a few months before Ted left me, our last Christmas as a married couple"). Now reexamine your story. How does giving away the ending affect it? Is the reader still motivated to read through to the end? Revise your story so it remains compelling even though you may well decide to return your ending to its original place.

### COLLABORATIVE

10. Each year in the back of the *Best American Short Stories* and *O'Henry Prize Stories*, the winning authors write a paragraph or two in which they discuss the genesis of their stories. Take a look at some of these, and then try it yourself. After your story has been workshopped, but before you've started the next draft, write a "contributor's note" similar to those in the back of the *Best American* or *O'Henry*. How did the story first occur to you? What intrigued you about it? How did the story evolve? Which of your plans changed, and why? What do you hope that readers will think the story is "about"? Read these contributors' notes aloud in class. Do they help you articulate the dramatic and thematic elements you wish to address in the revision process? Does your note illuminate the story or is it merely an explanation of what should be in the story, but hasn't yet made it there?

11. Spend about half an hour writing a scene that involves a conflict between two characters. Make a copy of what you write. Send the other copy home with a class member so he can write on it, making critical comments and suggestions. Keep the other copy for yourself, and take it home and rewrite it. When you get your reader's copy back, compare your impulses with those of your reader. Now, let everything sit for another day, so that you can "forgive" your reader and let yourself accept some of his ideas. On the day after that, rewrite the scene once more, incorporating the most intriguing of your reader's suggestions.

# APPENDIX A

# KINDS OF FICTION

What follows is a discussion of some kinds of fiction likely to be found in current books and magazines, which are also the kinds of contemporary narrative most likely to show up in a workshop. This is not by any means a comprehensive list, nor does it deal with the forms that represent the history of narrative—myth, tale, fable, allegory, and so forth—some of which are mentioned elsewhere in this book.

**Mainstream** refers to fiction that deals with subject matter with a broad appeal—situations and emotions common to and of interest to large numbers of readers in the culture for which it is intended. Mainstream fiction is **literary fiction** if its appeal is also lodged in the original, interesting, and illuminating use of the language; the term also implies a degree of care in the psychological exploration of its characters, and an attempt to shed light on the human condition. All of the stories in this volume fall under the general category of literary fiction.

Literary fiction differs from **genre fiction** fundamentally in the fact that the former is character-driven, the latter plot-driven. There is a strong tendency—though it is not a binding rule—of genre fiction to imply that life is fair, and to let the hero or heroine, after great struggle, win out in the end; and of literary fiction to posit that life is not fair, that triumph is partial, happiness tentative, and that the heroine and hero are subject to mortality. Literary fiction also strives to reveal its meaning through the creation of unexpected or unusual characters, through patterns of action and turns of event that will surprise the reader. Genre fiction, on the other hand, tends to develop character stereotypes and set patterns of action that become part of the expectation, the demand, and the pleasure of the readers of that genre.

Readers of the **romance** genre, for example, will expect a plucky-but-down-on-her-luck heroine, a handsome and mysterious hero with some dark secret (usually a dark-haired woman) in his background, a large house, some woods (through which the heroine will at some point flee in scanty clothing), and an eventual happy ending with the heroine in the hero's arms. These elements can be seen in embryo in the literary fiction of the Brontë sisters; by now, in the dozens of Harlequin and Silhouette romances on the supermarket rack, they have become **formulaic,** and the language is similar from book to book.

Like romance, most genres have developed from a kind of fiction that was at one time mainstream and represented a major social problem or concern. Early romance, for example, dealt with the serious question of how a woman was to satisfy the need for both stability and love in married life, how to be both independent and secure in a society with rigid sexual rules. The **detective story** evolved simultaneously with widespread and intense interest in science, an optimistic expectation that violence and mystery could be rationally explained. The **western** dealt with the ambivalence felt by large numbers of westward-traveling Euro-Americans about the civilizing of the wilderness, the desire to rid the West of its brutality, the fear that "taming" it would also destroy its promise of solitude and freedom. **Science fiction,** the most recently developed and still developing genre, similarly deals with ambivalence about technology, the near-miraculous accomplishments of the human race through science, the dangers to human feeling, soul, and environment. The surge in popularity of **fantasy fiction** can probably be attributed to nostalgia for a time even more free of technological accomplishment and threat, since fantasy employs a medieval setting and solves problems through magic, whereas science fiction is set in the future and solves problems through intelligence and technology. It is relevant that science fiction usually deals with some problem that can be seen to have a counterpart in the contemporary culture (space travel, international or interplanetary intrigue, mechanical replacement of body parts, genetic manipulation), whereas the plots of fantasies tend to deal with obsolete or archaic traumas—wicked overlords, demon interlopers, and so forth. Because of this contemporary concern, science fiction seems capable at this point in history of a deployment much more varied and original than other genres, and more often engages the attention of writers (and filmmakers) with literary intentions and ambitions. Among such writers are Octavia Butler, William Gibson, J. B. Ballard, Ray Bradbury, Ursula K. LeGuin, Philip K. Dick, and Doris Lessing.

In any case, the many other genres, including but not confined to **adventure, spy, horror,** and **thriller,** each have their own set of conventions of character, language, and events. Note again that the very naming of these kinds of fiction implies a narrowing; unlike mainstream fiction, they appeal to a particular range of interest.

Many—perhaps most—teachers of fiction writing do not accept manuscripts in genre, and I believe there's good reason for this, which is that whereas writing literary fiction can teach you how to write good genre fiction, writing genre fiction does not teach you how to write good literary fiction—does not, in effect, teach you "how to write," by which I mean how to be original and meaningful in words. Further, dealing in the conventions and hackneyed phrases of romance, horror, fantasy, and so forth, can operate as a form of personal denial, using writing as a means of avoiding rather than uncovering your real concerns. It may be fine to offer readers an escape through fiction, but it isn't a way to educate yourself as a writer, and it's also fair to say that escape does not represent the goal of a liberal education, which is to pursue, inquire, seek, and extend knowledge of whatever subject is at hand, fiction no less than science.

Partly because many college teachers of creative writing do not welcome genre fiction in the classroom, there has developed a notion of a "workshop story" that is realistic, sensitive, and small. I have never known a teacher who solicited such stories, or any particular sort of story. Leaps of imagination, originality, and genuine experimentation are in my experience welcome to both instructors and students. But it is true that often what seems wild and crazy to the student writer has occurred to others before. Stories set in dreams, outer space, game shows, heaven and hell, may seem strange and wonderful by comparison with daily life, but they are familiar as "experiments" and likely to be less startling to their readers than the author expects, whereas extreme focus on what the author has experienced may seem striking and fresh. **Realism**—the attempt to render an authentic picture of life, in such a way that the reader identifies with one or more characters—is a fair starting point for the pursuit of literary fiction. The writer's attempt at verisimilitude is comparable to the scientific method of observation and verification. Realism is also a convention, and not the only way to begin to write; but like the drawing of still life in the study of painting, it can impart skills that will be useful in more sophisticated efforts whether they are realistic or not. Many of the stories in this book are realistic; "A Serious Talk," "Royal Beatings," and "Keith," for example, might be seen as attempts to reveal in recognizable detail the drama of ordinary life.

**Experimental fiction** is always possible, however. It's more difficult by far to describe what is experimental in fiction than what is cliché, because by definition the experimental is the thing that nobody expects or predicts. There are, however, a number of kinds of experiment that have come to be recognized as subsets of literary fiction, and a few of these are worth mentioning.

**Magic realism** uses the techniques and devices of realism—verisimilitude, ordinary lives and settings, familiar psychology—and introduces events of impossible or fantastic nature, never leaving the tone and techniques of realism. Whereas fantasy will attempt to bedazzle its readers with the amazing quality of the magic, magic realism works in the opposite direction, to convince the reader that the extraordinary occurs in the context and the guise of the ordinary. David Lodge, in *The Art of Fiction*, interestingly points out that the practitioners of magic realism tend to have lived through some sort of historical upheaval—a political coup or terror, a literal war or gender war. Flight, he points out, is a central image in this fiction, because the defiance of gravity represents a persistent "human dream of the impossible." Columbian novelist Gabriel García Márquez, is a foremost practitioner of magic realism, and his novel *One Hundred Years of Solitude* is the best-known example of the genre. Interested readers might also look for *Labyrinths* by Jorge Luis Borges, who is often considered the father of this experimental mode.

**Metafiction** takes as its subject matter the writing of fiction, calls attention to its own techniques, and insists that what is happening is that a story is being written and read. Often the writing of the story is used as a metaphor for some other human struggle or endeavor.

**Minimalism** (also called miniaturism) refers to a flat, spare, and subdued style of writing, characterized by an accumulation of (sometimes apparently random) detail that gives an impression of benumbed emotion. The point of view tends to be objective or near-objective, the events accumulating toward a tense, disturbing—and inconclusive—conclusion.

**The short-short story** or **sudden fiction** is a fiction under 2,000 words; **microfictions** is a term sometimes used to distinguish stories under 250 words.

Such pieces, according to Nancy Huddleston Packer, "push to the limit the basic elements of all short stories—compression, suggestion, and change. They combine the intensity and lyricism of a poem with the dramatic impact and movement of a short story—these stories are so compressed, they explode." In a short-short story, change is often subtle, taking form as a moment of surprise or a shift in perception.

It's always comforting to have a good reference book on hand when an unfamiliar literary term comes up. Two I recommend are *The Fiction Dictionary* by Laurie Henry (Cincinnati: Story Press, 1995) and *The Bedford Glossary of Critical and Literary Terms* by Ross Murfin and Supryia M. Ray (Boston and New York: Bedford Books, 1997).

# APPENDIX B

# SUGGESTIONS FOR FURTHER READING

Like writing programs and writers' conferences, books on writing have proliferated in the last thirty years, and you can probably find a new one on the Internet or the library bookshelf for every week of the year. Browse for your own favorites—don't forget to write meanwhile. Here are some—most of them written by writers for writers—that have struck me as most useful, graceful, or original:

Alvarez, A. *The Writer's Voice*. New York & London: Norton, 2005. Alvarez has taken on the elusive and essential subject, and the result will become a classic. Alvarez shows how a writer's voice means—more than style—integrity, nuance, passion, aesthetic conscience, and the self itself. He demonstrates in every sentence his impeccable advice.

Alvarez, Julia. *Something to Declare*. Chapel Hill, NC: Algonquin Books of Chapel Hill, 1998. Part poetry, part prose, all inspiration, and not in any way a textbook, this beautiful collection of essays about Alvarez's life also includes pieces about the writing life, how paying attention to details can be the springboard for material, and how writing is a different process for everyone.

Aristotle. *The Poetics*. This is the first extant work of literary criticism and the essay from which all later criticism derives. There are numerous good translations.

Atchity, Kenneth. *A Writer's Time: A Guide to the Writer's Process from Vision through Revision*. New York: Norton, 1988. Atchity focuses on the problem every writer complains about most and offers startling perceptions and helpful directions for finding and apportioning time.

Barzun, Jacques. *On Writing, Editing, and Publishing*. Chicago: University of Chicago Press, 1986. Is it possible to be elegant, irascible, practical, and witty, all at the same time, at the full stretch of each? Read it and see.

Baxter, Charles. *Burning Down the House: Essays on Fiction*. St. Paul: Graywolf Press, 1997. Discursive, insightful, and large-minded, Baxter ruminates on craft in its relation to our culture. Some of his best passages convincingly and interestingly challenge traditional ideas laid down in *Writing Fiction*.

Bell, Madison Smartt. *Narrative Design: A Writer's Guide to Structure*. New York: Norton, 1997. Bell begins and ends with the assumption that all the elements of fiction are subservient to narrative form. His close readings of stories show how the authors have gone about making choices that contribute to overall design.

Benson, Angela. *Telling the Tale: The African-American Fiction Writer's Guide*. New York: Berkley Publishing Group, 2000. Wonderful all-around writing advice with helpful examples from African-American writers and culture. The exercises are designed to keep writers writing and are particularly helpful for fleshing out characters.

Bernays, Anne, and Pamela Painter. *What If? Writing Exercises for Fiction Writers*, 2nd Edition New York: Longman, 2003. Bernays and Painter identify more than seventy-five situations that a writer may face and provide exercises for each; included are student examples and clear descriptions of objectives. This book is useful and provocative.

Bly, Carol. *The Passionate, Accurate Story*. Minneapolis: Milkweed Editions, 1990. A genuine original, this book makes a thoughtful plea for value in writing and writing from your values. It combines the insights of literary technique, therapy, and ethics.

Brande, Dorothea. *Becoming a Writer*. Los Angeles: J. P. Tarcher, 1981. For those who are overmeticulous, or who have a hard time getting started, Brande's mind-freeing exercises may be enormously helpful.

Brown, Kurt, ed. *Writers on Life and Craft*. Boston: Beacon, 1994–96. This series culls the best of the lectures, talks, and keynote speeches from writing conferences around the country. It is various and thoughtful, and cheaper than travel.

Bunge, Nancy. *Master Class: Lessons from Leading Writers*. Iowa City: University of Iowa Press, 2005. *Master Class* is many classes in one—or rather, a patchwork-quilt comforter of good advice, surprises, wisdom, quirks, ponderables, and *aha!* moments. It can be read through or dipped into, both with benefit.

Burroway, Janet. *So, Is It Done? Navigating the Revision Process*. Chicago: Elephant Rock Productions, 2005. A DVD with interviews, exercises, and advice on revision from Rosellen Brown, Robert Olen Butler, Ron Carlson, Elizabeth Dewberry, Patricia Foster, Michael Martone, John McNally, Elizabeth Stuckey-French, and editor Holly Carver.

Busch, Frederick. *A Dangerous Profession: A Book about the Writing Life*. New York: St. Martin's Press, 1998. Busch pulls out all the stops as he explores some authors, himself included, driven to write despite the risks and discontents. He has also edited *Letters to a Fiction Writer* (New York: Norton, 1999), a rich compendium of advice from writers living and dead.

Checkoway, Julie. *Creating Fiction*. Cincinnati: Story Press, 1999. This book enables the reader to step into the minds of well-respected authors and teachers of the Associated Writing Programs and includes intelligent essays about the writing process with useful insights into characters, including a section on minor characters.

Chiarella, Tom. *Writing Dialogue*. Cincinnati: Story Press, 1998. Including a detailed breakdown of dialogue patterns, Chiarella provides tips and exercises to help re-create them effectively and realistically.

Danford, Natalie, and John Kulka, eds. *Best New American Voices*. New York: Harcourt Brace, ongoing. An ongoing series of short-story collections culled from workshops around the country by more than one hundred writing programs, it gives an opportunity to see what's new and what's best in college and conference writing.

Darnton, John, ed. *Writers on Writing: Collected Essays from* The New York Times. New York: Henry Holt and Company, 2001. A varied selection of essays from the popular weekly feature *The New York Times Book Review,* which publishes short pieces on craft, inspiration, and the writing process by the country's most respected literary authors.

Dillard, Annie. *The Writing Life*. New York: HarperCollins, 1989. This stunningly written account of "your day's triviality" touches drudgery itself with luminous significance. Every writer should read it. Also recommended is Dillard's *Living by Fiction* (New York: Harper, 1982).

Elbow, Peter. *Writing without Teachers*. New York and Oxford: Oxford, 1973. Elbow is excellent on how to keep going, growing, and cooking when you haven't the goads of teacher and deadline. *Writing with Power* (New York and Oxford: Oxford, 1981) is not aimed specifically at the imaginative writer, but still has useful advice and a good section on revising.

Forster, E. M. *Aspects of the Novel*. New York: Harcourt Brace Jovanovich, 1956. Forster delivered these Clark Lectures at Trinity College, Cambridge, England, in 1927. They are talkative, informal, and informative—still the best analysis of literature from a writer's point of view—a must.

Friedman, Bonnie. *Writing Past Dark*. New York: HarperCollins, 1994. Richly written ruminations on the writer's life illuminate this book. If you think writing is a lonely task, and you can afford only one book, buy this one.

Gardner, John. *The Art of Fiction: Notes on Craft for Young Writers*. New York: Alfred A. Knopf, 1991. *The Art of Fiction* is a new classic among books on writing. Gardner's advice is based on his experience as a teacher of creative writing and is addressed to "the serious beginning writer." The book is clear, practical, and a delight to read. Also recommended is Gardner's *On Becoming a Novelist* (New York: HarperCollins, 1985).

Gass, William. *Fiction and the Figures of Life*. Boston: David R. Godine, 1990. Gass writes of character, language, philosophy, and form, from acute angles in stunning prose—a joy to read.

Goldberg, Natalie. *Writing Down the Bones*. Boston: Shambhala, 1986. Also, *Wild Mind* (New York: Bantam, 1990). Goldberg is the guru of can-do, encouraging the writer with short, pithy, personal, and lively cheerings-on.

Hemley, Robin. *Turning Life into Fiction*. Cincinnati: Story Press, 1994. An excellent resource for turning life's situations into seeds for fiction writing, this book has an easy style with practical exercises to keep writers moving forward.

Hills, Rust. *Writing in General and the Short Story in Particular*. Boston: Houghton Mifflin, 1987. A former literary editor of *Esquire* magazine, Hills has written a breezy, enjoyable guide to fiction technique with good advice on every page.

Huddle, David. *The Writing Habit: Essays*. Layton, UT: Peregrine Smith Books, 1991. Huddle has a level voice and a sound sense of what it is to live with the habit. He is kind without being sentimental; this book is highly recommended.

Kaplan, David Michael. *Revision: A Creative Approach to Writing and Rewriting Fiction*. Cincinnati: Story Press, 1997. Kaplan convinces you that writing is revising, and that not only style and structure but meaning itself depends on the seeing-again part of the process.

Lamott, Anne. *Bird by Bird*. New York: Pantheon, 1994. Breezy, easy-reading, and full of witty, good advice, *Bird by Bird* (of which a chapter appears in this book) takes you from shitty first drafts through publication blues.

Le Guin, Ursula K. *Steering the Craft*. Portland, OR: The Eighth Mountain Press, 1998. Written by a master storyteller, this volume has a detailed chapter on point of view that includes helpful and explicit examples.

Lodge, David. *The Art of Fiction*. London: Penguin, 1992. A collection of Lodge's articles for British and American newspapers, this is not a how-to book but a work of short critical analyses. Nevertheless it crackles with insight and advice for writers.

Madden, David. *Revising Fiction: A Handbook for Fiction Writers*. New York: New American Library, 1995. Although it is too weighty to operate as a handbook, this volume shows the revision process convincingly and in full. Also useful as a reference tool is Madden's *A Primer of the Novel for Readers and Writers* (Lanham, MD: Scarecrow Press, 1980).

May, Rollo. *The Courage to Create*. New York: Bantam, 1984. May's book is a philosophic classic on the subject.

Nelson, Victoria. *On Writer's Block: A New Approach to Creativity*. Boston: Houghton Mifflin, 1993. Among the new breed of writers' books that use the insights of psychology and therapy, this is exceptionally helpful. Nelson is sensible as well as sensitive. Her suggestions work.

Olsen, Tillie. *Silences*. New York: Feminist Press at CUNY, 2003. *Silences* is comprised of eloquent essays, of which the title piece is a must.

Pack, Robert, and Jay Parini, eds. *Writers on Writing*. Middlebury, VT: Middlebury College Press, 1991. Described by the editors as a "celebration," this volume collects twenty-five eloquent essays by established writers who offer advice and experience that is practical, witty, confessional, flip, and moving and/or profound.

Rhodes, Jewel Parker. *Free Within Ourselves*. New York: Main Street Books, 1999. Encouraging exploration into the rich background of literary ancestors, Rhodes draws on her cultural resources as an African-American writer. In "My Best Advice," she shares her own tools for writing success.

Rico, Gabriele Lusser. *Writing the Natural Way*. Los Angeles: J. P. Tarcher, 1983. Rico describes in full the technique of clustering and offers useful techniques for freeing the imagination.

Seidman, Michael. *The Complete Guide to Editing Your Fiction*. Cincinnati: Writer's Digest Books, 2000. After a quick survey of the basic elements of writing, Seidman emphasizes the importance of revision in quality work and includes before-and-after case studies to illustrate the process of editing.

Shelnutt, Eve. *The Writing Room*. Marietta, GA: Longstreet Press, 1989. This is a wide-ranging, outspoken, often persuasive discussion of the crafts of fiction and poetry, with examples, analyses, and exercises.

Sloane, William. *The Craft of Writing*. Edited by Julia Sloane. New York: Norton, 1983. This book was culled posthumously from the notes of one of the great teachers of fiction writing.

Stafford, William. *Writing the Australian Crawl*. Edited by Donald Hall. Ann Arbor, MI: University of Michigan Press, 1994. The poet has affable and practical advice for fiction writers too. Also, *You Must Revise Your Life* (Ann Arbor, MI: University of Michigan Press, 1986) is an inspiriting potpourri of poems, essays, and interviews regarding writing.

Stern, Jerome. *Making Shapely Fiction*. New York: Norton, 2000. In this witty, useful guide, Stern illustrates various possible shapes for stories; he includes a cogent list of *don'ts* and discusses the elements of good writing in dictionary form so that you can use the book as a handy reference.

Strunk, William C., and E. B. White. *The Elements of Style*. 4th edition, New York: Pearson, 1999. Strunk provides the rules for correct usage and vigorous writing in this briefest and most useful of handbooks.

Ueland, Barbara. *If You Want to Write*. St. Paul: Graywolf Press, 1987. "Everybody is talented. Everybody is original," Ueland says, and she says it convincingly in this book that holds up very well since its first edition in 1938.

Welty, Eudora. *One Writer's Beginnings*. Cambridge, MA: Harvard Press, 1995. One of the best autobiographies ever offered by a writer, Welty's book is moving, funny, and full of insight.

Willis, Meredith Sue. *Personal Fiction Writing*. Rev. 2nd ed., 2000; *Blazing Pencils*, 1990; and *Deep Revision*, 1993, all published by Teachers & Writers Collaborative, New York. Willis teaches elementary to college-level and developmental workshops, both fiction and nonfiction, so her advice is a bit diffuse, but on the whole bears out her contention that "the heart of what happens in writing is shared by all writers, professional and avocational, adult and child." *Deep Revision*, especially, has many useful "do this" sections.

Wolitzer, Hilma. *The Company of Writers: Fiction Workshops and Thoughts on the Writing Life*. New York: Penguin Putnam, Inc., 2001. A guide to getting the most out of writing workshops, particularly outside the academic setting. The second half of the book is devoted to "focus sessions" designed to spark discussions of craft among workshop members.

Woodruff, Jay, ed. *A Piece of Work: Five Writers Discuss Their Revisions*. Iowa City, IA: University of Iowa Press, 1993. Poets and fiction writers (including Tobias Wolff and Joyce Carol Oates, whose stories are included in this volume) discuss their drafts, their writing processes, and much more.

Ziegler, Alan. *The Writing Workshop*. 2 vols. New York: Teachers & Writers Collaborative, 1981 and 1984. The author calls these useful books a "survey course" in writing. They are mainly intended for teachers of writing but can be adapted for use as a self-teaching tool; they're full of interesting practical advice.

Zinsser, William, ed. *Inventing the Truth: The Art and Craft of Memoir*. Boston: Houghton Mifflin, 1998. Although this series of talks, originally given at the New York Public Library, is not aimed at the fiction writer, it shines with hints on how to use the subject matter of your life from five fine writers: Annie Dillard, Toni Morrison, Russell Baker, Alfred Kazin, and Lewis Thomas.

## Services for Writers

Associated Writing Programs (Tallwood House, Mail Stop 1E3, George Mason University, Fairfax, VA 22030). Those enrolled in the creative writing program of a college or university that is a member of AWP are automatically members; others can join for a reasonable fee. AWP's services include a magazine, *The Writer's Chronicle*, a job placement service, an annual meeting, and a number of awards and publications. The organization can provide contact with other writers, as well as valuable information on prizes, programs, presses, and the ideas current in the teaching of writing. *The AWP Official Guide to Writing Programs* (published biannually in cooperation with Dustbooks) is a thorough guide to graduate and undergraduate creative writing programs in the United States, Canada, and the United Kingdom.

Poets & Writers, Inc. (72 Spring St., New York, NY 10012). Poets & Writers issues a bimonthly magazine of the same name that has articles of high quality and interest to writers; the magazine and organization also provide information on contests and on magazines and publishers soliciting manuscripts. The organization also has a number of useful publications that are periodically revised: the *Directory of American Poets and Fiction Writers*; *Literary Agents: A Writer's Guide*; *Author and Audience: A Readings and Workshops Guide*; and an annual listing called *Writers' Conferences*.

## *Writers' Guides*

*Directory of Small Press/Magazine Editors & Publishers 2005.* Edited by Len Fulton. Paradise, CA: Dustbooks, 1999 and ongoing. An exhaustive list of smaller book and magazine publishers for poetry, fiction, and nonfiction, this resource is an easy reference for writers looking for comprehensive information about the small-press industry, including helpful subject and regional indexes.

*The Portable Publishing Classroom for Fiction and Creative Non-Fiction Writers.* Audio-cassette produced by Poets & Writers, Inc. Amy Holman describes in detail the most efficient way to publish your writing by matching your style with the appropriate publication.

*2005/2006 Writer's Guide to Book Editors, Publishers, and Literary Agents.* Edited by Jeff Herman. Rockland, CA: Prima Publishing, 2000 and ongoing. Detailed chapters—about creating the perfect query letter and the drawbacks of sending unsolicited manuscripts as well as question-and-answer sections designed to take the mystery out of the publishing process—help writers understand the business side of writing.

*Writer's Market.* Cincinnati: Writer's Digest Books, ongoing. A new edition comes out each year with practical advice on how to sell fiction and nonfiction manuscripts as well as lists of book and magazine publishers, agents, foreign markets, and other services for writers.

# Credits

# Index